Creating Links and Innovative Overviews for a New History Research Agenda
for the Citizens of a Growing Europe

THEMATIC WORK GROUP 3

Religious and Philosophical Concepts

I

The Consortium

Karl-Franzens-Universität Graz (Austria)

Universiteit Gent (Belgium)

Sofiyski Universitet „Sveti Kliment Ohridski" (Bulgaria)

Univerzita Karlova v Praze (Czech Republic)

Panepistimio Kyprou (Cyprus)

Roskilde Universitetscenter (Denmark)

Tartu Ülikool (Estonia)

Turun Yliopisto (Finland)

Université Pierre Mendès-France, Grenoble II (France)

Université de Toulouse II - Le Mirail (France)

Universität Hannover (Germany)

Forschungszentrum Europäische Aufklärung (Germany)

University of Aberdeen (Great Britain)

Cardiff University (Great Britain)

University of Sussex (Great Britain)

Ethniko kai Kapodistriako Panepistimio Athinon (Greece)

Aristotelio Panepistimio Thessalonikis (Greece)

Debreceni Egyetem (Hungary)

Miskolci Egyetem (Hungary)

Háskóli Íslands (Iceland)

National University of Ireland, Galway/ Ollscoil na hÈireann, Gaillimh (Ireland)

Università di Bologna (Italy)

Università degli Studi di Milano (Italy)

Università degli Studi di Padova (Italy)

Università di Pisa (Italy)

Latvijas Universitāte, Riga (Latvia)

L-Università Ta' Malta (Malta)

Universiteit Utrecht (The Netherlands)

Universitetet i Oslo (Norway)

Uniwersytet Jagiellonski, Krakow (Poland)

Universidade de Coimbra (Portugal)

Universidade Aberta (Portugal)

Universitatea Babeş Bolyai din Cluj-Napoca (Romania)

Universitatea 'Stefan cel Mare', Suceava (Romania)

Moskowskij Gosudarstvennyj Oblastnoj Universitet (Russian Federation)

Slovenskej Akademie Vied (Slovakia)

Univerza v Mariboru (Slovenia)

University of KwaZulu-Natal (South Africa)

Universidad de Alcalá de Henares (Spain)

Universidad de Deusto (Spain)

Universidad Autónoma de Madrid (Spain)

Universitat de Valencia (Spain)

Universität Basel (Switzerland)

Orta Dogu Teknik Üniversitesi (Turkey)

Religion, Ritual and Mythology

Aspects of Identity Formation in Europe

edited by

Joaquim Carvalho

EDIZIONI

plũs
pisa university
press

Religion, ritual and mythology : aspects of identity formation in Europe / edited by Joaquim Carvalho
(Thematic work group)

940 (21.)
1. Europa - Civiltà   I. Carvalho, Joaquim

CIP a cura del Sistema bibliotecario dell'Università di Pisa

This volume is published, thanks to the support of the Directorate General for Research of the European Commission, by the Sixth Framework Network of Excellence CLIOHRES.net under the contract CIT3-CT-2005-006164. The volume is solely the responsibility of the Network and the authors; the European Community cannot be held responsible for its contents or for any use which may be made of it.

Volumes published (2006)

I. *Thematic Work Groups*

I.   Public Power in Europe: Studies in Historical Transformations
II.   Power and Culture: Hegemony, Interaction and Dissent
III. Religion, Ritual and Mythology. Aspects of Identity Formation in Europe
IV.   Professions and Social Identity. New European Historical Research on Work, Gender and Society
V.   Frontiers and Identities: Exploring the Research Area
VI.   Europe and the World in European Historiography

II. *Transversal Theme*

I.   Citizenship in Historical Perspective

III. *Doctoral Dissertations*

I.   F. Peyrou, La Comunidad de Ciudadanos. El Discurso Democrático-Republicano en España, 1840-1868

Cover: António Simões Ribeiro and Vicente Nunes, *Allegories of Honour and Virtue* (detail), University of Coimbra, Biblioteca Joanina, ceiling of the central room. Photo © José Maria Pimentel

© Copyright 2006 by Edizioni Plus – Pisa University Press
Lungarno Pacinotti, 43
56126 Pisa
Tel. 050 2212056 – Fax 050 2212945
info-plus@edizioniplus.it
www.edizioniplus.it - Section "Biblioteca"

ISBN 88-8492-404-9

Manager
Claudia Napolitano

Editing
Francesca Petrucci

Informatic assistance
Michele Gasparello

Contents

Preface

We are very pleased to present *Religion, Ritual and Mythology. Aspects of Identity Formation in Europe* to the academic and research community as well as to the general reader. It is the third of seven volumes in the first publication cycle of our pan-European Network of Excellence, CLIOHRES.net (www.cliohres.net). With this book, the Network's Thematic Work Group 3, on "Religious and Philosophical Concepts", launches its five year research plan.

The aim of the work group is to examine how religious ideas, organizations and practices – as well as general visions of the world and how it works – intertwine with other aspects of European history. In this first volume, the Group explores, or maps, the terrain. No one would doubt the power of belief in motivating human beings in their actions and moulding the way they organise their lives. But certainly, the effects and consequences of religious ideas and practices are even more varied and complex than appears on the surface.

In his lucid and wide-ranging Introduction Joaquim Carvalho locates and contextualises the general theme and explains how the Group has decided to define and approach their daunting task. This first 'mapping' volume provides a fascinating entrée into a world that emphasises ideas, beliefs and symbols, but without considering them to be separate from other aspects of human endeavour. The Group emphasises the 'faire' rather than the 'dire', and shows how historians investigate the many concrete, identifiable and even measurable ways in which 'Religious and Philosophical Concepts' affect the 'hic et nunc' and how they have been studied in the past as well as at present.

On the one hand, we find contributions on consolidated but not static traditions of religious history. Several chapters illustrate, catalogue or exemplify lines of study centring on particular religious manifestations, orders, missions and movements. Others look at the role of secularisation and its complex and contradictory effects. The obstacles to research on certain phenomena, personalities or movements because of political pressure or downright censorship are not forgotten. The subtitle of the volume speaks of identity, itself a complex and problematic concept. The choice is the result of the awareness that religion and religious practices are indeed one of the most obvious factors in forming and reinforcing collective identities and world views.

The challenge before the group is to carry out its part of the overall CLIOHRES.net agenda of rethinking current research practices and strategies in European history, by placing them in a broad analytical and comparative context, and using this juxtaposition to achieve a new level of critical understanding, necessary for an informed citizenship.

History is often thought of as remote and unconnected with daily life. It is usually absorbed in the form of general 'knowledge', and often assumes the form of generally shared convictions, orientations and prejudices which have their roots in national narratives.

These narratives took form everywhere in specific political and cultural contexts, but very few are aware of how and why they have taken the shapes they have. Our Network of Excellence is based on observations made over a number of years on the power of history in forming social and political attitudes, and in moulding our perceptions of ourselves and of others. Received ideas about the past influence each of us in our interaction with society and with other individuals, and in our decisions regarding actions to be taken and values to be observed or enforced. Such ideas form the foundation for the division of the world into ethnic or social groups, whose historical construction and maintenance serve as the basis for virtually all claims of national and other collective identities.

CLIOHRES.net began its work in June 2005, thanks to a five year research contract with the European Commission through the Sixth Framework Programme of its Directorate General for Research, under Priority 7, dealing with "Citizenship". As a matter of fact, CLIOHRES.net is an important result of the long term cooperation among a large number of European universities. Collaboration originally began with the ECTS History Network, which grew out of a pilot project launched at the end of the 1980s. Then the History Subject Area Group of the pilot project assumed the task of testing and developing methods of credit transfer and transparent rules for assessing performance in order to facilitate student mobility and recognition throughout Europe. At the outset, the ECTS History Network counted fifteen universities in eleven member states of the European Union; when the project ended in 1995, the Network had expanded to include 26 institutions in 16 EU and EFTA countries. In the following years, the partners developed two Socrates Curriculum development projects, the second of which, CLIOH ("Refounding Europe: Creating Links, Insights and Overviews for a new History agenda") was privileged to be able to include members from central and eastern Europe for the first time. CLIOH grew into CLIOHnet, the Erasmus Thematic Network for History (www.clioh.net), which at present has 80 partner institutions in 35 European countries, as well as a large number of associate partners. CLIOHnet has promoted inclusion and reciprocal knowledge and has extended its membership as fast as possible to partners from newly eligible countries and from various kinds of institutions. It is a sister Network, specialising in issues of higher education, and an essential complement to our research Network of Excellence.

CLIOHnet and CLIOHRES.net are intertwined with the remarkable social and political transformations which have taken place in Europe during the last twenty years, with the integration, consolidation and expansion of the European Union and the formation of a unique polity. The Networks correspond to a vision of what Europe is and should be. In this context, "excellence" does not mean a closed club of a few institutions of recognised prestige. "Excellence" means taking advantage of unique opportunities of cooperating across and beyond the European Union. It means finding ways for motivated and open-minded academics and researchers from many of the excellent universities and centres in Europe to collaborate, creating new knowledge and insights thanks to their very different points of view. Doing so means developing innovative teaching and research programmes, and requires that the two be tightly linked.

The CLIOHRES Network of Excellence builds on the experience gained to develop the field of historical and related research in an innovative way. Its name stands for "Creating

Links and Innovative Overviews for a New History Research Agenda for the Citizens of a Growing Europe". The Network is a consortium of 45 universities and research institutions in 31 countries. Each institution is represented by two senior researchers and two doctoral students, coming from various academic fields – primarily from history, but also from art history, sociology, archaeology, architecture, philology, political science, literary studies and geography. Thus the network serves as a platform for dialogue and debate, comparisons and cooperation across national, generational and disciplinary boundaries. The 180 researchers in the network are divided into six thematic work groups, each of which deals with a broadly designated research area – 'states, institutions and legislation', 'power and culture', 'religious and philosophical concepts', 'work, gender and society'; 'frontiers and identities' and, finally, 'Europe and the world'. Furthermore, the Network as a whole addresses 'transversal themes' of which one is emphasised each year. These are 'citizenship', 'identity', 'migration', 'gender', 'discrimination' and 'tolerance'. Each of the thematic work groups addresses these transversal themes from its specific point of view. During the first year, the theme addressed was 'citizenship', which is the topic of another volume included in the same publication cycle.

As a network of excellence, CLIOHRES is not an ordinary research project. It does not focus on a narrowly defined research question or on a set of specific questions. Rather it is conceived as a forum where researchers representing various national and regional traditions can meet and elaborate their work in new ways thanks to structured interaction with their colleagues. The objective is not only to transcend the national boundaries that still largely define historical research agendas, opening new avenues for research, but also to use those very national differences to become critically aware of how current research agendas have evolved.

In order to create a meaningful context for dialogue, the people engaged in it need to recognize both the similarities and marked differences between the various historical traditions in Europe. For this reason, the first phase of the project has been devoted to 'mapping', to exploring how the questions perceived as important for each thematic area appear in different national historiographies. In future years, further mapping will take place, while the groups proceed through the further stages of identifying research themes that can be of interest for all historiographies, comparing methodologies and sources, demonstrating how problems defined in one historiographical tradition can be developed in new contexts. In this way, in its five years of activity, the Network intends to create novel paradigms for European historical research.

In order to present the discussions and debates that take place in to Network to the wider public, CLIOHRES.net plans five publication cycles. Every year, the work groups will present at least one volume each, and the Network as a whole will treat one of the 'transversal' themes. This year's volumes vary in nature, but may be considered collections of working papers, documenting progress, rather than claiming to be the last word on the subject they deal with. They bring together scholars from very different stages in their professional careers. Some of the authors are doctoral students, while others are established professors with long experience of academic work. They also represent various discursive traditions, which is only appropriate, as history is perhaps the most heterogeneous scientific field that exists. CLIOHRES aims to facilitate dialogue between traditions and to open paths towards new critical understanding, but not to homogenize historical research in Europe. Diversity is intended and desired. History can be and is studied and narrated in many different ways – these ways in themselves being products of history, and worthy of investigation.

As the first year of this project comes to a close, we express our gratitude to the European Commission and its Directorate General for Research which has supported our Network generously through the Priority 7 of the Sixth Framework Programme. The grant awarded has given the Network the financial means to carry out its ambitious programme. Even more importantly, it is a recognition of the important role that history can play in shaping a better future for European citizens. We thank our project officers, Giulia Amaducci and Ioannis Kampolis. Their careful and knowledgeable support and advice has been of great importance.

Our thanks also go to the University of Pisa and to its Rector, Marco Pasquali. The University of Pisa supports the Network very generously in addition to giving great moral support. Without the understanding and backing of the coordinating institution, it would be impossible to carry out a programme of this kind. We thank the director of the central administration of the University, Dr Riccardo Grasso, for accepting the responsibilities connected with the management of the Network; Miriana Donati and Elisa Cascio for their special help; the Pisa team, Laura Burgisano, Adrian Marinescu and Pasquale Cuomo for their total immersion; and our student helpers Ileana Buzic, Lorenzo Gatti, Andreas Verdigi, Nicoletta Scapparone and Marina Cappelli, for their assistance in various different phases of the project.

Above all we are grateful to all members of the Network for a stimulating, challenging and productive year. We express our appreciation to the members of Thematic Work Group 3. The group has given an important contribution by writing the chapters in the present volume and participating in the debates and dialogues which have shaped it. Four of its members, Elena Brambilla, Joaquim Carvalho, Smiljana Gartner and Ivan Ilchev have made particularly significant contributions to the joint volume on the general or 'transversal' theme of "Citizenship".

Our special thanks go to the group's leader, Joaquim Ramos de Carvalho of the University of Coimbra, who is also the editor of this book, and to the other members of the Coimbra team. Joaquim Carvalho has kept motivation at a high level in TWG 3, thanks to his good humour and good organisation. Luisa Trindade and Ana Isabel Ribeiro not only have contributed significant studies to this volume, but have also helped very effectively to smooth the complexities of publishing a scientific work written by scholars from many countries, accustomed to varying discursive and typographical conventions. Roumen L. Genov of the St Kliment Ohridski University of Sofia is the reference person for TWG 3 in the CLIO-HRES.net Management Group. We are grateful for his help.

Ann Katherine Isaacs
Guðmundur Hálfdanarson

Coordinators, CLIOHRES.net

Pisa - Reykjavik, May 2006

Introduction

CLIOHRES.net AND TWG3: Aims, Phases and Methodology

This volume is the result of the first year of activities of the Thematic Working Group 3 (TWG3) of the CLIOHRES.net project. The group, one of six within the network, is dedicated to Religious and Philosophical concepts, and met three times: in Coimbra, in September 2005, in Pisa, during the plenary meeting of the project in December, and in Malta in early March 2006.

CLIOHRES.net does not correspond to a traditional type of research project, and the current volume can only be fully understood in its role as part of a process based on a specific model of organizing a large number of researchers from very different academic traditions around a set of overarching themes of great importance to the European historiographical agenda.

CLIOHRES.net is centred on the idea of placing people, already expert researchers, in a context where their previous knowledge and experience acquires a new meaning. The network provides a new type of environment designed to allow the emergence of new approaches on relevant historiographical themes. This is to be accomplished "in the interactive, finalised context of meetings designed around the presentation of research, the exchange of views and the mutual production of books and reports" with the goal of achieving a "common elaboration of new viewpoints, consigned to texts which in practice demonstrate interaction and broadening, and which can be widely distributed".

The project is structured as a progression of sub-goals and phases that provide a path of increasing integration and cross-fertilization of concepts, approaches and methodologies between the researchers involved. In this progression, the first year is defined as one of "recognition and mapping of how the questions perceived as important for the thematic area appear in the different national historiographies". This first phase will feed into the second year where the aim is "defining transversal problems which are relevant in a more general context, and investigating and illuminating the relation between the two levels".

The current volume therefore corresponds to the phase of "recognition" and "mapping". There were several possible interpretations of this goal. Our approach was that of widening the horizons by collecting contributions from all members of the group and welcoming a variety of topics, approaches and developments of the underlying research, while accepting the risk of a level of diversity that, in the context of this particular project, is not a handicap, but rather a necessary step. On the whole, our objective has been achieved, and very few researchers have been unable to participate in this stage.

Diversity, however, is not an asset *per se*. We are at the sowing stage, far from harvesting mature fruit, but it is important to try tentatively to produce an overview of the main questions and issues at hand and sketch a crude map of the most visible features of our misty territory.

RELIGION AND PHILOSOPHY IN CLIOHRES.NET

The original definition of the subject area of Thematic Workgroup 3 identifies the broad periods of the European history of ideas, adding contemporary interest to the connections between religion in national and ethnic identity:

> [the group] will consider the religious and philosophical achievements of the ancient world, and particularly the ways in which that patrimony has been given meaning in different political and cultural contexts from the medieval to the modern and contemporary world; it will examine the Reformation as a focal point for understanding and comparing different confessional and national approaches to the Reformation period; it will deal with Humanism and the Enlightenment; the emergence of lay philosophy and new religious movements, observing and contextualizing the different approaches to, and understandings of, such phenomena in different parts of Europe; it will examine the significance of religious identities as linked to national and ethnic sentiments.

Religion and philosophy belong to the realm of "ideas" or "concepts", mental constructs that frame the way people see the world. They are part of the worldviews shared by populations, which allow them to represent and operate with reality. As elements of the great mental frameworks, religion and philosophical concepts have reflected, shaped and interacted (the best verb is a matter for discussion) with other levels of social life and with other forms of conceptual representation of reality, from science to popular culture.

It is easy, sometimes irresistible, in this bird's-eye view of the development of mankind, to see the role of religion as tied inversely to the development of science, rational paradigms and the materialism of everyday life. Religion would be a primitive way to understand reality and to find values and goals in social interactions. As long as religion is considered in general terms as a way to understand reality, both natural and social, and as long as we believe that the rational and scientific comprehension of the world is cumulative and unlimited, the destiny of religious and philosophical concepts is already clear. In that sense, the history of religion is a part of the history of ideas, an area where broad and progressive chronological stages are easy to conceptualise. A clear progression seems to emerge, from the mythology of Antiquity through the dogmatic scholastic construction of medieval times, to the slow erosion and new construction brought about by Humanism, the Reformation, the Enlightenment and Lay Philosophies, with the unexpected revival of religious movements in the 19th and 20th centuries, puzzlingly against the current. August Comte put it very clearly in the great law of history, describing mankind moving through the theological, the metaphysical and, finally, the positivist state.

But the present shapes our view of the past. We live in a world where religion cannot possibly be considered a relic of a surpassed phase of human evolution, nor philosophy an ever-diminishing frontier around the lands not yet conquered by science. On the contrary, the social need to understand the omnipresence of religion, religious feeling and religious institutions has reached new heights in present times. At the same time, there is an unavoidable and almost daily need to question the concepts that are essential to our identity and sense of belonging, in the various non-concentic circles that delimit our daily life (gender, family, work, group, country, culture or civilization).

These intellectual urgencies are particularly relevant in the current European context, not because of the political need to custom-design a *post facto* identity, but, on the contrary, because of the necessity of understanding how the capacity for diversity (cultural, religious, political) has become, by paradox, one of the unifying references of the European ideal.

Any reference to the importance of religion, and the need for conceptual introspection on the values that constitute the European identity, normally triggers the evocation of the great and dramatic moments of recent times. We are faced with the need to question the inevitable progress of our world towards a better society based on rationality and tolerance and of our ability to face the threats of religious and ideological fanaticism, not only when they come from the outside but, more painfully, when they grow inside our own societies.

One could say that the historiography of religion is faced with a paradox: most long term historical evaluations of the role of religion would seem to point in the direction of decline, greater interiority or privatization, while the present seems to show the contrary, an extraordinary renewal of the importance of religious factors in the public as well as, in some countries, the private sphere. It is as if religion, in history, only seems to fade when looked upon from a distance. When watched at close range, it just seems to grow[1].

This paradox is not just the result of over simplistic views of the past and future in the heads of those few that try to rationalize the destiny of mankind. It has become part of what many of us consider to be the natural order of things. Some people feel puzzled or uncomfortable when faced with examples of well-educated, bright young people with very strong religious beliefs and corresponding practices. Education, material comfort and citizenship in democratic societies do not seem compatible with deep faith and beliefs in super-natural entities. It is as if progress, in the sense of knowledge, education and well-being, inevitably imply a decline of religious faith, associated with ignorance and political, social and economic exclusion.

One could also attribute this common conception to a tentative denial of the fear that the really significant lines of division of the planet are not, as they were a few years ago, those of the great ideological blocks, but those of religious choices. We were surprised and elated by the disappearance of the former great divide that had hung over our heads for decades, feeding the dark spectre of a possible Armageddon, and now we are shocked and reluctant to face the globalisation of a new Other and the returning nightmares about fingers on buttons. As before, we see the global divide cut through the inner space of our societies, and once again we face the tragic dilemmas of security and liberty.

These are matters that certainly deserve reflection and innovative approaches. While this is not the place for a lengthy discussion on the role of religion in society, either in the past or the present, it is worthwhile, in the spirit of the project, to raise a few questions that are relevant in this context, which can help us to appreciate the variety and diversity of the texts gathered here, and to envisage more clearly a future agenda for our undertakings.

Most of what follows concentrates on religion and not on philosophy, since, in fact, this first volume is almost exclusively centred on various manifestations of religion through history.

Understanding Religion: Widening the Horizon

All the chapters in this first volume from TWG3 are about religion or about phenomena where a religious dimension is present to varying degrees (the rituals around the commemoration of Tito's birthday provide perhaps the least obvious case, at first glance). The variety of topics, periods and phenomena is so wide that some questions certainly can be raised: What is the value of putting together such a diversity of subjects? Is there a common object in all this variety? Is it possible to define a field, however broadly, capable of attracting a coherent scientific endeavour?

These questions, together with the paradoxes and perplexities mentioned before, are partly determined by the complex usage patterns of the word "religion". In the European historiographic tradition, the word is commonly used at face value, precluding the need for formal definitions. Like all great words ("freedom", "progress", "happiness") everyone knows what "religion" means until a definition is attempted. Then the exceptions, qualifications and nuances multiply to such a point that no clear meaning remains. What exactly is "religion"? How can we define the concept in an operative way?

Régis Debray argued recently in a provocative and insightful book that the word should be avoided as a major epistemological obstacle[2]. He draws a parallel with the word "fire" that also seemed, at a certain point in time, to represent a clear phenomenon, present in everyday experience, naturally attracting the energy of thinkers and the imagination of countless minds. But only when "fire" was "de-objectified" and correctly identified as a particular manifestation of combustion, only when it was realized that there was nothing fundamental, intrinsic or elementary in the phenomenon, only then was it possible to move to a scientific discourse that actually explained what "fire" is[3].

Debray's proposal is to use the word "communion", a solution that is only understandable as part of his global argument that we use "religion" and derivatives for describing the basic mechanisms at work in the construction of human *communities*, the processes by which the "them" becomes "us". Religion is a sort of *ingénierie associative* [associative engineering] and the essence of the religious phenomenon lies less in its content than in the procedures that it encompasses. This is why, according to Debray, we find the same processes in every endeavour that attempts to draw together a group of individuals under a strong sense of identity and common belonging, from churches to new born nations, from revolutionary social experiments to dynamic organizations, all the way down to small teams and groups aiming to survive and succeed. In all of these situations we encounter the ideas of a common origin, narratives that place the contemporaries with regard to that common origin, a hierarchy and associated rituals that define roles for actors, and finally a membrane, which circumscribes the community and distinguishes the inside from the outside – the basic building blocks of group identity[4].

This approach is of interest to us here, because the path that TWG3 defined for itself from the first meeting, was to inquire into the way religion "works" in the context of multi-varied historical situations. In retrospect, we can say that this volume is, to use Debray's expressions, more about the *faire* than the *dire,* and more on *opérations* than on *représentations*.

This shift of focus from the "concepts" inscribed in the official title of the Group is less radical than it seems. Religious concepts are, by definition, "beliefs". And beliefs are mental processes intimately connected to action and the triggering of behaviour, a theme to which we will shortly and briefly return. So there is really no way to deal with religious concepts without matching them with the social practices they induce.

If we take religion as "social engineering", a toolbox of mechanisms and procedures that can be applied to all types of social interactions relevant to the construction of the identity of a community, then, in fact, we will find religion everywhere. And, inversely, whenever we look into religious processes at work, if properly contextualized, we will find the identity of communities being constructed and developed. The chapters in this book can be read profitably from this point of view, justifying the overarching title of *Religion, Ritual and Mythology: Aspects of Identity Formation in Europe.*

The intimate link between what is called "religion" and the basic processes of creation and maintenance of social groups implies more than just special attention to the concrete practices of social actors in historical situations. It also implies that religion and social life are inextricably tied and any theory of religion is, in a way, a theory of society, and any theory of society is bound to produce a theory of religion. The latter is, of course, very much confirmed by the facts, as we find a strong interest in religion from the founding fathers of sociological thought, including Comte, Durkheim, Weber and Marx. We also find the same interest in Freud and Jung. It can be argued that religion is one of the central issues in social theory, which is consistent with the "religion as social engineering" approach[5].

This poses fundamental theoretical questions that cannot of course be examined within the scope of this introduction. Nevertheless, it is important to stress the fact that the challenges of understanding the persistent role of religion in society, in the sense described above, has increasingly favoured approaches towards a "natural" grounding of religious behaviour. We have all read or heard countless times that religion corresponds to basic needs existing in human beings. We are now seeing attempts to demonstrate that "belief" or "religion" are part of the human "hardware", or that they emerge from the basic processes that are responsible for human societies[6]. Religion could be genetically determined, or be the product of an evolutionary process where beliefs evolve like organisms in symbiotic association with the human hosts who subscribe to them[7]. The widespread attention that religious issues attract nowadays makes these approaches suitable for broad public consumption.

It is in this context that the mission of TWG3 is progressively defined. As historians, we should welcome and answer as far as we can the renewed interest of our society in the historical roots of religious experience. This implies the careful analysis of religious processes in the past, in all their variety, complexity and different interactions with other aspects of social life. But it is also imperative that we do not lose sight of religion as being one of the most fascinating emanations of the human mind, one that particularly challenges history with the riddles of omnipresence in time and space.

The contributions

The chapters included in this volume vary widely in several ways. The group includes researchers from nine countries and ten different institutions, totalling 20 people of whom eight are doctoral students. Research interests range widely at various levels: chronological (from Antiquity to the late 20th century), thematic (from the sacrilization of rituals in an atheist state to urbanism and religious segregation in medieval towns) and geographic (from the Iberian Peninsula to the Balkans, from Malta to Ireland). The scope of the contributions is also varied, from early reviews of research topics and literature to bird's- eye views of a field and scholarly discussions of historiography in specific areas.

The volume is divided into four main sections. *Religious Communities and Urban Communities* brings together chapters that explore different ways in which religious communities interact with urban environments. *Religion and Mythology,* with contributions to identity in multi-cultural, multi-ethnic and multi-confessional societies is more closely related to the problem of identity, a pervasive topic that reappears throughout the volume. *Religion in Secularisation and Nation Building Rituals and Implementation of Religious and Political Power* approaches the ways in which religion and political power interact. Within each section the order of the contributions is chronological.

In the opening chapter of the first section, *Jean-Luc Lamboley* focuses on the role of religion in the urban development of new Greek colonial cities. His approach builds upon research of the last two decades of the 20th century which moved away from the political and institutional aspects of the foundation of cities to give more relevance to the religious dimension, especially the development of a common cult as the basis of the identity of the new communities, slowly replacing the particular devotions of the mixed population of original settlers. The archaeologist is able to retrace the emergence of the new identity through the effect of religion as a major structuring force of urban space. The poliad divinities, attached to the new city, become the unifying entity that organizes space, cultural references and activities.

The next three chapters give detailed overviews of the historiography of mendicant orders in urban contexts. *Dieter Berg* gives a detailed and scholarly overview of German historiography on the Franciscans, with a special focus on the relationship between the mendicant friars and the development of cities. The historiographical production is described in relation to a variety of topics: the wide-ranging interaction between the friars and the city involving the dimensions of urban topography, social status and prosopographical studies, and the role of the order in urban development, urban riots, urban economy and intellectual life. Other aspects included in the review are the relationships between the Franciscans and civil and ecclesiastical authorities in the cities, an aspect where privileges, property and prominence played a conflicting role. Berg's analysis also describes how historiographical interest in the Order shifted with historical context and researchers' backgrounds, from the interest after World War II in the original message of peace and reconciliation of St. Francis, the emergence of new approaches under the influence of French historiography of the 1970s, and the role of the political division of Germany in the shaping of different approaches to research.

Raphaela Averkorn provides a complementary approach to Berg's by focusing on the Dominicans rather than the Franciscans. The development of historiography in the field is closely connected to the emergence of a new regional history in the 1980s because the friars are obviously a central agent in the organization of territories. An overview of the research institutions in Germany is given. A number of recurrent topics of research emerge. The main themes deal with the perception of mendicants orders in medieval society by medieval people. Another is the involvement of Dominicans in church politics, relationship with bishops, local clergy and other monasteries as well as with local authorities and nobility. Averkorn also describes current research into the attitudes of the friars regarding preaching and pastoral care, and their relationship with various cultural areas. The gender dimension is also reviewed through the research on female monasteries (or convents) that developed from the 1980s onwards. The overview also refers to the work of German historians that have published work on the relationship of mendicant orders and citizenship outside Germany, i.e., in England, Scotland, Ireland, Italy, France, Aragon and Castile, showing the path towards the integrated study of mendicants in European society.

Rita Ríos de la Llave approaches the connections between mendicant orders and cities in another context, that of the medieval Castile and Léon. Ríos analyses the shift in historiography as the field opens to researchers from outside the Order. New topics emerge, including the relationships between the royal family and the order, the political role of the Dominicans, intellectual and academic development, religiousness and spirituality and urban growth. One of the main conclusions is that as long as studies of the mendicant orders and studies of medieval urban life remain as separate fields with little interaction and cross fertilization, true progress in both areas will be limited. The overview covers more specific themes, such as the communities of Dominican nuns in medieval Castile and Léon and the current issues of this emerging area. The last part of the chapter makes an inventory of open research topics related to Dominican communities and urban communities, among which we find the recurrent theme of conflicts with the secular clergy, with whom the friars were in a clear competition for souls and resources in the ecosystem of religious medieval life.

Luisa Trindade approaches the coexistence of different religious communities, a recurring theme in this volume. Here the angle is that of history of urbanism, or how multiple confessions coexist in the same urban area. The subject is the development of Jewish quarters in Portuguese towns. The spatial "identity" of the Jews is a construction of the 14th century, regulated by a royal decree of 1361. Trindade's interest lies in the difference between law and practice, or rather between the governed space and the lived-in space. The slow adoption of law, the local tensions, the constraints of urban space and different demographic rhythms created complex patterns over time until the abrupt expulsion/conversion of the Jews in the 15th century. The review of current research and open issues depicts an interesting picture of how religious identities, however clearly defined by dogma and ruled by law, had to coexist in everyday life with the down-to-earth realities of economic roles and urban daily life, which continuously eroded the attempts to delimit, through space, a well-connected Jewish community. This is a point we will see made again later on the volume, in connection with Sicily.

Victor Mallia-Milanes' paper on the Knights of St. John puts forward another important aspect of the role of religion in history: the relationship between religion and war, which he traces back to the famous sermon of Urban II in Clermont, 1095. The theme of the "Holy War" and the intellectual justification that makes it possible are very much at the centre of today's debates. For seven hundred years, the Knights of St. John brought about the intersection of religious ideals, military warfare and secular power that we find everywhere in Christianity, but rarely in such a condensed and circumscribed setting. One of the interesting points made on the review of the historiography is how a circumstantial answer to a need of professional military support becomes a persistent structure in time that was to last for centuries. It reminds us of the unmatched power of religion to hold together a community in a radically changing environment. It is fascinating to see the way the Hospitallers adapted their original mission, without ever really changing its essential aspects, by playing the card of the threat even when it was hardly credible, reinforcing the role of the hospital to make the flow of resources justifiable, and keeping alive the idea of crusade long after its historical time.

Emanuel Buttigieg presents research in progress on "growing up" in Hospitaller Malta, during the *Ancién Regime*. Growing up is of course a matter much concerned with religion, as age was the subject of precise regulations from canon law, touching aspects like autonomous will, capacity to take vows and decisions, etc… Buttigieg gives a brief overview of historical concepts of childhood before focusing on the way the question has been, or rather has not been, dealt with by Maltese historiography. The overview covers the exploitation of traditional sources like parish registers and information from medical institutions, while pointing at the same time to new approaches centred on the concept of "children's geographies". Travellers' accounts are used to reconstruct the way public space was the stage for children's activities in a society were men worked at sea and women ruled over the domestic space. The link between childhood and adolescence, and the charitable work of the Knights of St. John is made through a review of work related to the foundling hospital and to dowries for marriage.

Olga Dekhtevich's overview of the historiography of the Khlyst movement again raises the topic of the links between power, church and religious dissent. The Khlysts, or God's people, were a long-living sect founded in the 17th century with a significant following until the early 20th century. In the 19th century they became a threat to the Russian Orthodox Church. Like many other sects that short-circuited the carefully crafted symbiosis between the official church and the state, the Khlysts become the subject of persecution, and much of the early writing on the movement came from officials in charge of its persecution. *Dekhtevich* describes the existing literature, stressing that the secretive nature of the sect, which encouraged its followers to be good Orthodox Church members and keep their true faith a secret, together with biased accounts from interested parties, makes it difficult to have a clear picture of the facts. But in spite of the unreliable sources, an interesting topic emerges, that of the connections between religious sectarianism and social movements, together with the capacity of religion to aggregate the struggle of the deprived against the powerful institutions of the church and state.

The second section takes us from the urban setting to multi-cultural and multi-ethnical contexts.

Maria-Paola Castiglioni tackles the main recurring theme of this volume: the connection between the religious sphere and the construction of the identity of communities. Here the context is the Greek colonial cities and their foundational mythological narratives. Castiglioni opens with an extended review of the field of mythology before she moves to the more specific connections between myth, acculturation, frontiers and ethnic identity. Contrary to a strict structuralist approach, myth is put into the historical context where it lived and is taken as part of the history of the period. The example of the Illyrian myth of Cadmos, the hero from Thebes, is used by Castiglioni to show these symbolic mechanisms at work, integrating the mythic narrative with archaeological findings. The resulting analysis suggests that the local elites appropriated the Greek episode to anchor their power and status, leaving open many interesting questions on the ways the religious dimension is used in a multi-cultural setting.

Jean-Luc Lamboley, in his second paper in this volume, revisits the same theme of the connection of myth and identity. The setting is Taranto, a Spartan colony during the 8th century B.C. The Tarantine myth is a wonderful narrative that brings together a collective rite of passage with the foundation of a city. Lamboley's analysis goes one step further, demonstrating the role of the myth in asserting the right of the invading Greeks to the indigenous land they were occupying. By analysing the myth together with the archaeological evidence, it is possible to make sense of the particularities of the narrative and link them to the need to legitimise the appropriation of land that had a previous legitimate owner. The role of the myth as a resolution of basic conflicts of a culture is very well demonstrated. For the Greeks, the right to own land belonged to those that were born on it. Thus the occupation of other people's land posed a conceptual problem that the myth solves. A similar problem occurs in the re-colonization of territories occupied by Greek populations from another metropolis, which is also convincingly demonstrated in the case of Apollonia of Illyria.

Charles Dalli's chapter on medieval Sicily paints a vivid picture of the multiple combinations of religion, ethnicity and language that resulted from the Norman conquest of the island from 1060 onwards. The problem, from the new rulers' point of view, was how to deal with 250,000 Muslim subjects, and, on the side of the conquered, how to survive in the new regime, finding a path between "relegation and assimilation", through "dissimulation or rebellion". The Muslims had coexisted with Greek Christians and local Jews before the invasion, while the Normans brought new Greek and Latin immigrants from the continental territories under their control. The puzzle increased in complexity as the new lords choose Saracens both for high offices and court servants, while a new Latin feudal class emerged from the network of supporters of the new rulers. Dalli's review of sources and of current research highlights the complexity of the situation and the lack of correspondence between language, faith, ethnicity and social status until the policies of intolerance and ethnic clarification of the 13th century. We are again reminded that religious identities have to interact with different types of social constraints in complex ways.

Emőke Horváth's chapter is an example of approaching a frequently visited historiographical object and bringing in religion as a new angle. The Vandals' rule in Africa generated a stereotyped image, that of a people linked to violence and destruction, and persecutors of the Church. But the Vandals also had a religious element to their identity, that of following Arianism. According to Horváth, Arianism was a significant element of the identity of *gens vandalorum*. The Vandals were Christians, but by following Arianism they remained separate from the trinitarian world, including the Roman church. Horváth poses the question of the importance of religion to the Vandals, reviewing early medieval sources. Through the fragmentary evidence, there emerges a picture that stresses more the role of strategic constraints than an ethnic or religious specificity. A few thousand Vandals controlled a strategic territory, the most important harbour in the north of Africa and managed, as able seamen, to disrupt the main artery of commerce in the Mediterranean. The argument here is that religion, in this case Arianism, played an important role in forming the identity of the barbarian people. The religious intolerance of the Vandals derived from strategic choices rather than from special attention to dogmatic and spiritual subtleties. They persecuted the local Roman bishops because of their leadership role. Arianism was an important element of identity of a minority of rulers in a hostile world.

Thomas Ruhland reviews the literature on two pietist missions in India: the Dänish-Hallesche Mission and the Herrnbuter Brüdergemeine, the first of their kind. As two expressions of the same Protestant denomination inside an alien environment, it is striking to see how specific identities of practice and objectives are developed and sustained by both missionary communities. Conflicts within pietism, combined with different economic and administrative settings, manage to maintain a distinct individuality in the two enterprises. Both missions assume a holistic attitude towards their objectives regarding the local population: it is not just about conversion, but also about civilization and education. In consequence, the missionaries transmit the rational and scientific values of the Enlightenment. Ruhland reproduces the striking quote of missionary John: "Science and its spread are, as I take it, a part of religion and mission…". But each mission represents different trends inside the enlightened intellectual currents of the late 18th and early 19th centuries and different approaches towards the local population. Again we find identity and religion closely connected in unexpected ways.

In the third section, *Religion in Secularization and Nation Building*, we have interesting examples of the various ways in which the religious dimension is present in the process of the emergence of new nations.

Iwan-Michelangelo D'Aprile approaches the opposition between religious concepts and the new secular frameworks that arise from the Enlightenment in Europe. It is probably the contribution most clearly placed in the area of History of Ideas, focusing on an epoch where concepts were in fact discussed at the European level. D'Aprile revisits recent historiographical trends that can be evoked to deal with the topic in hand. The topographical turn of recent historiography finds an interesting historiographical subject in the city of Berlin, as it became an end point for Jewish emigration in Central Europe, a process favoured by the tolerant policies of Frederik II. The question of Jewish citizenship can be seen as a good subject for cultural transfer research because in the 18th century, it was clearly a trans-national European question. Other current trends in the historiography of the Enlightenment are reviewed in relation to D'Aprile's topic, namely the concept of a long 18th century, since the understanding of the evolution of the handling of Jewish citizenship in Germany is only comprehensible when seen in a long 18th century that culminates in the Napoleonic invasion of Prussia.

Michael Refalo describes the end of a half-century long establishment in Malta, one that saw the island under the dominant role of three papal institutions: the Order, the Church and the Inquisition. Napoleon ended the rule of the Hospitallers in 1798. Two years of French rule did not change much and the role of the church was reinforced by their participation in the expulsion of the French with the aid of the British. Refalo reviews the literature on the political and institutional aspects of the church and also inquires into the religious sentiments and experiences of the population in general. At the institutional level, the historiographical issues can be summarized in the conundrum "How could a Roman Catholic island in the middle of the Mediterranean be ruled fairly peaceably by an Atlantic Protestant nation?". It is very interesting to follow Refalo's overview of the careful British handling of religious affairs on the island, and the way the wider political issues of the relationship between the Crown and the Vatican shaped the ecclesiastical politics of Malta. Later, as a local political class emerged, religion became a weapon on the path to a new regime. In the last pages of the paper, Refalo reviews new approaches to the religious life of Malta, referring to research about the role of bell-ringing and belfries, which detects the complex role of religion in local identity and communications.

Giulia Lami looks into the role of religion in the sense of nationality in contemporary Ukraine. The divide between the Russian Orthodox Church and the other Orthodox denominations, created after independence in 1991, maps the political divide revealed worldwide by media coverage of the "Orange revolution". But Lami's picture is more complex, showing that religious confession, linguistic background and national identity do not map easily onto geographical and religious divides. Tracing the origins of the Ukrainian mosaic, Lami goes back to the disintegration of the Kyivan Rus' in the 13th century. The Greek-Catholic church, created in 1596 by the Union of Brest, becomes a factor of permanence and identity in an area of shifting borders all the way through to the 20th century. The review shows the intricate and sometimes unexpected ways in which national sentiments, religious denominations and the role of external powers interact. New perspectives and new methodologies are called for, especially trans-national comparative studies with a long time span, to respond to the need for historical knowledge in these changing times.

Borislav Mavrov's review of Irish historiography continues the exploration of the role of religion in historiographical discourse dealing with national identity. While in Ukraine we saw "a new need for history", in Ireland, the historiographical debate on the nature of national identity and the role of religion in the process has a long tradition. As Mavrov reviews the different schools and arguments on the specifics of the Irish national question, we are confronted with the fact that not only religion, but also history itself plays an important role in the foundation of identity processes, in a way similar to the foundation myths describe by Lamboley and Castiglioni.

In the last set of contributions, *Aleksey Klemeshov* reviews the Russian historiography on Roger Bacon, the famous Franciscan of the 13th century, whose works on grammar, philosophy, science and alchemy played a major role in medieval thought and the development of scientific thought. Klemeshov's review testifies to the difficulties of researching certain historical subjects in the Soviet era. The life and work of Bacon was either ignored or, probably worse, transformed into the "ideologist of the urban working classes, atheistic but inconsistent" when referred to in dictionaries and encyclopaedias. It was only in 1985 that the first solid and extensive work on Bacon, in the form of a doctoral thesis, appeared. Klemeshov's contribution constitutes the only chapter dedicated specifically to a significant religious thinker, which is somewhat surprising considering the number of important individuals that have shaped religious thought throughout the centuries.

The last two contributions introduce the role of rituals in the implementation of political power, an aspect that has been receiving growing attention in historiography.

Ana Isabel Ribeiro focuses on the question of ritual and symbolic representation in Portugal during the Anción Regime. This was one of religion's central roles in society. Reviewing the existing literature on the subject, Ribeiro stresses the bi-directional exchange of practices and symbols between secular power and the church. Consecration and funeral rites of the kings provide the major opportunities for the sacrilization of power, but other studies show the role played by special spaces shared by the secular and religious, and also the usage of representations of power originating from civil authorities by ecclesiastical dignitaries like bishops. In this context, the rituals mainly have a differentiating role of stressing hierarchies and the distance between rulers and the ruled.

Dimitar Grigorov's description of Tito's birthday celebrations shows that rituals also have a levelling and unifying function. It also demonstrates that in a secular context, theoretically freed of any explicit religious reference, we find a usage of symbols and ceremonies that are clearly drawn from the same toolbox that supports religious practices. The connection between the ritual celebrations and the sense of national unity is striking, and Grigorov's description quickly dismisses a simpler interpretation centred on personality cult. In fact, we were facing the symbolic construction of a supranational identity centred on one man, the founder, and the role of the rituals described is to show clearly, in an almost totemic way, the flow of faith from every member of the community converging towards this figure in the mystical nature of the last baton.

Conclusion

CLIOHRES.net, like all scientific endeavour, is not free from its "spontaneous ideology" to bring back the useful, if outdated, expression of French philosopher Louis Althusser. It is central to this "ideology" that the confrontation of different approaches, different academic traditions and different scientific objects will produce a positive decentring effect that will translate into innovative insights, new questions, and new methodologies and, in the end, into significant progress of scientific knowledge. The validation of this vision is the final object of the project, so at the current stage, it has to go under the label of a hopeful hypothesis. As a generic principle, it is in noble company, from the concept of the great advances in civilization that were connected to moments of increased multiculturalism (in Claude Lévi-Strauss), to the current basic dogma of biology: diversity promotes adaptation and evolution. In our view, this first volume constitutes a promising step in that direction.

Acknowledgments

Every book is the result of a confluence of efforts that extends beyond the time and knowledge of the direct contributors to the final text. Ana Isabel Ribeiro and Luisa Trindade, from the University of Coimbra, besides participating as authors, managed the flow of information towards the final result by organizing meeting materials, creating and updating the internal website of TWG3, and supporting the editorial process. Several of the members of the Group contributed to the volume prepared by the whole Network on the theme of "Citizenship". They are Elena Brambilla, Joaquim Carvalho, Ivan Ilchev and Smiljana Gartner. Victor Mallia-Milanes hosted an unforgettable meeting in Gozo, presenting the Group with just the right balance, an environment that was both very pleasant and conducive to hard work. Penelope Stonehouse David and Brian David led and coordinated an efficient and friendly team of language editors, to whom the final text owes much. Catarina Moleiro provided the flawless organizational support for the two meetings independently organized by the Group. Laura Burgisano, in Pisa, responsible for handling the administrative aspects of project, was permanently available, competent and knowledgeable in handling the many queries, doubts and bureaucratic imperfections flowing from TWG3 activities. To all of them, I extend our deep gratitude. Finally a very special word for the coordinators of CLIOHRES.net, Ann Katherine Isaacs and Guðmundur Hálfdanarson, whose courage, knowledge, talent and unending dedication made all this possible.

Joaquim Carvalho
University of Coimbra

NOTES

[1] However contemporary we may find the paradox of the present day importance of religion, it is, in fact, a recurrent theme that shows up frequently in the introduction of volumes on the subject. An example from the sixties: "One of the most intriguing intellectual phenomena of the mid-twentieth century is the widespread interest in religion at a time when there is also extensive agreement that religious belief, as traditionally understood, has markedly declined in its *intrinsic* significance for most members of modern societies". R. Robertson, *Sociology of Religion: Selected Readings,* Reading 1969, p. 11.

[2] R. Debray, *Les communions humaines. Pour en finir avec "la religion",* Paris 2005. See also, by the same author, *Le Feu sacré: fonction du réligieux,* Paris 2003.

[3] Debray, *Les communions* cit., p. 31.

[4] *Ibid.,* pp. 73-98.

[5] See S. Trigano, *Qu'est-ce que c'est la religion?,* Paris 2004, and R. Boudon, *Le sens des valeurs,* Paris 1999. Both provide a reflection on the role of beliefs in social theory that we feel is consistent with the perspectives put forward here. From the latter author, there is also a biased, but thought provoking review of the main classical authors' views on these topics: R. Boudon, *Études sur les sociologies classiques,* Paris 2000.

[6] L. Wolpert, *Six Impossible Things Before Breakfast. The Evolutionary Origins of Belief,* London 2006 and an earlier contribution: W. Burkert, *Creation of the Sacred: Tracks of Biology in Early Religions,* Harvard 1996.

[7] D. Dennet, *Breaking the Spell. Religion as a Natural Phenomenon*, London 2006.

Religious Space and Construction of Ancient Greek Civic Communities

Jean-Luc Lamboley
Université Pierre Mendès France, Grenoble II

Dans l'historiographie française, depuis l'ouvrage fondateur de Fustel de Coulanges, La Cité grecque, *les historiens de la Grèce ancienne se sont toujours intéressés au problème des origines de la* polis *(Cité-Etat). Toutefois à partir des années 70, une nouvelle approche qui s'est surtout développée à la suite des travaux de Pierre Vernant et Pierre Vidal Naquet grâce aux chercheurs du Centre Louis Gernet de Paris, a repris le problème en privilégiant le rôle de la religion, plutôt que les aspects institutionnels et politiques. Un ouvrage a marqué le résultat de ces travaux, celui de François de Polignac,* La naissance de la cité grecque, *publié en 1984 avec une seconde édition revue et mise à jour en 1995. Au même moment, le développement des recherches archéologiques, notamment dans les sanctuaires, a considérablement renouvelé nos connaissances et a permis de démontrer le rôle que les sanctuaires ont joué à la fois dans la structuration progressive de l'espace public des premières cités, et dans l'intégration des membres de la communauté civique en gestation. F. de Polignac a pu définir la cité comme étant d'abord une communauté cultuelle, et montrer que c'est à travers la participation à des fêtes religieuses que les premières sociétés grecques ont acquis leur cohérence communautaire et défini une forme primitive de citoyenneté en structurant un espace à la fois politique et religieux.*

Nous proposons dans cet article de présenter deux cas concrets: Mégara Hyblaea en Sicile et Marseille en Gaule, deux colonies fondées respectivement dans la seconde moitié du VIIIe siècle av. J.-C. par des populations doriennes, et à la fin du VIIe siècle av. J.-C. par des Ioniens. Dans le premier exemple, grâce aux fouilles archéologiques, on peut voir que la répartition des cultes et de l'espace public suit une évolution qui correspond à une urbanisation et à une intégration progressives des différents éléments composant la communauté civique mégarienne. Au moment de la fondation, les sanctuaires dessinent comme une couronne autour de la cité, avec en même temps, mêlés à l'habitat, des cultes à caractère familial, ce qui reflète une structure encore éclatée et indifférenciée correspondant à une société en voie d'homogénéisation. Au contraire, à la fin du VIIe siècle, les sanctuaires se concentrent autour de l'agora, et dans un grand sanctuaire au nord-ouest où se situe vraisemblablement le temple de la divinité poliade; on a ainsi une organisation beaucoup plus rationnelle et centrée, avec une hiérarchie des espaces publics qui touche aussi les premiers sanctuaires. La première phase correspond à l'arrivée des premiers colons de différentes origines (Mégariens, Chalcidiens et Doriens) qui créent des quartiers avec leurs propres cultes qu'ils ont importés. Avec le temps, ces populations mixtes fusionnent pour créer une véritable communauté civique et une entité urbaine bien structurée avec les cultes distribués entre l'agora et le principal sanctuaire poliade reliés entre eux par l'avenue principale de la cité.

Dans le cas de Marseille, on ne peut compter que sur les sources littéraires car la présence de la seconde ville et premier port de France, interdit aux archéologues une exploration systématique de la cité antique. Grâce à la description du géographe grec Strabon, nous savons que les temples des divinités poliades se situaient sur l'acropole et étaient consacrés à Apollon Delphinien et à l'Artémis d'Ephèse, qui n'étaient pas les divinités poliades de Phocée, la métropole ionienne, mais les deux divinités les plus honorées par l'ensemble des populations ioniennes d'Asie Mineure. Ainsi, à cause de la vocation commerciale et méditerranéenne de Marseille, les colons voulaient que leur cité apparût très ouverte, et ils se considéraient plus comme des Panioniens que comme des Phocéens. En conséquence, ils choisirent les cultes poliades qui pouvaient le plus attirer les marchands ioniens.

Ainsi, de Mégara en Sicile à Marseille en pays celtique, à travers les vestiges archéologiques comme à travers les témoignages littéraires, on mesure l'importance de la dimension religieuse dans la genèse d'une communauté civique en Grèce ancienne. L'évolution des espaces sacrés permet de suivre l'évolution d'une société naissante, et la monumentalisation de ces espaces religieux est le signe d'une Cité-Etat arrivée à sa maturité*.

Ever since *La cité grecque* (Paris 1864), the founding work by Fustel de Coulanges, historians of Ancient Greece, have always been interested in the origin of *polis* (the City-State). Fustel de Coulanges believed that religion played a key role in the formation of the civic community, the building block of the City. During the following century, the pivotal work was *Griechische Staatskund* (Munich 1920-1926) by G. Busolt and H. Swoboda, a direct inspiration for G. Glotz's manual *La cité grecque* (Paris, 1928), which remained in use into the 1960s. After M. Ventris updated our information about the Mycenaean civilisation by deciphering linear B, the following works came to light: V. Ehrenberg's *l'Etat grec* in 1957 (translated from German in 1976), H. Van Effenterre's, *La cité grecque des origines à la défaite de Marathon* (Paris 1985) and O. Murray's and S. Price's *La cité grecque d'Homère à Alexandre* (Oxford 1990), translated into French in 1992. All these works handled the issue essentially from the institutional and political perspectives. However, from the 1970s onwards, a new approach developed, following the findings of Pierre Vernant and Pierre Vidal-Naquet. Led by the researchers at the Louis Gernet Centre in Paris, it focused once more on the religious aspects of the City.

One work marked the result of these findings, François de Polignac's *La Naissance de la cité grecque*, published in 1984, republished and updated in 1995. It is not a return to Fustel de Coulanges' questioning, as these new findings owe much to the development of archaeological research, particularly in sanctuaries, which has renewed knowledge of the subject considerably, and shown the role played by sanctuaries in progressively structuring the civic space of early cities while at the same time integrating the members of the future civic community. Consequently, F. de Polignac was able to define the city as being a cult group, demonstrating that participation in religious festivals allowed early Greek societies to acquire their community coherence and define a primitive form of citizenship by structuring a space that was at the same time political and religious.

A word must be said about the spectacular development of archaeological science in the second half of the 20th century, because this phenomenon had important consequences for historiographical policies in all countries, particularly East-European countries that had, during this period, created archaeological institutes with considerable funding, on the condition that they contributed to the construction of the national identity. Many archaeological excavation and exploration programmes were launched which, when the publications were completed, gave the scientific community access to a considerable amount of new information. On the other side of the world, the United States was not to be outdone, and gave preference to chronological and typological study conditioned by a strong historio-culturalist tradition. At the end of the 1960s, L. Binford, professor at Chicago University, launched what was to become "new archaeology", emulating natural sciences. Using an anthropological rather than sociological approach, he attempted to form archaeology into an autonomous science capable of constructing its own rules and scientifically validating its results. This dimension was reinforced in the second half of the 20th century by the progress of archaeometry which, with its notably more sophisticated dating methods, was far more reliable than typological classifications and the advance of environmental studies. Despite the numerous debates between the advocates of contextual archaeology and those of processual and post-processual archaeology, archaeology became firmly established as a method of exploration of the past. This was a recognition of the pioneering work of Goldon Childe who, through a functionalist approach, was one of the first in Great Britain to propose a sociological and anthropological interpretation of Prehistory (*The Dawn of European Civilization*, 1929).

Progress in our knowledge of ancient history therefore depends a lot on the data obtained from archaeological excavations. At the same time, the attention given to physical traces favours a much more social vision. In this way, religion is no longer examined only from the angle of mythology or beliefs. It is also determined through the relics left by the men who practised it, and these religious practices in Greek cities were observed in public spaces created and reshaped by constantly evolving social structures. Among these practices, territorial distribution by the founder, at the time the settlement started, was a pivotal event which can be located by archaeological excavations, aerial photography or various searching techniques. In this way, the study of how space was allocated, taking into consideration the gods who received their *temenos* (sanctuary) and the men who received their *kleros* (the pieces of land allotted to the settlers), contributes to a very rational conception of the establishment of sanctuaries: the planning implemented by the founder immediately determined the arrangement between private and public spaces, assigned or reserved, with no regard for any sacred or emotional value attributed to a site (spring, rock marked by lightning, cave, river mouths, etc). The danger of such an approach is that the city appears to have come ready-made from the head of its founder, because it is only the progressive realisation of a preconceived, virtual and largely deterministic programme.

Even so, colonial cities, because they were new, are today a privileged field of observation for the study of these phenomena. They gave rise to a normative and assertive urbanistic policy, since settlers felt free to organise the space as they wished. Moreover, a colonial community was always a nascent community because of the very fact that the city was to be built. The original nucleus of colonists rarely represented more than two hundred men, and it therefore took several generations for the initial encampment to become a city and for the group of pioneers to become an urban community. Often from different hometowns, the colonists brought various traditions as well as religions specific to each of them. They had to then live together, honour the same poliad deities and participate in the same celebrations established by the city calendar. Such osmosis was not automatic, and through the slow evolutions identified by archaeology, it is possible for the historian to trace the formative stages of the social body. Chronology must also be taken into account. The earliest Greek colonial foundations came to light around the 8th century B.C. At that time, the major cities were still very young and still in development. The colonial phenomenon was itself a sign that this development was a difficult process, leading to segregation and exclusion. As a result, settlers did not reach their new territory with a ready-made, pre-established model. In this sense, colonial cities are a social laboratory worth observing.

Such a case was Megara Hyblaea, established on the eastern coast of Sicily, about thirty kilometres north of Syracuse (Fig. 1). According to Thucydides' chronology, which followed the tradition of the Syracusan historian Antiochus, it was founded in 728 B.C., a little after Syracuse and Leontini[1]. This foundation was completed at the end of a difficult process, mingling Greeks of different origins (Chalcidians from the island of

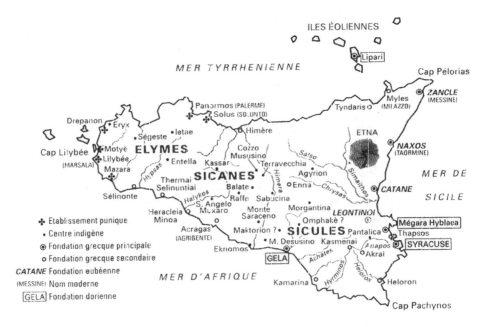

Fig. 1
Map of Sicily (from J.-L. Lamboley, *Les Grecs d'Occident*, Paris 1996).

Euboea, and other Ionians and Dorians, including some Megareans.). After a short stay in a port called Trotilon, located at a river mouth, the Megareans went to live with the Chalcidians from Leontini in a city a little further inland. They were later driven out by the Chalcidians and settled on the coast of Thapsos, where they were also chased away, very probably by the Dorians from Syracuse, who did not appreciate their being in such close proximity. Finally they were received by a native king, Hyblon, who gave them the territory where the city was founded, which subsequently took the name of Megara Hyblaea, a toponym evoking both the home town and the local setting. Literary sources also preserve the name of the founding father – Lamis, who died at Thapsos.

The idea that each colony was founded by a homogenous group of settlers from the same homeland is a fantasy, fashioned after recent European colonisations. In reality, the settlements were of a composite character with a multi-cultural dimension. It always ended, however, with the emergence of a dominant group, usually well-identified through the person of the founding father. In the case of Megara Hyblaea, with Lamis, there was definitely a specific Megarean contribution.

Archaeological data on the site is abundant following regular campaigns led by the French School in Rome since 1949, firstly with Fr. Villard and G. Vallet, and then with M. Gras and H. Tréziny, and the participation of architects Paul Auberson and Henri Broise. Their recent publication, dedicated to the ancient town, attempts to review and formulate hypotheses as to how the civic community coalesced from primitive nuclei and their religious traditions.

Traces of places of worship or sanctuaries are easily visible on the map (Fig. 2). One cluster is located in the north-west zone, with several votive offerings consisting of terracotta lamps and female statues (nos. 13 and 14). In the same area, there is the large sanctuary housing two temples, numbered 9 and 10, which has functioned since the origin of the city[2]. This sanctuary is situated on the site of an ancient Neolithic village, which may explain why this site was chosen by the settlers, who perhaps wanted to respect a place whose ancient usage was obvious. Another cluster is located to the east in the agora district (Fig. 3), easily identifiable by its trapezoidal form. Its southern side is bordered by two small buildings of worship (temples g and h), datable to the second half of the 7th century. At the north-eastern corner of the agora, building d is identified as a *herôon,* often regarded as the tomb of the founding father. Other buildings, such as building c to the east and building j to the north, seem to have had a religious function. In relation to temples A and B in the north-west zone, the buildings there are of smaller dimensions.

To the east of the city, on the seashore, excavations have unearthed three sanctuaries. One is temple C, to the north-east near the lighthouse, datable to about 570 (Fig. 2, no. 20), while a second is situated to the east, in the overhang of the depression which separates the northern and southern plateaux. Architectonic terracotta found in a well suggests the presence of a building of worship (no. 34). The third is placed to the southeast (no. 24), a sanctuary, active from the end of the 8th century and adorned with a small temple at the end of the 6th century.

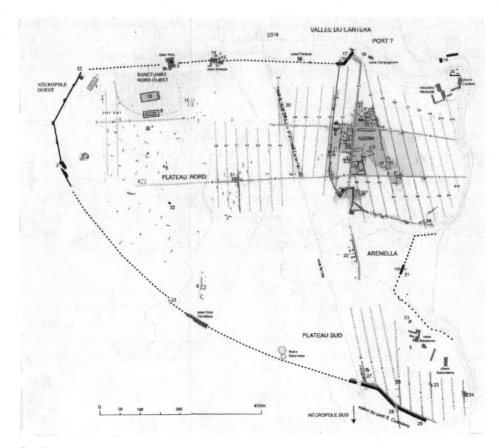

Fig. 2
General map of Megara Hyblaea (from M. Gras - H. Treziny - H. Broise, *Mégara Hyblaea 5. La ville archaïque*, Rome 2004).

To complete the survey, several places of worship discovered in the habitat or its periphery should also be noted. These are temple L to the south east of the agora (datable to the second half of the 7th century), temple K to the north of the agora, the small temple B, built at the end of the 6th century at the crossroad of roads B and E1 (no. 31), and temple E, situated outside of the area to the north of the city (no. 16).

Other important archaeological data relates to the organisation of the city in easily identifiable districts due to the orientation of the streets. To date, five districts have been identified. The agora was situated at the junction of two districts organised around the network of roads D and C, roads C1 and D1 converging where the northern gate of the city, or Marine gate, used to stand (Fig. 3). The small temple B (no. 31) is situated in the third district where E roads were oriented roughly north/south, an orientation similar to the large north-eastern sanctuary district. Finally, the southern gate (no. 28) is the nodal point between two different orientations, defined by roads 24, 25, and 26 to the east of the gate, and by roads 22 and 27 to the west.

It is interesting to note that these five districts may reflect the five primitive villages that formed the city. One of Plutarch's texts indicates that the Megareans lived in villages, and that the citizens were grouped into five sectors called Heraeis, Piraeis, Megaries, Kynosoureis and Triposiskoi[3]. From that, it is tempting to see, in the five districts of Megara, the duplication, within a smaller area, of the synoecism of the home town. However, caution should prevail as new excavations may bring new orientations and new districts to light. Nevertheless, it is still true that areas of worship were distributed

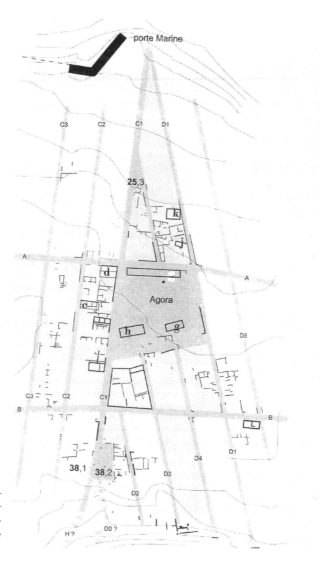

Fig. 3
Map of the agora of Megara Hy-
blaea (from G. Vallet - F. Villard -
P. Auberson, *Megara Hyblaea 1.
Le quartier de l'agora archaïque*,
Rome 1976).

Religious Communities and Urban Communities

among the districts and thereby constituted centripetal hubs from which urban space was structured. At the same time, the space reserved for the agora could convey the intention to create a civic space, also centripetal, competing with the autonomy of each district and symbolising the unity of the community of the new colony. The trapezoidal form of the agora, which was in no way influenced by terrain, has intrigued researchers. If we consider that it was formed by four main avenues, two of which converged at the Marine Gate, we observe that the intersections formed five points that could each symbolise the village of origin, if one concedes that the contingent of settlers reflected the metropolitan social structure from which the synoecism of five villages[4] came. As a result, the civic community of the new colony was structured gradually by tension between two antagonistic tendencies. Firstly, a family framework focused in the districts around areas of worship which can be linked to the phratries, which maintained the ancestral traditions of different groups of population from the home town, and secondly, the development of collective places of worship that cemented the new community in two public spaces that were reserved from the beginning. These were the poliad sanctuary and the agora. It is therefore men that make the city, and not walls, as Thucydides has Nicias say[5]. This structuring process was gradual, as the settlers, having different origins, did not arrive with a ready-made city pattern. Further to F. de Polignac's analysis one can propose a three-stage evolution[6].

1. From foundation until about the third quarter of the 7th century, peripheral sanctuaries designed like a crown of worship around the city prevailed, as was the case at Agrigento. At the same time, all over the city, there were more family-oriented places of worship, probably creating or reinforcing social relations within the districts.

This structure was still fragmented and undifferentiated, representing a composite society on a coalescing curve. Each district would have been provided with a central square of its own, and a specific sanctuary on its periphery. None of the religious spaces, even reserved spaces, played a cementing role in the civic community. So, during that period, the area reserved for the agora did not have any area of worship and no collective necropolis was offered outside the walls.

2. From the last third of the 7th century until about 580, the organisation was more centred. On one hand, there was the large north-east sanctuary, where the temple of the poliad deity was probably situated, and on the other hand, there was the agora and its different buildings of worship. The two constitutive hubs of any Greek city were formed this way, with monumental developments corresponding to the real urban planning of the city. This is when the *héröon* was erected in the north-eastern angle of the agora (building d), on the main road linking the agora to the sanctuary. If it corresponds to the tomb of the founding father, Lamis, more than a century after the settlement, it takes on a symbolic value as the town is only considered as founded when the civic community becomes aware of its own existence. Pausanias also cited at Megara, the hometown, the worship of the *prodomeis*, builder gods that were invoked before beginning construction and who had an altar-home[7]. Considering this from a town-planning perspective, the worship of these deities is entirely logical. It is to be noted that the

hérôon was perfectly integrated into the surface of a *kleros*, which was the smallest urban unit. There is a symbolic dimension which made this building the very expression of foundation at the time of the new organisation of the city, whether it was the cenotaph of the Founding Father or a *hérôon* of the builder gods.

3. The third and final phase was particularly characterised by the renovation of the orbital section of worship of the first phase. The entire northern part of the city shows clear evidence of the construction of much larger, monumental places of worship, such as temple A in the north-east sanctuary, and the temple in the lighthouse zone. The southern area, which is also the least explored, does not seem to have experienced this evolution. Small family places of worship, scattered in the habitat, also disappeared. These forms of worship, too strongly associated with a disconnected social organisation, were abandoned or absorbed by new forms of worship of a more civic nature.

The geometric division of the land, with allotments to settlers on arrival, must therefore not delude us. It did not create *ipso facto* a real urban unit. At first, the colonial society was still fragmented, and the settlement seemed more like the scale model of a synoecism, establishing equilibrium between the diversity of the components and the unity of the civic body. The different groups of founders remained quite autonomous, and the institutions necessary for running the community were not located in specific buildings in prestigious parts of the city. This urban pattern reflects, on a small scale, a system that must be quite close to that of *ethnè* federations, which was the social organisation of the Greeks before the City-State. From the beginning, the unity of this new society had to lie in the desire to live together, and having agreed to share the same destiny overseas. It takes at least three to four generations to see the creation of a true urban unit accompanying the construction of much larger, monumental places of worship and public spaces like the agora. This evolution enables us to assess the role played by religion and the distribution of sacred areas. Worship was not established once and for all, because its operation depended on the historical context. The poliad divinities only appeared progressively, and probably did not erase the original religions of early family solidarity. However, if there had not been the idea of a single urban network in the early stages of the settlement, the civic community may not have emerged at all. This is where one can best measure the originality and the richness of the Greek colonial experience.

We can therefore speak of a double foundation of the city. The first phase was on the settlers' arrival, sharing the land by equal distribution of lots to create an urban space that was both polycentric, with districts centred around their own areas of worship, and unitary, with an undeveloped space reserved for the agora. The second phase saw the genesis of the civic community. Family cults in the districts disappeared before the civic cults that materialised with the construction of temples gathered within two urban hubs connected by the main thoroughfare of the city, between the agora and the poliad deities' sanctuary. In both phases, religion played a crucial role because it was the constitutive element of identity, and therefore the binding catalyst. However, this religion evolved notably, and paradoxically, towards some sort of secularisation, changing from private family cults to public civic cults, and when the public trend towards the construction of much larger, monumental places of worship became visible, then one can say that the City-State was born. From the geometric foundation of the town to the genesis of the city, archaeology reveals to what extent sanctuaries remain privileged markers of social evolution.

The same idea is confirmed on reading literary sources, even though archaeological data is lacking. This is the case in the example of Marseille, a Phocaean colony founded in 600 B.C. The presence of the first French port on the site makes it very difficult to explore the city, which has to face all the problems of urban archaeology. There is no available map of the colony at its foundation, but the account of the geographer Strabo allows us to assess the importance of the religious element. This is how he describes the city:

> The town of Massalia is a Phocaean settlement. It occupies a rocky terrain and its port lies at the foot of a theatre-like cliff oriented towards the south, and is fortified with solid ramparts, as is the town. In the acropolis stand the Ephesium and the shrine of Apollo Delphinius. Worshipping this Apollo is common to all Ionians, while the Ephesium is the temple of Artemis, only revered at Ephesus. Indeed, they say that at the time when the Phocaeans left the shores of their homeland, an oracle told them to take the guide that they would receive from Artemis of Ephesus as head of their expedition. Having therefore set sail for Ephesus, they tried to find the guide prescribed by the goddess. Aristarcha, one of the most highly regarded women in this village, saw the goddess standing before her in a dream and ordering her to sail with the Phocaeans, taking a scale model of the shrine with her. She did so, and when the settlers reached their destination, they built the shrine and awarded Aristarcha the highest honour by making her priestess. In all the colonies of Marseille, Artemis is worshipped above all other divinities and her statue is shown in the same posture and worshipped with the same rituals as those observed in the hometown[8].

The poliad divinities of Marseille are clearly identified as Artemis and Apollo, who have their temple in the acropolis of the town, which was quite normal. However, Strabo's commentary points out that these divinities did not belong to Phocaea. That is surprising because settlers usually took the religion of their mother city with them. The rest of the text, which evidently had an aetiological function, gives the reason for this exception. The Phocaeans did not choose a Founding Father from among themselves. On the advice of an oracle, they stopped off at Ephesus, a little further south of Phocaea on the Ionian coast of Asia Minor , where a woman asked them to take the cult of Artemis of Ephesus with them. It is therefore a woman who, in a way, became the Founding *Mother* of the colony, a rare feat, and the only known case of a female guide on a colonial expedition. As a matter of fact, the impression is given that the goddess is the real founder of the city of Marseille, as the first act of the settlers was to erect the shrine devoted to her. As the shrine at Ephesus only had priestesses in the service of the goddess, it was normal that a woman should ensure the continuity of the cult at the other end of the Mediterranean. This importance of Artemis' worship at Marseille is also confirmed by the coinage chosen in the city, namely, the effigy of the goddess. Strabo's text does not tell us why the Massalians also chose to honour

Apollo Delphinius, but the author takes care to point out that this was not a deity exclusive to Phocaea, but rather a deity common to all Ionians living in Asia Minor and which originated in Miletus.

It is therefore clear that the identity of the Phocaean colony was not defined from the identity of the home city. Rather, the Ionian dimension is emphasized, an ethnic region much larger than one City. If this Artemis is that of Ephesus, her shrine, which in the Hellenistic age housed a temple that was one of the Seven Wonders of the World, knew greater fame than the city of Ephesus itself. All the Ionian peoples, and even the rest of Greece, went on pilgrimage to Ephesus to honour the deity, explaining the amazing wealth of this shrine, the most well-known in all Asia Minor, as the legend has it that when the Ionian peoples arrived, it was the town of Ephesus that welcomed Androcles, son of Codros, archegete of the Ionians.

It becomes clear that the Phocaean settlers wanted their city to have the image of an Ionian city, where any Ionian would feel at home in finding the two religions most important to him, rather than that of a strictly Phocaean colony. It must be remembered that Marseille is a port, and that the colony therefore had an essentially commercial vocation. Its wealth was not so much based on the exploitation of a territory, which remained limited for a long time, but on profits gained from commerce, and it was therefore vital for the new settlement to attract Greek merchants, especially in an era when the Persian conquest forced many populations from Asia Minor into exile. The position of a town completely isolated in a barbarian country far from any other Greek city can also explain the choice of Artemis who, in her very ancient Panhellenic dimension, was the deity of extremities on the borders between the savage world and the civilised world, and therefore the deity in the best position to manage relations between Greeks and Barbarians, as well as the situation of refugees, foreigners and supplicants. Major ports developed a population that was in general more cosmopolitan than the cities inland, as is still the case of Marseille today, and that enables us to understand the choice of titular deities likely to welcome strangers, for the proper integration of different elements of the population. Artemis of Ephesus and Apollo Delphinius fully met this need, and Strabo was quite aware that such was the secret of Marseille's success.

From Megara Hyblaea in Sicily to Marseille in Celtic country, through archaeological remains as well as literary accounts, we assess the importance of the religious dimension in the genesis of a Greek civic community. The evolution of sacred spaces enables the observer to follow the evolution of a nascent society, and when such religious spaces undergo the construction of much larger, monumental places of worship, it is proof that a City-State has come to full maturity. In conclusion, we can recall the reflections of F. de Polignac in his very innovative work on the Greek city: "What we call *polis* is the result of a progressive or rapid installation of social and hierarchical cohesions taking the form of a quest for harmony when choosing the mediatory religions, and the rituals defining a religious citizenship"[9].

Notes

* L'intégralité du texte en français est disponible sur le site: http://web.upmf-grenoble.fr/SH/Perso-Hist/Lamboley/Lamboley.html/. La traduction a été réalisée par Mme Hutchinson que je remercie personnellement.

1   Thucydides VI, 3-4. Information on the foundation of Megara Hyblaea is also available from other authors: Strabo VI, 1, 12 and VI, 2, 2 (Strabo, who cited Ephorus of Cyme, places the foundation of Megara before that of Syracuse); Pseudo-Scymnus v. 270-282 (the author underlines the predominance of the Ionian element over the Dorian element; Polyaenus V, 5, 1-2 (this is the author that gives the most details on the Megarean sojourn at Leontini and the manner in which they were driven out. He gives quite a negative image of the Chalcidians). The information is often contradictory and prevents the reconstitution of a single, coherent story. It is explained by the fact that these different colonies were founded in a very short period and were rivals from the beginning, which gave birth to partisan local traditions.

2   Temple no. 10, or temple B, is the oldest, and seems to have been consecrated to a female divinity (Artemis, Hyblaea or Hera). Temple no. 9, or temple A, constructed around the 7th century, corresponds to the construction of much larger, monumental places of worship in a religion that was only secondary at the beginning. The centre of the sanctuary remains marked by the location of temple B.

3   Plutarch, *Questions grecques* 17 = *Moralia* 295b.

4   See J. Svenbro, *A Mégara Hyblaea: Le Corps Géomètre*, "Annales ESC", 37, 1982 p. 953-964. The author remarks that while creating a unified city, this organisation of space into five distinct districts grouped around the agora respected the social organisation of the Megarean society.

5   Thucydides, VII, 77, 7.

6   F. de Polignac, *L'installation des dieux et la genèse des cités en Grèce d'Occident, une question résolue? Retour à Mégara Hyblaea*, in *La colonisation grecque en Méditeranée occidentale*, Coll. EFR 251, Rome 1999, p. 209-229.

7   Pausanias I, 42, 1.

8   Strabo, IV, 1, 4.

9   F. de Polignac, *La naissance de la cité grecque*, Paris 1995, p. 148.

Bibliography

Gras M. - Tréziny H. - Broise H., *Mégara Hyblaea 5. La ville archaïque*, Rome 2004.

Polignac de F., *La naissance de la cité grecque,* Paris 1995.

Polignac de F., *L'installation des dieux et la genèse des cités en Grèce d'Occident, une question résolue? Retour à Mégara Hyblaea*, in *La colonisation grecque en Méditerranée occidentale*, Coll. EFR 251, Rome 1999, pp. 209-229.

Vallet G., *Topographie historique de Mégara Hyblaea et problèmes d'urbanisme colonial*, "MEFRA", 95, 1983, pp. 641-647.

Vallet G. - Villard F. - Auberson P., *Mégara Hyblaea 3. Guide des fouilles*, Rome 1983.

Svenbro J., *A Mégara Hyblaea: le corps géometre*, in "Annales ESC", 37, 1982, pp. 953-964.

Mendicant Orders and Urban Life in the Middle Ages: the Franciscans. Aspects of German Historiography since World War II

DIETER BERG
University of Hannover

Die folgende Skizze verdeutlicht einerseits die Entwicklung der Franziskanerforschung nach 1945 auf institutioneller Ebene mit den wichtigsten Forschungseinrichtungen – von der Duns-Skotus-Akademie in Mönchengladbach bis zur „Forschungsstelle für Vergleichende Ordensforschung" in Eichstätt-Ingolstadt. Andererseits werden „Haupttrends" in der deutschen Mendikantenforschung aufgezeigt, die sich nach Krieg und Verfolgung durch die Nationalsozialisten zuerst der Grundlagenforschung zuwandte, die vorrangig das „Quellenfundament" einer zeitgemäßen „vita minorum" unter Rückgriff auf die frühesten Zeugnisse franziskanischen Lebens zu sichern suchte (mit Neuedition der Gründerschriften und Klärung der „Franziskanischen Frage"). Die bedeutendsten deutschen Franziskanerforscher aus dem Orden erwarben sich hierbei bleibende Verdienste, obwohl seit ca. 1980 die Grundlagenforschung zunehmend durch die italienische Mediävistik bestimmt wurde. Hinzu kam, daß sich seit Ende der 70er Jahre verstärkt „weltliche" Gelehrte in Deutschland mit Problemen der Ordensgeschichte beschäftigten und unter dem Einfluß der französischen Geschichtswissenschaft („Annales") andere und neue thematische Schwerpunkte entwickelten. Jüngere Forschergenerationen wandten sich intensiver modernen wirtschafts- und sozialwissenschaftlichen Themen zu, wobei sich die politische Spaltung Deutschlands mitunter in starken ideologischen Belastungen auch in den Studien zur Ordensgeschichte auswirkte. Seit den späten 70er Jahren beschäftigte man sich einerseits mit der „Mikrohistorie" einzelner Franziskanerkonvente und mit der Komplexität franziskanischen Wirkens in der jeweiligen Stadt; andererseits widmete man sich zunehmend der Mentalitätsgeschichte und der Historie der franziskanischen Bewegung im weiteren politischen und gesellschaftlichen Kontext von Städten und Territorien. Aus der Vielzahl an Detailstudien werden daher im Folgenden lediglich einzelne, als paradigmatisch zu betrachtende Einzeluntersuchungen vorgestellt.

PRELIMINARY REMARK*

This chapter will try to examine the essential features of historical research on the history of the Order of the Franciscans after the end of the Second World War, and especially the relationship between the Mendicants and citizenry, with regard to a historical research inventory for the geographical area of today's Republic of Germany. As the field of research "Mendicants and City" cannot be studied in isolation, the major tendencies of the development of Mendicant historical research will be outlined with respect to sources and basic research. As a result, the field of research of "Franciscans and Citizenry" can be documented in detail. In the first part, reference will be made to general literature and manuals in which the problem is mentioned, as well as monographs of the history of certain monasteries which directly address the problem area. Due to the vast numbers of different studies, only a representative choice of works will be presented. In the second part, the most important aspects, such as the history of the monasteries or special studies on certain topics, will be used to explain the major conventions of communication between the Franciscans and the citizens in the urban area.

IMPORTANT RESEARCH INSTITUTIONS IN EUROPE AND GERMANY IN PARTICULAR

The devastating occurrences of the Second World War inevitably had an impact on academic life both inside and outside the Order of the Franciscans. No major institution in the academic field worked just as an internal research and educational institution of the Order. The only two traditional research institutions of the community of the Franciscans in Europe that had supranational relevance and continued working were in Italy, and they tried to continue Franciscan research during the time of rapid rebuilding after the war. These two bodies were the Franciscan research institution near Florence and the University of Rome belonging to the Order of the Franciscans. Both institutions had been founded by the General Minister Bernardino dal Vago da Portogruaro in the 19th century. The "Collegio San Bonaventura", founded in 1877 in Quaracchi near Florence and transferred to Grottaferrata near Rome in 1971, was followed by the "Collegium S. Antonii Patavini in Urbe", which was used by the community of the Franciscans for an internal "studium generale" and renamed "Athenaeum Antonianum de Urbe" in 1938, and again in 2005, becoming "Pontificia Università Antonianum". Up to the present day, both institutions have dedicated themselves to the publication of Franciscan sources as well as to the research of the history of the several branches of the Franciscan family along with the updating of Franciscan thought[1].

Due to intensive rebuilding after the destruction of the Second World War, it was possible to re-establish the internal studies of the Order in the provinces of the Franciscans at the beginning of the 1950s. This happened in the province of Cologne and Saxony by way of founding centres of study in Paderborn, Münster and Mönchengladbach. An intensification of the pursuit of Franciscan history and theology was experienced by the "Duns-Skotus-Akademie" in Mönchengladbach at the beginning of the 1960s, and from 1968, in the inter-provincial academy of German-speaking Franciscans and the Rheinisch-Westfälische Province of the Capuchins. It was in these two research and educational institutions that the most famous German Franciscan scholars of their time worked, mainly shaping the development of research about the Order. In 1970, the "Institut für vergleichende Städtegeschichte" was founded by the "profane side". This institution examined the history of European cities, and in this context looked at the role of the Mendicants in German cities in an interdisciplinary and comparative way[2]. Since 1975, similar aims have been followed by Kaspar Elm at the Freie Universität Berlin when founding a major research field "Vergleichende Ordensforschung", and the publication of "Berliner Ordensstudien" within the "Berliner Historische Studien". This series of monographs is rich in material and contains important contributions to the history of the relationship between the Mendicants and the cities in the Middle Ages[3].

In 1988, the management of the Franciscan Province of Saxony decided to found its own research institution. Its objective was to document completely the history of the province in the context of the history of the whole Order, as well as the history of the cities and the country examined in its geopolitical areas. This task is being carried out by Dieter Berg at the "Institut für franziskanische Geschichte (Saxonia)", and, apart from editing several research series, the Institute has begun to publish the first complete portrayal of the history of the German Franciscan Province from the 13th to the end of the 20th century[4]. Then in the late 1990s, the "Deutsche Forschungsgemeinschaft" decided to establish a special research field "Institutionalität und Geschichtlichkeit", and within this a research project called "Institutionelle Strukturen religiöser Orden im Mittelalter" at the University of Dresden. Led by Gert Melville, this project is devoted to the investigation of institutional structures of religious orders in the Middle Ages within a range of comparative problems, the main one being the Mendicants and their role within German cities during the Middle Ages[5]. Since July 2005, these activities have been expanded through the creation of the "Forschungsstelle für Vergleichende Ordensgeschichte" at the University of Eichstätt-Ingolstadt. This research institution, which is mainly supported by the "Stifterverband für die Deutsche Wissenschaft", regards itself as a centre for coordination of international research of the Orders, striving to obtain a comparative analysis of the history of certain Orders with the inclusion of relevant partner science[6].

BASIC FRANCISCAN RESEARCH UNTIL CA. 1980

Publication of the Works of Francis of Assisi

The serious destabilisation of the Order of the Franciscans brought about by the Second World War and the National Socialist dictatorship of terror[7] led to a renewed compilation of the central aspects of Franciscan life. As on many occasions, the Order again faced the question about a modern shaping of the "vita minorum", this time from amongst the post-war rubble. The decision of many German Franciscans not only to find new ways to shape the life of the Order, but also to realise them, was typical of their determination. They decided on a new fundamental orientation through dedication to the very sources of the Order, especially to the rules of the community. In 1955, a working group led by Lothar Hardick published the *Werkbuch zur Regel des Hl. Franziskus*[8] with the support of the General Minister Augustin Sépinski. This work helped the

Franciscan brothers because of its thorough study and orientation. On the one hand it held important interpretative elements about the *Inhalt der Regel und die Ideale der Frühe* [Contents of the rule and the ideals of the early period], while on the other hand it contained a programme of the new academic edition of the Franciscan set of rules and regulations. Later, Lothar Hardick, David Ethelbert Flood[9], Engelbert Grau, and especially Kajetan Eßer devoted themselves to studies of the history of tradition and the critical edition of the works of the founder of the Order with particular emphasis on the early Franciscan rules. Their importance as the norm for the spiritual work a member of the Franciscan Order had to undertake in the 20th century was constantly emphasised[10]. After approximately 20 years of work, in 1976, Kajetan Eßer was able to publish a critical edition of the *Opuscula* of Francis of Assisi. This was followed by a revised text edition by Engelbert Grau in 1989[11]. Despite the objections which were made against Eßer's principles of editing and textual revision, a solid editorial basis had been established for the basic works of the Order of the Franciscans[12].

German Translations of Early Franciscan Works

Apart from the attempts to create a secure basis of the most important normative sources of the early Order of the Franciscans, the researchers mentioned above realised the necessity of allowing access to a broader public, and had the major Franciscan sources translated. Owing to the striving for a spiritual renewal, the important series of "Franziskanische Quellenschriften" was published. Mainly shaped by Lothar Hardick[13] and Engelbert Grau, this series not only tried to present the most important early Franciscan writings using a current translation, but also to experience the *Geist des Ordensstifters* [Spirit of the founder] and to respond to the challenges of modern times[14]. The objective was not so much the presentation of new research to a broad public, but more an introduction to Franciscan spirituality. Several annotated translations of early Franciscan sources served for this purpose, such as the vita of Aegidius of Assisi, the writings of Saint Antonius of Padua, the chronicles of foundations of Jordan of Giano and Thomas of Eccleston and the vita about Saint Francis of Saint Bonaventura and of Julian of Speyer – a publishing project which proved to be very successful[15]. Since the millennium, most of the texts of this ten volume series have served as the basis for the concept of a complete work of modern translations in German of all early Franciscan sources, which at the same time tried to allow access to Franciscan thought by a broader public[16].

Studies of Manuscript Tradition for Early Franciscan Historiography

A consequence of the new edition of the early Franciscan sources, including the sources of historiography, was the necessity for the German researchers to become intensively occupied with the *Franziskanische Frage* [Franciscan Question]. Since the publication of a critical biography of Saint Francis by Paul Sabatier in 1894[17], the aim had been to reveal the mutual dependence and the ties to specific times of the early sources of Franciscan historiography. As the historiography of the Order had been an important medium for the documentation of "true" Franciscan life since the early times, the official and critical works of Franciscan historiography played a key-role in the understanding of the history of the Mendicant communities until the late 14th century[18]. After decades of fruitless discussion between European researchers about the origin and objectives of the most important early Franciscan sources, the leading German researchers turned to the *Franziskanische Frage* [Franciscan Question] – problems concerning the history of manuscript tradition. Apart from Kajetan Eßer, it was mainly Sophronius Clasen and, after his death, Engelbert Grau who developed their own new system pertaining to the tradition of early Franciscan sources, following extensive studies into the manuscript tradition[19]. However, their conceptualised theories of manuscript tradition only received attention in German-speaking countries. After the death of Engelbert Grau († 1998), this discussion reached its temporary end in Germany, mainly due to basic research done by Italian scholars since the middle of the 1990s. Beginning with the 1970s, German research outside the Order on the studies of Franciscan historiography concentrated mainly on the questions of concept and mentality. This brought the community of the Mendicants closer in context to the changes of the Church and society of that time[20].

CITIZENRY AND THE ORDER OF THE FRANCISCANS IN HANDBOOKS OF GENERAL HISTORY ABOUT THE CHURCH AND THE ORDERS

The most important handbooks of ecclesiastical history and the history of the Orders focused on the Mendicants in cities during the Middle Ages, at least at a fundamental level. The huge and multi-volume ecclesiastical history works such as *Kirchengeschichte Deutschlands* by A. Hauck, *Handbuch der Kirchengeschichte* by H. Jedin, and *Geschichte des Christentums* in the High and Late Middle Ages by N. Brox, together with smaller presentations such as the ecclesiastical history by K. Bihlmeyer and H. Tüchle and the handbook of *Kirche in ihrer Geschichte* edited by K.D. Schmidt and E. Wolf, as well as encyclopaedic works about the medieval church by M. Borgolte and I.W. Frank, for example, documented the work of the Franciscans[21]. There are also monographs about the history of the Orders in the Middle Ages published by, among others, L. Holtz, L. Iriarte and J.R.H. Moorman, which appeared after the basic works of H. Holzapfel and M. Heimbucher[22]. Works covering several epochs of the history of certain regions or historical areas and their ecclesiastical history are also informative. Amongst these are studies about the history of the church in Westfalia by A. Schröer and the ecclesiastical history of Lower Saxony by H.-W. Krumwiede[23]. The vast collection of works "Germania Sacra" about the history of German bishoprics in the Middle Ages up to modern times, which was first published by P.F. Kehr from 1929 to 1944 and since 1956 by the Max-Planck-Institute for History in Göttingen, is also to be considered, as it gives information about the history of certain Franciscan monasteries[24]. Also to be taken into account are some volumes of the "Helvetia Sacra" which hold information about the history of the Mendicants in Switzerland[25]. Finally, one must not forget the regional "Klosterbücher", which contain information about spiritual institutions in certain regions and also about the relevant monasteries of the Franciscans. Some examples are the *Schleswig-Holsteinisches Klosterbuch*, the *Hessisches Klosterbuch*, the *Westfälisches Klosterbuch*, the *Württembergisches Klosterbuch* and the *Brandenburgisches Klosterbuch* (to be published). As these works are like handbooks, they are very informative and often contain important hints about the functions of the Mendicants in the urban world[26].

CITIES AND FRANCISCANS IN MONOGRAPHS OF CERTAIN PROVINCES OR REGIONS

The portrayals of the history of the Mendicant monasteries, mainly published by members of the Order of the Franciscans, within the provinces or a certain territory, are often richer in material than the regional descriptions mentioned above. Since the 19th century, Franciscan historians have concentrated primarily on the documentation of the history of their own province. Such studies are represented by K. Eubel about the "Oberdeutsche Minoriten-Provinz", R. Banasch on the monasteries of the Franciscans between the Weser and the Elbe, P. Schlager and K. Eubel on the province of Cologne, L. Lemmens and H. Hoogeweg on the Franciscan monasteries in the "Provincia Saxonia" (Lower Saxony), one by F. Jansen about the development of the province of Thüringen and one about Silesia by L. Teichmann. Although they are quite old, most of these works are still helpful today, especially because of their rich sources of material which has since been partly lost or destroyed[27]. After the Second World War, some Provinces continued this preoccupation with their own history and created large series of publications such as "Alemania Franciscana Antiqua" and "Bavaria Franciscana Antiqua". These document the history of the Provinces in a non-structured series of smaller monographs about single monasteries. Furthermore, these histories of the monasteries examine major aspects of Franciscan life in certain cities, thereby investigating the often intensive and fruitful cooperation between the Mendicants and the citizens. Later questions about the history of social matters or the history of mentality are often missing from these works which focus mainly on the chronology of events. However, they can be very useful as collections of material[28]. The series "Saxonia Franciscana" takes these later aspects of research into account. Apart from monographs about certain Franciscan monasteries in the area of the former "Provincia Saxonia", it includes investigations pursuing systematic and comparative research regarding the entire history of Saxonia and the relationship between the city and the Mendicants[29].

Since the 1980s, external authors, not belonging to the Order of the Franciscans, have turned towards the investigation of the history of certain provinces of the Franciscans. Such works include those by D. Berg and R. Nickel about the Franciscans in Westfalia, G. Streich about the Mendicant monasteries in Lower Saxony, H.J. Schmidt about monasteries in Brandenburg und Hessen, T. Berger about the Mendicants in the archbishopric of Mainz, L. Teichmann about the medieval Franciscan monasteries in middle and eastern Germany, M. Werner about the Mendicants in Thüringen, I. Ulpts about the Mendicants in Mecklenburg, A. Rüther about the Franciscans in Alsace, and B. Schmies and K. Rakemann about the "Provincia Saxonia". All the works mentioned above mostly examine several monasteries and document the efficiency of the Mendicants in a certain region based on the rich local sources of material[30].

CITIES AND FRANCISCANS IN MONOGRAPH STUDIES ABOUT SINGLE MONASTERIES

Since the end of the 1960s, non-Franciscan research in particular has devoted itself to the question regarding the position of the Mendicants in the medieval cities of the German Reich. While B.E.J. Stüdeli investigated the position of the Mendicants in the public life of the medieval city, and J.B. Freed the role of the Mendicant orders in society in several provinces, K. Elm published a series of important works about the position and efficiency of the Mendicant orders in urban society. Works on the sociology of the cities were added, for example, A. Herzig's report about the Mendicants and the ecclesiastical politics of the cities[31]. The publication of works concerning conflict and cooperation between the Franciscans and the citizenry was intensified at the beginning of the 1980s. Very often an attempt at comparative research was made, comparing different German cities[32]. A clear attempt at comparative research can be detected in certain monographs about certain Franciscan monasteries in German cities, and since the beginning of the 1980s the number of publications has increased. However, these have been more extensive in material as they have been based on case studies. In these investigations, whose number is too vast to allow mention of all the titles, all major aspects of Franciscan work in the cities or communities as well as conflicts and cooperation between the Mendicants and the citizenry are examined[33].

STUDIES ABOUT THE ROLE OF THE FRANCISCANS IN CERTAIN GERMAN CITIES IN DETAILED SURVEYS

Apart from the investigations mentioned above, which mainly document the history in a comparative manner, many monographs or detailed studies about the history of single monasteries examine a multitude of different aspects, although only a few of these can be noted. Many monographs on monasteries extensively described the history of the foundation of the convent. The latter is difficult to explain, as detailed constitutional rules and regulations of the community of the Franciscans are missing[34]. The phenomenon of finding the Mendicant monasteries mainly on the periphery of cities was investigated in the context of urban topography, as well as social status, in the city under examination[35]. Prosopographic research methods were increasingly used, and investigations were made into the personnel, the social background and the family of the "fratres" and their social status within the cities[36].

For a long time, research has paid great attention to the problem of the relationship between the Franciscans and the political authorities within the cities. This has been because of the personal relationships between the Mendicants and the leading community families, particularly those represented on the city councils. These relationships were intensified as a consequence of the strict postulate of poverty of the Order, as the Franciscans were dependent on the participation of the political authorities in the use and management of their properties. Additionally, there were often problems concerning the possession of pensions and donations to the Mendicants. Historical investigations also examined the economic status of the communities. Finally, the Franciscans were involved in riots and political unrest in several German cities, where their postulate of peace and its realisation in communal reality was investigated[37].

A different field of historical research concerns the relationship between the Franciscans and the bishop or the secular clergy of the towns. In the beginning, the Mendicants were welcomed by the leaders of the bishoprics, mainly because they improved the spiritual welfare in the communal centres. However, very soon, and especially as a consequence of intense papal privileges, a fierce rivalry developed between the Mendicants and the secular clergy, the latter seeing the Mendicants as a threat to their own economic income and therefore as annoying rivals. Hardly any city with Mendicant monasteries escaped rivalries or conflicts, which weighed heavily on the communities. Nevertheless, the spiritual welfare of the Franciscans and their activities in delivering sermons are an essential element of historical research because of their relevance to education within German cities[38]. The vast number of works on the importance of the Franciscans with regard to the reformation and the dissolving of Mendicant monasteries in certain cities, makes it impossible to discuss them in this essay. The same is also true for the innumerable monographs and studies on single members of the Orders, whose social and pastoral importance is often acknowledged in a glorifying and less critical way.

SUMMARY

After the war and the persecution of the Mendicants during the era of National Socialism, there was an attempt at renewal by the communities concerned. In German society after 1945, Saint Francis and his message of peace and reconciliation was a particular matter of investigation. This had an impact on German historical research, which sought a new start after the misuse of history by compliant scholars in the time of National Socialism[39]. In particular, German research on the Franciscans tried to resume the direction that it had taken at the beginning of the 20th century. However, this was not a radical change of paradigms, but a turn towards an investigation of the "true Saint Francis". In the first instance, it was an investigation of the objections of his "fraternitas" in the context of religious and social movements of that time, and in the second instance, it was admitted that basic research was needed for the analysis, which in turn required further research on the *Franziskanische Frage* [Franciscan Question]. developed by P. Sabatier in 1894. It mainly concerned the interdependence of early Franciscan historical writing and its credibility. Research also turned to the conceptual and jurisdictional fundamentals of the Order. These were the writings of the founder of the Order and, in particular, the regulations of the community.

Until the 1960s, research on Franciscan history, which had mainly been done by members of the Order, was concerned with the history of the Order in the context of religious development. This changed in about 1970 with the influence of historical research in Western Europe, the works of Jacques Le Goff and the French school of the "Annales" playing a particularly important role in shaping German medieval research[40]. Major research regarding the Mendicants and urbanisation were a role model for several German studies intensively occupied with the role of the Franciscans in the cities, about a decade later. Since approximately 1980, there have been not only the old studies about *Franziskaner und die soziale Frage* [Franciscans and the Social Question], but also the investigations on *Bettelorden und kommunale Entwicklung* [Mendicants and Urban Development], *Mendikanten und städtische Konflikte* [Mendicants and Urban Riots], *Mendikanten und die städtische Wirtschaft* [Mendicants and Urban Economy] and *Bettelorden im religiösen und geistigen Leben der Städte* [Mendicants and the Urban Religious and Intellectual Life]. Naturally, the political division of Germany has had an effect on the many areas of research concerning the Orders, and these areas have changed. For example, the communist historians in the GDR tried to describe the Franciscan movement as part of the class struggle and the early bourgeois revolution[41].

The basic research that had been carried out since the end of the war came to an end around 1980, mainly due to the fact that all the important German Franciscan researchers had died. Since then, research regarding the most important Franciscan sources has been continued primarily by Italians such as the group "Societá di Studi Francescani" (Chairman: Grado Merlo) in Assisi, who published important editions and translations, and the "Centro Interuniversitario di Studi Francescani" in Assisi which was founded later, and supports Franciscan research projects all over Europe. Since 1980 German historians have not played a major role in the field of research on Franciscan sources and manuscripts. However, lots of medievalists within the Federal Republic, though not being members of the Order, have begun to work on aspects of Franciscan history in the context of general social and urban history. Furthermore, broader research about the development of the Mendicants in certain regions of the German Reich has been continued, although this had already been partly done at the beginning of the 20th century, mainly by members of the Order. Newly founded research institutions like the "Institut für franziskanische Geschichte (Saxonia)" in Münster have played a major part in this research. For example, in this institute, sources from archives as well as several monographs about the relationship between the Mendicants and the citizenry of Saxony from the beginning of the Middle Ages until the 20th century, have been systematically collected. Additionally, an increasing number of studies about certain cities and their Mendicant monasteries have been published by secular historians. Communist historians of the GDR were especially interested in the role of the Mendicants in communal revolts and political unrest, identified in cities of Northern Germany from the middle of the 14th century. Most works of German medievalists are concerned with the history of single members of the Mendicant orders, examining such things as their activities in preaching within the cities, their theological relevance and their role within the Order etc.

Bearing in mind the development of German Franciscan research, a general trend in historical science can be established: on the one hand, the specialisation of research regarding certain people or single monasteries, and their social relevance, and on the other hand, the complete retreat from the area of basic research, which has been abandoned in the main to Italian researchers. An exception to this is the translation, currently being prepared, of the most important Franciscan sources, but even here German tardiness has been exposed as these texts have already been translated into the major languages of the world in great number and some time ago.

Notes

* I want to thank Ms Penelope Stonehouse David and Mr Arne Borstelmann for their help with the English translation.

1 *Il Collegio di San Bonaventura Quaracchi. Volume commemorativo del centenario della fondazione (1877-1977)*, "Archivum Franciscanum Historicum", 70, 1977, pp. 241-680; S. Gieben, *Centri ed organi di studi francescani*, "L'Italia Francescana", 52, 1977, pp. 293-405. – See the latest information about the Order on the Internet sites: http://www.fratiquaracchi.it and http://www.antonianum.ofm.org. – The most important series of publications of the collegium are: "Analecta Franciscana", "Bullarium Franciscanum", "Sinica Franciscana" and the periodical "Archivum Franciscanum Historicum".

2 A current overview about the different series of publications of the institute can be found on the Internet: http://www.uni-muenster.de/Staedtegeschichte/Institut.shtml.

3 An updated overview for the published volumes of the "Ordensstudien" can be found in the bibliography of K. Elm in F. J. Felten - N. Jaspert (eds.), *Vita Religiosa im Mittelalter. Festschrift für K. Elm zum 70. Geburtstag*, Berlin 1999, pp. 961-979.

4 Regarding the tasks and series of publications of the IFG ("Saxonia Franciscana", "Saxonia Franciscana – Beihefte", "Franziskanisches Leben") see http://www.dhm.de/gaeste/ifg_saxonia/books.htm as well as the short essay by D. Berg, *Franziskanisches Leben und franziskanische Geschichte in der Sächsischen Ordensprovinz. Zur Tätigkeit des „Institutes für franziskanische Geschichte (Saxonia)" in Bochum 1988-1991*, in "Vita Seraphica", 72, 1991, pp. 145-150.

5 A list of the publications of the members of staff in the SFB can be found at: http://rcswww.urz.tu-dresden.de/~ sfb537/teilprojekte/c/vc.htm.

6 Information regarding the perspectives of the research being presently done by this office, see: http://www.vita-religiosa.de/FOVOG.htm.

7 As an example of the Franciscan victims of the terror and dictatorship of Nationalist Socialism e.g. in the Saxonian Province: Patres Kilian Kirchhoff OFM, Elpidius Markötter OFM and Br. Wolfgang Rosenbaum OFM. See the short biographies of O. Mund, *Blumen auf den Trümmern. Blutzeugen der NS-Zeit*, Paderborn 1989.

8 *Werkbuch zur Regel des Heiligen Franziskus. Hrsg. v. den deutschen Franziskanern*, Werl 1955. Published at the same time as the series "Bücher franziskanischer Geistigkeit" (vols. 1 ff., Werl 1956). Here, General Minister Sépinski explained the attempt to get a systematic analysis of the Franciscan sources to discuss *Einzelfragen franziskanischer Geistigkeit* [special problems of Franciscan spirituality] and to point out their *Lebenswert für die Meisterung unserer heutigen Aufgaben* [importance for solving special problems nowadays] (vol. 1, Introduction p. 7).

[9] Cf. D.E. Flood, *Die Regula non bullata der Minderbrüder*, Werl 1967. Further studies based on different writings by K. Eßer, *Textkritische Untersuchungen zur Regula non bullata der Minderbrüder*, Grottaferrata 1974.

[10] See – apart from the basic studies of the sources – K. Eßer, *Das Testament des Heiligen Franziskus von Assisi* (Münster 1949) and the programmatic work of the same author: *Anfänge und ursprüngliche Zielsetzungen des Ordens der Minderbrüder*, Leiden 1966 – Added are several smaller investigations: K. Eßer - R. Oliger, *La tradition manuscrite des opuscules de Saint François d´Assise*, Rome 1972; K. Eßer (ed.), *Studien zu den Opuscula des Hl. Franziskus von Assisi*, E. Kurten - Isidoro de Villapadierna (eds.), Rome 1973.

[11] K. Eßer, *Die Opuscula des Hl. Franziskus von Assisi. Neue textkritische Edition*, Grottaferrata 1976; 2 revised edition, Grottaferrata 1989.

[12] For the acknowledgement of Eßer's works, cfr. H. Schneider (ed.), *Kajetan Esser – Leben und Werk*, Mönchengladbach 1998; A. Cacciotti (ed.), *Verba Domini Mei. Gli "Opuscula" di Francesco d´Assisi a 25 anni dalla edizione di K. Esser, OFM*, Rome 2003.

[13] The most important works by L. Hardick on historical tradition can be located in: D. Berg (ed.), *Spiritualität und Geschichte. Festgabe für L. Hardick zu seinem 80. Geburtstag*, Werl 1993.

[14] Preface to the 1st edition by K. Eßer - L. Hardick, in *Die Schriften des Heiligen Franziskus von Assisi. Einführung, Übersetzung, Auswertung v. K. Eßer, L. Hardick*, Werl 1951, p. 7.

[15] "Franziskanischen Quellenschriften", vols. 1 ff., Werl 1951 ff.

[16] The complete works will be published soon: *Die franziskanischen Quellenschriften deutsch*. Edited for the "Germanischen Provinzialen-Konferenz der Franziskaner" by D. Berg and L. Lehmann OFM Cap (vol. 1) as well as J. Schneider OFM (vol. 2).

[17] P. Sabatier, *Vie de S. François d´Assise*, Paris 1894.

[18] For the discussion about the "Franziskanische Frage" see *La "Questione francescana" da Sabatier a oggi*, Assisi 1974; D. Berg, *Armut und Wissenschaft. Beiträge zur Geschichte des Studienwesens der Bettelorden im 13. Jahrhundert*, Düsseldorf 1977, pp. 12 ff.; S. da Campagnola, *Le origini francescani come problema storiografico*, Perugia 1979; L. di Fonzo, *Questione francescana*, in"Dizionario degli Istituti di Perfezione", VII, Rome 1983, coll. 1133-1154; F. X. Bischof, *Die "Franziskanische Frage": ein ungelöstes historiographisches Problem*, "Münchener Theologische Zeitschrift", 41, 1990, pp. 355-382; E. Menestò - S. Brufani (eds.), *Fontes Franciscani*, S. Maria degli Angeli – Assisi 1995, pp. 1299 ff., 1395 ff.; M.P. Alberzoni - B. Bartoli Langeli (eds.), *Francesco d´Assisi e il primo secolo di storia francescana*, Turin 1997, esp. the papers of E. Menestò (pp. 117-143) and R. Rusconi (pp. 339-357); J.M. Arcelus Ulibarrena, *Floreto de Sant Francisco*, Madrid 1998, pp. 211 ff.; E. Pásztor, *Francesco d´Assisi e la "questione francescana"*, Assisi 2000, pp. 15 ff., 31 ff.; E. Kumka, *La "Compilatio Assisiensis". Una prova dell´analisi strutturale e concettuale*, "Miscellanea Francescana", 103, 2003, pp. 233-306; E. Caroli (ed.), *Fonti Francescane*, Padua 2004[2], pp. 221 ff.

[19] The fundamental study of S. Clasen, *Legenda Antiqua S. Francisci. Untersuchung über die nachbonaventurianischen Franziskusquellen, Legenda Trium Sociorum, Speculum Perfectionis, Actus B. Francisci et Sociorum Eius und verwandtes Schrifttum*, Leiden 1967. This was continued in several articles about the historical tradition, mainly published in the periodical "Wissenschaft und Weisheit", but never collected in a single volume. E. Grau continued the work of Clasen: E. Grau, *Franziskusbiographie*, in *800 Jahre Franz von Assisi*, Vienna 1982, pp. 64-78; Id., *Die Dreigefährtenlegende des Heiligen Franziskus von Assisi von Bruder Leo, Rufin und Angelus und Anonymus Perusinus*, Einführungen, Werl 1993, pp. 29 ff., 187 ff.

[20] Examples of the work by K. Elm - D. Berg, *Vitasfratrum. Beiträge zur Geschichte der Eremiten- und Mendikantenorden des zwölften und dreizehnten Jahrhunderts. Festgabe für K. Elm zum 65. Geburtstag*, edited by D. Berg, Werl 1994; D. Berg, *Armut und Geschichte. Studien zur Geschichte der Bettelorden im Hohen und Späten Mittelalter*, Kevelaer 2001.

[21] A. Hauck, *Kirchengeschichte Deutschlands*, 5 vol., Berlin 1911-1929[3-4]; H. Jedin (ed.), *Handbuch der Kirchengeschichte*, vol. 2/2, 3/1-2, Freiburg/B. 1966-1975; K.D. Schmidt - E. Wolf (eds.), *Die Kirche in ihrer Geschichte*, Faszikel E, F 1, G 1-2, H, Göttingen 1966 ff.; N. Brox (ed.), *Die Geschichte des Christentums*

(Deutsche Ausgabe), vol. 4-6, Freiburg/B. 1991-1994; M. Borgolte, *Die mittelalterliche Kirche*, Munich 1992; K. Bihlmeyer - H. Tüchle, *Kirchengeschichte*, vol. 2, Paderborn 1996[20]; I.W. Frank, *Kirchengeschichte des Mittelalters*, Düsseldorf 1997[4].

[22] H. Holzapfel, *Handbuch der Geschichte des Franziskanerordens*, Freiburg/B. 1909; M. Heimbucher, *Die Orden und Kongregationen der katholischen Kirche*, vol. 1, Paderborn 1933[3]; P.J. Hasenberg - A. Wienand (ed.), *Das Wirken der Orden und Klöster in Deutschland*, vol. 1, Cologne 1957; J.R.H. Moorman, *Medieval Franciscan Houses*, New York 1983; L. Holtz (ed.), *Männerorden in der Bundesrepublik Deutschland*, Zürich u.a. 1984; L. Iriarte, *Der Franziskusorden*, Altötting 1984; K.S. Frank, *Geschichte des christlichen Mönchtums*, Darmstadt 1988; H. Schneider, *Die Franziskaner im deutschen Sprachgebiet*, Werl 1988[2].

[23] A. Schröer, *Die Kirche in Westfalen vor der Reformation*, vol. 2, Münster 1967, esp. pp. 185 ff.; H.-W. Krumwiede, *Kirchengeschichte Niedersachsens*, vol. 1, Göttingen 1995, pp. 86 ff.

[24] Since 1929 published in three sections (vol. 1 ff., Berlin 1929 ff.), published in a New Series since 1962 by the Max-Planck-Institut (vol. 1 ff., Göttingen 1962 ff.).

[25] Cf. Helvetia Sacra, vol. 5/1: *Die Franziskaner, die Klarissen und die regulierten Franziskaner-Terziarinnen in der Schweiz. Die Minimen in der Schweiz*, edited by K. Arnold, Berne 1978.

[26] L. Schmitz-Kallenberg, *Monasticon Westfaliae*, Münster 1909; H. Kochendörffer, *Schleswig-Holsteinisches Klosterbuch*, Neumünster 1923; W. Dersch (ed.), *Hessisches Klosterbuch. Quellenkunde zur Geschichte der im Regierungsbezirk Kassel, im Kreis Grafschaft Schaumburg, in der Provinz Oberhessen und im Kreis Biedenkopf gegründeten Stifter, Klöster und Niederlassungen von geistlichen Genossenschaften*, Marburg 1940 (Reprint 2000[2]); K. Hengst (ed.), *Westfälisches Klosterbuch. Lexikon der vor 1815 errichteten Stifte und Klöster von ihrer Gründung bis zur Aufhebung*, vols. 1-3, Münster 1992-2003; W. Zimmermann - N. Priesching (eds.), *Württembergisches Klosterbuch. Klöster, Stifte und Ordensgemeinschaften von den Anfängen bis zur Gegenwart*, Ostfildern 2003; H.-D. Heimann u.a. (ed.), *Brandenburgisches Klosterbuch. Handbuch der Klöster, Stifte und Kommenden bis zur Mitte des 16. Jahrhunderts*, Berlin 2006.

[27] A. Koch, *Die frühesten Niederlassungen der Minoriten im rechtsrheinischen Bayern, Heidelberg 1880*; G.E. Friess, *Geschichte der österreichischen Minoritenprovinz*, "Archiv f. Österreichische Geschichte", 864, 1882, pp. 79-245; K. Eubel, *Geschichte der oberdeutschen (Straßburger) Minoriten-Provinz*, Würzburg 1886; R. Banasch, *Die Niederlassungen der Minoriten zwischen Weser und Elbe im dreizehnten Jahrhundert*, Breslau 1891; L. Lemmens, *Niedersächsische Franziskanerklöster im Mittelalter*, Hildesheim 1896; P. Minges, *Geschichte der Franziskaner in Bayern*, Munich 1896; P. Schlager, *Geschichte der Kölnischen Franziskaner-Ordensprovinz im Mittelalter*, Cologne 1904; K. Eubel, *Geschichte der Kölnischen Minoriten-Ordensprovinz*, Cologne 1906; P. Schlager (ed.), *Beiträge zur Geschichte der Sächsischen Franziskanerprovinz vom Hl. Kreuze*, vol. 1-6, Düsseldorf 1907-1913; H. Hoogeweg, *Verzeichnis der Stifter und Klöster Niedersachsens vor der Reformation*, Hannover-Leipzig 1908; L. Lemmens, *Die Franziskanerkustodie Livland und Preussen*, Düsseldorf 1912; F. Jansen, *Gründung und Entwicklung der Thüringischen Provinz*, "Franziskanische Studien", 10, 1923, pp. 127-141; H. Hoogeweg, *Die Stifter und Klöster der Provinz Pommern*, 2 vol., Stettin 1924-1925; A. Bürgler, *Die Franzikus-Orden in der Schweiz*, Schwyz 1926; L. Teichmann, *Die Franziskaner-Observanten in Schlesien vor der Reformation*, Breslau 1934.

[28] *Alemania Franciscana Antiqua (zur Geschichte der franziskanischen Männer- und Frauenklöster im Bereich der Oberdeutschen oder Straßburger Franziskaner-Provinz mit Ausnahme von Bayern)*, herausgegeben von der Bayrischen Franziskaner-Provinz (vol. 1 ff., Ulm 1956 ff.); *Bavaria Franciscana Antiqua (zur Geschichte der franziskanischen Männer- und Frauenklöster im Raum der Custodia Bavaria der ehemaligen Provincia Argentina)*, herausgegeben von der Bayrischen Franziskaner-Provinz (vol. 1 ff., Munich 1951 ff.). See also Bayerische Franziskanerprovinz. Ed. im Auftrag der bayrischen Franziskanerprovinz, Munich 1954.

[29] D. Berg (ed.), *Saxonia Franciscana*, (vol. 1 ff., Werl, später Kevelaer 1992 ff.); Id. (ed.), *Bettelorden und Stadt. Bettelorden und städtisches Leben im Mittelalter und in der Neuzeit*, Werl 1992; Id. (ed.), *Franziskanisches Leben im Mittelalter. Studien zur Geschichte der rheinischen und sächsischen Ordensprovinzen*, Werl 1994.

[30] *Fünfhundert Jahre Franziskaner der Österreichischen Ordensprovinz*, Vienna 1950; G. Haselbeck, *Die Franziskaner an der mittleren Lahn und im Westerwald*, Fulda 1957; C.G. M. Bak, *750 jaar minderbroeders in*

Nederland, vols. 1-3, Utrecht 1978-1983; D. Berg, *Franziskaner in Westfalen*, in G. Jászai (ed.), *Monastisches Westfalen*, Münster 1982², pp. 143-163; M. Vöckler, *Die Stellung und Wirksamkeit der Bettelorden in Thüringen von 1224 bis zum Beginn des 14. Jahrhunderts*, Diss. phil. masch. Jena 1987; R. Nickel, *Minoriten und Franziskaner in Westfalen vom 13. bis zum 17. Jahrhundert*, "Franziskanische Studien", 69, 1987, pp. 233-360; 70, 1988, pp. 3-43; 71, 1989, pp. 235-325; 72, 1990, pp. 1-29; G. Streich, *Klöster, Stifte und Kommende in Niedersachsen vor der Reformation*, Hildesheim 1986; K. Elm, *Mittelalterliches Ordensleben in Westfalen und am Niederrhein*, Paderborn 1989; H.-J. Schmidt, *Die Bettelorden und ihre Niederlassungen in der Mark Brandenburg*, in W. Schich (ed.), *Beiträge zur Entstehung und Entwicklung der Stadt Brandenburg im Mittelalter*, Berlin-New York 1993, pp. 203-225; H.-J. Schmidt, *Die Landgrafen von Hessen und die Bettelorden*, in D. Berg (ed.), *Könige, Landesherren und Bettelorden*, Werl 1998, pp. 127-152; T. Berger, *Die Bettelorden in der Erzdiözese Mainz und den Diözesen Speyer und Worms im 13. Jahrhundert*, Mainz 1994; L. Teichmann, *Die Franziskanerklöster in Mittel- und Ostdeutschland 1223-1993*, Hildesheim 1995; I. Ulpts, *Die Bettelorden in Mecklenburg*, Werl 1995; A. Rüther, *Bettelorden in Stadt und Land. Die Straßburger Mendikantenkonvente und das Elsaß im Spätmittelalter*, Berlin 1997; M. Werner, *Landesherr und Franziskanerorden im spätmittelalterlichen Thüringen*, in Berg, *Könige* cit. pp. 331-360; D. Berg (ed.), *Spuren franziskanischer Geschichte. Chronologischer Abriß der Geschichte der Sächsischen Franziskanerprovinzen von ihren Anfängen bis zur Gegenwart*. Bearbeitet v. B. Schmies - K. Rakemann, Werl 1999.

[31] B.E. J. Stüdeli, *Minoritenniederlassung und mittelalterliche Stadt*, Werl 1969; J.B. Freed, *The Friars and German Society in the Thirteenth Century*, Cambridge 1977; K. Elm (ed.), *Stellung und Wirksamkeit der Bettelorden in der städtischen Gesellschaft*, Berlin 1981; Id., *Reformbemühungen und Observanzbestrebungen im spätmittelalterlichen Ordenswesen*, Berlin 1989; Id., *Erwerbspolitik und Wirtschaftsweise mittelalterlicher Orden und Klöster*, Berlin 1992; A. Herzig, *Die Beziehung der Minoriten zum Bürgertum im Mittelalter*, "Die Alte Stadt", 6, 1979, pp. 21-53.

[32] To be mentioned as a paradigm the studies by R. Barth, *Argumentation und Selbstverständnis der Bürgeropposition in städtischen Auseinandersetzungen des Spätmittelalters [...]*, Cologne-Vienna 1974; N. Hecker, *Bettelorden und Bürgertum. Konflikt und Kooperation in den deutschen Städten des Spätmittelalters*, Frankfurt 1981; B.-U. Hergemöller, *Krisenerscheinungen kirchlicher Machtpositionen in hansischen Städten des 15. Jahrhunderts (Braunschweig, Lüneburg, Rostock, Osnabrück)*, in W. Ehrecht (ed.), *Städtische Führungsgruppen und Gemeinde in der werdenden Neuzeit*, Cologne-Vienna 1980, pp. 313-348; B.-U. Hergemöller, *Verfassungsrechtliche Beziehungen zwischen Klerus und Stadt im spätmittelalterlichen Braunschweig*, in *Rat und Verfassung im mittelalterlichen Braunschweig*, Braunschweig 1986, pp. 135-186; B.-U. Hergemöller, *Pfaffenkriege im spätmittelalterlichen Hanseraum*, Cologne-Vienna 1988; Berg, *Bettelorden* cit. (passim); Id., *Leben* cit. (passim).

[33] Examples of the history of monasteries and their relationship to the cities in the following chapter.

[34] See the vast number of detailed investigations about the foundation of Franciscan monasteries in Berlin, Dortmund, Halberstadt, Halle, Hamburg, Hannover, Hildesheim, Kiel, Münster, Osnabrück and Paderborn, in Berg, *Leben* cit. (*passim*).

[35] Cf. as an example Stüdeli, *Minoritenniederlassung* cit. ch. II/1; A. Mindermann, *Bettelordenskloster und Stadttopographie. Warum lagen Bettelordensklöster am Stadtrand?*, in Berg, *Könige* cit. pp. 83-103.

[36] Cf. S. Logemann, *Die Franziskaner im mittelalterlichen Lüneburg*, Werl 1996, ch. 3.

[37] Cf. B. Neidiger, *Mendikanten zwischen Ordensideal und städtischer Realität. Untersuchungen zum wirtschaftlichen Verhalten der Bettelorden in Basel*, Berlin 1981; H.J. Schmidt, *Bettelorden in Trier. Wirksamkeit und Umfeld im hohen und späten Mittelalter*, Trier 1986; I. Ulpts, *Zur Rolle der Mendikanten in städtischen Konflikten des Mittelalters. Ausgewählte Beispiele aus Bremen, Hamburg und Lübeck*, in Berg, *Bettelorden* cit. pp. 131-151; G. Wittek, *Franziskanische Friedensvorstellungen und Stadtfrieden. Möglichkeiten und Grenzen franziskanischen Friedewirkens in mitteldeutschen Städten im Spätmittelalter*, in Berg, *Bettelorden* cit. pp. 153-178; P. Müller, *Bettelorden und Stadtgemeinde in Hildesheim im Mittelalter*, Hannover 1994, ch. VI. – Especially the Marxist-influenced medieval research dedicated to the investigation of "revolutionäre kommunale Bewegungen" particularly "Bürgerkämpfen" and the role, which the Mendicants played in the

alleged "Klassenkämpfen", Cf. as an example K. Czok, *Zunftkämpfe, Zunftrevolutionen oder Bürgerkämpfe*, "Wissenschaftliche Zeitschrift der Karl-Marx Universität Leipzig, Gesell.gesch. Reihe", 8, 1958-1959, pp. 129-143; W. Mägdefrau, *Revolutionäre kommunale Bewegungen und spätmittelalterliche Bürgerkämpfe in den Städten des Thüringer Dreistädtebundes [...]*, Diss. phil. Jena 1971. Cfr. critics in the "bourgois capitalistic research": C. Reinecke, *Bürgerkämpfe und Stadtpolitik im mittelalterlichen Braunschweig*, Oldenburg 1984; R. Averkorn, *Les clercs face aux émeutes au bas moyen âge dans le nord-ouest, nord et nord-est de l'Allemagne*, in *Les clercs au Moyen Âge*. Colloque du CUER MA, Université de Provence, mars 1995, Aix-en-Provence 1995, pp. 9-29; W. Ehbrecht, *Hanse und spätmittelalterliche Bürgerkämpfe in Niedersachsen und Westfalen*, in W. Ehbrecht, *Konsens und Konflikt. Skizzen und Überlegungen zur älteren Verfassungsgeschichte deutscher Städte*, Cologne 2001, pp. 103-128; B. Kannowski, *Bürgerkämpfe und Friedebriefe - rechtliche Streitbeilegung in spätmittelalterlichen Städten*, Cologne 2001; R. Averkorn, *The Impact of the Religious Orders on Political Change in Medieval and Early Renaissance Europe*, in A. Cimdina (ed.), *Religion and Political Change in Europe*, Pisa 2004, pp. 33-56.

[38]   Cf. apart from the works already mentioned by Berg, *Armut* cit.; Id., *Leben* cit.; Berger, *Bettelorden* cit.; Ulpts, *Bettelorden* cit.; Logemann, *Franziskaner* cit.; Müller, *Bettelorden* cit. as well *Im Dienst an der Gemeinde. 750 Jahre Franziskaner-Minoriten in Würzburg, 1221-1971*, ed. Provinzialat und Konvent der Franziskaner-Minoriten in Würzburg, Würzburg 1972; M. Sehi, *Die Bettelorden in der Seelsorgsgeschichte der Stadt und des Bistums Würzburg bis zum Konzil von Trient*, Würzburg 1981; E. Schlotheuber, *Die Franziskaner in Göttingen. Die Geschichte des Klosters und seiner Bibliothek*, Werl 1996; R. Averkorn, *Die Bischöfe von Halberstadt in ihrem kirchlichen und politischen Wirken und in ihrer Beziehung zur Stadt von den Anfängen bis zur Reformation*, in D. Berg (ed.), *Bürger, Bettelmönche und Bischöfe in Halberstadt. Studien zur Geschichte der Stadt, der Mendikanten und des Bistums vom Mittelalter bis zur Frühen Neuzeit*, Werl 1997, pp. 1-79; W.L. Adam, *Friedberg in Hessen und die Franziskaner. Eine Symbiose von Stadt und Kloster im Mittelalter*, Michelstadt 2004.

[39]   Cf. K.F. Werner, *Das NS-Geschichtsbild und die deutsche Geschichtswissenschaft*, Stuttgart 1967; P. Lundgreen (ed.), *Wissenschaft im Dritten Reich*, Frankfurt 1985; E. Schulin - E. Müller-Luckner (eds.), *Deutsche Geschichtswissenschaft nach dem Zweiten Weltkrieg (1945-1965)*, Munich 1989; K. Schreiner, *Wissenschaft von der Geschichte des Mittelalters nach 1945. Kontinuitäten und Diskontinuitäten der Mittelalterforschung im geteilten Deutschland*, in Schulin, *Geschichtswissenschaft* cit., pp. 87-146; W. Schulze, *Deutsche Geschichtswissenschaft nach 1945*, Munich 1989; K. Schönwälder, *Historiker und Politik. Geschichtswissenschaft im Nationalsozialismus*, Frankfurt-New York 1992; W. Schulze - O.G. Oexle (eds.), *Deutsche Historiker im Nationalsozialismus*, Frankfurt/M. 1999; H. Duchhardt - G. May, *Geschichtsforschung um 1950*, Mainz 2002; F.-R. Hausmann (ed.), *Die Rolle der Geisteswissenschaften im Dritten Reich 1933-1945*, Munich 2002; J. Laudage (ed.), *Von Fakten und Fiktionen. Mittelalterliche Geschichtsdarstellungen und ihre kritische Aufarbeitung*, Cologne 2003; H. Lehmann - O.G. Oexle (eds.), *Nationalsozialismus in den Kulturwissenschaften*, 2 vol., Göttingen 2004; P. Moraw, *Kontinuität und später Wandel. Bemerkungen zur deutschen und deutschsprachigen Mediävistik 1945-1970/75*, in P. Moraw - R. Schieffer (eds.), *Die deutschsprachige Mediävistik im 20. Jahrhundert*, Ostfildern 2005, pp. 103-138. – For the historiographic traditions since the Deutsches Kaiserreich see N. Hammerstein, *Deutsche Geschichtswissenschaft um 1900*, Stuttgart 1988; D. Berg, *Mediävistik – eine "politische Wissenschaft". Grundprobleme und Entwicklungstendenzen der deutschen mediävistischen Wissenschaftsgeschichte im 19. und 20. Jahrhundert*, in W. Küttler - J. Rüsen - E. Schulin (eds.), *Geschichtsdiskurs*, vol. 1, Frankfurt 1993, pp. 317-330; O.G. Oexle, *Geschichtswissenschaft im Zeichen des Historismus. Studien zu Problemgeschichten der Moderne*, Göttingen 1996; P. Schöttler (ed.), *Geschichtsschreibung als Legitimationswissenschaft (1918-1945)*, Frankfurt 1997; H. Cymorek, *Georg von Below und die deutsche Geschichtswissenschaft um 1900*, Stuttgart 1998.

[40]   Basic studies by J. Le Goff, *Apostolat mendiant et fait urbain dans la France médiévale. L'implantation des ordres mendiants. Programme-questionnaire pour une enquête*, "Annales", 23, 1968, pp. 335-352; J. Le Goff, *Ordres mendiants et urbanisation dans la France médiévale. Etat de l'enquête*, "Annales", 25, 1970, pp. 924-946. In general M. Bloch, *Schrift und Materie der Geschichte. Vorschläge zur systematischen Aneignung historischer Prozesse*, edited by C. Honegger, Frankfurt 1977; M. Erbe, *Zur neueren französischen Sozialforschung*,

Darmstadt 1979; J. Revel, *Les paradigmes des Annales*, "Annales", 34, 1979, pp. 1360-1376; S. Clark, *The Annales Historians*, in Q. Skinner (ed.), *The Return of Grand Theory in the Social Sciences*, Cambridge 1985, pp. 177-198; K. Pomian, *L'heure des Annales*, in P. Nora (ed.), *Les lieux de mémoire*, vol. II/1, Paris 1986, pp. 377-429; H. Wesseling - J.L. Oosterhoff, *De Annales, geschiedenis en inhoudsanalyse*, "Tijdschrift voor Geschiedenis", 99, 1986, pp. 547-568; F. Dosse, *L'histoire en miettes. Des "Annales" à la "nouvelle histoire"*, Paris 1987; C. Fink, *Marc Bloch. A Life in History*, Cambridge 1989, ch. 7; H. Atsma - A. Burguière (eds.), *Marc Bloch aujourd'hui. Histoire comparée et sciences sociales*, Paris 1990; O.G. Oexle, *Was deutsche Mediävisten an der französischen Mittelalterforschung interessieren muß*, in M. Borgolte (ed.), *Mittelalterforschung nach der Wende 1989*, Munich 1995, pp. 89-127; U. Raulff, *Ein Historiker im 20. Jahrhundert: Marc Bloch*, Frankfurt 1995, pp. 25 ff.; P. Burke, *Offene Geschichte. Die Schule der "Annales"*, Frankfurt 1998; G. Bourdé - H. Martin, *Les écoles historiques*, Paris 2003².

[41] A. Fischer - G. Heydemann (ed.), *Geschichtswissenschaft in der DDR*, 2 vol., Berlin 1990, see esp. P. Segl, *Mittelalterforschung in der Geschichtswissenschaft der DDR*, vol. 2, pp. 99-147.

Bibliography

Alberzoni M.P. - Bartoli Langeli B. (eds.), *Francesco d'Assisi e il primo secolo di storia francescana*, Turin 1997.

Averkorn R., *Die Bischöfe von Halberstadt in ihrem kirchlichen und politischen Wirken und in ihrer Beziehung zur Stadt von den Anfängen bis zur Reformation*, in D. Berg (ed.), *Bürger, Bettelmönche und Bischöfe in Halberstadt. Studien zur Geschichte der Stadt, der Mendikanten und des Bistums vom Mittelalter bis zur Frühen Neuzeit*, Werl 1997, pp. 1-79.

Id., *Les clercs face aux émeutes urbaines au bas moyen âge dans le nord-ouest, nord et nord-est de l'Allemagne*, in *Les clercs au Moyen Âge*, Colloque du CUER MA, Université de Provence, mars 1995, Aix-en-Provence 1995, pp. 9-29.

Id., *The Impact of the Religious Orders on Political Change in Medieval and Early Renaissance Europe*, in A. Cimdina (ed.), *Religion and Political Change in Europe*, Pisa 2004, pp. 33-56.

Bak C.G.M., *750 jaar minderbroeders in Nederland*, vol. 1-3, Utrecht 1978-1983.

Barth R., *Argumentation und Selbstverständnis der Bürgeropposition in städtischen Auseinandersetzungen des Spätmittelalters* [...], Cologne -Vienna 1974.

Berg D., *Armut und Geschichte. Studien zur Geschichte der Bettelorden im Hohen und Späten Mittelalter*, Kevelaer 2001.

Id. (ed.), *Bettelorden und Stadt. Bettelorden und städtisches Leben im Mittelalter und in der Neuzeit*, Werl 1992.

Id., *Franziskanisches Leben im Mittelalter. Studien zur Geschichte der rheinischen und sächsischen Ordensprovinzen*, Werl 1994.

Id., *Mediävistik – eine "politische Wissenschaft". Grundprobleme und Entwicklungstendenzen der deutschen mediävistischen Wissenschaftsgeschichte im 19. und 20. Jahrhundert*, in W. Küttler - J. Rüsen - E. Schulin (eds.), *Geschichtsdiskurs*, vol. 1, Frankfurt/M. 1993, pp. 317-330

Id. (ed.), *Spuren franziskanischer Geschichte. Chronologischer Abriß der Geschichte der Sächsischen Franziskanerprovinzen von ihren Anfängen bis zur Gegenwart*. Bearbeitet v. B. - Schmies - K. Rakemann, Werl 1999.

Berger T., *Die Bettelorden in der Erzdiözese Mainz und den Diözesen Speyer und Worms im 13. Jahrhundert*, Mainz 1994.

Bourdé G. - Martin H., *Les écoles historiques*, Paris 2003².

Borgolte M., *Die mittelalterliche Kirche*, Munich 1992.

Burke P., *Offene Geschichte. Die Schule der "Annales"*, Frankfurt/M. 1998

Elm K. (ed.), *Erwerbspolitik und Wirtschaftsweise mittelalterlicher Orden und Klöster*, Berlin 1992.

Id. (ed.), *Reformbemühungen und Observanzbestrebungen im spätmittelalterlichen Ordenswesen*, Berlin 1989.

Id. (ed.), *Stellung und Wirksamkeit der Bettelorden in der städtischen Gesellschaft*, Berlin 1981.

Id., *Vitasfratrum. Beiträge zur Geschichte der Eremiten- und Mendikantenorden des zwölften und dreizehnten Jahrhunderts. Festgabe für K. Elm zum 65. Geburtstag*, edited by D. Berg, Werl 1994.

Eßer K., *Anfänge und ursprüngliche Zielsetzungen des Ordens der Minderbrüder*, Leiden 1966.

Fischer A. - Heydemann G. (eds.), *Geschichtswissenschaft in der DDR*, 2 vol., Berlin 1990.

Freed J. B., *The Friars and German Society in the Thirteenth Century*, Cambridge 1977.

Hausmann F.-R. (ed.), *Die Rolle der Geisteswissenschaften im Dritten Reich 1933-1945*, Munich 2002.

Hecker N., *Bettelorden und Bürgertum. Konflikt und Kooperation in den deutschen Städten des Spätmittelalters*, Frankfurt/M. 1981.

Hergemöller B.-U., *Krisenerscheinungen kirchlicher Machtpositionen in hansischen Städten des 15. Jahrhunderts (Braunschweig, Lüneburg, Rostock, Osnabrück)*, in W. Ehbrecht (ed.), *Städtische Führungsgruppen und Gemeinde in der werdenden Neuzeit*, Cologne -Vienna 1980, pp. 313-348.

Herzig A., *Die Beziehung der Minoriten zum Bürgertum im Mittelalter*, "Die Alte Stadt", 6, 1979, pp. 21-53.

Holzapfel H., *Handbuch der Geschichte des Franziskanerordens*, Freiburg/B. 1909.

Iriarte L., *Der Franziskusorden*, Altötting 1984.

Le Goff J., *Apostolat mendiant et fait urbain dans la France médiévale. L'implantation des ordres mendiants. Programme-questionnaire pour une enquête*, "Annales", 23, 1968, pp. 335-352.

Id., *Ordres mendiants et urbanisation dans la France médiévale. Etat de l'enquête*, "Annales", 25, 1970, pp. 924-946.

Logemann S., *Die Franziskaner im mittelalterlichen Lüneburg*, Werl 1996.

Lundgreen P. (ed.), *Wissenschaft im Dritten Reich*, Frankfurt/M. 1985.

Mindermann,A., *Bettelordenskloster und Stadttopographie. Warum lagen Bettelordensklöster am Stadtrand?*, in Berg, *Könige* cit., pp. 83-103.

Moorman J.R.H., *Medieval Franciscan Houses*, New York 1983.

Neidiger B., *Mendikanten zwischen Ordensideal und städtischer Realität. Untersuchungen zum wirtschaftlichen Verhalten der Bettelorden in Basel*, Berlin 1981.

Moraw P., *Kontinuität und später Wandel. Bemerkungen zur deutschen und deutschsprachigen Mediävistik 1945-1970/75*, in P. Moraw - R. Schieffer (ed.), *Die deutschsprachige Mediävistik im 20. Jahrhundert*, Ostfildern 2005, pp. 103-138.

Müller P., *Bettelorden und Stadtgemeinde in Hildesheim im Mittelalter*, Hannover 1994.

Nickel R., *Minoriten und Franziskaner in Westfalen vom 13. bis zum 17. Jahrhundert*, "Franziskanische Studien", 69, 1987, pp. 233-360; 70, 1988, pp. 3-43; 71, 1989, pp. 235-325; 72, 1990, pp. 1-29.

Rüther A., *Bettelorden in Stadt und Land. Die Straßburger Mendikantenkonvente und das Elsaß im Spätmittelalter*, Berlin 1997.

Schmidt J., *Bettelorden in Trier. Wirksamkeit und Umfeld im hohen und späten Mittelalter*, Trier 1986.

Schönwälder K., *Historiker und Politik. Geschichtswissenschaft im Nationalsozialismus*, Frankfurt/M. – New York 1992.

Schulin E. - Müller-Luckner E. (eds.), *Deutsche Geschichtswissenschaft nach dem Zweiten Weltkrieg (1945-1965)*, Munich 1989.

Schulze W., *Deutsche Geschichtswissenschaft nach 1945*, Munich 1989.

Schulze W. - Oexle O. G. (eds.), *Deutsche Historiker im Nationalsozialismus*, Frankfurt/M. 1999.

Stüdeli B. E. J., *Minoritenniederlassung und mittelalterliche Stadt*, Werl 1969.

Ulpts I., *Die Bettelorden in Mecklenburg*, Werl 1995.

Id., *Zur Rolle der Mendikanten in städtischen Konflikten des Mittelalters. Ausgewählte Beispiele aus Bremen, Hamburg und Lübeck*, in Berg, D. (ed.), *Bettelorden und Stadt. Bettelorden und städtisches Leben im Mittelalter und in der Neuzeit*, Werl 1992, pp. 131-151.

Mendicant Orders and Urban Life in the Middle Ages: the Dominicans. Aspects of German Historiography since World War II

RAPHAELA AVERKORN
University of Siegen

In dieser kommentierten Bibliographie, die keinen Anspruch auf Vollständigkeit erhebt, werden ausgewählte Werke zur Geschichte des Dominikanerordens sowie zu den Dominikanern und deutschen Städten im Mittelalter aufgeführt, die hauptsächlich von deutschsprachigen Forscherinnen und Forschern verfasst wurden. In einem Exkurs wird knapp auf die von deutschsprachigen Historikerinnen und Historikern publizierten Untersuchungen im Bereich Bettelorden und Städte in ausgewählten europäischen Ländern eingegangen, um zu zeigen, dass sich die Bettelordensforschung nicht auf den deutschsprachigen Raum beschränkt.

Die wesentlichen Themen, die in den vorliegenden Studien zu den Dominikanern in Deutschland und darüber hinaus zu den Bettelorden in europäischen Städten zumeist nach den Methoden der neuen Regionalgeschichte und der neuen Territorialgeschichte behandelt werden sind u. a. die Wahrnehmung der Bettelorden in der mittelalterlichen Gesellschaft, das Verhältnis zu den kirchlichen und weltlichen Autoritäten und anderen gesellschaftlichen Gruppen in der Stadt, die Analyse von Karrieremustern, Fragen der Seelsorge, der Caritas und der Memoria sowie des Schenkverhaltens und der Besitzerwerbung. Ebenso werden das Verhalten der Dominikaner in Zeiten städtischer Unruhen und Krisen und ihr Beitrag zur städtischen Kultur und zum Bildungswesen thematisiert. Weitere Forschungsschwerpunkte sind ebenfalls die Geschichte der Dominikanerinnen und ihr Verhältnis zur jeweiligen Stadt sowie Untersuchungen im Bereich der Kunstgeschichte zur Architektur des Ordens und ihrer Wirkung auf die Stadtentwicklung.

Die Tatsache, dass sich in den letzten Jahrzehnten und Jahren in Deutschland zahlreiche neue Forschungsgruppen zur interdisziplinären, komparatistischen Ordensgeschichte Deutschlands und Europas gegründet haben, zeigt die Aktualität dieses Themenbereichs.

INTRODUCTION

This chapter is a bibliographical survey of studies written by German speaking researchers that examine the relationship between the Mendicant Orders and certain aspects of urban life. The first part concentrates on the Dominicans, while the second briefly addresses the question as to whether German speaking historians in other European countries are also doing research work on Mendicant Orders (especially Franciscans and Dominicans) and urban life. Due to the limited space available, I have focused on selected examples and also indicated Internet resources which will allow the discovery of more exhaustive bibliographies. As research on the Mendicant Orders should be seen in a wider context, some indications of general literature and sources are also given.

It is important to note that research on the Mendicant Orders and citizenship has to be seen in close relationship with the development of regional and territorial history in Germany. After World War II, historians started a renewal in the field of regional and territorial history, especially in the area of medieval studies. One of the most famous institutions involved is the "Konstanzer Arbeitskreis für mittelalterliche Geschichte", which was founded in 1951. Traditional regional and territorial history was regarded as an old-fashioned way of writing history. A new orientation towards structural and social history can be noticed in the second half of the 1960s and, in the 1970s, in particular, German historiography was deeply influenced –especially in the area of Modern and Contemporary History – by the new currents of historical demography, social and economic history, and history of mentalities. Regional and territorial history did not change much at the beginning, but then the influence of urban history became more important. Since the second half of the 1970s, historians have used the term "regional history" instead of "territorial history" and started to include the new tendencies and aspects in their historiographical work. In the early 1980s, new aspects were included and the "construction of reality", "mental maps" and "regional culture" came to constitute interpretative keys. The "new regional history" was born. The old-fashioned territorial history no longer existed. A "new territorial history" was established using innovative methods and contents[1]. All these developments helped to create a revival of studies about the Mendicant orders and urban life, dealing with special case studies analysing German towns, regions and territories.

RESEARCH INSTITUTES

First of all, it is important to mention a research institution founded by the Dominican order in Germany. The "Institut zur Erforschung der Geschichte des Dominikanerordens im deutschen Sprachraum" is located in Bornheim-Walberberg (near Cologne) and was founded on the initiative of Professor Dr. Isnard W. Frank OP, himself a Dominican friar. After his retirement in 1999, the institute was placed on a new basis to increase its importance. It is supported by the Dominican province of Teutonia, which was founded in 1895. The institute is working on several projects, including "Orbis Dominicanus" (research on the history of the provinces and convents of the Dominican friars and nuns), research on the Inquisition, on the relationship between the Dominicans and the Reform and a bibliography on Dominican history by German speaking historians which is published in the annual "Dominican History Newsletter". The historians working in this institute are also collecting all available source material on the Order in the German provinces and building up a data-base on the members of the Orders in these provinces. This Dominican province is very interested in research on the history of the Order. It published the review "Archiv der deutschen Dominikaner" (4 volumes, 1937-1951) and edited the series "Quellen und Forschungen zur Geschichte des Dominikanerordens in Deutschland" (40 volumes up to 1951). Examples of famous researchers are Ulrich Horst OP and Isnard W. Frank OP[2].

It is also possible to find publications about the Dominicans in Germany in the series published by the "Institutum Historicum Ordinis Fratrum Praedicatorum/Istituto Storico Domenicano/Dominican Historical Institute", which is situated in Rome[3]. Among the most famous publications, it is worthwhile consulting the following series: "Monumenta ordinis fratrum Praedicatorum historica" (MOPH); "Dissertationes historicae" (DH) and the historical review of the Dominican Order "Archivum fratrum praedicatorum" (AFP). In 1992, the first issue of the "Dominican History Newsletter" (DHN) was published and it can be consulted online.

Furthermore, various lay research institutes, linked to universities, deal with urban history in this context, as well as with the history of the Dominican Order. One of the most important is the "Albertus-Magnus-Institut" in Bonn, which was founded in 1931 by the Archbishop of Cologne as a research organisation. It deals mainly with philosophical matters and ideas of the Dominicans, and has prepared a complete edition of the works of Albert the Great and edited a series entitled "Lectio Albertina".[4]

In 1970, the "Institut für vergleichende Städtegeschichte" (IStG) was founded in Münster and started its work in close relation with the University of Münster. In 2005, it was transformed into a private, non-profit company. Its main task is to analyse the history of German and European cities in a comparative manner. Therefore, various other publications are mentioned besides those dealing with the Dominican order and urban life. It is interesting to consult different series such as the "Städteforschung" (containing various subseries)[5] that have been published by the institute.

In Berlin, the historian Kaspar Elm, who holds a chair in medieval history at the Free University of Berlin (FU), constituted a research group to carry out comparative research on religious orders ("Vergleichende Ordensforschung"). This group has published a large number of books and monographs on different aspects, including contributions to the history of the Dominican order and citizenship. The most important series is the "Berliner Ordensstudien"[6].

About ten years later, "Institutionalität und Geschichtlichkeit", a special research group, was constituted at the University of Dresden and financed by the Deutsche Forschungsgemeinschaft. One of its subgroups is called "Institutionelle Strukturen religiöser Orden im Mittelalter" and has been directed since 1997 by Gert Melville. Its main goal is to do research into the institutional structures of medieval religious orders in a comparative manner. Many studies deal with the Mendicant orders and urban life and are published in a series called "Vita regularis"[7].

In 2005, a new research centre, the "Forschungsstelle für Vergleichende Ordensgeschichte" (FOVOG), which is linked to the Dresden centre and partly financed by the "Stifterverband für die Deutsche Wissenschaft", was created at the Catholic University of Eichstätt-Ingolstadt. It is directed by Gert Melville and aims to become an international coordination centre for monastic studies, dealing with comparative and interdisciplinary research into the monastic orders[8].

STUDIES ON THE DOMINICAN ORDER

This section concentrates on individual research results and subsequent publications about the order of the Dominicans in Germany. No internationally known source editions concerning material of the Dominican order were published by German speaking historians after World War II[9]. However, some editions of local source material can be found[10].

The most important manuals and monographs about the Dominican order, such as the studies by Vicaire on Saint Dominic, or by Hinnebusch, Bennett, Ashley and D'Amato on the history of the order, were not written by German speaking historians[11]. A short history of the Dominican order was recently translated into German[12]. Other studies by such people as Berger, Hertz and Müller and von Heusinger, which are also addressed to a wider public, should be briefly mentioned. Some studies deal with different members of the Dominican order in Germany[13].

In general, overviews of the Dominicans in the Middle Ages and different aspects of citizenship can be found in various manuals and handbooks about ecclesiastical history and Church history. Some examples are the *Kirchengeschichte Deutschlands* by A. Hauck, the *Handbuch der Kirchengeschichte* edited by H. Jedin, the *Geschichte des Christentums* by N. Brox and several other works[14]. It is also worthwhile consulting some general works on the monastic orders, not only the classic work by Hinnebusch on the Dominicans, but also those by such people as M. Heimbucher, P. J. Hasenberg and A. Viennaand, L. Holtz and K.S. Frank[15].

Basic information about the relationship between the Dominican friars and medieval cities is to be found not only in general works, but also in special manuals concerning church history of certain regions. The following are worth mentioning: studies about Lower Saxony by H.-W. Krumwiede, studies about Westfalia by A. Schröer and the various studies about German dioceses published in the series "Germania Sacra", which also deal with Dominican convents in different towns[16]. Switzerland publishes a similar series called "Helvetia Sacra"[17]. A couple of years ago, different groups of researchers started new projects dealing with the history of monasteries of different orders in various regions of Germany in particular, and aimed at the publication of a kind of handbook on monasteries called "Klosterbuch". At the moment, it is possible to consult, for example, manuals concerning Brandenburg, Schleswig-Holstein, Hesse, Westfalia and Württemberg[18].

After World War II, various historians started to publish on the history of the Mendicant Orders. It is interesting to note that only a minority of researchers belonged to the preaching Orders; most of them were lay people. Since 1970, and especially since 1980, more and more lay historians have dealt with the Dominican order and urban life on the basis of the ideas of a modern "regional" and "territorial" history[19].

First of all, some general works on the Mendicant orders and medieval society will be mentioned. In 1977, an American researcher, J.B. Freed, wrote a fundamental work on Mendicant Orders in German society in the 13th century[20], and German and Swiss historians also started to investigate the relationship between urban communities and Mendicant Orders, their foundation and settlement policy in general, the acquisition of property etc. This research group, situated in Berlin and directed by Kaspar Elm, published several studies, some of them dealing with the Mendicant Orders[21].

Last but not least, since the 1980s, individual researchers in both parts of Germany have concentrated on monographs concerning the Mendicant Orders and their relationship to certain towns or regions. Many of these works are doctoral theses. They especially deal with the Dominican and the Franciscan Orders and other mendicant orders. General and fundamental works have been written or published during the last few decades by such people as Schilp and Welzel, writing about Dortmund; by Rüther, writing about Straßburg and the Alsace region; by Ulpts, writing about Mecklenburg; by Berger, writing about the archdioceses of Mayence and the dioceses of Spire and Worms; by Berg, writing about various regions; by Schmidt, writing about Brandenburg and Hesse; by Elm, writing about Westfalia and the Rhine area; by Jászai, writing about Westfalia; by Streich, writing about Lower Saxony; by Voeckler, writing about Thuringia; by Gieraths, writing about Worms; by Lindow, writing about Prenzlau, and by Runne, writing about Warburg[22].

What are the main topics analysed in these studies and in further individual case studies of single convents or single towns? It is not possible to give an exhaustive overview concerning the contents of these studies but, in general, it is possible to enumerate a certain number of favoured topics.

In this context, one general aspect deals with the perception of the Mendicant orders in medieval society by medieval people[23]. Another main topic is the involvement of the Dominicans in church politics in the different towns, their relationship to the bishop in charge, the local clergy and other monasteries[24], and the career patterns of Dominican friars in towns, exploring such matters as how a friar could become a bishop[25].

On the same level, it is important to analyse the relationship to the lay seigneur of the town, as well as to the local authorities and the town government[26], and the different social groups in the towns[27]. In this context, one of the favourite research subjects is the behaviour of the Dominican order in situations of crisis and political conflict, riots etc., which is treated in several studies and in general studies about cities and crisis in the Middle Ages[28]. On the spiritual and practical level, several studies are dedicated to the Dominicans and their attitude towards preaching and pastoral care[29], to the memory of the deceased and to charity works, donations and the acquisition of property[30]. Another very interesting aspect is that relating to Dominicans and urban culture, not only to education and schools[31], but also to architecture, art, and the construction of churches and monasteries[32]. Schenkluhn has published widely known and well-received general works on the architecture of the Dominicans and the Franciscans in Europe, while Pieper has written a very interesting regional study about the churches of the Mendicant Orders in Westphalia[33]. Several art historians have published local studies about Dominican churches and monasteries[34].

Special emphasis should be given to gender history. It is especially interesting to note that, in this field, several historians, especially women, have dealt with monasteries of Dominican nuns since the late 1980s. These monographs treat such matters as the history of the monasteries, their settlement in urban communities, the importance of education, daily life in a monastery, charity work and many other aspects[35].

Research on the History of the Mendicant Orders and Citizenship Outside Germany After World War II by German Speaking Historians

Finally, in this section, I have added a small part on the work of German historians who deal with the above mentioned aspect of Mendicant orders in relation to other European countries. This is an important contribution to the comparative analysis of the history of the Mendicant orders. Many scholars have started research on these orders in different European countries. In general, the investigations focus on very different aspects, one of which looks at citizenship and the Mendicant Orders and which, therefore, should be mentioned here. It is not possible to give an exhaustive survey but, as an example, some studies concerning the above mentioned topic and the Mendicant Orders in England, Ireland, France, Italy, Spain and Portugal will be mentioned briefly.

Scholars such as Jens Röhrkasten, Annette Kehnle and Anne Müller have published studies on the Mendicant orders and urban life in England, Scotland and Ireland[36]. Researchers such as Dieter Berg regularly publish work about Mendicant orders in Italy and their relationship with authorities such as the emperor, the pope and city governments[37]. One theme favoured by German historians is France; the history of the Mendicant orders and French towns[38] is covered by researchers such as Annette Kehnle, Andreas Rüther, Ramona Sickert and Raphaela Averkorn.

Dieter Berg and Raphaela Averkorn[39] are investigating the relationship between urban authorities, kings and queens and the Mendicant orders in Aragon and Castile, while Averkorn is also looking at the impact of the Mendicant orders on society in various European countries in a more general sense[40].

Conclusion

Research on the Mendicant orders and urban life is still a very attractive topic. Since the introduction of a "modern and revised" regional and territorial history to German historiography, younger and, at the same time, more experienced established researchers continue to investigate in this area. It should be mentioned that more researchers are concentrating on the Franciscan rather than the Dominican order. This is often due to the available source material as well as the research possibilities offered by specialised institutions. Nowadays, the majority of the researchers dealing with these topics no longer belongs to one of the monastic orders. Most historians are laymen and come from different research fields such as urban history. The actuality of this topic and of the Mendicant Orders and religious orders in general can be seen in the fact that several new research groups and research centres have been created in the last few decades and even in recent years. Interdisciplinary and international comparative studies about religious orders will still be a promising and fruitful research area in the coming years.

Notes

[1]   M. Werner, *Zwischen politischer Begrenzung und methodischer Offenheit. Wege und Stationen deutscher Landesgeschichtsforschung im 20. Jahrhundert*, in P. Moraw - R. Schieffer (eds.), *Die deutschsprachige Mediävistik im 20. Jahrhundert*, Ostfildern 2005 (Vorträge und Forschungen 62), pp. 251-364, p. 251; W. Freitag, *Landesgeschichte als Synthese – Regionalgeschichte als Methode?*, "Westfälische Forschungen", 54, 2004, pp. 291-305; W. Köllmann, *Die Bedeutung der Regionalgeschichte im Rahmen struktur- und sozialgeschichtlicher Konzeptionen*, "Archiv für Sozialgeschichte", 15, 1975, pp. 43-50.

[2]   For further details, see the annual bulletins, p. ex. Institut zur Erforschung der Geschichte des Dominikanerordens im deutschen Sprachraum (IGDom), "Jahresbericht", 2, 2002, pp. 1-7.

[3]   For further information and general activities, see http://www.op.org/curia/storico/default/htm.

[4]   For publications and activities, see http://www.albertus-magnus-institut.de.

[5]   An overview of the publications can be found on the Internet: http://www.uni-muenster.de/Staedtegeschichte/Institut.shtml.

[6]   The most recent overview of the studies published in the series "Berliner Ordensstudien", a subseries of the "Berliner Historische Studien", can be found in the bibliography of K. Elm in F.J. Felten - N. Jaspert (eds.), *Vita Religiosa im Mittelalter. Festschrift für K. Elm zum 70. Geburtstag*, Berlin 1999, pp. 961-979.

[7]   A list of publications can be found at: http://rcswww.urz.tu-dresden.de/~sfb537/teilprojekte/c/vc.htm; a short description of the project at: www.vita-religiosa.de/presPrChtm. For individual publications, see below.

[8]   Information about this centre can be found on the Internet http://www.vita-religiosa.de/FOVOG.htm.alt.

[9]   As a bibliography of the writings of the order, consult Th. Kaeppeli (ed.), *Scriptores Ordinis Praedicatorum Medii Aevi*, 4 vol., Rome 1970-1993 and as examples p. ex. A. Walz (ed.), *Beati Jordani de Saxonia Epistulae*, Rome 1951; M.-H. Vicaire (ed.), *Saint Dominique et ses frères: évangile ou croisade? Textes du 13e siècle*, Paris 1967; S. Tugwell (ed.), *Early Dominicans: selected Writings*, Mahwah, N.Y. 1982.

[10]   For example, see Th. Zimmer (ed.), *Dominikanerinnenkloster St. Katharinen in Trier: Urkunden und Akten*, Düsseldorf 1995.

[11]   M.H. Vicaire, *Saint Dominic and His Times*, trans. by K. Pond, New York - Toronto - London 1964; M.H. Vicaire, *Dominique et ses prêcheurs*, Fribourg 1977, Id., *Histoire de saint Dominique*, 2 vol., Paris 1982; W.A. Hinnebusch, *The History of the Dominican Order*, 2 vol., New York 1966-1973; R.F. Bennett, *The Early Dominicans: Studies in Thirteenth-Century Dominican History*, Cambridge 1937, reprint in New York 1971; B. Ashley, *The Dominicans*, Collegeville, Min. 1990; A. D'Amato, *L'ordine dei Frati Predicatori*, Rome [1983]; in general about the Mendicant Friars, see C.H. Lawrence, *The Friars. The Impact of the Early Mendicant Movement on Western Society*, London 1994.

[12]   W.A. Hinnebusch, *Kleine Geschichte des Dominikanerordens*, Leipzig 2004 (English version: W.A. Hinnebusch, *The Dominicans. A Short History*, Dublin 1985, Staten Island, N.Y. 1975).

[13]   Albertus-Magnus-Akademie (ed.), *Dominikaner in Deutschland*, Düsseldorf 1951; F. Berger, *Kämpfer,*

Ketzer, Heilige. Die Dominikaner, St. Pölten 2000; A. Hertz, *Dominikus und die Dominikaner*, Freiburg 1981; F. Müller (ed.), *Dominikanerinnen und Dominikaner. Lebensbilder aus dem Predigerorden*, Freiburg 1988; I.W. Frank, *Albert der Große als Dominikaner seiner Zeit*, Augsburg 1981; S. von Heusinger, *Johannes Mulberg OP (+1414). Ein Leben im Spannungsfeld von Dominikanerobservanz und Beginenstreit*, Berlin 2000.

[14] A. Hauck, *Kirchengeschichte Deutschlands*, 5 vol., Berlin 1911[3-4]-1929; H. Jedin (ed.), *Handbuch der Kirchengeschichte*, vol. 2/2, 3/1-2, Freiburg/B. 1966-1975; K.D. Schmidt - E. Wolf (eds.), *Die Kirche in ihrer Geschichte*, issue E, F 1, G 1-2, H, Göttingen 1966ss.; N. Brox - J.M. Mayeur (eds.), *Die Geschichte des Christentums (Deutsche Ausgabe)*, vol. 4-6, Freiburg/B. 1991-1994; M. Borgolte, *Die mittelalterliche Kirche*, Munich 1992; K. Bihlmeyer - H. Tüchle, *Kirchengeschichte*, vol. 2, Paderborn 1996[20]; I.W. Frank, *Kirchengeschichte des Mittelalters*, Düsseldorf 1997[4].

[15] W.A. Hinnebusch, *The History of the Dominican Order*, 2 vol., New York 1966-1973; M. Heimbucher, *Die Orden und Kongregationen der katholischen Kirche*, vol. 1, Paderborn 1933[3]; P. J. Hasenberg - A. Viennaand (eds.), *Das Wirken der Orden und Klöster in Deutschland*, vol. 1, Cologne 1957; L. Holtz (ed.), *Männerorden in der Bundesrepublik Deutschland*, Zürich 1984; K.S. Frank, *Geschichte des christlichen Mönchtums*, Darmstadt 1988.

[16] A. Schröer, *Die Kirche in Westfalen vor der Reformation*, vol. 2, Munich 1967; H.-W. Krumwiede, *Kirchengeschichte Niedersachsens*, vol. 1, Göttingen 1995. The "Germania Sacra" collection has been published since 1929 in three sections (vol. 1ss., Berlin 1929ss.); a new series has been published since 1962 by the Max-Planck-Institut (Vol. 1ss., Göttingen 1962ss.).

[17] Cf. Helvetia Sacra, 4/5: *Die Dominikaner und Dominikanerinnen in der Schweiz*, edited by P. Zimmer - B. Degler-Spengler, Basel 1999.

[18] L. Schmitz-Kallenberg, *Monasticon Westfaliae*, Munich 1909; H. Kochendörffer, *Schleswig-Holsteinisches Klosterbuch*, Neumünster 1923; W. Dersch - K. Hengst (eds.), *Hessisches Klosterbuch. Quellenkunde zur Geschichte der im Regierungsbezirk Kassel, im Kreis Grafschaft Schaumburg, in der Provinz Oberhessen und im Kreis Biedenkopf gegründeten Stifter, Klöster und Niederlassungen von geistlichen Genossenschaften*, Marburg 1940 (reprint 2000[2]); *Westfälisches Klosterbuch. Lexikon der vor 1815 errichteten Stifte und Klöster von ihrer Gründung bis zur Aufhebung*, vol. 1-3, Munich 1992-2003; W. Zimmermann - N. Priesching (eds.), *Württembergisches Klosterbuch. Klöster, Stifte und Ordensgemeinschaften von den Anfängen bis zur Gegenwart*, Ostfildern 2003; H.-D. Heimann - K. Neitmann - W. Schich - E. Franke - Ch. Gahlbeck - P. Riedel (eds.), *Brandenburgisches Klosterbuch. Handbuch der Klöster, Stifte und Kommenden bis zur Mitte des 16. Jahrhunderts*, Berlin 2006.

[19] For the new research fields in German regional/territorial history, see Werner, *Zwischen politischer Begrenzung* cit., pp. 342-347 and concerning the development in the former East Germany, *ibid.*, pp. 348-362.

[20] J.B. Freed, *The Friars and German Society in the Thirteenth Century*, Cambridge 1977.

[21] For example, see the following studies K. Elm (ed.), *Stellung und Wirksamkeit der Bettelorden in der städtischen Gesellschaft*, Berlin 1981; Id. (ed.), *Reformbemühungen und Observanzbestrebungen im spätmittelalterlichen Ordenswesen*, Berlin 1989; Id. (ed.), *Erwerbspolitik und Wirtschaftsweise mittelalterlicher Orden und Klöster*, Berlin 1992.

[22] T. Schilp - B. Welzel (eds.), *Die Dortmunder Dominikaner im Späten Mittelalter und die Propsteikirche als Erinnerungsort*, Gütersloh 2006; G. Jászai (ed.), *Monastisches Westfalen*, Munich 1982[2]; M. Vöckler, *Die Stellung und Wirksamkeit der Bettelorden in Thüringen von 1224 bis zum Beginn des 14. Jahrhunderts*, Diss. phil. masch. Jena 1987; G. Streich, *Klöster, Stifte und Kommende in Niedersachsen vor der Reformation*, Hildesheim 1986; K. Elm, *Mittelalterliches Ordensleben in Westfalen und am Niederrhein*, Paderborn 1989; H.-J. Schmidt, *Die Bettelorden und ihre Niederlassungen in der Mark Brandenburg*, in W. Schich (ed.), *Beiträge zur Entstehung und Entwicklung der Stadt Brandenburg im Mittelalter*, Berlin-New York 1993, pp. 203-225; H.-J. Schmidt, *Die Landgrafen von Hessen und die Bettelorden*, in D. Berg (ed.), *Könige, Landesherren und Bettelorden*, Werl 1998, pp. 127-152; T. Berger, *Die Bettelorden in der Erzdiözese Mainz und den Diözesen Speyer und Worms im 13. Jahrhundert*, Mainz 1994; I. Ulpts, *Die Bettelorden in Mecklenburg*, Werl 1995; A.

Rüther, *Bettelorden in Stadt und Land. Die Straßburger Mendikantenkonvente und das Elsaß im Spätmittelalter*, Berlin 1997; G. Gieraths, *Die Dominikaner in Worms*, Worms 1964; A. Lindow, *Das Dominikaner-Kloster zu Prenzlau*, Munich 1995; B. Runne, *Die Dominikaner in Warburg. 1281-1993*, Warburg 1994[3].

[23] See p. ex. R. Sickert, *Wenn Klosterbrüder zu Jahrmarktsbrüdern werden. Studien zur Wahrnehmung der Franziskaner und Dominikaner im 13. Jahrhundert* (Vita regularis 28), Munich 2006 (at press).

[24] R. Averkorn, *Die Bischöfe von Halberstadt in ihrem kirchlichen und politischen Wirken und in ihren Beziehungen zur Stadt von den Anfängen bis zur Reformation*, in D. Berg (ed.), *Bürger, Bettelmönche und Bischöfe in Halberstadt. Studien zur Geschichte der Stadt, der Mendikanten und des Bistums vom Mittelalter bis zur Frühen Neuzeit* (Saxonia Franciscana 9), Werl 1997, pp. 1-80.

[25] See p. ex. J. Traeger, *Die Tätigkeit von Weihbischöfen aus dem Dominikanerorden im mittelalterlichen Bistum Schwerin*, "Archivum Fratrum Praedicatorum", 53, 1983, pp. 277-292.

[26] See p. ex. several case studies in D. Berg (ed.), *Könige, Landesherren und Bettelorden, Konflikt und Kooperation in West- und Mitteleuropa bis zur Frühen Neuzeit* (Saxonia Franciscana 10), Werl 1998 and p. ex. R. Butz, *Geschichtliche Grundzüge der Beziehungen zwischen den Landesherren und den Bettelorden im obersächsisch-meißnischen Raum bis zum Ausgang des 14. Jahrhunderts*, in Berg (ed.), *Könige, Landesherren und Bettelorden* cit., pp. 107-125; Chr. Römer, *Dominikaner und Landesherrschaft um 1300*, "Die Diözese Hildesheim in Vergangenheit und Gegenwart", 1981, 49, pp. 19-32.

[27] D. Berg, *Armut und Geschichte. Studien zur Geschichte der Bettelorden im Hohen und Späten Mittelalter* (Saxonia Franciscana 11), Kevelaer 2001; D. Berg (ed.), *Bettelorden und Stadt. Bettelorden und städtisches Leben im Mittelalter und in der Neuzeit* (Saxonia Franciscana 1), Werl 1992; D. Berg, *Zur Sozialgeschichte der Bettelorden im 13. Jahrhundert*, "Wissenschaft und Weisheit", 43, 1980, 43, pp. 55-64; D. Berg, *Bettelorden und Bildungswesen im kommunalen Raum. Ein Paradigma des Bildungstransfers im 13. Jahrhundert*, in J.O. Fichte (ed.), *Zusammenhänge, Einflüsse, Wirkungen. Versuch einer Bestandsaufnahme*, Tübingen 1986, pp. 414-425.

[28] See the case study by R. Averkorn, *Les clercs face aux émeutes urbaines au bas moyen âge dans le nord-ouest, nord et nord-est de l'Allemagne*, in *Les clercs au Moyen Age*, Colloque du CUER MA, Université de Provence mars 1995 (Sénéfiance 37), Aix-en-Provence 1995, pp. 9-29 and in general R. Barth, *Argumentation und Selbstverständnis der Bürgeropposition in städtischen Auseinandersetzungen des Spätmittelalters* [...], Cologne-Vienna 1974; N. Hecker, *Bettelorden und Bürgertum. Konflikt und Kooperation in den deutschen Städten des Spätmittelalters*, Frankfurt 1981; B.-U. Hergemöller, *Krisenerscheinungen kirchlicher Machtpositionen in hansischen Städten des 15. Jahrhunderts (Braunschweig, Lüneburg, Rostock, Osnabrück)*, in W. Ehbrecht (ed.), *Städtische Führungsgruppen und Gemeinde in der werdenden Neuzeit*, Cologne-Vienna 1980, pp. 313-348; B.-U. Hergemöller, *Verfassungsrechtliche Beziehungen zwischen Klerus und Stadt im spätmittelalterlichen Braunschweig*, in *Rat und Verfassung im mittelalterlichen Braunschweig*, Braunschweig 1986, pp. 135-186; B.-U. Hergemöller, *Pfaffenkriege im spätmittelalterlichen Hanseraum*, Cologne-Vienna 1988.

[29] See p. ex. J. Oberste, *Gesellschaft und Individuum in der Seelsorge der Mendikanten. Die Predigten Humberts de Romanis an städtische Oberschichten*, in G. Melville - M. Schürer (eds.), *Das Eigene und das Ganze. Zum Individuellen im mittelalterlichen Religiosentum* (Vita regularis 16), Munich 2002, pp. 497-527.

[30] See p. ex. D. Berg, *Armut und Geschichte. Studien zur Geschichte der Bettelorden im Hohen und Späten Mittelalter* (Saxonia Franciscana 11), Kevelaer 2001.

[31] D. Berg, *Armut und Wissenschaft. Beiträge zur Geschichte des Studienwesens der Bettelorden im 13. Jahrhundert*, Düsseldorf 1977; R. von Schlettstadt, *Historia memorabiles: zur Dominikanerliteratur und Kulturgeschichte des 13. Jahrhunderts*, Cologne-Vienna 1974.

[32] See the more general studies by G. Binding - M. Untermann, *Kleine Kunstgeschichte der mittelalterlichen Ordensbaukunst in Deutschland*, Darmstadt 1985; W. Braunfels, *Abendländische Klosterbaukunst*, Cologne 1985[5], 1976[1]; J. Fait, *Die norddeutsche Bettelordensbaukunst zwischen Elbe und Oder*, Greifswald 1954.

[33] W. Schenkluhn, *Ordines studentes. Aspekte zur Kirchenarchitektur der Dominikaner und Franziskaner im 13. Jahrhundert*, Berlin 1985; W. Schenkluhn, *Architektur der Bettelorden: Die Baukunst der Dominikaner und Franziskaner in Europa*, Darmstadt 2000; R. Pieper, *Die Kirchen der Bettelorden in Westfalen*, Werl 1993.

[34] Some regional studies are p. ex. R. Aulepp, *Die Predigerkirche von Mühlhausen — ein bedeutendes mittelalter liches Bauwerk der Dominikaner*, "Mühlhäuser Beiträge zu Geschichte und Kulturgeschichte", 3, 1980, pp. 79-85; K. Hillebrand, *Das Dominikanerkloster zu Prenzlau. Untersuchungen zur mittelalterlichen Baugeschichte*, Munich-Berlin 2003.

[35] P. Mai (ed.), *750 Jahre Dominikanerinnenkloster Heilig Kreuz Regensburg*, Munich-Zürich 1983; I. Grübel, *Bettelorden und Frauenfrömmigkeit im 13. Jahrhundert. Das Verhältnis der Mendikanten zu Nonnenklöstern und Beginen am Beispiel Straßburg und Basel* (Kulturgeschichtliche Forschungen 9), Munich 1987; A. Baumeister (ed.), *Caritas and scientia: Dominikanerinnen und Dominikaner in Düsseldorf*, Düsseldorf 1996; C. Halm, *Klosterleben im Mittelalter: Die Dominikanerinnen in Lemgo, von der Klostergründung bis zur Reformation*, Detmold 2004; M.-L. Ehrenschwendtner, *Die Bildung der Dominikanerinnen in Süddeutschland vom 13. bis 15. Jahrhundert*, Stuttgart 2004; C. Jäggi, *Frauenklöster im Spätmittelalter: die Kirchen der Klarissen und Dominikanerinnen im 13. und 14. Jahrhundert*, Petersberg 2006. The first general history of the Dominican nuns in Germany was published by H. Wilms, *Geschichte der deutschen Dominikanerinnen (1206-1916)*, Dülmen 1920.

[36] See p. ex. J. Röhrkasten, *The Mendicant Houses of Medieval London, 1221-1539*, Munich 2004; A. Kehnel, *The Narrative Tradition of the Medieval Franciscan Friars on the British Isles. Introduction to the Sources*, in R. Copsey - M. Robson (eds.), *The Mendicants and their World*, London 2004; A. Kehnel, *Regionale Ordnungen universaler Konzepte. Die Franziskaner auf den Britischen Inseln (13.-16. Jh.). Historische Fallstudie zu einer europäischen Gemeinschaft des Mittelalters* (masch. Habil.schr.), Dresden 2003; A. Kehnel, *Die Formierung der Gemeinschaften der Minderen Brüder in der Provinz Anglia*, in G. Melville - J. Oberste (eds.), *Die Bettelorden im Aufbau. Beiträge zu Institutionalisierungsprozessen im mittelalterlichen Religiosentum* (Vita regularis 11), Munich 1999, pp. 493-524, A. Müller, *Nationale Abgrenzung in universalen Verbänden? Zur Entwicklung und Autonomiebestrebung der schottischen Franziskaner im 13. und 14. Jahrhundert*, in R. Butz - J. Oberste (eds.), *Studia monastica. Beiträge zum klösterlichen Leben im christlichen Abendland während des Mittelalters* (Vita regularis 22), Munich 2004, pp. 261-285; A. Müller, *Internal Conflicts-External Control. The Franciscan Order between English Society and Irish Crown*, in "Francescani e la politica" (Palermo, 10-14 dicembre 2002), Atti del Convegno Internazionale di studi (at press). (In various studies, Müller also analyses the relationship between the Mendicant Orders and the Muslims and between the Mendicant Orders and their missions to Asia).

[37] D. Berg, *L'imperatore Federico II e i Mendicanti. Il ruolo degli Ordini mendicanti nelle controversie tra papato e impero alla luce degli sviluppi politici in Europa*, in G. Chittolini - K. Elm (eds.), *Ordini religiosi e società politica in Italia e Germania nei secoli XIV e XV* (Annali dell'Istituto storico italo-germanico in Trento. Quaderno 56), Bologna 2001, pp. 45-113; D. Berg, *Papst Innocenz IV. und die Bettelorden in ihren Beziehungen zu Kaiser Friedrich II.*, in F.J. Felten - N. Jaspert (eds.), *Vita religiosa im Mittelalter. Festschrift für Kaspar Elm*, (Berliner Historische Studien 31. Ordensstudien 13), Berlin 2000, pp. 461-481; D. Berg, *L'impero degli Svevi e il gioachimismo francescano*, in O. Capitani - J. Miethke (eds.), *L'attesa della fine dei tempi nel Medioevo*, Bologna 1990 (Annali dell'Istituto storico italo-germanico. Quaderno 28), Bologna 1990, pp. 133-167.

[38] A. Kehnle, *Rudolf von Habsburg im Geschichtswerk der Colmarer Dominikaner*, in R. Butz - J. Oberste (eds.), Studia Monastica, *Beiträge zum klösterlichen Leben im christlichen Abendland während des Mittelalters* (Vita regularis 22), Munich 2004, pp. 211-234; A. Rüther, *Bettelorden in Stadt und Land. Die Straßburger Mendikantenkonvente und das Elsaß im Spätmittelalter*, Berlin 1997; R. Sickert, *Dominikaner und Episkopat. Zur Etablierung des Predigerordens in südfranzösischen Bischofsstädten (1215-1235)*, in G. Melville - J. Oberste (eds.), *Die Bettelorden im Aufbau* (Vita regularis 11), Munich 1999, pp. 295-319; R. Averkorn, *Landesherren und Mendikanten in den burgundischen Territorien vom 13. bis zum 15. Jahrhundert*, in D. Berg (ed.), *Könige, Landesherren und Bettelorden. Konflikt und Kooperation in West- und Mitteleuropa bis zur frühen Neuzeit* (Saxonia Franciscana 10), Werl 1998, pp. 207-276.

[39] R. Averkorn, *Adlige Frauen und Mendikanten im Spannungsverhältnis zwischen Macht und Religion. Studien zur Iberischen Halbinsel im Spätmittelalter*, in C. Rabassa - R. Stepper (eds.), *Imperios sacros, monarquías divinas* (Col.leció Humanitats 10), Castellón de la Plana 2002, pp. 219-268; D. Berg, *Königshöfe und Bettelorden. Studien zu den Beziehungen der Mendikanten zu den aragonesischen und kastilischen Herrscherhöfen*

im 13. Jahrhundert, in C. Rabassa - R. Stepper (eds.), *Imperios sacros, monarquías divinas* (Col.lecció Humanitats 10), Castellón de la Plana 2002, pp. 129-160; D. Berg, *Mendikanten und Königtum. Beiträge zur Geschichte der Bettelordensprovinzen auf der Iberischen Halbinsel bis zum 14. Jahrhundert*, "Wissenschaft und Weisheit", 65, 2002, pp. 215-241.

[40] R. Averkorn, *Representing Nobility, Charity and Sainthood: Aspects of the European Movement of the Mendicant Orders in the 13th and 14th Centuries*, in P. Dupuy (ed.), *Histoire, images, imaginaire*, Pisa 2002, pp. 97-116; R. Averkorn, *The Impact of the Religious Orders on Political Change in Medieval and Early Renaissance Europe*, in A. Cimdiṇa (ed.), *Religion and Political Change in Europe*, Pisa 2004, pp. 33-56.

Bibliography

750 Jahre Dominikanerinnenkloster Heilig Kreuz Regensburg, edited by P. Mai, Munich-Zurich 1983.

Albertus-Magnus-Akademie (ed.), *Dominikaner in Deutschland*, Düsseldorf 1951.

Ashley B., *The Dominicans*, Collegeville, Minnesota 1990.

Averkorn R., *Adlige Frauen und Mendikanten im Spannungsverhältnis zwischen Macht und Religion. Studien zur Iberischen Halbinsel im Spätmittelalter*, in Rabassa C. - Stepper R. (eds.), *Imperios sacros, monarquías divinas* (Col.lecció Humanitats 10), Castellón de la Plana 2002, pp. 219-268.

Id., *Die Bischöfe von Halberstadt in ihrem kirchlichen und weltlichen Wirken und in ihrer Beziehung zur Stadt von den Anfängen bis zur Reformation*, in Berg D. (ed.), *Bürger, Bettelmönche und Bischöfe in Halberstadt. Studien zur Geschichte der Stadt, der Mendikanten und des Bistums vom Mittelalter bis zur Frühen Neuzeit* (Saxonia Franciscana 9), Werl 1997, pp. 1-79.

Id., *Landesherren und Mendikanten in den burgundischen Territorien vom 13. bis zum 15. Jahrhundert*, in Berg D. (ed.), *Könige, Landesherren und Bettelorden. Konflikt und Kooperation in West- und Mitteleuropa bis zur frühen Neuzeit* (Saxonia Franciscana 10), Werl 1998, pp. 207-276.

Id., *Les clercs face aux émeutes urbaines au bas moyen âge dans le nord-ouest, nord et nord-est de l'Allemagne*, "Les clercs au Moyen Age", Colloque du CUER MA, Université de Provence, mars 1995 (Sénéfiance 37), Aix-en-Provence 1995, pp. 9-29.

Id., *Representing nobility, charity and sainthood: aspects of the European movement of the Mendicant Orders in the 13th and 14th centuries*, in Dupuy P. (ed.), *Histoire, images, imaginaire*, Pisa 2002, pp. 97-116.

Id., *The impact of the religious orders on political change in Medieval and Early Renaissance Europe*, in Cimdina A. (ed.), *Religion and political change in Europe*, Pisa 2004, pp. 33-56.

Barth R., *Argumentation und Selbstverständnis der Bürgeropposition in städtischen Auseinandersetzungen des Spätmittelalters* [...], Cologne-Vienna 1974.

Baumeister A. (ed.), *Caritas and scientia: Dominikanerinnen und Dominikaner in Düsseldorf*, Düsseldorf 1996.

Bennett R.F., *The Early Dominicans: Studies in Thirteenth-Century Dominican History*, Cambridge 1937, reprint in New York 1971.

Berg D., *Armut und Geschichte. Studien zur Geschichte der Bettelorden im Hohen und Späten Mittelalter* (Saxonia Franciscana 11), Kevelaer 2001.

Id., *Armut und Wissenschaft. Beiträge zur Geschichte des Studienwesens der Bettelorden im 13. Jahrhundert*, Düsseldorf 1977.

Id. (ed.), *Bettelorden und Stadt. Bettelorden und städtisches Leben im Mittelalter und in der Neuzeit* (Saxonia Franciscana 1), Werl 1992.

Id., *Königshöfe und Bettelorden. Studien zu den Beziehungen der Mendikanten zu den aragonesischen und kastilischen Herrscherhöfen im 13. Jahrhundert*, in Rabassa C. - Stepper R. (eds.), *Imperios sacros, monarquías divinas*, (Col.lecció Humanitats 10), Castellón de la Plana 2002, pp. 129-160.

Id. (ed.), *Könige, Landesherren und Bettelorden, Konflikt und Kooperation in West- und Mitteleuropa bis zur Frühen Neuzeit* (Saxonia Franciscana 10), Werl 1998.

Id., *L'imperatore Federico II e i Mendicanti. Il ruolo degli Ordini mendicanti nelle controversie tra papato e impero alla luce degli sviluppi politici in Europa*, in Chittolini G. - Elm K. (eds.), *Ordini religiosi e società politica in Italia e Germania nei secoli XIV e XV* (Annali dell'Istituto storico italo-germanico. Quaderno 56), Bologna 2001, pp. 45-113.

Id., *L'impero degli Svevi e il gioachimismo francescano*, in Capitani O. - Miethke J. (eds.), *L'attesa della fine dei tempi nel Medioevo*, (Annali dell'Istituto storico italo-germanico. Quaderno 28), Bologna 1990, pp. 133-167.

Id., *Mendikanten und Königtum. Beiträge zur Geschichte der Bettelordensprovinzen auf der Iberischen Halbinsel bis zum 14. Jahrhundert*, "Wissenschaft und Weisheit", 65, 2002, pp. 215-241.

Id., *Papst Innocenz IV. und die Bettelorden in ihren Beziehungen zu Kaiser Friedrich II.*, in Felten F.J. - Jaspert N. (eds.), *Vita religiosa im Mittelalter. Festschrift für Kaspar Elm* (Berliner Historische Studien 31. Ordensstudien 13), Berlin 2000, pp. 461-481.

Id. (ed.), *Vitasfratrum. Beiträge zur Geschichte der Eremiten - und Mendikantenorden des zwölften und dreizehnten Jahrhunderts. Festgabe für K. Elm zum 65. Geburtstag* (Saxonia Franciscana 5), Werl 1994.

Berger F., *Kämpfer, Ketzer, Heilige. Die Dominikaner*, St. Pölten 2000.

Berger T., *Die Bettelorden in der Erzdiözese Mainz und den Diözesen Speyer und Worms im 13. Jahrhundert*, Mainz 1994.

Binding G. - Untermann M., *Kleine Kunstgeschichte der mittelalterlichen Ordensbaukunst in Deutschland*, Darmstadt 1985.

Braunfels W., *Abendländische Klosterbaukunst*, Cologne 1985[5], 1976[1].

Butz R., *Geschichtliche Grundzüge der Beziehungen zwischen den Landesherren und den Bettelorden im obersächsisch-meißnischen Raum bis zum Ausgang des 14. Jahrhunderts*, in Berg D. (ed.), *Könige, Landesherren und Bettelorden, Konflikt und Kooperation in West- und Mitteleuropa bis zur Frühen Neuzeit* (Saxonia Franciscana 10), Werl 1998, pp. 107-125.

D'Amato A., *L'ordine dei Frati Predicatori*, Rome [1983].

Schilp T. - Welzel B. (eds.), *Die Dortmunder Dominikaner im Späten Mittelalter und die Propsteikirche als Erinnerungsort*, Gütersloh 2006.

Ehrenschwendtner M.-L., *Die Bildung der Dominikanerinnen in Süddeutschland vom 13. bis 15. Jahrhundert*, Stuttgart 2004.

Elm K., *Mittelalterliches Ordensleben in Westfalen und am Niederrhein*, Paderborn 1989.

Id. (ed.), *Erwerbspolitik und Wirtschaftsweise mittelalterlicher Orden und Klöster*, Berlin 1992.

Id. (ed.), *Reformbemühungen und Observanzbestrebungen im spätmittelalterlichen Ordenswesen*, Berlin 1989.

Id. (ed.), *Stellung und Wirksamkeit der Bettelorden in der städtischen Gesellschaft*, Berlin 1981.

Fait J., *Die norddeutsche Bettelordensbaukunst zwischen Elbe und Oder*, Greifswald 1954.

Felten F.J. - Jaspert N. (eds.), *Vita Religiosa im Mittelalter. Festschrift für K. Elm zum 70. Geburtstag* (Berliner Historische Studien 31. Ordensstudien 13), Berlin 1999.

Frank I.W., *Albert der Große als Dominikaner seiner Zeit*, Augsburg 1981.

Freed J.B., *The Friars and German Society in the Thirteenth Century*, Cambridge 1977.

Gieraths G., *Die Dominikaner in Worms*, Worms 1964.

Grübel I., *Bettelorden und Frauenfrömmigkeit im 13. Jahrhundert. Das Verhältnis der Mendikanten zu Nonnenklöstern und Beginen am Beispiel Straßburg und Basel* (Kulturgeschichtliche Forschungen 9), Munich 1987.

Halm C., *Klosterleben im Mittelalter: Die Dominikanerinnen in Lemgo, von der Klostergründung bis zur Reformation*, Detmold 2004.

Hecker N., *Bettelorden und Bürgertum. Konflikt und Kooperation in den deutschen Städten des Spätmittelalters*, Frankfurt/M. 1981.

Hergemöller B.-U., *Pfaffenkriege im spätmittelalterlichen Hanseraum*, Cologne-Vienna 1988.

Hertz A., *Dominikus und die Dominikaner*, Freiburg 1981.

Heusinger S. von, *Johannes Mulberg OP (+1414). Ein Leben im Spannungsfeld von Dominikanerobservanz und Beginenstreit*, Berlin 2000.

Hillebrand K., *Das Dominikanerkloster zu Prenzlau. Untersuchungen zur mittelalterlichen Baugeschichte*, Munich-Berlin 2003.

Hinnebusch W.A., *Kleine Geschichte des Dominikanerordens*, Leipzig 2004.

Id., *The Dominicans. A Short History*, Dublin 1985, Staten Island, N.Y. 1975.

Id., *The History of the Dominican Order*, 2 vol., New York 1966-1973.

Jäggi C., *Frauenklöster im Spätmittelalter: die Kirchen der Klarissen und Dominikanerinnen im 13. und 14. Jahrhundert*, Petersberg 2006.

Jászai G. (ed.), *Monastisches Westfalen*, Munich 1982[2].

Kehnel A., *Die Formierung der Gemeinschaften der Minderen Brüder in der Provinz Anglia*, in Melville G. - Oberste J. (eds.), *Die Bettelorden im Aufbau. Beiträge zu Institutionalisierungsprozessen im mittelalterlichen Religiosentum* (Vita regularis 11), Munich 1999, pp. 493-524.

Id., *Regionale Ordnungen universaler Konzepte. Die Franziskaner auf den Britischen Inseln (13.-16. Jh.). Historische Fallstudie zu einer europäischen Gemeinschaft des Mittelalters* (masch. Habil.schr.), Dresden 2003.

Lawrence C.H., *The Friars. The impact of the early mendicant movement on western society*, London 1994.

Lindow, A., *Das Dominikaner-Kloster zu Prenzlau*, Munich 1995.

Moraw P., *Kontinuität und später Wandel. Bemerkungen zur deutschen und deutschsprachigen Mediävistik 1945-1970/75*, in Moraw P. - Schieffer R. (eds.), *Die deutschsprachige Mediävistik im 20. Jahrhundert*, Ostfildern 2005, pp. 103-138.

Müller F. (ed.), *Dominikanerinnen und Dominikaner. Lebensbilder aus dem Predigerorden*, Freiburg 1988.

Müller P., *Bettelorden und Stadtgemeinde in Hildesheim im Mittelalter*, Hannover 1994.

Müller R., *Nationale Abgrenzung in universalen Verbänden? Zur Entwicklung und Autonomiebestrebung der schottischen Franziskaner im 13. und 14. Jahrhundert*, in Butz R. - Oberste J. (eds.), *Studia monastica. Beiträge zum klösterlichen Leben im christlichen Abendland während des Mittelalters* (Vita regularis 22), Munich 2004, pp. 261-285.

Neidiger B., *Mendikanten zwischen Ordensideal und städtischer Realität. Untersuchungen zum wirtschaftlichen Verhalten der Bettelorden in Basel*, Berlin 1981.

Pieper R., *Die Kirchen der Bettelorden in Westfalen*, Werl 1993.

Röhrkasten J., *The Mendicant Houses of Medieval London, 1221-1539*, Munich 2004.

Römer Chr., *Dominikaner und Landesherrschaft um 1300*, "Die Diözese Hildesheim in Vergangenheit und Gegenwart", 49, 1981, pp. 19-32.

Runne R., *Die Dominikaner in Warburg. 1281-1993*, Warburg 1994[3].

Rüther A., *Bettelorden in Stadt und Land. Die Straßburger Mendikantenkonvente und das Elsaß im Spätmittelalter*, Berlin 1997.

Schenkluhn W., *Architektur der Bettelorden: Die Baukunst der Dominikaner und Franziskaner in Europa*, Darmstadt 2000.

Schenkluhn W., *Ordines studentes. Aspekte zur Kirchenarchitektur der Dominikaner und Franziskaner im 13. Jahrhundert*, Berlin 1985.

Schmidt H.-J., *Bettelorden in Trier. Wirksamkeit und Umfeld im hohen und späten Mittelalter*, Trier 1986.

Id., *Die Bettelorden und ihre Niederlassungen in der Mark Brandenburg*, in Schich W. (ed.), *Beiträge zur Entstehung und Entwicklung der Stadt Brandenburg im Mittelalter*, Berlin-New York 1993, pp. 203-225.

Id., *Die Landgrafen von Hessen und die Bettelorden*, in Berg D. (ed.), *Könige, Landesherren und Bettelorden*, (Saxonia Franciscana 10), Werl 1998, pp. 127-152.

Sickert R., *Dominikaner und Episkopat. Zur Etablierung des Predigerordens in südfranzösischen Bischofsstädten (1215-1235)*, in Melville G. - Oberste J. (eds.), *Die Bettelorden im Aufbau* (Vita regularis 11), Munich 1999, pp. 295-319.

Streich G., *Klöster, Stifte und Kommende in Niedersachsen vor der Reformation*, Hildesheim 1986.

Ulpts I., *Die Bettelorden in Mecklenburg*, Werl 1995.

Vicaire M.H., *Dominique et ses prêcheurs*, Fribourg 1977.

Id., *Histoire de saint Dominique*, 2 vol., Paris 1982.

Id., *Saint Dominic and his Times*, translated by Pond K., New York - Toronto - London 1964.

Vöckler M., *Die Stellung und Wirksamkeit der Bettelorden in Thüringen von 1224 bis zum Beginn des 14. Jahrhunderts*, Diss. phil. masch., Jena 1987.

Werner M., *Zwischen politischer Begrenzung und methodischer Offenheit. Wege und Stationen deutscher Landesgeschichtsforschung im 20. Jahrhundert*, in Moraw P. - Schieffer R. (eds.), *Die deutschsprachige Mediävistik im 20. Jahrhundert* (Vorträge und Forschungen 62), Ostfildern 2005, pp. 251-364.

Wilms H., *Geschichte der deutschen Dominikanerinnen (1206-1916)*, Dülmen 1920.

Urban Communities and Dominican Communities in Medieval Castile-León: a Historiographical Outline

RITA RÍOS DE LA LLAVE
University of Alcalá de Henares

Este trabajo pretende dar a conocer las principales líneas de investigación de la historiografía hispánica sobre la Orden de los Dominicos, y muy especialmente con relación a su vinculación con las comunidades urbanas de la Corona castellano-leonesa durante la Edad Media, al tiempo que se evidencian los aspectos que todavía deben ser objeto de un análisis más profundo.

En la primera parte se analiza de forma crítica la evolución de la historiografía hispánica sobre los frailes dominicos en la Corona castellano-leonesa, partiendo de un análisis crítico sobre el trabajo realizado por Vicente Beltrán de Heredia en 1965, seguido de una presentación de la producción posterior. Se puede afirmar que hubo un predominio de los trabajos de los historiadores pertenecientes a la propia Orden de los Dominicos hasta los años ochenta del siglo XX, cuando irrumpieron algunos historiadores ajenos a la misma.

La segunda parte del trabajo está dedicada a la historiografía hispánica sobre las monjas dominicas de Castilla y León, bastante limitada teniendo en cuenta el escaso interés generado por el desarrollo del conventualismo y del monacato femenino, sobre todo en lo referente a la época medieval.

A continuación se exponen los principales temas investigados con relación a la vinculación entre comunidades urbanas y comunidades de monjas y frailes dominicos de Castilla y León durante la Edad Media, como son los procesos de fundación e instalación en las diferentes ciudades castellano-leonesas, el papel de los frailes en las comunidades urbanas (promoviendo la conversión de musulmanes y judíos, colaborando en el desarrollo de la Inquisición, participando en las instituciones universitarias), y sobre todo, los conflictos existentes entre los dominicos y el clero laico de las ciudades.

El trabajo concluye con una presentación de aquellos aspectos que todavía deben ser objeto de investigación, tales como un análisis más completo de los procesos de fundación e instalación, pero relacionándolos con la transformación de las comunidades urbanas, el reclutamiento de monjas y frailes o la labor social de los miembros de la Orden hacia los pobres. Igualmente sería interesante estudiar el cuidado de las comunidades monásticas femeninas a cargo de frailes o clérigos urbanos, y el papel de las monjas en las ciudades medievales desde el punto de vista espiritual, económico y social. Finalmente, también sería necesario abordar la conflictividad entre dominicos y laicos, y sobre todo, profundizar en la evolución general durante la época bajo-medieval.

INTRODUCTION

The mendicant orders liked to establish themselves in urban settings in the Middle Ages, and the Dominican friars were no exception. According to the *De eruditione Praedicatorum* of Humbert of Romans, preaching was not only more effective in the cities, because there were more people, but also more necessary, given that behaviour was worse; moreover, preaching in town had an influence on the surrounding country-side, since the country tended to imitate the city[1].

In any case, religious orders that depended on organised mendicancy could be success-ful only in the cities. Country people had hardly enough for bare subsistence: the only places where there was a surplus that could be donated to the mendicant friars were the towns[2]. But there were some differences: the Franciscan friars liked smaller towns, while the Dominicans settled in the bigger cities. As the famous medieval poem said:

> Bernardus valles, montes Benedictus amabat,
> Oppida Franciscus, celebres Dominicus urbes[3].

Study of the mendicant communities is fundamental in understanding the evolution of the medieval urban world, and this paper examines earlier historiographical work, aim-ing to show some of the key aspects of this relationship in the kingdom of Castile-León, and focusing on the Dominicans, including their female branch. My main interest is to show the most important aspects that have been studied up till now, and the issues that are still waiting to be explored in greater depth.

HISTORIOGRAPHY ON DOMINICAN FRIARS IN MEDIEVAL CASTILE-LEÓN

Spanish historiography has paid very little attention to the mendicant order movement in general, and the Dominicans in particular; while this does not imply a lack of studies, those that exist are clearly insufficient. Vicente Beltrán de Heredia's interesting work (1965) was presented as a critical examination of Dominican historiography for the Province of Spain up till that time, mainly related to Castile[4]. But the article turned out to be a simple commentary on pre-19th century work, mostly a description of the context of the early historiography of the Dominicans in Spain, namely the concern of the general and provincial masters for the history of the whole Order of Preachers.

The first chronicles appeared during the 16th century, and their authors presented them as works related to the history of the whole Order, although they were in practice a compilation of assorted news related to the different kingdoms of the Iberian Penin-sula, including Castile-León. The most outstanding was the *Historia de la Orden de Santo Domingo* by Fray Hernando del Castillo, the first part published in 1584 and the second in 1592, with a continuation by Juan López appearing in 1613. The chronicle by Hernando del Castillo inspired the writers of the 17th, 18th and 19th centuries, who made few new contributions[5]. The material covered included hagiography, bib-liographical works of the Dominicans, biographies of different provincial masters, and publication of chapter acts. But relationships between the Dominican communities and the urban world were not reflected, even though the processes of foundation in Castilian cities have always been of interest.

Futhermore, Beltrán de Heredia´s article was not complete. He did not refer to the work of Martínez-Vigil, published at the end of the 19th century, following the traditional tendency of aiming to write the history of the whole Order[6]. Nor did he mention the important "La Ciencia Tomista", a theological review on Dominican history published since 1910, nor the most recent bibliography on Dominic de Guzman, the founder of the Order of Preachers, or other friars from the kingdom of Castile-León[7]. References to Aureliano Pardo Villar´s works on the Galician area were also missing[8]. But his main omission was the research that he himself, and Manuel María de los Hoyos, another Dominican, were doing from the middle of the 20th century[9]. These researchers was principally concerned with the reformation of the Order during the 15th and 16th centuries, the organization of the different provinces, and the foundation of the monastic communities in the cities.

Despite these efforts, trends in the historiography of the Dominican Order did not really develop, as far as we can see from research into historiographical works of the eighties and nineties. There were a few references to the Order of Preachers, for example Miguel Ángel Ladero Quesada's work on Spanish historiography between 1939 and 1984 related to the Middle Ages. There was also the bibliographical and methodological synthesis of monastic studies by Juan Ramón Romero (1987), and José Luis Martín's article on the historiography of the Church and the religious life (1999)[10]. Ladero Quesada's paragraph on ecclesiastical history did not mention studies on the Dominican Order. Romero, who assembled references to different monastic orders, barely mentioned new work on the processes of foundation[11], and José Luis Martín did not even quote the traditional historiography.

But there was an improvement, thanks to Dominicans such as Ramón Hernández Martín, who did important work on retrieval of sources, mainly the acts of the provincial chapters and some documents about the reformation of the Order, thus following the general trend. Venancio D. Carro, another Dominican friar, worked on Dominic de Guzman. But there were also some Franciscans, like José García Oro, who aimed at a comparative analysis between both Mendicant Orders, mainly with regard to reformation[12]. Finally the *Instituto Histórico Dominicano de San Esteban*, a Dominican institute for historical research, founded the review "Archivo Dominicano", a publication that has become the main dissemination channel for the history of the Order of Preachers in Spain since 1980.

Furthermore, some historians not involved in the Order became interested in the history of the Dominican friars. The first was Antonio Linaje Conde, who produced several works on the installation of the Mendicant Orders in the Iberian Peninsula, mainly the Dominicans. José Sánchez Herrero, a specialist in ecclesiastical history, also researched the Dominicans. María Teresa Barbadillo produced a doctoral dissertation on Dominic de Guzman, while several other scholars have produced monographs on particular monasteries[13].

These three historians show that a change was taking place around that time. Up to the end of the seventies and the beginning of the eighties, the history of the Order of Preachers had been the work of Dominican historians, and the main characteristic had been that they served some specific interests – to praise the main figures of the Order, to emphasise the characteristics of the Dominican way of life, to define the foundation process in the main cities and the provincial organization, and to describe the process of reformation in the Order. Concern with these issues gave rise to a history of the Order centred in itself, as if it had been an isolated institution without relationships with medieval society – as if the Dominican had lived apart. But the non-Dominican historians who were now beginning to research the topic brought about a change. They were still interested in the installation processes and in the history of some communities, but connected with the evolution of the surroundings, and that means bearing in mind the characteristics of the cities where the friars lived.

The outlook has been improving in the last fifteen years, thanks to lay historians interested in religious and ecclesiastical history, particularly in the history of the Dominicans. Work has increased, both on Dominic de Guzman and also on other Dominican friars who played an important role in medieval Castile[14].

Work on the Mendicant Orders as a whole has also improved, examples being the studies of Javier Peña Pérez, the different articles included in the *Proceedings* of the 6th Medieval Studies Week of Nájera, the study by Santiago Aguadé Nieto, or those by Ignacio Álvarez Borge, María del Mar Graña Cid and Rita Ríos[15]. Peña Pérez has approached the appearance of Franciscans and Dominicans in the general context of religious reformation during the High Middle Ages, and their installation in the main cities of Castile and León in the 13th century. While Aguadé has analysed the role of the different Castilian monarchs and members of the royal family in the processes of foundation, Álvarez Borge has dealt with Mendicant Orders and feudalism in Castile, and Rita Ríos has analysed their political role during the 13th century. The above mentioned *Proceedings* include a variety of subjects, including those related to urban communities, such as work on the processes of foundation from a regional point of view, the function of the monasteries in the urban setting and in architectural development, the role of the friars in intellectual and academic development, and the relationship between the friars and the spread of religiosity and spirituality, especially in the cities.

Some other scholars are only interested in the Dominicans, examples being José Salvador y Conde, who wrote a history of the Spanish Province, or Francisco García Serrano, who firstly analysed the relationship between the Dominicans and Don Juan Manuel, one of the main literary figures in medieval Castile, and later the relationship between Preacher friars and cities in Castile-León[16]. Serrano's main interest was the relation between the foundation processes of different communities and urban growth; he mentioned some of the conflicts caused by such processes, and also noted the contacts between Dominicans and the universities, urban oligarchies, the ecclesiastical hierarchy and the nobility, without, however, going deeply into these issues.

Some historians have studied not the whole of the kingdom of Castile, but particular regions. Such is the case of Jesús María Palomares Ibáñez, Carmen Manso Porto or María del Mar Graña Cid for Galicia, J. Toledano Galera, Álvaro Huerga and José María Miura Andrades for Andalusia, and Carlos Ayllón for Murcia[17]. Comparative analysis of Dominicans and Franciscans is the main characteristic of their studies, although interest settles again on the foundation processes of the different communities of friars. There are some differences, however. For example, Palomares offers some concrete data on the history of different monasteries, including documentary information, mainly on economic aspects, while Graña includes the conflicts between the friars and their surroundings, and their relationship with the monarchy. Miura presents a broad report of sources, a list of Dominican bishops and archbishops who occupied the palaces of Andalusia, and a roll of Andalusian friars assisting the monarchy; he also analyses Dominican privileges among the urban population, and their role in Andalusian cities (spiritual care for the Christian communities, missions to the Muslims, participation in war, custody of municipal documents), including conflicts related to services and pastoral care.

Finally we must mention that work devoted to specific communities of Dominican friars has increased in recent years. Studies tend to describe the social insertion processes in certain cities, architectural and artistic aspects, conflicts in the urban world, economic relationships, and cultural issues[18].

But much remains to be done. Beltrán de Heredia's lament of 1965 is still relevant, when he complained about the lack of a general history of the Dominican friars for the Spanish Province[19], not to mention a history of the Dominicans in Castile-León during the Middle Ages, or their role in the cities. We have seen that the historians of the Dominican Order were traditionally more interested in the relationships of each community with the Order in general, rather than in their links with the surroundings, despite the fact that cities were where Dominican communities were usually located. But this has been changing in recent years, and there is no doubt that this is the route that research must take.

At the same time we must abolish the boundary between historians working on religious issues and on those dealing with the transformations of the cities. A methodological change is also needed in research into the cities of the medieval Spanish kingdoms: this has largely ignored the development of monastic communities and the role of Dominicans in the cities. The *Proceedings* of the 29th Medieval Studies Week of Estella in 2003 are proof of this. They presented the work of a whole week devoted to urban societies in medieval Spain, but did not include even one article about urban monastic communities, not to mention the monasteries of Dominican friars, nor any reference to the problems caused by their installation, even though some of the papers refer specifically to urban conflicts[20].

The historians of the Order and the historians of the cities have worked in isolation until now, when it would be logical to work together to arrive at a thorough knowledge of the situation; for, as Juan Ramón Romero has said, "(un monasterio) es, ante todo, una reducción a escala del mundo circundante y una de las pocas instituciones que permite, gracias a la conservación de sus documentos, acercarse al conocimiento de ese mundo"[21] [(a monastery) is above all a reduction to scale of the surrounding world and one of the few institutions that allows us to approach the knowledge of this world through conservation of its documents]. So study of the Dominican friars' monasteries is an essential element in understanding the life of Castilian cities in the Middle Ages.

Spanish Historiography on Dominican Nuns' Communities in Medieval Castile-León

The first studies on women's history appeared in Spain in the seventies, and even though research into contemporary history predominated at the beginning, studies on other historical periods gradually appeared[22]. However, Spanish historians have touched little on some topics related to women's history, such as their role in the monastic world, a common problem with European historiography[23]. It seems incredible that these historians have tended to ignore the significance of the development of female spirituality in medieval Europe from the 12th century.

Little research has been carried out into female conventualism in Spain[24]. For example, there are no articles on this topic in the historiographical review of women's history by María Isabel del Val Valdivieso and others[25]. Only in two more recent works, by Margarita Cantera Montenegro and Isabel Morant, do we find some mention of studies devoted to the religious life of Spanish women[26] – and this despite some recent conferences on the history of female monasticism[27]. But there is no doubt that the insufficient impact of these conferences on research into medieval female monasticism result from chronological restriction (1492-1992), which clearly marginalized most of the work related to the Middle Ages.

However, there have been some essays improving this situation, especially in the case of the Dominican nuns of medieval Castile, and this despite the fact that access to sources is very difficult, given that a lot of the communities are still in existence and the nuns are reluctant to show their documents. But researchers must overcome this impediment if they want to understand the urban phenomenon, given the special relationship between the female institutions of the Dominican Order and their surrounding urban communities. This is mainly evident in the case of the smaller towns, because these were regularly chosen as sites for Dominican convents[28].

Clara Rodríguez Núñez has dedicated some studies to the Dominican nuns in Galicia, following the work of Aureliano Pardo, while José María Miura Andrades has studied Andalusian nuns, who were closely connected to the communities of Beguines, and Carlos Ayllón has researched the communities of Murcia[29]. But there is not as yet any work on Dominican nuns in the kingdom of Castile-León during the Middle Ages as a whole, largely because the local history of most of the female monasteries of the Order of Preachers has not been completed.

Historians have traditionally been interested in the first Dominican nuns' communities. The Convent of Santo Domingo el Real in Madrid has been most studied, with editions of sources, the origin of the institution, architecture and sculpture, comparative analyses between it and other mendicant communities, and more recently some studies that show the relationship with the urban surroundings from a economic and social point of view, such as Carlos Duart´s article on the relationships with the *alfoz* [medieval county borough], Manuel Montero´s research into the origin of the prioresses, the work by María Isabel del Val and Rita Ríos, and especially Juan Ramón Romero's doctoral dissertation[30].

There is also much detailed work on the Convent of Santa María la Real in Zamora – the third institution that the Dominican Order founded in Castile – analysing its origin, the relationships between it and the communities of *beatas* [Beguines], and conflicts with the religious authorities[31]. I shall omit here work on the Convent of Santo Domingo el Real in Caleruega, the second female monastery of the Dominican Order in Castile, given the rural character of its setting. But mention should be made of monographs and articles on other convents of Dominican nuns founded in Castilian cities during the Middle Ages, that have appeared more recently, mainly in the nineties[32].

The picture is slowly being completed, therefore, although some institutions are still awaiting research, while others that have been studied still have unsolved questions, like the origin of the nuns, or the recruitment of the friars and the clergy with responsibility for the *cura monialium*, a very important aspect related to the cloister. The processes of the creation and development of each monastic patrimony, the relationships between the communities and the urban population, lay or ecclesiastical, the religious, welfare and educational functions of each community, the conflicts caused by the installation processes or the fulfilment of those functions, are all issues to be analysed. All of these elements are useful for defining the influence of each community and its relationships, not only with the nearby city but also with others located in different parts of Castile and León.

Some Research Topics Related to Urban Communities and Dominican Communities

In spite of the lack of work on the relationships between monastic communities of the Dominican Order and the urban world of medieval Castile, some interesting topics can certainly be traced in the bibliography mentioned above.

The first interesting point for Spanish historians has been the establishment of a chronology for the foundation of the Dominican monastic communities in the main Spanish cities, starting with the arrival of the first friars in 1217 – an event which happened even before Fernando III united the two kingdoms in 1230 to form Castile-León. The chronology is rather confused, because most of the monasteries claimed to have been founded by Dominic de Guzman himself, in his travels around the Iberian Peninsula during the autumn of 1218. It is clear, however, that these monasteries were set up on the outskirts of flourishing cities, towns with political or cultural prestige, where industry and the trade were growing activities[33].

Royal patronage was very important during the 13th century, especially under Alfonso X, when the network of monasteries extended to the small towns as well; large monasteries were built here, especially for female communities. Some convents were also located in the cities of regions that had previously been left out, such as Galicia or Andalusia, where the expansion took place at the same time as the Spanish Christian Reconquest from the Muslims[34]. So when the Dominican Provincial Chapter met in 1299, the Order had 44 male monasteries located in the whole Iberian Peninsula, half of them in Castile[35]; but there were only three communities for nuns, those in Madrid, Caleruega and Zamora[36].

The situation during the 14th and 15th centuries has not much interested scholars up to now. The only figures for the Late Middle Ages are from Hoyos, who counted 65 male communities and 27 female ones in Castile-León[37]. But these figures must be checked, because at least 36 female communities have been located for the beginning of the 16th century[38].

Another topic of interest for Spanish historians has been the role of the Dominicans in Castilian urban communities during the Middle Ages, which they usually shared with the Franciscans.

Firstly the spiritual functions must be mentioned. It seems that the friars managed the main dioceses; they were responsible for the pastoral care of the Christian population, and also for the work of conversion of Muslims from the 13th century onwards. The Dominicans began to enlarge this activity to the Jews during the 15th century, when friars like Vincent Ferrer, a Dominican from Valencia, preached in the cities of Castile-León in an attempt to convert the Jewish population. Dominicans would later play a significant role in the treatment given to Jews and converts, and in the development of the Inquisition[39].

Dominican participation in the universities has also attracted the attention of scholars. The Preachers had *studia generalia* and provincial institutions in cities such as Salamanca, Santiago de Compostela, Burgos and Valladolid[40]. They did important work here, which benefited not only members of the Order but also other students. In this way, too, they could take part in university life; for example, the Dominican prior was a member of the court that solved disputes between the members of the University of Salamanca[41].

The most common topic of research in Spanish historiography is that related to the conflicts between the Dominicans and the secular clergy of the cities where they lived, in which laymen also sometimes participated. This was not a phenomenon unique to the

Castile-León kingdom, but was common to the whole of Europe[42]. But it was especially serious in Castilian cities, where the Church had lost wealth due to the agrarian crisis of the second half of the 13th century, so that that the friars had to compete with parish clergy, bishops, the clergy of the cathedrals and the older religious orders[43]. When the Dominican friars settled in the cities, the traditional clergy lost some of the gifts and the income from work done by priests, while the relationship between Dominicans and the urban population in non-religious matters was increasing. This situation was largely beyond the bishops' control, since the friars were under purely Papal jurisdiction[44]. The secular clergy blamed the Dominicans for the economic situation and the reaction was often very violent.

Spanish historiography has recorded numerous examples, mainly from the 13th century. The Dominicans of Palencia confronted Bishop Tello and the cathedral clergy in 1233[45]. There was also a dispute in Burgos, where conflicts between friars and cathedral clergy began in 1250, when Pope Innocent IV gave the Preachers permission to bury laymen in their churches and cemeteries; they also fought in subsequent years, because the Dominicans wanted to build their new monastery near the cathedral[46]. The bishop of Zamora, Suero Pérez de Velasco, defied the friars, who were not allowed to preach, to have relationships with laymen, or to minister to the Dominican nuns of the city; some nuns were also expelled from their convent[47].

There were also some conflicts in the cities in Galicia. The bishop of Tuy threatened those helping to build the Dominican monastery with excommunication, and the clergy of Lugo cathedral stopped the construction of the Dominican monastery and expelled the friars in 1276. The clergy of Santiago de Compostela cathedral rejected the appointment of Rodrigo González as archbishop, because he was the Dominican provincial master[48].

Finally it is interesting to mention the intervention of Pope Honorius IV in September 1285, when the Preachers of the Spanish Province complained about some bishops who persecuted them[49], and that of King Sancho IV, who had to place the Dominican communities of the Castile kingdom under the protection of the Monastery of *San Pablo* in Burgos in 1288, in order to avoid the improper attitudes of bishops and secular clergy[50].

Conclusion

This description of Spanish historiography on Dominican and urban communities in Castile-León shows that much work remains to be done.

Studies need to be carried out on the foundation and installation processes of Dominican monasteries and convents and their characteristics, including their relation to changes in urban communities. Another point of interest is the recruitment of nuns and friars. Historians have paid very little attention to Dominican duties such as social work with the poor, to the care of female communities by friars or urban clergy, or to the role of nuns in the medieval cities from a spiritual, economic and social point of view – all questions of great interest. Also requiring study are the conflicts between Preachers and laymen. Finally, although the situation during 13th century is quite well-researched, analysis of the situation in the following centuries, with the significant late medieval crisis, remains to be studied.

These new topics of research would help us to define the changes in the relationship between Dominicans and urban society. It would, in short, be a way to better understand the urban phenomenon in medieval Castile-León.

Notes

[1]   J. Le Goff, *Ordres mendiants et urbanisation dans la France médiévale*, "Annales E.S.C.", 25, 1970, p. 929.

[2]   C.H. Lawrence, *El monacato medieval. Formas de vida religiosa en Europa occidental durante la Edad Media*, Madrid 1999, pp. 304-305.

[3]   J. Le Goff, *Les ordres mendiants*, in *Moines et religieux au Moyen Age*, Paris 1994, p. 232.

[4]   V. Beltrán de Heredia, *Examen crítico de la historiografía dominicana en las Provincias de España y particularmente en Castilla*, "Archivum Fratrum Praedicatorum", 35, 1965, pp. 195-248.

[5]   The work of J. de Marieta, J. de la Parra and A. de Lorea stood out in the 17th century, those of J. Sarabia y Lezama, M. de Medrano, T. de Aróstegui and P. de Larrainzar in the 18th century, and finally those of M. Herrero and J. M. Suárez in the 19th century. They were all members of the Dominican Order.

[6]   R. Martínez-Vigil, *La Orden de Predicadores. Sus glorias, su santidad, apostolado, ciencias, artes y gobierno de los pueblos, seguidas del ensayo de una Biblioteca de Dominicos españoles*, Madrid-Paris 1884.

[7]   About Dominic de Guzman: L. González Alonso-Getino, *Vida de Santo Domingo de Guzmán escrita por el Beato Jordán de Sajonia*, Vergara 1916; Id., *Los nueve modos de orar del señor Santo Domingo*, "La Ciencia Tomista", 70, 1921; Id., *Origen del rosario y leyendas castellanas del siglo XIII sobre Santo Domingo de Guzmán*, Vergara 1925; Id., *Santo Domingo de Guzmán, prototipo del apóstol medieval*, Madrid 1939; Id., *Vida de Santo Domingo de Guzmán*, Madrid 1939; R. Castaño, *Santo Domingo de Guzmán*, Barcelona 1909; F. Díez Pardo, *Santo Domingo de Guzmán*, Vergara 1935; D. Díez de Triana, *Santo Domingo, apóstol universitario*, Barcelona 1945; R. Fernández Álvarez, *Santo Domingo de Guzmán. Consideraciones históricas sobre su vida*, Buenos Aires 1946; M. Gelabert - J.M. Milagro - J.M. de Garganta, *Santo Domingo de Guzmán visto por sus contemporáneos*, Madrid 1947; J.M. Macías, *Santo Domingo de Guzmán, fundador de la Orden de Predicadores*, Madrid 1979. About other Dominican friars: L. González Alonso-Getino, *Capítulos provinciales y priores provinciales de la Orden de Santo Domingo en España*, "La Ciencia Tomista", 13, 1916, pp. 67-96, 210-244; Id., *Dominicos españoles confesores de reyes*, "La Ciencia Tomista", 14, 1916, pp. 374-451; Id., *Vida y obra de fray Lope de Barrientos*, Salamanca 1927; M. Gaibrois, *Fray Munio de Zamora*, in *Abhandlungen aus dem Gebiete der mittleren und neueren Geschichte und ihrer Hilfswissenschaften. Eine Festgabe zum siebzigsten Geburtstag Geh. Rat Prof. Dr. Heinrich Finke*, Münster 1925, pp. 135-154.

[8]   A. Pardo Villar, *El convento de Santo Domingo de Tuy*, "Boletín de la Comisión de Monumentos de Orense", 14, 1941; Id., *Historia del convento de Santo Domingo de Pontevedra*, Pontevedra 1942; Id., *La orden dominicana en La Coruña*, La Coruña 1953; Id., *Los dominicos en Galicia*, Santiago de Compostela 1939; Id., *Los dominicos en Santiago. Los apuntes históricos*, Madrid 1953.

[9]   V. Beltrán de Heredia, *El convento de S. Esteban en sus relaciones con la Iglesia y la Universidad de Salamanca durante los siglos XIII, XIV y XV*, "La Ciencia Tomista", 84, 1926, pp. 95-116; Id., *Historia de la Reforma de la Provincia de España (1450-1550)*, Roma 1939; Id., *El intercambio hispano-lusitano en la historia de la Orden de Predicadores*, "Archivo Ibero-Americano", 16, 1944, pp. 521-554; Id., *Introducción a los orígenes de la observancia en España. Las reformas de los siglos XIV y XV*, "Archivo Ibero-Americano", 65, 1957, pp.

5-60; Id., *Los comienzos de la reforma dominicana en Castilla, particularmente en el convento de San Esteban de Salamanca y su irradiación a la provincia de Portugal*, "Archivum Fratrum Praedicatorum", 28, 1958, pp. 221-262; Id., *Miscelánea Beltrán de Heredia*, Salamanca 1971; M.M. de los Hoyos, *Primeras fundaciones dominicas en España*, "Boletín de la Institución Fernán González", 31, 1952, pp. 198-219; Id., *Registro documental. Material inédito dominicano español*, Valladolid 1961-1963; Id., *Registro historial de la Provincia de España*, Salamanca 1966-1968.

[10] M.A. Ladero Quesada, *Aproximación al medievalismo español (1939-1984)*, in V. Vázquez de Prada - I. Olábarri - A. Floristán Imizcoz, *La historiografía en Occidente desde 1945. Actitudes, tendencias y problemas metodológicos. Actas de las III Conversaciones Internacionales de Historia. Universidad de Navarra (Pamplona, 5-7 abril 1984)*, Pamplona 1985, pp. 69-86; J.R. Romero, *Los monasterios en la España medieval*, Madrid 1987; J.L. Martín, *Iglesia y vida religiosa*, in *La Historia Medieval en España. Un balance historiográfico (1968-1998). XXV Semana de Estudios Medievales. Estella, 14 - 18 July 1998*, Pamplona 1999, pp. 431-456.

[11] G. Arriaga, *Historia del insigne convento de San Pablo de la ciudad de Burgos y de sus ilustres hijos*, Burgos 1972; J.M. Miura Andrades, *Las fundaciones de la Orden de Predicadores en Andalucía durante el reinado de Juan I de Castilla (1379-1390)*, "Arquivo Histórico Português", 4, 1989, pp. 263-275; Id., *Las fundaciones de la Orden de Predicadores en Andalucía (1236-1591). Un análisis cronológico*, "Actas del Congreso Internacional sobre dominicos y el Nuevo Mundo", 1, 1988, pp. 73-99.

[12] R. Hernández, *Actas de la Congregación de la Reforma de la Provincia de España*, "Archivo Dominicano", 1, 1980, pp. 7-140, 1981, 2, pp. 5-118; Id., *Registro Antiguo de la Provincia de España I*, "Archivo Dominicano", 1981, 2, pp. 245-298; Id., *Actas de los Capítulos provinciales de la Provincia de España*, "Archivo Dominicano", 3, 1982, pp. 13-85; Id., *Pergaminos de Actas de los Capítulos Provinciales del siglo XIII de la Provincia Dominicana de España*, "Archivo Dominicano", 4, 1983, pp. 5-73; Id., *Las primeras Actas de los Capítulos Provinciales de la Provincia de España*, in *Archivo Dominicano*, 5, 1984, pp. 5-41; Id., *Repertorio documental*, "Archivo Dominicano", 7, 1986, pp. 287-292; Id., *La reforma dominicana entre los concilios de Constanza y Basilea*, "Archivo Dominicano", 8, 1987, pp. 5-50; Id., *Archivo antiguo del convento de San Esteban de Salamanca*, "Archivo Dominicano", 11, 1990, pp. 319-358, 12, 1991, pp. 205-231; Id., *Acta del Capítulo Provincial de Córdoba de 1464*, "Archivo Dominicano", 15, 1994, pp. 49-92; Id., *Santo Domingo de Guzmán, fundador de la primera orden universitaria, apostólica y misionera*, "La Ciencia Tomista", 220, 1946, pp. 5-81, 221, pp. 282-329; Id., *Caleruega, cuna de Santo Domingo de Guzmán*, Madrid 1952 - 1955; Id., *Caleruega, orígenes y monumentos: cuna de Santo Domingo*, Caleruega 1967; Id., *Santo Domingo de Guzmán. Historia documentada*, Madrid 1973. J. García Oro, *La reforma de los religiosos españoles en tiempo de los Reyes Católicos*, Valladolid 1969; Id., *Cisneros y la reforma del clero español en tiempo de los Reyes Católicos*, Madrid 1971; Id., *Conventualismo y observancia. La reforma de las órdenes religiosas en los siglos XV y XVI*, in *Historia de la Iglesia en España*, Madrid 1982; Id., *Viveiro en los siglos XIV y XV. La colección diplomática de Santo Domingo de Viveiro*, "Estudios Mindonienses", 3, 1987, pp. 11-131.

[13] A. Linage Conde, *Los dominicos*, in R. García-Villoslada, *Historia de la Iglesia en España*, Madrid 1982, pp. 136-142; Id., *De los monjes a los frailes. Notas sobre la implantación de la vida religiosa medieval en el territorio castellano-leonés*, in *El pasado histórico de Castilla y León, vol. 1: Edad Media*, Burgos 1983, pp. 263-274; Id., *El antiguo monacato en España a la hora de la implantación mendicante*, "Arquivo Histórico Dominicano Português", 3, 1983, pp. 81-114; Id., *Algunas particularidades de la Implantación Mendicante en la Península Ibérica*, "Arquivo Histórico Dominicano Português", 8/2, 1986, pp. 1-26; J. Sánchez Herrero, *Monjes y frailes. Religiosos y religiosas en Andalucía durante la Baja Edad Media*, in *Actas del III Coloquio de Historia medieval andaluza: grupos no privilegiados (Jaén, Nov.1982)*, Jaén 1984, pp. 405-456; Id., *Antecedentes Medievales de la Orden Dominica*, "Actas del Congreso Internacional sobre dominicos y el Nuevo Mundo", 1, 1988, pp. 29-71; M.T. Barbadillo de la Fuente, *Vida de Santo Domingo de Guzmán*, Madrid 1985. Dominican friars monasteries: J.M. Palomares Ibáñez, *Aspectos de la historia del convento de San Pablo de Valladolid*, "Archivum Fratrum Praedicatorum", 43, 1973, pp. 91-135; M. Espinar Moreno, *Convento de Santo Domingo (Monasterio de Santa Cruz la Real, 1492-1512)*, "Cuadernos de Estudios Medievales", 4-5, 1976-1977, pp. 73-87; J.L. Espinel Marcos, *San Esteban de Salamanca. Historia y Guía (siglos XII-XX)*, Salamanca 1978; J. Barrado, *El convento de San Pedro Mártir. Notas históricas en el V Centenario de su imprenta (1483-1983)*,

18, "Toletum", 1986, pp. 181-211; A. Rodríguez G. de Ceballos, *La Iglesia y el convento de San Esteban de Salamanca*, Salamanca 1987; M.C. Enríquez Paradela, *Colección diplomática del monasterio y convento de Santo Domingo de Ribadavia*, Ourense 1987.

[14] About Dominic de Guzman: L. Galmés Mas, *Juana de Aza y Domingo de Guzmán*, in *Santo Domingo de Caleruega. Jornadas de Estudios Medievales*, Salamanca 1994, pp. 325-339; B. Farrely, *¿Fue Santo Domingo de Guzmán canónigo premonstratense en el monasterio de Santa María de la Vida?*, "Archivo Dominicano", 16, 1995, pp. 155-198. Several papers in C. Aniz Iriarte - L.V. Díaz Martín, *Santo Domingo de Caleruega en su contexto socio-político, 1170-1221. Jornadas de estudios medievales. Caleruega 1992-1993*, Salamanca 1994; Id., *Santo Domingo de Caleruega. Contexto cultural. III Jornadas de Estudios Medievales. Caleruega, 1994*, Salamanca 1995; Id., *Santo Domingo de Caleruega. Contexto eclesial religioso. IV Jornadas de Estudios Medievales. Caleruega, 1995*, Salamanca 1996; C. Aniz Iriarte - J.M. Hernández, *Santo Domingo, canónigo de Osma. Presencia dominicana en la diócesis de Osma*, Salamanca 1997; Id., *Santo Domingo de Guzmán, canónigo de Osma*, Salamanca 1997; D. Iturgáiz, *Osma, plataforma espiritual de Santo Domingo de Guzmán*, "Archivo Dominicano", 17, 1996, pp. 231-250. About the Dominican friars: C. Manso Porto, *El obispo fray Pedro López de Aguiar, O.P. (1349-1390), reseña biográfica y aproximación a los principales acontecimientos en su diócesis durante el reinado de Pedro I*, "Archivo Dominicano", 14, 1993, pp. 43-67; P. Cátedra, *Sermón, sociedad y literatura en la Edad Media, San Vicente Ferrer en Castilla (1411-1412)*, Valladolid 1994; J.M. Nieto Soria, *Los proyectos de reforma eclesiástica de un colaborador de Juan II de Castilla: el obispo Barrientos*, "Cuadernos de Estudios Medievales y Ciencias y Técnicas Historiográficas", 21-23, 1995-1998, pp. 493-516.

[15] J. Peña Pérez, *Expansión de las órdenes conventuales en León y Castilla: franciscanos y dominicos en el siglo XIII*, in *III Semana de Estudios Medievales. Nájera, 3 - 7 August 1992*, Logroño 1993, pp. 179-198; *VI Semana de Estudios Medievales. Nájera, del 31 de julio al 4 de agosto de 1995. Espiritualidad y franciscanismo*, Logroño 1996; S. Aguadé Nieto, *Alfonso X y las órdenes mendicantes*, in D. Berg (ed.), *Könige, Landesherren und Bettelorden*, Werl 1998, pp. 277-302; I. Álvarez Borge, *Órdenes mendicantes y estructuras feudales de poder en Castilla la Vieja (siglos XIII y XIV)*, "Revista de Historia Económica", 17/3, 1999, pp. 543-578; M.M. Graña Cid, *Geografía de lo sagrado y creación de conventos: las órdenes mendicantes en Galicia (siglos XIII-XIV)*, "Miscelánea Comillas. Revista de teología y ciencias humanas", 57/110, 1999, pp. 169-196; R. Ríos, *The Role of the Mendicant Orders in the Political Life of Castile and León in the Later 13th Century*, in *Religion and Political Change in Europe: Past and Present*, Pisa 2003, pp. 21-32.

[16] J. Salvador y Conde, *Historia de la provincia dominicana de España*, Salamanca 1989-1994; F. García Serrano, *Don Juan Manuel and his connection with the Order of Preachers*, "Anuario de Estudios Medievales", 23, 1993, pp. 151-162; Id., *Preachers of the City. The Expansion of the Dominican Order in Castile (1217-1348)*, New Orleans 1997; Id., *Mundo urbano y dominicos en la Castilla medieval*, "Archivo Dominicano", 18, 1997, pp. 255-273.

[17] J.M. Palomares Ibáñez, *Aproximación histórica a la presencia de los dominicos en Galicia*, "Archivo Dominicano", 3, 1982, pp. 85-115; C. Manso Porto, *El códice medieval del Convento de Santo Domingo de Santiago*, "Archivo Dominicano", 3, 1982, pp. 117-164, 4, 1983, pp. 75-129, 5, 1984, pp. 43-90, 6, 1985, pp. 23-55, 7, 1986, pp. 59-76; Id., *Los cartularios medievales de Santo Domingo de Santiago*, "Archivo dominicano", 9, 1988, pp. 55-69; Id., *La arquitectura medieval de la Orden de Predicadores en Galicia*, "Archivo Dominicano", 11, 1990, pp. 5-68; Id., *Arte gótico en Galicia: los Dominicos*, La Coruña 1993; Id., *Las Órdenes Mendicantes en el Obispado de Mondoñedo. El convento de San Martín de Villaoriente*, Salamanca 1990; Id., *Franciscanismo y dominicos en la Galicia medieval: aspectos de una posición de privilegio*, "Archivo Ibero-Americano", 209-212, 1993, pp. 231-270; J. Toledano Galera, *Notas sobre la implantación de las órdenes mendicantes en Jaén en la Baja Edad Media*, "Instituto de Estudios Giennenses", 138, 1989, pp. 37-47; A. Huerga, *Los dominicos en Andalucía*, Sevilla 1992; J.M. Miura Andrades, *Las fundaciones de la Orden de Predicadores en el reino de Córdoba*, "Archivo Dominicano", 9, 1988, pp. 267-383, 10, 1989, pp. 231-389; Id., *Conventos y organización social del espacio. Fundadores y fundaciones dominicas en la Andalucía medieval*, "Historia Urbana", 2, 1993, pp. 85-111; Id., *La presencia mendicante en la Andalucía de Fernando III*, "Archivo Hispalense", 234-236, 1994, pp. 509-519; Id., *Frailes, monjas y conventos. Las Órdenes Mendicantes y la sociedad sevillana bajome-*

dieval, Sevilla 1998; C. Ayllón Gutiérrez, *La Orden de Predicadores en el Sureste de Castilla (Las fundaciones medievales de Murcia, Chinchilla y Alcaraz hasta el Concilio de Trento)*, Albacete 2002.

[18] Communities and cities: R. Martín Rodrigo, *El Monasterio de Santo Domingo de Piedrahíta*, Piedrahíta 1991; P. Linehan, *A tale of two cities: capitular Burgos and mendicant Burgos in the thirteenth century*, in D. Abulafia - M. Franklin - M. Rubien, *Church and City 1000-1500. Essays in honour of Christopher Brooke*, Cambridge 1992, pp. 81-110. J. Salvador y Conde, *Los conventos de Dominicos en Palencia*, Palencia 1997; A. Alcalde - I. Sánchez, *San Pedro Mártir el Real: Toledo*, Ciudad Real 1997. Disputes: E. Cal Pardo, *Pleito promovido por los frailes de Santo Domingo y San Francisco de Viveiro contra los curas de las parroquias de Santa María y Santiago de dicha villa... Santiago. Rupeforte, 10.V.1334*, "Estudios Mindonienses", 7, 1991, pp. 124-131. Economical relationships: A. Olivera Sánchez, *El lugar de Rascón. De dote de boda a manos de los dominicos de San Esteban*, "Archivo Dominicano", 13, 1991, pp. 147-153; L. Sastre, *Las propiedades del convento de Santo Domingo de la Coruña*, "Archivo Dominicano", 13, 1992, pp. 281-393. Architectonic, artistic and cultural issues: M.P. de Sena, *Los libros del convento de San Esteban en la Universidad de Salamanca*, "Archivo Dominicano", 12, 1991, pp. 233-277, 13, 1993, pp. 377-401; A. Castro Santamaría, *Sobre la fundación y construcción de la iglesia de San Esteban de Salamanca*, "Archivo Dominicano", 13, 1992, pp. 155-173; M.D. Barral Rivadulla, *Dos documentos para ampliar la historia del desaparecido monasterio de Santo Domingo de La Coruña*, "Archivo Dominicano", 13, 1992, pp. 245-251; L. García Ballester, *Naturaleza y ciencia en la Castilla del siglo XIII. Los orígenes de una tradición: los studia franciscano y dominico de Santiago de Compostela (1222-1230)*, "Arbor", 153, 1996, pp. 69-125; L. Lorente Toledo, *San Pedro Mártir el Real, conventual y universitario: siglos XIII-XIX, Toledo*, Ciudad Real 2002.

[19] Beltrán de Heredia, *Examen crítico* cit., p. 195.

[20] *XXIX Semana de Estudios Medievales. Estella, 15 - 19 July 2002. Las sociedades urbanas en la España medieval*, Pamplona 2003.

[21] Romero, *Monasterios* cit., p. 42.

[22] M.V. López-Cordón Cortezo, *Mujer e historiografía: del androcentrismo a las relaciones de género*, in J.L. de la Granja - A. Reig Tapia - R. Miralles, *Tuñón de Lara y la historiografía española*, Madrid 1999, pp. 260-266.

[23] P. l´Hermitte-Leclercq, *Las mujeres en el orden feudal (siglos XI y XII)*, in G. Duby - M. Perrot, *Historia de las mujeres en Occidente. 2: La Edad Media*, Madrid 1992, p. 286; J. Burton, *Monastic and Religious Orders in Britain, 1000-1300*, Cambridge 1994, p. 85.

[24] M.A. Ladero Quesada, J.M. Nieto Soria, *Iglesia y sociedad en los siglos XIII al XV (ámbito castellano-leonés). Estado de la investigación*, "En la España Medieval", 11, 1998, p. 144.

[25] M.I. Del Val Valdivieso - M.S. Tomás Pérez - M.J. Dueñas Cepeda - C. Cubo de la Rosa, *La historia de las mujeres: una revisión historiográfica*, Valladolid 2004.

[26] M. Cantera Montenegro, *Las órdenes religiosas*, "Medievalismo: Boletín de la Sociedad Española de Estudios Medievales", 13, 2004, pp. 113-126; I. Morant, *Historia de las mujeres en España y América Latina. Vol. I: De la Prehistoria a la Edad Media*, Madrid 2005.

[27] The first congress took place in León in 1992, the second in México in 1995, and the last in León in 2004.

[28] M.M. Graña Cid, *Frailes, predicación y caminos en Madrid. Un modelo para estudiar la itinerancia mendicante en la Edad Media*, in C. Segura Graíño, *Caminos y caminantes por las tierras del Madrid medieval*, Madrid 1994, p. 288.

[29] A. Pardo Villar, *El convento de Nuestra Señora de Valdeflores*, "Boletín de la Comisión de Monumentos de Lugo", 3, 1947; Id., *El convento de Santa María de Belvís*, "Boletín de la Comisión Provincial de Monumentos de Orense", 15, 1945-1946, pp. 32-78, 90-94; C. Rodríguez Núñez - M. Díez Tie, *La mujer gallega y los conventos dominicos (siglos XIV y XV). Aproximación documental e iconográfica*, in *Las mujeres en el cristianismo medieval*, Madrid 1989, pp. 303-315; C. Rodríguez Núñez, *Santa María de Belvís, un convento mendicante femenino en la Baja Edad Media (1305-1400)*, "Estudios Mindonienses", 5, 1989, pp. 335-485; Id., *El monasterio de dominicas de Belvís de Santiago de Compostela*, "Estudios Mindonienses", 5, 1990; Id., *Los conventos de dominicas en Galicia. La Orden de Predicadores y su papel institucionalizador de la religiosidad*

femenina bajomedieval, "Archivo Dominicano", 13, 1992, pp. 191-197; C. Rodríguez Núñez, *Los conventos femeninos en Galicia. El papel de la mujer en la sociedad medieval*, Santiago de Compostela 1993; Id., *El Monasterio de Nuestra Señora de Valdeflores de Viveiro*, El Ferrol 1994; J.M. Miura Andrades, *Beatas y beaterios andaluces en la Baja Edad Media; Su vinculación con la Orden de Predicadores*, in *Andalucía entre Oriente y Occidente (1236-1492). Actas del V Coloquio Internacional de Historia Medieval de Andalucía*, Córdoba 1988, pp. 527-536; Id., *Algunas notas sobre las beatas andaluzas*, in *Las mujeres en el cristianismo medieval*, Madrid 1989, pp. 289-302; Id., *Milagros, Beatas y Fundaciones de Conventos*, in *La religiosidad popular*, Barcelona 1989, pp. 443-460; Miura, *Frailes* cit.; Ayllón, *Orden* cit., pp. 98-109.

[30]   L. González Alonso-Getino, *Centenario y Cartulario de nuestra comunidad*, "La Ciencia Tomista", 19, 1919, pp. 15-20, 127-143, 253-272, 20, 1920, pp. 6-21; M.T. Carrasco Lazareno, *Santo Domingo el Real de Madrid. Estudio documental (1203-1284). Memoria de Licenciatura inédita*, Madrid 1990; Id., *La documentación de Santo Domingo el Real de Madrid (1284-1416). Tesis doctoral inédita*, Madrid 1994.; Id., *Los conventos de San Francisco y de Santo Domingo de la villa de Madrid (siglos XIII-XV). Breves consideraciones históricas, jurídicas y diplomáticas*, in *VI Semana de Estudios Medievales. Nájera, del 31 de julio al 4 de agosto de 1995. Espiritualidad y franciscanismo*, Logroño 1996, pp. 239-254; C. Duart Gaitero, *Relaciones económicas del monasterio de Santo Domingo de Madrid con el alfoz de la villa (1219-1474)*, in *I Jornadas de Estudios sobre la Provincia de Madrid. Ciudad Escolar Provincial. Madrid, 17- 19 December 1979*, Madrid 1980, pp. 628-631; J.M. Eguren, *Memoria histórico-descriptiva del monasterio de Santo Domingo de Madrid*, "Semanario Pintoresco Español", 15, 1850, pp. 33-35, 41-44, 50-52; M. Montero Vallejo, *Las prioras del monasterio de Santo Domingo el Real de Madrid durante la Edad Media*, "Anales del Instituto de Estudios Madrileños", 34, 1994, pp. 293-318; M.I. Pérez de Tudela y Velasco, *Madrid en la documentación de Santo Domingo el Real*, in *La ciudad hispánica durante los siglos XIII al XVI*, Madrid 1985, 2, pp. 991-1010; R. Ríos de la Llave, *La implantación de las órdenes mendicantes en Madrid en la Edad Media: Santo Domingo el Real. Memoria de Licenciatura inédita*, Alcalá de Henares 2000; J.R. Romero Fernández Pacheco, *Santo Domingo el Real de Madrid. Ordenación de un señorío conventual durante la Baja Edad Media (1219-1530). Tesis doctoral inédita*, Madrid 2004; A. Rull Sabater, *Del antiguo al nuevo convento de Santo Domingo el Real*, "Anales del Instituto de Estudios Madrileños", 35, 1995, pp. 389-402; G. Salteráin Díez, *El nuevo monasterio de Santo Domingo el Real*, "Anales del Instituto de Estudios Madrileños", 22, 1985, pp. 177-184; S. Tugwell, *St. Dominic´s Letter to the Nuns in Madrid*, "Archivum Fratrum Praedicatorum", 56, 1986, pp. 5-1; C.J. Vidal, *Breve reseña histórica del Convento de Santo Domingo el Real de Madrid. Desde su fundación por el mismo patriarca Domingo de Guzmán años del Señor de 1218*, Santiago de Compostela 1946.

[31]   A. Piñuela Ximénez, *Apuntes históricos del convento de Santa María la Real de las Dueñas de la Orden de Predicadores de la ciudad de Zamora*, Zamora 1988; Mª L. Bueno Domínguez, *Las mujeres de Santa María de las Dueñas: la realidad humana*, in *Las mujeres en el cristianismo medieval*, Madrid 1989, pp. 231-245; Id., *Santa María de las Dueñas de Zamora. ¿Beguinas o monjas? El proceso de 1279*, in *Historia. Instituciones. Documentos*, 1993, 20, pp. 43-97; P. Linehan, *The Ladies of Zamora*, Manchester 1997.

[32]   E. Abaigar, *El Convento de la Encarnación de Bilbao (Síntesis histórico-crítica)*, Bilbao 1971; F. Martínez Vázquez, *Reseña histórica y catálogo documental del monasterio de Quejana, 1374-1974, VI Centenario*, "Boletín de la Institución Sancho el Sabio", 19, 1975, pp. 5-180; P. Galindo Romeo, *Catálogo del Archivo del monasterio de Sancti Spiritus de Toro*, "Archivos Leoneses", 1976, pp. 205-236; C- Aniz Iriarte, *500 años de fidelidad: V centenario de la fundación del convento de Santa Catalina de Siena, Valladolid, 1488-1988*, Caleruega 1988; A. Bueno Espinar, *Monasterio de Santa Ana: la historia de las religiosas dominicas*, Murcia 1990; A. Rodríguez Palop, *V Centenario del Monasterio Dominicano de Santa Ana: Murcia (1490-1990): conferencias*, Murcia 1990; J. Méndez Varo, *Convento del Espíritu Santo y Palacio de las Cuevas del Becerro*, Écija 1990; M.J. Sanz Fuentes, *Documentos del Monasterio de Santa María la Real de Medina del Campo en la Biblioteca Universitaria de Oviedo*, "Historia. Instituciones. Documentos", 18, 1991, pp. 445-465; M.L. Fernández Baizán, *El Monasterio de Santamaría de las Dueñas «El Real» de la villa de Medina del Campo, también llamado de Santa María de los Huertos, en la baja edad media*, Madrid 1992; M.J. Sanz Fuentes, *Constituciones de la orden dominicana femenina en un manuscrito de la biblioteca universitaria de Oviedo*, in *I Congreso Internacional del Monacato Femenino en España, Portugal y América. 1492-1992*, León 1993, pp. 141-148; J. Enríquez Fernández, *Colección documental de los monasterios de Santo Domingo de Lequei-*

tio (1289-1520) y Santa Ana de Elorrio (1480-1520), Donostia 1993; J.M. Garrastachu, *Seiscientos años de aventuras: En el VI centenario de la fundación del monasterio de MM. Dominicas de Lequeitio [1368-1968]*, Bilbao 1968; C. Aníz Iriarte - L.V. Martín, *Real Monasterio de San Pedro Mártir de Mayorga: Fundación de la reina Catalina de Láncaster*, Salamanca 1994; M. Toribio Escobar - A. Lobato, *El monasterio de Madre de Dios de Sanlúcar de Barrameda*, Sanlúcar de Barrameda 1995; M.J. Vera Galán, *El monasterio de Santo Domingo el Real de Toledo*, Toledo 1991; J.L. Barrios Sotos, *Santo Domingo el Real y Toledo a fines de la Edad Media (1364-1507)*, Toledo 1997.

[33]   García Serrano, *Preachers* cit., pp. 4, 24, 40.

[34]   Aguadé, *Alfonso X* cit., pp. 286-287, 294, 302.

[35]   García Serrano, *Mundo* cit., p. 264; Hoyos, *Registro documental* cit., 2, p. 30.

[36]   M. M. de los Hoyos, *Doña María de Molina*, "Boletín de la Institución Fernán González", 51/180, 1973, p. 662.

[37]   Hoyos, *Registro documental* cit., 1, pp. 45-48, 68-69, 2, pp. 30-31.

[38]   R. Ríos de la Llave, *La implantación de las dominicas en Castilla durante la Edad Media: el Monasterio de Santo Domingo el Real de Caleruega. Tesis Doctoral inédita*, Alcalá de Henares 2003, p. 158.

[39]   Ladero, Nieto, *Iglesia* cit., p. 318.

[40]   García-Villoslada, *Historia* cit., 3/1, p. 228.

[41]   D. Mansilla Reoyo, *Iglesia castellano-leonesa y curia romana en los tiempos del rey San Fernando*, Madrid 1945, p. 263.

[42]   Lawrence, *Monacato* cit., p. 310. Linehan, *Tale* cit., p. 82. Le Goff, *Urbanisation* cit., p. 231.

[43]   P. Linehan, *La iglesia española y el papado en el siglo XIII*, Salamanca 1975, p. 195.

[44]   García Serrano, *Mundo* cit., p. 267.

[45]   Aguadé, *Alfonso X* cit., p. 282.

[46]   Linehan, *Tale* cit., pp. 83-88. García Serrano, *Preachers* cit., pp. 83-85. García Serrano, *Mundo* cit., p. 268.

[47]   Linehan, *Ladies* cit., pp. 2-3, 7, 11-23, 45-55, 60, 64, 78, 105.

[48]   Graña Cid, *Franciscanismo* cit., pp. 247-248.

[49]   Linehan, *Ladies* cit., p. 2.

[50]   Hoyos, *Doña María* cit., p. 655.

BIBLIOGRAPHY

Beltrán de Heredia V., *Examen crítico de la historiografía dominicana en las Provincias de España y particularmente en Castilla*, 35, "Archivum Fratrum Praedicatorum", 1965, pp. 195-248.

González Ollé F., *Manual bibliográfico de estudios españoles*, Pamplona 1976.

De la Granja J.L. - Reig Tapia A. - Miralles R., *Tuñón de Lara y la historiografía española*, Madrid 1999.

Ladero Quesada M.A., *Aproximación al medievalismo español (1939-1984)*, in V. Vázquez de Prada - I. Olábarri - A. Floristán Imizcoz, *La historiografía en Occidente desde 1945. Actitudes, tendencias y problemas metodológicos. Actas de las III Conversaciones Internacionales de Historia. Universidad de Navarra (Pamplona, 5-7 April 1984)*, Pamplona 1985, pp. 69-86.

Ladero Quesada M.A. - Nieto Soria J.M., *Iglesia y sociedad en los siglos XIII al XV (ámbito castellano-leonés). Estado de la investigación*, "En la España Medieval", 11, 1998, pp. 125-151.

Martín J.L., *Iglesia y vida religiosa*, in *La Historia Medieval en España. Un balance historiográfico (1968-1998). XXV Semana de Estudios Medievales. Estella, 14 - 18 July 1998*, Pamplona 1999, pp. 431-456.

Romero J.R., *Los monasterios en la España medieval*, Madrid 1987.

Sabín Rodríguez J.M., *Bibliografía Histórica. Cuadernos de Bibliografía Histórica. Historia de España. Historia de España Medieval*, Madrid 1999.

Del Val Valdivieso M.I. - Tomás Pérez M.S. - Dueñas Cepeda M.J. - de la Rosa Cubo C., *La historia de las mujeres: una revisión historiográfica*, Valladolid 2004.

XXIX Semana de Estudios Medievales. Estella, 15 - 19 July 2002. Las sociedades urbanas en la España medieval, Pamplona 2003.

Jewish Communities in Portuguese Late Medieval Cities: Space and Identity

LUÍSA TRINDADE
University of Coimbra

A cidade portuguesa foi, até 1496, um espaço multi-confessional partilhado por cristãos, muçulmanos e judeus. Essa coexistência assumiu, contudo, expressões diferentes no decorrer da Idade Média: lentamente, o sentimento de tolerância por parte da maioria cristã deu lugar a múltiplas formas de rejeição que tiveram no édito de expulsão o seu corolário.

O presente texto tem por objetivo a análise dos reflexos desse processo no espaço urbano, concretamente na forma como o espaço judaico evoluiu e interagiu com o todo da cidade cristã.

Avaliando o interesse que a questão específica do espaço tem suscitado na historiografia dedicada à presença judaica em Portugal, com relevo para os avanços registados a partir da década de oitenta do século XX, interessa-nos particularmente aferir dois aspectos fundamentais:

1. Apurar a forma como o relacionamento da maioria cristã com a minoria judaica se expressou no plano material, determinando transformações no espaço urbano de que os processos de ampliação, encerramento e deslocalização dos bairros judaicos são os mais visíveis. Alterações que, particularmente na segunda metade do século XV, se repercutiram para além dos limites e do funcionamento interno da comunidade, com implicações no tecido envolvente, criando impasses e alterando percursos cujos efeitos estão ainda por avaliar, determinando, com o rigor possível, graus de bloqueio ou permeabilidade. Num cenário de crescente tensão, ainda que sem o radicalismo assumido noutros reinos, importa também compreender a distância entre a lei e a prática quotidiana, distinguindo, por outras palavras, o espaço regulamentado do espaço vivido.

2. Avaliar, por confronto com a cidade cristã, o grau de expressão material da diferença, clarificando as linhas de continuidade ou o que possa ter sido, no domínio da cultura material, exclusivo à minoria. Domínio e marcação simbólica do espaço, implantação, propriedade do solo e caracterização do edificado adquirem neste âmbito um interesse fundamental para o entendimento do equilíbrio entre o que a comunidade assumia ser a sua identidade e as pressões externas a que se encontrava sujeita.

Until 1496, the Portuguese city was a multi-faith space, shared by Christians, Muslims and Jews alike. However, this coexistence changed as the Middle Ages progressed. In a gradual, but not necessarily violent manner, the Christian majority's feeling of tolerance was replaced by multiple forms of rejection that culminated in the edict which ordered the expulsion of the minorities. This article aims to analyse the repercussions that this process had on the city, specifically in terms of the way that the Jewish quarters evolved and interacted with the Christian city as a whole.

Medieval Portuguese society's tolerance of Judaism allowed for ways of life which, albeit subject to certain restrictions, helped to strengthen the ethnic and religious identity of the Jewish community, consolidating its position as a foreign body separate from the medieval city. Thus, the Jews had rights that were the direct result of their different creed and ethnic group, such as freedom of worship, the right to a different upbringing and the use of Hebrew. Moreover, in return for hefty taxation, Portugal's kings granted them a set of prerogatives that were of equal significance in establishing the differences. Under the local leadership of the rabbi, and national guidance of the chief rabbi, the Jewish communities enjoyed a broad degree of autonomy vis-à-vis the local authorities. This found political expression in their right to set up their own councils, and legal expression through their observation of Talmudic law, even though they were still ultimately subject to the general law of the land.

The ethnic and religious model of identity, reinforced in political and legal terms, was further entrenched in the middle of the 14th century by the imposition of a spatial "identity". The Jewish residential area, previously the result of the spontaneous permeable association that coexisted alongside non-congregated occupations throughout the urban network, was transformed by a royal decree from 1361 into a compulsory, restricted and exclusive space.

It is this Jewish residential area in comparison with the Christian part of the city which will be analysed below, examining and assessing signs of continuity between the two, as well as looking for evidence of material differences which might be exclusive to the minority. Matters such as control over and symbolic marking out of the space, location, land ownership and building characteristics are of fundamental interest in understanding the balance between what the community saw as its own identity and the external pressures to which it was subjected.

This analysis is underpinned by the evolution of the relationship between the Christian majority and the Jewish minority, expressed in material terms by concrete actions, the most significant being the expansion, closure and relocation of Jewish neighbourhoods. Such alterations, particularly in the final phase, had repercussions that extended beyond the limits and the internal functioning of the community, and impacted on the surrounding urban fabric, creating impasses and altering routes whose effects have yet to be assessed in terms of an accurate definition of the degree of blockage or permeability.

Although the background of growing tension never scaled the radical heights found in other kingdoms, it is equally important to understand the distance between the law and daily practice. In other words, a distinction must be made between the governed space and the lived-in space.

A BRIEF HISTORIOGRAPHICAL SURVEY

This interest in the Jewish space within the Portuguese medieval city is nothing new. Relevant material can be found in practically every book on the Jewish presence in Portugal. The main contributions deserve mention according to the nature and volume of the available data, the methodological decision taken and the focal point of the respective approaches.

Despite the clear signs of interest in the 19th century, this theme was only truly established as a research area in the 20th century. The previously published works had come out slowly and sporadically, and their main point of interest was the dissemination and criticism of document sources. Therefore, they are still essential reading as the documentary *corpus*. The reports paradigmatically gathered by Sousa Viterbo[1] and Gama Barros[2] present a cross-section of the Jewish presence in medieval Portuguese society, without ever touching on specific themes.

Around 1900, the Lisbon historian Vieira da Silva adopted the same methodological basis, but applied it specifically to the urban space. In his two articles on the Lisbon communities[3], especially the one on the old Jewish quarter, Vieira da Silva produced a seminal work on the physical structure of what was the most important Jewish quarter in Portugal. Despite his failure to contextualise, the use of a predominantly descriptive tone and the close adherence to the written documents, Vieira da Silva nonetheless wrote an in-depth analysis of place-names which, in conjunction with a range of historical maps, enabled him to locate streets and buildings in both space and time, thereby defining the borders of the Jewish community in the midst of the surrounding Christian parishes.

Lisbon's old Jewish quarter was the only one whose size and demographic density made it truly complex. Its relevance for any study of the mediaeval Portuguese Jewish communities further highlights the importance of Vieira da Silva's pioneering analysis. In addition to correcting errors, his text is a rich source of clues for other issues only picked up on and developed much later. Studies on other Jewish quarters followed Vieira da Silva's example such as the one on the quarter in Oporto by Barros Bastos[4], and on the quarter in Tomar by Santos Simões[5], which focuses mainly on the synagogue.

Due to specialisation and the development of an interest in material culture and life, the theme advanced, particularly in terms of ethnography, a field in which Leite de Vasconcelos' work was the cornerstone. Using archival documents and observation, as well as records of traditions and rituals in the Jewish communities that had returned to Portugal in the 19th century, Leite de Vasconcelos left a vast set of data that he had collected over several decades[6]. The theme was included in Volume IV of *Etnografia Portuguesa* [Portuguese Ethnography], published posthumously in 1958, appearing alongside work on the Moors, Mozarabs and Gypsies, and formed the basis for study regarding ethnic and historical hereditary factors in defining the Portuguese people. Leite de Vasconcelos detailed all aspects of the theme in some two-hundred pages that covered a broad time-span, embracing the communities and Jewish quarters, characterising customs and rituals, and recording examples of anti-Semitism in literature.

At that time, the theme was emerging as a research area in Portuguese universities. The first work, from 1948[7], was followed between 1959 and 1963 by three first-degree dissertations that focused on different areas from the 15th century[8]. Subsequently, Maria José Ferro Tavares published the first of her many works on this theme. Her dissertation *Os judeus em Portugal no século XIV* [The Jews in Portugal during the 14th Century], submitted to the University of Lisbon in 1969 and published in 1970 by the *Centro de Estudos Históricos do Instituto de Alta Cultura*, was a milestone in historiography on the theme, not only due to her in-depth approach, but above all to the methodology adopted.

The *Dicionário de História de Portugal* [Dictionary of the History of Portugal], a collective work directed by Joel Serrão and a fundamental tool in disseminating "New History", came out at around the same time (1963-1971). The impact on Portuguese historiography was similar to that of the *Annales* in France thirty years before. The section on the Jews, by Manuel Guerreiro, draws a simultaneously retrospective and forward-looking synthesis[9].

During the 1980s, the theme developed enormously. Once again, the fundamental work was by Maria José Ferro Tavares, who in this case focused on the 15th century[10]. Based on documentary sources and a vast international bibliography, she produced an in-depth and contextualised analysis of the theme. Alongside a general revision influenced "by the captivating methodological proposals from the new school of French historiography", her approach covered aspects that had hitherto been neglected, such as family structure, crime, education and how Jews and Christians saw themselves and others. The Jewish space formed a vital chapter for a topographic and toponymic survey of the main communities in Portugal, creating a comparative study that paid particular attention to public buildings.

Almost simultaneously, specialist articles started coming off the press, going further into specific themes or defining the case in question[11]. The most important works on the specific themes included Baquero Moreno's series of articles on anti-Jewish movements, highlighting the moments of greatest tension during the 15th century and establishing their causes, the scale of the movements and the reactions[12], all of which were fundamental for an understanding of the transformations imposed on the area. Meanwhile, the construction of this *corpus* of knowledge brought about the consolidation of works of synthesis included in general works, most notably those by Santos Silva, Ferro Tavares and Saul Gomes[13].

With the approach of 1996, the year that remembered the 500th anniversary of the expulsion of the minorities, historiography again focused on the Jews and Muslims. Portuguese and international meetings, seminars and exhibitions not only stimulated interest in the central topic of the expulsion, but also updated and expanded the debate to new horizons. Cultural questions, the comparative study of the two ethnic groups and the role of the Jews in Portuguese expansion, which was being commemorated at the same time, were of particular interest[14].

In the same decade, archaeology specialising in Jewish residential areas made significant advances in Portugal that had a direct impact on the field of the history of urbanism. Despite the limited number of excavations, the results achieved by Carmen Ballesteros in Castelo de Vide, Évora and Trancoso merit mention. In the first two cases, the work was carried out where the synagogues were located, while in Trancoso, it involved an exhaustive survey of Jewish religious symbols engraved on doorposts inside the town walls[15]. Following decades of surveys of the main archive sources, this study of the scarce Jewish material remains that had escaped destruction created new approaches for carrying out research into questions of urbanism.

To complete this brief survey of the development of historiography regarding the Jewish urban presence in mediaeval Portugal, the 1994 publication of the general work *A herança judaica em Portugal* [The Jewish Legacy in Portugal] combined a text of high academic quality with a particularly well-presented and attractive graphic appearance[16].

JEWISH QUARTERS IN PORTUGUESE LATE MEDIEVAL CITIES: SPACE AND IDENTITY

In contrast to the normal evolution of any consolidated urban centre, the Jewish urban space in the final centuries of the Middle Ages was clearly undergoing a transformation.

Within this context, 1361 was a fundamental milestone. By ordering the creation of separate neighbourhoods for groups numbering more than ten Jews[17], King Pedro I not only complied with the Church's orders that his predecessors had ignored, but also established the rules that, until the expulsion, dictated the evolution and characterisation of the Jewish urban space. However, this measure did not bring an immediate or radical alteration to the overall situation. Rather, all evidence suggests that it was applied through a slow and not always general process. The diverse forms that the Jewish presence took in Portuguese cities – dispersion, spontaneous association, special neighbourhoods and physically closed-off neighbourhoods, often concomitant – continued throughout the following century[18]. The weakness of the law, which has been overwhelmingly proven by documents, is the first of the three facts that underlie this study.

The significant change after 1361 was the added pressure that the then legitimised representatives of the people could exert on the monarch. This fact introduces the second critical factor: the restrictions imposed on the Jews were less a reflection of royal plans than of growing resentment among the Christian population, who mixed religious reasons with other more specific and petty issues, such as professional competition, as can clearly be seen from the content of the physical alterations that were insistently requested.

While never reaching the radical levels observable in other kingdoms, the demands increased in stridency during times of crisis (war, hunger and plague) and were essentially the result of the Jewish community's demographic growth. This peaked in Portugal during two specific periods, both of which were directly related to the instability and persecutions seen in the neighbouring kingdoms. The times in question were the late 14th and 15th centuries, and culminated in 1492 with the edict expelling the minority from Castile. The Jewish community in Portugal almost tripled[19] during the last decades of the 15th century, a fact that constitutes the third significant factor in this study.

The relationship between demographic growth and the increasing spatial definition of the Jewish quarters brought a range of consequences. Three are of specific relevance here, albeit with varying nuances in each case: the boom in the demographic density of Jewish quarters and the resulting pressure to expand them; the effects that this brought to the city's overall dynamic; the consolidation of demographically fragile structures, which is particularly clear in the perpetually under-populated towns in the border regions.

Documentary sources have confirmed the overpopulation of the pre-existing Jewish quarters. Besides enclosing the Jews, who had previously been dispersed throughout the urban structure, in a single space, they also received the many people who had crossed the frontier. The example of Évora at the end of the 14th century is among the most significant, and contemporary documents record the non-existence of any vacant housing and the consequent increase in prices[20].

In every case, after maximising the use of the attributed space by occupying unused land[21], extending the size of buildings or reducing the size of the streets, the expansion of the Jewish quarters through the incorporation of neighbouring roads emerged as a possible solution. In Lagos and Castelo Branco, it was enough to annex an alley or lane, but in other places such as Guarda and Évora, this expansion had to be on another scale. In the former case, the quarter expanded north and east towards *Praça de S. Vicente* [St. Vincent Square], while in the latter, six streets and alleys were added on. In other cases, the solution meant building a new Jewish quarter, as happened in Lamego and Lisbon. Indeed, this ultimately led to the coexistence of three such quarters in the capital.

Local councils often used the argument that there was a lack of space when proposing the transfer of the Jewish quarter to places that were normally described as "more appropriate"[22]. While additional motives such as forcible contact, disrespect for Christian rites and dirtiness were presented as arguments to the king, the accusations invariably had the underlying desire to move the Jews away from the centre of the town, thereby minimising the risks of competition. In fact, in Viana do Castelo, Montemor-o-Novo, Santarém, Lagos, Oporto, Lisbon, Setúbal and Guarda alike, whether dispersed or inside a community, the Jews were found along the main arterial roads – Rua Direita (Main Street) and Rua dos Mercadores (Merchant Street) – and in the squares and the churchyards, which were defined by the Christian majority as "honourable and frequented places"[23].

The number of requests to move the Jews was far higher than the number of actual relocations. Coimbra[24] and Braga[25] are examples where Jews were moved to less central areas which were, nonetheless, not totally on the periphery. The most revealing documentation concerns Lisbon, where the request approached head-on what was considered, from the Christian perspective, a subversion of the natural order between the superior, dominant majority and the subject, inferior minority. The council representatives complained to the king that "in some places of Your kingdoms, there are Jewish quarters in the best locations, and the Christians live in the worst". As Margarida Garcez Ventura emphasised, "the urban space cannot contradict the social hierarchy"[26].

It is more difficult to analyse the repercussions of closing off the Jewish quarters inside a city's overall network. Throughout the documents, there are references to gates to the Jewish quarters, some of which predate 1361 but most of which are from the 15th century. At the same time as the location of those that opened onto the busiest places was being challenged (as in Guarda, where the gateway opened directly onto the churchyard of S. Vicente), it was decided to reduce their number. A good example is in Covilhã, where five of the ten gateways to the quarter were closed[27].

In addition, the perimeter was also closed off, totally or partially covering the bays of the buildings "against Christianity". The process in Viseu is described in great detail: "...and as for the windows, we wish them to be closed in the following manner, with stone and lime, and like arrow-slits, with metal all along them in the middle, and these shall be high above the ground and so that there is no place to see through, and only to receive light, and not in any other way"[28]. The construction of fences, as recorded in several Jewish quarters in neighbouring kingdoms in Iberia[29], seems not to have been used in Portugal, although some doubts remain concerning Évora due to such expressions as the "wall of the Jewish quarter", "fencing of the Jewish quarter" and "fence around the Jewish quarter"[30].

With gateways sealed, the doors covered over and windows barred, the first impression of the Jewish space, which was kept under royal guard, is that of an inescapable ghetto.

However, even analysing the situation in terms of the rigorous application of the law, the evidence suggests that there never was an effective blockade. The Jewish quarters were only closed at night, just as the entire town or city closed its gates when the sun set. Until dawn, there was indeed a curfew, yet this practice had some exceptions in the form of safe-conducts and royal charters that granted privileges, namely for those involved in maritime activities or agriculture, mule-drivers and travelling salesmen and, above all, surgeons and doctors.

During the day, the Jews moved about freely. Their stalls and workshops were scattered across the city, but tended to be concentrated in the more central locations, where they were never banned. Equally, the male Christian majority had free access to the Jewish quarters. The only restriction, established by King Pedro and successively repeated, was for Christian women over 10 years old. Even so, they were allowed in, provided they were accompanied by a Christian adult[31].

Although conversation between the two creeds was only permitted in public spaces, the 15th century *Ordenações Afonsinas* (code of laws) clearly assume the disobedience of the law as a common practice: "seeing that conversation between Christians and Jews is prohibited... yet they never stopped speaking with the Christians..."[32]. Many typically Jewish professions, such as doctors, tailors, clothes-sellers, weavers, masons and carpenters, were not subject to the strict application of this measure.

In fact, the Jews' central role in the urban economy was a decisive factor in establishing a permanent loophole in any blockade. In 1460, the council representative of Viseu demanded that the Jews should attend the city market, and in 1462, when the king banned Sintra's Jewish community from using the gates that led to the Christian city, the issue in question was one of restricting physical contact rather than trade. He therefore authorised opening some "hatchways [in the doors] that reach up to a man's waist so that they can pass through the foodstuffs and other goods for sale"[33].

In sum, even when the law was fully complied with, the effects of the blockade were restricted, as the Jews could move freely in Christian territory and vice-versa. Moreover, the legal decisions were only observed at a late date, and even then neither generally nor strictly. The insistent demands made by the majority to the king that the laws be scrupulously observed date essentially from the second half of the 15th century, and led to the strict imposition of the law for a little over thirty years. Although the king established a deadline of two months to close the Jewish quarters in Lamego in 1456, the canons of the cathedral were still living alongside the Jews in the 1470s[34]. In 1466, Gonçalo Vasques, a clergyman at Braga Cathedral, was living in a house next to the synagogue[35], thereby confirming an ongoing situation that D. Diogo de Azambuja had fiercely criticised at the start of the century: "some Christian men and women live and wish to live in the Jewish quarters... and this causes much scandal among the other Christians, and those that do so put their souls in great peril"[36].

In any case, even assuming the law was rigorous followed, the impact that the physical limitation of the Jewish quarters had on the overall urban dynamic depended on the conjunction of two basic factors: the size of the quarter and its insertion into the urban network. The latter was particularly significant depending on how central it was, both in terms of intersecting or coinciding with the structural axial streets, and in relation to the gates and centres of trade and manufacture. Evidently, size was a decisive factor: the Old Jewish quarter in Lisbon, and those in Évora and Campo do Olival in Oporto each covered around one and a half hectares, occupying a significant area of the city as a whole. In contrast, those in other cities barely occupied more than a single street.

When considerable size was combined with a central location, the repercussions were naturally far higher, leading to the interruption of vital routes for a large number of users.

A comparison can be made between the Jewish quarters of Lisbon and those of Oporto. Both the Old and the New Jewish quarters occupied the very heart of Lisbon. They ran at a tangent to *Rua Nova* [New Street], the financial, trading and social centre, which monarchs and chroniclers alike considered to be the finest main street in the capital. The quarters stretched over three parishes (S. Julião, S. Nicolau and Madalena) and comprised a vast maze of main streets, cross streets and alleys. The main thoroughfares were *Rua do Picoto* (or *Mercadores*) and *Rua da Gibitaria*. In strict compliance with the law, the closure of the Jewish quarter cut off several important urban routes and forced travellers to skirt around the neighbourhood (Map 1).

In contrast, although the Jewish quarter in Oporto was of almost identical size, it occupied the northeast corner of the walled city and was bordered by two main urban

Map 1. Lisbon.

streets (*Rua de S. Miguel de Cima* and the route from *S. Domingos to Miragaia*) that guaranteed the basic necessity of movement from north to south and east to west. Each of these streets ended at one of the gates to the so-called Fernandine wall (Map 2). This system was fairly similar to the one in Guarda, where the location of the Jewish quarter did not interrupt the city's structural streets of *Rua de S. Vicente* (east to west) and *Rua Direita* (north to south), which intersected at the church and churchyard of S. Vicente (Map 3).

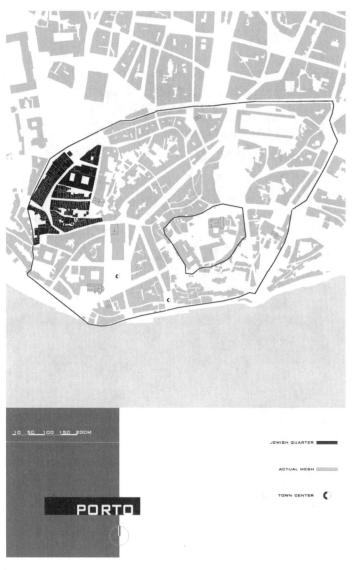

Map 2. Oporto.

Map 3. Guarda

Although the southern border (which had the main gate) of the old Jewish quarter in Coimbra opened directly onto *Rua da Calçada* – the axial trading street that crossed the entire lower part of the city – its location higher up and parallel to the walls left it on the borders of the main routes. Therefore, the Christian majority did not necessarily need to cross through the quarter. Bordered to the north and north-east by the land owned by the *Santa Cruz* Monastery, the structural axial street of the Jewish quarter led to an uninhabited slope that housed only the Jewish cemetery.

The location of the Jewish quarter in Évora raises other questions related to urban design. Despite its size and central position, the neighbourhood was located within a geometrical network bordered by *Rua de Alconchel* and *Rua do Raimundo*, straight axial streets that connected the gates to the main square and acted as the main routes for circulation. With a minimal detour, these streets could substitute the closed ones that ran parallel inside the Jewish quarter. In this case, the only problems concerned the transversal streets (Map 4).

Map 4. Évora.

However, in other cases, it was impossible to avoid crossing the Jewish space. The complaints made by the representatives of Santarém at the 1416 parliament explicitly refer to this. The Jewish quarter was located on the central street that linked *Rua da Sapataria* to the *Alcáçova* gate and Christians had no possible way of getting around it[37].

Finally, the consolidation of the urban fabric in demographically depressed towns was felt particularly strongly in the frontier area, a region that had undergone a sharp demographic decline since the 14th century. The first group of Castilian Jews reached Portugal in the aftermath of the Fernandine wars, when the crown felt an acute need to restore the peripheral areas, and in particular those that had felt the devastating effects of war after the previous damage inflicted by the plague. By settling the Jews there (a process that is particularly well-documented for the jurisdictional areas of Beira and Entre Tejo e Odiana[38]), the crown reinforced its complementary policy of encouraging repopulation of these areas by creating royal presidiaries[39].

The relative impact of this can be gauged by the example of Guarda. The two hundred convicts that King Fernando pardoned in 1371 in exchange for their settling in the city were still fewer in number than the Castilian Jewish immigrants who, according on different authors, totalled between 150 and 400 during the second half of the 15th century[40].

This growth became still more evident around 1492 with the arrival of the second large wave of refugees. In fact, most of the land-ports that the Portuguese crown defined as the places where Castilian Jews could enter the country had been granted the status of presidiaries during previous decades, demonstrating the fragility of the existing population, and exemplified by Melgaço, Bragança, Miranda, Arronches and Elvas. Even though most of the Castilian Jews only passed through, many others settled in the various frontier towns. Another contributing factor were the royal orders that tended to restrict the number of Jews that could leave the country, by encouraging them to convert, limiting the number of ports where they were authorised to sail from, or by the forced baptism of children and adolescents. In a country that had only very recently reversed the downwards demographic trend begun in 1348, every single man counted.

The same levels of growth can be observed in such places as Castelo Branco and Gouveia. In the former, the number of Jews doubled, while it tripled in the latter, justifying the construction of a new synagogue in 1496, just a few months prior to the expulsion. In similar fashion, the Jewish communities in Almeida, Belmonte, Sabugal and Celorico, whose incomes had been too low to appear on the list of donations, started to appear in documents from the late 15th century, confirming and establishing the demographic growth in those urban centres[41].

Many of the above facts provide an answer to the second question raised: assessing the extent of difference or continuity in the forms of the plots of land and buildings. The available evidence shows that the Jewish quarters did not differ from the surrounding Christian city in terms of the plots of land or the system of streets. This is confirmed by analysis of a small number of Jewish quarters, specifically those whose density and size are sufficient for such an analysis. This excludes all cases where a Jewish quarter was merely a single street or, at most, a street with an adjoining cross street, as exemplified by Guimarães, Barcelos, Vila Real, Tomar, Lagos and Miranda do Douro, amongst others.

A variety of factors contributed to this continuity in the urban fabric. First, there were issues of property. Without denying the abundantly proven existence of individual and community properties we can state, the Jews mainly rented. Among the bodies or authorities that traditionally owned urban land, the leading landlords in the Jewish quarters were the crown, chapterhouses and local councils.

Some examples are particularly enlightening. In the old Jewish quarter in Braga (and later in the new one), the houses belonged to the cathedral chapterhouse. In Lamego, the *Pedra* Jewish quarter was mainly established in the late 14th century on land owned by the cathedral. The same applied to the new Jewish quarter in Évora, where most of the land belonged to the bishop and the chapterhouse, while some other buildings were owned by the crown and the local council. Meanwhile, the Jewish communities in Guarda and Coimbra all rented their property from the crown. However, when the old Jewish quarter in Coimbra was closed down around 1360, the new location, near the Santa Cruz Monastery, was basically owned by that institution, while many other lands there belonged to the chapterhouse[42]. The three Jewish quarters in Lisbon were also mostly on crown property[43]. In Santarém, *Rua Nova* in the Jewish quarter (also called *Rua Direita de Alpram*), built in the late 14th century to extend the old Jewish quarter that was originally restricted to *Rua de S. João*, was mostly the property of the king, who had fifteen houses built there[44]. Likewise, the creation of the new Jewish quarter in Oporto saw the coffers of the council swell as, by order of the king, it leased Campo do Olival to the Jews in exchange for an annual payment of 200 old *maravedis*[45].

These examples make it clear that renting properties to Jewish communities was a significant part of the investment policy adopted by the leading owners of urban land. Above all, they reveal how the growth of the Jewish quarters from the end of the 14th century and/or the changes of location imposed on the minority were an opportunity to create lucrative real estate operations, make recent areas of expansion profitable, and allow the development of concerted strategies to acquire and upgrade urban properties.

From the perspective that is most relevant here, this demonstrates that the location of these quarters was largely conditioned by powers that were external to the community. The cases of Évora and Oporto are the best examples of this, both in terms of the scale of the undertaking and the coherence of the programme that was established. In both cases, the process was closely controlled and expressed in rational models, defining the principal axial streets, the cross streets and the marking out of the plots of land. In Évora, the location of the Jewish quarter was part of the global strategy to fill in a vast area of expansion that the *Cerca Nova* [New Walls] would soon integrate into the city.

The place-names reflect urban practices and models that were then common, such as the creation of a structure according to the system of *rua/travessa* [street/cross street][46], where one of the structural axial streets was often called *Rua Direita* [Main Street] or the new network was called *Vila Nova* [New Town], as exemplified by Évora. A terminology witch is commonly found in areas of Christian urban expansion in established cities and towns. In Oporto, the authorities' control of the process to urbanise Campo do Olival[47] is clear from the organisation of the plots of land in *Rua de S. Miguel*. In this case, the Jews received thirty plots of land that evidently corresponded to those that are still visible on today's land division.

The concept of urban continuity is confirmed by moving from the land partition to the buildings themselves. The scarcity of documentary sources that describe the Jewish residential space, the far-reaching transformations and destruction suffered by the Jewish quarters over the centuries and the limited number of archaeological excavations are all inescapable restrictions. However, based on other documents, parallels may be drawn with the results of recent research produced in Spain, namely the non-existence of any architecture that may be considered specific to the Jews during the Middle Ages[48].

As shown, not only were some of the buildings owned by Christian institutions, but in practice, they were used indiscriminately by Christians and Jews, regardless of whether the latter were living within "Christendom" or residing in the space defined as the Jewish quarter. The process of expanding Jewish quarters suggests the same absence of structural specificities. The adjacent arterial streets were incorporated in a process called "putting the street in the Jewish quarter", whereby the houses that the Christians left were immediately occupied by the excess Jewish population. Évora is the most striking of the many examples, as the quarter's expansion was approved by King João I in 1408: "and they asked us as a favour to extend the said Jewish quarter and we gave them for it some neighbouring streets, for they said that it would please the Christians or most of those whose houses were to be included in the Jewish quarter (...)"[49].

Despite having no impact in overall urban terms, there were some differences in detail. Recent studies[50] have demonstrated that the buildings inhabited by Jews were given a distinctive exterior mark – the *mezuzah* – that, according to the sacred texts, was a public statement that the inhabitants were Jewish. Set in the right side doorpost (or *mezuzah* in Hebrew) this is a longitudinal hollow measuring some 10 cm in length by 2 cm in width and depth that held the prayer of *Shema*, one the most important prayers in Jewish worship, inside a case. This discreet, yet easily recognisable, mark was associated with the ritual of kissing or touching the prayer with the right hand when crossing the threshold, while simultaneously invoking divine protection.

The same formal and apparent continuity seems to have characterised the public buildings that were an essential part of the community's daily life.

Obviously, the place where religious rules played a decisive role was the synagogue, which Jewish law required in any community comprising more than ten families. In functional terms, the synagogue was a complex structure, also acting as the community's meeting place and the space for communal justice. In smaller communities, it could also have acted as a study centre and house welfare institutions such as a brotherhood and hospital[51].

Religious Communities and Urban Communities

Although there was a set of norms that governed building a synagogue, observance was severely conditioned by the Christians, as construction depended on their authorisation. Working together, the kings and bishops imposed a series of restrictions that had the clear purpose of annulling any impact on the city. These restrictions included a ban on buildings rising above the height of the surrounding structures, especially any neighbouring church, and the imposition of strict controls on decorations. However, the minority managed to avoid such limitations by constructing the flooring inside the building at a lower level than the ground outside – as can be seen in the synagogue in Tomar – and only decorating the interiors.

The synagogues in Tomar and Évora[52], the only two that have been definitively identified so far, have the same almost anonymous exterior even if the internal structure differ. In both cases, the synagogues were built from scratch and use characteristics that can be integrated into the Sephardic model of sub-divided square ground-plan, with four columns dividing the space and defining the central area for the *Tevah*, the platform from which the Torah and other sacred texts were read a feature that was rather imperceptible from the outside. But similarity can also be found at ornamental level. The way in which the interior decoration of the synagogue in Tomar matches the general trends of the age proves it: the evident parallels with the crypt of Count Afonso of Ourém show that Mudejar motifs satisfied both the demands of the Jewish community and those of a Christian nobleman.

A third building, traditionally accepted as the synagogue of Castelo de Vide, a claim that is neither confirmed nor rejected by recent studies[53], only stands out from the surrounding structures by its somehow unusual size or the lack of original chimney. In fact it has no features that could attract attention or insult the Christian majority[54].

Furthermore not every community had the capacity to build a synagogue from scratch, adapting instead normal residences for the purpose. This is known to have been the case in Monchique, Tojal, Gouveia, Oporto and Guarda. In this case, by all accounts, their existence had no urban impact. Quite simply, once minimal requirements had been met, such as the prayer wall facing east, the existence of windows and the proximity of water, which was vital for ritual bathing, the Jewish faith did not demand a specific space to set up the synagogue. Any building that enabled the faithful to come together could be used[55].

Therefore, when abandoned or after being closed down, a sizeable number of the synagogues were converted into housing. In 1466, Diogo de Viana, from the chapterhouse of Braga, rented the building that had housed the synagogue in the old Jewish quarter after the religious institution was transferred to an existing house belonging to the cathedral inside the perimeter of the new Jewish quarter. The same fate befell the synagogues in Évora and Montemor-o-Novo, which the king respectively granted to the Bishop of Tangier and to Álvaro de Matos, a gentleman of the royal household[56].

Other structures from the Jewish quarters included baths, butchers' (or slaughterhouses), ovens and taverns. Although some religious rituals were associated with these buildings, they did not stand out from others used by the Christian majority, and in smaller communities would even be used by both.

The almost anonymous nature of these buildings meant that after the expulsion, traces of the Jewish presence in Portuguese cities soon faded. As had also happened some years earlier in Castile, the Jews' communally owned goods were confiscated and incorporated into crown property, and suffered a wide variety of fates. The synagogues were given to individuals, converted into chapels and in some cases churches, or converted into jails[57]. The cemeteries were often granted to the local authorities, as happened in Lisbon, where the king ordered that it be turned into a *rossio* [public open area], while the headstones were used to build the *Todos os Santos hospital*[58].

In a similar manner, the former Jewish quarters were integrated into "the Christian world". The neighbourhood gateways were knocked down, the doors that led onto neighbouring Christian streets were reopened, and the streets themselves were made accessible to all and given new names, the most common being "Rua Nova" and "Vila Nova". Many houses were never actually left vacant, as the inhabitants changed their faith rather than leave, and they were henceforth called converts or New Christians. Meanwhile, the houses that were abandoned due to the exodus were soon taken over by Christians.

CONCLUSION

Given the above, it can be concluded that the Jewish quarters had little impact on the urban structure of medieval Portuguese towns and cities, and practically none on the buildings themselves.

The permeable nature of the Jewish quarters was the result of a law that was not in itself very restrictive, was open to numerous exceptions and was only put into practice slowly and with difficulty. An atmosphere of acceptance and stability dominated until the 1480s[59] and was only sporadically interrupted by moments of tension that the crown promptly put a stop to. This undoubtedly contributed to the maintenance of a close coexistence between people of different creeds, one that was largely dictated by the effective participation of the Jewish communities in the kingdom's socio-economic life. In fact, rather than merely sharing in the material culture of the majority, the Jews acted as active agents in producing and developing that culture.

As has been shown for the other kingdoms of the Iberian Peninsula[60], the basis for Jewish specificity in Portugal was also spiritual culture[61]. The minority preserved its identity within the strict context of religious practice, in the objects for worship that were essentially used discreetly in the home, and to a lesser extent in the internal structure and decoration of some buildings. However, these were not necessarily exempt from external influences, and in general, the specificity of the buildings came from their ritual purpose rather than from individual architectural approaches.

Thus, the difference lay essentially in the religious division. The Jewish quarter was recognised and identified by all as a "different space" because it was inhabited by those who believed in Judaism, and not necessarily because it was a different physical space.

Notes

[1]   F. Viterbo, *Occorrencias da vida judaica*, in *Archivo Histórico Portuguez*, Lisbon 1904, II, pp. 176-200.

[2]   H. Barros, *Comunas de Judeus e comunas de Mouros*, "Revista Lusitana", 34, 1936, pp. 168-265, 35, 1937, pp. 161-238.

[3]   A. Silva, *As muralhas da Ribeira de Lisboa*, 2 vols., Lisbon 1900.

[4]   A. Bastos, *Os judeus no velho Porto*, Lisbon 1926.

[5]   J. Simões, *Tomar e a sua judiaria*, Tomar 1943.

[6]   J. Vasconcelos, *Etnografia Portuguesa*, IV, 1958.

[7]   J. Queirós, *Os Judeus em Portugal no século XV: subsídios para uma monografia*, Coimbra 1948.

[8]   M. Mendes, *Elementos para o estudo dos judeus em Portugal até aos fins de séc. XV*, Coimbra 1959; M. Martins, *Subsídios para o estudo dos judeus e dos mouros nos reinados de D. João I e de D. Duarte*, Lisbon 1961; A. Faria, *Análise sócio-económica das comunas judaicas em Portugal (1439-1496)*, Lisbon 1963.

[9]   M. Guerreiro, *Judeus, Dicionário de História de Portugal*, Lisbon 1963-1971.

[10]   M. Tavares, *Os Judeus em Portugal no século XV*, Lisbon 1982.

[11]   A. Andrade, *Judeus em Montemor-o-Novo*, Lisbon 1977; S. Gomes, *Os judeus de Leiria medieval como agentes dinamizadores da economia urbana*, "Revista Portuguesa de História", Coimbra 1993; S. Gomes, *A comunidade judaica de Coimbra medieval*, Coimbra 2003. In addition, the monographic studies on around twenty medieval cities, produced as part of the MA programme (directed by Oliveira Marques from 1980 to 1987) at the Faculty of Social and Human Sciences of Lisbon New University, was also decisive for knowledge of Portuguese Jewish communities.

[12]   The set of articles published in "Marginalidade e conflitos sociais em Portugal nos séculos XIV e XV: estudos de história", Lisbon 1985 is of particular relevance: *O assalto à Judiaria Grande de Lisboa em Dezembro de 1449*, pp. 89-131, *Movimentos sociais antijudaicos em Portugal no século XV*, pp. 79-87 e *Reflexos na cidade do Porto da entrada dos conversos em Portugal nos fins do século XV*, pp. 133-171.

[13]   M. Silva, *Judiarias, História de Portugal dos tempos Pré-históricos aos nossos dias*, Lisbon, 1993, III, pp. 337-340; M. Tavares, *Judeus e Mouros (séculos XII a XIV)*, in *História de Portugal dos tempos Pré-históricos aos nossos dias*, Lisbon 1993, III, pp. 341-349; S. Gomes, *Grupos étnico-religiosos e estrangeiros*, in *Nova História de Portugal*, Lisbon 1996, III, pp. 347-371.

[14]   *Judeus e Árabes da Península Ibérica: encontro de religiões, diálogo de culturas*, Lisbon 1994; *Os Judeus Portugueses entre os Descobrimentos e a Diáspora*, Lisbon 1994; *1º Colóquio Internacional da Associação Portuguesa de Estudos Judaicos*, 1995; *Os judeus portugueses em 500 anos de diáspora, (1496-1996): herança de uma nação, esperança de um povo: exposição documental*, Coimbra, 1996; *Os judeus portugueses e a expulsão: catálogo da exposição evocativa dos 500 anos da expulsão dos judeus de Portugal*, Lisbon 1996; *Os judeus sefraditas entre Portugal, Espanha e Marrocos* (Évora 1998), Lisbon 2004.

[15]   C. Ballesteros - J. Oliveira, *A judiaria e a sinagoga de Castelo de Vide*, "Ibn Maruán", 3, 1993, pp. 113-120; C. Ballesteros, *A judiaria e a sinagoga medieval de Évora*, in *Os judeus sefarditas entre Portugal, Espanha e Marrocos*, Lisbon 2004, pp. 191-218; C. Ballesteros - C. Santos, *Aspectos da Arqueologia Judaica em Trancoso*, in *Beira Interior, história e património*, Guarda 2000, pp. 331-342.

[16]   M. Tavares, *A herança judaica em Portugal*, Lisbon 1994.

[17]   *Cortes Portuguesas. Reinado de D. Pedro I (1357-1367)*, Lisbon 1986, p. 52.

[18]   Barros, *Comunas de Judeus* cit., pp. 256-265.

[19]   Tavares, *A herança* cit., p. 155.

[20]   G. Pereira, *Documentos Históricos da Cidade de Évora, 2ª parte*, Évora, 1887, pp. 10-11.

[21]   R. Gomes, *Um microcosmos citadino: a judiaria medieval da Guarda*, in *Guarda, história e cultura judaica*, Guarda, 1999, p. 112.

[22] Andrade, *Judeus* cit., pp. 18-19.

[23] Tavares, *Os judeus em Portugal no século XV* cit., p. 73.

[24] Gomes, *A comunidade* cit., pp. 16-22.

[25] A. Losa, *Subsídios para o estudo dos judeus de Braga no século XV*, "Congresso Histórico de Guimarães e sua colegiada", 5, 1982, pp. 97-126.

[26] M. Ventura, *Contributo para uma leitura social do espaço na Lisboa quatrocentista: o debate sobre a localização das judiarias*, "Revista Portuguesa de História", 36, I, 2002/2003, pp. 229-240.

[27] Barros, *Comunas de Judeus* cit., p. 260.

[28] Barros, *Comunas de Judeus* cit., pp. 259-260.

[29] We can find examples of Jewish quarters surrounded by fences at Maiorca, Zaragoza, Teruel or Pamplona. J. Lacave, *Juderías y sinagogas españolas*, Madrid 1992, p. 85, 100, 137 e 153.

[30] Ballesteros, *A judiaria e a sinagoga* cit., p. 202.

[31] *Chancelarias portuguesas. D. Pedro I*, Lisbon 1984, pp. 535-536.

[32] *Ordenações Afonsinas*, liv. II, tit. 66, pp. 421-423. About restrictions see Tavares, *Os judeus em Portugal no século XV* cit., pp. 400-403.

[33] Barros, *Comunas de Judeus* cit., pp. 264.

[34] A. Saraiva, *A inserção urbana das catedrais medievais portuguesas: o caso da catedral de Lamego*, "Revista Portuguesa de História", 36, 2002/2003, p. 261.

[35] Losa, *Subsídios* cit., p. 100; J. Marques, *As judiarias de Braga e Guimarães no século XV*, in *Xudeus e conversos na Historia*, Santiago de Compostela 1994, p. 353.

[36] Vasconcelos, *Etnografia* cit. p. 99.

[37] Tavares *Os judeus em Portugal no século XV* cit., p. 53.

[38] Tavares *Os judeus em Portugal no século XV* cit., p. 74.

[39] H. Moreno, *Elementos para o estudo dos coutos de homiziados instituídos pela coroa*, in *Os Municípios portugueses nos séculos XIII a XVI*, Lisbon 1986, pp. 93-138.

[40] Gomes, *Um microcosmos citadino* cit., p. 112 and M. Tavares, *Os Judeus na Beira Interior*, in *Guarda, história e cultura judaica*, Guarda, 1999, p. 117.

[41] Tavares, *Os Judeus na Beira* cit., pp. 117-123.

[42] Examples analysed respectively by Losa, *Subsídios* cit., p. 98; Saraiva, *A inserção urbana* cit., p. 260; A. Beirante, *Évora na Idade Média*, Lisbon 1995, pp. 71-72; Gomes, *Um microcosmos* cit., p. 111; Gomes, *A comunidade judaica* cit., p. 25.

[43] I. Gonçalves, *Aspectos económico-sociais da Lisboa do século XV estudados a partir da propriedade régia*, in *Um olhar sobre a cidade medieval*, Cascais 1996, p. 45.

[44] A. Beirante, *Santarém Medieva*, Lisbon 1980, p. 70.

[45] Tavares, *Os judeus em Portugal no século XV* cit., p. 65.

[46] The use of both terms street/transversal can be found in king João I document, dated from 1408, where the Jewish quarter new limits are described. Pereira, *Documentos Históricos* cit., pp. 222-223.

[47] Documentary sources record that "the said council representatives and judges assigned a certain place at the said Campo do Olival in order to built the said Jewish quarter, which had already begun using the divisions and marks established by the judges and councillors..."; Basto, *Os judeus* cit., p. 52. Tavares, *Os judeus em Portugal no século XV* cit., p. 65.

[48] R. Izquierdo Benito, *Arqueologia de una minoría: la cultura material hispanojudía*, in *El legado material Hispanojudío*, Cuenca 1998, p. 289; R. Izquierdo Benito, *Espacio y sociedad en la Sefarad medieval*, in *Juderías y sinagogas de la Sefarad medieval*, Cuenca 2003, p. 38.

[49] Pereira, *Documentos Históricos* cit., pp. 10-11.

[50] C. Ballesteros, *Marcas de simbologia religiosa judaica e cristã – para um levantamento prévio em povoações da raia portuguesa e espanhola*, "Ibn Maruán", 6, 1996, pp. 139-151.

[51] C. Ballesteros, *Das Sinagogas da Antiguidade às sinagogas medievais peninsulares. Origens e percursos de uma instituição*, in *Guarda, história e cultura judaica*, Guarda 1999, pp. 139-146; Cantera Montenegro, *Aspectos de la vida cotidiana de los judíos en la España medieval*, Madrid 1998, pp. 151-157.

[52] Ballesteros, *Das Sinagogas da Antiguidade* cit. pp. 143-144; Id., *A judiaria e a sinagoga medieval de Évora* cit., pp. 205-216.

[53] Ballesteros; Oliveira, *A judiaria e a sinagoga de Castelo de Vide* cit., pp. 113-120.

[54] In 1472, at the parliament session held in Coimbra, the council representatives complained about the way "some Jews, in their villages and communities, decorate and enrich their synagogues in an excessive manner, and it is prohibited by canon and religious law for them to build them either bigger or richer than they used to be". Tavares, *Os judeus em Portugal no século XV* cit. p. 365.

[55] Ballesteros, *Das sinagogas da Antiguidade* cit., p. 141.

[56] Losa, *Subsídios* cit., p.103; Andrade, *Judeus* cit., p. 27; Ballesteros, *A judiaria e a sinagoga medieval de Évora* cit., p. 204.

[57] The three Lisbon synagogues had different destinies: while the bigger one was sacred as Nossa Senhora da Conceição church, the other two were rented, the one in S. Julião street to Duarte Borges a converted tailor the other, in Alfama Jewish quarter, to Gonçalo Fernandes. Tavares, *Os judeus em Portugal no século XV* cit., pp. 385-386. The synagogue in Tomar was adapted to jail. Simões, *Tomar* cit., p. 52.

[58] Barros, *Judeus* cit., p. 180.

[59] Tavares, *Os judeus em Portugal no século XV* cit., p. 423.

[60] Izquierdo Benito, *Espacio y sociedad* cit., pp. 38-39; Id., *Arqueologia* cit., p. 273. Cantera Montenegro, *Aspectos de la vida* cit., p. 174.

[61] M. Tavares, *Judeus e Mouros: que cultura?*, in *Judeus e Árabes da Península Ibérica: encontro de religiões, diálogo de culturas*, Lisbon 1994, pp. 98.

BIBLIOGRAPHY

Andrade A., *Judeus em Montemor-o-Novo*, Lisbon 1977.

Ballesteros C., *A judiaria e a sinagoga medieval de Évora*, in *Os judeus sefarditas entre Portugal, Espanha e Marrocos*, Lisbon 2004, pp. 191-218.

Id., *Marcas de simbologia religiosa Judaica e cristã*, "Ibn Maruán", 6, 1996, pp. 139-152.

Id., *Das Sinagogas da Antiguidade às sinagogas medievais peninsulares. Origens e percursos de uma instituição*, in *Guarda, história e cultura judaica*, Guarda 1999, pp. 139-146.

Ballesteros C. - Oliveira J., *A judiaria e a sinagoga de Castelo de Vide*, "Ibn Maruán", 3, 1993, pp. 113-120.

Ballesteros C. - Santos C., *Aspectos da Arqueologia Judaica em Trancoso*, in *Beira Interior, história e património*, Guarda 2000, pp. 331-342.

Barros H., *Comunas de Judeus e comunas de Mouros*, "Revista Lusitana", 34, 1936, pp. 168-265, 35, 1937, pp. 161-238.

Cantera Montenegro E., *Aspectos de la vida quotidiana de los judíos en la España medieval*, Madrid 1998.

Gomes R., *Um microcosmos citadino: a judiaria medieval da Guarda*, in *Guarda, história e cultura judaica*, Guarda 1999, pp. 111-115.

Gomes S., *Os judeus de Leiria medieval como agentes dinamizadores da economia urbana*, "Revista Portuguesa de História", 28, Coimbra 1993.

Id., *A comunidade judaica de Coimbra medieval*, Coimbra 2003.

Guerreiro M., *Judeus* in *Dicionário de História de Portugal*, Porto 1985, III, pp. 409-414.

Izquierdo Benito R., *Arqueología de una minoría: la cultura material hispanojudía*, in *El legado material Hispanojudío*, Cuenca 1998, pp. 265-290.

Id., *Espacio y sociedade en la Sefarad Medieval*, in *Juderías y sinagogas de la Sefarad Medieval*, Cuenca 2003, pp. 29-55.

Losa A., *Subsídios para o estudo dos judeus de Braga no Séc. XV*, "Congresso Histórico de Guimarães e sua colegiada", 5, 1982, pp. 97-126.

Marques J., *As judiarias de Braga e Guimarães no século XV*, in *Xudeus e conversos na Historia*, Santiago de Compostela 1994, pp. 351-363.

Moreno H., *O assalto à Judiaria Grande de em Dezembro de 1449*, in *Marginalidade e conflitos sociais em Portugal nos séculos XIV e XV: estudos de história*, Lisbon 1985, pp. 89-131.

Id., *Movimentos sociais antijudaicos em Portugal no século XV*, in *Marginalidade e conflitos sociais em Portugal nos séculos XIV e XV: estudos de história*, Lisbon 1985, pp. 79-88.

Moreno Koch Y., *El espacio comunal por excelência: la sinagoga*, in *El legado material Hispanojudío*, Cuenca 1998, pp. 135-141.

Saraiva A., *A inserção urbana das catedrais medievais portuguesas: o caso da catedral de Lamego*, "Revista Portuguesa de História", 36, I, 2002/2003, pp. 241-265.

Silva A., *As muralhas da Ribeira de Lisboa*, Lisbon 1900.

Silva M., *Judiarias*, in *História de Portugal dos tempos Pré-históricos aos nossos dias*, Lisbon 1993, III, pp. 337-340.

Simões J., *Tomar e a sua judaria*, Tomar 1992.

Tavares M.J., *Os judeus em Portugal no século XIV*, Lisbon 2000.

Id., *Judeus e Mouros no Portugal dos séculos XIV e XV*, "Revista de História Económica e Social", 9, 1982, pp. 75-89.

Id., *Judeus e Mouros (séculos XII a XIV)*, in *História de Portugal dos tempos Pré-históricos aos nossos dias*, Lisbon 1993, III, pp. 341-349.

Id., *Judeus e Mouros: que cultura?*, in *Judeus e Árabes da Península Ibérica: encontro de religiões, diálogo de culturas*, Lisbon 1994, pp. 90-92.

Id., *Os Judeus na Beira Interior*, in *Guarda, história e cultura judaica*, Guarda 1999, pp. 117-123.

Id., *Os judeus em Portugal no século XV*, Lisbon 1982-1984.

Id., *A herança judaica em Portugal*, Lisbon 2004.

Vasconcelos J. - Guerreiro M., *Etnografia Portuguesa*, IV, Lisbon 1958.

Ventura M., *Contributo para uma leitura social do espaço na Lisboa quatrocentista: o debate sobre a localização das judiarias*, "Revista Portuguesa de História", 36, I 2002/2003, pp. 229-240.

Viterbo F., *Occorrencias da vida judaica*, in *Archivo Histórico Portuguez*, Lisbon 1904, II, pp. 176-265.

A Pilgrimage of Faith, War, and Charity.
The Order of the Hospital from Jerusalem to Malta

Victor Mallia-Milanes
University of Malta

The Hospitaller Order of St John, whose origins are traced back to the years before the First Crusade, began as a purely charitable institution in Jerusalem and, through the crusading movement and other related factors, gradually evolved into an exempt religious-military order of the Latin Church. Its two functions – to care for the sick and the poor and to fight for the Christian faith – were retained throughout its protracted pilgrimage from Jerusalem, through Acre, Cyprus, and Rhodes, to Malta. The French Revolution of 1789 and the Order's consequent eviction from the central Mediterranean island determined the need to rethink its constitution and to revert to its original charitable raison d'être. Its performance during this long pilgrimage constituted both a strong element of historical continuity and a powerful force of long-term change.

An Act of Love

Whatever the true political motives behind it were, Urban II's famous sermon, delivered in an open field outside Clermont on 27 November 1095, was an ingenious intellectual endeavour at reconciliation. He succeeded in bringing intimately together hitherto disparate realities to form a new conceptual phenomenon. Cloistered monastic life, chivalry, spiritual combat and worldly warfare, the traditional pilgrimage, the evangelical virtues of love and peace – all these realities had been for long distinct and incompatible. The emergence of the Cluniacs in the 11th century and the pervasive spiritual fervour of the 12th created the context which rendered changes in the general attitude towards these realities possible. Indeed their occurrence had already begun albeit at almost imperceptible rhythms. The 'emergence of a new ideal of Christian knighthood' was one such, the innovative fusion of the *miles Christi*, spiritually fighting the forces of evil, and the knight endeavouring to 'repel the enemies of Christ by material arms'[1]. Warfare was thus transformed into a holy activity and whoever participated in it was offered spiritual rewards in the form of indulgences for the remission of sins[2]. The alarmingly dangerous spread of Islam which 'had swept through Asia Minor and had almost reached Constantinople'[3], the persistent requests from Byzantium to the West for mercenaries and other military help, and the Latin Church's response to both consolidated the revolutionary drift in the shape and form assumed by the crusading movement which Urban II's long preaching tour round France had inaugurated.

Like the later crusades, the First Crusade was a holy war, with as much piety in it as there was adventure[4]. It was an armed pilgrimage for the liberation of a 'people' and 'a place' – to set free, says Jonathan Riley-Smith, both 'the baptized members of the Eastern churches ... from Muslim domination and tyranny,' and 'the Holy Sepulchre'[5]. Urban II succeeded in dramatically creating of the Muslim Turk a convincing image of 'Europe's most significant other'[6], a common enemy, one that had overrun 'an increasing amount of Christian territory on the frontiers [of the Byzantine world] ... ruining churches and ravaging the Kingdom of God'[7]. This was psychologically necessary and effective in seeking to promote solidarity in Latin Christendom. The Pope also succeeded in impressing on the European mind the importance and the urgency of fighting for the faith, an activity now transformed into a new Christian value, into 'an act of love'[8]. It was precisely this context, the social reality of a 'new vocation' and the ideals it inspired, that encouraged the charitable Hospitaller fraternity, then in its infancy, to develop into an institution not only with a significant military role to play, but also with considerably rich endowments to support it.

THE HOSPITALLER EQUATION

The concepts of faith, war, and charity explicitly convey the three major characteristics of the Order of the Hospital. Set up a few years before the preaching of the First Crusade, it came near to a complete collapse as a result of the great waves of revolutionary upheaval symbolically ushered in by the fall of the Bastille in Paris in 1789, seven hundred years later. Strongly professing an unshakeable belief in the authentic Christian truths, it was already in existence in Jerusalem in the 1080s as a small and humble hospice dedicated to St John the Baptist, inspired by a philosophy of evangelical love as expressed in the Holy Beatitudes – to care for the sick, the poor, and the needy, both men and women, to provide them with shelter and food, with clothing and decent Christian burial. Their 'suffering, injuries, sadnesses, and needs' were the brethren's main concern[9]. The innovative Hospitaller philosophy had transformed the humble folk into *quasi domini*, the Lords, with the entire fraternity at their service[10]. These were the original values which the institution retained unchanged in essence long after it had become involved in military activities. Its endeavour to contribute to the operations to wrest Christ's Tomb in Jerusalem from the Muslims and render it, along with the routes leading to it and the surrounding territories making up the Holy Land (where Christianity was believed to have first begun), free, safe, and accessible to devout Christian travellers and pilgrims, was a gradual process. The two distinct phenomena – the *servus pauperum* and the *miles Christi* – had been fused together to form the two sides of the Hospitaller equation. Perhaps the immediate driving forces behind this development were the powerful and pervasive influence of St Bernard, the personality and foresight of Raymond du Puy (died c.1160), and 'the predicament of a society they were serving' to which he was responding. The historian C.H. Lawrence sums up this dilemma as 'the military needs of *Outremer*' in the second decade of the 12th century, the 'urgent need' of 'a standing army of professionals' with which to have its 'defensive capability' reinforced[11].

The story of the Hospitallers constituted a true pilgrimage. Behind it lay the steady onslaught of the Seljuk Turks, followed by the consolidation and westward advance of the Ottoman Empire. Both Muslim phenomena dictated the physical transfer of the Hospitaller Convent from one place to another, both determined the Order's noble and chivalric response to changing realities. Begun at Jerusalem, it took them to Acre, Cyprus, and Rhodes, to Viterbo, Nice, and Malta[12]. But it was more than that: it was also a spiritual strength of will and mind, the Hospital's powerful resolve to continue to discharge elsewhere their primary obligations, the religious and the military, neither of which was allowed to detract from its original efficiency or importance. Like all living organisms, they evolved to respond to new pressures, to meet new demands.

Governed by their Augustinian Rule[13], the Hospitallers were fully-professed religious who took the three monastic vows of poverty, chastity, and obedience. Wherever they were, in Convent or on their European commanderies, they shared a common liturgical life – they prayed together, keeping the seven canonical hours of the divine office; they dined together in the refectory, retired to bed in their own cells at night, and rose for matins. Their style and pattern of life resembled much of 'western monastic life' in the later middle ages. Paschal II's *Pie postulatio voluntatis* of 15 February 1113 subordinated them to the master and the general-chapter[14]. From the mid-13th century, to qualify for admission into the Order, a brother knight had to be of legitimate birth and of immediate knightly ancestors[15]. Only brother knights could be elected master. For the execution of its mission and for the general up-keep of the Hospital, the Convent depended on the support it received from its landed estates in Europe. These varied in size and wealth, with the smallest unit of administration, the commandery or preceptory, consisting of a village, a hospice, a church, farms, and 'other lands lying close to one another[16], with a brother commander, or preceptor, entrusted with its government and answerable to the prior. These commanderies were originally spiritually-rewarding gifts the fraternity had been given by the faithful for its wide involvement in charitable activities. Administratively grouped into provinces or priories[17], each sent a third of its produce, in cash or kind, as *responsiones* to the conventual treasury every year. In the 14th century, a resident treasury official or receiver was attached to every priory, especially for the collection of such dues and other similar taxes[18]. The brotherhood consisted of knights, sergeants (at-service and at-arms), and chaplains. There were nuns, donats, and other lay associates or *confratres*, male and female. They built their own churches, had their own cemeteries, and were exempt from episcopal and secular jurisdiction.

CARING FOR THE SICK[19]

By the late 12th century the Order of St John was already functioning both as a hospice, which offered free shelter and comfort, physical and spiritual, to the homeless poor (*domus pauperibus*) and as a hospital, which extended free medical care and attention to the sick (*domus infirmis*). At every stage on their long pilgrimage from Jerusalem to

Malta, not only would the Hospitallers carry with them their crusading spirit, their holy relics, and their archives, their knowledge of government, administration, and fortress building, and their wide experience of medical practices, customs, and traditions[20]; they would set up a major functioning hospital within the Convent wherever they went, a living pious institution which owed much to the more advanced Arab theories and ideas[21]. Accompanying them on their military expeditions and (later) on board their naval squadrons were mobile hospitals to provide for those wounded during the campaigns. Moreover, an impressively remarkable network of similar institutions – hospitals, hospices, leprosies, and poorhouses – spread throughout their priories and commanderies in the West. Only in the eighteenth century, claims Christopher Toll, did Europe begin to surpass 'Arab surgical operations and instruments'[22]. The Hospitallers, with their long medical tradition, must have played a not insignificant role in this process of slow conversion.

The Rule, the statutes, and other treatises provide ample insight into the structure of the *palacium infirmorum* of St John at Jerusalem, the manner of its administration, and the nature of the charitable and medical activities that were performed in it. Great attention was given to the responsibilities of the physicians employed with the hospital and the quality of the service they vowed to administer to the patients. They visited the sick twice a day, checked urine and pulse regularly, diagnosed the nature of their disease, prescribed the right medicines to cure the infirmity, and issued appropriate dietary instructions. Lapidaries and herbals were used for their therapeutic qualities. Of similar importance were the type, quality, and quantity of the food and drink prescribed and served. Loving care too, we are told, was extended to the *filii beati Iohannis*, the abandoned infants. All poor and sick were admitted without discrimination – men and women, Christians and non-Christians, Muslims and Jews, free men and slaves. The Jerusalem hospital, according to one treatise, had eleven apparently general wards. When these were full, the brethren gave up their own cells and beds to the patients. Sick women had their own hospital. Under normal conditions, the hospital could accommodate some 1000 patients, with roughly six to seven patients per attendant, and four resident physicians – quite innovative by European standards, quite backward by traditional Muslim practice[23].

This pious commitment to 'our lords the sick and to the poor of Christ' became more distinct and pronounced during the long years the Hospitallers spent on Rhodes after c. 1310. On the Dodecanese island, their medical, sanitary, and other charitable institutions became better organized and more efficiently administered, almost assuming a near-permanent structure[24]. Responsibilities – like those of the Grand Hospitaller, who was the head of the Holy Infirmary; the infirmarian, the day-to-day administrator who 'visited the sick daily and saw that they had all the nourishment prescribed to them; that they behaved with great civility; that a sufficient number of servants was available to attend to the sick; and that the deceased received a decent burial'[25]; the *probi homines*; the 'learned and experienced' physicians[26]; the surgeons and pharmacist, the chaplain, the Commissioner for the Poor, the Health Commissioners or *do-*

mini sanitatis, and the Guardian of the Port – were defined with greater precision[27]. The Maltese phase of the Order's history (1530-1798) witnessed consolidation in this field. Notwithstanding the inherent difficulties which characterized the central Mediterranean island – general poverty; lack of natural resources; economic dependence on nearby Sicily; jurisdictional separatism; constant fear of outbreaks of plague; the recurrent threat of Muslim invasion; and the internal strife within the fraternity itself, reflecting 'the culmination of a period of great adjustment to the Order's changed position, its loss of territories, and the conflicts of Church and State in the 16th century'[28] – there was indeed marked expansion in several sectors. The negative conditions on late 16th-century Malta dictated the positive development of 'the hospital and the charitable role of the Order'. Both were, Ann Williams points out, re-emphasized, reinterpreted, and extended[29], apparently in the baroque spirit of the post-Tridentine Church. A larger hospital was constructed in the new city of Valletta in the 1570s. 'But the real change', she continues[30],

> does not come until the 1580s when the new hospital expanded under Verdalle and coordinated the charitable activities of the Order, the house for exposed infants, the hospital for women and the refuge for prostitutes, as well as treatment outside the hospital for less serious diseases, and for poor law relief for the Maltese and for the Rhodians who had loyally followed the Knights.

At every stage in its historical development, from the 12th century to the end of the 18th, the hospital played a significant role for the Order. In times of serious crisis, like the one of 1291, when the military Orders failed to stem the advance of Islam sweeping through Latin Syria, or that of 1522, when Rhodes, after more than two hundred years of Hospitaller rule, was lost to the Ottoman Turks, or indeed the fall in 1551 of the North African fortress of Tripoli, which had been entrusted to the Order twenty years earlier, on all these occasions the importance of the Hospitaller institution's charitable function became even more pronounced. If the Order had failed to realize its military objective or to maintain its military achievements, if the Order after the fall of Acre had become a political anachronism[31], or indeed irrelevant after Rhodes and Tripoli, were the revenues derived from its massive landownership in Europe, the equally wide patronage, and the vast and splendid array of privileges and exemptions it had been allowed to enjoy necessary and justified any further? The saving answer could well have been found in the hospital. By the time the Order had settled on Rhodes, says Anthony Luttrell, and indeed through the long 16th century, the hospital was more than 'a religious obligation'; it was more than 'a source of ideological strength'. It constituted, he claims, 'a show-piece to impress a visiting public which would transmit the resulting image throughout Latin Europe ...; the Conventual hospital was to some extent a public relations exercise'[32].

FIGHTING FOR THE FAITH

Like their active commitment to charity, the Hospitallers' professed hostility to Islam did not shrink over the centuries. Nor did changing geographical and political conditions succeed in weakening or diminishing its importance. Indeed, during their brief and uncomfortable stay on Cyprus, they had already begun to respond to the dictates of insularity by constructing a small naval force. This would open for them a vaster horizon of new forms of activity. On Rhodes, their mission was transformed into a profession of eternal war, waged on all fronts, against the infidel. Their naval and maritime activities in the eastern Mediterranean remained a constantly irritating source of nuisance to Ottoman lands surrounding the island, to Muslim pilgrims to Mecca, and to Muslim trade and shipping plying the area or crossing the important Alexandria – Constantinople caravan route[33]. Their participation in crusading ventures on land and by sea remained regular and consistent. Their services were nearly always ready on demand. The 1460s[34], to cite one example, saw the Hospitallers side by side with the Venetians at the siege of Negropont, defending the rights and privileges of the Adriatic Republic against Mahomet II in the east – as they would in the 1470s[35], at the turn of the century[36], and again and again throughout the early modern period[37].

After 1523 the Hospitallers sustained the same provocative activity, first during their eight-year odyssey in desperate search for a permanent home and then, after October 1530, from their new base on central Mediterranean Malta. The latter gave them the added strategic advantage of extending their holy war to the western portion of the sea and along the entire North African coast. Unshaken by the nascent spirit of nationalism and reluctantly compliant with the dictates of the papacy and of France's changing attitudes towards the Ottoman Empire, the Hospitallers were determined to uphold their policy of active hostility against Islam, to continue fighting for the faith and in defence of Christendom, a resolve that remained of considerable political relevance, like the image they promoted of their hospitaller activities. Endeavouring to keep the crusading ideal alive was necessary for their prolonged existence. The institution was unthinkable without European patronage which was eloquently realized in the dual form of great-power protection and the sustained regular flow of new recruits and revenue from their priories in Europe. The hospital, in its broadest charitable manifestations, as has been shown, in part justified their existence. And so did the consistency of their naval campaigns in early modern times. Hospitaller Malta, not unlike Hospitaller Rhodes, was transformed into a double fortress which combined the two vocations fairly intimately – one against Islam and one against the plague.

In harmony with such policy, the Hospitallers involved themselves in almost all the naval encounters between Christians and Muslims in the Mediterranean. On Malta, as on Rhodes, they joined holy leagues and consistently placed all their naval forces at the disposal of allied Christian fleets. In 1500 the Order's naval squadron fought along with those of Pope Alexander VI, Venice, Spain, Portugal, and France[38]. The role the Hospitaller galleys played in Pius V's holy league of 1571, culminating in Lepanto, is too well known to need description[39]. On several other occasions they contributed their entire galley squadron and other craft to Habsburg punitive expeditions against the infidel. Conforming to their institution's statutory provisions, they often acted too on their own in seasonal cruises, harassing Muslims on land and at sea, looting their towns and villages, and taking their men, women, and children into slavery. This latter form of anti-Muslim operations, already begun on Rhodes[40], would develop into a major industry on Malta. The naval historian Ubaldino Mori Ubaldini assigns the initial involvement of individual members of the Order in such formal operations to the early years of Spain's Golden Age[41]. The Hospitaller Inyogo Ayalla was, he claims, among the first participants in this massive activity which would reach its peak in the next century. On 24 November 1503, Grandmaster Pierre d'Aubusson allowed Ayalla to arm the Order's *barcia Sancta Maria* and venture on a corsairing expedition against the infidel in Levantine waters on condition that two-thirds of the booty would go to the Order's Treasury[42]. Even during the severe crisis of the post-1522 years, the Hospitallers were active in privateering ventures, either undertaken by the naval squadron or by individual brethren in their own private capacity. Such activity was designed as much to keep alive the innate warlike spirit against the infidel as to underscore the institution's relevance to the Christian West. It was in the Order's interests that naval feats against the infidel, the capture of hundreds of Muslim slaves, and the freeing of equally large numbers of Christian subjects of diverse European monarchies and principalities from slavery were given wide publicity. In 1524, for example, the Order's admiral Bernardino d'Airasca celebrated one such occasion with a pageant spectacle of a victory march displaying the trophies of battle along the principal streets of Rome. Ottoman flags and banners, convincing evidence of the triumph of the white eight-pointed cross over the crescent, decorated prominently the Hospital's temporary conventual residence at the church of San Faustino at Viterbo[43].

From October 1530 the monastic island-state of Malta began to assume the formidable task of being at the forefront of any Western Christian enterprise against Islam. During the earlier half of the 16th century alone, the Hospitaller galley squadron was present at Modon (1531)[44], Coron and Patras (1532)[45], Tunis (1535)[46], Corfu (1537)[47], Préveza (1538)[48], Otranto and Castelnuovo (1539)[49], at the conquest of Monastir and Susa (1540)[50], the sieges of Sfax[51] and Algiers (1541)[52], Mahdija (1550)[53], Djerba (1560)[54] – an infinitely long string of daring deeds, copiously and profusely provocative, that goes a long way to explain not only the skilful Muslim reprisals on Gozo and Tripoli in 1551[55], but also the abortive Ottoman siege of Malta in 1565[56]. The 'dazzling triumph'[57] of the Christian forces at Lepanto on 7 October 1571 would not be repeated, but the pattern of active performance in terms of courage, commitment, and naval technique that emerged in the 16th century would still characterize the story of the Hospital in the 17th and 18th centuries, though not perhaps on as large a scale as before.

A CHANGE OF DIRECTION AND FOCUS

Acre, the last crusader state in Latin Syria, fell to the Mamluks in 1291. With hindsight, after that loss there was no hope for the military orders of ever recovering the Holy Land. That development caused consternation, bitter resentment, and widespread disillusionment in the West, one which promoted severe criticism of the crusaders, the crusading movement, and the military orders[58]. Within the next two decades the Templars would be dissolved and the Teutonic Order would move to the Baltic[59]. For the Hospitallers, the fall of Acre, like the loss of Jerusalem before it, created a pattern of calculated response to hostile public opinion. It necessitated a change not only of direction on the pilgrimage they had undertaken, but also of focus, unless they wanted to allow themselves and their institution to be reduced to impotence. To survive, they needed to revisit their position – the ideas and ideals they had entertained, the structures they had worked in, and the conceptions they had been familiar with. The recovery of the Holy Tomb and the defence of the Holy Places were a thing of the past, albeit recent; they could no longer remain the focal point of their military activities. The Hospital acknowledged this new reality and turned its attention towards the new challenge. The security of the Latin West was at stake. Would the Turks overrun Europe? The threat of Islam was made to appear wider in magnitude and larger in scale than it really was, indeed ominous enough and frightening to shake the whole of Christendom on land and at sea. This was an impression which the Hospital sought deliberately to create in order to highlight its military worthiness, its indispensability, and its political and ideological relevance to Christian Europe. For subtly concealed beneath the failure to contain the Muslim threat lay the danger to its own continued existence. This approach was adopted not only after Acre. The strategically unnecessary building after 1407, for example, of the 'imposing and expensive' fortress of Bodrum[60] was a classic example. Bodrum, says Anthony Luttrell, 'allowed the Hospital to present itself to Western public opinion as being in direct contact and confrontation with the infidel'[61]. Similar methods were applied after the loss of Rhodes in 1523, after the fall of Tripoli in Barbary in 1551, and indeed at regular intervals during the Order's stay on Malta whenever the Hospital feared its raison d'être was in doubt. What contemporaries thought of the Hospitallers and especially the image their patrons (popes, emperors, and kings) entertained of them was a matter of no mean significance. Though clearly too extreme, the idea the order was trying to convey loud and clear at the end of the 13th century was reinforced by the dissension and internal strife that marked conditions in the West, a situation which strengthened the magnitude and gravity of the ever-growing threat from the East. At Manzikert in 1071, the Seljuk Turks had seized most of Asia Minor. Antioch fell in 1085. The power of Islam and the alarming pace with which it spread had helped create the military orders. After Acre it again in part determined the history of Europe; as it would after Rhodes. In 1789 the catalyst was no longer Islam but revolutionary France.

CONCLUSION

Historians of the Order tend to reiterate the popular view that the 18th century witnessed the decline and fall of the Order of the Hospital. This remains debatable. Dictionaries define decline as a natural process of gradual deterioration in quality, health, or character. It is a process coming from within. The eviction of the Order from Malta and its consequent crisis cannot, in this sense, be attributed to such process of disintegration, but rather to radical forces outside the institution's competence to contain or control. Changing patterns of international political, diplomatic, cultural, and commercial relations, the steady process of secularization, the pervasive influence of the French Enlightenment on European ideas, the force of rationalism – all challenged the principle of privilege on which the old order was established. This rendered the Hospital vulnerable, increasingly incompatible with the revolutionary spirit of the times. Few historians, if any, advance the saner argument that the institution had succeeded, against all odds, in nourishing the concept and spirit of the crusade for so long and in keeping its ideals alive through the entire 18th century. That was one of the Hospitallers' greatest achievements. With minor differences, every single privateering expedition organized seasonally by the Order as demanded by the statutes against the Muslim infidel in the Levant or on the long Maghrebi coast of North Africa was a campaign against the enemies of the faith, a holy war, a fusion of crusading piety and adventure[62]. In the late 1750s, shortly after the Hospitaller Massimiliano Buzzaccarini Gonzaga had settled on Malta as Venice's resident minister, he called the island 'so very necessary for the whole of Christendom'. Seven months before he passed away in 1776, he still entertained the idea that Hospitaller Malta, entrusted as it had been centuries earlier to the crusading Order by European sovereigns to protect Europe against the enemy of the Christian faith, was still performing that mission admirably[63].

This forms part of the Order's legacy to Europe. Though the subject still needs to be more carefully analysed, the Hospitallers' contribution must have been considerable. The crusading movement had widened the Order's function beyond its original charitable role and increased its reputation[64]. By allowing themselves to get so deeply involved in these massive migratory movements of populations, the Hospitallers were also in part responsible for the export or dissemination of 'Western and especially French culture beyond its own borders'[65]. But their legacy goes even further than that. At one level, through their charitable and military activities, the Hospitallers had fulfilled a 'great civilizing and defensive function in the development of Europe'[66], unwittingly contributing as much to the 'Christianization of Europe' as to the 'Christianization of warfare'[67]. At another level, the Hospitallers performed an intimately related and as equally remarkable social and economic function. Away from the theatre of war on land and at sea, outside the great halls and precincts of the hospital, and away from the remote Convent in Jerusalem or Acre, on Cyprus, Rhodes, or Malta, the Hospitallers for over seven hundred years resided on one of their Order's several European commanderies. In the long-term historical perspective, the intelligent administration of these massive estates, each of which played a wide range of useful and significant roles, constituted an unwittingly formative influence, a powerful force of continuity, and a constructive force in European civilization[68]. Today, as it had been at the start of its pilgrimage in Jerusalem, the Order's mission is to help that part of humanity that finds itself in distress. In the words of a recent French writer and critic, 'this institution holds sway over the world,' not through military force or political power, 'but through one sole act: that of charity'[69].

Religious Communities and Urban Communities

Notes

[1] J. Richard, *Introduction*, in M. Barber (ed.), *The Military Orders*, [I]: *Fighting for the Faith and Caring for the Sick*, Aldershot 1992, p. xxi.

[2] See C.H. Lawrence, *Medieval Monasticism: Forms of Religious Life in Western Europe in the Middle Ages*, 2nd edn, London 1989, p. 207.

[3] J. Riley-Smith, *What were the Crusades?*, 3rd edn, Hampshire 2002, p. 13.

[4] M. Bloch, *Feudal Society, II: Social Classes and Political Organization*, trans. by L.A. Manyon, London 1962, p. 295.

[5] Riley-Smith, *What were the Crusades?* cit., p. 13.

[6] P. Rietbergen, *Europe: A Cultural History*, London 1998, p. 114.

[7] Fulcher of Chartres's text of Urban II's sermon. Cited after *ibid.*, p. 115.

[8] J. Riley-Smith, *Crusading as an Act of Love*, "History", LXV, 1980, pp. 177-192.

[9] Cited after D. Selwood, *Knights of the Cloister: Templars and Hospitallers in Central-Southern Occitania c.1100 – c.1300*, Suffolk 1999, p. 51.

[10] A.T. Luttrell, *The Hospitallers' Medical Tradition: 1291-1530*, in M. Barber (ed.), *The Military Orders*, [I], cit., pp. 65, 71-72.

[11] Lawrence, *Medieval Monasticism* cit., p. 212.

[12] For the history of the itinerant Hospitaller Convent after the loss of Rhodes, V. Mallia-Milanes, *Charles V's Donation of Malta to the Order of St John*, "Peregrinationes Acta et Documenta", 2, 2001, pp. 23-33.

[13] Drawn up by Raymond du Puy, the second Master who had succeeded the Holy Gerard, the founder, it was confirmed by Pope Eugenius III.

[14] For the papal bull, National Library of Malta, Cod. 1126. See also J. Riley-Smith, *The Knights of St John in Jerusalem and Cyprus c.1050-1310*, London 1967, p. 342.

[15] H. Nicholson, *Templars, Hospitallers and Teutonic Knights: Images of the Military Orders, 1128-1291*, Leicester 1993, p. 4.

[16] Riley-Smith, *Knights of St John* cit., p. 341.

[17] In the thirteenth century, the priories were in turn grouped into larger geographical units called *langues*. The Order was made up of eight such *langues* – Provence, Auvergne, France, Italy, Aragon, England, Germany, and Castile.

[18] V. Mallia-Milanes, *The Hospitaller Receiver In Venice: A Late Seventeenth-Century Document*, "Studi Veneziani", n.s., XLIV, 2002, p. 310.

[19] This and the subsequent sub-headings are taken from the title of a conference on the military orders organized by the London Centre for the Study of the Crusades at the Museum of St John, St John's Gate, Clerkenwell, London, on 3-6 September 1992.

[20] Luttrell, *Hospitallers' Medical Tradition* cit., p. 64, and *passim*.

[21] S. Edgington, *Medical Care in the Hospital of St John in Jerusalem*, in H. Nicholson (ed.) *The Military Orders, II: Welfare and Warfare*, Aldershot 1998, pp. 27-33, especially p. 30.

[22] C. Toll, *Arabic Medicine and Hospitals in the Middle Ages: A Probable Model for the Military Orders' Care for the Sick*, in Nicholson (ed.), *The Military Orders*, II cit., p. 40.

[23] B.Z. Kedar, *A Twelfth-Century Description of the Jerusalem Hospital*, in *ibid.*, pp. 3-13. For a provisional edition of the treatise, *ibid.*, pp. 13-26.

[24] For details, see A. Williams, Xenodochium *to Sacred Infirmary: the Changing Role of the Hospital of the Order of St John, 1522-1631*, in Barber (ed.), *The Military Orders*, [I] cit., pp. 97-102.

[25] P. Cassar, *A Medical History of Malta*, London 1964, p. 40.

26 *Ibid.*, p. 41.

27 *Ibid.*, pp. 97-98.

28 *Ibid.*, p. 99.

29 *Ibid.*, pp. 100-101

30 *Ibid.*, p. 100.

31 Riley-Smith, *Knights of St John* cit., pp. 475-76.

32 Luttrell, *Hospitallers' Medical Tradition* cit., *passim*.

33 See N. Vatin, *L'Ordre de Saint-Jean-de-Jérusalem, l'Empire ottoman et la Méditerranée orientale entre les deux sièges de Rhodes (1480-1522)*, Paris 1994, pp. 294-307, 329-42.

34 U. Mori Ubaldini, *La Marina del Sovrano Militare Ordine di San Giovanni di Gerusalemme di Rodi e di Malta*, Rome 1971, p. 99.

35 *Ibid.*, pp. 99-100.

36 *Ibid.*, p. 100.

37 V. Mallia-Milanes, *Venice and Hospitaller Malta 1530-1798: Aspects of a Relationship*, Malta 1992, *passim*.

38 Mori Ubaldini, *La Marina del Sovrano Militare* cit., p. 106.

39 *Ibid.*, pp. 267-80.

40 L. Butler, *The Port of Rhodes under the Knights of St John (1309-1522)*, in *Les Grandes Escales: Receuils de la société Jean Bodin*, XXXII, Brussels 1974, pp. 339-345; A.T. Luttrell, *The Earliest Documents on the Hospitaller Corso at Rhodes: 1413 and 1416*, "Mediterranean Historical Review", X, 1995, pp. 177-188.

41 Mori Ubaldini, *La Marina del Sovrano Militare* cit., p. 108.

42 National Library of Malta, Cod. 80, *Liber Conciliorum*, fols. 74-75.

43 Mori Ubaldini, *La Marina del Sovrano Militare* cit., pp. 122-123; also A. Guglielmotti, *Storia della marina pontificia*, III-IV: La *guerra dei pirati e la marina pontificia dal 1500 al 1560*, Rome 1886-87, III, p. 228.

44 K.M. Setton, *The Papacy and the Levant (1204-1571)*, Philadelphia 1984, III, p. 352; E. Rossi, *Storia della marina dell'Ordine di S. Giovanni di Gerusalemme, di Rodi e di Malta*, Rome 1926, p. 36. In December 1531, the Venetian Marin Sanudo diarized the following observation: 'et si ben siegue che l'armata di questo Signor parte potria ussir et andar verso Malta contra il Gran Maestro di Rodi per vendicarsi di Modon'. M. Sanudo, *I diarii di Marino Sanuto*, edited by R. Fulin et al., Venice 1879-1903, LV, col. 518.

45 Rossi, *Storia della marina* cit., p. 37; Setton, *The Papacy* cit., III, pp. 366-67.

46 Setton, *The Papacy* cit., III, pp. 396-400.

47 *Ibid.*, pp. 170-72; Rossi, *Storia della marina* cit., p. 38-39; Setton, *The Papacy* cit., III, ch. 11, *passim*.

48 I. Bosio, *Dell'Istoria della Sacra Religione et Ill.ma Militia di S. Gio. Gierosolimitano*, III, Rome 1602, pp. 178-80; Rossi, *Storia della marina* cit., p. 39; Setton, *The Papacy* cit., III, pp. 445-449.

49 Bosio, *Dell'Istoria della Sacra Religione* cit., III, pp. 186-187.

50 *Ibid.*, p. 194; Rossi, *Storia della marina* cit., p. 39.

51 Bosio, *Dell'Istoria della Sacra Religione* cit., III, pp. 194-195; Rossi, *Storia della marina* cit., p. 39.

52 See Bosio, *Dell'Istoria della Sacra Religione* cit., III, pp. 199-200, pp. 205-211; Rossi, *Storia della marina* cit., pp. 40; also J.B. Wolf, *The Barbary Coast: Algiers under the Turks 1500 to 1830*, London 1979, pp. 27-30.

53 On the whole episode, Setton, *The Papacy* cit., III, pp. 533-535.

54 Rossi, *Storia della marina* cit., pp. 45-46; Moro Ubaldini, *La Marina del Sovrano Militare* cit., p. 201; Fern- and Braudel, *The Mediterranean and the Mediterranean World in the Age of Philip II*, trans. by Sian Reynolds, London 1972-73, pp. 977, 980.

55 Bosio, *Dell'Istoria della Sacra Religione* cit., III, p. 191; see also V. Mallia-Milanes, *Reflections on the Historiog-*

raphy of Hospitaller Gozo, in L. Briguglio (ed.), *Focus on Gozo*, Malta 1996, pp. 146-51. When Tripoli fell on 14 August 1551 to the besieging Ottoman forces, Henri II's French ambassador to the Porte, Gabriel de Luitz d'Aramon, was present with two galleys and a galliot. The Hospitaller Caspar de Villier, Marshall, of the French Langue of Auvergne, was governor. Setton, *The Papacy* cit., III, p. 555; Braudel, *The Mediterranean* cit., pp. 920-921. On Hospitaller Tripoli, E. Rossi, *Il dominio dei cavalieri di Malta a Tripoli (1530-1551) e i rapporti dell'Ordine con Tripoli nei secoli seguenti (1551-1798)*, "Archivum Melitense", VI, 2, 1924, pp. 43-85; A.P. Vella, *The Order of Malta and the defence of Tripoli, 1530-1551*, "Melita Historica", VI, 4, 1975, pp. 362-81; A. Williams, *Tripoli and the Knights of Malta Revisited*, in P. Xuereb (eds.), *Karissime Gotifride: Historical essays presented to Godfrey Wettinger on his seventieth birthday*, Malta 1999, pp. 96-102.

[56] For an evaluation of the significance of the siege, V. Mallia-Milanes, *The Birgu Phase in Hospitaller History*, in L. Bugeja et al. (eds.), *Birgu: A Maltese Maritime History*, Malta 1993, pp. 73-96.

[57] Braudel, *The Mediterranean* cit., p. 1088.

[58] See, for example, E. Siberry, *Criticism of Crusading 1095-1274*, Oxford 1985. Also N. Housley, *The Italian Crusades. The Papal-Angevin Alliance and the Crusades against Christian Lay Powers, 1254-1343*, Oxford 1982; H.E. Mayer, *The Crusades*, trans. by J. Gillingham, 2nd edn, Oxford 1988; H. Nicholson, *Templars, Hospitallers and Teutonic Knights: Images of the Military Orders, 1128-1291*, Leicester 1993.

[59] G. O'Malley, *The Knights Hospitaller of the English Langue 1460-1565*, Oxford 2005, p. 1; M. Barber, *The Trial of the Templars*, Cambridge 1978.

[60] O'Malley, *The Knights Hospitaller* cit., p. 5.

[61] A.T. Luttrell, *English Contributions to the Hospitaller Castle at Bodrum in Turkey: 1407-1437* in Nicholson H. (ed.), *The Military Orders*, II, cit., pp. 165-166.

[62] For such ventures, Mori Ubaldini, *La Marina del Sovrano Militare* cit., *passim*.

[63] See V. Mallia-Milanes, 'A Man with a Mission: A Venetian Hospitaller on Eighteenth-Century Malta', paper read in 'The Military Orders on Land and by Sea', The Fourth International Conference of the London Centre for the Study of the Crusades, the Military Religious Orders, and the Latin East', held at St John's Gate, London, 8-11 September 2005.

[64] P. Contamine, *War in the Middle Ages*, trans. by M. Jones, Oxford 1984, p. 75.

[65] Bloch, *Feudal* Society cit., p. 296.

[66] E. Schermerhorn, *On the Trail of the Eight-Pointed Cross: A Study of the Heritage of the Knights Hospitallers in Feudal Europe*, New York 1940.

[67] J. Le Goff, *The Birth of Europe*, trans. by Janet Lloyd, Oxford 2005, pp. 58, 94.

[68] Schermerhorn, *On the Trail of the Eight-Pointed Cross* cit., *passim*.

[69] B. Galimard Flavigny, *Histoire de l'Ordre de Malte*, Paris 2006, p. 10.

BIBLIOGRAPHY

Barber M., *The Trial of the Templars*, Cambridge 1978.

Bloch M., *Feudal* Society, II: *Social Classes and Political Organization*, trans. L.A. Manyon, London 1962.

Bosio I., *Dell'Istoria della Sacra Religione et Ill.ma Militia di S. Gio. Gierosolimitano*, III, Rome 1602.

Braudel F., *The Mediterranean and the Mediterranean World in the Age of Philip II*, trans. Reynolds S., London 1972-73.

Butler L., *The Port of Rhodes under the Knights of St John (1309-1522)*, Les Grandes Escales: Receuils de la société Jean Bodin, XXXII, Brussels 1974, pp. 339-45.

Cassar P., *A Medical History of Malta*, London 1964.

Contamine P., *War in the Middle Ages*, trans. by Jones M., Oxford 1984.

Edgington S., *Medical Care in the Hospital of St John in Jerusalem*, in Nicholson H. (ed.), *The Military Orders*, II: *Welfare and Warfare*, Aldershot 1998, pp. 27-33.

Galimard Flavigny B., *Histoire de l'Ordre de Malte*, Paris 2006.

Guglielmotti A., *Storia della marina pontificia*, III-IV: La *guerra dei pirati e la marina pontificia dal 1500 al 1560*, Rome 1886-87.

Housley N., *The Italian Crusades. The Papal-Angevin Alliance and the Crusades against Christian Lay Powers, 1254-1343*, Oxford 1982.

Kedar B.Z., *A Twelfth-Century Description of the Jerusalem Hospital*, in Nicholson H. (ed.), *The Military Orders*, II: *Welfare and Warfare*, Aldershot 1998, pp. 3-13.

Lawrence C.H., *Medieval Monasticism: Forms of Religious Life in Western Europe in the Middle Ages*, 2nd edn, London 1989.

Le Goff J., *The Birth of Europe*, trans. Janet Lloyd, Oxford 2005.

Luttrell A.T., *English Contributions to the Hospitaller Castle at Bodrum in Turkey: 1407-1437*, in Nicholson H. (ed.), *The Military Orders*, II: *Welfare and Warfare*, Aldershot 1998, pp. 163-72.

Id., *The Earliest Documents on the Hospitaller Corso at Rhodes: 1413 and 1416*, Mediterranean Historical Review, X, 1995, pp. 177-88.

Id., *The Hospitallers' Medical Tradition: 1291-1530*, in M. Barber (ed.), *The Military Orders*, [I]: *Fighting for the Faith and Caring for the Sick*, Aldershot 1992, pp. 64-81.

Mallia-Milanes V., *A Man with a Mission: A Venetian Hospitaller on Eighteenth-Century Malta*, paper read in "The Military Orders on Land and by Sea", The Fourth International Conference of the London Centre for the Study of the Crusades, the Military Religious Orders, and the Latin East', held at St John's Gate, London, 8-11 September 2005.

Id., *Charles V's Donation of Malta to the Order of St. John*, in *Peregrinationes Acta et Documenta*, II, 2 (2001), pp. 23-33.

Id., *Reflections on the Historiography of Hospitaller Gozo*, in *Focus on Gozo*, ed. L. Briguglio, Malta 1996, pp. 146-51.

Id., *The Birgu Phase in Hospitaller History*, in *Birgu: A Maltese Maritime History*, edited by L. Bugeja et al, Malta 1993, pp. 73-96.

Id., *The Hospitaller Receiver In Venice: A Late Seventeenth-Century Document*, in *Studi Veneziani*, n.s., XLIV (2002).

Id., *Venice and Hospitaller Malta 1530-1798: Aspects of a Relationship*, Malta 1992.

Mayer H.E., *The Crusades*, trans. J. Gillingham, 2nd edn, Oxford 1988.

Mori Ubaldini U., *La Marina del Sovrano Militare Ordine di San Giovanni di Gerusalemme di Rodi e di Malta*, Rome 1971.

Nicholson H., *Templars, Hospitallers and Teutonic Knights: Images of the Military Orders, 1128-1291*, Leicester 1993.

O'Malley G., *The Knights Hospitaller of the English Langue 1460-1565*, Oxford 2005.

Richard J., *Introduction* in M. Barber (ed.), *The Military Orders*, [I]: *Fighting for the Faith and Caring for the Sick*, Aldershot 1992, pp. xxi-xxvii.

Rietbergen P., *Europe: A Cultural History*, London 1998.

Riley-Smith J., *The Knights of St John in Jerusalem and Cyprus c.1050-1310*, London 1967.

Id., *Crusading as an Act of Love*, "History", LXV, 1980, pp. 177-92.

Id., *What were the Crusades?*, 3rd edn, Hampshire 2002.

Rossi E., *Il dominio dei Cavalieri di Malta a Tripoli (1530-1551) e i rapporti dell'Ordine con Tripoli nei secoli seguenti (1551-1798)*, in *Archivum Melitense*, VI, 2 (1924), pp. 43-85.

Id., *Storia della marina dell'Ordine di S. Giovanni di Gerusalemme, di Rodi e di Malta*, Rome 1926.

Sanudo Marino, *I diarii di Marino Sanuto*, edited R. Fulin et al., Venice 1879-1903.

Schermerhorn E., *On the Trail of the Eight-Pointed Cross: A Study of the Heritage of the Knights Hospitallers in Feudal Europe*, New York 1940.

Selwood D., *Knights of the Cloister: Templars and Hospitallers in Central-Southern Occitania c.1100 – c.1300*, Suffolk 1999.

Setton K.M., *The Papacy and the Levant (1204-1571)*, 4 vols., Philadelphia 1984.

Siberry E., *Criticism of Crusading 1095-1274*, Oxford 1985.

Toll C., *Arabic Medicine and Hospitals in the Middle Ages: A Probable Model for the Military Orders' Care for the Sick*, in Nicholson H. (ed.), *The Military Orders*, II: *Welfare and Warfare*, Aldershot 1998, pp. 35-41.

Vatin N., *L'Ordre de Saint-Jean-de-Jérusalem, l'Empire ottoman et la Méditerranée orientale entre les deux sièges de Rhodes (1480-1522)*, Paris 1994.

Vella A.P., *The Order of Malta and the defence of Tripoli, 1530-1551*, "Melita Historica", VI, 4, 1975, pp. 362-81.

Williams A., *Tripoli and the Knights of Malta Revisited*, in Xuereb P., *Karissime Gotifride: Historical essays presented to Godfrey Wettinger on his seventieth birthday*, Malta 1999, pp. 96-102.

Id., '*Xenodochium' to Sacred Infirmary: the Changing Role of the Hospital of the Order of St John, 1522-1631*, in Barber Malcolm (ed.), *The Military Orders*, [I]: *Fighting for the Faith and Caring for the Sick*, Aldershot 1992, pp. 97-102.

Wolf J.B., *The Barbary Coast: Algiers under the Turk*, Baltimore 2003.

Growing Up in Hospitaller Malta (1530-1798): An Overview

EMANUEL BUTTIGIEG
University of Malta

Wara li ntemm il-Konċilju ta' Trentu (1545-63), fl-1575 Ruma baghtet f'Malta lil Monsinjur Pietro Dusina bhala Vigarju Apostoliku sabiex jirraporta dwar l-istat tal-Knisja Maltija. Malta kienet ilha kważi hamsa u erbghin sena immexxija mill-Kavallieri ta' San Ġwann. Matul dawn is-snin, il-gżejjer Maltin sofrew żewġ attakki kbar (1551, 1565) mill-Imperu Ottoman; f'dan iż-żmien ukoll Malta rat il-bidu ta' process ta' urbanizazzjoni b'mod speċjali madwar il-Port il-Kbir. Dan l-iżvilupp urban kien xprunat mill-preżenza ta' l-Ordni li kellha biżżejjed riżorsi sabiex tibda u ssostni dan il-process. Il-preżenza ta' l-Ordni f'Malta fil-perjodu bikri modern fissret ukoll li Malta saret stat teokratiku, jiġifieri stat immexxi minn nies reliġjużi. Ghaldaqstant huwa fi hdan dan il-kuntest urban u reliġjuż li t-tema prinċipali ta' dan l-artiklu, jiġifieri, l-esperjenzi ta' kif wiehed kien jghix it-tfulija u l-adoloxxenza f'Malta fi żmien il-Kavallieri, tiżvolġi.

Dan l-artiklu jibda billi janalizza l-ideat ta' numru ta' filosofi u psikologi li matul il-milja tas-snin hallew impatt, permezz ta' hsibijiethom, fuq kif l-istoriċi – imma anke s-soċjeta inġenerali – harsu lejn il-proċessi tat-tfulija u l-adoloxxenza. Minn hemm nimxu biex naghtu harsa lejn l-istorjografija Maltija u barranija dwar dan is-suġġett. Fl-ahhar parti, l-artiklu jitratta l-komunitajiet urbani Maltin żviluppati mill-Kavallieri u kif, fi hdan dawn il-komunitajiet, tfaċċaw u nstabu soluzzjonijiet ghall-problemi soċjali bhalma kienu t-tfal abbandunati u n-nisa li ma setghux jiżżewġu minhabba n-nuqqas ta' dota.

INTRODUCTION

Following the Council of Trent (1545-63), in 1575 Rome sent Mgr Pietro Dusina as Apostolic Visitor to Malta to report on the state of the Maltese Church. By this time, Malta had been administered by the Order of St. John the Baptist of Jerusalem, also known as the Hospitallers, for forty-five years, in which time Malta had experienced the brunt of two major attacks (1551, 1565) by the Ottoman Empire, as well as witnessed the beginnings of a process of urbanization centred around its harbours (See Map 1). The Hospitallers, who were a religious-military community, had the dynamism and resources to drive the generation and expansion of urban communities that would thoroughly transform the social, economic and cultural dynamics of Malta. The juxtaposition of religion and urbanization was a fundamental feature of Hospitaller Malta, which was a theocratic state run by religious men – the Grand Master of the Hospitallers, the Bishop of Malta, and the Inquisitor – all of whom reported directly to the Pope. One way in which this intricate situation can be analysed is by looking at how religious concepts impacted on the experiences of children and adolescents growing up in the Hospitaller towns of early modern Malta, and how this was considered – or not – in the historiography.

RELIGIOUS AND PHILOSOPHICAL PERSPECTIVES ABOUT GROWING UP

Beginning with the philosophers of the ancient world, and continuing with the churchmen of the middle ages and the philosophers of early modern times, down through to contemporary psychologists, the human mind has tried to come to terms with the process of growing up. Over the centuries there has been an increasing level of complexity in ideas about young people, and this emerges in the summary of a sample of eight key thinkers from different eras presented in Table 1.

Aristotle was one of the first to describe specific time periods for stages of human development. He believed that at the onset of adolescence, individuals are unstable and impatient, lacking self-control to be a mature person. Self-control is however gained by the age of twenty-one[1]. Isidore of Seville adopted a framework very similar to that of Aristotle, where a distinction is made between three seven-year sub-ages within a person's lifespan[2]. Dante Alighieri believed that adolescence really begins at the age of

Age	Aristotle (384-322 B.C.)	Isidore of Seville (560-636), through Vincent de Beauvais (1184/94-1264)	Dante (1265-1321)	Rousseau (1712-1778)	Freud (1856-1939)	Piaget (1896-1980)	Erikson (1902-1994)	Santrock (*Adolescence*, 1998)
								Pre-natal period: from conception to birth.
0-1					Oral Stage: from birth to 18 months.	Sensorimotor Stage: from birth to 2 years.	Crises of Early Infancy.	Infancy: from birth to 18 or 24 months.
1			Infancy: from birth to 4 or 5 years.			Crises of Infancy.	
2				Anal Stage: from 1.5 to 3 years.		
3	Infancy: from birth to 7 years.	*Infantia*: from birth to 7 years.		Phallic Stage: from 3 to 6 years. Oedipus Complex occurs.	Preoperational Stage: from 2 to 7 years.		Early Childhood: up to 5 or 6 years.
4					Crises of Initiative vs. Guilt.
5						
6					
7					
8	Boyhood: from 7 to puberty.	*Pueritia*: from 7 to 14 years.		Savage: from 5 to 12 years.	Latency Stage: from 6 to puberty.	Concrete Operational Stage: from 7 to 11 years.		Middle and Late Childhood: from 6 to 11 years.
9						Systematic Learning.
10						
11					
12						Formal Operational Stage: from 11 to 15 years.
13				Stage 3: from 12 to 15 years.	
14			*Adolescentia*: from 8 to 25 years.		
15	Young Manhood: from puberty to age 21.					
16						Adolscence: from 10/13 years to 18/22 years.
17				Stage 4: from 15 to 20 years.	Crises of Late Adolescence.
18					
19					
20				Genital Stage: from puberty onwards.	
21		*Adolescentia*: from 15 to 28 years.			
22					
23					
24					
25					
26					
27					
28					

Table 1.
Age Stages According to a Sample of Eight Key Thinkers.

eight. According to Christiane Klapish-Zuber, this was because for Dante, the 'increasing of life' rather than referring to physical development, referred to a state of social and economic dependence characteristic of an age in which the chief virtue continued to be obedience[3].

Isidore's and Dante's ideas – and those of later philosophers and psychologists – seem to fall squarely within the Latin Christian tradition of considering the age of seven as the age of discretion, and therefore the time from which a child is capable of mortal sin and of receiving the sacraments of Penance, the Holy Eucharist, Confirmation, and so on[4]. The Christian tradition was in turn influenced by the ideas of Aristotle, by the *Pueri paidon agoges* [On the Education of Boys] generally attributed to Plutarch and by St. John Chrysostom's *On Vainglory and the Education of Children*[5]. Pre-Tridentine Christianity was marked by a certain fluidity with regards to age and the sacraments. This was a reflection of St. Thomas Aquinas' belief that "Age of body does not determine age of soul. Even in childhood man can attain spiritual maturity"[6]. The Council of Trent, in its drive to create uniformity and instill discipline, sought to regulate better the age at which sacraments could be received. Infant baptism was upheld, and Holy Communion and Confirmation, though not rigidly defined, could only be administered after a child was seven[7]. Boys under fourteen and girls under twelve could not marry[8]. Systems of novitiate for those taking religious vows were renewed or instituted, with sixteen being the minimum age to undertake one's profession[9]. According to Oliver Logan, Tridentine decrees viewed adolescence as a perilous age, and in order for a young child not to be over-taken by a sinful inclination later on life, small defects needed to be identified and eliminated at an early stage. Such a goal was to be achieved through formation, rather than repression, as a way to create a new generation of disciplined and obedient Catholics[10].

The theme of obedience was taken up in Thomas Hobbes's *Leviathan* (1660). In Hobbes's philosophy there is a natural link between the obedience that servants owe to masters, and the obedience that children owe to parents, especially to the father[11]. Hobbes rooted his obedience argument in the teachings of St Paul. It would therefore be interesting to see, in the light of the fact that the cult of St Paul developed into a symbol of Maltese identity[12] – because the saint is reputed to have been shipwrecked in Malta in 60 A.D. – whether the Maltese elites were particularly receptive to Hobbes's ideas.

The *Leviathan* was followed by John Locke's *Some Thoughts Concerning Education* (1693). In the introduction to his work, Locke says that he is publishing this work as a response to "...so many who profess themselves at a loss how to breed their children..."[13]. Locke used observations made about Malta in the travel account of Jean Du Mont in order to illustrate his ideas about children's clothes and the need not to overdress them so that their bodies could grow accustomed to the climate[14]. This in turn provides an unexpected source of information about childhood practices in Malta:

Malta is hotter than Rome, or any other place in Europe, ... The Peasants are as black as Egyptians; for they take no care to preserve themselves from the Sun; and the most scorching Heat is not able to drive 'em into their Houses, or even make 'em leave off working. This is an evident Demonstration of the Power of Nature in performing things that seem to be impossible: For there are few things which a Man may not suffer if he be accustom'd to 'em from his Infancy, as the Maltese are in this case, who inure the Bodies of their Children to Heat, by making 'em go stark naked, without Shirt, Drawers, or Cap, as soon as they are taken from their Mother's Breast, to the Age of Ten Years; so that their Skin grows as hard as Leather[15].

Locke's line of thought was later followed by Jean Jacques Rousseau. Similarly to Aristotle, Rousseau believed that development in childhood and adolescence occurs in a series of stages. In *Emile* (1762) he proposed greater freedom for children and advocated letting children run about idly up to the age of twelve. This is because during the 'Savage Stage', from five to twelve years of age, sensory development takes place. Sensory experiences such as play, sports and games should be the focus of education. However, whereas for Locke fables could be used as a bait to inculcate the love of reading in children, for Rousseau, such texts led to vice, not virtue[16].

These early modern philosophers were followed by an intellectual trio in the continuum represented by the psychologists Sigmund Freud, Jean Piaget and Erik Erikson. Their impact on ways of thinking about young people has not only fundamentally marked the modern age, but they have also informed historical interpretations of the past. According to Freud's psychoanalytic theories, development is primarily unconscious. This contrasts with Piaget's cognitive theories that emphasize conscious thoughts. Erikson, then, in his book *Young Man Luther* (1958), integrated Freudian ideas, history and his own direct observations of young people with emotional disturbances who were his patients. Erikson's word for 'stage' is 'crises', and his 'Five Stage Child Moulding Process by Crises' is according to him the process through which Martin Luther came to realise himself and ultimately break with the Catholic Church[17].

The richness of all of these theoretical frameworks means that our knowledge of young people's physiology and psychology has become much more thorough, complex, and refined. That is why, in the exposition of his ideas, John Santrock combines biological, cognitive and socio-emotional theories to present adolescence as a time of evaluation, of decision-making, of commitment, and of carving out a place in the world[18].

Overall, two main trends can be discerned in these theories about children and adolescents. Firstly, there is an intimate association of sexuality with children and adolescents; secondly, there is a tendency to dissect and compartmentalize the study of childhood and adolescence into stages or steps. Sexuality is seen to be an intrinsic part of every child's and adolescent's development, be it positive (in the sense of 'normal' biological development) or negative (in the sense of physical and psychological abuse by adults on younger people). From early modern times onwards, science and medicine vied increasingly with religion to influence such ideas, allowing for further specialisation in the vocabulary of age used to describe children and adolescents.

HISTORIOGRAPHICAL PERSPECTIVES ABOUT GROWING UP

The study of the history of childhood and adolescence – though quite 'young' as a field in itself – has grown enormously since the publication in France of Philippe Ariès's *L'Enfant et la Vie Familiale sous l'Ancien Regime* in 1960. The sheer amount and variety of work arising in response to Ariès spans the whole spectrum of classicists, medievalists, early modernists, modernists, art historians, anthropologists and archaeologists[19]. Neither these historiographical developments, nor the philosophical concepts mentioned above, have had any particular impact on Maltese historiography. According to Charles Cassar, the fundamental problem with the history of early modern Malta is that no major sustained research has been attempted; no institution or single scholar has undertaken a serious general statement based upon the extensive archival data available[20]. Keeping with this observation, there is no single work dedicated to the history of childhood and adolescence in Malta. There are, however, references to children and adolescents in broader historical works, and in works specialising in education, health and folklore, as well as undergraduate and graduate dissertations at the University of Malta[21].

Besides these, it should be noted that throughout the British colonial period (1800-1964) and since Independence, young people were often the focus of political, religious, literary and other movements. Throughout this period, children and adolescents who entered the slowly increasing number of schools throughout Malta and Gozo found themselves at the heart of the Malta Language Question, a cultural battle for the predominance of English or Italian as the language of instruction, justice and employment[22]. It was against this background that Maltese as the national language started coming to the front and this was reflected in an outpouring of literature in the vernacular in the late 19th and the early 20th centuries. This consisted of the writing down of legends that had been transmitted orally over the ages and the composition of a number of historical novels, many of them set in the days of the Hospitallers[23]. Such works bear relevance to the present study because many of them featured children. The 'young girl' in particular became a metaphor for Malta – for the island was always represented as a female – and its struggle to preserve her honour and freedom against the foreign coloniser – the lascivious Knight and the evil Turk in these stories served as veiled references to British rule in Malta[24].

The 19th and 20th centuries also saw the medicalisation of childhood as male doctors gradually sidelined traditional pseudo-religious healers (generally female) and began writing books and tracts in Maltese aimed at the wider population. Midwives were identified as a particular category that needed to be better instructed by doctors[25]. In more recent years, the introduction of compulsory education up to sixteen years of age, the ratification by the Maltese Parliament of the United Nations Convention on the Rights of Children in 1990, and the setting up of the National Commission for the Family and the Commissioner for Children, have meant the institutionalisation and secularisation of childhood and adolescence within the premise of them being representative of innocence and vulnerability. The murder of eight-year-old Twanny Aquilina in 1960 – allegedly by his own mother – is to-date still considered as "the murder of the century"[26].

In the historical field itself, it is in educational and medical history – long-time favourites among Maltese historians – that childhood and adolescence are generally dealt with. Most works analysing educational developments have generally adopted an institutional and statistical approach, where the humane aspect is missing and children appear only as names and numbers[27]. Charles Cassar and Charles Dalli, however, break away from this institutional approach. The former highlights two important points: firstly, he explores the divide between written and oral cultures; secondly, he points out the different mentalities that reigned in the harbour towns on the one hand, and in the countryside on the other, and how these impinged on the type and quality of education that were consequently available[28]. Dalli's work on medieval Malta distinguishes between formal institutionalised education, and the transmission of skills, techniques and values that constitute informal education. The pre-industrial household functioned as a repository of cultural values, modes of behaviour, skills and practices that were passed on across generations. This transmission took place either within the social context of the kin group or wider circle of friends and neighbours, or as part of an apprenticeship[29].

In 1964, Paul Cassar's *Medical History of Malta* was published, offering the first all-encompassing approach to the history of medicine in Malta over the ages. This was preceded in 1949 by Attilio Critien's study of foundlings under the Hospitallers[30]. These two pioneering works remain standard texts for anyone investigating medical history. Charles Savona-Ventura has also written extensively about the medical history of Malta. His works deal with medical institutions and their management, the treatment of orphans or foundlings, and especially the midwife profession. Midwives played an important role in traditional societies and their work and activities were closely scrutinised by the Roman Catholic Church. As early as 1575, Mgr Pietro Dusina enjoined parish priests to teach midwives the proper administration of the sacrament of baptism in cases of dire need. A license from the Episcopal Curia remained a requirement to

Map 1.
The Maltese Islands.

practise midwifery until 1906[31]. Other authors have written about the Holy Infirmary and other health-related institutions in early modern Malta[32].

Admittedly, unearthing source material on children and adolescents in the past is problematic. Children themselves leave few records, and artefacts designed for them, such as books and toys, have a poor survival rate[33]. Literary texts, polemics, biographies, diaries, letters, advice books, paintings and historical demography were the bedrock upon which the 'parents' of childhood history – Philippe Ariès, Peter Laslett, Lloyd de Mause, Edward Shorter, Lawrence Stone, Michael Anderson and Linda Pollock – developed the classical ideas which loom over the discipline[34]. With regards to Hospitaller Malta, biographical material of the like used by Stone and Pollock proves to be elusive, possibly due to a lack of access to the private archives of families pertaining to sectors of society generally expected to keep diaries at the time. With regards to historical demography, during the 1970s, Malta followed the lead of Great Britain, and a number of dissertations were carried out at the University of Malta, based on parochial registers, which provide a corpus of statistics, particularly for the first half of the 17th century. This work has of late been resuscitated at the same University[35]. The work of demographers has provided crucial evidence on such factors as age at marriage, number of children born and surviving, and the spacing between one birth and the other. These provide essential contours for the history of children and adolescents, but the facts of these matters do not unreservedly speak for themselves[36]. In the case of Hospitaller Malta it must also be noted that the amount of data extrapolated so far is limited.

Urban Communities

In 1575, while he was touring Valletta, Mgr Pietro Dusina remarked on the absence of children from the newly founded city[37]. The energy and assets of the Order soon rectified this situation, and it did not take long for the empty spaces of Valletta to fill up with people of all ages, especially young ones. By 1798, Valletta and the other harbour cities were a conurbation housing about thirty-seven percent of the population of Malta, and the overall population of the islands had increased from ca. 20,000 in 1530 to ca. 100,000 by the end of our period[38]. Children and adolescents filled the bustling streets of the harbour towns and roamed in the fields of the countryside as part of their play and recreation[39].

The 'street' is a key concept in the analytical framework developed by those who study the geography of childhood and stands for their concern with public space in general and the way young people relate to it[40]. This paper adopts the geographers' rendering of the 'street' as a metaphor for all outdoor spaces in which children are found[41]. At the same time the integration between the street and the home in the early modern context needs to be reiterated. The streets under investigation were generally urban, a slant determined by the sources and reflecting the overarching impact of the urbanisation of the harbour area on people's daily lives. Some streets become what Edward Soja has termed 'thirdspace', where young people can gather to affirm their sense of difference and celebrate their feelings of belonging[42]. Examples of such thirdspaces emerge in the sources – the square of Valletta, the staircase of a particular palace in Valletta, and the bastions of Senglea[43]. Whereas modern geographers seek to show how on contemporary streets gendered spaces are blurred and limited, the evidence for the streets of Hospitaller Malta shows them to have been quite rigidly gendered spaces. This needs to be tied in with perceptions of the body, and questions about age, social identity, and freedom of movement[44]. All these issues then need to be set against a background of a society with a generally violent and dangerous tenor of life.

Religious and ethnic conflicts in Maltese-Hospitaller urban communities could be seen in the fact that slaves were often the targets of children's teasing, as was the case of a slave wearing "a blazer and a red beret, and canvass trousers who was surrounded by boys shouting ["]This is a fugitive – let's tie him up[!"][45]. On the other hand, Patrick Brydone, who was in Malta in 1770, mentions a similar incident when he saw a group of boys disturb Turkish slaves who were worshiping in a mosque that had been built for them. The boys "were immediately sent to prison, and severely punished"[46].

Children, especially in their earlier years, tend to be associated much more with the female realm of the mother. In the harbour area of Malta, the environment tended to be particularly matriarchal as men worked at sea, while the women remained in Malta[47]. For example, in a district within Valletta known as *ta' Mundu il facchiu*, women sat in their doorways and worked with cotton, while children ran about playing. The close proximity of people was conducive to brawls breaking out and to many witnesses – including children – being present[48]. A very vivid description of a mother, terrified at the sight of her wounded and bleeding son, emerges from a particular case from Birgu in 1590. The thirteen-year-old Josepho removed a chair from beneath a stranger who was visiting his mother Joanna and made him fall to the ground. Offended at the boy's act, the said stranger unsheathed his sword and wounded Josepho in his left arm. Joanna, holding Josepho in her arms shouted and screamed at the perpetrator "you could have killed my son[!"][49]. Hearing the screaming, the female neighbours of Joanna, as well as male passers-by came to her house. Subtle details in the narrative point to this part of Birgu as having been a centre for prostitution[50]. Although religion may seem to feature but little in this incident and others that will follow below, it is important to remember

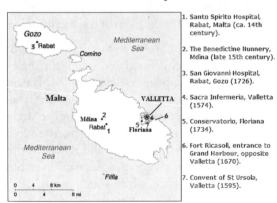

1. Santo Spirito Hospital, Rabat, Malta (ca. 14th century).

2. The Benedictine Nunnery, Mdina (late 15th century).

3. San Giovanni Hospital, Rabat, Gozo (1726).

4. Sacra Infermeria, Valletta (1574).

5. Conservatorio, Floriana (1734).

6. Fort Ricasoli, entrance to Grand Harbour, opposite Valletta (1670).

7. Convent of St Ursola, Valletta (1595).

Map 2.
Foundlings' Institutions.

that the Inquisition and the State Magistrates were never very removed from people's minds, and these examples are all derived from such courts of law.

FOUNDLINGS IN THE COMMUNITY

Throughout early modern Europe the phenomenon of child abandonment was very common, and Hospitaller Malta was no exception[51]. Nonetheless, the presence of the Hospitallers lent to it a certain particularity. In their individual capacities the Hospitallers were forbidden from taking care of any children, even if they were their relatives, and the penalties for breaking this rule were quite severe[52]. Such a measure seems to have been enacted in response to a number of cases where Hospitallers were being chosen as tutors to children[53]. Nonetheless as a community the Order was wholly dedicated to the care and welfare of children who were left to its care, as the following extract from their oath of investiture indicates:

> Question: Does thou promise to favour, and to show special concern for widows, for children, for orphans, and for all afflicted and troubled persons?
>
> Reply: With the aid of God our Lord, I swear to do so[54].

In the earliest Hospitaller communities in Jerusalem, many houses were double, containing sisters as well as brothers. These hospitaller sisters looked after children adopted by the Order, worked in the kitchen and inspected wet nurses[55]. However, by the time of the arrival of the Order in Malta in 1530, and especially after the Council of Trent, the role of the sisters was reduced to that of a secluded and contemplative life, so that responsibility for the care of the foundlings was left to the brothers[56]. From its earliest days in Malta, the Order took it upon itself to cater for foundlings. This it did within one of its most important institutions – the *Sacra Infermeria* [Holy Infirmary] – an all-round social institution to which people turned to in dire circumstances (Map 2 shows its location, as well as that of other similar or related institutions). In its role as caretaker of abandoned children, the Holy Infirmary became a socio-religious community, set within the wider urban community in which it was located.

While the Holy Infirmary was still in Birgu – up to 1574 – space and resources must have been somewhat limited. For this reason, when girls who were at the Holy Infirmary reached the age of three they were sent to stay with the cloistered nuns in Mdina until they reached "the age of marriage"[57]. Boys were kept at the Holy Infirmary until they were six, when they were apprenticed to learn some trade or other. The Treasury of the Order met all expenses in both cases. The Chapter General of 1578 confirmed these arrangements and in respect of boys, it was stated that "they were to be apprenticed to learn a trade in accordance with their own inclinations"[58]. This realization that people perform better when they are doing something that they enjoy, shows that the Hospitallers were familiar with the concept of aptitude, which was an important topic in Renaissance pedagogic thought[59]. In later years, when the Holy Infirmary in Valletta was well established, a more 'utilitarian' philosophy in respect of the foundlings seems to have developed, in that it was recognized that these children were a potential pool of labour that could be directed towards the needs of the Order itself. When boys reached the age of eight – later reduced to seven – they were moved to Fort Ricasoli, the great fortress at the mouth of the grand harbour, to be taken care of by the priest there, and where some form of military training was also provided[60]. A Commission that had been set up by the Council of the Order on 25 April 1796 to manage the Holy Infirmary was also empowered to keep an eye on those under age boys whose services were being employed by the Congregation for the Galleys, to see that both their physical and spiritual well-being were being taken care of[61]. Nonetheless the arrangement whereby boys were apprenticed according to their own inclinations was maintained[62]. The options for girls also increased as at eight – later seven – years of age, they were moved to the Conservatory of the Grand Master in Floriana until they were old enough to be married off or employment sought for them in the women's hospital[63]. The head of the women's hospital, the *Ospedaliera*, was duty bound to "instruct her pupils in those arts considered to be appropriate to their sex"[64].

Institutions similar to the Holy Infirmary in other parts of Europe are generally described with a certain feeling of doom. This is the impression which authors like Christiane Klapish-Zuber, Susan Steuer, Hugh Cunningham and Colin Heywood tend to give[65]. It is an impression derived from the terribly high mortality rates that were normal at such places. The figures at the Holy Infirmary itself were quite dismal. It has been estimated that in the twelve months 1787-88, there were 212 admissions and 121 deaths[66]. For those that survived, however, the Holy Infirmary seems not to have been such a bad place to be. On 14 December 1699, a certain Silvestro – who was described as an *alumnus* of the Holy Infirmary despite the fact that he was now twenty years old – was actually convalescing in the same Holy Infirmary because he was ill. His illness seems to have been serious as after he had received the final sacraments, he was drawing up his will. He nominated as his executor his master with whom he had been apprenticed by the Holy Infirmary some years before and his first wish was that the sum of ten *scudi* was to be given to Catharina – the woman who had been his wet-nurse – and her daughter Rosa, who were asked to pray for his soul[67]. Though this one case cannot be taken to be representative of the experiences of other foundlings who were farmed out to wet-nurses, it does provide a glimpse of love and affection.

RELIGION, MARRIAGE AND THE COMMUNITY

Although the Council of Trent affirmed the superiority of virginity to marriage, it also took marriage away from the hands of the laity and placed it under the strict supervision of the clergy[68]. One notable change in Notarial terminology with regards to marriage contracts had occurred by the 1590s. Whereas earlier marriage contracts were declared to be in accordance "with both the Greek as well as the Roman rite", by 1590 this was being replaced by the words "according to the mores and rituals of the holy and saintly Council of Trent and according to Roman usage"[69]. The concern evinced in the earlier formula was linked to an urge to guarantee the validity of a marriage in the light of the West-East Christian schism, and is explained away by Mgr Dusina's observation in 1575 of a plurality of rites being observed in Malta – Latin, Gallican and Greek[70]. The gradual introduction of this Tridentine formula over the course of the last part of the 16th century is indicative of the ways Catholic reforms were seeping down society and – at least on paper – being brought to the attention of people.

Families were very concerned with marrying off their children – especially daughters – and through dowries from both sides of the family the newly weds were assured a decent – and at times extremely rich – material base from which to set off on their life together. Age at marriage is a particularly important indicator of communal ideas and expectations about children, marriage and the family. In canon law, twelve was the minimum age of marriage for a girl, and fourteen for a boy[71]. The Council of Trent decided that marriages contracted by women under eighteen and men under twenty years of age without parental consent, were invalid[72]. A peculiarity of Hospitaller Malta was the common occurrence of child brides, which was in contrast to the European late marriage pattern[73]. For example, the doctor Domenico Leonardo Muriti presented a petition to Pope Paul III to be granted permission to marry off his fourteen-year-old daughter Johanna Muriti[74]. Demographic data for the parish of Porto Salvo in Valletta shows that the average age for male spouses was twenty-three, whereas that for women was seventeen to eighteen. However, beneath such averages, one then discovers girls who were getting married at the age of fourteen or even younger[75]. When she was twenty-one years old, Anna Maria Bonnici recalled how her mother had wed her to a fifty-year-old man when she was still fourteen or fifteen[76].

In Hospitaller Malta, it was the dowry that tangled the threads of a woman's fate[77]. The widow Petrissa Famigliomeno sold her slave Margerita for forty *scudi* to buy Tripolitanian soap which she was going to sell in order to make enough money for a dowry for her daughter Angela[78]. Both private individuals and organisations within the community sought to provide funds for dowries for girls whose families could not afford to provide them with one. In his will, Domenico Mifsud left sums of money to five men to be used as dowries for their individual daughters. This he did for the love of God and for the remission of his sins[79]. In preparing for his death, Domenico was reaching out to lay the foundations for five new family units on the strength of his dowries. Both the Noble Lady Margerita of Mdina and Isabella Sayd also made similar arrangements in their wills[80]. The Confraternity of the Holy Rosary in the Parish of Porto Salvo, Valletta, provided Gratia Schembri with her dowry[81]. Every year, the Grand Master, on the occasion of the anniversary of the Great Siege of 1565, sponsored six young, poor virgins by providing them with a dowry of 50 *scudi* each[82].

Besides the dowry, brides-to-be also received a *dodarium* from their future spouses. This custom, which was similar to the dower which English wives received, and which was also present in Roman Law, tended to consist of a sum of cash, and was a Maltese hybrid between the European *sponsalium*, or morning gift, and the Arab *mahr*, with a closer resemblance to the latter[83]. The *dodarium* was meant as a means of sustenance or as a second dowry in case the woman was widowed.

Conclusion

Hospitaller Malta was a special niche where the geographical reality of a central Mediterranean archipelago, merged with the peculiar institution that was the Order of St. John, to produce a set of logistics all of its own, but at the same time mirroring developments in the rest of Europe. The presence of the Order generated structural and social peculiarities similar only to other niche places such as Papal Rome or early modern Cambridge[84]. The whole period 1530-1798 was characterised by increasing urbanisation and migration – both internal and external. Population growth, the Reformation, the Counter-Reformation, the opportunities for work with the Order – both in service and on sea – drove many towards the harbour towns. As Paul Griffiths argues, there were many different ways of growing up in early modern society, and they were affected by religion, social class, gender, labour markets, urbanisation, and the responses of the young[85].

Religion permeated every aspect of life in Hospitaller Malta and by looking specifically at children and adolescents, this paper has sought to seek out information on several levels of a society undergoing change. People lived out their lives in an environment where religion and urbanisation overlapped at every corner. The example of the foundlings serves as a case study of how a 'community' – the Holy Infirmary – operated within the wider community to provide solutions for a social problem – that is, child abandonment – within a religious and urban framework. Marital dowries are another example of how individual components within a community – private individuals, families, confraternities, the Grand Master – inspired by religious concepts, would take action to address the problem of a lack of dowry that precluded a marriage from taking place.

Just as the history of Malta does not make sense when taken on its own and in isolation from wider developments, so its historiography needs to be considered alongside other national historiographies. The British connection – in the form of colonialism – created a nationalist/politicised historiography in which children and adolescents feature incidentally and act as a means to an end in the search for a national identity. More recent historiography – of which this paper is a part – seeks to recapture the experiences of people in the past, and in this quest a cultural history of religious concepts is crucial.

Notes

[1]   J.W. Santrock, *Adolescence*, Boston 1998, p. 8.

[2]   C. Klapish-Zuber, *Women, Family and Ritual in Renaissance Italy*, Chicago-London 1985, pp. 95-96.

[3]   Id. - C. Heywood, *A History of Childhood: Children and Childhood in the West from Medieval to Modern Times*, London 2001, p. 2.

[4]   G. Chapman, *Cathecism of the Catholic Church*, Avon 1994, p. 295; M. Quin (ed.), *Virtue's Catholic Encyclopedia*, London 1965, p. 11.

[5]   O. Logan, *Counter-Reformation Theories of Upbringing in Italy*, in D. Wood (ed.), *The Church and Childhood*, Oxford, U.K. and Cambridge, Massachusetts, pp. 277-278.

[6]   St Thomas Aquinas, *Summa theologiae*, III, 72, 8, ad 2, as quoted in Chapman, *Cathecism of the Catholic Church* cit., p. 295.

[7] M. Quin (ed.), *Virtue's Catholic Encyclopedia*, London 1965, p. 11; J.A. Coriden - T.J. Green - D.E. Heintschel (eds.), *The Code of the Canon Law: A Text and Commentary*, London 1985, p. 638.

[8] Quin, *Virtue's Catholic Encyclopedia* cit., p. 11.

[9] *Ibid.*; G. Aquilina - S. Fiorini (eds.), *Documentary Sources of Maltese History: Part IV – Documents at the Vatican, No. 1, Archivio Segreto Vaticano Congregazione Vescovi e Regolari Malta: Visita Apostolica No. 51 Mgr Pietro Dusina, 1575*, Malta 2001, p. 326.

[10] Logan, *Counter-Reformation Theories of Upbringing in Italy* cit., pp. 275-276, 283.

[11] D.G. Tannenbaum - D. Schultz, *Inventors of Ideas: An Introduction to Western Political Philosophy*, Boston and New York 1998, pp. 160-161.

[12] C. Cassar, *Society, Culture and Identity in Early Modern Malta*, Malta 2000, pp. 209-219.

[13] J. Locke, *'Some Thoughts',* [1693], in J.W. Yolton - J.S. Yolton (eds.), *Some Thoughts Concerning Education with Introduction*, Oxford 2000.

[14] *Ibid.*, p. 85.

[15] J. Du Mont, *A New Voyage to the Levant*, London, 1696. Although Locke quoted Du Mont, he did change a few words from this extract. Most notably he uses the word 'Gyspsies' instead of the original 'Egyptians', which two words were used interchangeably at the time.

[16] Santrock, *Adolescence* cit., p. 8. J.C. Steward, *British Art and the Origins of Modern Childhood*, 1730-1830, unpublished D.Phil Dissertation, University of Oxford 1997, p. 170.

[17] E.H. Erikson, *Young Man Luther: A Study in Psychoanalysis and History*, London 1958, p. 248.

[18] Santrock, *Adolescence* cit., p. 7.

[19] W. Coster, *Family and Kinship in England 1450-1800*, London 2001; J. Moore - E. Scott (eds.), *Invisible People and Processes: Writing Gender and Childhood into European Archaeology*, Leicester 1997.

[20] Cassar, *Society, Culture and Identity* cit., p. xxxv.

[21] F. Ciappara, *Society and the Inquisition in Early Modern Malta*, Malta 2001; C. Cassar, *Daughters of Eve – Women, Gender Roles and the Impact of the Council of Trent in Catholic Malta*, Malta 2002; J. Cassar-Pullicino, *Studies in Maltese Folklore*, Malta 1976; K. Gambin, *Popular Culture and the Inquisition, 1677-1678*, unpublished B.A. Hons. Dissertation, University of Malta, 1995; A. Camenzuli, *Maltese Social and Cultural Values in Perspective, 1771-1798*, unpublished M.A. Dissertation, University of Malta, 1999.

[22] J.M. Brincat, *The Language Question and Education: a Political Controversy on a Linguistic Topic*, in R. Sultana (ed.), *Yesterday's Schools: Readings in Maltese Educational History*, Malta 2001, pp. 137-158.

[23] S. Grima, *Il-Kavallieri fil-Klassi tal-Letteratura Maltija*, unpublished B.Ed Dissertation, University of Malta 2003, pp. 35-36, 64-65.

[24] Two such examples are the novels *Susanna* by Ġużè Muscat Azzopardi (Malta, 1946) and *Il-Leġġenda ta' Wied Speranza* as recorded by Victor Fenech, (Malta, 1983). See also Grima, *Il-Kavallieri fil-Klassi* cit.

[25] C. Savona Ventura, *L-Istorja tal-Mediċina fil-Gżejjer Maltin*, Malta 1999, pp. 48-50.

[26] E. Attard, *Delitti f'Malta: 200 Sena ta' Omiċidji, 1800-2000*, Malta 2001, pp. 43-87.

[27] P. Pecchiai, *Il Collegio dei Gesuiti in Malta*, "Archivio Storico di Malta", Fasc. II, 1939, pp. 129-169, 273-293; J. Cassar-Pullicino, *Pre-Jesuit Education in Malta*, "The Sundial", 6, IV, 1946, pp. 14-18; A.P. Vella, *The University of S. Maria Purtus Salutis*, "Journal of the Faculty of Arts", II, 1962, pp. 164-180; V. Borg, *Developments in Education Outside The Jesuit 'Collegium Melitense*, "Melita Historica", 3, 6, 1974, pp. 215-254.

[28] C. Cassar, *Education in Hospitaller Malta*, in R. Sultana (ed.), *Yesterday's Schools: Readings in Maltese Educational History*, Malta 2001, pp. 15-29.

[29] C. Dalli, *Education in Malta Before The Knights*, in Sultana (ed.), *Yesterday's Schools* cit., p. 1, p. 12.

[30] A. Critien, *The Foundlings Under the Order and After*, "Scientia", 1, XV, Malta, 1949, pp. 3-19, P. Cassar, *Medical History of Malta*, London 1964.

[31] C. Savona-Ventura, *The Influence of the Roman Catholic Church on Midwifery Practice in Malta*, "Medical History", 39, 1995, Malta, p. 26; *The History of Maternity Care in the Maltese Islands*, Malta 2003, pp. 12-13.

[32] M. Ellul, *The Holy Infirmary: The Hospitaller Vocation of the Knights of St John*, in T. Cortis - T. Freller - L. Bugeja (eds.), *Melitensium Amor: Festchrift in Honour of Dun Ġwann Azzopardi*, Malta 2002, pp. 149-162; S. Sciberras, *The Knights Hospitallers' Vocation: The Erection and Modification of Hospitals and Charitable Institutions in the Maltese Islands (1700-1750)*, "Sacra Militia", 3, 2004, pp. 44-51; S. Fiorini, *Santo Spirito Hospital at Rabat, Malta: The Early Years to 1575*, Malta 1989, pp. 35-38.

[33] Heywood, *A History of Childhood* cit., 6.

[34] P. Laslett, *Family Life and Illicit Love in Earlier Generations: Essays in Historical Sociology*, Cambridge 1977; L. de Mause, *On Writing Childhood History*, "The Journal of Psychohistory", 2, XVI, 1998; E. Shorter, *The Making of the Modern Family*, London 1976; L Stone, *The Family, Sex and Marriage in England, 1500-1800*, London 1977; M. Anderson, *Approaches to the History of the Western Family 1500-1914*, Cambridge 1980; L.A. Pollock, *Forgotten Children: Parent-Child Relations from 1500-1900*, Cambridge 1983.

[35] Two examples from each era are: R. Bowman - P. Sultana, *Marriages Between 1627-1650: A Study of the Records held in the Parish Church of Our Lady of Porto Salvo and St. Dominic at Valletta*, unpublished B.A. Gen. Dissertation, Royal University of Malta 1973, and A.P. Borg, *Migration and Mobility in Early Modern Malta: The Harbour-City of Valletta as a Case Study, 157-1650*, unpublished M.A. Dissertation, University of Malta 2003.

[36] H. Cunningham, *Children and Childhood in Western Society since 1500*, London-New York 1998, pp. 15-16.

[37] J. Cassar-Pullicino, *Il-Kitba tal-Malti sa l-1870*, Malta 2001, p. 47.

[38] Fiorini, *Demographic Growth and the Urbanization* cit, pp. 297-310; V. Mallia-Milanes, *Introduction to Hospitaller Malta*, in Id. (ed.), *Hospitaller Malta 1530-1798: Studies on Early Modern Malta and the Order of St John of Jerusalem*, Malta 1993, pp. 1-42.

[39] [N]ational [A]rchives of [M]alta, [M]agna [C]uria [C]astellaniae, [P]rocessi [C]riminali 92/04, Box 274, Doc. 2, ff.1rv, 27 July-28 October 1700.

[40] S.L. Holloway - G. Valentine, *Children's Geographies: Playing, Living and Learning*, in Ead. (eds.), *Children's Geographies: Playing, Living, Learning*, London-New York 2000, pp. 11-12.

[41] H. Matthews - M. Limb - M. Taylor, *The 'Street as Thirdspace'*, in Holloway - Valentine (eds.), *Children's Geographies* cit., p. 63.

[42] E. Soja, *Thirdspace: Journeys to Los Angeles and Other Real-and-Imagined Places*, Oxford 1996, as quoted in Matthews et al., *The 'Street as Thirdspace'* cit., p. 64.

[43] N.A.M., M.C.C., P.C. 92/04, Box 274, Doc. 10, n.p., 31 July 1700. M.C.C., P.C. 92/04, Box 334, Doc. 9, n.p., 22 August 1720. M.C.C., P.C. 92/04, Box 471, Doc. 12, n.p., 7 January 1760.

[44] J.S. Derevenski, *Children and Material Culture*, London and New York 2002, p. 11; M. Rhodes, *Approaching The History Of Childhood: Frameworks For Local Research*, "Family & Community History", 2, II, 2000, p. 131.

[45] [C]athedral [A]rchives of [M]dina, Malta, [A]rchives of the [I]nquisition [M]alta., A.C., Vol. 518, ff.260rv, undated, *"... in gilecco e berretta rossa, e calzoni di tela al quale in torno li ragazzi gridavano Questo e' fuggitivo – leghiamolo ...".*

[46] P. Brydone, F.R.S., *A Tour through Sicily and Malta in a Series of Letters to William Beckford, Esq. of Somerly in Suffolk*, Vol. I, London 1773, p. 331.

[47]   Cassar, *Daughters of Eve* cit., pp. 66-7. Borg, *Migration and Mobility* cit., pp. 42-44.

[48]   N.A.M., M.C.C., P.C. 92/04, Box 525, Doc. 112, f.5r, 7 November 1780.

[49]   N.A.M., M.C.C., P.C. 92/04, Box 27, Doc. 5, n.p., 9 September 1590, "... *elli potte amazati a mio figlio ...*".

[50]   N.A.M., M.C.C., P.C. 92/04, Box 27, Doc. 5, n.p., 9 September 1590. The lawyer described Joanna as "...*meritrice, cortegiana, puttana, cortegiana inhonesta, donna et puttana pubblica ...*".

[51]   Klapish-Zuber, *Women, Family and Ritual* cit., p. 104; Cunningham, *Children and Childhood*, cit., p. 93; Heywood, *A History of Childhood* cit., pp. 66-68.

[52]   R.A. de Vertot, *The History of the Knights of Malta*, London 1728, Vol. II, p. 111. [N]ational [L]ibrary of [M]alta, [A]rchives of the [O]rder of [M]alta 309, f.136v, Chapter General 1776.

[53]   [N]otarial [A]rchives [V]alletta, Malta., [Not]ary Nicolo de Agatiis, R202/11, ff.186-190, 555 March 1547.

[54]   N.L.M., A.O.M. 1663, f.47, 1784, "*Domanda: Promettete voi di favorire, e di aver particular cura delle vedove, di pupilli, degli orfani, e di tutte le persone afflitte, e tribolate? Risposta: Prometto di farlo coll'aiuto del Signor Iddio*".

[55]   J. Riley-Smith, *Hospitallers: The History of the Order of St John*, London 1999, pp. 61-62.

[56]   Ġ. Aquilina, *Is-Sorijiet Ġerosolomitani, il-Knisja u l-Monasteru ta' Sant'Ursola, Valletta*, Malta 2004.

[57]   N.L.M., A.O.M. 290, f.29rv, Chapter General 1574, "... *fin all'eta da maritarsi...*".

[58]   N.L.M., A.O.M. 292, f.63r, Chapter General 1578, "... *artem doceantur secudu eorum inclinationem...*".

[59]   Logan, *Counter-Reformation Theories of Upbringing in Italy* cit., p. 282.

[60]   N.L.M., A.O.M. 309, f.74v, Chapter General 1776. A.O.M. 1714, f. 34v, ca.1796.

[61]   N.L.M., A.O.M. 1714, f. 1r, ca.1796. A.O.M. 309, f.146r, Chapter General 1776. N.L.M., A.O.M. 1714, f. 38rv, ca.1796. The Congregation of the Galleys was the body responsible for the overall management of the Order of St John's fleet.

[62]   N.L.M., A.O.M. 309, f.74v, Chapter General 1776. N.L.M., A.O.M. 1714, f. 34v, ca.1796.

[63]   N.L.M., A.O.M. 309, f.74v, Chapter General 1776.

[64]   N.L.M., A.O.M. 1714, f. 35r, ca.1796, "...*istruire le sue alunne nelle arti proprie del loro sesso*".

[65]   Klapish-Zuber, *Women, Family and Ritual* cit., pp. 104-105; Steuer, *Family Strategies in Medieval London* cit.; Cunningham, *Children and Childhood* cit., pp. 93-94; Heywood, *A History of Childhood* cit., pp. 63-68.

[66]   Critien, *The Foundlings under the Order* cit., p. 3; Cassar, *Medical History of Malta* cit., pp. 352-353.

[67]   N.L.M., A.O.M. 1723, f.55, 14 December 1699.

[68]   Heywood, *A History of Childhood* cit., p. 45; F. Ciappara, *Marriage in Malta in the Late Eighteenth Century (1750-1800)*, Malta 1988, p. 117.

[69]   N.A.V., Not. Juliano Muscat, R376/11, ff.997v-1001v, (30.viii.1545), "... *ala greca seu ala romana ...*". Not. Antonio Scaglia, R431/4, ff.790v-793, (9.x.1590), "... *iuxta decta sacra santi concilj Tridentio ad morem ritum et consuetudinem Romanorum ...*".

[70]   J. Cassar-Pullicino, *Belief and Practices Relating to Birth and Infancy*, Malta 1976, pp. 228-229.

[71]   Heywood, *A History of Childhood* cit., p. 103.

[72]   R. Po-Chia Hsia, *The World of Catholic Renewal*, Cambridge 1998, pp. 22-23.

[73]   M. Mitterauer, *A History of Youth*, Oxford UK and Cambridge USA 1993, p. 20; P. Griffiths, *Youth and Authority: Formative Experiences in England, 1560-1640*, Oxford 1996, p. 5; Cunningham, *Children and Childhood* cit., p. 81.

[74]   N.A.V., Not. Nicolo de Agatiis, R202/8, ff.338-339, (4.vi.1544).

[75]   Borg, *Migration and Mobility* cit., pp. 51-53.

[76] C.A.M., A.I.M., [C]riminal [P]roceedings, Vol. 133C, Case 399, f.1240v, 20 January 1780.

[77] Cassar, *Society, Culture and Identity* cit., p. 148.

[78] N.A.V., Not. Placido Abela, R4, n.p., (16.xii.1557).

[79] N.A.V., Not. Ferdinando Zarb, R1145/4, ff.101-103v, (26.v.1611).

[80] N.A.V., Not. Brandano de Caxaro, R175/14, ff.87-88v, (11.x.1544). Not. Brandano de Caxaro, R175/42, ff.294v-299, (22.x.1554).

[81] N.A.V., Not. Petro Darmenia, R1649/58, ff.493-494v, (8.vii.1655).

[82] I. Bosio, *Dell'Istoria della Sacra Religione*, Vol. II, Rome 1602-1630, p. 732.

[83] S. Cachia, *The Family and the Land in Late Medieval Malta: A Study of the Acts of Notary J. Zabbara, 1486-1488*, Unpublished B.A. Hons. Dissertation, University of Malta 1999, p. 18; J. Goody, *Inheritance, Property and Women: Some Comparative Considerations*, in J. Goody - J. Thirsk - E.P. Thompson (eds.), *Family and Inheritance: Rural Society in Western Europe 1200-1800*, Cambridge 1976, p. 16; D.O. Hughes, *From Brideprice to Dowry in Mediterranean Europe*, in M.A. Kaplan (ed.), *The Marriage Bargain: Women and Dowries in European History*, London 1985, pp. 26-27; O. Spies, *'Mahr'*, in C.E. Bosworth - E. van Donzel - Ch. Pellat (eds.), *Encyclopaedia of Islam*, new edition, VI, Leiden 1991, p. 79.

[84] A. Shephard, *Meanings of Manhood in Early Modern England*, Oxford 2003, pp. 13-14.

[85] Griffiths, *Youth and Authority* cit., pp. 6-7.

BIBLIOGRAPHY

Anderson M., *Approaches to the History of the Western Family 1500-1914*, Cambridge 1980.

Aquilina Ġ. - Stanley F. (eds.), *Documentary Sources of Maltese History: Part VI – Documents at the Vatican, No. 1 Archivio Segreto Vaticano Congregazione Vescovi e Regolari Malta: Visita Apostolica No 51 Mgr Petrus Dusina, 1575*, Malta 2001.

Aquilina Ġ., *Is-Sorijiet Ġerosolomitani, il-Knisja u l-Monasteru ta' Sant'Ursola, Valletta*, Malta 2004.

Attard E., *Delitti f'Malta: 200 Sena ta' Omiċidji, 1800-2000*, Malta 2001.

Borg A.P., *Migration and Mobility in Early Modern Malta: The Harbour-City of Valletta as a Case Study, 1575-1650*, unpublished M.A. Dissertation, University of Malta, 2003.

Borg V., *Developments in Education Outside The Jesuit 'Collegium Melitense*, in "Melita Historica", 3, VI, 1974, pp. 215-254.

Bosio I., *Dell'Istoria della Sacra Religione*, vol. II, Rome 1602-1630.

Bowman R. - Sultana P., *Marriages Between 1627-1650: A Study of the Records held in the Parish Church of Our Lady of Porto Salvo and St. Dominic at Valletta*, unpublished B.A. Gen. Dissertation, Royal University of Malta 1973.

Brincat J.M., *The Language Question and Education: a Political Controversy on a Linguistic Topic*, in Sultana R. (ed.), *Yesterday's Schools: Readings in Maltese Educational History*, Malta 2001, pp. 137-158.

Brydone P. F.R.S., *A Tour through Sicily and Malta in a Series of Letters to William Beckford, Esq. of Somerly in Suffolk*, Vol. I, London 1773.

Cachia S., *The Family and the Land in Late Medieval Malta: A Study of the Acts of Notary J. Zabbara, 1486-1488*, unpublished B.A. Hons. Dissertation, University of Malta 1999.

Camenzuli A., *Maltese Social and Cultural Values in Perspective, 1771-1798*, unpublished M.A. Dissertation, University of Malta 1999.

Cassar C., *Daughters of Eve – Women, Gender Roles and the Impact of the Council of Trent in Catholic Malta*, Malta 2002.

Id., *Education in Hospitaller Malta*, in Sultana R. (ed.), *Yesterday's Schools: Readings in Maltese Educational History*, Malta 2001, pp. 15-29.

Id., *Society, Culture and Identity in Early Modern Malta*, Malta 2000.

Id., *Medical History of Malta*, London 1964.

Cassar-Pullicino J., *Belief and Practices Relating to Birth and Infancy*, Malta 1976.

Id., *Il-Kitba tal-Malti sa l-1870*, Malta 2001.

Id., *Pre-Jesuit Education in Malta*, "The Sundial", 6, VI, 1946, pp. 14-18.

Id., *Studies in Maltese Folklore*, Malta 1976.

Cavaliero R., *The Last of the Crusaders: The Knights of St John and Malta in the Eighteenth Century*, London 1960.

Chapman G., *Cathecism of the Catholic Church*, Avon 1994.

Ciappara F., *Marriage in Malta in the Late Eighteenth Century (1750-1800)*, Malta 1988.

Id., *Society and the Inquisition in Early Modern Malta*, Malta 2001.

Coriden J.A. - Green T.J. - Heintschel D.E. (eds.), *The Code of Canon Law: A Text and Commentary*, London 1985.

Coster W., *Family and Kinship in England 1450-1800*, London 2001.

Critien A., *The Foundlings Under the Order and After*, "Scientia", 1, XV, 1949, pp. 3-19.

Cunningham H., *Children and Childhood in Western Society Since 1500*, London-New York 1998.

Dalli C., *Education in Malta Before The Knights*, in Sultana R. (ed.), *Yesterday's Schools: Readings in Maltese Educational History*, Malta 2001, pp. 1-14.

Derevenski J.S., *Children and Material Culture*, London-New York 2002.

Ellul M., *The Holy Infirmary: The Hospitaller Vocation of the Knights of St John*, in Cortis T. - Freller T. - Bugeja L. (eds.), *Melitensium Amor: Festchrift in Honour of Dun Ġwann Azzopardi*, Malta 2002, pp. 149-162.

Erikson E.H., *Young Man Luther: A Study in Psychoanalysis and History*, London 1958.

Fildes V., *Wet Nursing: A History from Antiquity to the Present*, Oxford-New York 1988.

Id., *Demographic Growth and the Urbanisation of the Maltese Countryside to 1798*, in Mallia-Milanes V. (ed.), *Hospitaller Malta 1530-1798: Studies on Early Modern Malta and the Order of St John of Jerusalem*, Malta 1993, pp. 297-310.

Id., *Santo Spirito Hospital at Rabat, Malta: The Early Years to 1575*, Malta 1989.

Gambin K., *Popular Culture and the Inquisition, 1677-1678*, unpublished B.A. Hons. Dissertation, University of Malta 1995.

Goody J., *Inheritance, Property and Women: Some Comparative Considerations*, in Goody J. - Thirsk J. - Thompson E.P. (eds.), *Family and Inheritance: Rural Society in Western Europe 1200-1800*, Cambridge 1976, pp. 10-36.

Griffiths P., *Youth and Authority: Formative Experiences in England, 1560-1640*, Oxford 1996.

Grima S., *Il-Kavallieri fil-Klassi tal-Letteratura Maltija*, unpublished B.Ed Dissertation, University of Malta 2003.

Heywood C., *A History of Childhood: Children and Childhood in the West from Medieval to Modern Times*, London 2001.

Holloway S.L. - Valentine G., *Children's Geographies: Playing, Living and Learning*, in Holloway S.L. - Valentine G. (eds.), *Children's Geographies: Playing, Living, Learning*, London-New York 2000, pp. 1-26.

Hughes D.O., *From Brideprice to Dowry in Mediterranean Europe*, in Kaplan M.A. (ed.), *The Marriage Bargain: Women and Dowries in European History*, London 1985, pp. 13-58.

Klapish-Zuber C., *Women, Family and Ritual in Renaissance Italy*, Chicago-London 1985.

Laslett P., *Family Life and Illicit Love in Earlier Generations: Essays in Historical Sociology*, Cambridge 1977.

Livingstone E.A., *The Oxford Dictionary of the Christian Church*, Oxford 1997.

Locke J., *Some Thoughts*, [1693], in Yolton J.W. - Yolton J.S. (eds.), *Some Thoughts Concerning Education with Introduction*, Oxford 2000.

Logan O., *Counter-Reformation Theories of Upbringing in Italy*, in Wood D. (ed.), *The Church and Childhood*, Oxford, U.K.-Cambridge USA 1994, pp. 275-284.

Mallia-Milanes V., *Introduction to Hospitaller Malta*, in Mallia-Milanes V. (ed.), *Hospitaller Malta 1530-1798: Studies on Early Modern Malta and the Order of St John of Jerusalem*, Malta 1993, pp. 1-42.

Matthews H. - Limb M. - Taylor M., *The 'Street as Thirdspace'*, in Holloway S.L. - Valentine G. (eds.), *Children's Geographies: Playing, Living and Learning*, London-New York 2002, pp. 63-79.

Mause L. de, *On Writing Childhood History*, "The Journal of Psychohistory", 2, XVI, 1998, pp. 1-20.

Mitterauer M., *A History of Youth*, Oxford UK-Cambridge USA 1993.

Mont, J. Du, *A New Voyage to the Levant*, London 1696.

Moore J. - Scott E. (eds.), *Invisible People and Processes: Writing Gender and Childhood into European Archaeology*, Leicester 1997.

Pecchiai P., *Il Collegio dei Gesuiti in Malta*, "Archivio Storico di Malta", 1939, Fasc. II, pp. 129-169, pp. 273-293.

Po-Chia Hsia R., *The World of Catholic Renewal*, Cambridge 1998.

Pollock L.A., *Forgotten Children: Parent-Child Relations from 1500-1900*, Cambridge 1983.

Quin M. (ed.), *Virtue's Catholic Encyclopedia*, London 1965.

Rhodes M., *Approaching The History Of Childhood: Frameworks For Local Research*, "Family & Community History", 2, III, 2000, pp. 121-154.

Riley-Smith J., *Hospitallers: The History of the Order of St John*, London 1999.

Santrock J.W., *Adolescence*, Boston 1998.

Savona Ventura C., *L-Istorja tal-Mediċina fil-Gżejjer Maltin*, Malta 1999.

Id., *The History of Maternity Care in the Maltese Islands*, Malta 2003.

Id., *The Influence of the Roman Catholic Church on Midwifery Practice in Malta*, "Medical History", 39, 1995, pp. 18-34.

Sciberras S., *The Knights Hospitallers' Vocation: The Erection and Modification of Hospitals and Charitable Institutions in the Maltese Islands (1700-1750)*, "Sacra Militia", 3, 2004, pp. 44-51.

Shephard A., *Meanings of Manhood in Early Modern England*, Oxford 2003.

Shorter E., *The Making of the Modern Family*, London 1976.

Soja E., *Thirdspace: Journeys to Los Angeles and Other Real-and-Imagined Places*, Oxford 1996.

Spies O., *Mahr*, in Bosworth C.E. - van Donzel E. - Pellat Ch. (eds.), *Encyclopaedia of Islam*, New Edition, VI, Leiden 1991, pp. 75-89.

Steuer S.M.B., *Family Strategies in Medieval London: Financial Planning and the Urban Widow, 1123-1473*, "Essays in Medieval Studies", XII, 1995, pp. 126-145.

Steward J.C., *British Art and the Origins of Modern Childhood, 1730-1830*, unpublished D.Phil Dissertation, University of Oxford 1997.

Stone L., *The Family, Sex and Marriage in England, 1500-1800*, London 1977.

Tannenbaum D.G. - Schultz D., *Inventors of Ideas: An Introduction to Western Political Philosophy*, Boston-New York 1998.

Vella A.P., *The University of S. Maria Purtus Salutis*, "Journal of the Faculty of Arts", II, 1962, pp. 164-180.

Vertot R.A. de, *The History of the Knights of Malta*, London 1728, Vol. II.

The Historiography of the Khlyst Movement in Russia in the Second Half of the 19th and the 20th Centuries

Olga Dekhtevich
Moscow State Regional University

Статья посвящена изучению историографии хлыстовского движения в России во второй половине XIX – начале XX вв. Хлыстовство, известное также как "христовщина" или "хлыстовщина", представляло религиозную мистическую секту, признанную крайне вредной в Российской империи. Сектанты хранили свой культ в тайне и тщательно скрывались среди православных. Незнание всей правды о хлыстах рождало множество догадок и домыслов, при этом уровень интереса к сектантам был достаточно высок. Секта привлекала внимание различных исследователей, особенно представителей духовенства и чиновников. Однако, если о старообрядцах написано достаточно много серьезных работ, то о хлыстах их единицы. Многочисленные чиновники и сельские священники не часто заботились о качестве и достоверности информации и подчас просто переписывали друг у друга ложные сведения. Многочисленные публицисты в погоне за сенсацией тоже нередко сочиняли разные небылицы. При этом квалифицированных работ о хлыстах публиковалось крайне мало.

В связи с этим проблема историографии хлыстовского движения является актуальной и представляет большой интерес для исследования. Необходимость ее изучения заключается в том, что сектанты практически не оставили источников о самих себе. В таких условиях совокупность работ о хлыстах является незаменимым и практически единственным источником информации, с которым может работать исследователь.

Более или менее профессиональные исследования о хлыстах появляются лишь в начале XX века, когда проблема вероисповедной политики стояла в Российской империи наиболее остро. Понятно, что по идеологическим причинам тема хлыстовства крайне мало изучалась в СССР. Только конец 80-х – 90-е годы XX века можно отметить как время, когда все, что связано с мистикой, стало очень популярным. Тогда же многие исследователи возвращаются к теме русского сектантства, и в частности, к изучению хлыстовства. При этом подробное изучение историографии хлыстовского движения позволяет составить наиболее полное представление об этом явлении в русской религиозной жизни.

This chapter is devoted to the historiography of the Khlyst movement in Russia during the second half of the 19th century and the beginning of the 20th century. The Khlysts, who were known as *Khlystovshina* or *Bozhii ludi* [God's People], were a mass religious movement. The sect, which was formed in the 17th century, existed until the 20th century, and their great development did not go unnoticed. Over the course of several centuries, the Khlysts attracted the attention of a great number of researchers, mostly clerics and various officials whose work brought them into contact with the Sectarians.

During the second half of the 19th century and the beginning of the 20th century, the problem of Sectarianism grew. It was a matter of concern not only for researchers, but also for ordinary people. There were a lot of rationalist and mystic sects in the territory of the Russian empire, and Old Believers and Sectarianism were becoming a serious danger to the Russian Orthodox Church, which commanded a position of strength, not susceptible to weakness. The overdue formation of a religious policy, coupled with repressive measures taken to solve the Sectarian problem, made people hostile to the state and Orthodoxy. Harsh conditions, discontent with their spiritual life, and semi-illiteracy were responsible for people joining the sect. For over three centuries, Russian Sectarians had attracted great attention from other people. Many mysterious rituals and strange beliefs were attributed to the Khlysts, and they were regarded as followers of either an alien religious movement or an original rural Russian belief system. They were also thought to be the most dangerous sect, and were attacked in all possible ways, being accused of debauchery, the ritual murder of children and other bloodthirstiness. The greatest strength of the Khlyst sect was drawn from its mystery, and that was the reason why its original leaders had insisted that its members should strictly obey the rules of the Orthodox Church, often encouraging them to be over-zealous in their obedience in order not to give the sect away.

The researchers of the 19th century knew more about the Khlysts than we do now. Although they never managed to make a full and objective analysis of the movement, a variety of opinions about the sect tells us how important the issue was for the people during our period of study. For this reason, the historiography of the Khlyst movement is very topical, representing an extensive sphere of research.

During the 19th to the beginning of the 20th century, the attitude of researchers towards the Sectarians was quite biased; they simply copied the attributes of the Khlysts mechanically from each other, without any proper investigation. Research of a more professional nature only appeared at the beginning of the 20th century, when the problem of a religious policy became more marked. For clear ideological reasons, the Khlysts were insufficiently studied in the USSR, although the period at the end of the 1980s going into the 1990s can be noted as the time when everything connected with mysticism became very popular.

Scientists have paid greater attention to the history of the movement in the 17th and 18th centuries, and as a result, the study of the history of the movement during the second half of the 19th century and the beginning of 20th century has suffered. The historiography of the Khlyst movement represents a very interesting field for research because, while there were a lot of volumes devoted to the Old Believers, because many historians were interested in researching this movement, only very few studied the Khlyst sect. The history of its study is in itself interesting and special. On the one hand, there are many volumes devoted to how it came into existence, but on the other hand, the main aspects of most of this research concern rituals, beliefs and folklore. These works are devoted to the history of the sect in the 17th century, the time when it first appeared. There are, however, exceptions to this type of research, as reports by missionaries and priests, published in theological magazines, usually contain quite useful information about the sect.

Most materials traditionally used by researchers concerning the Russian mystic sects were collected and published during the second half of the 19th century and the beginning of the 20th century.

One of the first works devoted to this sect was a note by the Kaluga priest Ivan Sergeev. Entitled *Iz"yasneniye raskola, imenuemogo khrystovshina ili khlystovshina* [The Explanation of the Schism Called Khrystovshina or Khlystovshina], it was submitted to the Synod in 1809. Sergeev had been admitted to the community and participated in *radenya* [divine service assembly]. He was also one of the first to write about the sect and supply the authorities with necessary information[1].

The works devoted to the Khlysts started to appear in the early 1860s. The first researchers of the sect were officials of the Home Office, among them the professor of law N.V. Varadinov, who had written the history of the Home Office. This eighth, additional book was devoted to a history of decrees on the schism[2]. Using the facts, Varadinov showed the attitudes between the Church and power structures on the one hand, and the Church and the Khlysts on the other. Being an expert on the history of law, he managed to collect and analyse a significant number of documentary sources – decrees and decisions connected with the schism. He also showed and characterised the stages of the government's activity regarding the Old Believers.

Theological researches contributed greatly to investigating *khlystovshina*. They were the first to draw public attention to the sect and the fact that it was so widely spread. They began to write about it actively. One of the first was a professor of the Kazan Spiritual Academy I.M. Dobrotvorskiy, whose monograph *Lyudi Bozh'i. Russkaya sekta tak nazyvaemykh dukhovnykh khristian* [People Divine. Russian Sect of So-called Spiritual Christians] was published in Kazan in 1869.

The work of Dobrotvorskiy received some criticism. In his book, he designated "the doctrine about mysterious death and mysterious revival" as ostensibly typical for the Khlyst sect. But this was based only on the letters and notes of Vasiliy Radaev, who, as Dobrotovskiy stated in his book, was the Khlyst's prophet. He also wrote about the depravity of the Khlysts. However, the great merit of Dobrotvorskiy's work was the publication of 85 Sectarian church motets which had been collected by him[3].

Dobrotovkiy's work was preceded by some other publications by church authors. However, they involved a minimal quantity of additional material. For example, G. Protopopov's *Opyt istoricheskogo obozreniya misticheskikh sekt v Rossii* [Experience of a Historical Review of Mystic Sects in Russia] (1867)[4], suggested that the Russian sects should be divided into the following groups: "mystic" ('Khlysts', 'Castratos', 'Napoleonits', 'Racers' and 'Montans') and "rationalist" ('Molokans', 'Dukhobors')[5]. According to the book, the Khlysts was a dangerous sect, and the author declared that it was crucial for the church and the government to fight it.

N.I. Barsov's report, *Russkiy prostonarodnyi mistitsizm* [The Russian Demotic Mysticism], published in 1860-1870, is of some interest, along with his collection of Sectarian motets (103 texts)[6]. The advantage of his works lies in the critical approach to P.I. Melnikov's works *Taynye sekty* [Secret Sects] and *Belye golubi* [White Pigeons], and Dobrotovkiy's *Lyudi Bozhii. Russkaya sekta tak nazyvaemykh dukhovnykh khristian* [Divine People. Russian Sect of So-called Spiritual Christians][7]. In his works, Barsov detailed the contents of all the communications concerning the Khlysts that he was aware of, although he repeated an old mistake of his predecessors. He also wrote that Vasiliy Radaev was a Khlyst, and he made some reasonably practical remarks about the genesis of the Khlysts as well as writing about the prospects for research on the sect's folklore. Moreover, following the priest Sergeev, he tried to see a certain theological doctrine behind the tradition of the sect.

F.V. Livanov devoted a whole series of writings to the Khlysts and the Eunuchs. He described a history of the Tatarinova sect with its divine service cult[8]. However, he did not check the information. He expressed confidence that the Khlysts was a political organization which posed danger to the state and society, and basically focused on the sect's history and ceremonial practice. However, the style of the book *Dissenters and Jailers* can hardly be called scientific, as it was written in a non-academic, popular style. When reading Livanov's works, one might think that he must have written them for ordinary illiterate people with the purpose of making them afraid of the Khlysts. As a result, his book is of little scientific value and the information in his works should be carefully checked.

One of the best-known researchers of the schism was the writer P.I. Melnikov. He showed his writing talent in the third part of the novel *Na gorakh* [On Mountains]. He was also famous for his non-academic, popular works such as the articles *Taynye sekty* [Secret Sects] and *Belye golubi* [White Pigeons], published in *Russkiy byulleten'* [The Russian Bulletin] in 1868 and 1869, as well as his scientific research about the Castratos, which was published along with documentary materials in the archive of the Home Office. Later, it was included in the collected works of Melnikov[9].

As a writer, Melnikov based his research about the Khlysts on oral communications without checking their reliability. One can forgive a writer for using of unchecked information, but as long as Melnikov was a researcher and an official of special orders, he should have chosen his sources of information more carefully. Unfortunately, he made the same error when writing *Otchet o sostoyanii raskola v Nizhegorodskoy gubernii* [The Report on the Condition of the Schism in the Nizhniy Novgorod Province], for the Home Office. This certainly reduces the quality of his work considerably[10].

His articles *Tainye sekty* [Secret Sects] and *Belye golubi* [White Pigeons] did not show a methodical approach to the stated facts, but as these products are literary, rather than scientific, their usage for research of the Khlysts is considerably limited in any case. However, the author probably did not aim to write a scientific work and so frequently altered the facts. The facts given in the novel *Na gorakh* [On Mountains] are even less reliable

A.P. Shchapov's volumes are of great interest. In 1858, his thesis *Russkiy raskol staroobryadchestva* [Russian Schism of the Old Believers] was published[11]. He considered the schism to be not only religious, but also a historical, domestic and social phenomenon. Later he developed the ideas in his book *Zemstvo i raskol* [Zemstvo and Schism][12].

Shchapov's approach to the problem of Sectarianism was the best thought out and compared very favourably with all his contemporaries. His ideas on the genesis of the Russian Khlysts are still of scientific interest. In trying to present the Russian schism of the 17th century as a reaction of regional and federal tendencies to growing state centralization, he assumed that the collision resulted in mass and local religious creativity becoming more intense. He noticed, quite reasonably, that there was some kind of new belief which was distinct from official Orthodoxy in the rural environment, and, in his opinion, the reason for it was the lack of knowledge about Christianity, and semi-illiteracy among the people. The suppression of the Russian peasants generated religious imposture; that is, the occurrence of imaginary 'Christs' and 'prophets'.

Nevertheless, the quality of Shchapov's research was much better than that of those who followed. Unfortunately, he never continued his work on the Khlyst movement.

One of the researchers of the 1860s was V.I. Kelsiev. His research was followed by the publication of the four-volume *Sbornik pravitelstvennykh svedeniy o raskolnikakh* [Collection of Government Data on Dissenters] (London, 1860-1862) and the two-volume *Sobraniye postanovleniy po chasti raskola* [Assembly of Decisions in Connection with the Schism] (London, 1863). It was one of the largest publications of sources on the history of the schism.

The second edition of *The Collection of Decisions in Connection with Schism* contained materials about the Khlysts. It included a communication from the participants of the 1852 expedition who took part in research on the schism in the Nizhniy Novgorod, Kostroma and Yaroslavl provinces. It also included a classification of the dissenting movements which fell into three categories: Orthodox, Molokanstvo and the belief of the 'Divine People'. He referred to the Khlysts as Divine People, saying that there was not much known about them[13].

In 1867, a series of articles entitled *Sviatorusskie dvoeveri* [Double-faith Believers of Holy Russia] was published in the magazines of Saint Petersburg[14]. Kelsiev's work has advantages such as the publication of some important documents as well as quite a few stories about the Khlysts' bloodthirstiness, albeit without any proper facts that could prove these statements.

In 1872, another government work about the Khlysts was published[15], written by the Moscow official of the Ministry of Justice, N.V. Reutsky. He actively used documents from the Moscow archives: "authentic sources and original papers", which were practically unknown to previous researchers. However, neglect of reference to the documents considerably reduces the quality of his work, although he pointed out in his research that the attitude towards the legend about the Khlyst's "Sabaof" Danila Philippovich should be changed to a critical one.

Ten years later, in 1882, Reutskiy published an original addition to the monograph – the article that contained a history of the Khlyst movement in Moscow in the first half of the 19th century[16].

B.V. Andreev was one of the followers of Schapov's ideas. Andreev tried to find a new approach to the question of Sectarianism and his attempt does deserve approval, although he worked with unreasonably narrow frameworks of research, which was certainly a drawback. Andreev followed the basic idea of many researchers who tried to find the roots of the Khlyst movement anywhere but in the Russian environment, presenting these religious movements as an alien phenomenon. Moreover, he stated in his work that the Khlysts were predecessors of the Castratos, which gives rise to a number of objections.

In the eighties and nineties of the 19th century, interest in the Khlyst sect increased considerably. Hundreds of research works and articles devoted to the Khlysts were published. They were the works of seminary students such as K.V. Kutepov, I.G. Ayvazov, N.G. Vysotsky, T.I. Butkevich, N.I. Ivanovsky etc.

The thesis of the teacher of the Kazan spiritual academy, the archpriest K.V. Kutepov, is of great interest. For example, in the monograph *Sekty khlystov i skoptzov* [Sects of the Khlysts and Castratos][17], the author was not too anxious to criticize any sources, and tried to unify all the data known to him about the Khlysts, but he aimed to show the harmful affect which the Khlysts had had. In 1900, Kutepov's 'research' was republished without any changes, which emphasized the unwillingness of the author to change his approach to the problem of the sect.

In 1908, D.G. Konovalov published the monograph *Religiozniy ekstaz v russkom misticheskom sektantstve* [Religious Ecstasy in the Russian Mystic Sectarianism][18]. The views in the book were different to those of other research. In his work, he did not rank Radaev as a Khlyst, whereas he had previously been considered to be almost the ideologist of debauchery, though he was not a Sectarian at all. That has been proved and confirmed by experts from the Moscow Spiritual academy. Another advantage of Konovalov's work was that he proved that the *12 Commandments* of Danila Philippovich were of a later origin than previously thought[19].

However, the works of Konovalov contain a number of drawbacks. In spite of the fact that he found a new approach to the problem of Sectarianism, he did not manage to fully develop his ideas. Nevertheless, it should be noted that Konovalov's ideas were more progressive than those of many of his colleagues.

I.G. Aivazov and N.G. Vysotsky were of a theological orientation. In 1910, Aivazov published some archival materials about the Khlysts and the Castratos[20]. Unfortunately, he did not bother to order the documents he used, or make comments about them. This, as well as the irreconcilability of Aivazov to Sectarianism, means we cannot trust the information in his work completely. Therefore, his research should be subject to strict criticism.

In 1915, a book by Professor and Archpriest T.I. Butkevich entitled *Obzor russkikh sekt i ikh tolkov* [The Review of Russian Sects and Their Significance] was published[21]. The author gave a detailed description of the Khlysts as a fanatical and extremely harmful sect. This publication served as a reference book for missionary work for a long time. Nearly all sects which were known about at that time were described in it. The author offered a detailed analysis of Khlyst doctrines, representing them as unequivocal. The ideas of Butkevich were typical of the majority of historians and theologians. He could not be reconciled to Sectarianism and wrote about the real need to fight it. Therefore, it is necessary to treat such research carefully.

In 1912, N.I. Ivanovskiy, Professor of the Kazan Spiritual Academy and official Councillor of State, had his book entitled *Rukovodstvo po istorii i oblicheniyu staroobryadcheskogo raskola* [The Manual of the History and Censure of the Old Believers' Schism] published[22]. It was a textbook for missionaries and priests. Ivanovskiy was more constrained in his ideas on the sect. In the articles published in the Ministry of Justice's magazine, he weighed all the 'pros' and 'cons' of the Khlysts, fairly assessing and criticizing the new legislation[23].

A.S. Prugavin was one of the best known historians of the schism. From 1877, he was known as an ethnographer and a publicist. He worked on the history of the Old Believers and Sectarianism as well as the problems of a religious policy in the Russian Empire. Prugavin's works on the Khlyst movement are of great interest to us[24]. In his opinion the Khlysts were a very advanced group of people

Prugavin's *Bunt protiv prirody* [The Revolt Against Nature] is completely devoted to the Khlysts of the Samara province, a place where he had lived for some years owing to his work. According to him, the Khlysts were innocent victims of prosecutions by the authorities, and especially by the clergy.

Prugavin compared the Khlysts to the Mormons, in the way that they were thought of in society at that time. In his opinion, the Khlysts were the sanest of people, and he denies all rumours concerning general debauchery, while admitting that if there had been any instances, they would have been exceptions.

V.D. Bonch-Bruevich also contributed to the scientific development of the problem of Sectarianism. He saw huge revolutionary potential in Sectarians who resisted oppression and repression by the state. In his opinion, the Khlyst sect was the most united against the state. He wrote that the Khlysts supported revolutionary movement in the Russian villages[25].

In the multi-volume edition *Materialy po istorii sektantstva i staroobryadchestva* [Materials on the History of Sectarianism and Old Believers], Bonch-Bruevich expressed the same point of view on the schism. However, his research did not result in anything new.

Among the researchers of the Soviet period, it is necessary to pay attention to A.I. Klibanov, whose teacher was V.D. Bonch-Bruevich (1960-1970). Klibanov published the whole series of monographs, articles and literary sketches devoted to the history and public role of Russian heretical movements and sects, including the Khlysts[26]. However, his works on the history of *khristovery,* as he called them, were mostly based on the research of previous authors.

In 1950-1960 Klibanov organized and led sociological and historical expeditions for studying "modern religious beliefs" (and, in particular, sectarianism) in central areas of Russia. However they did not discover much. In 1959 in Tambov regional center Rasscazovo managed to get acquainted with several *postniki* – followers of one of the khlyst's branches, formed in 1820th by peasant Abakum Kopylov[27]. But, anyhow, Klibanov's works were, as a matter of fact, unique within the framework of the Soviet religious studies of a post-war period. Unfortunately, they actually did not bring anything new in studying of the sect in the second half of the 19th and the beginning of 20th century.

When speaking about research of the history and culture of Russian Sectarians in latter years, it is necessary to note A.M. Etkind and A.A. Panchenko.

A. Etkind's book entitled *Khlyst: sekty, literatura i revolyutsiya* [Khlyst: Sects, Literature and Revolution][28] (his thesis for his doctoral degree at the University of Helsinki), is devoted to Russian religious communities during the 19th and 20th centuries, and the influence of their ideas and collective forms of life on intellectuals and literature. Communal sects in Russia paved the way for the victory of Bolshevism. The author traced the destiny of Russian communal Sectarianism during the Soviet period. The archival materials he collected, together with the facts testifying to the interaction of communistic Sectarianism and Bolsheviks in construction of a new society, are valuable. He also considered the display of *Khlystovstvo* in the creation of figures in literature during the period known as the "silver age" as an innovation in native science.

A. A. Panchenko's monograph called *Khrystovshina i scopchestvo: folklor i traditzionnaya kultura russkikh misticheskikh sekt* [Khrystovshina and Scopchestvo: The Folklore and Traditional Culture of Russian Mystic Sects] represented the first regular research of cultural tradition of the two mass religious movements from the 18th century to the beginning of the 20th century. Panchenko considered the folklore and rituals of *Khrystovshina* and *Scopchestvo* (Castratos) in the wider context of the religious culture of the common people from the 17th to the 20th centuries. However, he hardly studied *Khrystovshina* in the 19th century at all, limiting it to a brief summary. As a whole though, Panchenko's work is worthy, and has great scientific interest[29].

In conclusion, it is necessary to note that the historiographic review allows us to create a representation of the development of Khlyst research in Russia. Lack of sources left by the Sectarians makes the research more complicated, and for this reason, we have to turn to numerous articles, brief literary sketches, and textbooks by missionaries on the subject of the schism, in our search for information. There has been quite a lot of research in this area, although we need to bear in mind that most of it is of poor quality. The historiography is a very important aspect of studying this religious movement, and its study is a priority.

NOTES

[1] К.В. Кутепов, *Секты хлыстов и скопцов* [Sects of Khlysts and Castrati], Kazan 1883.

[2] Н. Варадинов, *История министерства внутренних дел. Восьмая, дополнительная книга. История распоряжений по расколу* [History of the Home Office. Additional. History of the Decrees on the Schism], Book 8, Saint Petersburg 1863.

[3] И.М. Добротворский, *Люди Божьи. Русская секта так называемых духовных христиан* [Divine People. Russian Sect of So-called Spiritual Christians], Kazan 1869.

[4] Г. Протопопов, *Опыт исторического обозрения мистических сект в России* [Experience of a Historical Review of Mystical Sects in Russia], "Труды Киевской духовной академии" [Works of the Kiev Spiritual Academy], 10, 11, 1867.

[5] *Ibid.*

[6] Н.И. Барсов, *Русский простонародный мистицизм* [Russian Mysticism of Common People], "Христианское чтение" [Christian Reading], 9, 1869.

[7] Н.И. Барсов, *Исторические, критические и полемические опыты* [Historical, Critical and Polemic Experiences], Saint Petersburg 1879.

[8] See: Ф.В. Ливанов, *Раскольники и острожники* [Dissenters and Extremely scarces], vol. I-IV, Saint Petersburg 1868-1873.

[9] П.И. Мельников (Андрей Печерский), *Собрание сочинений* [The Collected Works], vol. 1-6, Moscow 1863.

[10] И.М. Добротворский, *К вопросу о людях Божьих* [To a Question on Divine People] "Православный собеседник" [The Orthodox Interlocutor], 1, 1870, pp. 19- 20, pp. 25-29.

[11] А.П. Щапов, *Русский раскол старообрядчества* [Russian Schism of the Old-Believers], Kazan 1859.

[12] А.П. Щапов, *Земство и раскол* [Zemstvo and Schism], Saint-Petersburg 1862.

[13] В.И. Кельсиев, *Сборник правительственных сведений о раскольниках* [The Collection of the Governmental Information on Dissenters], London 1861.

[14] В.И. Кельсиев, *Святорусские двоеверы* [Double-faith Believers of Holy Russia], "Заря" [Dawn], 10, 1869.

[15] Н.В. Реутский, *Люди Божии и скопцы. Историческое исследование (Из достоверных источников и подлинных бумаг)* [Divine People and Castrati. Historical Research (From Authentic Sources and Original Papers)], Moscow 1872.

[16] Н.В. Реутский, *Московские Божии люди во второй половине XVII и XIX столетии* [Moscow "Divine People" in the Second Half of XVIII and in the XIX centuries], "Русский вестник" [The Russian Bulletin], 5, 1882.

[17] Кутепов, *Секты хлыстов и скопцов* cit.

[18] See: Д. Коновалов, *Религиозный экстаз в русском мистическом сектантстве* [Religious Ecstasy in the Russian Mystical Sectarianism], Sergiev Posad 1908.

[19] Д. Коновалов, *Религиозные движения в России. I. Секта хлыстов.* [Religious Movements in Russia. I. Sect of Khlysts], "Ежемесячный журнал литературы, науки и общественной жизни" [The Monthly Magazine of the Literature, Science and a Public Life], 1, 1914.

[20] И.Г. Айвазов, *Материалы для исследования русских мистических сект, I, Христовщина* [The Materials for Research of Russian Mystical Sects, I, Khristovshina], vol. 1-3, Petrograd 1915l, И.Г.Айвазов, *Первое следственное дело о христовщине* [The first Investigation Affair Devoted Khrystovshina], "Миссионерское обозрение" [The Missionary Review] 7, 8, 11, 1916, pp. 360-386, pp. 641-661; Н.Г. Высотский, *Критический обзор мнений по вопросу о происхождении хлыстовщины* [The Critical Review of Opinions Concerning an Origin of Khlystovshina], "Миссионерское обозрение" [The Missionary Review], 13, 1903, pp. 311-325, 14, pp. 438-454, 16, pp. 703-714.

[21] Т.И. Буткевич, *Обзор русских сект и их толков с изложением их происхождения и вероучения и с опровержением последнего* [Review of Russian Sects and Their Senses With a Statement of Their Origin, Distribution and Dogma and With a Refutation of the Last], Petrograd 1915.

[22] See: Н.И. Ивановский, *Руководство по истории и обличению старообрядческого раскола* [The Manual on a History and Accusation of Old Believe Schism], vol. III, Kazan 1912.

[23] Н.И. Ивановский, *Судебная экспертиза о секте хлыстов* [Judicial Examination about Sect of Klysts], "Журнал Министерства юстиции" [Magazine of the Ministry of Justice], 1, 1896, pp. 79-108.

[24] See: А.С. Пругавин, *Программа для собирания сведений о русском расколе или сектантстве* [Program for Collecting Information on Russian Schism or Sectarianism], Moscow 1881; А.С. Пругавин, *Религиозные отщепенцы (Очерки религиозного сектантства)* [Religious Turncoats. (Sketches of Modern Sectarianism)], vol. 1-2, Sanct-Petersburg 1904; А.С. Пругавин, *Раскол и сектантство в русской народной жизни* [Schism and Sectarianism in Russian National Life], Moscow 1905; А.С. Пругавин, *Бунт против природы. (О хлыстах и хлыстовщине)* [Revolt Against the Nature. (About the Khlysts and Khlystovshina)], vol. 1, Moscow 1917.

[25] В.Д. Бонч - Бруевич, *Среди сектантов. Статья 2* [Among the Sectarians. Article 2], "Жизнь" [The Life], 2, 1902, pp. 297-298.

[26] See: А.И. Клибанов, *Реформационные движения в России* [The Reformation Movements in Russia], Moscow 1960; А.И. Клибанов, *История религиозного сектантства в России* [A history of Religious Sectarianism in Russia], Moscow 1965; А.И. Клибанов, *Религиозное сектантство и современность* [The Religious Sectarianism and the Present], Moscow 1969; А.И. Клибанов, *Проблемы изучения и критики религиозного сектантства* [Problems of Studying and Criticism of Religious Sectarianism], Moscow 1971.

[27] А.И. Клибанов, *Религиозное сектантство в прошлом и настоящем* [The Religious Sectarianism in the Past and the Present], Moscow 1973, pp. 181-183.

[28] А. Эткинд, *Хлыст: секты, литература и революция* [Khlyst: Sects, the Literature and Revolution], Moscow 1998.

[29] А.А. Панченко, *Христовщина и скопчество: фольклор и традиционная культура русских мистических сект* [Khrystovshina and Scopchestvo: the Folklore and Traditional Culture of Russian Mystical Sects], Moscow 2002.

Bibliography

Айвазов И.Г., *Материалы для исследования русских мистических сект, I, Христовщина* [The Materials for Research of Russian Mystical Sects, I, Khristovshina], voll. 1-3, Petrograd 1915.

Id., *Первое следственное дело о христовщине* [The first Investigation Affair Devoted Khrystovshina], "Миссионерское обозрение" [The Missionary Review], 7, 8,11, 1916.

Барсов Н.И., *Исторические, критические и полемические опыты* [Historical, Critical and Polemic Experiences], Saint Petersburg 1879.

Id., *Русский простонародный мистицизм* [Russian Mysticism of Common People], "Христианское чтение" [Christian Reading], 9, 1869.

Бонч - Бруевич В.Д., *Среди сектантов. Статья 2* [Among of the Sectarians. Article 2], "Жизнь" [The Life], 2, 1902.

Буткевич Т.И., *Обзор русских сект и их толков с изложением их происхождения и вероучения и с опровержением последнего* [Review of Russian Sects and Their Senses With a Statement of Their Origin, Distribution and Dogma and With a Refutation of the Last], Petrograd 1915.

Варадинов Н., *История министерства внутренних дел. Восьмая, дополнительная книга. История распоряжений по расколу* [History of the Home Office. Additional. History of the Decrees on the Schism], Book 8, Saint Petersburg 1863.

Высотский Н.Г., *Критический обзор мнений по вопросу о происхождении хлыстовщины* [The Critical Review of Opinions Concerning an Origin of Khlystovshina], "Миссионерское обозрение" [The Missionary Review], 13, 14, 16, 1903.

Добротворский И.М., *К вопросу о людях Божьих* [To a Question on Divine People], "Православный собеседник" [The Orthodox Interlocutor], 1, 1870, pp. 19-20, 25-29.

Id., *Люди Божьи. Русская секта так называемых духовных христиан* [Divine People. Russian Sect of So-called Spiritual Christians], Kazan 1869.

Ивановский Н.И., *Руководство по истории и обличению старообрядческого раскола* [The Manual on a History and Accusation of the Old Believer Schism], vol. III, Kazan 1912.

Id., *Судебная экспертиза о секте хлыстов* [Judicial Examination About Sect of Klysts], "Журнал Министерства юстиции" [Magazine of the Ministry of Justice], 1, 1896.

Кельсиев В.И., *Сборник правительственных сведений о раскольниках* [The Collection of the Governmental Information on Dissenters], London 1861, 2.

Id., *Святорусские двоеверы* [Double-faith Believers of Holy Russia], "Заря" [Dawn], 10, 1869.

Клибанов А.И., *История религиозного сектантства в России* [A history of Religious Sectarianism in Russia], Moscow 1965.

Id., *Религиозное сектантство в прошлом и настоящем* [The Religious Sectarianism in the Past and the Present], Moscow 1973.

Id., *Религиозное сектантство и современность* [The Religious Sectarianism and the Present], Moscow 1969.

Id., *Реформационные движения в России* [The Reformation Movements in Russia], Moscow 1960.

Id., *Проблемы изучения и критики религиозного сектантства* [Problems of Studying and Criticism of Religious Sectarianism], Moscow 1971.

Коновалов Д., *Религиозные движения в России. I. Секта хлыстов.* [Religious Movements in Russia. I. Sect of Khlysts] "Ежемесячный журнал литературы, науки и общественной жизни" [The Monthly Magazine of the Literature, Science and a Public Life], 1, 1914.

Id., *Религиозный экстаз в русском мистическом сектантстве* [Religious Ecstasy in the Russian Mystical Sectarianism], Sergiev Posad 1908.

Кутепов К.В., *Секты хлыстов и скопцов* [Sects of Khlysts and Castrati], Kazan 1883.

Ливанов Ф.В., *Раскольники и острожники* [Dissenters and Extremely scarce], vol. I-IV, Saint Petersburg 1868-1873

Мельников П.И. (Андрей Печерский), *Собрание сочинений* [The Collected Works], vol. 1-6, Moscow 1863.

Панченко А.А., *Христовщина и скопчество: фольклор и традиционная культура русских мистических сект* [Khrystovshina and Scopchestvo: the Folklore and Traditional Culture of Russian Mystical Sects], Moscow 2002.

Протопопов Г., *Опыт исторического обозрения мистических сект в России* [Experience of a Historical Review of Mystical Sects in Russia], "Труды Киевской духовной академии" [Works of the Kiev Spiritual Academy], 10, 11, 1867.

Пругавин А.С., *Бунт против природы.(О хлыстах и хлыстовщине)* [Revolt Against the Nature. (About the Khlysts and Khlystovshina)], vol. 1, Moscow 1917.

Id., *Программа для собирания сведений о русском расколе или сектантстве* [Program for Collecting Information on Russian Schism or Sectarianism], Moscow 1881.

Id., *Раскол и сектантство в русской народной жизни* [Schism and Sectarianism in Russian National Life], Moscow 1905.

Id., *Религиозные отщепенцы (Очерки религиозного сектантства)* [Religious Turncoats. (Sketches of Modern Sectarianism)], vol. 1–2, Saint-Petersburg 1904.

Реутский Н.В., *Люди Божии и скопцы. Историческое исследование (Из достоверных источников и подлинных бумаг)* [Divine People and Castrati. Historical Research (From Authentic Sources and Original Papers)], Moscow 1872.

Id., *Московские Божии люди во второй половине XVII и XIX столетии* [Moscow "Divine People" in the Second Half of XVIII and in the XIX centuries], "Русский вестник" [The Russian Bulletin], 5, 1882.

Щапов А.П., *Земство и раскол* [Zemstvo and Schism], Saint Petersburg 1862.

Id., *Русский раскол старообрядчества* [Russian Schism of the Old-Believers], Kazan 1859.

Эткинд А., *Хлыст: секты, литература и революция* [Khlyst: Sects, the Literature and Revolution], Moscow 1998.

Myth as an Instrument for the Study of Greek and Indigenous Identities I: Greek Myths in the Illyrian Area

Maria Paola Castiglioni
Université Pierre Mendès-France, Grenoble II

Le mythe constitue pour l'historien de l'Antiquité un instrument irremplaçable pour l'approche et pour la compréhension de la civilisation grecque: expression fondamentale, avec le rite et les représentations figurées du divin, de la religion hellénique, le mythe en partage la complexité et la présence dans tous les aspects de la vie publique et sociale de l'homme grec.

Etudié depuis l'Antiquité, le concept de mythe a été pendant des siècles au centre d'un débat pluridisciplinaire et international enrichi par des contributions hétérogènes et antithétiques qui font aujourd'hui de l'ensemble des récits légendaires hellènes une clé de lecture indispensable pour déchiffrer l'univers grec.

L'itinéraire pluriséculaire de la mythologie (dans son sens étymologique de "discours – donc étude – sur les mythes") connut un début proprement scientifique et une lecture libérée des préjugés moralistes à partir de la moitié du XIXe s. Les apports complémentaires, souvent nourris de points de vue divergents et polémiques, des linguistes de l'école de mythologie comparée, des représentants de l'école anthropologique anglaise, des philologues allemands, des symbolistes, des fonctionnalistes et, à une époque plus récente, des structuralistes, ont promu une définition progressive du concept de mythe et une prise de conscience de son importance pour la compréhension non seulement du monde grec, mais, plus généralement, de l'univers mental humain. Les dernières recherches fournissent encore des impulsions profitables et efficaces pour une réflexion plus approfondie sur les aspects et les utilisations multiples du discours mythique.

A partir des années soixante-dix du XXe s., grâce aux découvertes archéologiques et à la progression des études anthropologiques, le mythe joue un rôle fondamental dans la compréhension des mécanismes identitaires déclenchés par le phénomène de la colonisation grecque. Les chercheurs ont en effet mis en évidence l'intensité de l'impact social et politique du mythe dans les contextes coloniaux helléniques: le mythe est ici mis au service du renforcement du sentiment d'appartenance commune des colons, de la légitimation de la possession du territoire colonial et de la médiation du contact avec les indigènes, notamment avec les élites. Le processus d'acculturation provoque parfois chez ces dernières une réception des thèmes mythiques d'origine grecque.

Dans le cadre de cette approche, l'Illyrie constitue un terrain privilégié d'enquête: en effet cette région, dont la colonisation grecque remonte à la fin du VIIe s. av. J.-C., est évoquée dans les attestations littéraires comme la terre d'élection de nombreux épisodes mythiques d'origine grecque. L'exemple le plus caractéristique est offert à ce propos par le destin illyrien du héros thébain Cadmos.

J.-P. Vernant affirmed some years ago that "Greek religion ... is a domain where the researcher has to think holistically, embracing religion and politics, anthropology and history, morality and daily life"[1]. This phrase effectively summarizes the complexity of approaching the Hellenic religious world, a vast symbolic construction interwoven in all areas of public and social life, in which the myth constitutes, beside ritual practices and the figurative representation of the divine, the fundamental mode of expression[2]. However, this critical concept, the origin of which has been attributed to the Greeks themselves and which later became one of the preferential themes, if not the principal one, of cultural anthropology, has been the subject of a reflection punctuated by heterogeneous and sometimes antithetical contributions, of a long and tormented intellectual itinerary ending in provisional and hypothetical conclusions, fruits of an international and polyphonic dialogue whose origins go back to ancient times and whose most original developments took place in the age of the Enlightenment.

From the beginning of studies on myths, the role of French scholars has been critical and prolific. However, it must be emphasised that this area is nurtured and continues to be enriched by contributions from enquiries and discussions which have never known the compartmentalization of national frontiers. Our analysis, therefore, will seek to underline the principal stages of the progression of this knowledge by concentrating on French research, but will not fail to register the role that other schools and specialists have played within the framework of mythological studies. In addition, equal emphasis will be given to the fact that this itinerary is of a multidisciplinary nature, where history is only one component of a global enquiry bringing together anthropologists, linguists, philologists and even psychoanalysts. Nevertheless, it is thanks to this multiplicity of outlooks and levels of interpretation that accurate historical knowledge of the Greek past has been able to advance. The Hellenic scholar of today knows that myth was generated by a social environment that influenced this collective framework. He does not hesitate therefore to use this incomparable decoding instrument. In particular, studies conducted on the theme of modes of contact between Greek and non-Greeks, notably in the colonial setting, clearly show how crucial mythical discourse is to understanding this historical reality. One will observe that the tools and procedures already used by historians in the case of southern Italy are also suitable to the Illyrian region, one of the new horizons still partly unexplored by historiographical research of the ancient world.

BIRTH AND DEVELOPMENT OF A SCIENCE OF MYTHS[3]

A point of reference for religious and social life in ancient times, paradoxically myth has been submitted, since the times of Xenophanes of Colophon and of Thucydides up to

Plato and Aristotle, to polemic exegesis and a shocked scrutiny which underscored, in particular, its irrational character and its fantastic and erroneous content[4]. Considered for a long time as "fabulous stories of gods, demigods, and heroes of Antiquity", or "a confusing mixture of fantasy, philosophical ideals and fragments of ancient history" whose "analysis is impossible"[5], the idea that myth was a mode of thought as well as a narrative tool was only integrated into studies at the beginning of the 18th century.

The early beginnings of a science of myth are strictly linked to the exploration of the New World and the discovery of customs and fables of American peoples: the publication in 1724, of the essay of French and Jesuit traveller J.-F. Lafitau, *Mœurs des sauvages américains comparées aux mœurs des premiers temps* [Habits of American Savages Compared to Customs of Antiquity], by establishing a parallel between the beliefs of ancient Greeks and the superstitions of American Indians and by recognising a convergence between the stories of the Hellenes and those of inhabitants of the New World, laid the foundation of an early comparative mythology. In the eyes of the priest, the two peoples had a pre-Christian religious level in common, and shared a condition of religious primitiveness, of which the myth constituted a decadent and crude expression[6].

Still hindered by an ethical and moralising interpretation, where the myth is nothing but a narration of atrocity, incest, parricide, adultery, murder and acts of cannibalism, there were no new developments in mythological study until the second half of the 19th century, and then further development was due to the progress of linguistics and comparative grammar, which form the base of the reflections of Max Muller, founder of the school of comparative mythology. For this Indianist, the myth is only a pathology of language, a kind of metaphoric perversion in the development of language, the result of a journey in three stages which sees, after the formation of words of the language and the development of grammatical structures, the expression of the mythopoetic phase, where the original sense of words is obliterated, ceases to be clear to the speakers and denotes mythical figures[7].

At the end of the 19th century, the English anthropological school, founded by E.B. Taylor and A. Lang, opposed Muller's linguistic model, often too fanciful in its linguistic and etymological reconstructions, objecting to it as being irrational: how could one give an explanation for the savage nature of myths, a feature still quite present within so-called primitive civilizations? Taylor's response no longer mobilised language, but the human spirit, in which the myth constitutes the early stage of evolution and the primordial state: man "mythologizes" spontaneously in his early days, before attaining the age of reason and philosophy, in ancient Greece as well as among "savage peoples"[8]. A vestige of times past, the myth therefore represents the savage state of thought. This point of view encouraged the revival of comparativism and places this approach within the framework of a real ethnological science: it was in the wake of this study that J.G. Frazer embarked upon the immense task of a parallel interpretation of myths of classical civilizations and primitive peoples which ended in the publication, from 1890, of the twelve volumes of *The Golden Bough*, an enormous synthesis an evolutionist approach[9].

Religion and Mythology

The reaction to the English thesis, notably to the generalisations provoked by an anthro-pological confrontation with other cultures judged as excessive, was not long in coming and, at the beginning of the 20th century, the German school of historical philology called for the return of classical mythological studies to the monopoly of philology. The contributions of L. Deubner, M.P. Nilsson and O. Gruppe, through the collection and the classification of classical mythic data, have provided indispensable work tools, even if their purely literary analysis led to an ignorance of the specificity of the myth[10].

Meanwhile, in Germany, within the sphere of influence of the philosophy of E. Cas-sirer[11] and those dedicated like him to the "tautegorical" approach to myth (the mean-ing of the myth is in what it recounts and not in another object) designated by F.W. Schelling[12], S. Freud likened the myth to other forms of symptomatic expressions of unconscious desires (dreams, *lapsus linguae*, subconscious deliberate mistakes), thereby creating the basis of his vast psychoanalytical construction; C.G. Jung recognized arche-typical images organized in the collective unconscious in mythical stories; K. Kerényi considered myth to be "the myth of man", as a modality of knowledge and creation specific to man. The religious phenomenology of F.W. Otto pursued this reflection on the symbolism of myths finding a force that shapes the culture of man[13].

The functionalists did not hesitate to oppose the position of the German symbol-ists: the criticisms of B. Malinowski underlined the absence, in the interpretation of symbolists, of all consideration of the social and institutional role of the myth, which is taken completely out of its context[14]. The studies of this Polish ethnologist placed myths in their social environment: they served to maintain social stability and pre-served, by the repetition of its language and symbols, respect for norms and hierarchies. It played a role in studying the function of a social institution or individual behaviour. The same perspective was shared by E. Durkheim, the head of the French School of So-ciology: Durkheim's reflection conceded a primary role to myth (no longer separated from religion) because it is at the origin of fundamental notions of science and major forms of culture ("Toutes sont comme vêtues et enveloppées de quelque figure issue du mythe"[15]).

It is on these foundations, and with the desire to integrate limits within them, that the research of the anthropologist M. Mauss, the sinologist M. Granet and the Hellenist L. Gernet was added[16]. The latter insisted, in particular, on what related to the Greek domain, on the unity and continuity between mythic symbols, institutional practices and language events. The specificity of the mythic story is read in the light of the insti-tutional and conceptual system of which it constitutes a particular expression. Thought is therefore a "total social fact" which involves economic and political dimensions, as well as ethics and aesthetics at the same time[17].

After G. Dumézil's research on the functional tripartition of sovereignty, war and fer-tility myths, which revealed the deep structural analogies in Indo-European myths[18], the most sensational advances took place between 1958 and 1964, again in France and more precisely at the Ecole Pratique des Hautes Etudes, an eminent place of religious research, thanks to the Americanist C. Levi-Strauss. By looking on the one hand to the studies of Mauss, Gernet and Dumézil, and on the other to his knowledge of a vast number of Amerindian myths of oral tradition, the founder of structuralism defined myth as a story structured in episodes, told on particular occasions, often sacred, and reproduced through different stories without breaking down its general structure. Only the latter counts for analysis, which is done by picking out the constitutive elements of the story, the mythemes, short phrases in themselves devoid of meaning (like pho-nemes in language) but the combination of which gives narrative sense to the mythic story through the interaction of opposition and homology. Therefore, myth possesses an apparent narrative level, but also a more profound level that mythemes allow them to reach. In order to understand it completely, "Il ne doit jamais être interprété seul, mais dans son rapport avec d'autres mythes qui, pris ensemble, constituent un groupe de transformations" and "par reference à l'ethnographie des sociétés dont ils provien-nent"[19], which amounts to recognizing the importance of the skills of the historian in the case of Greek myths[20].

Submitted to methods of structural analysis, myth has earned a legitimate place in the domain of History: not only for the fact that it is part of History and that its "formal dynamic reflects by a collection of logical transformations the historical evolution of societies", but also because it helped to detect in civilisations "the presence of such or such a concrete element" which revealed, for example, the existence, otherwise unsus-pected, of contacts and exchanges between several societies[21].

Inspired by the work of this distinguished predecessor, the research of French Hellenists of the Ecole Pratique des Hautes Etudes has adopted and adapted the Levi-Straussian procedures to the Greek domain: J.-P. Vernant, M. Detienne and P. Vidal-Naquet have enriched mythic knowledge and interpretation with essential contributions to several aspects of Greek culture and spirituality. Their work has stimulated an international reflection, the results of which are still relevant today[22].

Conscious of the fundamental contribution of myth to the knowledge of the Greek man and of his social, political and cultural concerns, Hellenists today dedicate them-selves to discerning, behind the richness of mythic discourses, their deeper meaning and their relationship with History.

MYTH IN THE PERIPHERY: ACCULTURATION, FRONTIERS, ETHNIC IDENTITY

Today, the long exercise of "unravelling" myth makes it an essential tool for studying the multiple facets of the Greek universe. Mythic stories, a mode of expression of the mental organisation of the Greek man, of his reference systems and values, therefore provides an essential contribution to the study of cultural and social processes triggered off by contacts between Greeks and non-Greeks: the relationship between the Other and the complex dynamics aroused in the context of social intercourse with Greeks or their occupation of peripheral territories (*emporia* and colonies) can be better grasped thanks to the acknowledgement of the role played by the myth.

The Greek colonial phenomenon earned a place in ancient studies in the relatively recent past: the development of archaeological sites in southern Italy since the 1960s and the spread of a more general thought pattern – linked to the effects of decolonisation – of re-evaluation and re-valorisation of cultures other than 'Western', have produced a new interest in the encounters and interferences between Greek culture and "Barbarian" cultures.

Once again, this process is indebted to the experience of anthropological studies: the reflections developed in studies on American Indians in the late 19th century have led to the introduction into the vocabulary and the field of scientific research of the word and notion of "acculturation"[23], that is "the collection of phenomena resulting from direct and continued contact between groups of individuals from different cultures with subsequent changes in the cultural types of one group or the other"[24]. Later contributions, especially from the 1930s, have permitted the introduction of new hypotheses, a better definition of working methods and an early classification of the types of itineraries and acculturative agents[25].

This anthropological approach, elaborated particularly in the framework of a study of modern and contemporary colonial contexts, has therefore been applied to the Greco-Roman world. The now outdated label used in the beginning of "Hellenisation" and "Romanisation" was followed by the definition, more "politically correct" and more satisfying from an epistemological point of view, of "modes of contact and transformation processes"[26]. This new formula was also the title of a meeting held in Cortona in 1981, a key colloquium in the debate on the problems of cultural exchange in ancient societies[27]. This important scientific step has in reality been the outcome of a fruitful dialogue between Italian and French researchers that started as early as the 1960s, and of which the founding moments have been, in 1961, the first Congress on Studies of Greater Greece at Taranto, *Greci e Italici in Magna Grecia* and, in 1963, the 8th International Congress on Classical Archaeology, *Le rayonnement des civilisations grecque et romaine sur les cultures périphériques*[28]. Again in 1971, ten years after the first meeting, the annual rendezvous in Taranto highlighted the problem of non-Hellenic inhabitants in Magna Graecia (*Le genti non greche in Magna Grecia*) as a key issue.

In 1967, the Centre Jean Bérard, a research team associated with the CNRS, was created in Naples, becoming a joint emanation from the CNRS and the French School of Rome (Ecole française de Rome) from 1999: a research platform for French and Italian researchers working on southern Italy and Sicily. By means of archaeological excavations organised in Southern Italy and its numerous publications, the Centre Jean Bérard has considerably enriched the knowledge of the colonial realities of Magna Graecia and Sicily, by allowing a better comprehension of the social, economic and religious phenomena linked to the Greek colonial presence[29].

In 1997, the researchers who met at Taranto became interested in the frontier territories in the western Greek world, in the context of new research originating from concepts of *Frontier History* and *Ethnicity*, two notions coined by Anglo-American historiography that met with great success among Hellenists from the 1990s onwards and which today constitute the pivot of the historiographical debate in favour or against a Helleno-centric vision of ancient history[30].

The frontier, both geographical and cultural, is the place of difference, and therefore the space, both physical and psychological, where the question of identity manifests itself most violently with two corollary consequences: a more acute sense of belonging to one's own community and its values, and a clearer perception of the Other and of his Otherness[31].

Highlighted by G. Pugliese Carratelli, the frontier is also a meeting point. It is not an impassable boundary but a permeable field of reciprocal ethnic interrelations and transmissions. Thus, sometimes Greek myths originally "projected" on non-Hellenic environments used a conceptual and expressive code shared by the indigenous peoples themselves (or by a group, often the elite, of the native community) which could therefore be used to assert their own identity and values. In this case, the myth was often perceived as a vector of prestige and therefore as an essential power factor: its social and political impact was such that it contributed to the "heroisation" of indigenous aristocracies. In these instances, one can witness the phenomenon of mythic reception.

For a definition of identities and, more generally, for the illustration of the themes of acculturation, myth has been taken into consideration in southern Italy and Sicily more than in any other region affected by Greek colonisation. This is partly by virtue of a "high degree of acculturation in the indigenous societies, likely to participate in an identical common imagination (with the Greek) and perhaps also by reason of "a Mycenaean tradition taking root in the societies of the Dark Ages"[32]. Here, we are indebted to the exemplary exploitation of an archaeological and, in particular, iconographical document capable of offsetting the lack of more explicit evidence. We refer to the contributions gathered after the international colloquium in Rome on *Le mythe grec dans l'Italie antique*. In particular, the communication of F.-H. Massa-Pairault with his remarkable interpretation of the Etruscan recovery of the Athenian myth of Erichthonius, the mythical founder of the autochthonous Athenian identity, a legendary story that metamorphoses into the foundation myth of the *nomen etruscum* identity in the middle of the 4th century B.C.[33]. This is an exemplary case of reception of a Greek myth.

Finally, each study of a myth requires a thorough awareness of the historical context in which the myth in question was produced: I. Malkin defined this "mythic-historical" approach and emphasized that, rather than considering the myth as bearers of a "core of truth" relative to the past that they narrated, it is necessary to see them "as an integral part of the history of the period in which it was told"[34]. This interpretation allows for a better understanding of the links that united the Greeks to colonised territories and the responses that they gave to the confrontation with the Other. After having travelled the mythic path which accompanied colonial foundation, the Israeli researcher applied his methodology, in particular, to the myths about Ulysses' return in order to better define the period of Greek proto-colonisation[35]. The originality of his approach, nurtured by a multi-disciplinary effort, has opened new influential and stimulating paths of exploration for specialists.

GREEK MYTHS IN ILLYRIA: HISTORIOGRAPHICAL REVIEW OF ILLYRIAN STUDIES

Today, taking advantage of solid theoretical and methodological bases, research is more and more oriented towards investigating other territories also involved in the encounter with the Hellenic world, thanks to discoveries by archaeologists attracted to new research terrains. Among these, there is the Illyrian region, namely the eastern Adriatic coast and its surroundings: Croatia, Montenegro, Serbia and Albania (Fig. 1).

If the difficult political situations that these countries have gone through have prevented sufficient in-depth research in the past and if, even today, it is still complicated to have direct access to materials brought to light in excavations (that began, in some cases, in the first half of the 20th century), the enormous archaeological capital of the region can interest historians once again. In fact, activity has resumed in the last few years now as researchers from nations concerned with the excavations participate in archaeological missions. For example, in Albania, France has archaeologists working at Apollonia and at Byllis, Italy at Phoinike and the United Kingdom at Butrint. These missions aim to complete topographical and archaeological knowledge of the Albanian sites and permit the conservation and improvement of a heritage of rare value. The examination of the evidence uncovered will permit new chapters to be added to the history of colonisation and contacts between Greeks and non-Greeks, even though it will be necessary to wait several years before the results are compiled into an entirely satisfying syntheses.

Outside, and before, research on the terrain, the interest in Illyria is part of the larger framework of growing attention to the Adriatic space. After the pioneering studies of R. L. Beaumont on the Adriatic and, a little later, the contributions of D. Rendić-Miočević, it was necessary to wait until the 1970s to see a realization of the impact exerted by the Adriatic *koinè*[36] and the Adriatic "traffic" on the development of ancient civilisations[37]. The book *Grecità adriatica* by L. Braccesi, published in 1971, followed by the 1973 congress *L'Adriatico tra Mediterraneo e penisola balcanica nell'Antichità* , has opened a new and fruitful debate over this space[38]. If Braccesi's attention is concentrated on the eastern part of the Adriatic, and particularly on the Syracusan colonial presence in the Adriatic, P. Cabanes' studies, originally oriented to the region of Epirus, now focuses on the southern Illyrian region.

These two researchers, operating with two, sometimes far distant, approaches and questionings, have been able, through their dynamism and enthusiasm, to promote scientific initiatives that continue to enrich the knowledge of the Adriatic space and its history with new contributions: the Italian scholar through the periodic publication of *Hesperia* and his French colleague with the organisation and publication of international colloquia on southern Illyria and Epirus in Antiquity[39].

Fig. 1
The Illyrian tribes.

In their research, the two teams have included the problem of colonial and indigenous identities and have tackled it, in part, through the interpretation of myths[40], which happen to find a particularly fertile terrain in ancient Illyria and Epirus. Literary sources in the Greek and Latin languages record the presence of numerous characters and episodes belonging to the Hellenic tradition, where there is a pervasive presence of heroes from *nostoi*, the return voyages from the Trojan War: Diomede, Helenus and Andromache, Aeneas, Antenor and above all Elephenor. The link with Troy is developed to such a point it would seem that a real Trojan tradition existed.

The Dorian hero par excellence, Heracles, also had close relations with this region. The Argonauts hugged the eastern shores of the Adriatic on their way to Corinth after capturing the Golden Fleece.

The Theban hero, Cadmus, emigrated there with his spouse Harmonia as serpents, and reigned over the local tribe of Enchelians: this legend is without doubt the most entrenched in the Illyrian territory and seems to have been, more than others, taken up by the indigenous royalty. Indeed, numerous literary sources locate the legend of Cadmus-serpent on the Oriental Adriatic slopes between the rivers Neretva and Drin and around Lake Ohrid at the frontiers between Albania and Macedonia. There, according to Strabo's account (VII, 7-8), the sovereigns of one indigenous tribe, the Enchelians, claimed to be descendants of the Theban couple (Fig. 2).

The appropriation of the Cadmean myth, suggested by this literary passage, would be later confirmed by two pieces of iconographic: two belt clasps of Illyrian manufacture. One was found at Selca e Poshtme (Albania) and the other at Gostilj (Montenegro), both date back to the Hellenistic age and representing a quasi-identical battle scene which can, without doubt, be linked with the Illyrian episode of the myth of Cadmus (Fig. 3).

Therefore, it would appear to be an example of myth absorption, obviously favoured by the existence of a strong cultural substratum in Illyria, probably going back to the prehistoric age, in which the sacred nature of the serpent was well established.

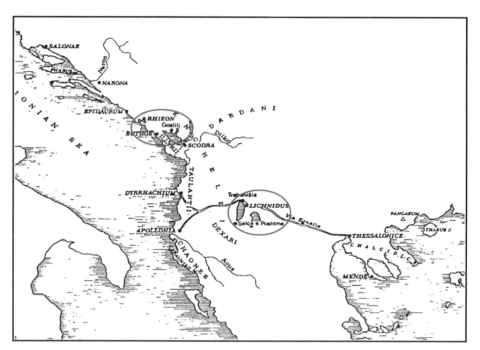

Fig. 2
Cadmus and Harmonia in Illyria: peoples and places mentioned in the texts.

Fig. 3
Selca's and Gostjli's belt buckles.

It must be admitted that these legends, unquestionably the result of Greek contacts with the Illyrian world, have been frequently modified, embellished and transformed according to circumstances. Certain mythic data does not fall far short of real propaganda, as is the case with the legend of Illyrios, related by Appian (*Illyriké*, II, 3-4), or the story about the origin of the name *Ionios kolpos*, the Adriatic Sea, also recorded by Appian (*Bellum Civile*, II, 39). This aspect of traditional narrative sometimes makes it difficult to establish the original version of the myth and to distinguish later additions, especially if one considers the chronological span of literary traces.

Probably because Illyrian research is so recent, these myths have been the subject of only a few articles, the most convincing of which remain M. Šašel Kos's contributions, but these have never been read thoroughly or with a view to synthesizing their entire significance[41].

Only the detailed study of the historical context, along with a careful textual exegesis and the support of the available archaeological material, will permit the correct interpretation of these mythical stories and make them a precious tool for the definition of the acculturative alchemies that arose from the contact between Greeks and Illyrians. Therefore, the research is still far from its conclusion, but the necessary tools have been prepared.

The centuries-long research on the myth, after rendering the modes of expression intelligible, continues today, and will continue in future to provide historians with new tools to understand the Ancients. The objective will be to shed light on a crucial dimension within studies that are supposed to be humanistic: forms of thought, mentalities, awareness of the self and perception of the Other by the Antique Man, considered as an individual and as a member of a community, his inner history and his social and cultural environment, of which he is both an actor and a creator.

NOTES

[1]   Interview with the "Nouvel Observateur" (May 5 1980), words recorded by J.-P. Enthoven and J. Julliard.

[2]   See J.-P. Vernant, *Mythe et religion en Grèce ancienne*, Paris 1990, pp. 34-35

[3]   This entire section benefits from the contribution of several readings and therefore constitutes a synthetic review of more detailed reconstitutions than one can obtain in: J.-P. Vernant, *Mythe et religion en Grèce ancienne*, Paris 1974; Id., *Enciclopedia del Novecento*, vol. IV, Istituto della Enciclopedia Italiana, Rome 1979, in the article "Mito", pp. 350-367; M. Detienne, *L'invention de la mythologie*, Paris 1981; Id., *Les Grecs et nous, Une anthropologie comparée de la Grèce ancienne*, Paris 2005; C. Calame, *Mythe et histoire dans L'Antiquité grecque, La création symbolique d'une colonie*, Lausanne 1996.

[4]   For a more complete overview of the perception of Greek myths by the ancients, see P. Veyne, *Les Grecs ont-ils cru à leur mythes? Essai sur l'imagination constituante*, Paris 1983. See also: C. Ginzburg, *Mito*, in *I Greci. Storia, cultura, arte e società*, I: *I Greci e noi*, Turin 1996, pp. 197-237.

[5]   Quotation from the article "Mythologie" of the *Encyclopédie ou dictionnaire raisonné des arts et des métiers*, X, Neuchâtel 1765, pp. 924-926.

[6]   J.-F. Lafitau, *Mœurs des sauvages américains comparés aux mœurs des premier temps*, 4 vols., Paris 1724. Lafitau's point of view is shared in part by another Frenchman, B. Le Bouyer de Fontenelle, author of the treatise *De l'origine des fables*, published in Paris en 1724; for him, fables and myths are only irrational and inventions. Contrary to the Jesuit, he considered them not as a deteriorated form of a religious spirit, but as embryonic manifestations of a phenomenon that would transform itself into a religion.

[7]   M. Müller, *The science of language*, London 1861-1863 and Id., *Lectures on the science of language. Second series*, London 1863.

[8]   E.B. Taylor, *Primitive culture. Researches into the development of Mythology, Philosophy, Religion, Language, Art and Custom*, London 1903[4]; A. Lang, *La mythologie*, Paris 1886; Id., *Modern Mythology*, London 1897; Id., *The making of religion*, London 1909[3].

[9]   J.G. Frazer, *The Golden Bough. A study in magic and religion*, 12 vols., London 1890-1915.

[10]   M.P. Nilsson, *Greek popular religion*, New York 1940; Id., *Geschichte der Griechischen Religion*, vol. I, Munich 1967[3], vol. II, 1961[2]; O. Gruppe, *Griechische Mythologie und Religionsgeschichte*, Munich 1906; Id., *Geschichte der klassichen Mythologie und Religionsgeschichte, während des Mittelalters im Abendland und wahrend der Neuzeit*, in *Ausführliches Lexicon der griechischen und römischen Mythologie* (Roscher), suppl., Leipzig 1921.

[11]   E. Cassirer, *Philosophie der symbolischen Formen*, 3 vols., Berlin 1923-1929.

[12]   F.W. Schelling, *Einleitung in die Philosophie der Mythologie*, 2 vols., Stuttgart-Augsburg 1856-1857.

[13]   S. Freud, *Totem und Tabu*, Leipzig-Vienna 1913; C.G. Jung, *Zur Psychologie westlicher und östlicher Religion*, Zurich 1963; C.G. Jung - K. Kerenyi, *Einführung in das Wesen der Mythologie*, Amsterdam-Leipzig 1941; K. Kerenyi, *Die Mythologie der Griechen*, 2 vols., Munich 1951; W.F. Otto, *Die Götter Griechenlands. Das Bild des Göttlichen im Spiegel des griechischen Geistes*, Frankfurt/Main 1947.

[14]   B. Malinowski, *Argonauts of the Western Pacific*, New York-London 1922; Id., *Myth in primitive psychology*, London 1926.

[15]   "Everything is clothed in and enveloped by some figure originating from myth".

16   M. Mauss, *Œuvres. Vol. II., Représentations collectives et diversité des civilisations*, Paris 1969; M. Granet, *Danses et légendes de la Chine ancienne*, 2 vols., Paris 1926; Id., *La pensée chinoise*, Paris 1934; Id., *La religions des Chinois*, Paris 1951; L. Gernet, *Recherches sur le développement de la pensée juridique et morale en Grèce*, Paris 1917; Id., *Anthropologie de la Grèce antique*, Paris 1968.

17   See *ibid.*, p. 131.

18   G. Dumézil, *Mythe et épopée*, vol. I, *L'idéologie des trois fonctions dans les épopées des peuples indo-européens*, Paris 1968 et vol. II, *Types épiques indo-européens: un héros, un sorcier, un roi*, Paris 1971.

19   "It should never be interpreted alone, but in relation to other myths which, taken together, constitute a group of transformations" and "by reference to the ethnography of the societies from which they came". C. Lévi-Strauss, *Religions comparées des peuples sans écriture*, in *Annuaire de l'EPHE*, Paris 1961, p. 5.

20   C. Lévi-Strauss, *Anthropologie structurale*, Paris 1958; Id., *La geste d'Asdiwal*, in *Annuaire de l'EPHE*, Paris 1958; Id., *Mythologiques*, vol. I, *Le cru et le cuit*, Paris 1964; vol. II, *Du miel au cendres*, Paris 1966; vol. III, *L'origine des manières de table*, Paris 1968; vol IV, *L'homme nu*, Paris 1971.

21   See F. Keck, *Claude Lévi-Strauss, une introduction*, Paris 2005.

22   As a comprehensive list would be too long, this list is limited to the major titles: J.-P. Vernant, *Les origines de la pensée grecque*, Paris 1962; Id., *Mythe et pensée chez les Grecs, Etudes de psychologie historique*, Paris 1965; *La mort dans les yeux. Figures de l'autre en Grèce ancienne*, Paris 1985; Id., *L'individu, la mort, l'amour. Soi-même et l'autre en Grèce ancienne*, Paris 1989; J.-P. Vernant - P. Vidal-Naquet, *Mythe et tragédie en Grèce ancienne*, Paris 1972; J.-P. Vernant - M. Detienne, *Les ruses de l'intelligence. La métis des Grecs*, Paris 1974; M. Detienne, *Les jardins d'Adonis. La mythologie des aromates en Grèce*, Paris 1972; P. Vidal-Naquet, *Le chasseur noir, Formes de pensée et formes de société dans le monde grec*, Paris 1981.

23   The first person to use the word "acculturation" was the American ethnologist Powell. (J.W. Powell, *Introduction to the study of Indian languages*, Washington 1880, p. 46).

24   R. Redfield - R. Linton - M. Herskowits, *Memorandum for the Study of Acculturation*, "American Anthropologist", 38, 1936, pp. 149-152.

25   See R. Bastide, *"Acculturation"*, *Encyclopedia Universalis*, Paris 1968, vol. 1, pp. 102-107; Id., *Le prochain et le lointain*, Paris 2001; N. Wachtel, *L'acculturation*, in P. Nora (ed.), *Faire de l'Histoire. Nouveaux problèmes*, Paris 1974, t.1, pp. 124-146.

26   Useful, for a reading of methodological problems, an article by C. Gallini, *Che cosa intendere per ellenizzazione. Problemi di metodo*, in "Dialoghi di archeologia", 1973, 7, pp. 175-191, where the phenomenon of Hellenisation of the Roman world is interpreted in light of Marxist dynamic structure-superstructure.

27   *Modes de contacts et processus de transformation dans les sociétés anciennes, Actes du colloque de Cortona (24-30 mai 1981)*, Rome 1983.

28   One can also cite, but in a philological rather than a historical context, the encounter eloquently entitled *Grec et Barbares*, Interview with the Hardt foundation in 1961.

29   As an example, we will cite: A. Mele, *Il commercio greco arcaico. Prexis ed emporie*, Naples 1979; *Recherches sur les cultes grecs et l'Occident. 1.*, Naples 1980 and *Recherches sur les cultes grecs et l'Occident. 2.*, Naples 1984; *Contribution à l'étude de la société et de la colonisation eubéennes*, 1975 and *Nouvelle contribution à l'étude de la société et de la colonisation eubéennes*, Naples 1982; B. D'Agostino - M. Bats (ed.), *Euboica. L'Eubea e la presenza euboica in Calcidica e in Occidente, Actes du Colloque International (Naples 1996)*, Naples 1998, (co-edited with l'Istituto Universitario Orientale).

30   *Confini e frontiera nella Grecità d'Occidente, Atti del trentasettesimo convegno di studi sulla Magna Grecia, Taranto 3-6 ottobre 1997*, Taranto 1999.

31   See W. Nippel, *La costruzione dell'"altro"*, in W. Nippel, *I Greci. Storia, Cultura, Arte, Società*, I: *Noi e i Greci*, Torino 1996, pp. 165-183; F. Hartog, *Mémoire d'Ulysse. Récits sur la frontière en Grèce ancienne*, Paris 1996; G. Vanotti - C. Perassi (eds.), *In limine. Ricerche su marginalità e periferia nel mondo antico*, Milan 2004.

[32] P. Lévêque, *L'Italie des mythes*, in *Le mythe grec dans l'Italie antique, fonction et image, Actes du Colloque international, Rome, 14-16 novembre 1996*, Rome 1999, p. 637.

[33] F.-H. Massa-Pairault, *Mythe et identité politique, l'Etrurie du IVe siècle à l'époque hellénistique*, in *Le mythe grec dans l'Italie antique, fonction et image, Actes du colloque international, Rome, 14-16 novembre 1996*, Rome 1999, pp. 521-554.

[34] I. Malkin, *La Méditerranée spartiate, Mythe et territoire*, Paris 1999, p. 23.

[35] I. Malkin, *Religion and colonisation in Ancient Greece*, Leiden 1987; *The Return of Odysseus. Colonisation and ethnicity*, Berkeley 1998.

[36] Common space.

[37] R.L. Beaumont, *Greek influence in Adriatic Sea before the fourth century B.C.*, "JHS", 61, 1936, pp. 159-204; D. Rendić-Miočević, *I Greci in Adriatico*, "Studi romagnoli," 12, 1962, pp. 39-56.

[38] See in particular: M. Pallottino, *Considerazioni sul problema della funzione storica dell'Adriatico nell'Antichità*, in *L'Adriatico tra Mediterraneo e penisola balcanica nell'Antichità (Lecce-Matera, 21-27 ottobre 1973)*, Taranto 1983, pp. 11-21; E. Lepore, *Problemi storici dell'area adriatica nell'età della colonizzazione greca*, in *L'Adriatico tra Mediterraneo e penisola balcanica nell'Antichità (Lecce-Matera, 21-21 ottobre 1973)*, Taranto 1983, pp. 127-145

[39] The collection *Hespéria, Studi sulla Grecità d'Occidente* was published from 1990. Today, there are twenty monographs in the collection, which however are not all dedicated to Adriatic problems. The international colloquia on meridional Illyria and Epirus take place every six years. The first and the second took place in Clermont-Ferrand in 1984 and 1990, the third in Chantilly in 1996. The most recent one, the fourth, was held in Grenoble in 2002 and was organised and edited by P. Cabanes and J.-L. Lamboley.

[40] See, as an example, P. Cabanes, *La présence grecque sur la côte orientale de l'Adriatique en Illyrie du Sud*, in *Greek influence along the East Adriatic Coast, Proceedings of the International Conference held in Split from September 24th to 26th 1998*, Split 2002, pp. 51-62; L. Braccesi, *Diomedes cum Gallis*, "Hesperìa", 2, 1991, pp. 90-102.

[41] M. Šašel Kos, *Cadmus and Harmonia in Illyria*, "Arheološki vestnik", 44, 1993, pp. 113-136; Id., *Mythological stories concerning Illyria and its name*, in P. Cabanes - J.-L. Lamboley (eds.), *L'Illyrie méridionale et l'Epire dans l'Antiquité – IV, Actes du IV° colloque internationale de Grenoble (10-12 octobre 2002)*, Paris 2004, pp. 493-504.

BIBLIOGRAPHY

Bastide R., *"Acculturation"*, *Encyclopedia Universalis*, Paris 1968, vol. 1, pp. 102-107.

Beaumont R.L., *Greek influence in Adriatic Sea before de fourth century B.C.*, "JHS", 61, 1936, pp. 159-204.

Braccesi L., *Grecità adriatica*, Bologna 1971.

Cabanes P. (ed.), *L'Illyrie Méridionale et l'Epire dans l'Antiquité, Actes du colloque international de Clermont-Ferrand (22-25 octobre 1984)*, Clermont-Ferrand 1987.

Cabanes P. (ed.), *L'Illyrie Méridionale et l'Epire dans l'Antiquité II, Actes du IIe colloque international de Clermont-Ferrand (25-27 octobre1990)*, Paris 1993.

Id. (ed.), *L'Illyrie Méridionale et l'Épire dans l'Antiquité-III, Actes du IIIe colloque international de Chantilly (16-19 octobre 1996)*, Paris 1999.

Id. (ed.), *Histoire de l'Adriatique*, Paris 2001.

Id., *La présence grecque sur la côte orientale de l'Adriatique en Illyrie du Sud*, in *Greek influence along the East Adriatic Coast, Proceedings of the International Conference held in Split from September 24th to 26th 1998*, Split 2002, pp. 51-62.

Confini e frontiera nella Grecità d'Occidente, Atti del XXXVII convegno di studi sulla Magna Grecia, Taranto 3-6 ottobre 1997, Taranto 1999.

Contribution à l'étude de la société et de la colonisation eubéennes, Napoli 1975.

Detienne M., *L'invention de la mythologie*, Paris 1981.

Id., *Les Grecs et nous, Une anthropologie comparée de la Grèce ancienne*, Paris 2005.

Frazer J.G., *The Golden Bough. A study in magic and religion*, 12 vols., London 1890-1915.

Gallini C., *Che cosa intendere per ellenizzazione. Problemi di metodo*, "Dialoghi di archeologia", 7, 1973, pp. 175-191.

Gernet L., *Anthropologie de la Grèce antique*, Paris 1968.

Ginzburg C., *Mito*, in *I Greci. Storia, cultura, arte e società*. I: *I Greci e noi*, Turin 1996, pp. 197-237.

Greci e Italici in Magna Grecia. Atti del I Convegno di studi sulla Magna Grecia, Taranto, 4-8 novembre 1961, Naples 1962.

Grecs et Barbares, Entretient de la fondation Hardt du 1961.

Hall J.M., *Ethnic identity in Greek Antiquity*, Cambridge 1997.

Hartog F., *Mémoire d'Ulysse. Récits sur la frontière en Grèce ancienne*, Paris 1996.

Le genti non greche in Magna Grecia. Atti dell'undecimo Convegno di Studi sulla Magna Grecia, Taranto 10-15 ottobre 1971, Naples 1972.

Lévi-Strauss C., *Anthropologie structurale*, Paris 1958.

Id., *Mythologiques*, vol. I, *Le cru et le cuit*, Paris 1964; vol. II, *Du miel au cendres*, Paris 1966; vol. III, *L'origine des manières de table*, Paris 1968; vol. IV, *L'homme nu*, Paris 1971.

Malkin I., *The Return of Odysseus. Colonisation and ethnicity*, Berkeley 1998.

Massa-Pairault F.-H., *Introduction*, in *Le mythe grec dans l'Italie antique, fonction et image*, Actes du colloque international, Rome, 14-16 novembre 1996, Rome 1999, pp. 1-8.

Modes de contacts et processus de transformation dans les sociétés anciennes, Actes du colloque de Cortona (24-30 mai 1981), Rome 1983.

Mele A., *Il commercio greco arcaico. Prexis ed emporie*, Naples 1979.

Moscati-Castelnuovo L. (ed.), *Identità e prassi storica nel Mediterraneo greco*, Milan 2002.

Vernant J.-P., *Mythe et société en Grèce ancienne*, Paris 1974.

Id., *Enciclopedia del Novecento*, vol. IV, Istituto della Enciclopedia Italiana, Rome 1979, article "Mito", pp. 350-367.

Veyne P., *Les Grecs ont-ils cru à leurs mythes? Essai sur l'imagination constituante*, Paris 1983.

Myth as an Instrument for the Study of Greek and Indigenous Identities II: Myths in Western Greek Colonies

JEAN-LUC LAMBOLEY
Université Pierres Mendès France, Grenoble II

Des études récentes sur la notion d'ethnicité ont montré que l'identité d'un peuple ou d'une communauté peut se construire à partir d'éléments culturels différents et hétérogènes. Ce sont les acteurs sociaux eux-mêmes qui déterminent les critères qui les différencient dans leur relation aux autres. Ces critères peuvent varier dans le temps et dans l'espace, mais ils fournissent toujours les limites définissant les frontières entre les différents groupes ethniques qui se font face. Ainsi, il peut y avoir étanchéité des ethnies sans étanchéité des cultures. En Grèce ancienne, le problème est assez différent car les Grecs ne reconnaissent pas d'autre culture que la leur, et sont donc incapables de penser l'altérité ou la diversité culturelle en dehors du couple antithétique Grec/Barbares. Cela crée un système de relation à l'autre totalement dissymétrique. Néanmoins, en milieu colonial les Grecs se retrouvent en situation particulière parce que leurs voisins sont précisément des populations non grecques avec lesquelles ils sont contraints d'établir des relations quotidiennes normalisées. Ils doivent alors produire pour eux-mêmes une représentation de ces autres, et pour ce faire, ils utilisent le mythe sous la forme d'un récit de fondation. En conséquence, l'étude de ces mythes nous permet de saisir la perception que les Grecs ont du monde étranger qui les entoure et de leurs propres expériences dans cette relation aux autres. Le récit mythologique apparaît ainsi comme un instrument privilégié pour comprendre comment les Grecs ont construit leur propre identité et celle des autres.

On se propose ici d'étudier deux récits de fondation, celui de la cité de Tarente dans le sud de l'Italie, et de la cité d'Apollonia en Illyrie, à travers les témoignages d'auteurs anciens (Justin pour Tarente, et Pausanias pour Apollonia). Il s'agit donc essentiellement d'une étude de documents. On verra que dans les deux cas, en dépit des variantes dues à des contextes locaux évidemment différents, le problème des colons est de justifier l'appropriation d'un sol qui ne leur appartient pas, et par voie de conséquence, de normaliser leur rapport avec les populations indigènes auxquelles ils ont volé une partie du territoire. En Grèce propre, à Athènes par exemple, le mythe de l'autochtonie pouvait fonctionner, et c'était la base de la citoyenneté et de l'identité civique ; dans les colonies c'était plus difficile du fait du contexte multiethnique, mais le mythe conserve la même fonction identitaire*.

The foundation of a Greek colony generally gives rise to narratives preserved by literary tradition, all using a mythical discourse because it entails speaking of origins. The value of these stories is significant, as they justify the very existence of the colony and determine its principal identity traits. Several versions of such narratives often exist, the origins of which are not always easy to explain because they reflect the antagonistic interests of different groups involved in the colonial process. The difficulty in comprehending these myths lies especially in the fact that as stories that became impressive when and where they were told, they should not be detached from their context. This context, which refers to a very remote past, is still little known to us. However, studying these myths enables us to throw some light on the history of the colonial world by highlighting the cultural paradigms which allowed the Greeks to conceive the colonial phenomenon and, indeed, even models of action.

A case in point is the story of how Tarentum was founded, as conveyed by the Latin writer Justin. Tarentum was established about 706 B.C. by Spartan colonists on the gulf known as Tarentum on the Ionian coast of southern Italy, situated on the remote borders of Oenotria and Apulia. Not much is known about Justin as an author. Some place him in the 2nd century A.D., others in the 4th. He abridged a monumental work which would otherwise have been lost, the *Philippic Histories* by Pompeius Trogus, a Roman historian of Gallic origin living in the Augustinian era. This Universal History in 44 books compiled information from different Greek sources and, as a result, it should contain a combination of all traditions relative to one given theme. It is evidently difficult to know what Justin preserved or discarded from the original, but in the abridgement he presents, the different versions are fairly obvious. Here is the unabridged version of his story (Book III, chapter 4):

Thanks to its morals, Sparta was soon so strong that when they declared war on the Messenians who had outraged their daughters during a ceremonial sacrifice, they swore by the most fearsome oath not to return home before taking Messenia, so much did they count on their strength or luck. This was the beginning of dissension between Greeks and the cause of an internal war. But they were mistaken in their predictions and remained six years outside the walls of the city. Recalled by the complaints of their wives, who were tired of such a long widowhood, they feared that this determination to wage war would be more fatal to them than for the Messenians. Indeed, they compensated for the losses that war caused amongst the youth through the fertility of their women, while combat caused the Spartans continual losses that the fertility of their wives, in the absence of their husbands, could not recoup. Consequently, they chose young men from relief troops after the pledging of the oath and sent them back to Sparta with permission to indiscriminately mate with all women, convinced they would conceive more quickly if each of them tried with several men. The children born as a result of this policy were called Partheniae, as a reminder of the dishonour of their mothers. When reaching the age of thirty, fearing destitution, because none of them had a father they could hope to inherit from, they took Phalantus, the son of Aratus, who had advised the Spartans to send the youth back to father children, as their leader. As they owed their very existence to the advice of the father, they hoped to find support for their expectations and their honour in the son.
Without taking leave of their mothers, who they regarded as tainted with the infamy of adultery, they left in search of a settlement, and after being tossed about for a long time in diverse adventures, they seized the citadel of Tarentum, captured the former inhabitants and established

themselves in the town. But after many years, Phalantus, their leader, was banished by sedition. He retired to Brundusium, where the Tarentinians had taken refuge after being chased from their country. In his final moments, he persuaded them to grind his bones and final remains and to scatter them in secret in the agora of Tarentum because, he told them, the oracle at Delphi had declared that they could recover their homeland through such action. Believing that he had revealed the destiny of his fellow citizens to avenge himself, they followed his recommendations, but the prophecy had an entirely contrary meaning. The god had actually promised perpetual possession and not the loss of the town, and this is how, through the counsel of the exiled leader and the intervention of their enemies, the possession of Tarentum was forever assured to the Partheniae. In memory of this, they awarded Phalantus divine honours.

The narrative is organised around two distinct periods: the war between Spartans and Messenians, and the departure of the Partheniae and their difficult occupation of Tarentum[1]. There is, of course, a very close unity between the two periods. Firstly, due to the filiation of Aratus and Phalantus, and secondly, due to the logical relation which made the episode of the adulterous coupling the cause of the departure of the Partheniae. The first part is evidently dependent on the local tradition of Sparta because it revolves around the war against the Messenians – an episode regarded as historical – and the inferior status of the Partheniae in relation to the *homoioi* or citizens with full rights. The context is therefore quite easily identified here.

The term 'Partheniae' is in itself interesting, because it conjugates the masculine of the article with the feminine form of the noun. This formation is a product of the rites of symbolic inversion linked with the initiation practices which structured Spartan society. The most well known is the *crypteia*, which allowed the passage from the ephebe class to that of adult citizens. It is clear that the Partheniae represented a social category that could not acquire citizenship because firstly of their fathers who, not being bound by the oath, were not fully-fledged warriors and therefore could not transmit complete citizenship, and secondly, because of the infamy of adultery as underlined in Justin's account. We also know that in Spartan society, the possession of a *kleros* that allowed contribution to the *syssitia* was a condition of citizenship. The Partheniae could not receive *kleros*, since they were of unknown fathers. Although Justin put the economic aspect in the foreground – they feared destitution – in a strictly Spartan context, the handicap was mainly political. The real problem of the Partheniae was that they could not attain full rights of citizenship, and their only remaining hope was to leave and form another city. Their departure was also a condition for the proper functioning of Spartan society, where the number of inferiors could not be allowed to increase without endangering the very status of the *homoioi*.

The first episode that awaited the Partheniae was war. In a rare occurrence, they did not found a new town, but took an indigenous city by force. The war episode and military victory constituted the first stage of reinstated citizenship, as the Partheniae had to first prove they were capable of being real warriors. It is interesting to note that in other traditions, the oracle of Delphi, who was consulted before the departure of the colonists, expresses itself in these terms:

Here: I offer you Satyrion as a gift
And also allow you to people the region
Of lush Tarentum, and to be the plague
That must wreak havoc on the Iapygian[2].

Installation in Tarentum, or the foundation process, is therefore presented as the last episode that terminated a crisis caused by the estrangement of a whole generation. We have here the three characteristic moments of rites of passage with inversion of status and exile from the original community, the phase of wandering and banishment, and then the acquisition of a new status, the foundation in this case equating to a process of integration. If it is possible for the rites of initiation to furnish a paradigm for foundation stories, it is because the two phenomena can be described in accordance with the same sequence.

However, this scenario is not the only one. Justin's story also integrates another event: that of the banishment of Phalantus and his return to the agora of Tarentum by means of his dispersed ashes. The action unfolded as two parallels: after the Partheniae had to leave Sparta, the exile of the founding father having to leave Tarentum to take refuge at Brundusium seems to be the same ordeal repeated. Therefore, a new etiological story is brought into play in a context which is no longer that of Sparta but of Tarentum in its relations with the locals. It is very likely that Justin follows the Tarentum tradition here. This story was not tacked on to the preceding one. Justin's text is skilfully constructed and only comes to an end with the death of Phalantus, whereas it began with his father Aratus. The latter originated the Partheniae, and the son, assuming his father's responsibility, as was the case in archaic societies, had to put an end to the Partheniae. The father had created inferior citizens who had to live in exile and the son had to durably establish fully-fledged citizens. But why was this new story necessary?

In actual fact, the first episode restores the Partheniae to their status of authentic warriors and accomplished adults entitled to claim full citizenship. They are in a position to found a city, but the capture of Tarentum does not amount to a real foundation. Rather, it is an act of war which in itself does not justify the appropriation of a territory, and that is why they needed another rite to secure the foundation of the city on a long term basis. This rite did not appear to be a Greek rite, but an indigenous one. Indeed, incinerating corpses and dispersing the ashes was not a Greek funeral custom. This is why, since its origin, the Tarentum necropolis has only provided burial tombs. On the other hand, it seems that this was the practice peculiar to the neighbouring Iapygian population, also called Messapians. In fact, archaeological research in their territory has not found any burial sepulchre before the 6th century B.C., a date when, according to other evidence such as the use of the Tarentum alphabet or the Greek mythological scenes on representative vases, Hellenic influence began to impact on local culture. Messapian habitats had existed from at least the 8th century. If the necropolises left no trace, it is because there was not any burial, which confirms the rite of incineration and dispersion of ashes.

It is therefore necessary to wonder why the myth needs to resort to non-Greek practices. In actual fact, Phalantus' stratagem to secure the foundation of his town was to translate the Greek routine of the foundation ritual into an indigenous version. The Greek version envisages the institution of worship of the founding father with a tomb in the agora. At the end of the text, the worship is well-established – the sign itself of an authentic foundation – but through a dispersion of ashes that refers to an indigenous ritual. Therefore, the indigenous ritual serves as mediation to restore the Greek heroic figure. It is at this point that the reference to the oracle of Delphi is made, without which there is no authenticated colonisation. Normally, in these stories, the oracle intervenes earlier, before the colonists depart for their new destination. One finds the figure of the cunning and clairvoyant hero capable of understanding the enigma of the oracle, a feature common to all founding fathers, but what is original is that the oracle makes the indigenous people intervene for its fulfilment. In other words, one has the impression that it was the indigenous people themselves who founded the Greek city by conceding their land in spite of themselves, seeing that they had been fooled by Phalantus who deceived them about the meaning of the oracle. Once again, we are faced with symbolic inversions. We have an exile and barbarians, the very two faces of 'the anticitizen' which established the civic community. At the end of the text, there is clearly a return to a stable situation after a crisis phase. Phalantus, an exile and a political refugee among the indigenous peoples, comes back to his homeland and receives the worship that is due to him. But this worship can only be established once the city has really been founded. What is made legitimate here is the appropriation of indigenous land by the Greeks. The right of the victor, far too prosaic, is not enough. The Greeks could only obtain this legitimate character as a gift from the legitimate owners. Consequently, the introduction of a native funeral ritual of territorial appropriation by dispersing ashes in the agora allowed a violent occupation to become perpetual concession. This resolved the contradiction that literary traditions have preserved well – the presence of a Greek founding hero, Phalantus, along with that of a native eponymous hero, Taras. It was not easy for Greeks to assume a mixed or mingled identity. Only the myth, rooted in a very particular ethno-cultural context, allowed this.

This problem of legitimate right to the land where the colony was founded is recurrent, and all foundation narratives aim at establishing this legitimacy. Indeed, for the Greeks, only indigenousness ensured inalienable right to the land. That was valid for a metropolis, but for colonies it was difficult to claim that the colonists were returning to the land of a former homeland[3]. The most extreme case is probably that of Apollonia of Illyria. The colony was founded about 600 B.C. by colonists, led by Gylax, from Corinth and Corfu. The town was allegedly called Gylakeia, before taking the name of the god. There is no actual foundation narrative available, but an Olympia inscription on an *ex voto*, erected by the Apollonians after a victory over a neighbouring city, alludes to the foundation of the city in these terms:

"We are dedicated in memory of Apollonia, which long-haired Phoebus founded in the Ionian Sea. Those who have conquered the borders of the land of the Abantide have erected this monument here with the help of the gods as a tribute to Thronion"[4]. Pausanias's text further annotates this inscription as follows:

Religion and Mythology

the country called Abantide and the city of Thronion were part of the Thesprotie of Epirus along the Ceraunian Mountains. The Greek fleets having been scattered on their return voyage from Troy, the Locrians from Thronion, at the mouth of the Boagrios river, and the Abantes of Euboea, each with their eight ships, were swept along toward the Ceraunian Mountains. They settled there, founded the city of Thronion, and by a mutual accord gave the name Abantide to all the portion of territory that they shared. But later, they were expelled from it after having been defeated in war by their Apollonian neighbours.

Pausanias's text is very clear. The Apollonians settled in a region that did not belong to them, as the first Greeks to disembark there were the Euboeans (the Abantes), on returning from the Trojan War. This tradition is also attested to by Apollodorus:

> After the sacking of Ilion (Troy), Menestheus, Pheidippos, Antiphos, the companions of Elephenor and Philoctetes navigated in convoy up to Mimas... Elephenor, according to him, died at Troy, but his companions, who were carried away to the Ionian Gulf, settled at Apollonia in Epirus[5].

The Abantes and the character of Elephenor are well known to Homer, who mentions them in the Catalogue of Vessels.

> Those who honoured Euboea, the Abantides radiating ardour, Chalcis, Eretria and Histiaea of abundant grapes, Cerinthus on the seaside and the high citadel of Dion, those who honoured Carystus and those who honoured Styra, these were led by Elephenor, the offspring of Ares, descendant of Chalcodon, the kind-hearted leader of the Abantes. He is the one who followed the swift Abantes who had long hair at the back of his head[6].

The tradition is therefore unanimous in recognising in the Abantes, the Euboeans of Elephenor, who came to settle in Epirus in the Apollonian region after the fall of Troy.

The Olympia inscription claims that the founder of the town was not a man, heroic or otherwise, but Apollo himself. One could believe that it exists only to explain the origin of the name of the town, but the inscription also refers to the country of the Abantes, and to 'long-haired' Apollo, which calls to mind the hair of the Abantes of the *Iliad*, this connection signifying that Apollo, founder of Apollonia, is also Apollo protector of the Abantes, which is a priori paradoxical[7]. But why remember the foundation of the town by a military event that took place a century and a half later? Also, why remember that this land was that of another Greek population that had arrived there well before the Corinthians who, therefore, had no legitimate right to occupy it? The answer is in the text itself. It is Apollo himself who decided. In fact, only he could be the founder of the town. The Apollonians could not be unaware of the very solidly established tradition of a Euboean presence in the region before their arrival. Neither could they erase their Corcyra-Corinthian origin and, consequently, it was very difficult for them to justify the conquest of land to which they had no legitimate right. They had two remaining solutions. One, they claimed to be descendants of the first Trojans that arrived in the area, but this Trojan identity card had already been taken by the Molossians and the Chaonians living in Epirus and nothing connected the Apollonians to these two peoples, and two, they shifted the heavy responsibility over to a divinity. If, in addition, this god happened to be the same one that protected the conquered people and territory, there could be no better alibi!

It was in this manner that the Apollonians came to be at home on the territory of the Abantes. They even had the right to increase its size (if this was not the case, how would the gods have granted them victory?), because Apollo was home there and was the Archegete, as in the case of Naxos for the Euboeans. The tradition which keeps the memory of the name change of the colony must therefore be taken seriously. It is impossible to know when the change took place, although it was probably before the conquest of Thronion, which occurred in the course of the 5th century. This name change corresponds to a foundation myth, the echo of which is found in the Olympia inscription.

The difference between the story of Justin, who had to stage two different episodes to legitimise the foundation of Tarentum, and the three lines of the Olympia inscription, using a simple name change to justify the foundation of Apollonia, seems huge. However, it is still the myth that is at work, because it alone can feed the narrative of origins that supports the appropriation of a territory and grants durable identity.

Notes

[*] L'intégralité du texte en français est disponible sur le site: http://web.upmf-grenoble.fr/SH/Perso-Hist/Lamboley/Lamboley.html/. La traduction a été réalisée par Mme Hutchinson que je remercie personnellement.

[1] The second period is itself divided into two episodes: the capture of the village and expulsion of its inhabitants, and the exile of Phalantus and the return of his ashes.

[2] Oracle kept by Strabo (VI, 3, 2) who quoted the historian Antiochus. The Iapygia are the indigenous peoples who, in Justin's text, found refuge at Brindisi, a town situated about sixty kilometres from Tarentum on the Adriatic coast. As regards Satyrion, it concerns an Iapygian site identified by archaeological digs and located on the Ionian coast about twelve kilometres south of Tarentum.

[3] The myths of autochthony are numerous: just as with Thebes, Cadmus sowed the teeth of the local dragon in the soil from which the *Spartoi* were born (= the sown ones, those who were born from the soil) at the origin of the Thebans. As a first king, Athens had Erichthonius, who was born from the sperm of Hephaestus which had fallen on the land of Attica. Legend says that Erichthonius had a body that ended in the tail of a serpent, which is normal for creatures born from the Earth. The Spartans called themselves descendants of Heracles, whose homeland was the Peloponnese.

[4] Inscription read and preserved by Pausanias, V, 22, 2-4.

[5] Apollodorus, *Epitome* VI, 15b. The verb used by Apollodorus is *oikein*, which means "to live, reside" and not *oikizein*, which is used for colonial foundations. We are, therefore, not in a colonial context, which is normal as the episode is placed after the fall of Troy, well before the colonial period. The Abantide is, therefore, viewed as the new homeland of the Euboeans.

[6] Homer, *Iliad*, 2, 536-543.

[7] Excavations on the site at Eretria have shown that the main sanctuary of this town was consecrated to Apollo. Furthermore, the first Euboean foundation in Sicily, on the site at Naxos, was constructed under the protection of Apollo Archegete, founder of the town (Thucydides VI, 1, 3). This makes clear the importance of this divinity to the Euboean peoples.

BIBLIOGRAPHY

Corsano M., *Sparte et Tarente: le mythe de fondation d'une* colonie, "Revue d'Histoire des Religions", 196, 1979, pp.113-140.

Dougherty C., *The poetics of Greek colonization*, Oxford 1993.

Lamboley J.-L., *Légendes troyennes d'une rive à l'autre du canal d'Otrante*, in *Le canal d'Otrante et la Méditerranée antique et médiévale*, Bari 2005, pp. 15-22.

Lombardo M., *Tombe, necropoli e riti funerari in Messapia. Evidenze e problemi*, "Studi di antichità", 7, 1994, pp.25-45.

Malkin I., *Myth and Territory in the Spartan Mediterranean*, Cambridge 1994.

de Polignac F., *Mythes et modèles culturels de la colonisation grecque archaïque*, in *Mito e Storia in Magna Grecia*, Atti del trentaseiesimo convegno di stui sulla Magna Grecia (Taranto 4-7 ottobre 1996), Taranto 1997, pp. 167-187.

From Islam to Christianity: the Case of Sicily

CHARLES DALLI
University of Malta

L-istorja ta' Sqallija mis-seklu disgħa sas-seklu tnax intisġet madwar sensiela ta' ġrajjiet li bidlulha darba għal dejjem il-karattru tagħha. Sakemm ħakmu l-gżira minn idejn il-Biżantini, l-Għarab damu mis-sena 827 sas-sena 902. Il-kontroll ta' l-ikbar gżira Mediterranja tahom is-setgħa li jikkolonizzawha, u dan wassal sabiex l-ilsien, it-twemmin u l-kultura tad-dinja Għarbija rabbew l-għeruq bis-saħħa tal-klassi ġdida mexxejja u ta' parti mdaqqsa mill-popolazzjoni li waslet hekk kif il-gżira saret parti minn Dar l-Islam. Madankollu, fi Sqallija tas-seklu ħdax kien għadhom jgħixu eluf ta' nsara Griegi, kif ukoll għadd imdaqqas ta' Lhud. Il-ħakma Normanna ta' Sqallija ġabet magħha bidla kbira fil-ġerarkija politika u soċjali tal-pajjiż. Minn tmiem is-seklu ħdax il-gżira ssiehbet ma' l-Ewropa Latina, u dan nissel tibdil mill-qiegħ fl-istrutturi tal-ħajja u fl-identitajiet individwali u kollettivi ta' saffi differenti. Fis-seklu tnax Sqallija kellha sehem ewlieni fit-tfassil tas-Saltna Normanna, u l-belt ewlenija tagħha, Palermo, nbidlet minn metropoli Għarbija f'belt kapitali rjali. Dan l-istudju qasir jifli l-iżviluppi li seħħew taħt in-Normanni, u jingħaqad ma' storiċi ta' żmienna li leħħnu dubji dwar il-kwadru pożittiv ta' tolleranza reliġjuża u etnika fl-istorjografija tradizzjonali ta' Sqallija minn Ruġġieru II sa Federiku II. Minflok, qegħdin joħorġu iżjed ċari t-tensjonijiet u l-firdiet bejn komunitajiet differenti Sqallin skond twemmin reliġjuż u nisel etniku. Sa nofs is-seklu tlettax, il-popolazzjoni Musulmana ta' Sqallija kienet għebet għal kollox, bl-aħħar ftit eluf itturufnati fil-belt ta' Lucera; fil-waqt li l-kultura nisranija Griega ġiet imwarrba, u l-Għarbi baqa' mitkellem biss mill-minoranza Lhudija, flimkien man-nies ta' Malta, Għawdex u Pantellerija. L-iSqalli ta' tmiem is-seklu tlettax ftit li xejn kellu x'jaqsam ma' l-imgħoddi Għarbi tal-gżira, bħallikieku l-istorja ta' Sqallija bdiet fl-1091.

The history of high medieval Sicily bears all the hallmarks of a regional crossroads which, between the 9th and 11th centuries, exchanged hands between three major civilizations[1]. The island's political upheavals, military confrontations, social change and cultural transformations read like an index page to central Mediterranean history[2]. The fall of Muslim Palermo to the Norman conquerors in 1072 was a landmark in the high medieval wave of Latin Christian expansion across the Mediterranean world[3]. The defeat of the island's Muslim rulers was completed within twenty years of the fall of the capital city, but the last Muslims of Sicily left the island one hundred and eighty years later, towards the end of Frederick II's reign[4]. Beyond the formal political chronology, three, more or less equal, yet distinct epochs, mark the transition from Muslim to Latin Christian Sicily: 1072 to 1130, during which period the Norman conquest of the island, launched in 1060, became first a feasible reality, then a political fact consolidated with the establishment of the Regno[5]; 1130 to 1190, when the relationship between the island's Christian rulers and inhabitants and the subject Muslim populations was gradually entrenched in terms of feudal bondage[6]; and 1190 to 1250, which was marked by Muslim armed resistance, the setting up of a rebel polity under the last Muslim leader of Sicily, and Frederick II's 'extermination' of Islam[7].

Sicily's 'disengagement' from the world of Islam was lived out by a population caught in the grips of a tumultuous historical transformation which it itself had helped author. It was a transition marked by contrasting, rather than complementary, identities, which can only be reconstructed in the coarse brushstrokes permitted by a fragmentary and frequently partial documentation. In the early decades of Norman conquest, the Latin lord took his place alongside newly installed western Christian bishops in wielding power and authority over a fledgling community of settlers. Gradually these settlers emerged from the margins of Sicilian society to become the mainstream community, pushing subject Muslim populations to the edges of the social framework. For native Christian populations, most of whom were Greek speaking, social and cultural integration within the new dominant Latin environment beckoned. Cutting across linguistic boundaries, recent historiography has 'rediscovered' the Arab Christian, and the Arabic-speaking Jew of Sicily. And, in contradistinction to the inexorable decline of the native Muslim population into land bound servitude, exile or deportation, the all-powerful, foreign-born caste of 'palace saracens' take their exclusive place at the heart of the island's Norman regime, and disappear only with its downfall. Their artificially engineered identity symbolizes the predicament of non-Christian subjects faced with the choice of assimilation or relegation, to which they replied with dissimulation or rebellion.

The present survey provides an overview, rather than a comprehensive discussion, of the historiography of Sicily's transformation from a province of Dar al-Islam into a Latin Christian society[8]. Whether one agrees or not with the epithet of *terra senza crociati* [a land without crusaders][9], the island's experience constituted an important chapter in the history of military confrontations between Christian and Muslim forces extending from the Latin East to the Spanish peninsula and beyond[10]. Nonetheless, it was also part of a wider phenomenon of Latin Christian expansion across the Mediterranean world which was not to be reduced to a chronology of military victories, nor its effects confined to newly conquered territories opened up for Christian settlement and colonization at the expense of Islam[11]. According to some estimates, Frederick II deported around twenty-five thousand Muslims to Lucera in the 1220s to 1240s; these deportees made up only one-tenth of the quarter of a millions Muslims subjected to Christian rule in 1091[12]. 'Deislamicization', the other side to 'Latinization', was not simply a soldier's achievement. "Conquest, colonization, Christianization: the techniques of settling in a new land, the ability to maintain cultural identity through legal forms and nurtured attitudes, the institutions and outlook required to confront the strange or abhorrent, to repress it and live with it, the law and religion as well as the guns and ships"[13].

An outpost of the eastern Roman empire until the 9th century, the island bore the brunt of Muslim raids across the strategic sea channels separating it from the north African mainland throughout the 700s[14]. The Muslim conquest of Sicily, under way from 827, climaxed with the fall of its capital, Syracuse, in 878, but was only completed in 902 with the storming of Taormina[15]. Arab control of Sicily paved the way for its integration into Dar al-Islam. The influx of Muslim settlers from north Africa did not cancel the presence of Greek Christian and other populations, which were transformed into subject communities[16]. The island became an outpost of the Fatimid empire, governed from around 950 by emirs belonging to the Kalbite family, who transformed Palermo into the thriving capital city described by the Iraqi traveller Ibn Hawqal[17]. Muslim resistance frustrated Constantinople's vain efforts, particularly under Michael IV (1034-41), to restore Byzantine rule in Sicily, but it proved ineffective against the Norman forces empowered by the support of the Roman Church and the material resources of their southern Italian bases[18].

According to some Arab accounts of the Norman conquest of Sicily, it was one of the Muslim chiefs of the island, Ibn al-Thumna lord of Syracuse who treacherously appealed to Robert Guiscard and his brother Roger for their help against rival faction leaders[19]. The Normans had already established their control across southern Italy, and in 1059 obtained the Church's blessing for their next major venture, the annexation of Muslim Sicily. The discord among the Arabs of Sicily was no secret[20]. No central force had emerged to fill the power vacuum created by the downfall of the Kalbite emirate. Contrary to the rapid advance by the Byzantine invasion of Sicily in 1038-40, which was called off by Constantinople, the Norman conquest spanned a much longer period of three decades, between 1060 and 1090, but in the end produced a permanent regime change[21]. The island's Muslim populations, largely made up of Arabs, Berbers, and native converts to Islam, capitulated and pledged their tribute and obedience[22]. Those who could leave, apparently did so, seeking refuge in North Africa[23]. The rest were forced to live under Christian overlordship[24].

The island conquered by the Normans was a multicultural world[25]. Local Greek Christian communities, which had survived especially in north-eastern Sicily as *dhimmi* under Muslim rule, generally welcomed the new Christian rulers[26]. Perhaps the best known sign of their status as *dhimmīyūn* was their obligation to pay the *jizya*, or poll tax, and the *kharāj* or land tax. Under Arab rule there were different categories of *jizya* payers, but their common denominator was the payment of tribute as a mark of subjection to alien rule[27]. As Sicily was also home to substantial Jewish communities (about 1,500 Jewish residents in the capital alone, according to the traveller Benjamin of Tudela) who were similarly burdened by precise fiscal obligations, it was a subjection shared across religious boundaries[28]. The Latin Christian conquerors came across a vast population of *ahl al-dhimma*, made up of non-Muslim communities subjected to their erstwhile Muslim rulers. The radical change in the balance of power after 1091 transformed this reality, but it did not dissolve it. Different categories of subjection tended to merge over time, but a complex variety of factors determined the manner in which the individual would bear his burdens, and the extent to which he would be able to position himself to survive. It was the turn of the Muslim inhabitants to be subjected to 'dhimmitude', but their one-time subjects did not necessarily fare better. Although forms of bondage varied in degree and kind, in many cases the servitude of Greek villagers subjected to the feudal lordship of the principal landlord families and establishments remained a fact under Norman rule. Bondage was not limited to the non-Latin peasantry, for different categories of town dwellers were also burdened by payments and corvées. The Jewish example remained the classic one. Regarded as royal property, the Jews were denoted as *servi camere regie* (loosely translatable as servants of the Crown) and, under Frederick II, this ambiguous Latin phrase was extended to Muslim subjects at Lucera, in a clear effort to underline absolute royal authority over them.

The Norman annexation opened the way for Greek-speaking, as well as Lombard, immigrants from Norman-held lands in southern Italy, but these were joined by 'Latin' settlers from all over the Italian peninsula and beyond[29]. As early as the 1090s, the right to settle at the *castrum* of Patti was offered only to *homines quicumque sint Latine lingue*, excluding Greek and Arabic speakers[30]. But this policy could hardly have been applied across the chequered board of a conquered society. Norman policy was based on "a formula of unequal coexistence"[31]. Nevertheless, for decades the Norman creation outwardly seemed to overcome the challenges posed by its composite character. The "Kingdom of Sicily", established officially from 1130 onwards with Roger II's coronation, also comprised the whole of southern Italy[32]. The new framework of Latin Christian rule encompassed a network of communities as characterized by their diverse ethnic, linguistic and cultural identities as by their distinct religious affiliations[33]. In the 1140s, Roger II extended his overlordship across central Mediterranean waters into the eastern Maghrib, but this Latin Christian expansion was checked and reversed by 1160 when the Almohad conquest of North Africa was completed[34]. His successors William I 'the Bad' (1154-66), and William II 'the Good' (1166-89) had to face open baronial rebellions, urban revolts, as well as the enmity of emperors both east and west. Outbursts of ethnic and religious strife, denoted by chroniclers as *perturbationes*, seemed to spell the end of the mirage of Sicilian *convivencia*.

That the regime survived all of these threats testifies to the ampleness of its resources and the loyalty of its skilled servants, soldiers and administrators. As conqueror of Sicily, Roger retained large parts of the island as his personal domain, but loyal supporters were granted fiefs in reward for their services, creating a Latin feudal class. Beyond the dazzling urban spectacle of royal rule under Roger II, there evolved a feudal countryside where authority was exercised as much by the main baronial families and powerful religious establishments, as by royal governors. Nonetheless, the size of the royal domain and the efficiency of their administrative machinery guaranteed the Norman rulers the means to govern Sicily and to embark on ambitous foreign ventures.

Besides the material means which reportedly aroused the jealousy of their royal counterparts in Europe, the kings at Palermo also commanded the loyalty of some brilliant servants with colourful biographies. The emir Christodoulos, also known as ʿAbd al-Rahmān, moved from his native Calabria to serve Roger II eventually becoming his chief minister. His protegee George of Antioch started his career in the Byzantine East and Zīrid Ifrīqiya before settling in Sicily. Possibly arranging his mentor's downfall, George rose to become Roger II's chief minister, designing the royal dīwān (administration) and commanding the expeditions against North Africa[35]. Maio of Bari rose from a lowly administrative rank to become William I's 'great admiral' and chief minister, only to be assassinated by the baronial rebels in 1160. Peter, a qāʾid (leader), royal eunuch and 'palace saracen' of possible Djerban origin, commanded the fleet and acted as chief minister to Queen Margaret at William I's death until his defection to the Almohads. Another qāʾid and eunuch, the 'palace saracen' Martin, led the royal reprisal against the rebels of 1160-61, while qāʾid Richard led opposition to Stephen of Perche, archbishop of Palermo.

The royal court was characterized by a numerous caste of 'palace saracens', including eunuchs, slave-girls and concubines. Drawing their identity from their attachment to the palace, on which they were completely dependent, these saracens fulfilled diverse tasks. Some of them worked in the royal factories, kept the king's animals, ran his kitchen and formed his personal guard. A number of them advanced to top administrative posts, or were even entrusted with military command and admitted as royal familiars. Royal generosity could quickly turn to wrath at the least hint of disloyalty. A top palace saracen, Philip of al-Mahdīya, commander of an attack on Bône, was burnt at the stake at the end of 1153 According to Ibn al-Athīr, Philip was executed for showing clemency to the people of Bône, but in Romuald of Salerno's account he was accused of practising Islam in private whilst professing Christianity in public. Many palace saracens were massacred in 1161 by supporters of the rebel barons, among them a young Tancred of Lecce, an event described vividly by 'Hugo Falcandus'. Yet twenty-four years later Ibn Jubayr was astonished at discovering black Muslim slaves guarding William II, and a royal staff made up of Muslim slave-girls, eunuchs and concubines.

From the 1160s, the internal stability which had characterized much of Roger II's reign in Sicily was torn apart by baronial revolt against royal rule, and by Latin Christian attacks on Muslim communities[36]. The island's kings, Roger II, William I 'the Bad' (1154-66), and William II 'the Good' (1166-89) managed this problem in contrasting ways[37]. In the last decades of the 12th century, the island's remaining rural populations of Muslim peasants were to be found mainly serving as bondsmen on the estates of leading Church establishments and feudal landholding families[38]. The crisis of the dynastic state after the death of William II in 1189, during which Tancred's troubled tenure of the Sicilian throne was openly contested by Henry VI of Germany, was exacerbated by a large scale Muslim rebellion which broke out in 1190. A new chain of events triggered by organized resistance and systematic reprisal marked the final chapter of Islam in Sicily[39]. The Muslim problem characterized Hohenstaufen rule in Sicily under Henry VI (1194-97) and his son Frederick II (1197-1250)[40]. In the 1220s, in order to stamp out the Muslim rebellion, Frederick adopted a programmatic extermination of Sicilian Islam, marked by expulsion and forced deportation to the Apulian town of Lucera[41]. The annihiliation of Sicilian Islam was completed by the late 1240s, when the final deportations to Lucera took place[42].

The 'father of Sicilian historiography' the Dominican friar Tommaso Fazello viewed the Arabs of Sicily as foreign occupiers of rightfully Christian land. His was a prevalent opinion shared by many erudite authors both in Sicily and beyond[43]. Arabic epigrapical, numismatic, monumental, and other archaeological remains aroused antiquarian interest. This material was often included unsystematically in geographical dictionaries[44]. Nevertheless, the turning point was reached in the late eighteenth century. Much has been written about the notorious fabrication of a 'Sicilian Arab' codex by an eighteenth century Maltese forger with powerful backers at court, Abate Giuseppe Vella[45]. In reaction to Vella's inventions, the scholar Rosario Gregorio published a learned rebuttal[46]. Fortunately, the study of medieval Sicily proceeded apace, undeterred by Vella's charlatanism, in the scientific direction established by Gregorio's meticulous research[47].

Students of the island's tectonic movement from one civilization to another stand on the solid, if not altogether secure, shoulders of giants: the publication of substantial collections of narrative and administrative sources in the nineteenth and early twentieth centuries provided a vital stimulus to the island's historiography[48]. The Latin narratives include the texts of Geoffrey Malaterra, William of Apulia, Amatus of Montecassino, Romuald of Salerno, Richard of San Germano, and 'Hugo Falcandus'[49]. Scholars still rely on Del Re's edition for basic Latin narrative sources, such as Falco of Benevento's *Chronicon*, the *Gesta Rogerii Regis Siciliae* by Alexander of Telese, Niccolo Jamsilla's history of Frederick II and his children, and the *Rerum Sicularum Historia* by Saba Malaspina[50]. By contrast, there are no native Greek and Arab histories of Sicily, though the island and its affairs featured in Greek historians such as Michael Psellus and John Skylitzes, Niketas Choniates and John Kinnamos[51].

The study of Muslim and Norman Sicily still benefits from the towering achievement of the nineteenth century achievement of Michele Amari. His collection, of over one hundred texts, entitled *Bibliotheca Arabo-Sicula*, compiled principal Arabic narrative sources for Muslim and Norman Sicily like Ibn Hawqal, al-Idrīsī, Ibn Jubayr, Yāqūt, Qazwīnī, Ibn al-Athīr, al-Tījānī, al-Nuwayrī, Ibn Khaldūn, Ibn Hamdīs, and ʿImād al-Dīn[52]. Amari's corpus of texts, complemented by his ephgraphical studies, remains the major reference work, and his three-volume history of Muslim Sicily continues to command study of the period. Nevertheless, important additions have considerably expanded knowledge of these periods, including the discovery of a cosmographical treatise 'without precedent' entitled *The Book of Strange Arts and Visual Delights* composed around the mid-eleventh century[53], the poetry of Ibn Qalāqis[54], as well as the later medieval geographical dictionary of al-Himyarī[55].

It has been noted how, during the Muslim and Norman periods, there were frequent opportunities for Arabic-Greek bilingualism, while Arabic-Latin bilingual intercourse is attested in the later Norman and Hohenstaufen epochs[56]. The collection of charters in the three administrative languages of Norman Sicily by Salvatore Cusa and his students remains, to date, "an essential tool for researchers" despite containing some serious errors and the fact that the planned translations and annotations of the documents were never published[57]. These charters – forty-six in all, dating between 1093 and 1242 – were composed in Arabic, together with Greek and/or Latin. The elegant creation of the royal Dīwān, they frequently noted land grants to the new class of Latin owners, some registering the ancient boundaries (*dafātir al-hudūd*), others providing a list – a *jarīda* or *plateia* – naming the Muslim and Greek cultivators bound to the estates (*jarā'id al-rijāl*). Beyond their utilitarian purpose, they came to symbolize the Norman administration they were designed to serve[58]. These charters symbolized, in a powerful way, autocratic royal authority over all subjects making up Sicily's *populus trilinguis*[59].

For scholars who, since the days of Charles Haskins[60] upheld 'the Norman achievement' in 12th century Europe the documents were powerful reminders of a unique society created under the aegis of the Norman conquerors, marked by an exceptional multicultural coexistence. It was an achievement mirrored as much in the pragmatic adoption and application by the rulers of institutions from subject communities, as in the transmission of knowledge enabled by Sicilian translator. It was reflected as much in Roger II's *Assizes*, as in the monumental statements made by the Palatine Chapel, the Martorana, and the churches at Monreale and Cefalù. Critics of this approach do not deny the remarkable cross-fertilization which took place in Sicily – but they question its extent, and indeed its relevance beyond the palatial walls of the Norman regime, down the social strata of the island's communities[61].

Until their expulsion in 1492, the Jews of Sicily were an Arabic speaking minority with different types of contacts all over the Mediterranean world, as well as constituting a living link with the island's long gone Muslim past. Goitein's systematic investigation of their network of contacts in the Cairo Geniza documents sheds vital new light on Sicilian Jews and their country, bridging the last decades of Islamic rule and the Norman period[62]. In his comprehensive study of Sicilian Jewry, Bresc makes ample use of the Geniza material to underline the originality of these communities which remained 'anchored' in their Arabic and Norman past, whilst adopting in later medieval times the 'European' material culture of their Christian counterparts[63].

One proponent of the Norman achievement was forced to admit, "Norman and Lombard, Greek and Saracen, Italian and Jew – Sicily had proved that for as long as they enjoyed an enlightened and impartial government, they could happily coexist; they could not coalesce"[64]. Comparisons between the two insular kingdoms under Norman rulers seem tenuous at best, and recent scholarship has generally discarded the concept of a 'Norman achievement' in Europe as a historiographic tool. This historical rethinking has been marked, over the past four decades, by a remarkable increase in teaching, research, and scholarly output on Norman and Hohenstaufen history, both in Italy and abroad. For instance, the acts of the *Giornate di Studi* organized, since 1973, by the "Centro di studi normanno-svevi" at the University of Bari, form a veritable encyclopedia on the Norman and Hohenstaufen south. The ongoing publication of the Latin charters from the chancelleries of the Norman rulers in the *Codex diplomaticus regni Siciliae*[65] provides a vital tool for the study of Norman Sicily.

Royal patronage of the Church and religious establishments provided the regime with an efficient manner to legitimize an authority acquired by conquest, and to consolidate it. Count Roger, who claimed legatine powers throughout his conquered realm, established Latin bishoprics and Churches, providing them with substantial endowments. His successors emulated his example. Religious establishments became powerful agents of the feudal regime. In a famous example, King William II established Monreale Abbey in 1174 and over the next twelve years endowed it with more than 1,200 square kilometres of land in western Sicily cultivated by around 1,200 Muslim serfs who dwelled in some one hundred villages[66]. Lighter forms of Muslim serfdom – called *muls* as distinguished from the strict bondage of the *hursh* – were done away with. This 'Muslim reserve' was closely encircled from the rest of Sicily by a network of castles[67].

The Norman regime owed less to the institutions which preceded it than previously thought, although one can hardly cast doubt on its pragmatic ability to reconcile disparate elements. The very continuity between the administrative system of Muslim Sicily and the Arab clerks who staffed the Norman dīwān has been questioned. Titles and practices were consciously imported from Fāṭimid Egypt and then adapted to the local situation. By emulating the Egyptian model, argues Johns, the Norman rulers hoped to underline their royal authority in no uncertain way[68]. The pragmatic approach is also evident in the different management of territories across the Mediterranean. Contrary to 'Norman Africa', where Roger II governed the communities subjected to his overlordship via their own local Muslim leaders, the 'Palace Saracens' serving the Crown in Sicily were royal dependants, not community leaders[69]. Johns argues that all the eunuchs at court were foreign slaves, unrelated to the island's Muslim population and therefore unfettered by any obligation towards family and community. "It was their social isolation and their utter dependence upon the king, as much as the act of castration, that distinguished the eunuchs"[70].

By contrast, native Muslims of noble birth were given little political space. In 1185 Ibn Jubayr met Muhammad Abū l-Qāsim ibn Hammūd, a qāʾid in royal administration who was regarded by Sicilian Muslims as their hereditary leader. The Muslim traveller was moved to tears at ibn Hammūd's confession that he would rather be sold with his family into slavery in some foreign land, so that he might one day reach a Muslim country, than continue to bear the tyranny of the Christian ruler. "Were he to convert to Christianity", reported Ibn Jubayr, "there would not remain a single Muslim on the island, who would not do as he did"[71]. The same Arab author remarked about ibn Hammūd's wealth and generosity. The rich Muslim possessed substantial property in Palermo and Trapani, and was known for his charitable help to the poor and to pilgrims. His loyalty was convincing enough to have been employed in the royal dīwān, but there were reports that a pilgrim who had benefited from his generosity conveyed the Sicilian's appeal to Saladin to come to his brethren's help. Ibn Jubayr dismissed as false the allegation that ibn Hammūd had asked the Almohads for their aid, but it was one of the charges which led to his house arrest[72].

In the early decades of Norman rule Greek Christians 'kept the balance between Christian and Muslim on which the whole future of Norman Sicily depended'. They also helped counterbalance the claims of the Roman Church with regard to Sicily, with Nilus Doxopatrius, Archimandrite of Palermo, dedicating a treatise to Roger II in 1143 upholding the primacy of the Patriarch of Constantinople[73]. Open royal patronage of basilian communities on both sides of the Straits was matched by large-scale employment of Greeks in royal service. Greek Christians played a key role in mediating between the upper class of Latin lords and the subject populations of Muslim serfs[74].

Apart from their Christianity which they shared with the Latin ruling class, Greek Christians enjoyed a decisive strategic advantage over their Muslim neighbours. The Greek communities formed part of a much larger Greek world which extended across the Regno's southern Italian mainland, and could rely on the support of their numerous brethren. On the other hand, the Muslims of the Regno were confined to Sicily and the smaller islands (that is, before the making of Muslim Lucera), and could not appeal beyond their king and community without committing treason. It goes unsaid that the Jewish condition was even worse, for a Muslim qā'id might appeal to a Saladin, while the Jews had no one to turn to.

Faced sternly with the choice of departure or subjection to Christian rule, many Muslims will have chosen the former option, provided they were able to do so. Indeed, Muslims were prohibited from living under non-Muslim rule if they could help it. "The transformation of Sicily into a Christian island", remarks Abulafia, "was also, paradoxically, the work of those whose culture was under threat"[75]. According to Ibn Jubayr, many of William II's Arab servants were secretly Muslim and practised *taqiya*, (that is, pretending to be Christian), and Muslim slave-girls at court even managed to convert Christian women to Islam. Ibn Jubayr's testimony could not have been altogether unbiased; but his reference to sons and daughters accepting baptism to escape the authority of their Muslim parents rings true, if only with reference to teenage rebellion.

Despite the presence of an Arab-speaking Christian population, it was Greek churchmen who seemed to have attracted Muslim peasants to accept baptism. Arab converts normally adopted Greek Christian names; in several instances, Christian serfs with Greek names listed in the Monreale registers had living Muslim parents[76]. Contrary to Malta, where an Arab-speaking Christian population was created as a result of conversion from Islam, the descendants of Sicilian converts from Islam do not seem to have retained their language[77]. Nonetheless, onomastic evidence has been compiled to make the case for rural, as well as town-dwelling, Christian Arab communities[78].

How 'Greek' were the island's 'Greek Christians'? "Latin sources tended to separate 'Latin' Catholic Christians from the 'Greeks' of the Eastern church on confessional/linguistic lines", remarks Metcalfe. "As such, it was possible for the Latin sources to refer to the Christians as 'Greeks' even when some of them lived in amongst Arabic-speaking Muslim communities, and were likely to have been Arabic speakers or Arabic-Greek speakers themselves"[79]. This is not to deny that the interplay between the different eth-

Religion and Mythology

nic groups was probably too constricted by social, economic, religious and linguistic barriers to stimulate their fusion. "The immigrant Latin and indigenous Arab communities of Sicily", affirms Johns, "were separated from each other by a cultural barrier which, if anything, grew less permeable with time; and the manner in which the Greek community acted as an intermediary between the Latin and the Arab may even have increased their distance from each other"[80]. Norman success in fusing together the disparate elements of their kingdom was, at best, limited.

Christianization did not necessarily lead to Latinization, as shown by the Maltese case[81]; nevertheless, it might be retorted that the isolated southerly example of Malta is the exception which proves the rule. Moreover, it is easy to forget that Latinization was ongoing not only in Sicily, but also across the mainland half of the Regno, where Greek lost ground to 'Italian' dialects. The advance of Latinization ultimately took place at the expense of the other elements; but survival strategies were devised, including "the option of either feigning conversion or of making a social realignment that was sufficient to smudge the defining margins of one's identity and thus benefit from the protection that might offer...it was relatively easy for Muslims to slip into the guise of Arabic-speaking Christians"[82]. In other words, their response to the threat of assimilation was the strategy of dissimulation.

This strategy might guarantee individual survival, but it could not be a long-term solution. The dividing line between Muslims and Christians in Sicily became increasingly geographical in the final decades of Norman rule. 'Lombard' pogroms against Muslims had taken place since the 1160s. In the years after Ibn Jubayr's visit to Sicily, the island's Muslims were mainly confined behind an internal frontier which divided the south-western half of the island and the Christian north-east. An unfree and subjected population, Sicilian Muslims depended on the mercy of their masters and, ultimately, on royal protection. When this was removed, hell broke loose. King William's death in 1189 opened the way for widespread attacks against the island's Muslims. The author of the *Epistola ad Petrum* remarked that "it would be difficult for the Christian population not to oppress the Muslims in a crisis as great as this, with fear of the king removed" and predicted that Muslims would respond by occupying mountain strongholds[83].

History proved the anonymous author right. The turning point of 1189-90 destroyed any lingering hope of coexistence, however unequal that might have been. Henry VI's death in 1197, followed by that of his wife Constance a year later, plunged the Regno into a deep crisis. With 'fear of the king removed', to echo the author of the *Epistola*, and with Frederick II still an infant in papal custody, the Regno became a battleground for rival German and papal forces. The island's Muslim rebels sided with German warlords like Markward von Anweiler; declaring a crusade, Innocent III alleged that Markward had made an alliance with the Saracens of Sicily: "he called on their help against the king and the Christians; and so as to stimulate their spirits more keenly to the slaughter of our side and to increase their thirst, he has spattered their jaws already with Christian blood and exposed captured Christian women to the violence of their desire"[84] Yet in 1206 the same pope addressed a letter to the Muslim leaders and the whole Saracen population of Sicily urging them to remain loyal towards Frederick. By this time the Muslim's strongholds included Jato, Entella, Platani and Celso, all mentioned in the letter. Other records mention also Muslim control of Calatrasi, Corleone (taken in 1208), Guastanella and Cinisi. In other words, the Muslim revolt extended throughout a whole stretch of western Sicily. The rebel polity was led by Muhammad Ibn ʿAbbād, who called himself 'prince of believers', minted his own coinage, and sought Muslim help from abroad.

Frederick II's response to this internal challenge was determined. In a series of campaigns against the Muslim rebels, launched in 1221, the forces of the Hohenstaufen ruler faced the resolute defenders of Jato, Entella, and the other fortresses. In 1223, the first deportations to the Muslim garrison town of Lucera started in earnest. A year later, expeditions were sent against Malta and Djerba, to establish royal control and prevent their Muslim populations from helping the rebels. Frederick II Hohenstaufen "was not a Sicilian, nor a Roman, nor a German, nor a *mélange* of Teuton and Latin, still less a semi-Muslim: he was a Hohenstaufen and a Hauteville"[85]. The chronichler Matthew Paris famously described him as "stupor quoque mundi et immutator mirabilis", or 'wonder of the world and its astonishing transformer'. It befell him, as *immutator mundi*, to sever the roots of Sicilian Islam and reclaim the legacy of its Norman conquerors.

Sicily's total 'Christianization' would almost seem, from the vantage point of historical hindsight, a foregone conclusion. Nevertheless, cautioned by the evidence, one realizes that its character need not have been so all-embracing, its conclusion so rapid, its legacy of irreversible change so everlasting, but for the extraordinary conjuncture of events which trapped the islanders of the *populus trilinguis* in the vortex of historical change. Across the island, individual and collective identities were shaped and reshaped, its social fabric undone and redone. That its Christianization proved to be so final also testifies to the strength of its Latinization. It was an achievement at the expense of competing cultural identities, and its price was high. By paying it, a new Latin Christian people could claim the home, if not the inheritance, of the vanquished society to which it traced its troubled ancestry.

NOTES

[1] D. Abulafia, *The two Italies. Economic relations between the Norman kingdom of Sicily and the northern communes*, Cambridge 1977, especially chapters 5-6 by John Pryor and Michel Balard respectively.

[2] D. Mack Smith, *A History of Sicily: Medieval Sicily 800-1713*, London 1968; A. Ahmad, *A History of Islamic Sicily*, Edinburgh 1975; I. Peri, *Uomini città e campagne in Sicilia dall'XI al XIII secolo*, Bari 1990; D. Matthew, *The Norman Kingdom of Sicily*, Cambridge 1992.

[3] H. Bresc - G. Bautier-Bresc (eds.), *Palermo 1070-1492. Mosaico di popoli, nazione ribelle: l'origine della identità siciliana*, Palermo 1996.

[4] M. Amari, *Storia dei Musulmani di Sicilia*, 1854-72, rev. ed. C.A. Nallino, 3 vols., Catania 1933-9; D. Abulafia, *The end of Muslim Sicily*, in J.M. Powell (ed.), *Muslims under Latin Rule 1100-1300*, Princeton 1990.

[5] G.A. Loud, *The Age of Robert Guiscard: southern Italy and the Norman Conquest*, Harlow 2000.

⁶ A. Nef, *Conquêtes et reconquêtes médiévales: la Sicile normande est-elle une terre de réduction en servitude généralisée?*, in *Mélanges de l'École Française de Rome (Moyen Âge)*, 2000; J. Johns, *Arabic Administration in Norman Sicily. The Royal Dīwān*, Cambridge 2002.

⁷ F. Maurici, *L'emirato sulle montagne*, Palermo 1987; Id., *Breve storia degli arabi in Sicilia*, Palermo 1995.

⁸ H. Bresc, *La formazione del popolo siciliano*, in *Tre millenni di storia linguistica della Sicilia*. Atti del Convegno della Società italiana di Glottologia (Palermo 1983), Pisa 1985.

⁹ F. Giunta - U. Rizzitano, *Terra senza crociati*, Palermo 1967.

¹⁰ J.J. Norwich, *The Normans in Sicily. The magnificent story of 'the other Norman Conquest'*, London 1992.

¹¹ H. Bresc, *Mudéjars des pays de la couronne d'Aragon et sarrasins de la Sicile normande: le problème de l'acculturation*, in *X Congreso de Historia de la Corona de Aragon: Jaime I y su epoca (Zaragoza 1975)*, 3, Zaragoza 1980; Powell (ed.), *Muslims under Latin Rule 1100-1300* cit.

¹² Abulafia, *The end of Muslim Sicily*, in Powell (ed.), *Muslims under Latin Rule 1100-1300* cit., p. 104; Peri, *Uomini città e campagne in Sicilia* cit., p. 160.

¹³ R. Bartlett, *The Making of Europe. Conquest, Colonization and Cultural Change 950-1350*, London 1993, pp. 313-314.

¹⁴ Maurici, *Breve storia degli arabi* cit.

¹⁵ Ahmad, *A History of Islamic* cit.; Amari, *Storia dei Musulmani di Sicilia* cit., vol 1.

¹⁶ Amari, *Storia dei Musulmani di Sicilia* cit., vol 1.

¹⁷ Ibn Hawqal's account in M. Amari, *Biblioteca arabo-sicula*, 2 vols., Turin-Rome 1880-81, vol. 1, ch. 4.

¹⁸ Norwich, *The Normans in Sicily* cit.; Loud, *The Age of Robert Guiscard* cit.

¹⁹ Ibn al-Athīr's account in Amari, *Biblioteca arabo-sicula* cit., vol. 1, ch. 35; Ibn al-Thumna's deal with Roger of Hauteville, dated 1052 by al-Athīr, at pp. 447-448.

²⁰ Amari, *Storia dei Musulmani di Sicilia* cit., vol 3.

²¹ Geoffrey Malaterra's account in E. Pontieri (ed.), *Geoffrey Malaterra, De rebus gestis Rogerii Calabriae et Siciliae comitis et Robertis Guiscardi ducis fratris eius*, "Rerum Italicarum Scriptores", 5/1, Bologna 1927-28; K.B. Wolf (trans), *The Deeds of Count Roger of Calabria and Sicily and of His Brother Duke Robert Guiscard by Geoffrey Malaterra*, Ann Arbor 2005.

²² Amari, *Storia dei Musulmani di Sicilia* cit., vol 3; Malaterra, books 3-4; L. Gatto, *Sicilia Medievale*, Rome 1992.

²³ Abulafia, *The end of Muslim Sicily* cit.; A. Nef, *Géographie religieuse et continuité temporelle dans la Sicile normande (XIe-XIIe siècles): le cas des évêchés*, in P. Henriet (ed.), *À la recherche de légitimités chrétiennes - Représentations de l'espace et du temps dans l'Espagne médiévale (IXe-XIIIe siècles) (Madrid 2001)*, Lyon 2003.

²⁴ A. Nef, *Conquêtes et reconquêtes médiévales: la Sicile normande est-elle une terre de réduction en servitude généralisée?*, in *Mélanges de l'École Française de Rome (Moyen Âge)*, Rome 2000.

²⁵ Giunta - Rizzitano, *Terra senza crociati* cit.; A. Nef, *Fortuna e sfortuna di un tema: la Sicilia multiculturale*, in F. Benigno - C.Torrisi (eds.), *Rappresentazioni e immagini della Sicilia tra storia e storiografia*, Atti del Convegno di Studi, Caltanissetta-Rome, 2003.

²⁶ V. von Falkenhausen, *Il monachesimo greco in Sicilia*, in C.D. Fonseca (ed.), *La Sicilia rupestre nel contesto delle civiltà mediterranee*, vol 1, Lecce 1986; J. Johns, *The Greek church and the conversion of Muslims in Norman Sicily?*, "Byzantinische Forschungen", 1995.

²⁷ Johns, *Arabic Administration* cit., pp. 56-7, pp. 146-147.

²⁸ S.D. Goitein, *Sicily and southern Italy in the Cairo Geniza documents*, "Archivio Storico per la Sicilia Orientale", 67, 1971; M. Gil, *Sicily 827-1072, in the light of the Geniza documents and parallel sources*, in *Italia Judaica. Gli ebrei in Sicilia sino all'espulsione del 1492 (Palermo 1992)*, Rome 1995; N. Bucaria, *Sicilia Judaica*, Palermo 1996; H. Bresc, *Arabes de langue, Juifs de religion: L'évolution du judaïsme sicilien dans l'environnement latin, XIIe-XVe siècles*, Paris 2001.

[29] H. Bresc, *Féodalité coloniale en terre d'Islam. La Sicile (1070-1240)*, in *Structures féodales et féodalisme dans l'Occident méditerranéen (Xe-XIIIe siècles): Bilan et perspectives de recherches*, Rome 1978; Bresc, *La formazione del popolo siciliano* cit.; H. Houben, *Normanni fra Nord e Sud. Immigrazione e acculturazione nel Medioevo*, Rome 2003.

[30] A. Metcalfe, *Muslims and Christians in Norman Sicily. Arabic speakers and the end of Islam*, London 2003, pp. 78-79.

[31] Maurici, *Breve storia degli arabi* cit.

[32] Matthew, *The Norman Kingdom* cit.; H. Houben, *Roger II of Sicily. A Ruler between East and West*, Cambridge 2002.

[33] E. Jamison, *Admiral Eugenius of Sicily. His life and work and the authorship of the 'Epistola ad Petrum' and 'Historia Hugonis Falcandi Siculi'*, London 1957; H. Houben, *Mezzogiorno Normanno-Svevo. Monasteri e castelli, ebrei e musulmani*, Naples 1996.

[34] D. Abulafia, *The Norman kingdom of Africa and the Norman expedition to Majorca and the Muslim Mediterranean*, in R. Allen Brown (ed.), *Anglo-Norman Studies 7. Proceedings of the Battle Conference 1984*, London 1985; J. Johns, *Malik Ifrīqiya: the Norman kingdom of Africa and the Fātimids*, "Libyan Studies", 1987.

[35] L-R. Ménager, *Amiratus – Ἀμηρᾶς. L'émirat et les origines de l'amirauté (XIe – XIIe siècles)*, Paris 1960.

[36] *Hugo Falcandus* in G.B. Siragusa (ed.), *'Hugo Falcandus', La Historia o Liber de Regno Sicilie e la Epistola ad Petrum Panormitane Ecclesie Thesaurarium*, in *Fonti per la Storia d'Italia*, Rome 1897, 22 and G.A. Loud - T. Wiedemann (trans.), *The History of the Tyrants of Sicily by 'Hugo Falcandus' 1154-69*, Manchester 1998; Abulafia, *The end of Muslim Sicily* cit.; Maurici, *Breve storia degli arabi* cit.

[37] R.J.C. Broadhurst (trans.), *Ibn Jubayr, The travels of Ibn Jubayr*, London 1952.

[38] Bresc, *Féodalité coloniale* cit.; J. Johns, *The Monreale Survey: Indigenes and invaders in medieval west Sicily*, in C.Malone - S.Stoddart (eds.), *Papers in Italian Archaeology IV. The Cambridge Conference*, vol. 4, Oxford 1985; A. Nef, *Anthroponomie et jarā'id de Sicile: Une approche renouvelée de la structure sociale des communautés arabo-musulmanes de l'île sous les normands*, in M. Bournin - J-M. Martin - F. Menant (eds.), *L'Anthroponomie: document de l'histoire sociale des mondes méditerranéens médiévaux*, in *Mélanges de l'École Française de Rome (Moyen Âge)*, 108/2, Rome 1996.

[39] Maurici, *L'emirato sulle montagne* cit.

[40] D. Abulafia, *Frederick II: a medieval emperor*, London 1988.

[41] P. Egidi, *Codice Diplomatico dei Saraceni di Lucera*, Rome 1917; Abulafia, *The end of Muslim Sicily* cit.; D. Abulafia, *Monarchs and Minorities in the Christian Western Mediterranean around 1300: Lucera and its Analogues*, in S.L. Waugh - P.D. Diehl (eds.), *Christendom and its Discontents. Exclusion, Persecution and Rebellion, 1000-1500*, Cambridge 1996.

[42] Maurici, *Breve storia degli arabi* cit.; A.T. Luttrell, *The Making of Christian Malta: From the Early Middle Ages to 1530*, Aldershot 2002.

[43] T. Fazello, *De Rebus Siculis Decades Duae*, Palermo 1558; G.F. Abela, *Della Descrittione di Malta*, Malta 1647; R. Pirro, *Sicilia Sacra*, 2 vols, rev. ed. A. Mongitore, Palermo 1733.

[44] G. Bellafiore, *Architettura in Sicilia nelle età islamica e normanna, 827-1194*, Palermo 1990; A. Molinari, *La Sicilia islamica: riflessioni sul passato e sul futuro della ricerca in campo archeologico*, in *Mélanges de l'École Française de Rome (Moyen Âge)*, 116/1, Rome 2004; F. D'Angelo, *La ceramica islamica in Sicilia, archeologico*, in *Mélanges de l'École Française de Rome (Moyen Âge)*, 116/1, Rome 2004.

[45] G. Vella, *Codice diplomatico di Sicilia sotto il governo degli Arabi*, Palermo 1789-92; A. Baviera Albanese, *L'arabica impostura*, Palermo 1978.

[46] R. Gregorio, *Rerum arabicarum quae ad historiam siculam spectant ampia collectio*, Palermo 1790.

[47] R. Gregorio, *Considerazioni sopra la storia di Sicilia dai tempi normanni sino ai presenti*, 6 vols., Palermo 1805-16.

[48] V. D'Alessandro, *I parenti scomodi. Fra storici e storie*, Palermo 2005.

[49] E. Pontieri (ed.), *Geoffrey Malaterra, De rebus gestis Rogerii Calabriae et Siciliae comitis et Robertis Guiscardi ducis fratris eius*, "Rerum Italicarum Scriptores", 5/1, Bologna 1927-8 and K.B. Wolf (trans.), *The Deeds of Count Roger of Calabria and Sicily and of His Brother Duke Robert Guiscard by Geoffrey Malaterra*, Ann Arbor 2005; M. Mathieu (ed.), *William of Apulia, La Geste de Robert Guiscard*, Palermo 1961; V. De Bartholomaeis (ed.), *Amatus of Montecassino, Storia dei Normanni*, "Fonti per la Storia d'Italia", 76, *Mélanges de l'École Française de Rome (Moyen Âge)*, 1935; C.A. Garufi (ed.), *Romuald of Salerno, Chronicon*, "Rerum Italicarum Scriptores", 7/1, 1914-35; Id. (ed.), *Richard of San Germano, Chronicon*, "Rerum Italicarum Scriptores", 7/2, 1937-8; Siragusa (ed.), *'Hugo Falcandus'* cit. and Loud - Wiedemann (trans.), *The History of the Tyrants* cit.

[50] G. Del Re, *Cronisti e scrittori sincroni napoletani editi e inediti*, 2 vols., Naples 1845-1868.

[51] E. Jamison, *Admiral Eugenius of Sicily. His life and work and the authorship of the 'Epistola ad Petrum' and 'Historia Hugonis Falcandi Siculi'*, London 1957; F. Giunta, *Bizantini e bizantinismo nella Sicilia Normanna*, Palermo 1974.

[52] Amari, *Storia dei Musulmani* cit.

[53] Johns, *Arabic Administration* cit.; Id., *Una nuova fonte per la geografia e la storia della Sicilia dell'XI secolo. Il Kitāb Ġarā'ib al-Funūn wa- Mulah al-ʿUyūn*, in *Mélanges de l'École Française de Rome (Moyen Âge)*, 116/1, Rome 2004. The manuscript is now kept at the Bodleian Library, Oxford.

[54] A. De Simone, *Splendori e misteri di Sicilia in un'opera di Ibn Qalāqis*, Messina 1996.

[55] A. De Simone, *La descrizione dell'Italia nel Rawd al-Miʿtār di al-Himyarī*, Mazara del Vallo 1984; Id., *Nella Sicilia 'araba' tra storia e filologia*, Palermo 1999.

[56] Metcalfe, *Muslims and Christians* cit., p. 180.

[57] S. Cusa, *I diplomi greci e arabi di Sicilia*, 2 vols., Palermo 1868-82; Metcalfe, *Muslims and Christians* cit., pp. 221-224; Johns, *Arabic Administration* cit., pp. 7-8.

[58] H. Takayama, *The Administration of the Norman Kingdom of Sicily*, Leiden 1993; Johns, *Arabic Administration* cit.

[59] The phrase was used by Peter of Eboli in *Carmen de rebus Siculis*: Johns, *Arabic Administration* cit., pp. 284-300; Peri, *Uomini città e campagne in Sicilia* cit., pp. 63-71.

[60] C.H. Haskins, *The Normans in European history*, Boston-New York 1915.

[61] G.A. Loud, *How "Norman" was the Norman Conquest of southern Italy?*, "Nottingham Medieval Studies", 1981; Id., *The Gens Normannorum. Myth or reality?*, in R.A. Brown (ed.), *Proceedings of the Fourth Battle Conference on Norman Studies*, Woodbridge 1982.

[62] S.D. Goitein, *A Mediterranean Society. The Jewish Communities of the Arab World as portrayed in the documents of the Cairo Geniza*, 6 vols., Berkeley-Los Angeles-London 1967-93; Goitein, *Sicily and southern Italy in the Cairo* cit.

[63] Bresc, *Arabes de langue, Juifs de religion* cit.

[64] Norwich, *The Normans in Sicily* cit., p. 751.

[65] H. Zielinski, *Tancredi et Willelmi III regum diplomata*, in *Codex diplomaticus Regni Siciliae*, Cologne-Vienna 1982; T. Kölzer, *Constantiae imperatricis et reginae Siciliae diplomata, 1195-98* in *Codex diplomaticus Regni Siciliae*, Cologne-Vienna 1983; C.R. Brühl, *Rogerii II regis diplomata latina*, in *Codex diplomaticus Regni Siciliae*, Cologne-Vienna 1987; H. Enzensberger, *Guillelmi I regis diplomata*, in *Codex diplomaticus Regni Siciliae*, Cologne-Vienna, 1996.

[66] Johns, *The Monreale Survey* cit.; Maurici, *Breve storia degli arabi* cit.; Id., *Arabic Administration in Norman Sicily* cit.

[67] Maurici, *Breve storia degli arabi* cit., pp. 141-142.

[68] Johns, *Arabic Administration* cit., pp. 280-281.

[69] *Ibid.*, pp. 289-292.

[70] *Ibid.*, p. 250.

[71] Broadhurst (trans.), *Ibn Jubayr* cit., pp. 358-360.

[72] Johns reconstructs his biography at pp. 234-242; for appeal to Saladin, p. 241.

[73] Norwich, *The Normans in Sicily* cit., pp. 450-452; Abulafia, *The end of Muslim Sicily* cit., p. 123.

[74] Johns, *Arabic Administration* cit., pp. 4-5.

[75] Abulafia, *The end of Muslim Sicily* cit., p. 109.

[76] J. Johns, *The Greek church and the conversion of Muslims in Norman Sicily?*, "Byzantinische Forschungen", 21, 1995; for Greek Christianity in Sicily see also V. von Falkenhausen, *Il monachesimo greco in Sicilia*, in C.D. Fonseca (ed.), *La Sicilia rupestre nel contesto delle civiltà mediterranee*, vol. 1, Lecce 1986.

[77] Abulafia, *The end of Muslim Sicily* cit., pp. 109-112; Metcalfe, *Muslims and Christians* cit., pp. 174-187.

[78] Metcalfe, *Muslims and Christians* cit.

[79] *Ibid.*, p. 178.

[80] Johns, *Arabic Administration* cit., p. 4.

[81] C. Dalli, *A Muslim Society Under Christian Rule*, in T. Cortis - T. Freller - L. Bugeja (eds.), *Melitensium Amor. Festschrift in honour of Dun Gwann Azzopardi*, Malta 2002; Luttrell, *The Making of Christian Malta* cit.

[82] Metcalfe, *Muslims and Christians* cit., p. 179.

[83] Johns, *Arabic Administration* cit., p. 285; Siragusa (ed.), *'Hugo Falcandus'* cit., p. 172.

[84] Abulafia, *Frederick II* cit., p. 99.

[85] *Ibid.*, p. 439.

BIBLIOGRAPHY

Abdul-Wahab H.H. - Dachraoui F., *Régime foncier en Sicile aux IXe-Xe siècles*, in *Etudes d'Orientalisme dédiées à la mémoire de Lévi-Provençal*, vol. 2, Paris 1962, pp. 401-444.

Abela G.F., *Della Descrittione di Malta*, Malta 1647.

Abulafia D., *The two Italies. Economic relations between the Norman kingdom of Sicily and the northern communes*, Cambridge 1977.

Id., *The Norman kingdom of Africa and the Norman expedition to Majorca and the Muslim Mediterranean*, in Allen Brown R. (ed.), *Anglo-Norman Studies 7. Proceedings of the Battle Conference 1984*, London 1985, pp. 26-49.

Id., *Frederick II: a medieval emperor*, London 1988.

Id., *The end of Muslim Sicily*, in Powell J.M. (ed.), *Muslims under Latin Rule 1100-1300*, Princeton 1990, pp. 103-133.

Id., *Ethnic variety and its implications: Frederick II's relations with Jews and Muslims*, in Tronzo W. (ed.), *Intellectual Life and the Court of Frederick II Hohenstaufen*, Washington D.C. 1994, pp. 213-26.

Id., *Monarchs and Minorities in the Christian Western Mediterranean around 1300: Lucera and its Analogues*, in Waugh S.L. - Diehl P.D. (eds.), *Christendom and its Discontents. Exclusion, Persecution and Rebellion, 1000-1500*, Cambridge 1996, pp. 234-263.

Id. (ed.), *The Mediterranean in History*, London 2003.

Id., *The Italian Other: Greeks, Muslims, and Jews*, in Abulafia D. (ed.), *Italy in the Central Middle Ages*, Oxford 2004, pp. 215-236.

Agius D., *Siculo Arabic*, London-New York 1996.

Ahmad A., *A History of Islamic Sicily*, Edinburgh 1975.

Amari M., *Storia dei Musulmani di Sicilia*, 1854-1872, rev. ed. Nallino C.A., 3 vols., Catania 1933-39.

Id., *Biblioteca arabo-sicula*, 2 vols., Turin-Rome 1880-1881.

Arezzo C.M., *De situ insulae Siciliae libellus*, Messina 1542.

Bartlett R., *The Making of Europe. Conquest, Colonization and Cultural Change 950-1350*, London 1993.

Baviera Albanese A., *L'arabica impostura*, Palermo 1978.

Bellafiore G., *Architettura in Sicilia nelle età islamica e normanna, 827-1194*, Palermo 1990.

Bresc H., *Pantelleria entre l'Islam et la chrétienté*, "Cahiers de Tunisie", 19, 1971, pp. 105-127.

Id., *Féodalité coloniale en terre d'Islam. La Sicile (1070-1240)*, in *Structures féodales et féodalisme dans l'Occident méditerranéen (Xe-XIIIe siècles): Bilan et perspectives de recherches*, Rome 1978, pp. 631-647.

Id., *Mudéjars des pays de la couronne d'Aragon et sarrasins de la Sicile normande: le problème de l'acculturation*, in *X Congreso de Historia de la Corona de Aragon: Jaime I y su epoca (Zaragoza 1975)*, 3, Zaragoza 1980, pp. 51-60.

Id., *La formazione del popolo siciliano*, in *Tre millenni di storia linguistica della Sicilia*, Atti del Convegno della Società italiana di Glottologia (Palermo 1983), Pisa 1985, pp. 243-265.

Id., *Politique et société en Sicile, XIIe-XVe siècles*, Aldershot 1990.

Id., *Arabes de langue, Juifs de religion: L'évolution du judaïsme sicilien dans l'environnement latin, XIIe-XVe siècles*, Paris 2001.

Bresc H. - Bautier-Bresc G. (eds.), *Palermo 1070-1492. Mosaico di popoli, nazione ribelle: l'origine della identità siciliana*, Palermo 1996.

Bresc H. - Nef A., *Les Mozarabes de Sicile (1100-1300)* in Cuozzo E. - Martin J.-M. (eds.), *Cavalieri alla conquista del Sud. Studi sull'Italia normanna in memoria di Léon–Robert Ménager*, Bari 1998, pp. 134-156.

Brett M., *Ibn Khaldun and the Medieval Maghrib*, Aldershot 1999.

Broadhurst R.J.C. (trans.), *Ibn Jubayr, The travels of Ibn Jubayr*, London 1952.

Brühl C.R., *Diplomi e cancelleria di Ruggero II*, Palermo 1983.

Id., *Rogerii II regis diplomata latina*, in *Codex diplomaticus Regni Siciliae*, Cologne-Vienna 1987.

Bucaria N., *Sicilia Judaica*, Palermo 1996.

Caracausi G., *Arabismi medievali di Sicilia*, Palermo 1983.

Id., *Lessico Greco della Sicilia e dell'Italia Meridionale (secoli X-XIV)*, Palermo 1990.

Id., *Dizionario Onomastico della Sicilia. Repertorio storico-etimologico di nomi di famiglia e di luogo*, 2 vols., Palermo 1993.

Caspar E.L.E., *Roger II (1101-1154) und die Gründung der normannisch-sicilischen Monarchie*, Darmstadt 1963.

Chalandon F., *Histoire de la domination normande en Italie et en Sicile*, 2 vols., Paris 1907.

Cuozzo E. - Martin J.-M. (eds.), *Cavalieri alla conquista del Sud. Studi sull'Italia normanna in memoria di Léon–Robert Ménager*, Bari 1998.

Cusa S., *I diplomi greci e arabi di Sicilia*, 2 vols., Palermo 1868-82.

Dalli C., *A Muslim Society Under Christian Rule*, in Cortis T. - Freller T. - Bugeja Lino (eds.), *Melitensium Amor. Festschrift in honour of Dun Gwann Azzopardi*, Malta 2002, pp. 37-56.

D'Alessandro V., *Storiografia e politica nell'Italia Normanna*, Naples 1978.

Id., *I parenti scomodi. Fra storici e storie*, Palermo 2005.

D'Angelo F., *La ceramica islamica in Sicilia*, in *Mélanges de l'École Française de Rome (Moyen Âge)*, 116/1, Rome 2004, pp. 129-143 .

De Bartholomaeis V. (ed.), *Amatus of Montecassino, Storia dei Normanni*, "Fonti per la Storia d'Italia", 76, 1935.

De Simone A., *Palermo nei geografi e viaggiatori arabi del medioevo*, "Studi Maghrebini", 2, 1971, pp. 128-189.

Id., *Spoglio antroponomico delle giaride arabo-greche dei diplomi editi da Salvatore Cusa*, Roma 1979.

Id., *La descrizione dell'Italia nel Rawd al-Miʿṭār di al-Himyarī*, Mazara del Vallo 1984.

Id., *Salvatore Cusa arabista siciliano del XIX secolo*, in *La conoscenza dell'Asia e dell'Africa in Italia nei secoli XVIII e XIX*, vol. 1, Naples 1984, pp. 593-617.

Id., *I diplomi arabi di Sicilia*, in *Giornata di studio: testimonianze degli arabi in Italia*, Rome 1988, pp. 57-75.

Id., *Splendori e misteri di Sicilia in un'opera di Ibn Qalāqis*, Messina 1996.

Id., *Nella Sicilia 'araba' tra storia e filologia*, Palermo 1999.

Id., *Ancora sui "villani" di Sicilia: alcune osservazioni lessicali*, in *Mélanges de l'École Française de Rome (Moyen Âge)*, 116/1, Rome 2004, pp. 471-500.

Del Re G., *Cronisti e scrittori sincroni napoletani editi e inediti*, 2 vols., Naples 1845-1868.

Delogu P., *I Normanni in Italia. Cronache della conquista del regno*, Naples 1984.

Egidi P., *Codice Diplomatico dei Saraceni di Lucera*, Rome 1917.

Enzensberger H., *Guillelmi I regis diplomata*, in *Codex diplomaticus Regni Siciliae*, Cologne-Vienna, 1996.

Falkenhausen V. von, *Il monachesimo greco in Sicilia*, in Fonseca C.D. (ed.), *La Sicilia rupestre nel contesto delle civiltà mediterranee*, vol. 1, Lecce 1986, pp. 135-174.

Fazello T., *De Rebus Siculis Decades Duae*, Palermo 1558.

Garufi C.A. (ed.), *Romuald of Salerno, Chronicon*, in *Rerum Italicarum Scriptores*, 7/1, Città di Castello - Bologna 1914-35.

Id. (ed.), *Richard of San Germano, Chronicon*, in *Rerum Italicarum Scriptores*, 7/2, Bologna 1937-38.

Gatto L., *Sicilia Medievale*, Rome 1992.

Gil M., *Sicily 827-1072, in the light of the Geniza documents and parallel sources*, in *Italia Judaica. Gli ebrei in Sicilia sino all'espulsione del 1492 (Palermo 1992)*, Rome 1995, pp. 96-171.

Giunta F., *Bizantini e bizantinismo nella Sicilia Normanna*, Palermo 1974.

Giunta F. - Rizzitano U., *Terra senza crociati*, Palermo 1967.

Goitein S.D., *A Mediterranean Society. The Jewish Communities of the Arab World as portrayed in the documents of the Cairo Geniza*, 6 vols., Berkeley-Los Angeles-London 1967-93.

Id., *Sicily and southern Italy in the Cairo Geniza documents*, "Archivio Storico per la Sicilia Orientale", 67, 1971, pp. 9-93.

Gregorio R., *Rerum arabicarum quae ad historiam siculam spectant ampia collectio*, Palermo 1790.

Id., *Considerazioni sopra la storia di Sicilia dai tempi normanni sino ai presenti*, 6 vols., Palermo 1805-16.

Haskins C.H., *The Normans in European history*, Boston-New York 1915.

Houben H., *Mezzogiorno Normanno-Svevo. Monasteri e castelli, ebrei e musulmani*, Naples 1996.

Id., *Roger II of Sicily. A Ruler between East and West*, Cambridge 2002.

Id., *Normanni fra Nord e Sud. Immigrazione e acculturazione nel Medioevo*, Rome 2003.

Jamison E., *Admiral Eugenius of Sicily. His life and work and the authorship of the 'Epistola ad Petrum' and 'Historia Hugonis Falcandi Siculi'*, London 1957.

Johns J., *The Monreale Survey: Indigenes and invaders in medieval west Sicily*, in Malone C. - Stoddart S. (eds.), *Papers in Italian Archaeology IV. The Cambridge Conference*, vol. 4, Oxford 1985, pp. 215-223.

168 Charles Dalli

Id., *I titoli arabi dei sovrani normanni di Sicilia*, "Bollettino di Numismatica", 6-7, 1986, pp. 11-54.

Id., *Malik Ifrīqiya: the Norman kingdom of Africa and the Fātimids*, "Libyan Studies", 18, 1987, pp. 89-101.

Id., *The Greek church and the conversion of Muslims in Norman Sicily?*, "Byzantinische Forschungen", 21, 1995, pp. 133-157.

Id., *Arabic Administration in Norman Sicily. The Royal Dīwān*, Cambridge 2002.

Id., *Una nuova fonte per la geografia e la storia della Sicilia dell'XI secolo. Il Kitāb Ġarā'ib al-Funūn wa- Mulah al-ʿUyūn*, in *Mélanges de l'École Française de Rome (Moyen Âge)*, 116/1, Rome 2004, pp. 409-449.

Kamp N., *Kirche und Monarchie im staufischen Königreich Sizilien*, Munich 1973-82.

Kehr K.A., *Die Urkunden der normannisch-sicilischen Könige. Eine diplomatische Untersuchung*, Innsbruck 1902.

Kölzer T., *Constantiae imperatricis et reginae Siciliae diplomata, 1195-98*, in *Codex diplomaticus Regni Siciliae*, Cologne- Vienna 1983.

Lagumina B. - Lagumina G., *Codice diplomatico dei giudei di Sicilia*, 3 vols., Palermo 1884-1909.

Loud G.A., *How "Norman" was the Norman Conquest of southern Italy?*, "Nottingham Medieval Studies", 25, 1981, pp. 3-34.

Id., *The Gens Normannorum. Myth or reality?*, in Brown R.A., *Proceedings of the Fourth Battle Conference on Norman Studies*, Woodbridge 1982, pp. 104-116, 204-209.

Id., *Conquerors and Churchmen in Norman Italy*, Aldershot 1999.

Id., *The Age of Robert Guiscard: southern Italy and the Norman Conquest*, Harlow 2000 .

Loud G.A. - Metcalfe A. (eds.), *The Society of Norman Italy*, Leiden 2002.

Loud G.A. - Wiedemann T. (trans.), *The History of the Tyrants of Sicily by 'Hugo Falcandus' 1154-69*, Manchester 1998.

Luttrell A.T., *The Making of Christian Malta: From the Early Middle Ages to 1530*, Aldershot 2002.

Mack Smith D., *A History of Sicily: Medieval Sicily 800-1713*, London 1968.

Mallette K., *The Kingdom of Sicily, 1100-1250: A Literary History*, Pennsylvania 2005.

Mathieu M. (ed.), *William of Apulia, La Geste de Robert Guiscard*, Palermo 1961.

Matthew D., *The Norman Kingdom of Sicily*, Cambridge 1992.

Maurici F., *L'emirato sulle montagne*, Palermo 1987.

Id., *Breve storia degli arabi in Sicilia*, Palermo 1995.

Ménager L-R., *Amiratus – Αμηρᾶς. L'émirat et les origines de l'amirauté (XIe – XIIe siècles)*, Paris 1960.

Metcalfe A., *Muslims and Christians in Norman Sicily. Arabic speakers and the end of Islam*, London 2003.

Mira G., *Bibliographia siciliana*, 2 vols., Palermo 1873.

Molinari A., *La Sicilia islamica: riflessioni sul passato e sul futuro della ricerca in campo archeologico*, in *Mélanges de l'École Française de Rome (Moyen Âge)*, 116/1, Rome 2004, pp. 19-46.

Nef A., *Anthroponomie et jarā'id de Sicile: Une approche renouvelée de la structure sociale des communautés arabo-musulmanes de l'île sous les normands*, in Bournin M. - Martin J-M. - Menant F. (eds.), *L'Anthroponomie: document de l'histoire sociale des mondes méditerranéens médiévaux*, in *Mélanges de l'École Française de Rome (Moyen Âge)*, 108/2, Rome 1996, pp. 123-142.

Id., *Conquêtes et reconquêtes médiévales: la Sicile normande est-elle une terre de réduction en servitude généralisée?*, in *Mélanges de l'École Française de Rome (Moyen Âge)*, 112, 2000, pp. 579-607.

Id., *Géographie religieuse et continuité temporelle dans la Sicile normande (XIe-XIIe siècles): le cas des évêchés*, in Henriet P. (ed.), *À la recherche de légitimités chrétiennes - Représentations de l'espace et du temps dans l'Espagne médiévale (IXe-XIIIe siècles) (Madrid 2001)*, Lyon 2003, pp. 177-194.

Id., *Fortuna e sfortuna di un tema: la Sicilia multiculturale*, in Benigno F. - Torrisi C. (eds.), *Rappresentazioni e immagini della Sicilia tra storia e storiografia*, Atti del Convegno di Studi, Caltanissetta-Rome, 2003, pp. 149-170.

Id., *Peut-on parler de 'politique linguistique' dans la Sicile du XIIe siècle? Quelques réflexions préliminaires*, in Dakhlia J. (ed.) *Trames de langues - Usages et métissages linguistiques dans l'histoire du Maghreb*, Paris 2004, pp. 41-58.

Id., *Jalons pour de nouvelles interrogations sur l'histoire de la Sicile islamique: les sources écrites*, in *La Sicile islamique. Questions de méthode et renouvellement récent des problématiques*, in *Mélanges de l'École Française de Rome (Moyen Âge)*, 116/1, 2004, pp. 7-17.

Norwich J.J., *The Normans in Sicily. The magnificent story of 'the other Norman Conquest'*, London 1992.

Peri I., *Il villanaggio in Sicilia*, Palermo 1965.

Id., *Uomini città e campagne in Sicilia dall'XI al XIII secolo*, Bari 1990.

Pirro R., *Sicilia Sacra*, 2 vols., rev. ed. Mongitore A., Palermo 1733.

Pontieri E. (ed.), *Geoffrey Malaterra, De rebus gestis Rogerii Calabriae et Siciliae comitis et Robertis Guiscardi ducis fratris eius*, "Rerum Italicarum Scriptores", 5/1, 1927-28.

Powell J.M. (ed.), *Muslims under Latin Rule 1100-1300*, Princeton 1990.

Rizzitano U., *Storia e cultura nella Sicilia saracena*, Palermo 1975.

Romeo R. (ed.), *Storia della Sicilia*, 10 vols., Naples 1979-81.

Siragusa G.B. (ed.), *'Hugo Falcandus', La Historia o Liber de Regno Sicilie e la Epistola ad Petrum Panormitane Ecclesie Thesaurarium*, "Fonti per la Storia d'Italia", 22, 1897.

Id. (ed.), *Peter of Eboli, Carmen de rebus Siculis*, "Fonti per la Storia d'Italia", 39-40, 1905-06.

Takayama H., *The Administration of the Norman Kingdom of Sicily*, Leiden 1993.

Varvaro A., *Lingua e storia in Sicilia*, Palermo 1981.

Vella G., *Codice diplomatico di Sicilia sotto il governo degli Arabi*, Palermo 1789-92.

White L.T., *Latin Monasticism in Norman Sicily*, Cambridge, Mass. 1938.

Wolf K.B., *Normans and their Historians in Eleventh-century Italy*, Pennsylvania 1995.

Id., (trans.), *The Deeds of Count Roger of Calabria and Sicily and of His Brother Duke Robert Guiscard by Geoffrey Malaterra*, Ann Arbor 2005.

Zielinski H., *Tancredi et Willelmi III regum diplomata*, in *Codex diplomaticus Regni Siciliae*, Cologne-Vienna 1982.

The Role of Arianism in the Vandal Kingdom

EMŐKE HORVÁTH
University of Miskolc

A tanulmány a vandál állam történetére vonatkozó alapvető forrásokat az arianizmus és ortodoxia viszonyán keresztül mutatja be. Közismert tény, hogy a barbár államok közül egyedül a vandálok voltak mindvégig ellenségesek az ortodox rómaiakkal szemben. Vajon mi indította őket arra, hogy ilyen intoleráns magatartást tanusítsanak a fennhatóságuk alatt élő rómaiakkal, közülük is elsősorban a papsággal és a nemeséggel szemben. Alapvetően politikai és gazdasági jellegű indítékok húzódtak meg a vandál uralkodók intézkedései mögött. A források sok szenvedésről, rémtettről és „esettanulmányról" számolnak be, melyek alapján úgy tűnik, a vandálok kegyetlenkedéseikkel tudatosan meg akarták félemlíteni a rómaiakat. Ez az "erős kéz politikája" a nagy multú afrikai ortodox egyház jelenlétére adott kihívó válasz volt. A kis létszámú vandál nép nem tudta volna megőrizni vezető szerepét, ha nem határolódik el az Észak-Afrikában élő római lakosságtól és nem törekszik mindenáron identitásának megőrzésére. Identitásuk legfőbb kifejeződését pedig új vallásukban, az arianizmusban látták. Az arianizmus megvilágította másságukat, biztosította összetéveszthetetlenségüket a rómaiakkal. Az észak-afrikai ortodox püspökök fizikai megsemmisítésével javaik megszerzése is együtt járt. A papság mellett a nemesség is hasonló sorsra jutott, ami azt jelzi, hogy a gazdasági motívumok legalább olyan erősek voltak, mint a vallási indittatás.

The word 'Vandal' has had a long 'career' over the centuries. Since being used initially to denominate a people, it has been degraded, and gained negative attributes that qualify a certain attitude. Behind the changes in meaning are *topoi* developed in the historical literature of Roman and Byzantine authors. Later, these *topoi* became widespread and common knowledge. Inevitably, on the basis of these beliefs, the image of senseless devastation has been interwoven with the Vandals for all time. Is it fair for succeeding generations to remember the Vandals in this way? To answer this question fully, the history of the Vandals would have to be investigated from many viewpoints. However, my study will focus on one point: what was the role of religion in the development of the above mentioned beliefs and in the preservation of the true identity of the Vandals? In searching for the answer to my question, I have relied on the historiographical works from the Early Middle Ages, because recent church historical studies do not cover the viewpoints sufficiently, and only emphasize the religious intolerance of the Vandals. In my opinion, the contrast between Arianism and Catholicism was a dominant factor in the development of the identity of *gens vandalorum,* and this subject requires a thorough examination.

THE HISTORICAL BACKGROUND

Vandals founded their independent state with its centre in Carthage, North Africa. Although the Roman Empire lost a significant part of its territory to the Vandals, the Romans suffered a greater blow when the Vandals became adept seaman. After occupying Carthage and a part of the Proconsularis provinces, the Vandals obtained important strategic territories in Africa. The new territories allowed them to take the initiative against Rome. As a consequence, a new power evolved beside Rome on the Mediterranean Sea. The Vandals occupied significant islands, including Corsica, Sardinia and the Balearics, and ruled the Western part of Sicily. As each strategically important territory of the Mediterranean Sea fell under their military control, the Vandals became a more powerful enemy of the Eastern Roman Empire. A brand new situation arose for the Vandals and Romans when the Vandals settled in Africa. The Vandals were separated from the Western Barbarian Kingdoms in the course of their migration and had to face the challenge of the Roman Empire alone. Also, the Vandals' relationship with the native Berbers was ambivalent. They occasionally fought together against the Romans, but most of the time they remained enemies. The Vandals maintained their rule of Africa for one hundred years, only to disappear without trace after 534.

Africa was also significant from the perspective of Christianity for economic and other reasons. Alexandria, with its Hellenistic traditions, became one of the most important intellectual centres, and its theological debates had a powerful effect on other territories. When the Vandals appeared, the area had already become Christian, and the idea of monasticism was spreading out from Africa through Western Europe[1]. Prominent ecclesiastics like Cyprian, Fulgentius or Facundus were active in this continent, but the most notable was Augustine. His personality and works had a lasting effect on the era of the Late Antique and the Early Medieval Catholic Church. His role and importance grew beyond Hippo and the African province. He was to be a determinative personality for the Catholic Church throughout subsequent centuries. In spite of this, paganism survived, and it is well known there were still representatives of the pagan traditions in Italy and Spain in the 7th century[2].

Before the Vandals arrived on the Iberian Peninsula, they had been pagans. They were acquainted with Arianism through the Visigoths, and had become followers of Arius by the time they appeared in Africa. A conversion of religions took place between 409 and 429, a very short period, and could not have made far-reaching changes in the religious rituals for members of the *gens.*

Arianism derives from Alexandria, where Arius started to preach his subordinating thesis, for which he was excommunicated by the Canons of the Council held there in 318. Soon, many people were influenced by Arianism and, as a consequence, most of the East was divided into two factions. The quarrel became so passionate that the Roman Emperor had to mediate, and he called the first universal Council in Nicea in 325, where the ideas of Arius were, again, condemned. In spite of the condemnation, Arius' dogmas were still alive and, moreover, they reached the Germans. The Germans were acquainted with Arianism through the missionary work of Wulfila.[3] Wulfila created the Gothic alphabet and translated the Bible into the Gothic language. In other words, he created the intellectual basis of the Arian Church. According to the sources, numerous crowds were converted by his missionary activity.[4] Arianism was spread among Germans by the Goths. The Germans established their own church, where holy services were held in vernacular languages, and the ecclesiastical hierarchy was simple.

The adoption of Arianism provoked many changes. On one hand, the Vandals became closer to the Romans, and on the other, they became farther removed from them because of other changes. Although the Romans rejected paganism, it encompassed the possibility of conversion to Catholicism, and the chance of developing a Roman alliance. That is, it provided advantages the Romans could exploit. Although Arianism represented Christianity, it was considered a heretical form, and therefore radically separated the Vandals and the Romans. As the Arians were considered degraded Christans, whose religion could not be accepted by the officially Catholic Rome, a yawning gap was created between them, just as if the Vandals had remained pagans. Romans considered paganism a 'child's disease' which could be treated easily, but they regarded Arianism as a harmful infection. This 'illness' devastated the West. We think of St. Ambrose, and how he struggled against Arianism in Milan. Roman authors identified the figures of the Arian and the Catholic with the Barbarian and the Roman, respectively. The questions is, did the Barbarians consider their religion to be as important as the Romans did? Was it a conscious limitation for them? To answer these questions, we can only seek the help of the Early Medieval sources.

SALVIAN'S *DE GUBERNATIONE DEI*

To take the first step, it is worth studying the work *De Gubernatione Dei*, written by Salvian. In this book, different people are merged into one big crowd and characterized in a general manner. The author rarely mentions a *gens* by name. The monk of Lerinum, who had personally experienced the invasion of Gaul, was surprisingly indulgent, understanding and almost cordial to the Barbarians. He thought they were heretics because their knowledge was defective. They did not have a written culture, were ignorant of all literature, and knew only what they heard from their teachers[5]. They were not knowingly heretics. On the contrary, they were heretics because they were ignorant. They lived in error, but they erred with a good heart, not in hatred, but in the love of God, believing that they trusted and loved God. The above mentioned thoughts confirm the assertion that the author did not represent the Barbarians with the usual hostility, but described them as pure and uncontaminated 'savages' in an almost romantic way. The entire book emphasized the contrast between the pure morals of the Barbarians and the corrupted Romans. Salvian commented on events of the epoch when he interpreted the German attacks as divine punishment for the sins committed by the Romans. He thought Christians lived an improper life: they frequented the circus and theatre[6] which embodied pagan morals, and injustice and greed were everywhere.[7] According to him, charity should have been learned from pagans, as they believed they should live together in goodwill and purity.[8] In Salvian's opinion, the simplicity of the Barbarians was a mark of their goodwill, and he believed they were the tool of punishment in the hand of God, and that savageness and cruelty did not originate from them although they devastated the Roman Empire. According to his interpretation, the Vandals appeared in Africa as a divine punishment to stop the sins committed by the Christians.[9] It seems clear that Salvian did not share in shaping a negative image of the Vandals. On the contrary, he excused them for their behaviour against the Romans. His fundamental reason for not examining the attitudes of the Barbarians was his interest for the other side of the situation, in scourging the moral faults of the Christians. The Barbarians were important to him as a tool with which he could criticize the Romans. In counterpoint, his creation of the Barbarian image as a spiritual whip emphasized a more positive view of them. However, in spite of Salvian's own viewpoint, the Vandal state in Africa became synonymous with cruelty and savagery in subsequent historical works and public opinion.

The Works of Victor of Vita and Procopius

We should study Africa if we want to understand the conditions which evolved after the Vandals arrived. There were very few sources available on the Vandals. Our guides can be Victor of Vita and Procopius, who investigated the history of the Vandal state. Victor of Vita was a native African ecclesiastic, the Bishop of Vita. He experienced the Vandal invasion and the reign of Geiserich and Hunerich, and was, therefore, a witness to historical events. His personal experiences are recalled in his work *Historia Persecutionis Africanae Provinciae*. Procopius was a Byzantine intellectual and worked as a secretary to Belisarius, the commander of Emperor Justinian. He went to Africa, where his duty was to record the history of the Vandalic War. Based on their writings and on our knowledge of words and events, we can stress two important events which have influenced the opinions of contemporaries and succeeding generations. One of them is the devastation of the Roman towns, and the other is the Vandals relentless persecution of the Catholic Church. We can get closer to the 'riddle of the Vandals' if we examine these two subjects. If we view the first topic, we can obtain more information from Procopius. He wrote that Geiserich had the walls of every town, except Carthage, pulled down. The author not only noted the demolition itself, but commented on the events surrounding it as well. We can conclude there was no hatred or sudden anger behind the destruction of the towns: rather it was a conscious act, because Geiserich wanted to prevent further resistance from the towns, by pulling down their walls[10]. Later, this order helped Belisarius to occupy the Vandals' towns[11]. It is clear that Geiserich's guiding principles were deliberate and strategic, rather than aimless or random, before he had the walls pulled down. However, he did not think of everything, and did not count on the possibility of an external attack. Procopius noted scornfully that after the successful Byzantine attacks, Geiserich became an object of contempt when what had appeared to be wisdom turned out to be foolishness[12]. Despite such remarks, the author did not represent Geiserich as a blood-thirsty savage, but as a leader who erred in his military calculations. In his work, Procopius gave an explanation of the relationship between cause and effect which was missing from other medieval writers. On the basis of the Byzantine author, we can exempt the Vandals from charges of senseless devastation. In contrast, senseless devastation was represented as an aim in the work of Victor of Vita. According to him, the Vandals almost took delight in destroying the walls and buildings, and, as a token of their savageness, he remarks: "the former beauty of the towns cannot be deduced from what they look like now"[13]. It is strange that a clergyman counted the pulling down of the theatre in Carthage amongst the sad losses, while other clergy considered these institutions the bulwark of paganism[14]. Think of Salvian and how he spoke contemptuously of those immoral Christians who visited theatres and circuses. In all likelihood, the Bishop of Vita did not ascribe to such a love of the theatre, but was taking every opportunity to charge the Vandals with cruelty and devastation. Therefore, he was not afraid of protecting profane pagan buildings and customs. He disclosed his prejudices through this method, showing his hostility towards the Vandals. He was surely affected by the difficulties he and the other clergy met, but it is disputable whether the events took place as they were depicted in his work. Obviously, we cannot refute his work *per se,* and archaeological researchers can help to clarify the issue[15].

To explore the second event, I must briefly introduce some historical facts . The Vandals were able to occupy Carthage in 439 when Aetius' interest was captivated by the Goths and the Burgundians, resulting in a new situation in which their presence in Africa became constant thereafter. In 442, Emperor Valentinian III had no other choice but to acknowledge the Vandal domination over the occupied area which extended to the territories of the Africa Proconsularis (with Carthage), Byzacena and a part of Numidia (with Hippo Regius). With the conquest of Carthage, which played an important strategic role both in supplying corn to the Roman Empire and as a significant harbour, the Vandals were able to drive Rome into a corner and close the western part of the Mediterranean Sea. Although Roman rule included some territories in Africa, the area's most important harbour and its surroundings were under the Vandals' control, and so Rome became defenceless and threatened by extortion. At the same time, the Vandals also became defenceless, as they were surrounded by Roman and Berber enemies. There is no exact data on the population of the Vandals when they settled in Africa. Sources mention about eight thousand people, but it can be hypothesised that their number must have been insignificant in comparison to that of the Romans and the natives[16], a fact which would point to the Vandals, extreme vulnerability.

According to Victor of Vita, the army of Geiserich, after occupying Carthage, pulled the bishops out of their churches and the nobles out of their homes, forcing them to flee naked[17]. Quodvultdeus, the bishop of Carthage, and most of the priests were forced into exile. Geiserich gave away the Restituta church and the Arians received the Celerina and Scillitani basilicas as well[18]. Possidius asserted that only three churches remained in the possession of the Catholics: Carthage, Hippo and Cirta[19]. Vandals robbed the Catholic churches and took away gold and silver devotional objects, set the holy buildings on fire, and tortured, humiliated and exiled the clergy. Victor of Vita gives accounts of the horrible tortures[20]. According to Geiserich's orders, only Arians could fill court offices[21]. In 456/457, after the death of Deogratis, the Bishop of Carthage, Geiserich would not allow the bishopric to be filled. Only under the rule of his son, with the protection of Emperor Zeno, was it possible to fill this position in 480/481. As far as we know, Hunerich was crueler to the Catholics, because he used violence to force them to become Arians[22]. Those who resisted were burnt, or their tongues were cut out[23]. Finally, in 483, Hunerich issued an edict for an assembly of bishops and called upon the Catholic clergy to take part in a religious debate with the Arians[24]. This debate was held, but it was unsuccessful for the Arians because Catholic bishops kept on resisting. All these events show that, from the beginning of their settlement, the Vandals had an uncooperative attitude towards the Roman inhabitants, especially the clergy and nobles. It is obvious that the Vandals were not really interested in dogmatic issues. Rather, their guiding principle when they formed their connection with the Romans was political practicality. Their small population and limited area of rule kept them in a state of uncertainty. In spite of that, they gained a key position which gave them an opportunity for maritime expansion. The Vandals took every chance they had when crossing the sea to attack towns and seize ships which they could plunder as *pirati* on the Mediterranean. This plundering generated income for the state and, at the same time, forced Rome to realize that the Barbarians had grasped the artery of Roman wealth by controlling Eastern and Western shipping on the Mediterranean.

In investigating religious persecution, we are supported by the above mentioned works. The work of Victor of Vita assists us because, in spite of the author's bias and involvement in the events, it is a relevant and standard work. However, the influence of other writers can be seen in pieces of the text of the *Historia Persecutionis Africanae Provinciae*. I think the Vandal persecution of the bishops and nobles is an accurate representation of the epoch on the whole, albeit with some exaggeration of details which cannot always be accepted as authentic. For example, Victor of Vita described the sufferings of Romans with expressions adopted from Victor of Aquileia in the first chapter of the first book. Victor also adopted the sentences of Rufinus on the siege of Jerusalem.[25]

THE PERSECUTIONS AND THEIR AIMS

Arianism became significant in the political development of the Barbarian Kingdoms. The importance of religion was emphasized primarily by Roman authors. I believe, after Emperor Valens had let the Goths inside the *limes*, the concepts of 'outsider' and 'preventability' could no longer be linked to the Barbarians, so Romans had to change their defence strategy against them. By ending physical separation, the conflict was transferred to the spiritual sphere. Actually, the Romans gave a 'national' character to Arianism. The Germans accepted it and their states kept this character for a long time. It is the general opinion that the Barbarian Kingdoms pursued a policy of religious tolerance towards the Romans, save for some periods, disregarding the Vandals. What can the reason for the relentless cruelty of the Vandals be? If we review the assertions of the historical sources, we can verify that the Vandal rulers had an intolerant attitude primarily towards two groups: the bishops and the landowner nobles. While the state provided considerable support for Arianism, Catholicism was under strict state restrictions and forced into the private sphere. When Victor of Vita described these events, he almost always emphasized the brutality of the devastation. The fiercest persecutions took place between 440 and 490. The *Historia Persecutionis Africanae Provinciae* mentioned by name the bishops that had to suffer long exiles, torture or both. It is striking that most persecutions were endured by the bishops of religious orders. We can find the reason easily in the surviving practices in Africa, where bishops are regarded as the only fit servants of the Eucharist. They were the leaders of the communities and therefore their numbers were considerably bigger than those in the religious orders of Western Europe. The relentless retaliation against Roman clergy can be interpreted in many ways. By removing the bishops, the Vandals acquired their possessions and estates, and could also seize the valuable textiles and precious metals from the churches which they closed. In addition to economic gain, there was the more important aspect of eliminating and defacing the Roman intellectual elite. As a consequence of executions and deportations, the Romans were deprived of their intellectual leaders. They were symbolically beheaded. We could say that the Catholic Church built up a kind of mental wall around Northern Africa and then the Vandals collapsed it by removing its most important pillars, the bishops. At the same time, the danger of resistance to the Vandals was decreasing because the role of bishops in the administrative governance of the towns was determinant; removing them resulted in vacancies in those positions. We can say that the Vandals pulled down the town walls both in a physical and figurative sense, the latter being regarded as the greater loss. In addition to prompt economic profit, powerful representation of Arianism became an important fact of consciousness in the Vandal Kingdom. This does not mean that Arianism became a determinant spiritual experience for all of the Vandal people, but it does mean that the Vandal ruler was able to handle the religious question as useful propaganda. We can state, almost positively, that after twenty to thirty years of religious change, only an insignificant minority of people were alienated from pagan customs, and the new faith was represented primarily by the court. This does not mean that the elite were staunch adherents of the new religion, but that it seemed to be useful to them. They were not guided by dogma, but they persisted in their faith to the utmost for political reasons. We should not forget that the Vandals had to face a difficult Roman challenge because those territories in North Africa which were now under Vandal rule had had serious Christian traditions. These traditions inspired the Vandals to give a definitive response. Perhaps their firmness of purpose was exaggerated. Beside the desire to seize material goods, they were inspired by the constant struggle for their survival. The danger of a threatened existence developed a religion, the most important means of inheriting an identity. The Vandals did not have a written literature, but their legends and myths survived by oral tradition which could be said to confirm a consciousness of inheritance and origin. These roots of the pagan past are not appropriate when applied to Arianism. The Vandals had to find a new common bond which provided a different identity from the Romans and they managed to find it in their religion.

Notes

[1]   Hermit settlements of Sketis and Nitria acquired such a significant reputation that the fathers of the desert were visited by many western lay persons. Among them were Cassian and Rufinus who saw this area, and their experiences were recorded in their works *Collationes* and *Lausica*.

[2]   J.N. Hillgarth, *Popular Religion in Visigothic Spain*, in J. Edward (ed.), *Visigothic Spain: new approaches*, Oxford 1980, pp. 3-60.

[3]   Jordanes, *Getica*, ed. MGH AA, V, 1 53-138, p. 267.

[4]   *Ibid.*, p. 267.

[5]   Salvian, *De Gubernatione Dei*, V, 2 edited by Pauly F., Vienna 1883.

[6]   *Ibid.*, VI, 3.

[7]   *Ibid.*, V, 11.

[8]   *Ibid.*, V, 11.

[9]   *Ibid.*, VII, 13.

[10]   Procopius, *De bello vandalico*, III, V, 8, in Procopius, *Wars*, ed. Dewing, Procopius 1-5, Cambridge, Mass. 1914-1928.

[11]   *Ibid.*, V, 9.

[12]   *Ibid.*, V, 10.

[13]   Victor Vitensis, *Historia persecutionis africanae provinciae sub Geiserico et Hunirico regibus. Wandalorum*, I, 8.

[14]   See Augustine, *Confessiones*; Salvian, *De Gubernatione Dei* cit.

[15]   The basic literature on the history of the Vandal state: C. Courtois, *Les Vandales et l'Afrique*. Paris 1955.

[16]   Victor Vitensis, *Historia persecutionis africanae* cit., I, 1; Procopius, *De bello* cit.

[17]   *Ibid.*, I, 14.

[18]   *Ibid.*, I, 9; I, 15.

[19]   Possidius was the secretary of Augustine and later on he became Bishop of Hippo. He wrote the biography of Augustine. Vita Augustini, 30.

[20]   e.g. I, 37: "the servants of God were to have their feet bound behind the backs of four running horses and perish together in the thorny places of the woods, the bodies of those innocent ones, as they were dragged to and fro, being cut to pieces by the thorn bushes in the woods."; I, 33: "...strong cudgels were to be made with jagged edges like palm branches,....as these beat upon their [priest's] backs they would not only break their bones but, as the spikes bored through them, would remain inside them".

[21]   Victor Vitensis, *Historia persecutionis africanae* cit., I, 43.

[22]   Procopius, *De bello* cit., III, VIII, 3-4.

[23]   *Ibid.*, III, VIII, 4.

[24]   Victor Vitensis, *Historia* cit., II, 39.

[25]   P. Wynn, *Rufinus of Aquileia's Ecclesistical History and Victor of Vita's History of the Vandal Persecution*, "Classica et mediaevalia", 41, 1990, pp. 187-198, p. 189.

BIBLIOGRAPHY

Primary sources

Isidore, *Historia Gothorum, Wandalorum et Suevorum*, edited by C. Rodriguez, León 1975.

Jordanes, *Getica*, edited by MGH AA, V, 1 53-138.

Procopius, *Wars*, ed. Dewing, Procopius 1-5, Cambridge, Mass. 1914-1928.

Rufinus, *Historia Ecclesiastica*, PL 21.

Salvian, *De Gubernatione Dei,* edited by F. Pauly, CSEL 8, Vienna 1883.

Victor Vitensis, *Historia persecutionis africanae provinciae sub Geiserico et Hunirico regibus Wandalorum*, E. Halm, 1879

Secondary works

Catalogue of the Coins of the Vandals, Ostrogoths and Lombards and the Empires of Thessalonica, Nicea and Trebizond in the British Museum.

La marina vándala: los silingios de España [The Vandal Fleet: the Silings in Spain], Barcelona 1969.

Clover F. (ed.), *The Late Roman West and the Wandals*, Aldershot 1993.

Courtois Ch., *Les Vandales et l'Afrique*, Paris 1955.

Collins R., *Early Medieval Spain, Unity and Diversity, 400-1000*, London 1983.

Gil M.E., *África en tiempos de los vándalos: continuidad y mutaciones de las estructuras sociopolíticas romanas* [Africa at the Time of the Vandals: Continuity and Changes of the Roman Social Structure], Alcalá de Henáres 1998.

González Salinero R., *Poder y conflicto religioso en el norte de África* [Power and Religious Conflict in North Africa], Madrid 2002.

Hefele C.J., *Conciliengeschichte*, II, 2. vols., 1875.

Hillgarth J.N., *Popular Religion in Visigothic Spain*, in Edward J. (ed.), *Visigothic Spain: new approaches*, Oxford 1980, pp. 3-60.

Markus R.A., *The End of Ancient Christianity*, Cambridge 1998.

Merills A. (ed.), *Vandals, Berbers and Romans: New Perspectives on Late Antique Northen Africa*, Aldershot 2004.

Miles R. (ed.), *Constructing identities in Late Antiquity*, London-New York 1999.

Souza Ph., *Piracy in the Graeco-Roman World*, Cambridge 1999.

Thompson E.A., *The Visigoths in the Time of Ulfila*, Oxford 1966.

Warmington B.H., *The North African Provinces from the Diocletian to the Vandal Conquest*, Westport, Conn. 1971.

New Perspectives for Comparative Investigations on Identity in Protestant Missions in 18th-Century South India

Thomas Ruhland
University of Potsdam

Religiöse Gemeinschaften und die Frage nach dem Fundament ihrer Identität sowie dem Identitätsverständnis ihrer Mitglieder bilden den Kern dieses Beitrages. Ausgangspunkt dafür ist der Konflikt innerhalb des deutschen Pietismus. Das 300-jährige Jubiläum des Beginns einer organisierten protestantischen Missionstätigkeit wird genutzt, um einen Überblick über die Literatur zur Dänisch-Halleschen Mission und der Mission der Herrnhuter Brüdergemeine in Südindien im 18. Jahrhundert zu geben. Das Ziel ist es, neuere Forschungsansätze für eine vergleichende Betrachtung nutzbar zu machen, um die Identitätsgrundlagen der beiden Missionen unter besonderer Beachtung ihrer gegenseitigen Wahrnehmung mit dem Prozess der Aufklärung in Beziehung zu stellen. Zu diesem Zweck werden mehrere Themenkomplexe miteinander verknüpft.

An Hand der Historiographiegeschichte wird die unterschiedliche Bewertung der beiden Missionen erörtert. Dabei ist eine eklatante Vernachlässigung bzw. pauschale Verurteilung der Herrnhuter Brüdergemeine als Folge der Missionsapologetik des späten 19. Jahrhunderts zu erkennen. Die Bewertung des Unterganges der Dänisch-Halleschen Mission ist eng verknüpft mit der Debatte um das Verhältnis zwischen Aufklärung und Mission innerhalb des Pietismus. Diese Problematik wird an Hand mehrerer Beiträge zum Schulwesen der Dänisch-Halleschen Mission diskutiert. Sie alle verfolgen den neuen Ansatz, Mission als die Begegnung zweier unterschiedlicher Kulturen zu verstehen, um vor allem die wechselseitigen Aneignungsprozesse zu fokussieren. So kann z. B. gezeigt werden, dass indische Intellektuelle durch ihre Prägung im Schulwesen der Mission zu Beginn des 19. Jahrhunderts pietistische Vorstellungen von Frömmigkeit und Wissenschaftlichkeit des frühen 18. Jahrhunderts mit den neuesten naturwissenschaftlich rationalistischen Erkenntnissen verbanden. Damit ist nicht nur die herkömmliche Dichotomie von „Glauben und Wissenschaft" in Frage gestellt; auch die gängigen Annahmen hinsichtlich des Selbstverständnisses der Missionare sind dahingehend zu überprüfen.

Der Unterschied zwischen der „Halleschen Theologen-Mission" und „Herrnhuter Handwerker-Mission" verweist nicht nur auf unterschiedliche Identitätsgrundlagen der beiden Gemeinschaften, sondern offenbart verschiedene Missionskonzepte. Ihre Veränderungen in Folge der Aufklärung und die Verknüpfung mit hegemonialen Zivilisationstheorien zeigen ihre Bedeutung für Untersuchungen über Identität und Fremdwahrnehmung am Beginn der europäischen Moderne.

Introduction

For nearly two millennia, Christianity has been a firm component of European history. Its changes in the course of time have led to a variety of confessions which have often stood, and still stand, in conflict with each other. The world-wide preaching of the gospel reflects these tensions and raises the question, 'What shaped the identity of the carriers of this Christian mission?' Was it their affiliation to their special denomination, the overall uniting community of the faith in Jesus Christ, the contrary effects of the Enlightenment, or the reference to one, at least culturally and politically relatively similar origin – Europe? Investigations into these subjects promise interesting insights into the current discussions about identities within a European framework and their relationship to Christianity and Enlightenment, as well as the process of the variation of identities.

The year 2006 marks the 300th anniversary of the beginning of organised Protestant missionary work. Personally carried out and ideologically inspired by the Halle Pietism, the *Dänisch-Hallesche Mission* [Danish-Halle Mission (thereafter DHM)][1], also known as the *Tranquebarmission* [Tranquebar Mission], started its work in the Danish colony Tranquebar [Tarangambadi] in South India in June 1760. In a tension-loaded relationship, it had to compete there again with the other Protestant, and likewise Pietistic, missionary community of the 18th century – the *Herrnhuter Brüdergemeine* [Moravian Brethren (thereafter MB)][2]. As a result, conflicts within European Pietism, obvious in the radical demarcation in relation to differing theological doctrines, were transformed into an intercultural context, gaining expression in different concepts of mission.

Developments in the science of history, the so called "performative turn", in connection with the question about the contribution of religion to identity in multi-denominational and multi-ethnical societies, open a broad field of investigation[3]. Two aspects are therefore of interest. Martschukat convincingly carries out the "productive and meaning-constituent power of human behaviours in history" can be followed with the help of performative theoretical approaches[4]. Through such human behaviour, the "changing of cultural configurations" can be investigated[5]. Assuming, in addition, that the generation of meaning takes place *in actu*, it seems possible to attain access to this process and its change through the reconstruction of identity[6]. Applied to the members of both missions, it is possible on the one hand to examine the secular effects of the Enlightenment and its rationalism on religious communities and their identity, and on the other hand their reaction to it. This seems to be more interesting for the two missionary communities, as the duration of their activities coincides with the appearance of arguments based on theories of civilisation in the perception of the cultural 'other' and the theory of mission, which were some of the bases for the colonial policy of the 19th century, and thus also for the formation of the European modernity[7].

This chapter discusses new approaches within the research literature of both missions with regard to the points mentioned above and attempts to make them useful for further investigations on identity. To produce a history of historiography in the given framework would be an almost presumptuous intention. Whereas a multiplicity of monographs and special investigations exist for the history of the DHM, it is a different matter with the MB's mission in Tranquebar, about which, surprisingly, very few texts exist. Furthermore, comparative research on both missions with regard to investigations about their mutual perception is almost non-existent. However, special attention is given to this point in the review of the literature undertaken here, because it can provide information about the identity of the missionaries. While only the most important works from the older literature can be briefly highlighted, a few recent works and a short comparative analysis of both missions indicate developments over the last few years. Finally a comment on recent research on the Moravian autobiographies is given. As an example, performative concepts are presented here with emphasis on writing, community formation and identity in their functional mode for the constitution of the Moravian Brethrens as a world-wide missionary community.

THE DANISH-HALLE MISSION AND THE MISSION OF THE MORAVIAN BRETHREN IN SOUTH ASIA IN CONFESSIONAL HISTORIOGRAPHY

Danish-Halle Mission

Shortly after its foundation in 1706, the DHM came to the attention of the European public[8]. The most important reason for this was the publication of the *Hallesche Berichte* [Halle Reports][9] by the *Frankeschen Stiftungen* [Francke Foundation] of Halle – one of the intellectual centres of German Pietism, and supporting institution of the mission. With Bartholomäus Ziegenbalg (1682-1719), known through Erich Beyreuter as "Pioneer of the World Mission", stands as an example for later generations of Protestant missionaries[10].

In 1843, Ferdinand Fenger wrote the first complete history of the mission in Danish, which is a classic on the subject[11]. His critical approach to the sources is remarkable, even through he only had access to Danish archives. The first person who was able to work with the material held at the archives of the Franke Foundation in Halle (hereafter AFS), as well as the documents from Tranquebar itself, was William Germann. Having worked himself as a missionary in Tamil Nadu in South India, he edited source publications and published a few works which represent not only the results of the evangelisation, but also the linguistic and scientific achievements of the most important missionaries[12]. Representing the 20th century, it is necessary to mention the works of Arno Lehmann, himself a former missionary in the region of the old *Tranquebarmission* and a known dravidologist[13]. Because of the incompleteness of the aforementioned studies, the work by Anders Nørgaard has to be examined in more detail, which, even without a special focus on the Tamil culture and its interaction with the mission, marks a new beginning in the research of DHM history[14].

Nørgaard brings the fundamental incompatibility of mission and trade into discussion, thus characterising the DHM by the pragmatic use of the Lutheran *Zwei Reiche*

Lehre [Two-Empire Doctrine] as standing in a reserved relationship with the colonial authorities. This became the model for many later Protestant missionary societies[15]. He describes the general history of the DHM in three phases: foundation, established mission and fall[16]. Nørgaard, like Lehmann and previous analysts, describes the end of the DHM as a decay. According to this interpretation, the inspired missionary fervour, so apparent at the beginning, changed to a rationalistically diminished attitude towards preaching the gospel, focusing only on general public education through which "the entire mission sermon [should be] replaced"[17]. The rationalism of the last missionaries, particularly Johann Peter Rottler (1749-1836), Christoph Samuel John (1746-1813) and August Friedrich Caemmerer (1767-1837), seems to have caused the decay of the mission from this point of view[18]. Indeed, the relationship between Pietism and Enlightenment in the DHM is far more complex, and still requires a comparative analysis of the beginning and the end of the mission[19]. Gita Dharampal-Frick takes the attitude of the already mentioned Ziegenbalg as an "acknowledgment of a relative historical simultaneousness between pre-industrial Germany and India before the beginning of the *British Raj*, a diagnosis which differs remarkably from the hegemonial theories and the assumption of a strictly different timing in the later colonialistic discourse"[20]. Andreas Nehring points out that the condemnation of these missionaries is due to the apologia of the 19th century mission, and is connected with the take-over of this mission field by the successor to the DHM, the *Leipziger Mission* [Leipzig Mission], which was committed to the New Lutheranism, and mostly engaged in the historiography of the DHM. Indeed, the final stage of the DHM needs further consideration in the contextualisation of its theology, thereby including the "challenges which the Enlightenment drew upon the theological thinking of the outgoing 18th century"[21]. Missionary John, for example, understood mission activities as a basic contribution to social change. On one hand "the best means to improve the local inhabitants [would be] if one wins its heart by instruction for Jesus", on the other hand, he thereby expected a social and economic improvement for all castes[22]. Also in accordance with this premise, the ecumenical expansion of the activities of the mission took place in the form of intensification of the collaboration with the SPCK, already in existence since 1710, especially in educational matters, and with the East India Company, the prevailing power in South India at this time[23]. The educational work carried out by the missionaries, and by native catechists and schoolmasters[24], was decried as a waste of power and time by the critics in the early 19th century, as well as by confessional historiography later on. Even in direct connection with the beginning of the DHM, it had changed in substance. The old Pietist concept of sin was no longer the reason for the 'depravity' of the Indians and therefore the initial point for Christian introduction, but a social category, differentiating between Christian and Indian society[25]. As a result, Christianity became part of a theory of civilisation, positioning itself to the fore[26]. Consequently, the mission itself became an instrument of civilisation, and the Christian education system, although with narrow reference to domestic tradition, the means by which it was carried out.

Mission of the Moravian Brethren

Literature about the history of the MB in Tranquebar, also known as *Nikobarenmission* [Nicobar Mission], is rare, although unique ethnological, linguistic, as well as missiological material exists[27]. One comprehensive work was written by Hermann Römer in 1921[28]. On the basis of the sources of the UA, it describes the history of the efforts to preach the gospel on the Nicobar Islands in the Bay of Bengal. At the same time, it discusses the conflicts with the DHM over the set up and the maintenance of the necessary South Indian mainland station, the *Brüdergarten* near Tranquebar, from the arrival of the first Moravians in 1760 up to their final departure in 1803. Unfortunately, this account contains almost no references, but does provide some important sources.

Römer's description of the relationship between MB and DHM is based on a mission understanding which existed at the beginning of the 20th century. He states that "today the Moravian missionaries would have... strong doubts... if Anglo-Saxon Methodists were to set up a community somewhere in one of their old mission fields"[29]. Hereby, he uses a concept of mission which is linked to the confessions, and assumes a mutual competition with one another which does not cover the impetus of the beginnings

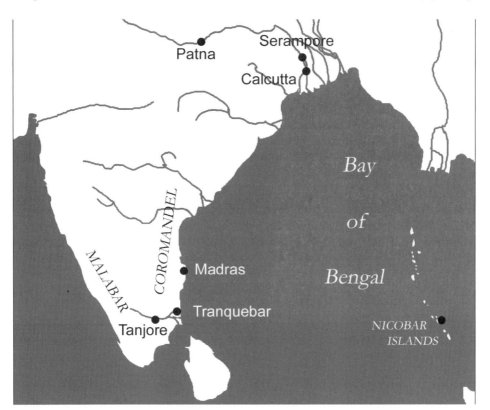

Map 1.
Protestant Missions in 18th-Century India

of the Protestant mission[30]. From that, his negative evaluation of the establishment of the Moravian mission in an already existing Protestant mission field arises. With this opinion Römer repeats the contemporary statements and views of some of the DHM members, that the MB should not have operated a mission in Tranquebar, which had caused fundamental problems to the existence of the *Brüdergarten*, despite a differently-phrased Royal Reskript dated January 12th 1759[31].

Arno Lehmann, 30 years later, used the statements of Römer for his own negative judgments of the Moravian mission in Tranquebar, which appeared to him to be only a wilful interference in the Halle activities in Tranquebar[32]. These old evaluations of the Moravian activities are examples of the way the conflict between the Pietism of Moravian and Halle was handled, which continued in the mission historiography. So far no research has been carried out that would cover all available sources as well as the self-perception of the missionaries of both sides. Therefore, it is difficult to compare both missions in their shared field of activity adequately. Greater insight could be gained from the examination of the waning, limited successes in the evangelisation of the heathens by the MB[33], compared to the considerable successes of the DHM, in the 18th century in South India, in contrast to the healthy survival of the MB mission worldwide, together with the downfall of the DHM, in the 19th century[34].

BETWEEN CULTURAL HISTORY AND MISSIOLOGY

The Education System of the DHM – European Impact and its Effects

In the following section, more recent works with a focus on the relationship between the mission and the native population will be discussed. They have a similar approach in their emphasis on the changes of social spheres and social mobility through the expansion of Christianity and the development of the education system introduced by the DHM and continued in the time of British colonial rule[35]. At the same time, the mission is understood to be a convergence of different cultures with increasing awareness of the differentiated indigenous achievements in the appropriation of western values in relation to the intended transfer interests[36].

Daniel Jeyaraj tries to remedy the fact that most European works had no reference to the way of life of the Tamil people by using, to a large extent, the existing Tamil sources. He succeeds in clarifying the process of adoptions between European missionaries and the South Indian population, in displaying the communication of these meetings, where he illustrates the clash of different identities, and shows their variation and/or the development of the new identity of the Tamil Lutheran Christians from these identities[37]. The analysis of this process, with a focus on the intercultural dimension, illuminates the identity structures of the DHM missionaries further and provides insights into the mission methods when the mission started. At the same time, Jeyaraj also works out details of the missionaries' perception of the Tamil people and culture, without explicitly focusing on that particular aspect.

The significance of the mission schools as "important social areas of intercultural encounter and communication", beyond the purpose of implementing the Christian faith and recruiting a new generation of native assistants, is shown by Heike Liebau[38]. She regards "education and upbringing in the missionary context as processes of dealing with norms, traditions, knowledge and experiences of different cultural and religious origin"[39]. Liebau explains the educational policy of the DHM as resulting from their dependence on the pedagogic principles of August Hermann Franke (1663-1727), the founder of the Franke Foundation: "The bringing up of pious, virtuous and hard working young people, who lived and worked in the Pietist sense" with "religious education in the foreground"[40]. There was no special institution for training the missionaries. Their own study of theology at the University of Halle, as well as their teaching activity at one of the schools of the Franke Foundation, was fundamental to their way of teaching in India and for their identity as missionaries of the DHM. With August Hermann Niemeyer (1754-1828) as the head of the Franke Foundation since 1784, "also the ideas of the Enlightenment became a component of the educational policy"[41]. These changes became a challenge for future missionaries, who had to combine Pietist devoutness and scientific interpretation of the world, especially through the close connection with the University of Halle[42]. Missionary John was able to say with missionary fervour: "science and its spread are, as I take it, a part of religion and mission and its promotion is my liability"[43]. The introduction of scientific subjects into the curriculum of the mission schools since the 1770s has to be seen in this context, whereas religious content dominated further. With the plans to introduce a mixed European-Indian school, a change can also be observed in the social status of the students in relation to the missionaries, and to each other: "The European children stand with the teacher, the Malabarian children must kneel and serve the European during the meal"[44]. This expression of 'European superiority' shows the beginning of the adoption of elements of a theory of civilisation within the mission.

On the basis of the mission education system, Indira Viswanathan Peterson examines the development of a new Christian and European scientifically-educated social group in South India[45]. With the example of the Tamil Poet Vedanāyakam Sāstri (1774-1864) and King Serfoji II of Tanjore [Thanjavur] (1777-1832), both students of the famous DHM missionary Christian Friedrich Schwarz (1726-1798)[46] and of John, Caemmerer and Rottler, the adoption of "'natural theology' ... as an integral aspect of Franke's Pietist theology" into South Indian literature and the intellectual life of the early 19th century is illustrated[47]. For this purpose, an analysis of the bases of Francke's conception of education and science has been undertaken. "Halle Pietists became leaders in the Enlightenment enthusiasm for pushing back the frontiers of scientific learning, and the *HKNK* [(*Hallesche Kunst- und Naturalienkammer*) Halle Cabinet of Objects from Nature and Art] was emblematic of their commitment to this ideal"[48]. Considering, in the contemporary context, the very modern pedagogic methods (here we may mention the *Realienunterricht* [Instruction on Objects]), it becomes clear that Francke used the idea of the European *Kunst- und Wunderkammer* [Cabinet of Objects from Art and

Curiosities], strongly questioned by the Enlightenment, for his own purposes to clarify empirically the omnipotence of the one creator God[49]. At the same time, it appears that the "ideology of natural theology or physico-theology" remained a basic concept during the entire existence of the DHM, but was nevertheless absorbing elements of the changing sciences in the course of the further Enlightenment[50]. This is apparent, for example, in the adoption of the Linnéi classification scheme for the famous plant collection of missionary Rottler[51]. Nehring suggests that it is wrong to locate this appropriation of enlightened scientific concepts, like the former mission historiography, under the "dichotomy of faith and science"[52]. Rather, the structural order of nature reveals the organizing God, and proves the plausibility of the Christian faith in discussions with the heathens[53]. The works of the two protagonists illustrate that the rationalistic scientific achievements reached India through the instruction of the German missionaries. At the beginning of the 19th century, the two South Indian intellectuals reproduced an "early-18th century Pietistic vision of science"[54] connected with the "reception of European models of classification and epistemology"[55]. The criticism of having subordinated the mission to the ideas of the Enlightenment, ignores not only the benefit which the missionaries hoped to gain from the scientific interpretation of the world for the propagation of the glory of God, but also the missionary impetus while transmitting these scientific insights. Consequently, it becomes clear why the works of Sāstri, the "Evangelical poet of Tanjavur"[56], "based on the coherent universe of Pietist Christianity", encompassed the newest geographical and astronomical achievements of Europe at that time[57].

The Moravian Brethren in the Social Structure of Tranquebar

Martin Krieger is the first to use documents of the Rigsarkivet Copenhagen [National Archives of Copenhagen], in addition to sources from Herrnhut, for his work on the MB in Tranquebar and on the Nicobar Islands, which is, as far as I can see, the only one in recent decades[58]. The declared emphasis lies on an investigation of the relevance of the dichotomy between the mission and the authorities. Its argument follows Nørgaard and comes to the conclusion that this opposition is recognisable for the DHM. Contrary to this, regarding the MB, he points out that "such a conflict was not institutionalised, but resulted from the subjective attitude to life of the respective missionaries"[59]. At this point it is important to look at Römer's valuation regarding the points of conflict around the agency of the MB. "On the part of the Danish government and the *Asiatisk Kompagni* [Asiatic company] the station of the MB in Tranquebar was meant only as a base for the Nicobar Islands and should not become a mission field of the MB, as the Danish mission [DHM] had already been active there for 50 years"[60]. The exact interpretation of the interests and intentions of all involved in the settlement of the MB is a controversial matter. Krieger imputes, unlike Römer, that the *Asiatisk Kompagni* had a large, economically based interest in a long-term agency of the MB, not only on the Nicobar Islands, but also in Tranquebar[61]. Convincingly, he describes the rapid integration of the small MB community into the colonial Indo-European social structures, their religious tolerance contributing significantly to it[62]. Their practice-oriented attitude to life brought both the population and the company substantial profit and medical care. As Krieger shows, after brief contacts at the beginning, no further communication took place with the missionaries of the MB and the DHM. The Moravians were anxious to defuse "every potential upcoming conflict"[63]. Unfortunately, their exact relationship with the DHM and the decades of the inevitability of living together with the DHM missionaries and their Lutheran protégés does not lie in his focus.

The moment of the mutual benefit of the mission-willing Moravians and the colonist-seeking *Asiatisk Kompagni* appears clearly in the departure to the Nicobar Islands in 1768. Here, in addition, the one-sided dependence of the MB on the company leadership and its governors became clarified. In the case of the cancellation of the company ships, no contact between the islands and the mainland existed partly for years, which means the Moravians on the Nicobar Islands had "no further economical value for the Danish Asia trade"[64]. Nevertheless, later on the company obligatorily appointed some Moravians as royal residents to maintain the Danish claims on the Nicobar Islands. Their desperate economic situation, connected with the lack of success in their attempts to preach the gospel to the natives, in connection with the high loss of human life caused by unfavourable climatic conditions, forced the Moravians to give up their mission station *Tripjet* on the Nicobar Islands in 1786. The Moravians did not apply for new mission concessions for Danish or other territories in India after that. Therefore the *Brüdergarten* lost its function as a basic station. In Tranquebar itself, as a result of their complicated relationship with the DHM and the *Asiatisk Kompagni*, which was not interested in conversion activities, the Moravians never did implement their missionary work to any great extent. In 1795, the European authorities came to a decision regarding its solution. Krieger comprehensively describes the MB as liberating itself from the position of being an instrument of the *Asiatisk Kompagni*, and constructing its own identity, especially on the basis of its independent gainful occupation[65].

The Concept of Mission and Identity

Hermann Wellenreuther analyses the relationship of Pietism and mission as well as the continuity of Pietist traditions in the Protestant mission until the beginning of the 20th century[66]. He points out a basically different characterisation of the missions of the MB and the DHM. Whereas mission was "one of many enterprises but never the central component of the Halle self understanding", it was the main target of the worldwide activities of the MB[67]. The fundamental difference between the "*Halleschen Theologen-Mission* [Halle theologian-mission], and the *Herrnhuter Handwerker-Mission* [Moravian craftsman-mission]" with their obligation for general priesthood, is reflected in the strictly Lutheran understanding of their position as priests and theologians of the first in opposition to a shared intention to live and work in a community in order to give an account for one's own conversion to God in expression of the ideal of serving as an example and model with one's own life brought about by *Zeugentrieb* [witness impulse][68]. Thus Wellenreuther describes the fundamental characteristics of identity of the two missions. These differences also appear in the concepts of mission and the term of penance, so controversially discussed on both sides. The generally long training period for catechumens illustrates that, within the DHM, conversion was understood as a process, shaped according to the *Frankisches Bußkampfmodell* [Franke's model of struggle of penance][69], whereas the MB set theological instruction aside and expected, in contrast to this, a spontaneous emotional acceptance of Jesus Christ. Wellenreuther obtains this concise characterisation mainly from the comparison of the DHM in Tranquebar with the North American Indian mission of the Moravians under the well-known missionary David Zeisberger[70]. Therefore, he is not able to make statements about effects and implications of these differences in a shared local context, or draw conclusions as to the success of the missionary work. However, he provides an outstanding insight in order to place the theological background of the different concepts of oneself and of the others of both missionary communities in relation to the change in the course of the Enlightenment. "At the end of the 18th century, the Moravian mission theology was surprisingly in conformity with intellectual and cultural currents that were to determine European thinking at the beginning of the 19th century, whereas on the contrary, the theological thinking of Halle Pietism, because of the rationality of the Enlightenment, was pushed to the theological and intellectual periphery"[71]. His statement gains importance in consideration of the worldwide longevity of these two characteristic types of Protestant mission. Likewise, the process of the *Bußkampf* appears within the guise of a theory of civilisation, "since a strict break with the heathen religious world forced the adoption of a European-civilised religiosity"[72].

The Moravian Brethren – Autobiographies and Identity

A characteristic feature of the MB since the 1750s is the *Lebensläufe* [autobiographies] of its members[73]. These personal records only recently came to the notice of the scientific research of a most different provenance[74]. Slowly, the rush judgment of uniformity and "typically Pietistic" begins to be revised, corresponding to the complexity and the extent of the archive material[75]. Irina Modrow concludes, "that the Pietist attestations of self should be recognised as important documents of individual self-depiction and religious reflection"[76]. However, she holds the view that only to a small extent can the self-perception of the group be derived from this representation of the so-called *innere Welt* [inner world]. According to this opinion, the "value of the autobiographies in the course of reconstruction of the production of identity is limited"[77]. On the contrary, Susanne Hose emphasised the "communicative function" of the autobiographies and their role for the constitution of the community, pointing out "the high information value" for, and the "model effect" on, the MB as a worldwide community[78]. In doing so, she accentuates the pedagogic and thus the *Werte-Kodex* [value-code] of the community-conserving effect of the *Lebensläufe*, arguing implicitly against Modrow, whose article she does not seem to have noticed[79].

An article by Christine Lost stresses the connection between a life as service to the community and at the same time as a model for the other community members[80]. Consequently, the autobiographies are placed within a narrow functional connection to those "educational principles and community mechanisms, which have ensured the specific form of existence of this community up to the present", providing a "reservoir for the stability and the developmental capacity of the community"[81]. Hence, they serve as "*Lehrtext*" [training text]. They are "example, account, experience and apprenticeship" with an "as clear as possible connection between the individual and the community"[82]. In this context, two special aspects are mentioned. First of all, the learning of reading and writing was a basic component of the life of the MB, through which a high level of communicative capability was achieved. Secondly, Lost stresses the aspect of "disciplining the community members" which, in connection with the basic demand to make all individual power available for the community, constitutes the "total community" as the normative frame for the development of personality and identity[83]. "The individual biography becomes the internalised community and thereby is given back to the community as accountability and experience"[84]. Thus, the autobiographies offer the possibility of tracing the changes which the MB underwent in the course of the Enlightenment. And thus should provide statements about the concepts of mission and the modi of perception of the other as well as their changes, and help to demonstrate the self-perception of the South Indian community of the MB in the context of the conflict with the DHM.

Conclusion

The examination of the present state of research on the Moravian Brethren and the Danish-Halle Mission in South Asia reveals a fundamental lack of a comparative investigation, which is remarkable, considering their historic importance as the first Protestant missions. However, various single investigations offer long-range approaches to the constitutions of both mission organisations, to the identity of their members, to their perception of the Indian culture and of their "mission objectives", as well as placing these perceptions in relation to the changes in the course of the Enlightenment. The conflicts within Pietism, which found their continuation in partially one-sided representations by the confessional mission historiography, were transferred into a multicultural context. Together with different ways of means of subsistence, they form the foundation for the identity of the missionaries. On the basis of the education system of the DHM as well as the *Lebensläufe* of the MB, the effects of the changes in Europe on the missionaries in India can be detected. Therefore, it becomes clear that simple opposition of Pietism versus Enlightenment makes it difficult to focus on the changes in the identity and the self-perception of the missionaries as well as their perception of the Indian culture. On the contrary, a direct confrontation of the beginning and the final phase of the two missions seems to provide a solid foundation in order to examine the identity of religious communities and their perception of the cultural other in their relationship with the emergence of hegemonic theories of civilisation at the beginning of the European modernity.

Notes

[1]   For names of Indian people and places, I have adopted the spelling common in the mission records. Where possible, the modern common version is given in square brackets. All translations from the German in this

chapter are mine. When necessary, the original text is given in footnotes. German proper names are written in italics and, when possible, followed by an English translation in square brackets the first time. Abbreviations are given in round brackets.

2   Other German names are *Unitas Fratrum* or *Brüder-Unität*. Names in English are also *The Moravian Church* and *The Church of the United Brethren*.

3   J. Martschukat - S. Patzold (eds.), *Geschichtswissenschaft und "performative turn". Ritual, Inszenierung und Performanz vom Mittelalter bis zur Neuzeit*, Köln-Weimar-Wien 2003.

4   ["Produktiven und bedeutungskonstituierenden Kraft von menschlichen Handlungsweisen in der Geschichte"]: J. Martschukat - S. Patzold, *Geschichtswissenschaft und "performative turn": Eine Einführung in Fragestellung, Konzepte und Literatur*, in Martschukat - Patzold (eds.), *Geschichtswissenschaft und "performative turn"*. cit., pp. 1-31, p. 11.

5   ["sich wandelnden kulturellen Figurationen"]: *ibid.*, p. 11.

6   *Ibid.*, pp. 10ff.

7   H. Wellenreuther, *Pietismus und Mission. Vom 17. bis zum Beginn des 20. Jahrhunderts*, in H. Lehmann (ed.), *Geschichte des Pietismus Bd. 4: Glaubenswelt und Lebenswelten*, Göttingen 2004, pp. 166-193.

8   H. Obst, *Missionsberichte aus Indien im 18. Jahrhundert: Eine Einführung in den missionsgeschichtlichen Kontext*, in M. Bergunder (ed.), *Missionsberichte aus Indien im 18. Jahrhundert: ihre Bedeutung für die europäische Geistesgeschichte und ihr wissenschaftlicher Quellenwert für die Indienkunde*, Halle 1999, pp. 1-6.

9   *Der Königlich Dänischen Missionarien aus Ost-Indien eingesandte ausführliche Berichte* [Reports of the Royal Danish Missionaries from East-India], 9 vol., 108 cont., Halle 1710-1767 (thereafter HB) and continuing: *Neuere Geschichte der evangelischen Missions-Anstalten zu Bekehrung der Heiden in Ostindien aus den eigenhändigen Aufsätzen und Briefen der Missionarien herausgegeben* [New Reports from the Protestant Attempt to Convert the Heathens in East-India], 8 vol., 95 cont., Halle 1776-1848 (thereafter NHB).

10   E. Beyreuter, *Ziegenbalg, Bahnbrecher der Weltmission*, Suttgart 1968.

11   J.F. Fenger, *Geschichte der Trankebarschen Mission*, Grimma 1845.

12   W. Germann, *Die wissenschaftliche Arbeit unserer alten Tamulen=Missionare mit Berücksichtigung neuerer Leistungen*, "Missionsnachrichten der Ostindischen Missionsanstalt zu Halle", 17, 1865, pp. 1-26, 53-81, 85-119; the same, *Ziegenbalg und Plütschau. Die Gründungsjahre der Trankebarschen Mission. Ein Beitrag zur Geschichte des Pietismus nach handschriftlichen Quellen und ältesten Drucken*, Erlangen 1868.

13   A. Lehmann, *Es begann in Tranquebar: Geschichte der ersten evangelischen Kirche in Indien*, Berlin 1955.

14   A. Nørgaard, *Mission und Obrigkeit: Die Dänisch-hallische Mission in Tranquebar 1706-1845*, Gütersloh 1988.

15   *Ibid.*, pp. 243 f.

16   *Ibid.*, p. 10.

17   ["die ganze Missionspredigt ersetzt"]: Lehmann, *Es begann* cit., p. 300. Cf. Nørgaard, *Mission* cit., pp. 229 ff.

18   Lehmann, *Es begann* cit., pp. 293 ff. Cf. also Nørgaard, *Mission* cit., p. 29. Their periods of residence in India: Rottker 1776-1803, from 1803-1833 he served as a missionary for the Society for Promoting Christian Knowledge (thereafter SPCK); John 1771-1817; Caemmerer 1791-1937. The dates according to the biographical database of the AfS (www.francke-halle.de).

19   A. Nehring, *Orientalismus und Mission: Die Repräsentation der tamilischen Gesellschaft und Religion durch Leipziger Missionare 1840-1940*, Wiesbaden 2003, p. 59.

20   ["Anerkennung einer relativen geschichtlichen Gleichzeitigkeit zwischen dem vorindustriellen Deutschland und Indien vor dem Beginn des *British raj*, in einer Diagnose also, die sich von hegemonialen Theorien und von der Annahme einer strikten Ungleichzeitigkeit im späteren kolonialistischen Diskurs bemerkenswert unterscheidet"]: G. Dharampal-Frick, *Malabarisches Heidenthum: Bartholomäus Ziegenbalg über Religion und Gesellschaft der Tamilen*, in Bergunder (ed.), *Missionsberichte* cit., pp. 126-152, pp. 126f.

21 ["Herausforderungen, die die Aufklärung an das theologische Denken des ausgehenden 18. Jhd. stellte"]: Nehring, *Orientalismus und Mission* cit., p. 80.

22 ["das beste Mittel, die hiesigen Einwohner zu verbessern, [...] wenn man ihr Herz durch Unterricht für Jesum gewinnt"] John in "NHB", 1827, 6, 62, p. 189. Cf. Nehring, *Orientalismus und Mission* cit., p. 67.

23 The handing over of the country communities from the DHM to the SPCK in 1820, and the following transfer to the Society for the Propagation of the Gospel (SPG) in 1825 in connection with their conversion to the Church of England, is one reason for the negative judgements of this ecumenical collaboration, and also casts a shadow on the evaluation of the education system of the late DHM. Lehman, *Es began* cit., p. 301.

24 H. Liebau, *Country Priests, Catechists, and Schoolmasters as Cultural, Religious and Social Middlemen in the Context of the Tranquebar Mission*, in R.E. Frykenberg (ed.), *Christians and Missionaries in India: Cross-Cultural Communication since 1500*, Cambridge 2003, pp. 79-92.

25 Nehring, *Orientalismus und Mission* cit., p. 72.

26 *Ibid.*, pp. 77 ff.

27 So to mention the diaries of the different mission stations, letters and autobiographies and probably the first Nikobaren – German dictionary as well as a translation of the gospel of Mathew in Nikobar. Thanks to Dr. Köger, director of the *Unitätsarchiv Herrnhut* [Moravian archives, thereafter UA], for his enormous help.

28 H. Römer, *Geschichte der Brüdermission auf den Nikobaren und des ,Brüdergartens' bei Trankebar*, Herrnhut, 1921.

29 ["*Dass heut zu Tage die Brüdermissionare ... schwere Bedenken ... hegen würden, wenn irgendwo in eines ihrer alten Missionsgebiete angelsächsische Methodisten eine Gemeinde setzten*"]: *ibid.*, p. 15.

30 For the ecumenical tendencies at the beginning of both missions. Cf. Nehring, *Orientalismus und Mission* cit., p. 63.

31 Second Reskript of Settlement for the Moravian Brethren by King Friedrich V of Denmark, 12. 01. 1759, UA, R.15.T.a.1.20.

32 Lehmann, *Es begann* cit., pp. 281-290.

33 Note that the mission of the MB, even in the 18th century, had quite a number of proselytes, but not in South Asia. Cf. D. Meyer, *Zinzendorf und Herrnhut*, in M. Brecht - K. Deppermann (eds.), *Geschichte des Pietismus Bd. 2: Der Pietismus im achtzehnten Jahrhundert*, Göttingen 1995, pp. 34-40, 68-74.

34 Wellenreuther, *Pietismus und Mission* cit., p. 172.

35 H. Liebau, *Über die Erziehung "tüchtiger Subjekte" zur Verbreitung des Evangeliums: Das Schulwesen der Dänisch-Halleschen Mission als Säule der Missionsorganisation*, in A. Bogner - B. Holtwick - H. Tyrell (eds.), *Weltmission und religiöse Organisationen. Protestantische Missionsgesellschaften im 19. und 20. Jahrhundert*, Würzburg 2004, pp. 427-458; H. Liebau, *Country Priests, Catechists, and Schoolmasters* cit. and I.V. Peterson, *Tanjore, Tranquebar, and Halle: European Science and German missionary education in the lives of two Indian intellectuals in the early nineteenth century*, in Frykenberg (ed.), *Christians and Missionaries in India* cit., pp. 93-126.

36 D. Jeyaraj, *Inkulturation in Tranquebar: der Beitrag der frühen dänisch-halleschen Mission zum Werden einer indisch-einheimischen Kirche (1706 – 1730)*, Erlangen 1996, p. 39; H. Liebau, *Tamilische Christen im 18. Jahrhundert als Mitgestallter sozialer Veränderung: Motivation, Möglichkeiten und Resultate ihres Wirkens*, in P. Heidrich - H. Liebau (eds.), *Akteure des Wandels: Lebensläufe und Gruppenbilder an Schnittstellen von Kulturen*, Berlin 2001, pp. 19-44, pp. 19 f. To the indigenous appropriation of the Gospel cf. R.F. Young, *Singer of the 'Sovereign Lord'; Hindu Pietism and Christian Bhakti in the Conversions of Kanapati Vattiyar, 18th-century Tranquebar Tamil 'Poet'*, contribution at the 2nd International Congress for Pietism studies in Halle 2005 (to be published).

37 Jeyaraj, *Inkulturation* cit., pp. 37 ff.

38 ["Wichtige soziale Räume interkultureller Begegnung und Kommunikation"]: Liebau, *Erziehung* cit., p. 427.

39 ["Bildung und Erziehung im missionarischen Kontext als Prozesse des Aufeinandertreffens von Normen, Traditionen, Wissen und Erfahrungen unterschiedlicher kultureller und religiöser Provenienz"]: *ibid.*, p. 446.

40 ["Die Heranbildung von frommen, tugendhaften und arbeitsamen jungen Menschen, die im pietistischen Sinne lebten und arbeiteten", "Religionsunterricht im Vordergrund."]: *ibid.*, pp. 433f.

41 ["Wurden auch die Ideen der Aufklärung zu einem Bestandteil der Bildungspolitik der Frankeschen Stiftungen"]: *ibid.*, p. 434.

42 *Ibid.*, p. 432; Peterson, *Tanjore, Tranquebar, and Halle* cit., pp. 96 f.

43 ["Wissenschaft und die Ausbreitung derselben halte ich für einen Theil der Religion und Mißion und deren Förderung als meine Pflicht"]: cf. Liebau: *Erziehung* cit., p. 437.

44 ["Die europäischen Kinder stehen mit dem Lehrer, die Malabarischen Kinder müssen Knien und bedienen die europäischen beim Essen..."]: NHB, 1790, 3, 30, p. 707. Cf. Liebau, *Erziehung* cit., p. 440.

45 I.V. Peterson, *Science in the Tranquebar Mission Curriculum: Natural Theology and Indian Response*, in Bergunder (ed.), *Missionsberichte* cit., pp. 175-220.

46 Period of residence in India: 1750-1778, from 1778-1798 he served as a missionary for the SPCK.

47 Peterson, *Science in the Tranquebar Mission Curriculum* cit., p. 186.

48 *Ibid.*, pp. 188 f. cf. also Peterson, *Tanjore, Tranquebar, and Halle* cit., pp. 97 ff.

49 Peterson, *Science in the Tranquebar Mission Curriculum* cit., pp. 119, 216, 218.

50 *Ibid.*, p. 185.

51 C.S. Mohanavelu, *German Tamilology: German contribution to Tamil language, literature and culture during the period 1706-1945*, Madras 1993, p. 151.

52 ["Dichotomie von Glauben und Wissenschaft"]: Nehring, *Orientalismus und Mission* cit., p. 76.

53 *Ibid.*, pp. 70, 76 ff.

54 Peterson, *Science in the Tranquebar Mission Curriculum* cit., p. 203.

55 *Ibid.*, p. 196.

56 *Ibid.*, p. 178.

57 *Ibid.*, p. 218; Cf. Peterson, *Tanjore, Tranquebar, and Halle* cit., pp. 105 ff.

58 M. Krieger, *Vom ‚Brüdergarten' zu den Nikobaren. Die Herrnhuter Brüder in Südasien*, in S. Cornermann (ed.), *Der indische Ozean in historischer Perspektive*, Hamburg 1998, pp. 209-244.

59 ["daß ein derartiger Konflikt eben nicht institutionalisiert war, sondern daß er sich aus der subjektiven Lebenseinstellung der jeweiligen Missionare ergab"]: *ibid.*, p. 209.

60 ["Von Seiten der dänischen Regierung und der Asiatischen Kompanie war die Niederlassung der Brüder in Trankebar nur als Stützpunkt für die Mission auf den Nikobaren gemeint, nicht aber sollte auch Trankebar ein Missionsfeld der Brüder werden, weil dort schon die dänische Mission seit 50 Jahren tätig war"]: Römer, *Geschichte* cit., p. 14.

61 Krieger, *Vom 'Brüdergarten' zu den Nikobaren* cit., pp. 221, 229. Römer does not really extend the economic issue to Tranquebar itself: Römer, *Geschichte* cit., pp. 71 f. But Nørgaard already mentioned this fact: Nørgaard, *Mission und Obrigkeit* cit., p. 179.

62 Krieger, *Vom 'Brüdergarten' zu den Nikobaren* cit., p. 227.

63 ["Jedes sich bietende Konfliktpotential zu entschärfen"]: *ibid.*, p. 231, see also pp. 229 ff.

64 ["Keinen ökonomischen Wert mehr für den dänischen Asienhandel"]: *ibid.*, p. 237.

65 *Ibid.*, p. 241.

66 Wellenreuther, *Pietismus und Mission*, cit.

67 ["Als eines von vielen Unternehmungen... nie zentraler Bestandteil des halleschen Selbstverständnisses"]: *ibid.*, p. 168.

68   ["Halleschen Theologen-Mission... Herrnhuter Handwerker-Mission"]: *ibid.*, p. 170.

69   For the differences between Franke and the MB regarding the *Bußkampf* cf. E. Geiger, *Zinzendorfs Stellung zum Halleschen Bußkampf und zum Bekehrungserlebnis*, in "Unitas Fratrum", 49/50, 2002, pp. 13-22.

70   Wellenreuther, *Pietismus und Mission* cit., p. 170, notes 22, 23.

71   ["Am Ende des 18. Jahrhunderts war die Herrnhuter Missionstheologie erstaunlicherweise im Einklang mit geistigen und kulturellen Strömungen, die zu Beginn des 19. Jahrhunderts europäisches Denken bestimmen sollten, während umgekehrt das theologische Denken Halles wegen der Rationalität der Aufklärung an die theologische und intellektuelle Peripherie gedrängt wurde"]: *ibid.*, p. 172.

72   ["Denn Bruch mit der Heidnisch religiösen Welt erzwang die Annahme einer europäisch-zivilisierten Religiosität"]: *ibid.*, p. 182.

73   23,000 autobiographies are accessible in the database at the UA (01. 07. 2004).

74   M. Friedrich, *Herrnhutische Lebensläufe als Quellen der Sozial- und Mentalitätsgeschichte: Ein Hinweis auf neuere schwedische Forschungen*, in "Unitas Fratrum", 2002, 49/50, pp. 202-213.

75   ["typisch pietistisch"]: I. Modrow, *Religiöse Erweckung und Selbstreflexion. Überlegungen zu den Lebensläufen Herrnhuter Schwestern als einem Beispiel pietistischer Selbstdarstellung*, in W. Schulze, *Ego Dokumente: Annäherung an den Menschen in der Geschichte*" Berlin 1996, pp. 121-129, p. 121.

76   ["Daß die pietistischen Selbstzeugnisse als wichtige Dokumente individueller Selbstbetrachtung und religiöser Schau Beachtung finden sollten"]: *ibid.*, p. 128.

77   ["Rekonstruktion der Produktion von Identität... ihr Aussagewert... eingeschränkt"]: *ibid.*, p. 128.

78   ["Kommunikative Funktion", "den hohen Informationswert", "Vorbildwirkung"]: S. Hose, *„Für die Stunde meines Begräbnisses": Zur kommunikativen Funktion von Lebensbeichten in der Herrnhuter Brüdergemeine; Ein Beitrag zum Zinzendorf-Jahr*, "Lĕtopis", 47/2, 2000, pp. 78-94, 78, 91.

79   *Ibid.*, p. 91.

80   C. Lost, *Die Herrnhuter Tradition der Lebensberichte – Das Leben als Dienst und Lehre*, in "Mitteilungen & Materialien, Zeitschrift für Museum und Bildung", 53, 2000, pp. 24-36.

81   ["Erziehungsprinzipien und Gemeinschaftsmechanismen, die die spezifische Existenzform dieser Gemeinschaft bis zur Gegenwart gesichert haben", "ein Reservoir für Bestandserhaltung und Entwicklungsfähigkeit der Gemeine"]: *ibid.*, pp. 25 f.

82   ["Lehrtext", "Beispiel, Rechenschaft, Erfahrung und Lehre", "möglichst klaren Verbindung zwischen dem einzelnen und der Gemeinschaft"]: *ibid.*, pp. 24 ff.

83   ["Disziplinierung der Gemeinschaftsmitglieder", "totale Gemeine"]: *ibid.*, p. 30. To the term "total community" see: H.-W. Erbe, *Erziehung und Schulen der Brüdergemeine*, in M.P. van Buijtenen - C. Dekker (eds.), *Unitas Fratrum: Herrnhuter Studien*, Utrecht 1975, pp. 315-351, p. 319.

84   ["Die individuelle Biographie wird zur verinnerlichten Gemeinschaft und an die Gemeinschaft als Rechenschaft und Erfahrung zurückgegeben"]: Lost, *Herrnhuter Tradition der Lebensberichte* cit., p. 32.

BIBLIOGRAPHY

Bergunder M. (ed.), *Missionsberichte aus Indien im 18. Jahrhundert: ihre Bedeutung für die europäische Geistesgeschichte und ihr wissenschaftlicher Quellenwert für die Indienkunde*, Halle 1999.

Beyreuter E., *Ziegenbalg, Bahnbrecher der Weltmission*, Suttgart 1968.

Dharampal-Frick G., *Malabarisches Heidenthum: Bartholomäus Ziegenbalg über Religion und Gesellschaft der Tamilen*, in Bergunder M. (ed.), *Missionsberichte aus Indien im 18. Jahrhundert: ihre Bedeutung für die europäische Geistesgeschichte und ihr wissenschaftlicher Quellenwert für die Indienkunde*, Halle 1999, pp. 126-152.

Erbe H.-W., *Erziehung und Schulen der Brüdergemeine*, in van Buijtenen M.P. - Dekker C. (ed.), *Unitas Fratrum: Herrnhuter Studien*, Utrecht 1975, pp. 315-351.

Fenger J.F., *Geschichte der Trankebarschen Mission*, Grimma 1845.

Friedrich M., *Herrnhutische Lebensläufe als Quellen der Sozial- und Mentalitätsgeschichte: Ein Hinweis auf neuere schwedische Forschungen*, "Unitas Fratrum", 49/50, 2002, pp. 202-213.

Frykenberg R.E., *The Halle Legacy in Modern India: Information and the Spread of Education, Enlightenment, and Evangelisation*, in Bergunder M. (ed.), *Missionsberichte aus Indien im 18. Jahrhundert: ihre Bedeutung für die europäische Geistesgeschichte und ihr wissenschaftlicher Quellenwert für die Indienkunde*, Halle 1999, pp. 6-29.

Germann W., *Die wissenschaftliche Arbeit unserer alten Tamulen=Missionare mit Berücksichtigung neuerer Leistungen*, "Missionsnachrichten der Ostindischen Missionsanstalt zu Halle", 17, 1865, pp. 1-26, 53-81, 85-119.

Id., *Ziegenbalg und Plütschau. Die Gründungsjahre der Trankebarschen Mission. Ein Beitrag zur Geschichte des Pietismus nach handschriftlichen Quellen und ältesten Drucken*, Erlangen 1868.

Hose S., *"Für die Stunde meines Begräbnisses": Zur kommunikativen Funktion von Lebensbeichten in der Herrnhuter Brüdergemeine; Ein Beitrag zum Zinzendorf-Jahr*, "Lětopis", 47/2, 2000, pp. 78-94.

Hudson D.D., *Protestant Origins in India: Tamil Evangelical Christians, 1706-1835*, Cambridge 2000.

Jeyaraj D., *Inkulturation in Tranquebar: der Beitrag der frühen dänisch-halleschen Mission zum Werden einer indisch-einheimischen Kirche (1706 – 1730)*, Erlangen 1996.

Juneja M., *Begegnung, Kommunikation, Sinnbildung. Deutsche Pietisten und Südindische Tamilen im 18. Jahrhundert*, in Grandner M. - Komlosy A. (eds.), *Vom Weltgeist beseelt: Globalgeschichte 1700-1815*, Wien 2004, pp. 221-242.

Krieger M., *Vom ,Brüdergarten' zu den Nikobaren. Die Herrnhuter Brüder in Südasien*, in Cornermann S. (ed.) *Der indische Ozean in historischer Perspektive*, Hamburg 1998, pp. 209-244.

Liebau H., *Über die Erziehung „tüchtiger Subjekte" zur Verbreitung des Evangeliums: Das Schulwesen der Dänisch-Halleschen Mission als Säule der Missionsorganisation*, in Bogner A. - Holtwick B. - Tyrell H., (eds.) *Weltmission und religiöse Organisationen. Protestantische Missionsgesellschaften im 19. und 20. Jahrhundert*, Würzburg 2004, pp. 427-458.

Liebau H., *Country Priests, Catechists, and Schoolmaster as Cultural, Religious and Social Middlemen in the Context of the Tranquebar Mission*, in Frykenberg R.E. (ed.), *Christians and Missionaries in India: Cross-Cultural Communication since 1500*, Cambridge 2003, pp. 79-92.

Liebau H., *Tamilische Christen im 18. Jahrhundert als Mitgestalter sozialer Veränderung: Motivation, Möglichkeiten und Resultate ihres Wirkens*, in Heidrich P. - Liebau H. (eds.), *Akteure des Wandels: Lebensläufe und Gruppenbilder an Schnittstellen von Kulturen*, Berlin 2001, pp. 19-44.

Lehmann A., *Es begann in Tranquebar: Geschichte der ersten evangelischen Kirche in Indien*, Berlin 1955.

Lost C., *Die Herrnhuter Tradition der Lebensberichte – Das Leben als Dienst und Lehre*, "Mitteilungen und Materialien, Zeitschrift für Museum und Bildung", 53, 2000, pp. 24-36.

Martschukat J. - Patzold S. (eds.), *Geschichtswissenschaft und „performative turn". Ritual, Inszenierung und Performanz vom Mittelalter bis zur Neuzeit*, Cologne-Weimar-Vienna 2003.

Martschukat J. - Patzold S., *Geschichtswissenschaft und „performative turn": Eine Einführung in Fragestellung, Konzepte und Literatur*, in Martschukat J. - Patzold S. (eds.), *Geschichtswissenschaft und "performative turn". Ritual, Inszenierung und Performanz vom Mittelalter bis zur Neuzeit*, Cologne-Weimar-Vienna 2003, pp. 1-31.

Meyer D., *Zinzendorf und Herrnhut*, in Brecht M. - Deppermann K. (eds.), *Geschichte des Pietismus Bd. 2: Der Pietismus im achtzehnten Jahrhundert*, Göttingen 1995, pp. 3-106.

Modrow I., *Religiöse Erweckung und Selbstreflexion. Überlegungen zu den Lebensläufen Herrnhuter Schwestern als einem Beispiel pietistischer Selbstdarstellung*, in Schulze W., *Ego Dokumente: Annäherung an den Menschen in der Geschichte*, Berlin 1996, pp. 121-129.

Mohanavelu C.S., *German Tamilology: German contribution to Tamil language, literature and culture during the period 1706-1945*, Madras 1993.

Nehring A., *Orientalismus und Mission: Die Repräsentation der tamilischen Gesellschaft und Religion durch Leipziger Missionare 1840-1940*, Wiesbaden 2003.

Id., *Natur und Gnade: Zur Theologie und Kulturkritik in den Neuen Halleschen Berichten*, in Michael Bergunder (ed.), *Missionsberichte aus Indien im 18. Jahrhundert: ihre Bedeutung für die europäische Geistesgeschichte und ihr wissenschaftlicher Quellenwert für die Indienkunde*, Halle 1999, pp. 220-245.

Nørgaard A., *Mission und Obrigkeit: Die Dänisch-hallische Mission in Tranquebar 1706-1845*, Gütersloh 1988.

Obst H., *Missionsberichte aus Indien im 18. Jahrhundert: Eine Einführung in den missionsgeschichtlichen Kontext*, in Bergunder M. (ed.), *Missionsberichte aus Indien im 18. Jahrhundert: ihre Bedeutung für die europäische Geistesgeschichte und ihr wissenschaftlicher Quellenwert für die Indienkunde*, Halle 1999, pp. 1-6.

Peterson I.V., *Tanjore, Tranquebar, and Halle: European Science and German missionary education in the lives of two Indian intellectuals in the early nineteenth century*, in Frykenberg R.E. (ed.), *Christians and Missionaries in India: Cross-Cultural Communication since 1500*, Cambridge 2003, pp. 93-126.

Id., *Science in the Tranquebar Mission Curriculum: Natural Theology and Indian Response*, in Bergunder M. (ed.), *Missionsberichte aus Indien im 18. Jahrhundert: ihre Bedeutung für die europäische Geistesgeschichte und ihr wissenschaftlicher Quellenwert für die Indienkunde*, Halle 1999, pp. 175-220.

Römer H., *Geschichte der Brüdermission auf den Nikobaren und des 'Brüdergartens' bei Trankebar*, Herrnhut, 1921.

Wellenreuther H., *Pietismus und Mission. Vom 17. bis zum Beginn des 20. Jahrhunderts*, in Lehmann H. (ed.), *Geschichte des Pietismus Bd. 4: Glaubenswelt und Lebenswelten*, Göttingen 2004, pp. 166-193.

Young R.F., *Singer of the 'Sovereign Lord'. Hindu Pietism and Christian Bhakti in the Conversions of Kanapati Vattiyar, 18th-Century Tranquebar Tamil 'Poet'*, contribution at the 2nd International Congress for Pietism studies, Halle 2005 (to be published).

The Role of Religious Minorities in European Nation Building Processes around 1800: The Discussion Concerning Citizenship for the Jews in Prussia

Iwan-Michelangelo D'Aprile
University of Potsdam

Mit dem vorliegenden Artikel werden zwei Zielsetzungen verfolgt. Zum einen werden kurz vier Trends oder Entwicklungen der jüngeren historischen Forschung bzw. der Aufklärungsforschung in Deutschland vorgestellt: (1) Die sogenannte „topographische Wende", d. h. die kulturräumliche Differenzierung von Aufklärungsbewegungen und die damit verbundenen methodologischen Vorgaben, wie z. B. die synchrone Betrachtung von Gleichzeitigkeiten (anstatt traditioneller „großen Erzählungen" von diachron aufeinander folgenden Epochen) oder die Verbindung ideengeschichtlicher Fragestellungen mit ihrer materialen (institutionellen, sozialen, medialen) lokalen Basis. (2) Die Kulturtransfer- bzw. Kulturvergleichsforschung, d. h. die Erweiterung des Bezugsrahmens über den traditionellen nationalgeschichtlichen Rahmen hinaus. (3) Die Erweiterung des historischen Bezugsrahmens über den europäischen Kontext hinaus zu globalen Fragestellungen in der sog. „Neuen Weltgeschichtsschreibung" und schließlich (4) die Betrachtung der Aufklärungsepoche des 18. Jahrhunderts als Gründungsgeschehen der Moderne und die Untersuchung der Wirkungen der Aufklärung in den Staatsbildungsprozessen des frühen 19. Jahrhunderts. Anschließend wird jeweils skizziert, wie sich diese methodischen Vorgaben auf einen bestimmten historischen Gegenstand, nämlich die Debatten um die Staatsbürgerschaft der Juden in Preußen um 1800, anwenden ließen.

This chapter has two goals: on the one hand it deals with the historical program of citizenship for religious minorities, in this case the Jewish minority in Brandenburg-Prussia around 1800, which is also an important part of the Prussian nation building process after the breakdown of the ancien régime in 1806. In addition I shall present some general methodological and heuristical trends of recent German historiography, foremost Enlightenment research. Thus I will briefly present four trends and innovations of contemporary research; these methods then will be applied to the historical subject mentioned above.

The topic is particularly significant for two reasons, when we take into account his torical and contemporary issues surrounding the unification process of Europe: first, it is of the highest importance that in the debates about the emancipation of the Jews the question of citizenship is inextricably linked to questions of cultural and religious identity. That means that the progressive contributors to that debate call for civil rights for the Jews *as* Jews – and they do not presuppose the traditional condition of assimila-tion by or even conversion to Christianity. In other words, in addition to the common human rights of life, peace, property, freedom, justice and so on, the human right of cultural identity is one basic demand of those representatives of the Enlightenment. Next, the debate about emancipation of the Jews is a transnational (and, of course, also prenational) debate concerning the whole of Europe in which the standards of treat-ing a minority, which is discriminated against as "non-European" (with the argument that they are "non-Christians"), are discussed. Maybe it is a lesson of history that this minority in the 19th and early 20th centuries was one of the main representatives of European high culture.

THE "TOPOGRAPHICAL TURN"

The concepts of "Topographical turn" and "Area Studies" are being used more and more in historiography to examine synchronic and spatial phenomena of culture op-posed to the diachronic approach of the great narratives of traditional historiography. One important work which paradigmatically exemplifies that method and which has been discussed in the last years in Germany is Karl Schlögels "Im Raume lesen wir die Zeit"[1] ["In Space We Read History"]. Schlögel's main area of interest is 19th- and 20th-century Russian history: for example Schlögel looks at the inhabitants of one single house at a particular time on a particular street in St. Petersburg. But his method can be applied to other areas of history. For example, we can differentiate individual Enlight-enment centres in the 18th century as well as different cultural/spatial manifestations of the Enlightenment.

Berlin in the 18th century was a very specific cultural place, characterized by the density of different cultures: German, French, Jewish, Polish. It is this cultural hybridity that is a significant property not only of Berlin but more or less of all of Central and Eastern Europe, where modern state building processes were slower, more heterogeneous and more complex than in France or Great Britain. In his recent doctoral dissertation Matt Erlin describes this hybridity of 18th-century Berlin as follows: "The real significance of representation of late 18th-century Berlin lies in their explicit or implicit engage-ment with [...] hybridity, a hybridity that challenges commentators to develop new frameworks for conceptualizing the origins and implications of modern urban phe-nomena"[2].

 The politics of tolerance and settlement of people from different countries with dif-ferent religions has a long Brandenburgian tradition since the Great Elector who tried to compensate for the losses in the Thirty Years War (1618-1648) with a proactive policy of *Peuplierung* [Populization]. From the beginning, the politics of tolerance in Brandenburg-Prussia was granted to Christian (Lutherans, Calvinists, Catholics) and non-Christian denominations. For example, Friedrich II stated in the middle of the 18th century: "Alle Religionen seindt gleich und guth, wann nuhr die leute, so sie profesieren, Ehrlige leute seindt, und wen Türken und Heihden kämen und wollten das Land pöplieren, so wollen wir sie Mosqueen und Kirchen bauen." ["All religions are equal and good, as long as the people who profess to be honourable indeed are so. If Turks and heathens came here to populate the country, we would want to build mosques and churches for them"][3]. But especially during the reign of Friedrich II there was a gap between the official doctrine and ideology of tolerance, and the concrete *Realpolitik*. In particular, the policies against the Jewish minority were full of restrictions and discrimination.

It was thus not by chance that this contradiction was laid bare to the public by the reform elements within the Prussian bureaucracy only at the end of Friedrich's reign in the 1780s. Before this, the discourse was conducted only in the field of literature: for example by Gotthold Ephraim Lessing in his play *The Jews* in the 1750s (and later in *Nathan the Wise*). And many of the reform treatises are dedicated to the prince and designated king Friedrich Wilhelm II, for example Mirabeau's *Lettre remise à Fréderic Guillaume II, roi régnant de Prusse, le jour de son avènement au trône* [Open Letter to Friedrich Wilhelm II][4] or Christoph Goßlers *Versuch über das Volk. Zum Besten der Armen* [An Essay about the People: For the Benefit of the Poor][5]. Indeed, at the beginning of the reign of Friedrich Wilhelm II there are some improvements for the Jewish citizens: for example Markus Herz was called as the first Jewish professor to the Prussian Academy of Science. But this springtime of reforms ended suddenly with the King's fear of a supposed danger of revolution after 1789 (see also part 4).

Although, by our modern standards, the official Prussian immigration politics concerning the Jews would then seem restrictive, Berlin was becoming at the end of the 18th Century a European Centre of the Jewish Enlightenment (*Haskala*). Until then Berlin had been, compared e.g. to traditional cities of Jewish culture as Frankfurt/M. or Prague, a completely unimportant place[6]. This change of significance is expressed for example in the foundation of the first *Jüdische Freyschule* [Jewish Public School] (1778), the founding of groups such as the *Gesellschaft der Erforscher der hebräischen Sprache* [Society for Hebrew Language Research] (1782) or the *Gesellschaft der Freunde* [Society of Friends] (1792), as well as the debut of the first Hebrew enlightenment journal *HaMe'assef* (*Der Sammler* [The Collector]) in 1783, from 1787 edited in Berlin). The best known institutions of Jewish-Prussian culture are, of course, the Jewish *salons* which were a meeting place for almost the whole Prussian cultural elite – gentiles as well as Jewish citizens; noblemen as well as bourgeois.

In its social structure the Berlin Jewish community can be characterized by mainly two groups: on the one hand, there are the wealthy bankers, merchants and proto-industrialists, who are often direct successors of the so called "court Jews", like Ephraim Veitel, Isaac Daniel Itzig, Lazarus Bendavid or Saul Ascher. They represent the class

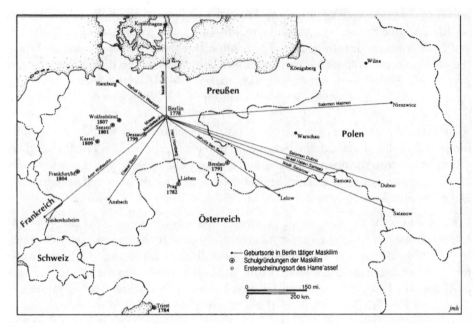

Fig. 1
Migration of Jews to Berlin in the 18th Century, from M. A. Meyer et al. (eds.), *Deutsch-jüdische Geschichte in der Neuzeit*, vol. 1, Munich 1996, p. 280.

of the upper "bourgeoisie" in Berlin. A far larger part of the Jewish community, however, are poor immigrants from all over Central and Eastern Europe. The living conditions of this second group are expressed in literature, for example in Salomon Maimon's autobiography "Description of my Life" (*Salomon Maimons Lebensbeschreibung*)[7].

Not only for these discussions on 'civic improvement' for the Jews are the enlightened circles and societies of the highest importance; it was in this milieu that new forms of class-transcending interaction in the public sphere[8] were constituted. In the Berlin "Mittwochsgesellschaft" [the Wednesday Society] for example the most important contributors were meeting weekly – Moses Mendelssohn, as well as Christian Dohm or even the French visitor Mirabeau. And the main points of the discussions in the "Mittwochsgesellschaft" were immediately published in the "Berlinische Monatsschrift".

Concluding points: as a melting pot, Berlin can be seen as the concrete background of multicultural experiences on which the discussions about citizenship for the Jews take place. To use Pierre Bourdieu's term one could say the city is the *field* in which specific forms of *habitus* are developed. The topographical approach thus allows to link questions of the history of ideas with those of the history of institutions, social formations, and the media.[9]

"Cultural Transfer Research" (*Kulturtransferforschung*)

This kind of research has been developed since the 1980s, especially in works concerning the Franco-German relationships in history. Historians to be named here are Michel Espagne, Michael Werner, Hans-Jürgen Lüsebrink and Etienne François. They all try to expand or even replace the national paradigm of historiography with the examination of transnational processes, relationships, hybridities. These processes of transfer can be examined on different levels: as transfers of knowledge, of technology, products, books, and of course ideas[10].

The achievement of citizenship for the Jews in Europe is a typical case of a transfer process where different agents all over Europe were involved. The debate can only be adequately understood if one takes into consideration the whole of Europe. Authors from different countries who were living in different historical-social systems took part in it: for example, the early Enlightenment figures Manasseh ben Israel with the *Rettung der Juden* [Salvation of the Jews][11], or John Toland with his *Reasons for Naturalizing the Jews in Great Britain*[12]; the champions of the Jewish enlightenment, of course, such as Moses Mendelssohn, Lazarus Bendavid, David Friedländer, Naphtali Hirz Wessely and others; parts of the clergy in the Austrian and Prussian "Enlightened Absolutism" such as Joseph von Sonnenfels, Christian Dohm, Heinrich Friedrich Diez, Christoph Goßler, Kaspar Friedrich von Schuckmann, Wilhelm von Humboldt; and last but not least French Revolutionaries like Mirabeau.

The discussion I am examining started with pogroms against the Jews in Alsace who sent a *Mémoire sur l'état des Juifs en Alsace* to Moses Mendelssohn in Berlin and asked him for help because he was a well-known philosopher. Mendelssohn ordered the Prussian clerk Christian Dohm to write an enquiry on this topic. Dohm then published in 1781 the political program of citizenship for the Jews under the title: *Über die bürgerliche Verbesserung der Juden* [Concerning the Civic Improvement of the Jews]. In his *Mémoire*, the anonymous author demands not only the elimination of all employment restrictions, through which the Jews are strictly limited to trading in a very restricted class of goods. Touching on the contemporary discussions about "Natural Rights", he then calls for rights of cultural identity, autonomy of the Jewish community and free practice of religion. He links this to an appeal for tolerance and cosmopolitism: because, as he maintains, to be part of a religion has nothing to do with birth, education or tradition but only with the free decision by a rational and reasonable individual.

So in the Alsatian *Mémoire* we can already find many of Dohm's arguments, for example Dohm's main point against the current prejudices against the Jews, that they are not based on natural characteristics but only on the consequences of the history of anti-Jewish politics of European governments: "Alles, was man den Juden vorwift, ist durch die politische Verfassung, in der sie itzt leben, bewirkt, und jede andre Menschengattung, in dieselben Umstände versetzt, würde sich sicher eben derselben Vergehungen schuldig machen". [Everything that people accuse the Jews of is a consequence of the political circumstances in which they live. Any other group of people forced into the same conditions would end up in the same unfortunate state][13].

The fact that Christian Dohm, as a Prussian clerk and colleague of the Minister Graf von Herzberg (and thus as a half-official speaker of the Prussian government), could go to the public with such theses under the broadly known anti-Jewish attitude of the king at all, is due to the competition between Prussia and Austria over hegemony in the territory of the old Holy Roman Empire. Thus, according to the ruling ideology of 'enlightened absolutism' in both states, this was a contest to see who was more reformist. So it is then not by chance that shortly before the Dohmian Treatise some plans were published by the Habsburg Monarch Joseph II, in the context of his "Josephenian Reforms", concerning the improvement of the situation of the Jews in Austria. For example, on 13 May 1781 the emperor published suggestions on how to "make so many members of the Jewish nation more useful to the state" by abandoning "all humiliating and spiritually repressive laws which force Jewish people to an unnecessary difference in clothing and other externals"[14]. In addition to that, the Jewish subjects should be allowed to work in agriculture and professional trades, which had been forbidden to them up till then[15]. In the Prussian press these suggestions are immediately celebrated, for example in the article by Naphtali Hirz Wessely under the title *Worte der Wahrheit und des Friedens an die gesammte jüdische Nation. Vorzüglich an diejenigen, so unter dem Schutze des glorreichen und großmächtigsten Kaysers Joseph II. wohnen. Aus dem Hebräischen* [Words of Truth and Peace to the Entire Jewish Nation. Foremost on Those Living under the Protection of the Glorious and Most Mighty Emperor Joseph II. From the Hebrew][16]. For the harbingers of the Prussian Enlightenment, this public celebration of the traditional enemy, Austria, becomes one important strategy to make their own government act[17].

Moses Mendelssohn himself took part in the debate in early 1782, when he published together with Markus Herz a translation of the English original of Manasseh ben Israels' *Rettung der Juden*. The translation contained a foreword where Mendelssohn and Herz point out the parallels between the appeal by the Amsterdam Rabbi Manasseh ben Israel to Oliver Cromwell in 1651 to give sanctuary to the Jews and their own situation. Mendelssohn and Herz try to show that, despite all the progress in the enlightened 18th century, many anti-Jewish prejudices were still virulent and that the danger of persecution campaigns remained undiminished.

The transfer of the debate back to France, where it started in Alsace, is first of all the work of Honoré Gabriel Victor Riqueti, Comte de Mirabeau. Mirabeau stayed in Berlin from January 19, 1786 to April 17, 1786 and again from July 21, 1786 to January 19, 1787 as a secret agent of the French Secretary of Foreign Affairs to report on the political tendencies in the context of the expected death of Friedrich II and the foreseen succession. Here he actively took part in the discussions of the "Berlin Enlightenment", was a guest member of the "Berliner Mittwochsgesellschaft" and was in almost daily contact with his main adviser, Christian Dohm. Immediately after his Berlin stay Mirabeau then published his work *Sur Moses Mendelssohn, sur la réforme politique des juifs: Et en particulier sur la révolution tentée en leur faveur en 1753 dans la Grande Bre-*

tagne[18], which contains in the first part a biography of Moses Mendelssohn, and in large sequences of the second part an adaption of Dohms "Bürgerlicher Verbesserung".

With this work, Mirabeau is the initiator of a debate in France about the civic improvement of the Jews, which for example leads to the competition of the Royal Academy of Sciences in Metz concerning the question *Est-il un moyen de rendre les Juifs plus utile et plus heureux en France?* (1787). In their essays, all three prize-winners follow the Mendelssohn/Dohm/Mirabeau-theses: Abbé Grégoire with his *Essai sur la régénération physique, morale et politique des Juifs*[19], Adolphe Thiéry with the *Dissertation sur cette question: Est-il des moyens de rendre les Juifs plus utile et plus heureux en France?*[20] and the Jewish immigrant Zalkind Hourwitz, who came from Poland to France via Berlin, with his *Apologie des Juifs*[21].

But even more importantly, during the French Revolution, Mirabeau was the speaker of the Third Estate and played an important role in the implementation of the constitution in France, which for the first time in European history gave full civil rights to the Jews (28 January, 1790: citizenship was granted to Jews, 27 September 1791: all Jews could become active citizens)[22].

On the other hand this did not go unnoticed in Prussia: given the proclamation of human rights in the French Revolution, in Prussia there also were totally new possibilities to further the aim of civic improvement of the Jews. It was mostly the Jewish heralds of the Enlightenment in Berlin who translated and published the French developments in this field for Germany, for example Lazarus Bendavid *Sammlung der Schriften an die Nationalversammlung, die Juden und ihre bürgerliche Verbesserung betreffend. Aus dem Französischen* [Collections of Works Concerning the Jews and their Civic Improvement for the French National Assembly][23], David Friedländers translation of the *Antwort der Juden in der Provinz Lothringen auf die der Nationalversammlung von der sämmtlichen Stadtgemeinde zu Straßburg überreichte Bittschrift* [Response of the Jews in Lorraine] in the "Berlinischen Monatsschrift"[24] or Moses Hirschel *Apologie der Menschenrechte. Oder philosophisch kritische Beleuchtung der Schrift: Ueber die physische und moralische Verfassung der heutigen Juden* [A Defence of Human Rights. Or a Philisophical-Critical Examination of the Work: Concerning the Physical and Moral State of the Jews][25].

And when Napoleon then started his invasion of Europe and brought the French constitution to Germany too, Christian Dohm worked as a minister for Napoleon in the occupied Kingdom of Westphalia to implement the *Code Civil*. In Prussia, Dohm's former pupil Wilhelm von Humboldt, who led during the whole time an intense correspondence with Dohm, fought for civil rights for the Jews in Prussia as well, rights which were, at least to some extent, given to them during the Prussian reforms in the "Edict of Emancipation" (*Emanzipationsedikt*) on 11 March 1812.

EUROPE AND THE NON-EUROPEAN WORLD

The general trend of contemporary historiography towards a "New Global History" also has an impact on Enlightenment research. Two examples of this expansion of perspective are the works of the historian Jürgen Osterhammel[26] and the recent collection of essays by Felicity A. Nussbaum[27]. As Hegel had already stated, the global perspective was not of such importance for German history because, unlike for example Portugal, Spain, France, Holland or England, during the Ancient Regime the German principalities never had colonies. As Hegel puts it, the German journeys went into the unknown continent inside us instead of into foreign and far away continents. Starting with the coincidence of the events around the crucial year 1500 – the discovery of America and the appearance of Luther, Hegel asserts (not free of the prejudice of the German *Kulturnation*): "Während die übrige Welt hinaus ist nach Ostindien, Amerika, – aus ist, Reichthümer zu gewinnen, eine weltliche Herrschaft zusammenzubringen (...) ist es ein einfacher Mönch, der das Dieses, das die Christenheit vormals in einem irdischen, steinernen Grab suchte, vielmehr in dem tieferen Grabe der absoluten Identität alles Sinnlichen und Äußerlichen, in dem Geiste findet, und dem Herzen zeigt". [While the other nations are going to East-India, America to get rich and become powerful.., it is a simple monk who finds all this in the spirit and the heart][28]

It is interesting, in this context, that the prejudices and stereotypes against the Jews are in many respects similar to those against Moslems in our day and age. The Jews were depicted as being religious fanatics with strange religious rites, funny clothes, beards and hairstyles, and it was held that they tend to violence and even blood murders. This parallel can be also shown also by the fact that the discourse of Jewish emancipation is part of the academic subject of *Orientalistik* (not 'orientalism' in the sense of Edward Said). For example, one of the most famous anti-Dohmean and anti-Jewish articles in the debate stems from the most important professor of *Orientalistik* of his time, Johann David Michaelis. In his reaction to Dohm's *Bürgerlicher Verbesserung* in the 19th part of the *Oriental and exegetic library* (*Orientalische und exegetische Bibliothek*)[29], a journal which was edited by Michaelis himself, Michaelis tries to 'prove' all the traditional prejudices against Jews as scientific facts.

THE LONG 18TH CENTURY

Whereas in earlier historiography, talk was often of the "long 19th century" (from the French Revolution to the beginning of World War I), currently one hears more and more of the continuity of the developments of Enlightenment in the late 18th century and the modern nation building processes in early 19th century. The social developments up to the Revolution of 1848 can then be seen as a manifestation, popularisation, and continuation of the Enlightenment (see for example the works of Rudolf Vierhaus and Jürgen Osterhammel)[30].

For the historical situation in Prussia, this thesis of continuity is obvious: not only the Prussian Reforms continued and completed Friedrich the Great's reforms but also the agents of both reforms were the same. It is interesting here to see how historical progress is more a thing of "long durée" than of single events. And, at least in the case we discuss here, they develop more under the surface, in the continuity of the Prussian administration, than through decisions of the crown. It was already mentioned that Friedrich II, in contrast to his self-description as 'enlightened', had many prejudices against Jews. If the "Age of Enlightenment" in Prussia is then what Kant defined as the "Age of Friedrich the Great", Jewish emancipation processes took place after that age. Nonetheless it should have become clear that they have their roots in that period.

Also the successor of Friedrich, Friedrich Wilhelm II had not fulfilled the expectations which people had of him (see part 1). On the contrary, already in the year 1791 all public debates on the topic were outlawed; in the same year it was forbidden to deal with all topics concerning Human Rights, and on May 7, 1792, the reform of civic laws for the Jews was suspended. In the course of the national movement of early Romanticism, there was a rising anti-Semitism leading up to Carl Wilhelm Friedrich Grattenauer's polemic article: *Wider die Juden. Ein Wort der Warnung an alle unsere christlichen Mitbürger* [Against the Jews. A warning to all Christian citizens] from 1803. By a police act of September 20, 1803, and by a *Cabinets-Ordre in Ansehung der Druckschriften wider und für die Juden*[Orders of the Cabinet considering publications against and in support of the Jews] of October 1, 1803 the whole debate was closed by the state[31].

It was only after the collapse of the *Ancien Régime* and the Napoleonic occupation that it was possible again to deal with this subject, from 1808 onward. Now the reform project was supported again by many *Denkschriften* which led to the *Emanzipationsedikt* of March 11, 1812[32]. The more conservative faction in the Prussian clergy, like Leopold von Schroetter, maintained many restrictions on Jewish citizenship: for example he demanded that the Jews absolutely erase (*vertilgen*[plow under]) their cultural identity and assimilate to the Christian majority. On the other hand the liberal faction around Wilhelm von Humboldt and Friedrich von Schuckmann called for full civil rights for Jews. It is exactly this group – including Wilhelm von Humboldt's mentor Christian Dohm – that had initiated the debate 30 years before in the 1780s.

NOTES

[1]   K. Schlögel, *Im Raume lesen wir die Zeit. Über Zivilisationsgeschichte und Geopolitik*, Munich 2003.

[2]   M. Erlin, *Berlin's Forgotten Future. City, History, and Enlightenment in Eighteenth-Century Germany*, 2004, p. 169.

[3]   W. Schulze, *Einführung in die Neuere Geschichte*, Stuttgart 2002, p. 214.

[4]   H.-G. de Riquetti comte de Mirabeau, *Lettre remise à Frédéric Guillaume II, roi régnant de Prusse, le jour de son avènement au trône* [Open Letter to Friedrich Wilhelm II], Berlin 1787.

[5]   C. Goßlers, *Versuch über das Volk. Zum Besten der Armen* [An Essay about the People: For the Benefit of the Poor], Berlin 1786.

[6]   Ch. Schulte, *Die jüdische Aufklärung in Berlin. Eine Bewegung aus Migranten und Autodidakten*, in I. D'Aprile (ed.), *Europäische Ansichten. Brandenburg-Preußen um 1800 in der Wahrnehmung europäischer Reisender und Zuwanderer*, Berlin 2004, pp. 192-194.

[7]   S. Maimon, *Salomon Maimons Lebensbeschreibung* [Description of my Life], Berlin 1793.

[8]   J. Habermas, *Strukturwandel der Öffentlichkeit*, Neuwied 1962.

[9] G. Lottes, '*The State of the Art*', *Stand und Perspektiven der 'intellectual history*', in F.-L. Kroll (ed.), *Neue Wege der Ideengeschichte. Festschrift für Kurt Kluxen zum 85. Geburtstag*, 1996.

[10] H.-J. Lüsebrink (ed.), *Kulturtransfer im Epochenumbruch Frankreich – Deutschland 1770 bis 1815*, vol. 1-2, Leipzig 1997.

[11] Manasseh ben Israel, *Rettung der Juden* [Salvation of the Jews], 1651.

[12] J. Toland, *Reasons for Naturalizing the Jews in Great Britain*, 1714.

[13] Ch. Dohm, *Ueber die bürgerliche Verbesserung der Juden*, Berlin-Stettin 1781, p. 35.

[14] *Die "so zahlreichen Glieder der jüdischen Nation dem Staate nützlicher zu machen", indem "alle demütigende[n] und den Geist niederschlagende[n] ZwangsGesetze, die den Juden einen Unterschied der Kleidung und Tracht, oder besondre äußerliche Zeichen auflegen" abgeschafft werden.*

[15] G. Heinrich, *"...man sollte itzt beständig das Publikum über diese Materie en haleine halten". Die Debatte um die 'bürgerliche Verbesserung der Juden' 1781-1786*, in U. Goldenbaum, *Appell an das Publikum. Die öffentliche Debatte in der deutschen Aufklärung 1687-1796*, 2 vols., Berlin 2004, vol. 2, p. 830.

[16] N. Hirz Wessely, *Worte der Wahrheit und des Friedens an die gesammte jüdische Nation. Vorzüglich an diejenigen, so unter dem Schutze des glorreichen und großmächtigsten Kaysers Joseph II. wohnen. Aus dem Hebräischen* [Words of Truth and Peace to the Entire Jewish Nation. Foremost on Those Living under the Protection of the Glorious and Most Mighty Emperor Joseph II. From the Hebrew], Berlin 1782.

[17] Heinrich, *"...man sollte itzt beständig das Publikum"* cit., pp. 830 ff.

[18] H.-G. de Riquetti comte de Mirabeau, *Sur Moses Mendelssohn, sur la réforme politique des juifs: Et en particulier sur la révolution tentée en leur faveur en 1753 dans la Grande Bretagne*, London-Berlin 1787.

[19] Abbé Grégoire, *Essai sur la régénération physique, morale et politique des Juifs*, Metz-Paris 1789.

[20] A. Thiéry, *Dissertation sur cette question: Est-il des moyens de rendre les Juifs plus utile et plus heureux en France?*, Paris 1788.

[21] Z. Hourwitz, *Apologie des Juifs*, Paris 1788.

[22] C. Jones, *The Longman Companion to the French Revolution*, London-New York 1990, pp. 255 f.

[23] L. Bendavid, *Sammlung der Schriften an die Nationalversammlung, die Juden und ihre bürgerliche Verbesserung betreffend. Aus dem Französischen* [Collections of Works Concerning the Jews and their Civic Improvement for the French National Assembly], Berlin 1789.

[24] D. Friedländers (trans.), *"Antwort der Juden in der Provinz Lothringen auf die der Nationalversammlung von der sämmtlichen Stadtgemeinde zu Straßburg überreichte Bittschrift"* [Response of the Jews in Lorraine], "Berlinischen Monatsschrift", October 1791, pp. 365-392.

[25] M. Hirschel, *Apologie der Menschenrechte. Oder philosophisch kritische Beleuchtung der Schrift: Ueber die physische und moralische Verfassung der heutigen Juden* [A Defence of Human Rights. Or a Philisophical-Critical Examination of the Work: Concerning the Physical and Moral State of the Jews], Zurich 1793.

[26] J. Osterhammel - N.P. Petersson, *Geschichte der Globalisierung. Dimensionen, Prozesse, Epochen*, München 2003; J. Osterhammel, *Die Entzauberung Asiens. Europa und die asiatischen Reiche im 18. Jahrhundert*, Munich 1998.

[27] F.A. Nussbaum (ed.), *The Global Eighteenth Century*, Baltimore 2003.

[28] G.W.F. Hegel, *Sämtliche Werke. Jubiläumsausgabe in 20 Bänden*, edited by H. Glockner, 4th edition, Stuttgart 1964, 11, p. 522.

[29] J.D. Michaelis, *Orientalische und exegetische Bibliothek* [Oriental and exegetic library], 1782, p. 4 ff.

[30] R. Vierhaus, *Deutschland im 18. Jahrhundert. Politische Verfassung, soziales Gefüge, geistige Bewegungen. Ausgewählte Aufsätze*, Göttingen 1987; R. Vierhaus, *Frühe Neuzeit – frühe Moderne? Forschungen zur Vielschichtigkeit von Übergangsprozessen*, Göttingen 1992; J. Osterhammel, *Die Entzauberung Asiens. Europa und die asiatischen Reiche im 18. Jahrhundert*, Munich 1998.

[31] L. Geiger, *Geschichte der Juden in Berlin*, 2 vols., Leipzig 1988 (1871 reprint), vol. 2, pp. 301-312.

[32] I. Freund, *Die Emanzipation der Juden in Preußen unter besonderer Berücksichtigung des Gesetzes vom 11. März 1812. Ein Beitrag zur Rechtsgeschichte der Juden in Preußen*, Berlin 1912, vol. 1, pp. 103-226, vol. 2, pp. 207-248, pp. 336-339.

BIBLIOGRAPHY

Battenberg F., *Das europäische Zeitalter der Juden. Zur Entwicklung einer Minderheit in der nichtjüdischen Umwelt Europas*, 2 vols., Darmstadt 1990.

Dohm Ch., *Ueber die bürgerliche Verbesserung der Juden*, Berlin-Stettin 1781.

Erlin M., *Berlin's Forgotten Future. City, History, and Enlightenment in Eighteenth-Century Germany*, 2004.

Freund I., *Die Emanzipation der Juden in Preußen unter besonderer Berücksichtigung des Gesetzes vom 11. März 1812. Ein Beitrag zur Rechtsgeschichte der Juden in Preußen*, Berlin 1912.

Geiger L., *Geschichte der Juden in Berlin*, 2 vols., Leipzig 1988 (1871 reprint).

Grab W., *Der deutsche Weg der Judenemanzipation 1789-1938*, Munich 1991.

Gronau W., *Christian Wilhelm von Dohm nach seinem Wollen und Handeln. Ein biographischer Versuch*, Lemgo 1824.

Guggisberg H.R., *Religiöse Toleranz. Dokumente zur Geschichte einer Forderung*, Stuttgart-Bad Canstatt 1984 (a collection of sources concerning the discussion on 'tolernace' from Nicolaus v. Cues to the French Revolution).

Habermas J., *Strukturwandel der Öffentlichkeit*, Neuwied 1962.

Hegel G.W.F., *Sämtliche Werke. Jubiläumsausgabe in 20 Bänden*, edited by H. Glockner, 4th edition, Stuttgart 1964.

Heinrich G., *"…man sollte itzt beständig das Publikum über diese Materie en haleine halten". Die Debatte um die "bürgerliche Verbesserung der Juden" 1781-1786*, in Goldenbaum U., *Appell an das Publikum. Die öffentliche Debatte in der deutschen Aufklärung 1687-1796*, 2 vols., Berlin 2004, vol. 2, pp. 813-896.

Herzig A., *Jüdische Geschichte in Deutschland. Von den Anfängen bis zur Gegenwart*, Munich 1997.

Hsia R. - Po-Chia-Lehmann, H. (eds.), *In and Out of the Ghetto. Jewish-Gentile Relations in Late Medieval and Early Modern Germany*, Cambridge 1995.

Jones C., *The Longman Companion to the French Revolution*, London, New York 1990.

Katz J., *Aus dem Ghetto in die bürgerliche Gesellschaft. Jüdische Emanzipation 1770-1870*, Frankfurt/M. 1986.

Lottes G., *'The State of the Art'. Stand und Perspektiven der ,intellectual history'*, in Kroll, F.-L. (ed.), *Neue Wege der Ideengeschichte. Festschrift für Kurt Kluxen zum 85. Geburtstag*, 1996, pp. 27-45.

Lüsebrink H.-J. (ed.), *Kulturtransfer im Epochenumbruch Frankreich – Deutschland 1770 bis 1815*, vols. 1-2, Leipzig 1997.

Nussbaum F.A. (ed.), *The Global Eighteenth Century*, Baltimore 2003.

Osterhammel J., *Die Entzauberung Asiens. Europa und die asiatischen Reiche im 18. Jahrhundert*, Munich 1998.

Osterhammel J. - Petersson, N.P., *Geschichte der Globalisierung. Dimensionen, Prozesse, Epochen*, Munich 2003.

Rürup R., *Emanzipation und Antisemitismus. Studien zur "Judenfrage" der bürgerlichen Gesellschaft*, Frankfurt/M. 1987.

Schlögel K., *Im Raume lesen wir die Zeit. Über Zivilisationsgeschichte und Geopolitik*, Munich 2003.

Schmale W. - Stauber, R. (eds.), *Menschen und Grenzen in der Frühen Neuzeit*, Berlin 1998.

Schulte Ch., *Die jüdische Aufklärung in Berlin. Eine Bewegung aus Migranten und Autodidakten*, in D'Aprile I. (ed.), *Europäische Ansichten. Brandenburg-Preußen um 1800 in der Wahrnehmung europäischer Reisender und Zuwanderer*, Berlin 2004, pp. 191-208.

Schulte Ch., *Die jüdische Aufklärung*, Munich 2003.

Schulze W., *Einführung in die Neuere Geschichte*, Stuttgart 2002 (4th edition), pp. 58-91.

Vierhaus R., *Deutschland im 18. Jahrhundert. Politische Verfassung, soziales Gefüge, geistige Bewegungen. Ausgewählte Aufsätze*, Göttingen 1987.

Vierhaus R., *Frühe Neuzeit – frühe Moderne? Forschungen zur Vielschichtigkeit von Übergangsprozessen*, Göttingen 1992.

Present (and Past) Concerns, Future Directions: Religion and the Church in the Writing of 19th-Century Maltese History

MICHAEL REFALO

University of Malta

Bil-miġja tal Ingliżi f'Malta, twieldet kollaborazzjoni bejn Stat u Knisja illi kienet komda għat-tnejn. L-istorjorgrafija Maltija tas-Seklu Dsatax tagħmel aċċent fuq il-livell politiku-istituzzjonali. Għaldaqstant, din il-kitba issegwi l-istess tendenza. Pero` fit-tieni parti tagħha, tipprova turi illi hemm triq oħra illi twassal sabiex nifhmu aħjar ir-rwol tar-reliġjon u tal Knisja f'Malta fis-seklu dsatax.

Storiċi Maltin li jiktbu dwar dan il-perjodu, ġeneralment jibbażaw il-kitbiet tagħhom fuq mill-anqas waħda minn tlett premessi: (a) il-proċess ta' modernizzazzjoni; (b) il-proċess ta' awto-determinazzjoni; u (c) l-integrazzjoni ta' Malta f'perspettiva Ewropea. Tema fundamentali oħra hija dik illi tittratta r-relazzjoni bejn gvern Protestant u l-Knisja Kattolika fil-kuntest ta' poter u l-intriċċji konnessi miegħu.

Il-presenza Ingliża f'Malta tara l-bidu tagħha fit-talba ta' rappresentanti Maltin għall-protezzjoni Ingliża. Minn dak il-fatt storiku l-istorjografija tittratta dawk l-episodji illi juru kif il-Gvern kolonjali u l-Knisja Kattolika żvolġew ir-relazzjonijiet ta' bejniethom matul iż-żmienijiet. Normalment kienet teżisti armonija f'dawn ir-relazzjonijiet. Imma minn żmien għal ħmien kienu jqumu kwestjonijiet illi juru illi beżgħat u suspetti kienu jeżistu taħt il-kalma apparenti. Fost dawn, ta' min isemmi dawk marbuta mal-immunitajiet ekkleżjastiċi, id-dritt ta' santwarju, il-liġi tal Manomorta, u dik rikorrenti dwar in-nomina tal Isqof ta' Malta. Imma l-akbar kwestjoni bejn iż-żewġ naħat kienet dik marbuta ma' l-attentat Ingliż għal introduzzjoni ta' leġislazzjoni biex tirregola iż-żwiġijiet imħallta. Dawn kollha juru illi minkejja l-protesti Ingliżi illi dejjem irrispettaw ir-reliġjon tal pajjiż, xorta waħda kienu jqumu konflitti bejniethom. Fl'aħħarnett pero` kien hemm il-konsapevolezza illi posizzjoni riġida minn xi waħda mill-partijiet setgħet tkun ta' detriment għal-influwenza eġemonika tagħhom f'Malta.

Fuq il-bazi soċjali wieħed ma jistax jinsa illi l-viċinanza ta' Malta lejn l-Italja tar-Risorgimento u l-użu tal gżira bħala bażi militari u navali Ingliża kienu jikkontribwixxu għal presenza ta' numru konsiderevoli ta' barranin. Dawn bilfors kellhom effett fuq il-ħajja ta' kuljum tal popolazzjoni lokali u loġikament fuq kif tiġi elaborata ir-relazzjoni mar-reliġjon u mal Knisja.

Sabiex l-istorja tar-reliġjon u tal Knisja f'Malta matul is-seklu dsatax tkun aktar kompleta hemm bżonn illi l-attenzjoni tal istoriċi tiffoka ukoll fuq l-aspett soċjali. Hemm bżonn għalhekk illi jittieħed pass l-isfel biex nimxu 'l quddiem lejn stampa iżjed shiħa dwar is-suġġett. Diġa jeżistu eżempji ta' dan fit-trattament ta' l-attitudni tal Maltin lejn l-Enċiklika Rerum Novarum u fil kotba dwar Manwel Dimech. Pero ' l-eżempju illi juri b'mod l-aktar dirett id-direzzjoni futura huwa dak illi jittratta l-ħwejjeġ tal ħajja ta' kuljum bħad-daqq tal qniepen. Huwa biss b'dan il-mod illi nistgħu nifmu ir-relazzjonijiet bejn il-massa tan-nies, il-Knisja, u l-Gvern Kolonjali bl-armoniji u l-konflitti illi fil-livell soċjali kienu parti shiħa mill-ħajja ta' kuljum.

For over two hundred and sixty years the Maltese Islands were ruled by the Order of St. John answerable to the Pope. The Pope was also head of the two other institutions that played a dominant role over life in Malta: the Church and the Inquisition. The presence of these three institutions within the circumscribed territory that are the Maltese Islands, led to frequent disputes over jurisdiction and areas of influence. At the same time, it also helped to entrench religion in the mentality, mores and habits of the people[1]. This pervasive influence of religion and Church on all levels of social and civil life was, in a certain sense, new. Of course, the Maltese population had been Catholic for centuries. However, the Church did not enjoy the same influence in civil life during the late middle ages. As a general rule, the clergy "seem to have been almost entirely preoccupied with their religious duties and, perhaps with keeping body and soul together for themselves and for their dependents. Their incursions into politics were few and far between ... and they only attended meetings of the town council on the rarest occasions when specially invited, usually only when matters affecting them were on the agenda"[2]. As Dominic Fenech[3] rightly observes there seems to have been a temporal inversion in so far as Church involvement in civil and political matters are concerned: the term medieval is more appropriate to the attitude of the Church from early modern times onwards: "the penetration of the Church in Maltese public life occurred in reverse order of time". Hospitaller rule thus ushered in Malta a period when the church was to occupy an important, hegemonic, influence over the political, institutional and social life of the tiny Mediterranean archipelago. This did not change when Britain took over Malta in the first decade of the 19th century. Ironically enough it was the confluence of interests of the Roman Catholic Church and the Protestant coloniser that reinforced and solidified this state of affairs.

Hospitaller rule ended abruptly in 1798 with the arrival in the Maltese port of Napoleon and his fleet. The two-year French rule although overtly secular was not long enough to change the structural parameters upon which Maltese society had moulded itself during the previous two centuries or so. Indeed, the clergy participated actively in the revolt against French rule and in the ultimate expulsion of the French from the islands with the aid of the British and Portuguese navies.

This chapter reviews some of the more important writings on religion and the Church in 19th-century Malta. Since the balance is in large measure tipped in favour of the institutional, political aspect, it inevitably follows this course. However, it also seeks to review departures from the mainstream. Hence, in its second, shorter, part, it looks towards the alternative view – the 'bottom up' approach. In doing that it aspires to show that by descending a few steps down the social scale one can advance towards a more complete picture of 19th- and early 20th-century life on the islands. The field of religion was a contested area where the various players acted out their part sometimes in harmony but sometimes not. The pressures brought to bear upon this field did not originate in the field of politics alone. What these were and how these affected the daily lives of the people is for future study to uncover.

The historiography on the subject generally owes its basis to at least one of three theoretical premises: (a) the process of modernisation; (b) the progress towards self-determination; and (c) integration of the Maltese Islands with a wider, European perspective.

In pursuance of the first premise, it has been asserted that during the first few decades of British rule, an attempt was made *by the colonial master* to bring the local church in line with the practices obtaining in other parts of Catholic Europe. "Other than in remote Quebec", writes Harrison Smith, "the British had not – perhaps never would – encounter a Church medieval, a Church militant, and a Church that had lived under a theocracy long after the era of the nation-state had modified the feudalism of Europe"[4]. Furthermore, and in accordance with the second premise, relations between Church and lay authorities were generally bilateral (local church or Rome and Governor or London) in the early stages. Subsequently, and gradually, the voice of a local interlocutor representing, whether in fact or in perception, the general population would play a part in the issue. Finally, some historians have placed the relations between the Maltese church and the colonial masters within a wider international perspective. These have successfully managed to show that the way problems in Malta arose and how these were solved had, or may have had repercussions elsewhere in the empire.

Apart from these general considerations there is another theoretical construct, not always explicit, but nonetheless present. This is relevant for a proper understanding of Church-State relations in Malta in general and for its historiography in particular: the relationship of power existing between a political master and a dominant religion within a confined geographic territory. The weaving of this 'web in power', not always explicit, provides the answer to the conundrum of how a Roman Catholic island in the middle of the Mediterranean could be ruled fairly peaceably by an Atlantic Protestant nation. Even where implicit, most histories of the period have concentrated on the ups and downs of this relationship. They have elaborated on one or more instances where Church and State were on the verge of a clash and then retreated from entrenched positions in the respective interest. Only on one occasion during the 19th century did this clash threaten to become nasty and when similar occasions arose in the 20th the British authorities played a minor role: the real conflict was between the church and local, not foreign, politicians.

Religion in Secularization and in Nation Building

Fitting Malta within the wider geo-political strategies of an Imperial power did not require only the refurbishment of its port and the building of fortifications but also keeping the local population acquiescent. Some British politicians, starting from the Duke of Wellington, considered the island a man-of-war[5]. The best method to ensure acquiescence was through collaboration with the Roman Catholic Church. In the early decades of the century,

> "The Protestant population did not exceed 700 excluding the garrison; of the remaining 120,000 inhabitants, 1020 were clergymen, the rest staunch Catholics. In Malta and Gozo there were 17 male convents and 5 nunneries and a total of over 250 churches and chapels. The Ecclesiastical Establishment was supported independently of the local government. The life of the people was centred in their church, they began the day's work by hearing Mass and their main recreation was centred in religious festivals. In these circumstances an anti-Catholic policy was impossible of success, in fact the tranquillity of the island was seen in 1825 as a consequence of British policy of non-interference in religious matters"[6].

It is no wonder then that the British "not only respected the liberty of the Church but also, to some extent, protected it from proselytising"[7]. "Public religious ceremonies held by non-Catholics could be banned whenever the government expected a disturbance of the peace ..."[8]. Not only were the British careful not to tread upon the toes of an all-powerful church, but they were also willing to offer honours and privileges to it and its leader. Commissioner Ball assured the Maltese that they would henceforth (from 1807) no longer have foreigners as bishops. The British also ensured that the Diocese of Malta would be separated from the Metropolitan See of Palermo (1831); and as early as 1801 the Maltese bishop "was given the right to receive the military honours of a Brigadier"[9]. Despite the protestations of the Anglican bishop (of Malta and Gibraltar) no such honour was bestowed upon him. The difference in treatment is also evident from the delay in erecting an Anglican church in Valletta. For Henry Frendo[10] it was only just that there should be an Anglican Church in the capital city of a British colony. Until 1844 however, the only Protestant place of worship was a small chapel in the Governor's palace (previous used for a variety of purposes including as a kitchen). In the early years, an attempt had been made to turn the Conventual Church of the Order of St. John – formerly belonging to the Order but now contended between the secular and ecclesiastical authorities – into an Anglican church. However, that attempt was quashed by London[11]. The government still claimed ownership of the church, which had been declared a Co-Cathedral in 1798 (but made definitive only in 1925). A *modus vivendi* was found with the throne formerly occupied by the Grandmaster reserved for the British sovereign (and hence kept always vacant) and another one placed on the left hand side reserved for the Archbishop[12]. Another attempt was made to take over the former Jesuit Church adjoining the University. Once again London demurred[13]. It was only twelve years later that funds became available to build the Protestant church, and these were not forthcoming from the public coffer but from a private donation made by Queen Adelaide, Victoria's aunt[14].

The treatment accorded to the Catholic religion was not unique to Malta. Canada and some other colonies had been similarly treated[15]. Generally, however, historiography prefers to base this relationship upon a petition made by a number of persons, claiming to act on behalf of the local population, that requested British protection in 1802.

In that year, persons chosen "to represent them [the Maltese] on the important manner of ascertaining our rights and privileges"[16] asked for British protection and recognised the English King as "lawful Sovereign" of the islands. They made this request subject to a number of qualifications of which the sixth read:

> That His Majesty the King is the protector of our holy religion, and is bound to uphold and protect it as heretofore; and without any diminution of what has been practised since these Islands have acknowledged His Majesty as their Sovereign to this day.

This declaration and Britain's repeated protestations that it adhered by it – particularly during the early decades – have found their way in most writings about the period[17]. At the same time, historians have highlighted the early attempts (often successful) made by the British in order to change some of the practices then current within the local church. These were considered detrimental to the smooth running of the local administration; in some cases hindering the proper exercise of justice. There was little in common between Malta and Britain. As Frendo says, the two islands had a different language, religion and temperament. But above all one could command and the other could only obey[18].

The early measures which the British sought to reform were the right of sanctuary and ecclesiastical immunities. Both required the consent of Rome. "It was realised that obedience to the proposed Government regulations would demand from the people action contrary to certain Papal Bulls; and that such an offence merited excommunication. Obviously the difficulties of executing the regulations under such circumstances would be almost insuperable"[19]. Rome's consent was negotiated, and, for Hilda Lee[20] "this material change ... [was] favourably received by the population at large". Frendo sees these measures as essentially aimed at greater centralisation. Henceforth, he says, civil and criminal law became applicable to all the subjects of the Crown in the same way with exceptions depending upon Government. He also sees in them traces of secularisation and modernity because of the consequent equality before the law[21]. For Bezzina, on the other hand, the Vatican yielded easily, though unwillingly, to British diplomatic pressure "due to an eagerness to avoid any obstacles in the promulgation of the Emancipation Act [in the UK]"[22].

One other problem concerned the vast land ownership of the local church. Mortmain law, in terms of which "the Church or other pious or religious institutions could not acquire immovable property, except under the condition that it should be sold or disposed of within one year; if it was not, the property would be forfeited to the Government *ipso facto*"[23] was introduced in 1828. That law was intended to restrict the temporal power of the church, owner of approximately one third of the land[24]. Koster argues that "the Maltese had on various occasions asked for legal remedies against this situation [i e. the fact that the church owned one third of the property]". He goes on to say that probably it was the landed class who had asked for these remedies because "these became burdened with a relatively more substantial part of the taxes as the Church was exempt from tax-paying"[25].

There was another, more important matter that needed to be solved between the British and the Vatican: the choice of bishop for the island. As successors of the Order of St. John, the British claimed a right to indicate their preference. Hence when Bishop Mattei died (1829), they proposed their candidate Archdeacon Caruana. Caruana had been one of the leading insurgents against the French and had been favoured by the British also in 1807. Although Rome did not oppose this nomination, the King of Naples, in virtue of tenuous pretensions which in reality could never be asserted, still claimed the right to nominate.

The choice of Caruana established a precedent. Such decisions were to be made in Rome after taking into consideration the recommendations of the British government. No other party had a stake. "This was, therefore, another step in virtue of which the Crown could continue to consolidate its power over Malta and its population; through the maintaining of good relations with the ecclesiastical leaders of the country"[26]. And yet disagreements between Rome and London on the matter recurred. In 1841, for example, it was through the intervention of the Irish Catholic members of the House of Commons that an impasse was resolved[27]. When the problem cropped up again (1888) things had changed. With the grant of a form of representation to the Maltese, firstly as nominated by the Governor and then on an elective basis a new actor enters the scene. The local representative, then a politician, now in the process of becoming a political party, henceforth plays a role in the relationship between church and state. That role is hardly ever determinant during the period. And yet the local politician could make his voice heard and could move public opinion.

This is not the place to recount in detail the constitutional vicissitudes of the Maltese Islands under British rule[28]. They can, however, be summarised in the words of Jeremy Boissevian, "Constitutional development in Malta has been a painful and slow process; for it is not a simple matter to give representative government to a fortress"[29]. The first constitution under which elections were held was granted in 1849. Despite a limited franchise and repeated protests, that constitution remained in force until 1887. Henceforth, discussions held in the Council of Government found members supporting the government (usually the so-called 'official members' being nominated by the Governor) as well as an opposition (almost always all the elected members). This meant that matters affecting the Church and religion could now be used by these individuals and by the political parties that followed them, to castigate the government and, often, to make political mileage out of it.

The so-called 'Marriage Question' is such a case. Briefly, the problem concerned the validity of marriages celebrated in Malta when one of the parties was a non-Catholic. The Roman Catholic Church enjoyed absolute power over marriages in Malta. This matter, together with other topical issues, formed the agenda of a meeting in Rome between the former Governor of the island, Sir Lintorn Simmons and Cardinal Rampolla for the Vatican[30]. "Sending a diplomatic mission to the Vatican was not a decision that the British Government took lightly", says Dominic Fenech[31]. Indeed the respective interests of the two sides – the desire to establish diplomatic ties following the loss of temporal power on the Roman side; and the advantage of papal support in Ireland on the British side – made this a reality.

If some sort of working agreement was reached on the future appointment of Maltese bishops, no such agreement was forthcoming on marriages. Although civil legislation was necessary in order to regulate the civil validity of marriages

> the Vatican had no wish to diminish Church influence by undermining the civil force of canon law … After several consultations with the Maltese Archbishop, Cardinal Rampolla in January 1890 presented Simmons with the only formula that the Vatican would accept. The Holy See would not object to civil legislation stipulating that the form established by the Council of Trent was the only valid form of all marriages when at least one of the spouses was a Catholic[32].

Matters became complicated in 1892 when the British Parliament enacted the Foreign Marriages Act which "validated marriages contracted in the presence of the colonial governor anywhere in the empire"[33]. The Maltese bishop was assured that the law would be suspended in Malta's case until a decision (on the conflict between this law and the agreement reached with the Vatican) was forthcoming by the highest court of the land.

It is interesting to compare the two main writings on the subject. Henry Frendo's *Party Politics in a Fortress Colony: The Maltese Experience*[34] is devoted to the rise of political parties in Malta and covers the crucial period between 1880 and 1921. By the latter date fully-fledged political parties would contest elections to a Legislative Assembly entrusted with wide, albeit limited, legislative powers. Within this context, the 'Marriage Question' forms part of the larger picture of political parties, political figures, and political opportunism. Frendo illustrates the intertwining of politics and religion in the local setting: how politicians made use of the dispute to further political ends; how these attracted huge crowds to their meetings – called 'monster meetings' – by appealing to the religious sentiments of the people and how ultimately the British backed down. The position in so far as marriages in Malta were concerned was laid to rest for another eighty years: in fact, it was only in 1975 that Catholic celebration ceased to be the only accepted form of marriage in Malta. The incident was to herald an era of "the politics of religion"[35] – religion in the hands of Maltese politicians was to become a weapon with which to beat a political adversary; the church would accompany the rise of the Maltese political party but would also claim the right to guide, to interfere, to punish whenever it felt that the dictates of religion so demanded. Further elaboration on that would take us well into the 20th century.

Dominic Fenech places the discussions in Rome which preceded the dispute within the wider perspective of Anglo-Vatican relations. Referring to official papers and correspondence, he asserts, "The question of Maltese Episcopal appointments was the major issue, especially for the Vatican. It had served as the subject of communication between Britain and the Vatican more than any other single issue in the past"[36]. He asserts that because of the way events developed "[a]s far as Malta was concerned, the outcome of the mission was worse than useless"[37].

What about the Church itself? How did it fit within the colonial framework? What were its fears, its hopes, its aspirations?

Although Protestant colonial rule may have suited the Maltese church better than the double nuisance of Grandmaster and Inquisitor, some measure of suspicion (and perhaps fear) remained. If Church and bishop were generally respected and honoured this does not mean that antipathies and fears did not, from time to time, surface.

Governor Stewart (1843-1847), "a Governor who made very obvious his personal prejudices against the Roman Catholic Church"[38], had attempted to interfere with the administration of pious legacies and a clash was averted only when the Bishop pre-empted the Ordinance enacted by the Governor[39]. The 'Marriage Question' has already been mentioned; and other incidents were generally smoothed over due to the willingness of both sides to avoid, as much as possible, serious clashes which would render life on the islands difficult for both. As a general rule, Maltese historians have stressed this fact. Thus, for example, most writings on the period allude to the willingness of the British to curb proselytising by Protestant missionaries on the island. "The activities of Protestant missionaries … were often frowned upon and restricted by the British administrators"[40]. The possibility of Protestantism spreading in Malta was a major preoccupation of both the 19th-century church as well as 20th-century historians. "[W]ith the lapse of time and with the increase of English residents, Protestant propaganda and attempts at proselytism had to start" says Arthur Bonnici[41]. The curtailment of activities of the (Protestant) Missionary Society and the restriction on distribution of translations of the bible are mentioned as proof of British reluctance to irritate the local church[42]. It was, above all, the lifting of press censorship that exercised the minds of the Maltese Bishop. It was feared that henceforth anyone could criticise the church of the land. Freedom of the press was granted in 1839. That this coincided with the landing in Malta of Italian refugees augmented Church suspicions.

For Henry Frendo the delay in the lifting of press censorship is attributable to the reservations that the local church had against the potential spread of Protestant teachings[43]. Indeed, both the local bishop and Rome had protested against the possible introduction of freedom of the press as early as 1836. In 1837 Rome informed Bishop Caruana that it would never approve of the lifting of press censorship even if laws against possible abuse were enacted[44]. One can understand the Church's objection to a liberal press, says Adrianus Koster, "if the reader remembers that it has always been the policy of the Church to monopolise the means of orientation. The lifting of censorship made 'free' competition in the sector possible"[45].

The presence in Malta of Italian refugees, fleeing from persecution in the Italian States – including the Papal States – in the wake of the reaction against revolts occurring there since 1848 and culminating in the *Risorgimento*, alarmed the Catholic Church in Malta. Newspapers critical of the temporal power of the pope and of absolutist monarchs were being published regularly in Malta. No doubt, the presence of these persons and their publications could only have, in the eyes of the church, a detrimental effect. "Il giornalismo di Malta, passato quasi completamente nelle mani degli emigranti italiani … raggiunse nell'Isola una sviluppo quasi prodigioso. Dopo otto mesi di libera stampa si potevano contare ben ventotto fogli, mentre alla fine del primo semestre del 1846, i giornali pubblicati a Malta superavano la sessantina"[46]. It is no wonder then that the Church did its utmost to keep these Italian refugees at bay. These refugees, particularly those who arrived in Malta during the period 1839-1848, were more active than those that preceded them. They encountered the opposition of the Jesuits and the Catholic population of the island. The British, on their part, were sympathetic to the cause of Italian unification but at the same time felt that peace on the island could be disturbed[47]. In fact, the Roman Catholic Irish Governor of the islands, More O'Ferrall, frequently refused permission for refugees to land in Malta, even if this exposed him "to a great deal of criticism"[48].

Protestantism, freemasonry and dissent in general were the main preoccupations of the local church and this is reflected constantly in the writings on the period by local – and foreign – historians. As a general rule there is an assumption, valid (at least until the last decade of the 19th century) that it was the 'foreigners' who were the problem. Whether these were the Italian refugees or the ever-increasing British soldiers and sailors on the island, the local voice of dissent is hardly ever mentioned. It was only towards the end of the century that a different voice – local, maybe isolated, but certainly powerful enough to ruffle the Episcopal feathers – could be heard.

Emanuel [or Manwel] Dimech, son of lower class parents, accused of complicity in murder and then of false currency, had educated himself in prison, ironically under the guidance of the spiritual director but also aided by protestant ministers. He rose to fame – or should one say notoriety – as a critic of an old-fashioned church and of imperialism.

Dimech was ignored by historians for over half a century. Starting from the 1970s a number of books have been published about him. Henry Frendo's *Birth Pangs of a Nation. Manwel Dimech's Malta (1860-1921)*[49] was followed by two others of which the first reports Dimech's pronouncements on various subjects and the second attempts a biographical reconstruction of the controversial figure[50]. If Frendo's book steers clear of "certain aspects of Dimech's life, such as his criminal court cases, his imprisonment period, his years in exile and his family life"[51], a new biography is not as reticent[52]. This latter publication not only examines in detail Dimech's life but also attempts a psychological reconstruction of his character and his actions. It is not possible to comment extensively on the work. What concerns us are two main things, namely the historical aspect of a person who managed to attract a discreet following (its exact entity being unknown, but it certainly fluctuated in relation to the Bishop's actions against him) and the set of events surrounding his notoriety in a colony considered totally faithful to the Roman Catholic religion; and the historiographical aspect. In connection with the latter it is interesting to note that starting from the 1970s, secularisation in Malta became more prevalent. Furthermore, relations between Church and State (now independent of Britain and, from 1974, a republic) became strained. The newly elected Labour Government (MLP) embarked upon a process of net separation between church and state. Dimech thus assumed a topicality when the previous decades preferred to leave dormant such a controversial figure. Mark Montebello, a Dominican friar, but not completely 'in tune' with the Church hierarchy, 'resurrects' Dimech in a decade when secularisation and dissent no longer shock the psyche of the population.

Montebello views Dimech as a beacon of light in a dark, church-dominated society where the population is "predominantly fanatical and conditioned by the utterances of others [the clergy]"[53]. Dimech incurred the wrath of the Archbishop by his writings, critical of the church hierarchy. Furthermore, he was considered to have Protestant leanings because of his fierce criticism of processions and feasts[54] which he considered to be tools for the alienation of the people. Predictably, he attracted the suspicion of the imperial government because of his writings in favour of the Maltese language, of independence and of a republic of Malta. For Montebello, Dimech was engaged in a battle for the minds of a gullible, illiterate people. Despite a number of followers, Montebello goes on, "the embedded solidity of the clergy was too strong for him; he was alone"[55]. The stream of criticism which Dimech levelled at Archbishop Pace led to his excommunication and the sanctioning of his newspaper[56]. Although Dimech was later to retract his offensive comments and the Bishop was to pardon him, he remained suspect. Indeed, for the author, Dimech is transmuted from an enemy of the church to an enemy of imperial interests in Malta[57]. On the eve of the First World War such a person was uncomfortable for both Church and Government. He was hurriedly deported from Malta in 1914 and died in exile in 1921.

If the books dealing with the political history of Malta highlight the institutional level, Montebello's biography recounts the story of a man of lower class origins, perhaps a misfit, perhaps a visionary and definitely out of tune with the prevailing circumstances of the times. Montebello portrays Dimech in a David and Goliath struggle which the former could not win. "What Dimech had not understood despite his abilities was that he could neither penetrate to the basis of that phenomenal myth nor could he match the prestige of the exponents of that myth"[58]. The hegemonic influence of the church, the collusion with the government authorities were forces which however much, one tried could not be defeated.

One other aspect of that biography is the author's portrayal of his hero as the first person who created an organization[59] that transforms relations of charity into ones based on justice[60]. It is a constant of Maltese historiography of the 19th and early part of the 20th centuries to stress the charitable activities of the church. This, accompanied by the reiteration of the devotion of the people towards their church, may be considered a recurring theme in all writings concerning the 19th century Maltese church[61]. One book, however, published in 1991, analyses the social consciousness of the Maltese church immediately before and after the promulgation of *Rerum Novarum* in 1891[62]. There, the author stresses that during the period "the local church had alleviated the worker and his dependents in their social distress principally through her practice of Christian charity"[63]. He mentions, as does Montebello, one of the first mutual aid societies to be founded in Malta. It was the intention of the founder – Angelo Caruana – to form "a workers' society based purely on trade unionistic lines"[64]. This met with the opposition of the church. Some members of the clergy believed that "the aim of the society was to spread Protestantism in Malta"[65]. Caruana was eventually convinced by the church authorities to convert his union into a mutual aid society, to insert the word "Cattolica" in the name and to have a Curia-appointed spiritual director for the society[66].

Agius says that the papal encyclical *Rerum Novarum* "had in fact been given due importance by the leading newspapers of the time"[67]. It was published in Italian and in English almost immediately. Similarly articles discussing 'the social problem' started appearing[68] And yet "[h]ardly any article was written about the local social conditions of the working classes and how workers' rights could be improved in the light of the social document"[69]. Agius, himself a cleric, justifies the lack of initiative of the Maltese church in this regard "on account of certain problems facing it at that particular moment, namely the involvement in the aftermath of the Simmons-Rampolla controversy"[70].

In synthesis: Maltese historians have concentrated primarily upon the relations between the local church and the British masters. They accept that the original request made by the Maltese and its affirmation by the British formed the basis of a mutually convenient relationship. This notwithstanding, that relationship passed through moments of crisis but it behove both parties to settle them amicably. On the other hand, the two texts mentioned above steer away from the institutional-political field. If one is openly critical of the way religion was used to dispose of an uncomfortable person, the other seeks to patch up the inadequacies of the local church to deal with social matters during the 19th century. None however – as far as can be perceived – attempt to descend the social ladder in order to examine *how* religion was practised. Indeed, there seems to be an implicit assumption that all the people, all the time, were deeply faithful to their church; that life centred round their church; that religion permeated social and domestic life. Undoubtedly this is true to a very great extent. But the cosmopolitan nature of Maltese urban society and the presence of a foreign (Protestant) master need to be re-elaborated into the story of 19th-century religion in Malta. Thus, for example, we are told that many of the Italian refugees in Malta during the *Risorgimento* gave private lessons "to the children of the better Maltese families". Some of them mixed with the Maltese upper classes: the nobility, the professionals, some merchants and part of the clergy[71]. Most of these refugees were openly critical of the temporal power of the pope and if they published newspapers with an anti-clerical bent, it is very unlikely that they did not have some influence on their hosts.

Similarly, during the second half of the century, British presence on the island increased substantially. This was accompanied, from 1869 onwards, by an influx of naval vessels on their way to the east through the newly opened Suez Canal. Research[72] shows that the local population eagerly awaited the British navy in port because that meant greater spending, more profits. But research also shows that antagonism between the Maltese and the British sailor or soldier could sometimes end up in bloody fights. When the religious sensibilities of the population were hurt, as they sometimes were, the effect of religious belief upon ordinary men and women stands out. They fight, and beat – or get beaten by – sailors or soldiers who interrupt religious processions. They show intolerance when religious practices are not respected. But they are also critical of some priests; they refuse to accept parish priests imposed upon them by the Bishop, or insist on their replacement; they fight over their patron saints. If on one level there existed an institutional Church that dealt with the colonial authorities, on another level there existed the village church that dealt with the local villagers.

There is one pointer towards future directions. John Chircop's *Bell-Ringing in Maltese History 1800-1870s. Language, Regulator and Weapon*[73] is, according to the historian, "the preliminary section of a lengthier study which inquires on customary bell-ringing in the Maltese Islands, during these last two hundred years"[74]. Bells, bell towers and bell ringing are not only a manifestation of religious belief. Indeed, they are "instruments of communication ... impart[ing] social routines in the villages and towns ... they occupied the central space of the village square which was the permanent *locus* containing and channelling the daily social flow"[75]. As instruments "structuring and sustaining the lives of the people," bells were appropriated by "the fundamentalist Catholic Church [which] reinforced ... cultural values through the official interpretation of bell-ringing"[76]. On the other hand, bell-ringing was viewed by "the civilising colonialist mind" – Protestants who objected to the pervading influence of the Catholic Church – as "an expression of the 'corrupt state of morals' existing in the people under Popish rule"[77]. There is a further facet to bell-ringing: "although the Archbishop commanded the Church, he did not control and had no rights of ownership over the belfries"[78]. In this sense, therefore the bells become an instrument of protest, of assertion of rights by 'the ordinary people'. The incident referred to concerns the limitations on bell-ringing ordered by the Archbishop on a number of occasions in 1865. This offended not only the proprietary rights of the parishioners but was also understood as an encroachment of "the people's inherited rights"[79].

John Chircop is critical of the '*High History*' approach highlighted in the earlier part of this essay. For him these only serve for a "fabrication of a *homogeneous national identity*"[80].

An approach "from the bottom" serves to illustrate that religion in 19th-century Malta was not a paradigm that applied throughout without crease or tear. Whether it was the relationship of the people with ecclesiastical or civil authority, whether it was the contact with foreigner or whether it was the simple human urge to assert oneself, the correct approach should encompass both 'high' and 'low'. Only in this way can a proper understanding of the past be attained. If historical circumstances placed an island population which is neither fully Latin not totally Arab under Anglo-Saxon domination; if it served the interests of both secular and clerical rulers to join forces, this does not mean that history should concern itself solely with this fact. Whether it is religion or politics or social structure, the theme can only be correctly analysed and presented in correct historical terms by paying attention to all levels. At the lowest level one discovers areas of conflict, of compromise and of harmony that are hidden from view when looking from the top. Our knowledge of the past is enriched and our understanding of ourselves can only be achieved by starting from the ground before taking flight.

Notes

[1] For a comprehensive survey of 18th-century religious practices and malpractices see F. Ciappara, *Society and the Inquisition in Early Modern Malta*, Malta 2001.

[2] G. Wettinger, *Early Maltese Popular Attitudes to the Government of the Order of St. John*, "Melita Historica", VI, 1976, pp. 255-278.

[3] *The Concordat Turned Sour: the Simmons-Rampolla Agreement of 1890* in P. Xuereb (ed.), *Karissime Gottifride*, Malta 1999; pp. 135-145.

[4] H. Smith, *Britain in Malta. Volume 1. Constitutional Development of Malta in the 19th Century*, Malta 1953.

[5] H. Frendo, *Party Politics in a Fortress Colony: The Maltese Experience*, Malta 1991, p. 3.

[6] H.I. Lee, *British Policy Toward the Religion, Ancient Laws and Customs in Malta, 1824-1851*, "Melita Historica", XV, 1963, pp 1-14.

[7] J. Bezzina, *L-Istorja tal Knisja f'Malta*, Malta 2002, p. 144. See also A. Koster, *Prelates and Politicians in Malta*, Assen 1984, p. 39.

[8] Koster, *Prelates* cit., p. 40.

[9] *Ibid.*, p. 41.

[10] *Storja ta' Malta. Is-Seklu Dsatax. Zmien l-Inglizi* , Malta 2004, p. 110.

[11] A. Bonnici, *Thirty Years to Build a Protestant Church*, "Melita Historica", XXV, 1973, pp. 183-191.

[12] Bezzina, *L-Istorja* cit., p. 181. For a slightly different version see Frendo, *Storja* cit., p. 111.

[13] Frendo, *Storja* cit., p. 111.

[14] *Ibid.*, pp. 111-113.

[15] Lee, *British Policy* cit.

[16] *Declaration of Rights of the Inhabitants of the Islands of Malta and Gozo* (1802), in *Maltese Political Development 1798-1964: Selected Readings Edited, Annotated and Introduced by Professor Henry Frendo*, Malta 1993, pp 55-56.

[17] See, for example, Lee, *British Policy* cit.; Bezzina, *L-Istorja* cit., pp. 177-178; Frendo, *Is-Seklu* cit., pp. 23-26.

[18] Frendo, *Is-Seklu* cit., p. 75.

[19] Lee, *British Policy* cit.

[20] *Ibid.*

[21] Frendo, *Is-Seklu* cit., pp. 81-82.

[22] *Religion and Politics in a Crown Colony: The Malta-Gozo Story 1798 – 1864*, Valletta 1985, p. 146. The Catholic Emancipation (Relief) Act was enacted by the British Parliament in 1829 and made Roman Catholics eligible for most public offices.

[23] Koster, *Priests* cit., pp. 44-45.

[24] Frendo, *Is-Seklu* cit., p. 79.

[25] Koster, *Priests* cit., p. 44.

[26] Frendo, *Is-Seklu* cit., p. 83 (*Mela dan kien pass iehor sabiex il Kurunu tkompli tikkonsolidda s-setgha taghha fuq Malta u niesha, billi tassigura kemm tista' relazzjonijiet tajba u kordjali mal-mexxeja ekkleziastici fuq il-post.*). See also Bezzina, *L-Istorja* cit., pp. 184-185 and Lee, *British Policy* cit.

[27] Bezzina, *L-Istorja* cit., p. 184.

[28] For an exposition of the early constitutions see J.J. Cremona, *Malta and Britain: The Early Constitutions*, Malta 1996.

[29] J. Boissevian, *Saints and Fireworks: Religion and Politics in Rural Malta*, New York 1965, p. 7.

[30] See H. Frendo, *Party Politics in a Fortress Colony: The Maltese Experience*, Malta 1991, pp. 71 ff.

[31] *A Concordat Turned Sour: The Simmons-Rampolla Agreement of 1890* in P. Xuereb (ed.), *Karissime Gotifride*, Malta 1999, pp. 135-145.

[32] Fenech, *The Concordat* cit., p. 137.

[33] *Ibid.*, p. 141.

[34] Malta 1991.

[35] Fenech, *The Concordat* cit., p. 74.

[36] *Ibid.*, p. 138.

[37] *Ibid.*, p. 140.

[38] Lee, *British Policy* cit., p. 4.

[39] See, for example, Bezzina, *L-Istorja* cit., pp. 182-183.

[40] Koster, *Priests cit.*, p. 40.

[41] Bonnici, *History of the Church in Malta. Volume IV 1800-1975*, Zabbar 1975, p. 189.

[42] See, for example, Koster, *Priests* cit., p. 41; Bezzina, *L-Istorja* cit., p. 178; Frendo, *Is-Seklu* cit., p. 102. A dissentient voice is that of Bianca Fiorentini, for whom Britain attempted to subject Malta to its own religion (quoted in Koster, *Priests* cit., p. 39).

[43] Frendo, *Is-Seklu cit.*, p. 103.

[44] Bezzina, *L-Istorja* cit., p. 182; Frendo, *Is-Seklu* cit., p. 104. In his autobiographical chronicle of the 20th century, Herbert Ganado (*Rajt Malta Tinbidel*, vol. 1, Malta 1977, p. 114) adds that we should not judge the Vatican decision to oppose press freedom at all costs from today's perspective.

[45] Koster, *Priest* cit., p. 46

[46] B. Fiorentini, *Il Giornalismo a Malta durante il Risorgimento Italiano,* in V. Bonello - B. Fiorentini - L. Schiavone (eds.), *Echi del Risorgimento a Malta*, Malta 1963, pp. 21-111. Journalism in Malta passed almost entirely in the hands of the Italian immigrants. Within eight months from the lifting of press censorship there were twenty eight papers, and by the first half of 1846, papers published in Malta exceeded sixty.

[47] L. Schiavone, *Esuli italiani a Malta durante il Risorgimento* in Bonello - Fiorentini - Schiamone (eds.), *Echi* cit., pp. 113-164.

[48] C. Cassar, *A Concise History of Malta*, Malta 2000, p. 161.

[49] Malta 1972. The book was preceded by another one in Maltese also by H. Frendo on which the latter work is based: *Lejn Tnissil ta' Nazzjon, it-twemmin socio-politiku ta' Manwel Dimech*, Malta 1971.

[50] G. Azzopardi, *X'Garrab Manwel Dmech*, Valletta 1975 and, by the same author, *Ghajdut Manwel Dimech*, Valletta 1978.

[51] Frendo, *Birth Pangs* cit., p. 8.

[52] M. Montebello, *Dimech (1860-1921) Bijografija*, Malta 2004.

[53] *Ibid.*, p. 341 [*Fuq il-mohh ta' popolazzjoni predominentement fanatika u dipendenti fuq kliem hadiehor*].

[54] *Ibid.*, p. 349.

55 *Ibid.*, p. 344.

56 *Ibid.*, p. 371

57 *Ibid.*, p. 435

58 *Ibid.*, p. 376 [*Dak li jidher li ma fehmx Dimech kien li bil-hila tieghu kollha u ma setax ilahhaq sal bazi ta' dak il-mit fenomenali u anki prestigjuz ta' l-Awtoritajiet li kienu qeghdin imexxu l-mit*].

59 Called *ix-Xirka tal Imdawwlin* – Society of the Enlightened.

60 Montebello, *Dimech* cit., pp. 453-454.

61 See, for example: A. Bonnici, *History of the Church in Malta. Vol. IV. 1800-1975*, Zabbar 1975; Bezzina, *Istorja* cit., but also a number of books dedicated to monasteries, communities or religious and lay persons who devoted their lives to charity or education of the children of the poor. Some examples of the latter are A. Azzopardi, *Jesuit Schools in Malta,* vol. I: *1592-1907*, Malta 2002; A. Bonnici, *Is-Sorijiet tal-Karità u l-Hidma Taghhom f'Malta*, Malta 2002; L.A. Grasso, *Fra Diegu Bonanno 1831-1902*, Malta 1995.

62 E. Agius, *Social Consciousness of the Church in Malta 1891-1921. The Impact of Rerum Novarum*, Malta 1991.

63 *Ibid.*, p. 18.

64 *Ibid.*, p. 22.

65 *Ibid.*, p. 23.

66 *Ibid.*, p. 23.

67 *Ibid.*, p. 28.

68 *Ibid.*, pp. 29-32.

69 *Ibid.*, p. 33.

70 *Ibid.*, p. 37.

71 H. Ganado, *Rajt Malta Tinbidel*, vol. 1, Malta 1977, p. 112.

72 I am carrying out research in this area in connection with my doctoral thesis under the (provisional) title *Social Class in Malta 1870-1914*.

73 Published in *Karissime Gotifride*, Malta 1999, pp. 147-158.

74 Footnote to title.

75 Chircop, *Bell-Ringing* cit., p. 148.

76 *Ibid.*, p. 149.

77 *Ibid.*, p. 151.

78 *Ibid.*, p. 155.

79 *Ibid.*, p. 155.

80 *Ibid.*, p. 147.

BIBLIOGRAPHY

Agius E., *Social Consciousness of the Church in Malta 1891-1921. The Impact of* Rerum Novarum, Malta 1991.

Azzopardi G., *X'Garrab Manwel Dimech*, Malta 1975.

Id., *Ghajdut Manwel Dimech*, Malta 1978.

Bezzina J., *Religion and Politics in a Crown Colony. The Gozo-Malta Story 1798-1864*, Valletta 1985.

Id., *L-Istorja tal Knisja f'Malta*, Malta 2002.

Id., *The Church in Malta: An Indelible Imprint upon the Nation's History and Character*, in *Malta: Roots of a Nation. The Development of Malta from an Island People to an Island Nation*, Malta 2004.

Boissevain J., *Saints and Fireworks: Religion and Politics in Rural Malta*, New York 1965.

Bonello, V. - Fiorentini B. - Schiavone L. (eds.), *Echi del Risorgimento a Malta*, Malta 1963.

Bonnici A., *The Church and Freedom of the Press in Malta*, "Melita Historica", VII, 1957.

Id., *British Assurances to Protect the Roman Catholic Religion in Malta*, "Melita Theologica", IX, 1959.

Bonnici A., *Protestant Propaganda in Malta (1800-30)*, "Melita Theologica", XIII, 1961.

Id., *Mixed Marriages in Malta (1800-1900)*, "Melita Theologica", XX, 1968.

Id., *Thirty Years to Build a Protestant Church*, "Melita Historica", XXV, 1973.

Id., *History of the Church in Malta, 1800-1975*, vol. 3, Malta 1975.

Cassar C., *A Concise History of Malta*, Malta 2000.

Chircop J., *Bell-Ringing in Maltese History 1800-1870s*, in Xuereb P. (ed.), *Karissime Gottifride. Historical Essays presented to Godfrey Wettinger on his seventieth birthday*, Malta 1999.

Cremona J.J., *Malta and Britain. The Early Constitutions*, Malta 1996.

Fenech D., *Birgu during the British Period*, in Bugeja L. - Buhagiar M. - Fiorini S. (eds.), *Birgu: a Maltese Maritime City*, L Msida 1993

Id., *A Concordat Turned Sour: The Simmons-Rampolla Agreement of 1890* in Xuereb P. (ed.), *Karissime Gottifride. Historical Essays presented to Godfrey Wettinger on his seventieth birthday*, Malta 1999.

Fiorentini B., *Malta Rifugio di Esuli e Focolare Ardente di Cospirazione Durante il Risorgimento Italiano*, Malta 1966.

Frendo H., *Birth Pangs of a Nation. Manwel Dimech's Malta (1860-1921)*, Malta 1971.

Id., *Party Politics in a Fortress Colony: The Maltese Experience*, Malta 1991.

Id., *Maltese Political Development 1798-1964. Documentary History. Compiled and Edited with Introductory Notes*, Malta 1993.

Id., *Life during the 'British' Period: Strains of Maltese Euopeanity*, in *Malta: Roots of a Nation. The Development of Malta from an Island People to an Island Nation*, Malta 2004.

Id., *Storja ta' Malta. Zmien l-Inglizi. Is-Seklu Dsatax*, Malta 2004.

Ganado H., *Rajt Malta Tinbidel*, vol. 1, Malta 1977.

Harding H., *Maltese Legal History under British Rule (1801-1836)*, Malta 1968.

Koster A., *Prelates and Politicians in Malta. Changing Power-balances between Church and State in a Mediterranean Island Fortress*, Assen 1984.

Lee H.I., *British Policy Towards Religion, Ancient Laws and Customs in Malta 1824-1851*, "Melita Historica", XV, 1963.

Montebello M., *Dimech (1860-1921) Biografija*, Malta 2004.

Smith H., *Britain in Malta Volume 1. Constitutional Development of Malta in the 19th Century*, Malta 1953.

Religion and Nation in Ukraine during the 19th and 20th Centuries: a Short Survey

Giulia Lami
University of Milan

Uno dei cambiamenti più significativi sulla carta politica europea è la presenza dell'Ucraina, diventata indipendente nel 1991, come nuovo stato che viene a collocarsi fra l'ex-Unione Sovietica e l'Unione Europea allargata.

Come tutte le "neo" repubbliche post-sovietiche, l'Ucraina attraversa ancora un periodo di transizione, punteggiato di difficoltà economiche, sociali e politiche. Essa ha comunque avviato un processo di affermazione nazionale e di riscoperta/rielaborazione del proprio passato, che si è variamente intrecciato al più ampio processo di revisione storico-politica vissuto dal mondo comunista nel suo complesso.

In questo capitolo ho indagato il rapporto fra religione e nazione/nazionalità sotto il profilo di una ricomposizione dell'identità ucraina, che è parte essenziale del processo di costruzione nazionale che il paese sta ancora compiendo. Dopo una rapida panoramica della situazione attuale che vede la presenza sul suolo ucraino di cinque diverse Chiese e di altre storiche comunità religiose (Armeni, Ebrei, Musulmani, Protestanti) che hanno specifiche istituzioni di riferimento, mi sono soffermata sui principali studi apparsi negli ultimi quindici anni.

La mia attenzione si è concentrata in particolare sul periodo a cavallo fra Ottocento e Novecento, quando si concretizzano le aspirazioni all'unità ed all'indipendenza che troveranno una parziale realizzazione nel periodo 1917-1921 e sul periodo successivo, che ha comportato nell'Ucraina sovietica diverse forme di persecuzione religiosa e nazionale, il cui peso è ancora d'ostacolo nella vita dell'Ucraina attuale.

Ho richiamato quindi la necessità di implementare gli studi sul XIX e XX secolo, esaminando in modo comparativo e sul lungo periodo i rapporti fra religione e nazione/nazionalità nelle differenti regioni ucraine; di riservare la dovuta attenzione al periodo rivoluzionario (1917-1921); di seguire il destino della Chiesa sotto il regime sovietico; di analizzare le relazioni esistenti fra le varie religioni presenti in Ucraina nei loro rapporti reciproci e verso lo stato; di tenere in considerazione il ruolo e l'influenza delle Chiese e delle comunità emigrate sulla realtà ucraina; di analizzare il ruolo della "Chiesa del silenzio" nel contesto del fenomeno del dissenso in Ucraina e in Unione Sovietica; di esaminare i materiali archivistici in Ucraina ed all'estero, non trascurando le fonti vaticane che sono consultabili almeno fino al 1922.

In conclusione si può dire che in questi anni si è assistito ad una innovazione in campo storiografico a livello di fonti, metodi e problematiche che senz'altro apre una nuova e feconda fase nello sviluppo degli studi storici ucraini, nello specifico ed in generale.

The changes that have occurred in Eastern Europe in the last fifteen years have reshaped the political map of the whole continent. One of the most interesting new realities is an independent Ukraine, whose presence halfway between East and West has given a new outline to European borders. But western knowledge about this country is still deficient in many ways.

The reasons of this lack of knowledge are deeply rooted in the past. Ukraine has been considered for centuries as a part of the multinational states or empires to which it has belonged (Polish-Lithuanian Commonwealth, Austrian and Russian Empire, Soviet Union) and, to a great extent, has been deprived of the opportunity to have its own history and culture recognized. Nevertheless, Ukraine has a history and a specific culture, worthy of study. Being positioned at the crossroads of various, often contrasting influences, Ukraine is in many ways a frontier region between East and West, not only from a geopolitical standpoint, but also from a cultural and religious one[1].

Historically, Ukraine has been placed at the core of a trade network, but has also been turned into a battlefield. This situation continues to have consequences even now: the Orange revolution has demonstrated once again the difficulties Ukraine meets in finding its position between Russia – which is ready to satellitise it – and Europe – which is having trouble considering the extension of its eastern borders beyond the limits of the former Soviet Union. Apart from the political and strategic problems menacing the newly acquired independence, I would like to stress the need that Ukraine has to recreate its self-perception, to reinterpret the collective memory and to consolidate civil democratic life.

In this difficult on-going transition process, culture undoubtedly has a great role to play. With this in mind, I would like to focus attention on the crucial problem of the interplay between religion and nation, because this is traditionally a central issue in the building of Ukrainian self-perception, an old-new problem that deserves great attention.

Generally speaking, the topics of Nation and Religion have acquired prominence in scholarly consideration of Eastern Europe since the fall of communism and the reopening of unsolved questions[2]. Ukraine can be a very interesting case study because of the co-presence on its soil of many religions and competing Churches[3]. The problem of identity has not been solved and, in many ways, this identity problem is connected with religious denomination. Ukraine is a country that is still undergoing a process of nation building. It is obvious to all observers, both inside and outside the country, that religion and nation and/or nationality raise difficult issues and problems. The goal would be that of building a secular state which supports all religions and national minorities with tolerance: we cannot forget that in Ukraine there are consistent communities of Protestants, Jews and Muslim aspiring to have their rights preserved and confirmed in everyday life.

The actual situation is very complex. Undoubtedly, with the end of communism and the inception of independence, Ukrainian religious life was able to emerge onto the surface. In the beginning, there were three Churches of Eastern Byzantine tradition, and one Church of Western Latin tradition: the Ukrainian Catholic Church, also called the Uniate[4] or Greek-Catholic Church (UGCC), the Ukrainian Autocephalous Orthodox Church (UAOC), the Russian Orthodox Church (ROC) and the Roman Catholic Church. The first two Churches (UGCC and UAOC) had undergone severe persecution during the twenties and thirties, and their properties had been confiscated and transferred to the Russian Orthodox Church (ROC). Notwithstanding the officially professed atheism, Moscow privileged, in accordance with the long tsarist tradition, the Russian Orthodox Church as a tool of Russification against possible concurrent nationalisms. The first conflict involving the three Eastern Churches broke out during the first few years after independence (1991) and concerned the issue of the confiscated properties. The Russian Orthodox Church, in accordance with the Soviet government, had administrated these properties[5]. Later, another serious conflict broke out inside the Orthodox world itself, that eventually gave birth to three branches of the Orthodox Church as a whole: the Ukrainian Orthodox Church-Moscow Patriarchate (UOC-MP), the Ukrainian Orthodox Church-Kyivan Patriarchate (UOC-KP), and the Ukrainian Autocephalous Orthodox Church (UAOC). Other historical religious communities (Armenians, Jews, Muslims, Protestants) have their religious institutions on Ukrainian territory, where there are around seventy different officially registered religions.

It is worth noting that both the conflict between Uniate and Orthodox, and the conflict within Orthodoxy itself, are focused on the question of the country's identity and history. These conflicts are less theological than cultural or political. This judgement was widespread among the commentators of the Orange Revolution: at that time, it was very common to read or hear that the country was divided into two halves, following a cultural and confessional inner borderline. From this perspective, commentators and analysts located a block faithful to the Russian Orthodoxy in the east and the south, and a block faithful to the Ukrainian Autocephalous Orthodox Church, the Ukrainian Greek-Catholic Church and the Latin (Roman)-Catholic Church in the west. Politically, this division was meant to be an indicator of a pro-Russian attitude versus a pro-western one. In reality, the situation doesn't correspond to this easy schema. The believers of the Greek-Catholic Church, the Ukrainian Autocephalous Church, and the Roman Catholic Church (belonging generally to Polish or Hungarian linguistic minorities) consider themselves to be Ukrainians as much as the believers of the Ukrainian Orthodox Church-Moscow Patriarchate and the Ukrainian Orthodox Church-Kyivan Patriarchate do. Eventually, the Ukrainian identity can cohabit with a Russian or post-Soviet identity. This complex situation is due to the historical division of the Ukrainian lands among the neighbouring States which has existed since the medieval period. The Ukrainian question dates back to Kyivan Rus', the common point of origin of the present Eastern Slavs, the Russians, the Ukrainians and the Belarusians.

Christianised in 988 in accordance with the Greek rite, the Kyivan Rus' disintegrated in the 13th century because of domestic conflicts and the Mongol invasion. The

Ukrainian lands that had been part of Kyivan Rus', following a period of independence centred around the Kingdom of Galicia-Volhynia, were incorporated along with the Belarusian ones, mostly into the Grand Duchy of Lithuania. When Lithuania united itself with the Kingdom of Poland in 1569, creating the Polish- Lithuanian Commonwealth (*Rzeczpospolita*), the major part of Ukrainian lands came under Polish rule. In 1596, the religious Union of Brest was signed, founding the Uniate Church which was also called Greek-Catholic because it conserved the traditional Byzantine liturgy and rites, while recognizing the Pope as its head. This Union, nevertheless, did not prompt the disappearance of the Orthodox Church, but gave rise to the co-presence of two rival Byzantine Churches, namely the Greek-Catholic and the Orthodox, in a territory where the Latin-Catholic Church retained a dominant position. In the 17th century, the Cossacks became the champions of the Orthodox cause, especially under the leadership of the Hetman Bohdan Khmelnytsky: in 1654, owing to the Union of Pereiaslav between the Cossack Host and Russia, the territories of the Dnepr's Left Bank – called Hetmanate – came under Russian sovereignty; from 1772 to 1795, and, as a result of the partitioning of the Polish-Lithuanian Commonwealth, the Dnepr's Right Bank came under Russian rule as well. In the meantime, the regions further to the west, i.e. Galicia and Transcarpathia, were incorporated by the Absburg empire that already possessed Bukovina, the northern part of Moldavia, inhabited by Romanians and, partially, by Ukrainians. After World War I, the western Ukrainian territories – Galicia, Transcarpathia, Bukovina – were divided among Poland, Czechoslovakia and Romania, while the Russians' central and eastern territories already formed the new Ukrainian Soviet Republic. After World War II, owing to Stalin's conquests, Ukraine regained the major part of the western territories, thereby acquiring its present geo-political demarcation. A very important moment in this story is the 1917-1921 period, when an independent Ukrainian Republic was founded. For a short while, it realized the 19th century's nationalistic dream of creating a state for all Ukrainians from west to east[6]. Only now has that dream become a reality.

The points on the historical research agenda regarding Ukraine are many and controversial. Even though historians are independent from the political necessities of the day, it is clear that the end of communism and the renewed independence finally allowed the restarting of a series of studies interrupted during the Soviet era. In Ukraine, as in Russia, since *glasnost*, the desire to fill in the blank spaces of national history has provoked a request for "more history" from civil society. Historians, either from the West or from the East, have tried to fulfil this demand[7], even though cultural operators independent from the academic world, such as journalists and publicists, have very often preceded them, especially during the first years of independence. Whatever the case may be, we have seen the renewal of historical studies that have also involved western historiography, which during the soviet period very often did not touch upon sensitive problems or enlarge its research perspective sufficiently, notwithstanding the freedom it enjoyed.

The historiographical interest for the genesis and the developments of the Union of Brest is vital. As Sophia Senyk wrote, "literature about the Union of Brest began to appear almost immediately after the Synod of October 1596 that confirmed it. Defenders and opponents took pen in order to promote or hinder this success. This polemical bent of literature about the Union has persisted to the present day. Polemics is seldom original; polemics about the Union has repeated certain statements so often that they tend to be accepted on faith even by scholars, not needing verification"[8]. In the last decade, scientific works studying the problem from different points of view in accordance with the different national historiographical traditions have appeared[9]. The result is encouraging because it demonstrates the attempt to offer the present discussion a solid base.

The status and existence of the Greek-Catholic Church is still contested by intransigent Russophile Orthodox, in Ukraine and, of course, in Russia: following a long tradition of self-preservation from external influences, they see the Greek-Catholic Church as a tool in the hands of the Vatican, or their Catholic neighbour, Poland. We have to take into account that the moral and organizational crisis experienced by the Orthodox Church, due to its long coexistence with an atheistic and totalitarian power like the Soviet regime, fuelled the fear that the concurrent Churches could gain a moral primate and material help from abroad, as in the case of the Uniate Church, formally linked to the Vatican. This suspicion, coupled with hostility towards everything coming directly or indirectly from abroad, was extended to the Protestant groups which flourished in the new liberal situation. They were seen as modern Westernised elements, very capable of pursuing social programs, a field in which all the Ukrainian Churches lacked experience, because social work had been prohibited under the Soviet regime. The problem of the pastoral separation between the hierarchy and the flock was a great problem for all the Churches in Ukraine. They could gain favour with the people by reinforcing their symbolic image, resting on history and tradition, but the Greek-Catholic Church and the Ukrainian Autocephalous Church were in a better moral position because of their suffering during the Soviet period and their clandestine activity.

During the Soviet period, the Uniates suffered from severe repression, and their Church survived underground or abroad[10]. When it reappeared on the surface, enthusiasm for its renewal was undoubtedly great. Cardinal Lubomyr Husar decided to transfer the Metropolitan see from Lviv, in Galicia, to Kyiv, where Greek Catholics are relatively few: this symbolic act, approved by the Vatican, governed by a Polish Pope, was seen as a Catholic provocation, and embittered the relationship between the two confessions. In a series of interviews given by Cardinal Husar, edited together with other texts by Antoine Arjakovsky, the Ukrainian primate explained the important reason that lay behind this move. First of all, the fact that even the Greek-Catholic Church belongs to the Kyivan tradition, no less than the other Orthodox Churches: in the light of this truth, the Greek-Catholic Church has a right to be present in Kyiv, the capital of the State, the centre of the original Metropolitanate of Kyiv and all Rus', and the centre of Ukrainian religion and spirituality from the earliest times. Cardinal Husar stressed the necessity to reconsider the relationship between religion and nation in a larger Christian perspective. In his words:

Nous sommes des Ukrainiens, nous sommes des chrétiens, nous sommes de tradition orientale, et nous sommes aussi en communion avec le siège apostolique de Rome. Cela signifie qu'être dans cette communion ne fait pas de nous des êtres moins ukrainiens, moins chrétiens, moins orthodoxes dans le sens d'appartenance à la tradition Byzantine. Ceci a toujours été impensable pour les patriarches de Moscou et pour beaucoup d'autres églises orthodoxes. Et je pense que cela devient excessif. Cela doit être dépassé.

> We are Ukrainians, we are Christians, we are of the Eastern tradition, and we are also in communion with the Apostolic See in Rome. To belong to this communion does not make of us a group of beings who are less Ukrainian, less Christian, less Orthodox in the sense of belonging to the Byzantine tradition. This has always been inconceivable for the patriarchs of Moscow and for many other orthodox churches. And I think that this has become exaggerated, and has to be overcome [11].

Cardinal Husar explained his ecumenical purpose, which appeared quite unrealistic in the troubled Ukrainian context. At the same time, he aspired to have an official Patriarchy for the Greek-Catholic Church instituted by the Pope, in accordance with an old request that could not be satisfied in the last century because of the difficult relationships between the Roman Church and the Orthodox World[12]. The Orthodox establishment fears the proselytism of the Greek-Catholic Church and stigmatises its presence in eastern and southern Ukraine as an aggressive move, although the Greek-Catholic Church also has a lot of believers in those parts of Ukraine and other parts of the former Soviet Union owing to the persecution and forceful re-location of the Western Ukrainian Greek-Catholic flock in different regions under the Soviet regime. These believers, or their descendants, are calling for a parish Greek-Catholic presence. Once again the burden of history plays its role in the present polemics.

Historically, the Greek-Catholic Church is rooted in the former Austrian part of the former Polish-Lithuanian Commonwealth, because its relative presence in the Russian part was erased definitively during the 19th century between 1839 and 1875 (Chełm diocese)[13] by the Tsarist government. As illustrated above, Ukrainian lands were always divided into different States: because they were mainly part of the Polish-Lithuanian Commonwealth, they came under Russian or Austrian rule after its partition. In the Austrian part, the existence of the Greek-Catholic Church was permitted even though the Latin-Catholic Church was, owing to the Polish dominant influence, always strong. During the 19th century, the Greek-Catholic Church became the guardian of Ukrainian self-perception. In the Russian part of the former Polish-Lithuanian Commonwealth there was no room for the Greek-Catholic Church: it was seen as a schismatic phenomenon to be suppressed and reincorporated into the main confession[14]. After World War II, when the lands that had fallen under Polish rule after World War I, i.e. Galicia, and under Czechoslovakian rule, i.e. Subcarpathian Rus', were reclaimed by the Soviet Union, the Greek-Catholic Church was suppressed (in Galicia in 1946 and in Subcarpathian Rus' in 1949[15]) and absorbed by the Russian-Soviet Orthodox Church.

Generally, in the Russian Empire, the Orthodox Church was conceived as an instrument of Russian centralism. As a result of the Pereiaslav agreement of 1654[16], any attempt to preserve a specific Ukrainian identity, even though Orthodox, in the Ukrainian lands under the Tsarist rule, was severely inhibited[17], as the absorption of the Kyivan Metropolitanate by the Moscow Patriarchate since the late seventeenth century well demonstrates[18]. This move responded to the idea of the primacy of Russia as the unique heir of Kyivan Rus'[19].

During the Soviet period, the Bolshevik power played *divide et impera* with the various confessions in the context of the struggle against religions, in accordance with its atheistic ideology. At first, when it wanted to defeat the Russian Orthodox Church, it helped to establish the Ukrainian Autocephalous Church; during the 1920s and 1930s, it began to persecute this Church as well; during the war, when the Church-State partnership was in place, only the Russian Orthodox Church was tolerated and, in a certain way, promoted, because once again it helped to support the imperial attitude of the political centre. The crisis of the Soviet Union and its further developments questioned that supremacy.

It is now possible to have an open discussion on these crucial points, and the collection of articles written by Serhii Plokhy and Frank E. Sysyn, scholars of the Canadian Institute of Ukrainian Studies (CIUS), and published under the title *Religion and Nation in Modern Ukraine*[20], is very interesting regarding this matter.

Serhii Plokhy is the author of another distinguished study on the interplay between secular and religious ideas in Ukrainian history. In this case, attention is focused on the crucial period 1561-1654 when the Cossacks arose as defenders of Orthodoxy in a movement culminating with the famous Khmelnytsky uprising. As Plokhy wrote: "The use of religious slogans, most notably appeals to fight for the rights of persecuted Orthodoxy, gave Cossackdom a unique opportunity to legitimise its rebellions not only as a defence of the rights and privileges of its own estate but also as a vindication of the rights of the whole Ruthenian nation"[21]. The consequences were enormous:

> having declared the Orthodox Church dominant on the territory of the Cossack polity and prohibited, or greatly complicated, the presence within its boundaries of organized communities of Catholics, Uniates, Protestants, and Jews, Cossackdom effectively renounced the principle of religious toleration professed by Orthodox of the previous age and took on the project of building a monoconfessional state. (...) The Council of Pereiaslav and Khmelnytsky's acceptance of the Muscovite protectorate also could not fail to strengthen the Cossack officers' resolution to establish a purely Orthodox Cossack state[22].

But, as Plokhy stressed, because the Orthodox religion bonded Cossack Ukraine with Tsarist Muscovy and later with the Russian Empire, the religion, over the long period, did not help the growth of a Ukrainian sense of distinctiveness as was the case in the western part of Ukraine that was socially and culturally dominated by Poles. This difference between the eastern part and the western part of Ukraine was felt during the 19th century, when a specific Ukrainian nationalism arose. For this reason, the Greek-Catholic Church in Galicia – and to a lesser extent in the Carpathian Rus' – were able to play a major role in the development of a national Ukrainian identity. As John Paul Himka demonstrated in his works dedicated to the western Ukraine, religion and nationality were tied here in several ways[23]. This kind of study is very precious in order to evaluate the situation in all Ukrainian lands over the last two centuries, even though it is always necessary to look up to the Early Modern Age in order to understand the complexity of inherited questions. The historiographical panorama of the last ten years presents a wealth of interesting perspectives to be further developed in many directions. Of course, the contemporaneousness attracts attention, because the religious situation in Ukraine is still very fluid, and the possibility of openly following one's chosen religion is still not taken for granted by many. From a historical point of view, we have to remark upon the need to pursue historical research apart from the compelling necessities of the present. One of the most promising trends is that of comparative studies. In the case of Ukraine, a comparative approach is absolutely necessary because the partition among different countries during its past has determined different developments in various cultural and political contexts. In general, a comparative analysis is required for historians dealing with the vicissitudes of Eastern Central Europe, where the boundaries – ethnic, national, religious etc. – changed so often and abruptly, frequently leaving the population in a situation of uncertainty with regard to their real identities. Some questions arise: how is the discourse of proto-national identity connected with the discourse of confessional identity in Europe's Christian culture? How did confessional and ethnic traditions shape cultural identities in Europe? How did these discourses influence the construction of the national identity during the 19th and 20th centuries under the dominating secular trend of development of the European societies? Are the differences between East and West really so deep as would appear at a first glance? And with regard to the East, what are the differences within the different countries? This is a rich field of study which has already attracted some groups of researchers, and the results would be undoubtedly of great interest. I would like to stress that Ukrainian studies are developing in several centres in Europe, in Canada, in the United States and in Israel. In this context, many researchers are also studying religious problems in all their complexity as well as organizing seminars, congresses, courses and publications. Of course, the domain of Ukrainian studies encounters some difficulties gaining recognition in the academic world as a distinct field within the traditional structure of Slavic studies – both historical and literary – but things are changing quite rapidly.

Here, I would like to adapt some general historiographical considerations to a more limited object of study. As I wrote above, the year 1991 can be seen as a watershed in the historiography concerning Eastern Europe and Russia. Dealing with the Ukrainian case study obliges us to consider the broader context of post-Soviet historiography regarding Church and Religion[24]. In Soviet times, the topic of religion was neglected or subordinated to the standpoint of Marxism-Leninism, which excluded *a priori* a long series of important questions. Now the field of research is undoubtedly as large as it has been in the West and new methods, approaches and perspectives are entering the post-Soviet historiography, including Western historiography post-1991. Even though the field of study is not so rich as one might suppose, the volume of publications has increased greatly compared to the previous period, thanks to the opening-up of archives.

In particular, it is interesting to notice that several studies are currently examining the Russian Orthodox Church, in order to review stereotypes of the previous period. The image of this Church as the "handmaiden of the state"[25] has been seriously challenged, stressing the moment of conflict with the Russian government during the last period of the old regime; the impact of modernization processes and urbanization on religion has been considered together with the attitudes of different strata of Russian society *vis-à-vis* religion, paying special attention to rural and popular religion; the trends of secularisation during the 19th and 20th centuries have been examined, comparing the Western world with that of Russia; a gender approach to religious history has been instigated; the study of religious minorities in Russia, i.e. Jews, Muslims, Catholics, Protestants, Old Believers, Sectarians etc. has been reconsidered; the relationship between ethnic identity, nationality and religion has been investigated. As I. Mukhina concludes, regarding the rich survey of historiography on Church and Religion in Imperial Russia, "the study of religion is still poorly developed and not comparable with the historiography of religion in Western European countries", even though it is worth noting the improvement accomplished in the last fifteen years[26]. If, at the beginning of the historiographical renewal, historians in every part of the former Soviet system felt compelled to investigate the "blank spaces" or "dark holes" of their country's history, now they can concentrate on other topics, not immediately related to the needs of the society. They can explore new topics, or reconsider traditional topics of national and religious history in a different light, thanks to access to well-developed methods and themes in Western historiography, from social history to gender studies, from history of mentality to the "post-modern" approaches. If we consider Ukraine, I think that we must not neglect the necessity of integrating its history into the history of the multiethnic and multi-confessional empires dominating its lands for centuries. For this reason, the issue of Religion and Nation in Ukraine has to be considered in a broader context, i.e. Polish-Lithuanian, Russian, Austrian, former-Austrian, and Soviet. This approach involves certain difficulties, but it is the most fruitful in perspective, in order to avoid any distorted form of "regionalism" or "nationalism" so frequent in post-Soviet historiography, as a sort of *revanche* for the long subjugation to the "centre" in political, economic and cultural terms. In this respect, Ukraine shares the general problems common to the former-Soviet realities in search of emancipation[27].

It is worth remembering that a perspective of "longue durée" always has to be taken into consideration; the early modern and the modern ages are very important in understanding a series of dynamics in the context of Ukrainian lands up to the 20th century. Nevertheless, we need to implement the studies of the 19th and 20th centuries, examining, in a comparative approach, the relationship between religion and nation in the different Ukrainian regions; to pay attention to the revolutionary period, when the two Russian revolutions coincided with a revolutionary situation in Ukraine that developed into the foundation of the first Ukrainian State (1917-1921); to follow the destiny of the Church, in a broader sense, under the Soviet regime, differentiating the periods, i.e. from Lenin up to Gorbachev, because it is senseless always to speak about a "Soviet period" in a generic way; to analyse the relationships existing between the various Ukrainian religions in their reciprocal attitudes and in their attitude toward the State; to take into account the role and the influences of emigrated Churches or religious communities on Ukrainian reality, even during the Soviet period; to analyse the question of the underground Church, of the Church of "silence" in its connection with the general movement of "dissent" in Ukraine and the Soviet Union; to examine the archival material in Ukraine and abroad, not neglecting the Vatican archival resources, which are very rich and not yet deeply examined, even though they are consultable only up until 1922.

Notes

[1]   This point of view was deeply developed by the specialists of Ukraine convened in Gargnano (18-20 November 2004) for the ESF International Workshop on *The re-integration of Ukraine in Europe: a historical, historiographical and politically urgent issue*. See G. Brogi - G. Lami (eds.), *The re-integration of Ukraine in Europe: a historical, historiographical and politically urgent issue*, Alessandria 2005.

[2]   We have had some general works such as: G.A. Hosking (ed.), *Church, Nation and State in Russia and Ukraine*, Edmonton, Alberta 1990; S.K. Batalden, *Seeking God: The Recovery of Religious Identity in Orthodox Russia, Ukraine, and Georgia*, DeKalb, Ill. 1993; W.H. Swatos, *Politics and Religion in Central and Eastern Europe: Traditions and Transitions*, Westport, CT 1994; M. Bourdeaux (ed.), *The Politics of Religion in Russia and the New States of Eurasia*, Armonk, N.Y. 1995; P.G. Danchin - E.A. Cole (eds.), *Protecting the Human Rights of Religious Minorities in Eastern Europe*, New York 2002; S. Ferrari - W.C. Durham jr. - E.A. Sewell (eds.), *Diritto e religione nell'Europa post-comunista*, Bologna 2004.

[3]   C.M. Hann, *Religion and Nationality in Central Europe: The Case of the Uniates*, "Ethnic Studies", 10, 3, 1993, pp. 201-213; H. Johnson, *Religio-Nationalist Subcultures under the Communists: Comparisons from the Baltics, Transcaucasia and Ukraine*, "Sociology of Religion", 54, 3, 1993, pp. 237-255; G. Gee, *Geography, Nationality and Religion in Ukraine: A Research Note*, "Journal for the Scientific Study of Religion", 34, 3, 1995, pp. 383-391; S. Plokhy, *Church, State and Nation in Ukraine*, "Religion in Eastern Europe", 19, 5, 1999, pp. 1-28.

[4]   Commonly the word "united" is substituted by "uniate" that has been overlaid with pejorative connotation: in any case I will use here the term "uniate" because it is extensively used in English.

[5]   On this first period see: D. Little, *Ukraine. The Legacy of Intolerance*, Washington, D.C. 1991.

[6]   G. Lami, *La questione ucraina fra '800 e '900*, Milan 2005.

[7]   Articles on current religious and national problems in independent Ukraine: P. Herlihy, *Crisis in Society and Religion in Ukraine*, "Religion in Eastern Europe", 14, 2, 1994, pp. 1-13; M. Tomka, *The sociology of religion in Eastern and Central Europe: Problems of teaching and research after the breakdown of communism*, "Social Compass", 41, 3, 1994, pp. 379-392; J. Casanova, *Incipient Religious Denominationalism in Ukraine and Its Effects on Ukrainian-Russian Relations*, "The Harriman Review", 9, 1-2, 1996, pp. 38-42; O.W. Gerus, *Church Politics in Contemporary Ukraine*, "Ukrainian Quarterly", 52, 1, 1996, pp. 28-46; B. Gudziak - V. Susak, *Becoming a Priest in the Underground: The Clandestine Life of the Ukrainian Greco-Catholic Church*, "Oral History", 24, 2, 1996, pp. 42-48; A. Krawchuk, *Religious Life in Ukraine: Continuity and Change*, "Religion in Eastern Europe" , 16, 3, 1996, pp. 16-26; C. Lapychak, *Rifts Among Ukraine's Orthodox Churches Inflame Public Passions*, "Transition", 2, 7, 1996; T. Kuzio, *In Search of Unity and Autocephaly: Ukraine's Orthodox Churches'*, "Religion, State and Society", 25, 4, 1997, pp. 393-415; D. Wojakowski, *Life in Religious Pluralism: The Religious Situation in the Polish-Ukrainian Borderland*, "Religion, State and Society", 27, 3-4, 1999, pp. 343-354; A. Kolodniy, *Traditional Faiths in Ukraine and Missionary Activity*, "Religion in Eastern Europe", 20, 1, 2000, pp. 20-45; M. Marynovitch, *Toward Religious Freedom in Ukraine: Indigenous Churches and Foreign Missionaries*, "Religion in Eastern Europe", 20, 5, 2000, pp. 1-14; G. Fagan - A. Shchipkov, *Rome is not our Father, but neither is Moscow our Mother: Will There be a Local Ukrainian Orthodox Church?*, "Re-

ligion, State and Society", 29, 3, 2001, pp. 197-205; G. Fagan - A. Shchipkov, *The Ukrainian Greek Catholics in an Ambiguous Position*, "Religion, State and Society", 29, 3, 2001, pp. 207-213; N. Mitrokhin, *Aspects of the Religious Situation in Ukraine*, "Religion, State and Society", 29, 3, 2001, pp. 173-196; G. Stricker, *On a Delicate Mission: Pope John Paul II in Ukraine*, "Religion, State and Society", 29, 3, 2001, pp. 215-225; M. Tataryn, *Russia and Ukraine: Two Models of Religious Liberty and Two Models for Orthodoxy*, "Religion, State and Society", 29, 3, 2001, pp. 155-172; C. Wanner, *Advocating New Moralities: Conversion to Evangelicalism in Ukraine*, "Religion, State and Society", 31, 3, 2003, pp. 273-87.

[8]   S. Senyk, *The Ukrainian Church in the Seventeenth Century*, "Analecta ordinis s. Basilii magni", XV (XXI), 1996, pp. 339-374, p. 339.

[9]   Among the major works on this controversial issue see: S. Senyk, *The Background of the Union of Brest*, "Analecta ordinis s. Basilii magni", XV (XXI), 1996, pp. 104-144; R. Łużny - F. Ziejka - A. Kępiński, *Unia brzeska: geneza, dzieje i konsekwencje w kulturze narodów słowiańskich: praca zbiorowa*, Cracow 1994; H. Diłągowa, *Dzieje Unii Brzeskiej (1596-1918)*, Warsaw-Olsztyn 1996; A. Mironowicz, *Kościół prawosławny v dziejach dawnej Rzeczypospolitej*, Białystok 2001; M. Dmitriev, *Meždu Rimom i Car'gradom; genezis brestskoj cerkovnoj unii 1595-1596 gg.*, Moscow 2003. See also J. Borzecki, *The Union of Lublin as a Factor in the Emergence of Ukrainian National Consciousness*, "Polish Review", 41, 1, 1996, pp. 37-61; B.A. Gudziak, *Crisis and Reform. The Kyivan Metropolitanate, the Patriarchate of Costantinople, and the Genesis of the Union of Brest*, Cambridge, MA 1998, pp. 139-142; see also chapter I of B.R. Bociurkiw, *The Ukrainian Greek Catholic Church and the Soviet State (1939-1950)*, Edmonton - Toronto 1996.

[10]   Bociurkiw, *The Ukrainian Greek Catholic Church and the Soviet State* cit.

[11]   A. Arjakovsky, *Entretiens avec le Cardinal Lubomir Husar. Vers un christianisme post-confessionel*, s.l. 2005, p. 58.

[12]   For more details see: S. Plokhy, *Between Moscow and Rome: Struggle for the Greek Catholic Patriarchate in Ukraine*, "Journal of Church and State", 37, 4, 1995, pp. 849-867.

[13]   Diłągowa, *Dzieje Unii Brzeskiej* cit.

[14]   Generally, there was no room in the Russian empire as a whole. On forced conversion of Uniate Ukrainians to Russian Orthodoxy see the innovative study: B. J. Skinner, *The Empress and the Heretics: Catherine II's Challenge to the Uniate Church, 1762-1796 (Russia, Ukraine, Belarus)*, PhD., Georgetown University 2001; see also: G.L. Bruess, *Religion, Identity and Empire: A Greek Archbishop in the Russia of Catherine the Great*, New York 1997. B.J. Skinner analized the bloody Ukrainian uprising called Koliivshchyna (1768) in the context of Uniate-Orthodox conflict, demonstrating how "cross-border influences complicated and intensified confessional tensions": B. Skinner, *Borderlands of Faith: Reconsidering the Origins of a Ukrainian Tragedy*, "Slavic review", 64, 1, 2005, pp. 88-116. On the concept of religious frontier see: E. Andor - I. G. Toth (eds.), *Frontiers of Faith. Religious Exchange and the Constitution of Religious Identities. 1400-1750*, Budapest 2001; D. Tollet (ed.), *La frontière entre les chrétientés grecque et latine au XVIIème siècle. De la Lithuanie à la Russie subcarpathique*, "XVIIème siècle", 220, 2003. A very interesting publication in several volumes on the Catholic Church Unions in Central and Eastern Europe is *Polska-Ukraina. 1000 lat sąsiedztwa* (Poland-Ukraine. 1000 years of neighbourhood), Przemyśl 1990.

[15]   A.B. Pekar, *The History of the Church in Carpathian Rus'*, Fairview, NJ 1992.

[16]   A new study on this crucial topic is: J. Basarab, *Perejaslav 1654. A Historiographical Study*, Edmonton, Alberta 2003.

[17]   N.L. Chirovsky, *The Church: Defender of Ukrainian National Identity*, "Ukrainian Quarterly", 46, 1, 1990, pp. 45-58.

[18]   Gudziak, *Crisis and Reform. The Kyivan Metropolitanate, the Patriarchate of Costantinople, and the Genesis of the Union of Brest*, cit.

[19]   J. Pelenski, *The Context of the "Kievan Inheritance" in Russian-Ukrainian Relations: The Origins and Early Ramifications*, in P.J. Potichnyj (ed.), *Ukraine and Russia in Their Historical Encounter*, Edmonton, Alberta 1992, pp. 3-19.

[20]   S. Plokhy - F.E. Sysyn, *Religion and Nation in Modern Ukraine*, Edmonton, Alberta 2003.

[21]   S. Plokhy, *The Cossacks and Religion in Early modern Ukraine*, Oxford 2001, p. 341. On the early modern period see also: S.H. Baron - N. Shields Kollmann (eds.), *Religion and Culture in Early Modern Russia and Ukraine*, DeKalb, Ill. 1997.

[22]   *Ibid.*, p. 339.

[23]   J-P. Himka, *Religion and Nationality in Western Ukraine: the Greek Catholic Church and the Ruthenian National Mouvement in Galicia, 1867-1900*, Montreal 1999.

[24]   A very useful historiographical survey is given by I. Mukhina, *Church and Religion in Imperial Russia. A Review of Recent Historiography*, "Marburg Journal of Religion", 9, 2, 2004. A survey on a more specific topic is: G.L. Freeze, *Recent scholarship on Russian Orthodoxy: a Critique*, "Kritika", 2, 2001, pp. 269-278. It is impossibile here to list all the works edited in these last years. Because my short survey concentrates on 19th and 20th century Ukraine I mention only some works: E.N. Cimbaeva, *Russkoe katolicizm*, Saint Petersburg 1998; D.J. Dunn, *The Catholic Church and Russia: Popes, Patriarchs, Tsars, and Commissars*, Aldershot 2004; R.P. Geraci - M. Khodarkovsky (eds.), *Of Religion and Empire: Missions, Conversions, and Tolerance in Tsarist Russia*, Ithaca 2001; V.A. Kivelson - R.H. Greene (eds.), *Orthodox Russia: Belief and Practice Under the Tsars*, University Park, Penn. 2003; H. Kirimli, *National Movements and National Identity among Crimean Tatars. 1905-1917*, New York 1996; C. Worobec, *Death ritual among Russian and Ukrainian Peasants*, in S. Frank - M. Steinberg, *Cultures in Flux: Lower-Class Values, Practices and Resistance in Late Imperial Russia*, Princeton 1994.

[25]   G. Freeze, *Handmaiden of the State? The Church in Imperial Russia Reconsidered*, "Journal of Ecclesiastical history", 36, 1985, pp. 82-102.

[26]   Mukhina, *Church and Religion* cit.

[27]   See the interesting conclusive essay of T. Sanders (ed.), *Historiography of Imperial Russia: The Profession and Writing of History in a Multinational State*, Armonk, N.Y.-London 1999 about the actual research of a new paradigm for post-soviet historiography. For a better understanding of the Ukrainian historiographical background see also Z. Kohut, *The Development of a Ukrainian National Historiography in Imperial Russia*, *ibidem*, pp. 453-477.

BIBLIOGRAPHY

Volumes:

Andor E. -Toth I. G. (eds.), *Frontiers of Faith. Religious Exchange and the Constitution of Religious Identities. 1400-1750*, Budapest 2001.

Arjakovsky A., *Entretiens avec le Cardinal Lubomir Husar. Vers un christianisme post-confessionel*, s. l. 2005.

Baron H. - Shields Kollmann N. (eds.), *Religion and Culture in Early Modern Russia and Ukraine*, DeKalb, Ill. 1997.

Basarab J., *Perejaslav 1654. A Historiographical Study*, Edmonton, Alberta 2003.

Batalden S. K., *Seeking God: The Recovery of Religious Identity in Orthodox Russia, Ukraine, and Georgia*, DeKalb, Ill. 1993.

Bociurkiw B.R., *The Ukrainian Greek Catholic Church and the Soviet State*, Edmonton - Toronto, 1996.

Bourdeaux M. (ed.), *The Politics of Religion in Russia and the New States of Eurasia*, Armonk, N.Y. 1995.

Brogi G. - Lami G. (eds.), *The re-integration of Ukraine in Europe: a historical, historiographical and politically urgent issue*, Alessandria 2005.

Bruess G.L., *Religion, Identity and Empire: A Greek Archbishop in the Russia of Catherine the Great*, New York 1997.

Cimbaeva E.N., *Russkoe katolicizm*, Saint-Petersburg 1998.

Diląngowa H., *Dzieje Unii Brzeskiej (1596-1918)*, Warsaw-Olsztyn 1996.

Dmitriev M., *Meždu Rimom i Car'gradom; genezis brestskoj cerkovnoj unii 1595-1596 gg.*, Moscow 2003.

Dunn D.J., *The Catholic Church and Russia: Popes, Patriarchs, Tsars, and Commissars*, Aldershot 2004.

Ferrari S. - Durham W.C. jr. - Sewell E.A. (eds.), *Diritto e religione nell'Europa post-comunista*, Bologna 2004.

Frank S. - Steinberg M., *Cultures in Flux: Lower-Class Values, Practices and Resistance in Late Imperial Russia*, Princeton 1994.

Geraci R.P. - Khodarkovsky M. (eds.), *Of Religion and Empire: Missions, Conversions, and Tolerance in Tsarist Russia*, Ithaca 2001.

Gudziak B.A., *Crisis and Reform. The Kyivan Metropolitanate, the Patriarchate of Costantinople, and the Genesis of the Union of Brest*, Cambridge, MA 1998.

Himka J-P., *Religion and Nationality in Western Ukraine: the Greek Catholic Church and the Ruthenian National Mouvement in Galicia, 1867-1900*, Montreal 1999.

Hosking G.A. (ed.), *Church, Nation and State in Russia and Ukraine*, Edmonton, Alberta 1990.

Kirimli H., *National Movements and National Identity among Crimean Tatars. 1905-1917*, New York 1996.

Kivelson V.A. - Greene R. H. (eds.), *Orthodox Russia: Belief and Practice Under the Tsars*, University Park, Penn. 2003.

Lami G., *La questione ucraina fra '800 e '900*, Milan 2005.

Little D., *Ukraine. The Legacy of Intolerance*, Washington, D. C. 1991.

Łużny R. - Ziejka F. - Kępiński A., *Unia brzeska: geneza, dzieje i konsekwencje w kulturze narodów słowiańskich: praca zbiorowa*, Cracow 1994.

Mironowicz A., *Kościół prawosławny v dziejach dawnej Rzeczypospolitej*, Białystok 2001.

Pekar A.B., *The History of the Church in Carpathian Rus'*, Fairview, NJ 1992.

Plokhy S., *The Cossacks and Religion in Early modern Ukraine*, Oxford 2001.

Plokhy S. - Sysyn F.E., *Religion and Nation in Modern Ukraine*, Edmonton, Alberta 2003.

Potichnyj P.J. (ed.), *Ukraine and Russia in Their Historical Encounter*, Edmonton, Alberta 1992.

Sanders T. (ed.), *Historiography of Imperial Russia: The Profession and Writing of History in a Multinational State*, Armonk, N.Y.-London 1999.

Skinner B.J., *The Empress and the Heretics: Catherine II's Challenge to the Uniate Church, 1762-1796 (Russia, Ukraine, Belarus)*, PhD., Georgetown University 2001.

Swatos W. H., *Politics and Religion in Central and Eastern Europe: Traditions and Transitions*, Westport, CT 1994.

Articles:

Borzecki J., *The Union of Lublin as a Factor in the Emergence of Ukrainian National Consciousness*, "Polish Review", 41, 1, 1996, pp. 37-61.

Casanova J., *Incipient Religious Denominationalism in Ukraine and Its Effects on Ukrainian-Russian Relations*, "The Harriman Review", 9, 1-2, 1996, pp. 38-42.

Chirovsky N. L., *The Church: Defender of Ukrainian National Identity*, "Ukrainian Quarterly", 46, 1, 1990, pp. 45-58.

Fagan G. - Shchipkov A., *Rome is not our Father, but neither is Moscow our Mother: Will There be a Local Ukrainian Orthodox Church?*, "Religion, State and Society", 29, 3, 2001, pp. 197-205.

Fagan G. - Shchipkov A., *The Ukrainian Greek Catholics in an Ambiguous Position*, "Religion, State and Society", 29, 3, 2001, pp. 207-213.

Freeze G., *Handmaiden of the State? The Church in Imperial Russia Reconsidered*, "Journal of Ecclesiastical history", 36, 1985, pp. 82-102.

Gerus O.W., *Church Politics in Contemporary Ukraine*, "Ukrainian Quarterly", 52, 1, 1996, pp. 28-46.

Gudziak B. - Susak V., *Becoming a Priest in the Underground: The Clandestine Life of the Ukrainian Greco-Catholic Church*, "Oral History", 24, 2, 1996, pp. 42-48.

Herlihy P., *Crisis in Society and Religion in Ukraine*, "Religion in Eastern Europe", 14, 2, 1994, pp. 1-13.

Kolodniy A., *Traditional Faiths in Ukraine and Missionary Activity*, "Religion in Eastern Europe", 20, 1, 2000, pp. 20-45.

Krawchuk A., *Religious Life in Ukraine: Continuity and Change*, "Religion in Eastern Europe", 16, 3, 1996, pp. 16-26.

Kuzio T., *In Search of Unity and Autocephaly: Ukraine's Orthodox Churches'*, "Religion, State and Society", 25, 4, 1997, pp. 393-415.

Lapychak C., *Rifts Among Ukraine's Orthodox Churches Inflame Public Passions*, "Transition", 2, 7, 1996.

Marynovitch M., *Toward Religious Freedom in Ukraine: Indigenous Churches and Foreign Missionaries*, "Religion in Eastern Europe", 20, 5, 2000, pp. 1-14.

Mitrokhin N., *Aspects of the Religious Situation in Ukraine*, "Religion, State and Society", 29, 3, 2001.

Mukhina I., *Church and Religion in Imperial Russia. A Review of Recent Historiography*, "Marburg Journal of Religion", 9, 2, 2004.

Plokhy S., *Between Moscow and Rome: Struggle for the Greek Catholic Patriarchate in Ukraine*, "Journal of Church and State", 37, 4, 1995, pp. 849-867.

Senyk S., *The Background of the Union of Brest*, "Analecta ordinis s. Basilii magni", XV (XXI), 1996, pp. 104-144.

Senyk S., *The Ukrainian Church in the Seventeenth Century*, "Analecta ordinis s. Basilii magni", XV (XXI), 1996, pp. 339-374.

Skinner B., *Borderlands of Faith: Reconsidering the Origins of a Ukrainian Tragedy*, "Slavic review", 64, 1, 2005, pp. 88-116.

Stricker G., *On a Delicate Mission: Pope John Paul II in Ukraine*, "Religion, State and Society", 29, 3, 2001, pp. 215-225.

Tataryn M., *Russia and Ukraine: Two Models of Religious Liberty and Two Models for Orthodoxy*, "Religion, State and Society", 29, 3, 2001, pp. 155-172.

Tollet D. (ed.), *La frontière entre les chrétientés grecque et latine au XVIIème siècle. De la Lithuanie à la Russie subcarpathique*, "XVIIème siècle", 220, 2003.

Tomka M., *The sociology of religion in Eastern and Central Europe: Problems of teaching and research after the breakdown of communism*, "Social Compass", 41, 3, 1994, pp. 379-392.

Wanner C., *Advocating New Moralities: Conversion to Evangelicalism in Ukraine*, "Religion, State and Society", 31, 3, 2003, pp. 273-87.

Wojakowski D., *Life in Religious Pluralism: The Religious Situation in the Polish-Ukrainian Borderland*, "Religion, State and Society", 27, 1999, nos. 3-4, pp. 343-354.

The Irish Nationalist and Unionist Philosophy at the Beginning of the 20th Century: a Historiographical Approach

Borislav H. Mavrov
St. Kliment Ohridski University of Sofia

С Акта но обединение от 1800 г. се създава нова държава Обединено кралство на Великобритания и Ирландия, в което се включват Англия, Уелс, Шотландия и Ирландия. Последната губи правото да има свой национален парламент за сметка на възможността да избира и изпраща свои представители директно в централизирания имперски парламент в Уестминстър. За по-голямата част от ирландците този акт е неприемлив и накърняваш националното им достойнство, и в крайна сметка се оказва първопричина за зараждането на ирландския национализъм и съответно на ирландския национален въпрос. За другата, по-малка част от тях пък, Съюзният акт поставя началото на един желан и особено полезен Съюз, защитата на който ще се превърне в основен приоритет. Това вътрешно ирландско противопоставяне между противниците- националистите (в голямото си мнозинство католици) и защитниците-юнионистите (преобладаващо протестанти) на Обединено кралство на Великобритания и Ирландия се трансформира в отчетлива разделителна линия, която бележи и определя ирландската национална съдба не само през XIX, но и през целия XX век, та до ден днешен. В този смисъл може да се обобщи, че на ирландската историческа сцена ясно се открояват две враждуващи и същевременно допълващи си концепции – национализъм и юнионизъм. Противопоставянето между тях е обусловено от сложен набор от религиозни, социални, икономически и политически причини и се превръща в определящ и неизменен фактор за съдбата на ирландската нация.

Настоящето изследване цели да даде обща представа за това как тези две философии са анализирани от историографска гледна точка и дали и до каква степен е изследвана взаимовръзката между тях. То изгражда пъстра картина на многообразието от интерпретации и тяхната еволюция във времето и ясно очертава ключовите им характеристики и особености.

At the end of the 19th century and the beginning of the 20th century, two hostile, and yet at the same time two complementary, concepts – Nationalism and Unionism – were clearly outlined in Ireland. The opposition between them has been conditioned by a complex set of religious, social, economic and political causes and turned into a decisive factor for the fate of the Irish nation. This internal Irish contradiction between the Nationalists (predominately Catholics) and the Unionists (predominately Protestants) divided the country into two distinct sides, marked and determined the Irish national fate from that time onward until the present day.

The current survey aims to give a general notion of how these philosophies have been interpreted from a historiographical point of view and whether, and to what extent, the interaction between them has been analysed and explored.

In a great number of countries, the founders of professional historical science have been the leaders of the national revival. This renders the histories they construct subject to a large extent to mythical features and national idealism. In this context, Ireland is no exception in that Prof. Eoin MacNeill, the 'father' of modern Irish historiography, was a Vice President of the Gaelic League, President of the Irish Volunteers and the first Minister of Education of the independent Irish state. As a result, historiographical interpretations until the 1930s were dominated by the *Nationalist* trend. The key concept for the representatives of this idea was the presentation of Irish history as a continuous struggle between the fledgling Irish nation and the 'tyrannical imperialism' of the English. In those early studies, the role of individuals was explored along with their contribution to the period.

According to the traditional Nationalist concept, a separate Irish nation, based on the *Gaelic* language and culture, existed even before the first English invasion in the 12th century. From that moment the Irish people were systematically deprived of their historical rights while the English interests were always guaranteed. That is why the Irish people had a moral right to fight for its political, economic, social and cultural independence. The Nationalist historiography subordinates the historical truth to the interests and needs of the nation, basing itself on historical myths and mythology, mixing fact and fiction in a non-scientific approach[1].

The use of these methods by Nationalist historians was responsible for the appearance at the end of 1930s and the beginning of the 1940s of the first doubts about the objectivity of the orthodox Nationalist interpreters, and concern about the way they presented their own Irish national history. The school of the *Revisionists* was established. T.W. Moody[2], D.B. Quinn, R. Dudley Edwards (people with varying religious backgrounds, but representatives of the academic communities of Trinity College Dublin, University College Dublin and Queen's University Belfast, respectively) set themselves the task of revealing the real Irish past, clearing away the myths and writing in a purer and more scholarly way. They were united in their purpose in the academic periodical *Irish Historical Studies* which represented a joint publication of two academic and seminar-like forums – the *Ulster Society for Irish Historical Studies* and the *Irish Historical Society*[3], the result of which was the revision of the details and facts of the national heroes and national movements of Irish history, and their representation in a revolutionary way with respect to aims, methods and style.

"We have before us two main tasks – the one constructive, the other instrumental", declared the Revisionist programme of Moody and Edwards. They offered a neutral and thorough history, free from extreme emotions and historical interpretation, and setting aside partiality to the Nationalist viewpoint and the production of myths: "History is a matter of facing the facts of the Irish past, however painful some of them may be; mythology is a way of refusing to face the historical facts"[4]. According to the Revisionists, one cannot argue with a myth, but historians can argue with one another and only in this way can knowledge be extended and understanding deepened. At the same time they admit that the mental war of liberation from servitude to the myth is a very hard and almost endless process.

There are two main myths, which proved to be destructive with respect to the interpretation of Irish history. The first – the separatist myth - is associated with the Ulster Unionists, and the second – the Nationalist myth – is characteristic of their opponents, the Republicans. The spread of these myths concerning Ireland's past undermines its present and makes its future vulnerable.

With regard to the myths in the analyses of modern Irish history at the end of the 19th and beginning of the 20th centuries, some of the leading revisionists (Moody, O`Hegarty) gave as the best example, that of the *predestined nation*. At its foundation lies the understanding that the Irish nation had successfully survived through an eight century epic struggle with England, coming out of its underground period and discovering every aspect of its national life subjected to the will and interests of the British. According to them, this wide-spread myth sounds unreasonable, bearing in mind that Irish history was not wholly a history of conflict and opposition. Nationalist politics had not generally been dominated by the concept of continual war with Britain until the complete separation between the two nations was achieved. In practice, the leading factor in Nationalist life during these years was the moderate and constitutional home rule movement rather than the extreme one of achieving absolute independence through physical force. It was not until the eve of the First World War and especially in 1916 (The Easter Rising), when the real transfer from parliamentary to radical revolutionary Nationalism started to change the character of Irish politics.

The revisionists encourage the research of unused sources and unexplored topics. The preferred mode of writing is the historical monograph, based on thorough archival research, critical analysis, careful contextualisation and rigorous documentation of sources[5]. A very specific characteristic of the new historic approach from the late 1930s has been the ambition to widen the academic readership of Irish history and to provoke greater international interest through the organisation of a series of international conferences.

The Revisionist school entered a new period of its development from the beginning of the 1970s with the outburst of violence in the Northern Ireland. Though some historians consider that the conflict after 1969 simply coincided with this new phase, while the real impulse for its emergence is the partial opening of the official Irish archives and a growth of interest in social and economic history, undoubtfully the events in the Northern Ireland established a totally new environment for the researchers. The Ulster conflict gave additional motivation to those 'revising' the Nationalist approach as it created a sense that Irish people desperately needs liberation from the mythology, which according to them caused the eruption of troubles at the end of 1960s and 1970s. This explains why nationalist heroes and movements came under "even more aggressive, critical scrutiny"[6].

In this new political context the revisionists writings turned into an important factor in the public and political debate in the country, especially concerning the issue of Anglo-Irish relations and Northern Ireland. In this connection it is intriguing to quote Ronan Fanning, one of the most prominent revisionists from the period, citing Bernard Lewis in his turn:

> Those who are in power control to a very large extent the presentation of the past and seek to make sure that it is presented in such a way to buttress and legitimize their own authority, and to affirm the rights and merits of the group which they lead.

And on this Fanning comments:

> One could scarcely find a more succinct statement of what motivated the Irish political establishment after 1969 to adopt the interpretation of Modern Irish history, commonly described as "revisionist"[7].

Prof. Fanning proved himself as one of the most energetic and strict revisionists, defending his colleagues` efforts to write in accordance with the rules of the academic history, overbearing the settled myths and legends both of Irish Nationalism and Unionism, regarding without exceptions the available historical evidence. This trend was categorically supported during the 1980s by respected historians as Michael Laffan, John Murphy and Tom Dunne, through the columns of the intellectual journals as *The Crane Bag* and *The Irish Review*.

In the 1970s, having succeeded in their enterprise to subvert the Nationalist approach, the revisionists faced the challenge of contributing to the writing of a new, general, voluminous synthetic history of Ireland. In actuality, this had happened at the very end of the 1960s and the beginning of 1970s when T.W. Moody[8] and F.S.L. Lyons[9] had each tried to reach a wider audience. However, the culmination and new synthesis built on the achievements of the revisionist historiographical approach was made by Roy Foster with his popular and provocative *Modern Ireland, 1600-1972*[10]. What was so characteristic about this survey was its author's style – lucid, highly polished and full of self-confident judgments and explanations. It became the standard history of the period from about 1600 onwards and, although this book is most often represented as the "the consolidation of the current phase of Revisionist historiography", combining all its virtues and vices[11], its publication provoked a new phase in the historians' debate about the history and nature of Irish identity. In fact, the appearance of Roy Foster's work established the demarcation line between Revisionism and its opponent school – anti-Revisionism.

Almost simultaneously with the appearance of *Modern Ireland, 1600-1972*, at the end of the 1980s, this already-established approach was severely criticized by Brendan Bradshaw in an article published, by an irony of fate, in the revisionist publication *Irish Historical Studies*[12]. This particularly intensified the controversy among historiographical circles in Ireland, and marked the beginning of a new and more profound discussion concerning the ways in which the Irish past has been interpreted.

The main variance emphasized by Bradshaw was connected with the application by the revisionists of the 'value free' approach, expressed in their interpretation of some of the key developments of the Irish historical experience, and especially in the march of national self-expression. They were accused of writing a history disconnected from the popular historical consciousness and of neglecting the social task and mission of the historian. The attack was levelled at the neglect of the human suffering in the tragic past of the country, which in turn led to the creation of a false historical reconstruction. According to Bradshaw, that was the reason why one of the main tasks of the historian should be to reconstruct the past with empathy. He alluded to the well-known historian and philosopher R.G.Collingood and particularly to his theory of 're-enactment of the past':

> This re-enactment... is not a passive surrender to the spell of another's mind... The historian not only re-enacts past thought, he re-enacts it in the context of his own knowledge and therefore, in re-enacting it, criticizes it, forms his own judgment of its value, corrects whatever errors he can discern in it[13].

In fact, according to the anti-revisionists, a pro-British and loyalist approach was hidden behind the pretension for objectivity and the neutral pursuit of demythologising. One of the main accusations of the anti-revisionist school was connected with servitude to the political establishment. According to them, the way the past was presented proves to be decisive in legitimising the authority of those in power. In this context, Desmond Fennell, one of the Bradshaw`s most energetic followers, describes how the revisionists interpret some of the key understandings in the history of Ireland:

> A retelling of Irish history which seeks to show the British rule of Ireland was not, as we have believed a *bad* thing, but a mixture of necessity, good intentions and bungling; and that the Irish resistance to it was not as we have believed a *good* thing, but a mixture of wrong-headed idealism and unnecessary, often cruel violence. The underlying message is that in our relations with Britain on the Irish question, the Irish have been much at fault. This is the popular image of historical Revisionism[14].

The anti-revisionists were not opposed in general to the research techniques and methodology of their colleagues. Nor were they opposed to the discovery of new historical facts and the revision of some tenets of traditional Irish Nationalism. However, they definitely stood against the 'new moral interpretation' and the 're-allocation' of the major facts concerning the Irish Nationalist tradition and British rule. The anti-revisionists criticize the neglect of women's history and the tendentious disregard of the Irish language sources. According to Desmond Fennell, the revisionists applied a threefold approach when discrediting the Nationalist tradition. Firstly, they attacked the key Nationalist interpretation that the British rule of Ireland was 'morally wrong' and that the

Irish resistance to it was 'morally right'; secondly, they sought to discredit the 'Republican' wing rather than the genuine Nationalist one, because of its ultimate aim of the establishment of a nation-state; and thirdly, they undermined the main achievement of that republican tradition – the Irish Revolution itself[15].

Despite the above, a definition of a common standard and a coherent categorization of the anti-revisionist school of thought are hardly feasible. This is because of the existence of some divergences in defining a single standard for the representatives of this school, as for example between B. Bradshaw and Kevin Whelan[16] there is a certain disbalance in respect to audience, targets and contents of critics against the revisionists. But what is valid in general about Bradshaw and the other anti-revisionists, is the fact that they gave expression to public opinion in Ireland, the larger part of which at the end of the 1980s and the beginning of 1990s, continued to show a keen interest in the deeds of its historic leaders and be proud of its past.

The unifying element among the majority of the historiographical studies is the opinion that, despite the serious debate, an artificial and relative opposition among the Nationalists, revisionists and anti-revisionists is being created[17]. Behind it, a thorough and detailed investigation of documents and resources (the greater part of which were not available to the historians of the early years) is being carried out and new research theories and methods are being applied. To sum up, it could be said that after the 1940s there was a tangible process of broadening of the base of knowledge concerning the Irish past, rather then a revision of the ways of its interpretation. In this context, Roy Foster`s evaluation "we are all revisionists now" sounds particularly suitable.

In a similar manner to the historiography of Nationalism, the interpretations of Unionism varied, and were dependant to a significant extent on the developments of political debates. A reflection of this tendency is Lord Rosebery`s comment that "the Irish question has never passed into history because in has never passed out of politics"[18]. The fragmentary character of Irish Unionism provoked a tendency to produce a kind of a simplified historical creed which emphasises periodic changes in accordance with political necessity and agenda.

The first Unionist interpreters were the so called 'Unionist historians'. Their profile is of Unionists engaged in the writing of history, active in the interests of Unionism or just revealing political sentiments, although not all of them participated in Unionist developments. Logically, the early Unionists' writings, from the end of the First World War to the 1940s, were generally characterized by their apologist character. The leading institution connected with Unionist historical scholarship was Trinity College, Dublin. As a predominantly Protestant and landowning institution, it became one of the most influential suppliers of lawyers and historians to the Unionist movement, giving it its ideological substance.

At the beginning of the 20th century, Lecky, as the most distinguished representative of the Trinity intellectual elite, started actively investigating the Unionist tradition in Ireland. Together with Falkiner and Ball, he focused on the main values and achievements of Anglo-Irish political practice, giving a predominantly Anglo-centric viewpoint. The character of the literature produced during the period of the foundation of Northern Ireland was far from being professional, logically partitionist, or orientated towards the necessities of the Ulster community and its elite.

The most prominent example of this early stage from the development of the Unionist historiography was Ronald McNeil's book[19] "Ulster's Stand for Union". It represented a substantial and thoroughly documented account of the movement written by one of its active participants, giving a new approach from the traditional partitionist one and becoming a harbinger of A.T.Q.Stewart's contribution a few decades later. The first example of professional scholarly interpretation of Unionism appeared in 1967. Stewart`s *The Ulster Crisis*[20] differed substantially from anything produced before in respect of methodology and research technique, but resembled its precursors in the partial and pro-Unionist presentation of the founders of Northern Ireland, rendering their actions in heroic dimensions. This approach was valid for all the representatives of the early Unionist historiography who, like their colleagues from the Nationalist school, glorified and mythologized historic figures and events.

This tendency started to change in 1969 when the outbreak of violence in Northern Ireland created a different environment for the study and research of Unionism. The so called 'historian of Unionism' (differing from the already mentioned 'Unionist historian') emerged, providing a more comprehensive and broader examination of the history of the movement. The new historiographical tradition was connected with the involvement of external comments and analysis as well as the production of more weighty literature, even including some less scholarly contributions. Not surprisingly, more was written in the twenty year period after 1969 than had been written in the preceding fifty years. A rediscovery of the long neglected Southern Unionism can be observed. Patrick Buckland was responsible for renewing interest in the study of Southern Loyalism, and he made a substantial contribution to both the North and South in the pre-partition period[21]. He was supported by J.C. Beckett[22], who also put some emphasis on the debate on Southern Unionism through his *The Anglo-Irish Tradition*. F.S.L. Lyons and D.C. Savage focused on Unionism during some of the key phases of its evolution from 1885-1886 and 1904-1905, while Andrew Gailey in his *Ireland and the Death of Kindness*[23] explored the Ulster Loyalist – British connection. Of course, many aspects have still not been researched or at least not extensively studied.

The new approach allows criticisms and redefinitions of some of the key concepts and the previously created myths spread in the 'apologetic' interpretation of Unionism. Of course, this does not mean that the promotion of the loyalist tradition has ceased. On the contrary, in 1985, the *Ulster Society* was created "to promote an awareness and appreciation of our distinctive Ulster-British culture"[24]. It was connected with the production of well-illustrated, cheap and attractive editions, designed for the mass market, eternalising the merits of the loyalist tradition.

The literature on Unionism during these years became even more diverse and heterogeneous. The reason is that a certain number of issues provoked intellectual debates among the historians dealing with it. The key one is partition and its historical background. According to A.T.Q. Stewart[25] the conflict in Northern Ireland dates back to the 16th, 17th and 18th centuries where the roots of the problem lay. In other words the developments in the early 20th century Irish history and especially the partition and the Nationalist/Unionist clash in Ulster was something inevitable, irrespectively of circumstances, which *de facto* is more a symptom of the problem than its cause. Against this interpretation came Brian Walker's thesis that the role the past plays in the present in Northern Ireland is not unique and that the current situation is not linked in a distinctive way to the past:

> The conflict in Northern Ireland is not an age-old one...other parts of Europe have also faced and still do face similar problems. As elsewhere, leaders and people in Ireland, both north and South, have a vital role to play in determining the shape of their own society, and are not just helpless victims of a turbulent past[26].

The historiography in the period after 1969 is mainly characterized by its diverse character, combining both old and new approaches, but remaining predominantly influenced by the specifics of the political debate. The political controversy has had an immense impact on those researching Unionism and it could be concluded that the evolution of the Unionist historiography is a reflection of the evolution of the Unionism itself.

Among the historiographical interpretations on the Irish history at the beginning of the 20th century there is another parallel approach – the Marxist one. The latter is comparatively similar to the one revealed among the traditional historians, writing on the problems of Irish Nationalism and Unionism, especially in respect to the internal division and controversy among the Marxist academics. Similarly to the revisionist/anti-revisionist debate here we can talk about a Marxist/neo-Marxist divergence.

The early representatives of the traditional Marxist historiography on Ireland stuck to the classical tenets of the founders of the school, Marx and Engles. Marx and Engles had even greater impact on their colleagues, as they both made a certain personal contribution, turning into one of the few non-Irish writers on Irish affairs. The Irish Marxists presented the Irish Nationalism as a 'pure' and 'centuries-old heroic' Nationalist struggle against foreign oppression[27]. Consequently, they found themselves close to the first Nationalist historians' writings, in exhibiting a very sympathetic manner towards the cause of the Irish Nationalism and a negative one towards the Unionists. Starting from the very first attempt to interpret the country's history in classical Marxist terms made by the prominent Irish labour activist James Connolly, passing through the works of Erich Strauss and C. Desmond Greaves and finishing with T.A. Jackson[28] – all Irish Marxists revealed the English involvement in Ireland (at that time under the form of partition) as the prime reason for the country's troubles[29].

Since the 1960s, in parallel and to some extent within the developing revisionist criticism, a new generation of neo-Marxist or Marxist-revisionists historians has emerged (Paul Bew, H. Patterson and P.Gibbon). They have questioned the contribution of the older Marxist tradition, and revised the main concepts of the classical tradition, basing their approach on newly available archive material and using freer and more informal language. Practically drifting apart from the traditional Marxist emphasis, they set a new agenda for their project. They speak against the role of Imperialism in Ireland and reject the traditional approach based on Lenin's "rights of nations to self-determination". Bew, Patterson and Gibbon[30] defend "The State in Northern Ireland" and particularly the Protestant working class, which according to them is a key actor and determinant social force in the various crises of the Northern state. Contradictory to the classical tenets, the Marxist revisionists wish to reinforce artificially created national boundaries, reassure the architects of a sectarian state and foreign investors that Imperialism is not under threat.

Irish Unionism and Irish Nationalism are mutually connected and inductive concepts, proper understanding and analysis of which is impossible without a detailed exploration of this complicated interaction. Most historians have focused on either the development of Nationalism with its various dimensions or on the internal dynamics of Unionist resistance to home rule. Until now, the full scope and the actual interaction of Ulster Unionism and Irish Nationalism has been systematically neglected. Knowledge of the two traditions has increased, but there has been no attempt to combine them in a scholarly analysis based on primary sources from both the North and the South.

NOTES

[1]   N. Curtin, *Varieties of Irishness: Historical Revisionism, Irish Style*, "The Journal of British Studies", 35, 2, Revisionisms, 1996, p. 195.

[2]   T.W. Moody, *Irish History and Irish Mythology*, in C. Brady (ed.), *Interpreting Irish History*, Dublin 1994, pp. 71-86.

[3]   C. Brady, *'Constructive and Instrumental': The dilemma of Ireland's First 'New Historians'*, in Brady (ed.), *Interpreting Irish History* cit., Dublin 1994, p. 4.

[4]   Moody, *Irish History and Irish Mythology* cit., p. 84

[5]   R.W. Foster. *History and the Irish Question*, "Transactions of the Royal Historical Society", xxxiii, 1983, pp. 188-189.

[6]   Curtin, *Varieties of Irishness* cit., p. 195.

[7]   R. Fanning, *The Great Enchantment*, in Brady (ed.), *Interpreting Irish History* cit., Dublin 1994, pp. 156-7.

[8]   T.W. Moody, *A New History of Ireland*, Oxford 1976.

[9]   F.S.L. Lyons, *Ireland after the Famine*, London 1971.

[10]   R.W. Foster, *Modern Ireland, 1600-1972*, London 1988.

[11]   Curtin, *Varieties of Irishness* cit., p. 196

[12]   B. Bradshaw, *Nationalism and Historical Scholarship in Modern Ireland*, "Irish Historical Studies", 26, 1989.

[13]   Quoted in D.G. Boyce - A. O'Day, *'Revisionism' and the 'revisionist' controversy*, in D.G. Boyce - Alan O'Day (eds.), *The Making of Modern Irish History*, London 1996, p. 11.

[14]   D. Fennel, *Against Revisionism*, in Brady (ed.), *Interpreting Irish History* cit., pp. 184-185.

[15]   *Ibid.*, p. 186.

[16] K. Whelan, *Come All You Staunch Revisionists: towards a Post-revisionist Agenda for Irish History*, "Irish Reporter", 2, 1991 and K.Whelan, *The Recent Writing of Irish history*, "U.C.D. History review", 1991.

[17] Brady (ed.), *Interpreting Irish History* cit.; Boyce - O`Day (eds.), *The Making of Modern Irish History* cit.; Curtin, *Varieties of Irishness* cit.

[18] A. Jackson, *Unionist history*, in Brady (ed.), *Interpreting Irish History* cit., p. 256.

[19] R. McNeil, *Ulster's Stand for Union*, London, 1922.

[20] A.T.Q. Stweart, *The Ulster Crisis*, London 1967.

[21] P. Buckland, *Irish Unionism, 1885-1923*, Belfast 1973 and P. Buckland, *Ulster Unionism and the Origins of Northern Ireland, 1886-1922*, Dublin 1973.

[22] J.C. Beckett, *The Anglo-Irish Tradition*, London 1976.

[23] A. Gailey, *Ireland and the Death of Kindness: the experience of constructive unionism, 1890-1905*, Cork 1987.

[24] A. Jackson, *Unionist history*, in Brady (ed.), *Interpreting Irish History* cit., p. 264

[25] A.T.Q. Stewart, *The Narrow Ground: Aspects Of Ulster, 1609-1969*, London 1977.

[26] B. Walker, *Dancing to History's Tune: History, Myth and Politics in Ireland*, Belfast 1996, p. 158.

[27] A. Coughlan, *Ireland's Marxist Historians*, in Brady (ed.), *Interpreting Irish History* cit., Dublin 1994, p. 288.

[28] T.A. Jackson, *Ireland Her Own, An Outline History of the Irish Struggle*, London 1947 – this represented the first comprehensive history of Ireland from Marxist standpoint.

[29] A.Coughlan, *Ireland's Marxist Historians*, in Brady (ed.), *Interpreting Irish History* cit., p.29

[30] P. Bew, P.Gibbon and H.Patterson, *The State in Northern Ireland, Political Forces and Social Classes*, Manchester 1979.

BIBLIOGRAPHY

Beckett J.C., *The Anglo-Irish Tradition*, London 1976.

Bew P. - Gibbon P. - Patterson H., *The State in Northern Ireland, Political Forces and Social Classes*, Manchester 1979.

Boyce G.D. - O`Day A. (eds.), *The Making of Modern Irish History*, London 1996.

Bradshaw B., *Nationalism and Historical Scholarship in Modern Ireland*, "Irish Historical Studies", 26, 1989.

Brady, C. (ed)., *Ideology and the Historians*, in *Irish Conference of Historians*, held at Trinity College Dublin, June 1989, Dublin 1991.

Id. (ed.), *Interpreting Irish History*, Dublin 1994.

Buckland P., *Irish Unionism, 1885-1923*, Belfast 1973.

Id., *Ulster Unionism and the Origins of Northern Ireland, 1886-1922*, Dublin 1973.

Clarke A., *Robert Dudley Edwards (1909-1988)*, "Irish Historical Studies", XXVI, 1988-9.

Collins P. (ed.), *Nationalism and Unionism – Conflict in Ireland, 1885-1921*, Belfast 1994.

Curtin N., *Varieties of Irishness: Historical Revisionism, Irish Style*, "The Journal of British Studies", 35, 2, Revisionisms, 1996.

Dooge J. (ed.), *Ireland in the Contemporary World. Essays in Honor of Garret FitzGerald*, Dublin 1986.

Edwards R.D., *T.W. Moody and the Origins of Irish Historical Studies*, "Irish Historical Studies", XXVI, 1988-9.

Ellis S., *Historiographical Debate: Representations of the Past in Ireland: Whose Past and Whose Present?*, "Irish Historical Studies", XXVII, 1990-1.

Fanning R. *The Meaning of Revisionism*, "Irish Review", IV, 1988.

Foster R., *History and the Irish Question*, "Transactions of the Royal Historical Society", XXXIII,1983.

Id., *Modern Ireland, 1600-1972*, London 1988.

Id., *The Problem of Writing Irish History*, "History Toady", XXXIV, 1988

Id., *We are All Revisionists Now*, "Irish Review", I, 1986.

Gailey A., *Ireland and the Death of Kindness: the Experience of Constructive Unionism, 1890-1905*, Cork 1987.

Garvin T., *Nationalist Revolutionaries in Ireland, 1858-1928*, Oxford 1987.

Id., *The Return of History: Collective Myths and Modern Nationalisms*, in "Irish Review", IX, Autumn 1990.

Hutton S. - Stewart P. (eds.), *Ireland's Histories: Aspects of State, Society and Ideology*, London and New York 1991.

Jackson T.A., *Ireland Her Own, An Outline History of the Irish Struggle*, London 1947.

Kearney H., *The Irish and their history*, "Irish Historical Studies" XXVI, 1989.

Lyons F.S.L., *Ireland after the Famine*, London 1971.

McNeil R., *Ulster's Stand for Union*, London 1922.

Moody T.W., *A New History of Ireland*, Oxford 1976.

Moore J., *Historical Revisionism and the Irish in Britain*, "Linen Hall Review", Autumn 1988.

Mulvey H.F., *Theodore William Moody (1907-1984): an Appreciation*, "Irish Historical Studies", XXIV, 1984-5.

O'Brein C.C., *States of Ireland*, London 1972.

O'Neill K., *Revisionist Milestone*, "Irish Literary Supplement",VIII, 2, 1989.

Ó Snodaigh P., *Two Godfathers of Revisionism*, Dublin 1991.

Show F., *The Cannon of Irish history: a challenge*, in Irish Historical Studies, XIV, 1972.

Stweart A.T.Q., *The Narrow Ground: Aspects Of Ulster, 1609-1969*, London 1977.

Id., *The Ulster Crisis,* London 1967.

Walker B., *Dancing to History's Tune: History, Myth and Politics in Ireland,* Belfast 1996.

Whelan K., *Come All You Staunch Revisionists: towards a Post-revisionist Agenda for Irish History*, Irish Reporter, 2, 1991.

Id., *The Recent Writing of Irish history*, "U.C.D. History review", 1991.

Whyte J., *Interpreting Northern Ireland*, Oxford 1990.

Roger Bacon's Life and Ideas in Russian Historiography

ALEKSEY KLEMESHOV
Moscow State Regional University

В статье рассматриваются тенденции и пути изучения жизни и идей религиозного философа и ученого XIII в. Роджера Бэкона в российской историографии. Личность этого выдающегося францисканского мыслителя привлекали внимание российских авторов в течение двух столетий, начиная с XVIII в.

В исследованиях биографии и воззрений Бэкона можно выделить несколько этапов. В XVIII в. он становится известен в России как маг и выдающийся алхимик. Такой образ сформировался под влиянием зарубежных публикаций XVII-XVIII столетий и оказался столь живучим, что просуществовал до начала XX века. Однако уже во второй половине XIX в. российские историки составляют общее представление о судьбе и идеях мыслителя, основываясь на зарубежных публикациях и изучая уже имеющийся в библиотеках Петербурга и Москвы "Великий труд" (Opus majus), главное сочинение Бэкона, в издании XVIII в.

В советской историографии необходимо отметить две важных тенденции: с одной стороны, активно развивалось появившееся в западноевропейской историографии XIX в. представление о Бэконе как о борце за свободу мысли и развитие науки, пострадавшем за свои убеждения, которые резко выделялись на фоне средневековой схоластической мысли. С другой стороны, в это время внимание историков привлекают частные аспекты взглядов Роджера Бэкона, прежде всего его алхимические и географические представления. Появляются переводы фрагментов трудов мыслителя. Кроме этого, труды Бэкона изучались в контексте более широких исследований.

Интерес к западноевропейской средневековой мысли усиливается в российской историографии в 1980-х гг. К этому периоду относится защита докторской диссертации и публикация статей Г.П. Елькиной (Алма-Ата, Казахский государственный университет), посвященных идеям развития научного знания и учению об "опытном знании" в сочинениях францисканского ученого.

В 1990-х – начале 2000-х гг. начинается новый этап в российской медиевистике. Для него характерны освоение широкого круга литературы и источников, усиление внимания к ранее не поднимавшимся проблемам и слабо освещенным вопросам, в том числе в истории средневековой мысли. Публикуются новые переводы сочинений Роджера Бэкона, в 2005 г. отдельной книгой выходит под редакцией И.В. Лупан-

дина перевод избранных трудов францисканца. Однако, за исключением нескольких
работ, посвященных важным аспектам его воззрений, многие стороны бэконовской
мысли остаются слабо освещенными в российской историографии.

Roger Bacon, a Franciscan philosopher and scientist who lived in the 13th century (the actual dates of his birth and death are unknown, but it is possible to calculate that he was born around 1210 and died in 1294), was one of the outstanding medieval thinkers. His life and views have attracted the attention of Russian historians for two centuries, and the aim of this paper is to review the impact of Bacon and his ideas on Russian historiography.

Until recently, religious and philosophical thought of the 13th century had featured very little in Russian historiography, partly due to the difficulty of working with the sources. Until the early 20th century, there were no critical publications of many of Bacon's important works. There are, however, two complete editions of the *Opus Majus* [The Great Work], the philosopher's principle writing. Samuel Jebb published the first and best edition of this work in 1733, in London, and it was republished in 1750, in Venice[1]. Between 1897 and 1900, J.H. Bridges published the second edition using different manuscripts with his own introduction[2]. In spite of the low quality of the second edition, together with the fact that Jebb's edition was available in Russian libraries, most Russian historians only used Bridges' edition.

After the Russian Revolution, many Russian historians could not use the libraries and archives of Western Europe and the USA. The ideological factor was of great importance, too. Until the early 20th century, research about Catholic religious and philosophical thought was not very popular in orthodox Russia. Even the widely-available works of Thomas Aquinas have not received worthy mention in the works of Russian historians.

In Soviet Russia, the official atheistic and anti-clerical ideology did not cause the total interruption of the research of medieval thought, although the investigation of many very important problems was suspended and only resumed in the 1970s.

Notwithstanding this, the situation regarding research of Bacon's ideas was comparatively fortunate as historians took more of an interest in his thought in Soviet Russia than in Tsarist Russia. Even so, the number of publications dedicated to Bacon does not compare favourably against the hundreds published about him in American and Western European historiography. Despite this, the research in Russia regarding Bacon's views is of interest for its own sake, and for its appearance at all in Russian medieval studies.

Russia's first acquaintance with Roger Bacon took place in the 18th century when papers about European philosophers and mystics began to be published in the journals *Truten'* [The Bumble-Bee], *Zhivopisets* [The Painter] and *Utrenniy Svet* [The Morning Light], edited by the famous N.I. Novikov. At the same time, European publications began to appear in Russian private libraries, and Bacon was mentioned among the famous medieval thinkers. However, the information about him portrayed Bacon as a mythological character, and this image as a magician and famous alchemist spread in Russia. This was caused by the portrayal of Bacon in French and English historical works such as *The Famous Historie of Fryer Bacon* published "at London by E.A. to Francis Groue in 1630". The tradition of this image had begun in the 14th century when Bacon's alchemical and astrological ideas, together with the burning mirrors and other admirable things described by him in his writings, gave rise to such fantastic representations of the man. For centuries, Roger Bacon grew as a legendary person with ludicrous details attached to his life. The appearance of these representations in Russian popular publications began to occur at the end of the 19th and the beginning of the 20th centuries, one unknown source even proclaiming that Bacon died in an explosion in his laboratory. N.A. Morozov, a famous writer and author of alternative and incredible approaches to world history, who was held prisoner in the Petropavlovskaya fortress, portrayed Bacon as an expert alchemist, and noted Bacon's alchemical achievements in his work *V poiskakh filosofskogo kamnya* [In Search of the Philosopher's Stone]. Morozov concluded that Bacon's alchemical books were the first texts in medieval alchemical tradition, "authenticity of which is undoubted"[3].

This more rational point of view had already begun to gain popularity in Russia by the middle of the 19th century. By studying unpublished sources, some European researchers, such as E. Charles[4] and his followers, showed Bacon's views as being unique in medieval thought and that Bacon was one of the few medieval thinkers who supported the experimental investigation of nature and the wide practical inculcation of scientific achievements. In his *Pis'ma o Prirode* [Letters about Nature], A.I. Gertsen[5], a famous Russian writer and publicist, maintained that Bacon was a unique, outstanding phenomenon in the general development of scholastic thought, although unable to change the general intellectual situation in 13th century. Overall, these one hundred and fifty years may be considered to be a united period when the representations of Bacon in Russia were echoing what had happened previously in West European historiography.

At the end of the 19th century, Russian historians had better information about Bacon's life and his views. At this time they made acquaintance with the newest European publications (a few general works were translated into Russian and were published in the late 19th and early 20th centuries[6]) and with some sources edited in the 18th and 19th centuries. Russian medieval studies had been developing actively, and a good illustration of this process can be found in papers in different dictionaries. In the first papers dedicated to Bacon in Brockgause and Efron's *Entsiklopedicheskiy Slovar'* [The Encyclopaedic Dictionary] and *Entsiklopedicheskiy Slovar'. Biografii* [The Encyclopaedic Dictionary. The Biographies], the main facts of Bacon's life and works were detailed, together with a description of publications and their translations.

Noviy Entsiklopedicheskiy Slovar' [New Encyclopaedic Dictionary] also placed K.M. Miloradovich's lengthy paper about the philosopher with a list of publications about him. At the same time, some very successful research was produced into the Franciscan

Order of the 13th century and medieval religious and philosophical representations. We also need to note the works of S.A. Kotlyarevskiy, such as his monograph *Frant-siskanskiy Orden i Rimskaya Kuriya v XIII i XIV Vekakh* [Franciscan Order and Roman Curia in the 13th and 14th Centuries][7]. The relationship between the Franciscans and the Pope was described in a vast historical, cultural and intellectual context in this work, but Kotlyarevskiy did not attract attention to Bacon. With the exception of the dictionary papers, there were no works dedicated to Bacon's ideas.

The next period is from 1917 to 1950. At this time, few special publications appeared about Roger Bacon, and there were no sound works among them. It is possible to identify two main trends.

Firstly, as in the previous fifty years, dictionary papers continued to be published, using European works and previous Russian publications[8] as a basis, and popular information was often repeated in them. At the same time, in accordance with active atheistic propaganda and general ideological influence on historical studies, interest was limited to medieval religious and philosophical thought.

Secondly, in parallel with this trend, some researchers studied particular aspects of Bacon's views in greater depth. V.P. Zubov, an outstanding historian and philosopher, was among them, though unfortunately only part of his work was published. In 1924, for the fist time, Zubov addressed Bacon's heritage when he made a report about optical representations[9]. Furthermore, Zubov used Bacon's writings (first of all, *Opus Majus*) when learning of the athomistic representations in medieval calendars – computes, medieval architectural theory, optical concepts and magnetism. The same author wrote a paper about Bacon for *Filosofskaya Entsiklopediya* [The Philosophical Encyclopaedia]. Zubov's works are distinguished by their solid study of sources, although Bacon's ideas were not the subject of special interest for Zubov. Bacon's name was noted in general works about the history of chemistry, too.

In previous periods, Bacon's works were accessible to Russian researchers only in Latin and in English translation by R. Burke, but now the first Russian translations began to appear. In 1932, M.P. Alekseev included a small part of *Opus Majus* with a short introduction in his compendium of medieval texts on the theme of Siberia[10]. In the introduction, he repeated the popular point of view of the time. As Alekseev wrote, Roger Bacon, "who had the misfortune to join... the Franciscan Order, lived in the terrible struggle for the right to scientific thought" and tried to illuminate the "obscurity reigning at that time in European science"[11].

By the middle of the 20th century, the situation with the edition of Bacon's texts was better than a hundred years previously. During the last century, *Opus Tertium* [The Third Work], *Opus Minus* [The Minor Work] and other works were published by J. Brewer, E. Charles, R. Steele, A.G. Little and other editors. However, Russian historians during the first half of the 20th century mostly did not use these editions.

From the fifties to the seventies, the trend which had started in Soviet historiography in the first half of the 20th century developed enormously, and Bacon's name continued to be used for the aims of atheistic propaganda. This point of view, introduced into European historiography in the 19th century, had been developing. In papers published in Soviet popular science journals, Bacon was shown as a fighter for freedom of thought and the triumph of science, as well as a thinker who suffered for his ideas.

These publications, which had little in common with the scientific works, presented extraordinary facts about him. These facts are found even in dictionaries. An example of such material was printed in the 400,000 copies of *Filosofskiy Slovar'* [The Philosophical Dictionary], which was edited by M.M. Rozental and P.F. Yudin[12]. It included the paper about Bacon[13] in which he was named as "the thinker-innovator, the predictor of the experimental science of modern times, the ideologist of the urban working classes", who "detected the feudal morality, ideology and politics" and "was distanced in 1277 from the teaching in Oxford University because of his views, and was held in the monastery prison in accordance with the orders of the Church authorities". The author of the paper said Bacon was "atheistic but inconsistent" and asserted that Bacon's aim for all sciences was "the extension of human power over nature".

The same characteristics of the philosopher appeared in other publications such as V. Khinkis' childish book about Bacon and his papers, the popular A. Belov's book *Obvinenie v Eresi* [The Condemnation of Heresy], and in the papers *Doctor Mirabilis* ("Admirable Doctor", as Bacon was named in late-medieval Europe) by K. Reydemeyster and *Rasskaz ob Angliyskom Monakhe Rodzhere Becone* [The Story of the English Friar Roger Bacon] by V. Lunkevich[14].

Of course, we cannot look upon these publications as scientific works, but they formed the image of Bacon. A more solid and objective characterisation of Bacon's views was given by O.V. Trakhtenberg in his *Ocherki po Istorii Zapadnoevropeyskoy Filosofii* [Outlines of History of West European Philosophy][15]. This period produced the most informative and representative review of Bacon's life and views for a vast readership. From the list of Bacon's published works and the studies about him, O.V. Trakhtenberg could only use *Opus Majus* and two works – the popular Bacon biography by F.W. Woodruff and E. Charles' work of 1861. In spite of these limitations, O.V. Trakhtenberg shed light on Bacon's views, including the concept of the experimental study of nature and the perspectives of scientific progress used for the good of the Church, the State and society.

However, this work was not free from ideological influence. With limited sources and the use of old research, Trakhtenberg's estimations of Bacon's thought lacked objectivity, leading him to conclude that Bacon characterized the aggressive politics of the Church which viewed "infidels" negatively. Bacon actually spoke about the excessive energy of "servants of God", but in *Opus Majus* and other writings he also insisted on the conversion of infidels to the "true religion" and said that in the near future, all infidels who persisted in their ways would have to be destroyed. Moreover, Bacon proposed to the Pope different ways and means not only for conversion, but also for the destruction of infidels, including the burning mirrors, powder and poison gas[16].

During this period, Bacon's views were groundlessly modernized, but we have to bear in mind that it was a time of great scientific and technical progress, and the desire to find in Bacon a prophet of this progress was normal.

During the 1970s, Soviet historiography had two ways of studying special aspects of Bacon's views, which were interesting and would be developed in the 1980s. They were the studies of the alchemical medieval traditions and Bacon's geographic representations. V.L. Rabinovich looked at Bacon's alchemical views in the context of medieval alchemical tradition, but it is possible to dispute some of his conclusions[17]. Also, he used works ascribed to Bacon, although their authorship by Bacon is very unlikely.

We need to note the *Istoriya Printsipov Fizicheskogo Eksperimenta* [The History of Principles of the Physical Experiment] by A.V. Akhutin[18], in which the Oxford scientific school's ideas were contemplated, and problems which were discussed in this work are related to Bacon's concept of experimental science and to his views in general, because he was a follower of many of the ideas of Robert Grosseteste, Bishop of Lincoln and outstanding representative of the Oxford school.

New translations continued to be published. In 1979 V.I. Matuzova included several fragments of *Opus Majus* in her reliable compendium of sources of the 11th to 13th centuries[19] (including the fragment which was translated by M.P. Alekseev). This publication was accompanied by an introduction, a parallel Latin text, based on J.H. Bridges' edition, a list of the bibliography from the early 19th century up to 1969, an index of publications and Russian translations of *Opus Majus*, sources, manuscripts and a commentary. Matuzova's introduction was short, but most objective and trustworthy.

There were some other translations of Bacon's works. Several important fragments of *Opus Majus* were included in the second part of the first volume of the *Antologiya Mirovoy Filosofii* [The Anthology of World Philosophy]. The translation was made by A.Kh. Gorfunkel', based on J.H. Bridges' edition[20]. The small fragments of *Opus Majus* and *Opus Tertium* [The Third Work], in which Roger Bacon described his ideas about music, were included in the compilation *Muzykal'naya Estetika Zapadnoevropeyskogo Srednevekov'ya i Vozrozhdeniya* [The Musical Aesthetic of Medieval and Renaissance Western Europe][21].

In the next period, the eighties, the trends which characterized the previous period, such as the using of Bacon's ideas (often in a distorted manner) for anticlerical propaganda continued. For example, in the work *Svobodomyslie i Ateizm v Drevnosti, Srednie Veka i v Epokhu Vozrozhdeniya* [The Freedom of Thought and Atheism in the Ancient World, the Middle Ages and the Renaissance], not only were Bacon's life and writings described with serious errors, but also the conclusions regarding Bacon's views reminded one of the noted *Filosophskiy Slovar'*. Bacon was named as one who "fought against Catholicism" and, as if he was an author of the concept, "caused the negation of Church and Christianity". Moreover, the work claimed that Bacon's natural studies were "quietly contradictory to the medieval religious image of mind".

However, these historiographic myths were a thing of the past. In works of this period, Bacon's thought was characterized in the context of the medieval intellectual situation. Among the most important works is V.V. Sokolov's textbook *Srednevekovaya Filosofiya* [The Medieval Philosophy][22], which includes a review of the problems of the Franciscan thinker's life and the character of his views. Sokolov describes Bacon's social ideas and the relationship between theology and philosophy. The historian used J.H. Bridges' edition of *Opus Majus* and the translation by A.Kh. Gorfunkel. Although the textbook isn't the place for discussion, Sokolov was able to illustrate the disputable topics in the study of Roger Bacon's thought.

Throughout the whole of this period, from the 1960s to the 1980s, greater acquaintance with the foreign studies of medieval religious and philosophical thought was made. The Russian translations of works of famous medievalists such as E. Garin and reports of E. Gilson's works were published.

However, the most important appearance at this time was the first solid work dedicated solely to Bacon, the doctoral dissertation of G.P. El'kina, which was defended in 1985 at the Kazakhstan State University[23].

El'kina analysed the concept of the development of scientific knowledge in Bacon's philosophy. The undoubted merit of this work was the sources – *Opus Majus* and *Opus Tertium*. El'kina also used everything that was accessible for her foreign studies. In this dissertation, the focus was on the development of scientific knowledge in Bacon's writings, but the author also included a brief description of Bacon's life in the preface. She was interested in Bacon's concept of experimental science (*scientia experimentalis*), one of his most interesting concepts, and published three papers about it. In the first, El'kina thinks that for Bacon, the term "experiment" included all that could be gleaned by empirical observation of common life. The researcher believed that Bacon often used the term "experience" to mean observation. El'kina concluded that for Bacon, the term "experiment" meant the sensual experience and experience of life, although it seems to be improbable[24].

We can see that one of the trends in research during the fifties to the eighties was the representation of Bacon primarily as a philosopher and scientific theorist.

From the 1990s until the early 2000s, the problems of medieval religious and philosophical thought began to be studied actively. A.M. Shishkov published papers about Robert Grosseteste's concept of light metaphysics. O.S. Voskoboynikov studied the astrological, magical and scientific ideas in the court of Emperor Frederick II and in the Papal court[25]. During this period, there was a resurgence of interest in medieval thought and history in general. This was caused, on the one hand, by the serious changes in Russian society which influenced Russian historical science, and on the other hand, from the seventies to the nineties, by an essential advance in the studies of the problems of medieval history in general and of medieval studies in particular. In this period, the problems in the studies of intellectual, scientific and religious history were studied actively in research about ancient and medieval West European and Arab history. At first, there were the works of V.P. Gaydenko and G.A. Smirnov, P.P. Gaydenko, A.Ya. Gurevich, I.D. Rozhanskiy, O.F. Kudryavtsev and A.V. Sagadeev.

In the brief period of the last fifteen years, progress seems to be being made in the studies of the problems of medieval intellectual history, an area which had been insufficiently studied in previous periods. However, as far as Bacon is concerned, these achievements are not very serious. At first, progress was in the publication of the Russian translations of Bacon's works. In 1999, Bacon's *Introductio* [Introduction], published by him in the treatise *Secretum Secretorum* [The Secret of Secrets], was translated by A.V. Vashestov with his introduction and commentaries[26]. This translation was inserted in a compilation of texts about magic, germetism and natural philosophy from the Ancient World to the Modern Time. Unfortunately, this translation was poor and it contained many serious errors. In 2002, in Saint-Petersburg, *Antologiya Srednevekovoy Mysli. Teologiya i Filosofiya Evropeyskogo Srednevekov'ya* [The Anthology of Medieval Thought. The Theology and Philosophy of Medieval Europe] was published, containing a translation of a large part of *Opus Tertium* by A.B. Apollonov. The most recent Russian translation is the edition of Bacon's selected works with the parallel Latin text, published in Moscow in 2005. The editor is I.V. Lupandin[27].

Among the research about Bacon, there are only introductions and commentaries for these translations and some other papers. A chapter about the Franciscan thinker was included in the popular review *Estestvennonauchnye Predstavleniya v Srednevekovoy Evrope* [The Natural Scientific Representations in Medieval Europe] by S.M. Marchukova[28]. The philosopher V.V. Bibikhin wrote a paper about Bacon for *Novaya Filosofskaya Entsyklopediya* [The New Philosophical Encyclopaedia], which was published in 2001. In same year, a paper about Bacon's optical concept was published in the journal *Voprosy Filosofii* [Philosophical Questions][29]. In my two papers and the candidate dissertation on the problems of studying Bacon's concept of experimental science, the thinker's concept of ideal state, *respublica fidelium* [the state of truth] and his social and political views were examined[30].

To conclude, although it is possible to see progress in the research into Bacon's life and views, the achievements are disproportional. Russian medievalists have only begun to research many of the problems of studying Roger Bacon's concepts.

NOTES

[1] S. Jebb (ed.), *Fratris Rogeri Bacon... Opus majus ad Clementem IV pontificem maximum* [Friar Roger Bacon, The Great Work to Pope Clement IV], London 1733 (reprinted in Venice in 1750). These two editions are in the Russian State Library in Moscow.

[2] J.H. Bridges (ed.), *The "Opus Majus" of Roger Bacon*, Edinburg 1897-1900, vols. I-III.

[3] Н.А. Морозов, *В поисках философского камня* [In Search of the Philosopher's Stone], Saint Petersburg 1909, pp. 98-114.

[4] See E. Charles, *Roger Bacon: sa vie, ses ouvrages, ses doctrines*, Paris 1861.

[5] А.И. Герцен, *Письма об изучении природы* [Letters about Nature], in А.И. Герцен, *Сочинения* [The Writings], Moscow 1985, vol. I, p. 337.

[6] For example, A. Stöckl's *Geschichte der Philosophie des Mittelalters* (Mainz, 1866) [The History of Medieval Philosophy], published in 1912 in Moscow.

[7] S.A. Kotlyarevskiy, *Frantsiskanskiy Orden i Rimskaya Kuriya v XIII i XIV Vekakh* [Franciscan Order and Roman Curia in the 13th and 14th Centuries], Moscow 1901.

[8] See В. Ивановский, *Бэкон Роджер* [Roger Bacon], in *Большая советская энциклопедия* [The Great Soviet Encyclopaedia], Moscow 1927, vol. 8, pp. 364-366.

[9] We have no information about publication of this report.

[10] *Роджер Бэкон о Сибири* [Roger Bacon about Siberia], in М.П. Алексеев, *Сибирь в известиях западноевропейских путешественников и писателей* [Siberia in Information from West European Travellers and Writers], Irkutsk 1941, pp. 23-27.

[11] *Ibid.*, p. 21.

[12] M.M. Rozental - P.F. Yudin (eds.), *Filosofskiy Slovar'* [The Philosophical Dictionary], Moscow 1963.

[13] *Философский словарь*, pp. 59-60.

[14] В.А. Хинкис, *Необычный монах. Страницы жизни Роджера Бэкона...* [Uncommon Friar. Pages of Roger Bacon's Life], "Наука и религия" [Science and religion], 1, 1971, pp. 73-83; 2, pp. 64-75; 3, pp. 75-84; Id., *Жизнь и смерть монаха Роджера Бэкона...* [The Life and Death of Friar Roger Bacon...], Moscow 1972; А.В. Белов, *Обвинение в ереси* [The Condemnation in Heresy], Moscow 1972; К. Рейдемейстер, *Доктор Мирабилис* [The Admirable Doctor], "Знание – сила" [Knowledge is Power], 6, 1955, pp. 12-18; В. Лункевич, *Рассказ об английском монахе Роджере Бэконе, который призывал к опытному изучению природы...* [The Story about English Friar Roger Bacon who called for the Experimental Study of Nature...], "Наука и жизнь" [Science and life], 11, 1974, pp. 131-135.

[15] O.V. Trakhtenberg, *Ocherki po Istorii Zapadnoevropeyskoy Filosofii* [Outlines of History of West European Philosophy], Moscow 1957.

[16] See, for example, J. Brewer (ed.), *Roger Bacon, Opus tertium*, London 1859, p. 46; *Roger Bacon, Opus majus*, vol. II, p. 221. For Bacon's condemnation of the Teutonic Order's aggression against infidels see: *Roger Bacon, Opus majus*, vol. III, p. 122.

[17] В.Л. Рабинович, *Теоретическое предвидение и его интерпретация. По алхимическим трактатам Р. Бэкона* [Theoretical Prevision and Its Interpretation. On the alchemical treatises of Roger Bacon], in *Научное открытие и его восприятие* [Scientific Discovery and Its Interpretation], Moscow 1971, pp. 146-155; Id., *Концептуальная историография европейской алхимии* [The Conceptual Historiography of European Tradition], in *Герметизм и формирование науки* [Germetism and the Formation of Science], Moscow 1983, pp. 173-228; Id., *Созерцательный опыт Оксфордской школы и герметическая традиция* [The Contemplative Experience of the Oxford School and the Germetic Tradition], "Вопросы философии" [Philosophical questions], 7, 1977, pp. 137-147.

[18] A.V. Akhutin, *Istoriya Printsipov Fizicheskogo Eksperimenta* [The History of Principles of the Physical Experiment], Moscow 1976.

[19] Р. Бэкон, *Великое сочинение* [The Great Work], in В.И. Матузова, *Английские средневековые источники IX-XIII вв. Тексты, переводы, комментарии* [The English Medieval Sources IX-XIII Centuries. Texts, translations, commentaries], Moscow 1979, pp. 189-232. *Antologiya Mirovoy Filosofii* [The Anthology of World Philosophy], Moscow 1969. The translation was made by A.Kh. Gorfunkel', based on J.H. Bridges' edition.

[20] J.H. Bridges (ed.), *Antologiya Mirovoy Filosofii* [The Anthology of World Philosophy], trans. by A.Kh. Gorfunkel, Moscow 1969.

[21] Р. Бэкон, *Opus majus. Opus tertium. Отрывки из трактатов* [The Great Work. The Third Work. The

Fragments of Treatises], in *Музыкальная эстетика западноевропейского средневековья и Возрождения* [The Musical Aesthetic of Medieval and Renaissance Western Europe], Moscow 1966, pp. 54-78.

[22] V.V. Sokolov, *Srednevekovaya Filosofiya* [The Medieval Philosophy], Moscow 1979.

[23] See Г.П. Елькина, *Идеи развития научного знания в философии Роджера Бэкона. Диссертация на соиск. уч. ст. докт. филос. наук* [The Ideas on the Development of Scientific Knowledge in the Philosophy of Roger Bacon. Ph.D. Dissertation], Alma-Ata 1985.

[24] Г.П. Елькина, *Роджер Бэкон об опытном пути познания* [Roger Bacon on the Experimental Approach to Knowledge], "Известия АН Каз. ССР. Серия 'Общественные науки'" [The News of Academy of Sciences Kaz. SSR. Series "Social Sciences"], 2, 1982, pp. 29-30.

[25] We need to note that the acquaintance with the works of Agostino Paravicini-Bagliani played an important role in the study of the relationship between Roger Bacon's medical ideas and the concepts of health in the Papal court.

[26] Р. Бэкон, *Введение к трактату псевдо-Аристотеля "Тайная тайных"* [The Introduction to the Pseudo-Aristotle's Treatise "The Secret of Secrets"], in *Герметизм, магия, натурфилософия в европейской культуре 13-19 вв.* [Germetism, Magic, and Natural Philosophy in European Culture – 13th to 19th Centuries], Moscow 1999, pp. 41-69.

[27] Р. Бэкон, *Избранное* [Selected works], edited by I.V. Lupandin, Moscow 2005.

[28] С.М. Марчукова, *Естественнонаучные представления в средневековой Европе* [The Natural Scientific Representations in Medieval Europe], Saint Petersburg 1997, pp. 114-116.

[29] А.А. Белый, *Ценностная компонента науки и становление оптики (от Августина до Леонардо да Винчи)* [The Value Component in Science and the Development of Optics (from Augustin to Leonardo da Vinci)], "Вопросы философии" [Philosophical questions], 10, 2001, pp. 114-128.

[30] А.С. Клемешов, *Понятие опыта у Роджера Бэкона* [The Concept of Experience in Roger Bacon's Thought], in *Диалог со временем. Альманах интеллектуальной истории* [Dialogue with Time. Intellectual History Review], Moscow 2002, vol. 9, pp. 231-239; Id., *Учение о "государстве верных" Роджера Бэкона* [The Roger Bacon's Concept of the "state of truths"], in *Общественная мысль в контексте истории культуры: Сб. в честь А.Э. Штекли* [Social Thought in the Context of Cultural History. Studies in Honour of A.E. Stökli], Moscow 2004, pp. 51-65.

Bibliography

Russian translations of Roger Bacon's works (except quotations in books and papers of researchers):

Бэкон Р., *Роджер Бэкон о Сибири* [Roger Bacon about Siberia], translated by Alekseev M.P., in Алексеев М.П., *Сибирь в известиях западноевропейских путешественников и писателей* [Siberia in Information from West European Travellers and Writers], Irkutsk 1941, pp. 23-27.

Id., *Великое сочинение* [The Great Work], in Матузова В.И., *Английские средневековые источники IX–XIII вв. Тексты, переводы, комментарии* [The English Medieval Sources IX–XIII Centuries. Texts, translations, commentaries], Moscow 1979, pp. 183-232.

Id., *Opus majus. Opus tertium. Отрывки из трактатов* [The Great Work. The Third Work. The Fragments of Treatises], translated by Zubov V.P., in *Музыкальная эстетика западноевропейского средневековья и Возрождения* [The Musical Aesthetic of Medieval and Renaissance Western Europe], Moscow 1966, pp. 54-78.

Id., *Большое сочинение* [The Great Work], translated by Gorfunkel' A.Kh., in *Антология мировой философии* [The Anthology of World Philosophy], Moscow 1969, vol. I, part II, pp. 862-877.

Id., *Введение к трактату псевдо-Аристотеля "Тайная тайных"* [The Introduction to the Pseudo-Aristotle's Treatise "The Secret of Secrets"], translated by Vashestov A.V., in *Герметизм, магия, натурфилософия в европейской культуре 13-19 вв.* [Hermetism, Magic, and Natural Philosophy in European Culture – 13th to 19th Centuries], Moscow 1999, pp. 41-69.

Id., *Третий труд* [The Third Work], in *Антология средневековой мысли. Теология и философия европейского средневековья* [The Anthology of Medieval Thought. The Theology and Philosophy of Medieval Europe], translated by Apollonov A.B., Saint Petersburg 2002, vol. II, pp. 81-121.

Id., *Избранное* [Selected works], edited by Lupandin I.V., Moscow 2005.

Bibliography:

Елькина Г., *Идеи развития научного знания в философии Роджера Бэкона* [The Ideas on the Development of Scientific Knowledge in the Philosophy of Roger Bacon], Ph.D. Dissertation, Alma-Ata 1985.

Клемешов А., *Роджер Бэкон и его учение об "опытном знании"* [Roger Bacon and his concept of 'experimental science'], Candidate of Sciences in History Dissertation, Moscow 2003, pp. 31-40.

Матузова В., *Английские средневековые источники IX-XIII вв. Тексты, переводы, комментарии* [The English Medieval Sources IX-XIII Centuries. Texts, translations, commentaries], Moscow 1979, pp. 189-193.

The Use of Religion in the Ceremonies and Rituals of Political Power (Portugal, 16th to 18th Centuries)

ANA ISABEL RIBEIRO
University of Coimbra

As cerimónias, as festas e os rituais enquanto expressão do poder régio e instrumento da sua afirmação têm sido o objecto de inúmeros estudos no contexto da historiografia portuguesa, especialmente dos anos 90 do século XX Embora alguns destes estudos se debrucem sobre a monarquia medieval e dos inícios da Época Moderna, a maioria centra a sua análise no tempo e no processo de construção da monarquia absoluta, especialmente nos reinados de D. Pedro II e D. João V.

Neste artigo procuraremos explicitar de que forma alguns desses trabalhos interpretam especificamente a questão da utilização da religião e da linguagem do sagrado na afirmação do poder régio e na construção da imagem do príncipe e dos fundamentos do seu poder ao longo da Época Moderna. Ressalte-se que a maioria destes estudos não contempla exclusivamente esta perspectiva, integrando-a numa análise que tenta descodificar os diversos instrumentos e linguagens do poder – sagrados ou profanos.

Assim, procuraremos num primeiro momento percorrer os principais estudos e a abordagem que fazem desta problemática, seguindo-se a análise de alguns trabalhos operam uma inversão de perspectiva, ou seja, o da utilização pelo poder religioso de rituais e cerimónias do poder temporal.

Finalmente tentaremos apontar algumas linhas de análise que pensamos merecerem algum aprofundamento e estudos mais sistemáticos, nomeadamente a da relação das elites protagonistas do poder local com o universo cerimonial religioso e a utilização que fazem deste nas suas estratégias de afirmação social e política.

Ceremonies, festivities and rituals, while being both an expression of regal power as well as an instrument of its affirmation, have been the subject of innumerable studies in the context of Portuguese historiography, especially during the final decade of the 20th century[1]. Although some of these studies focus on the medieval monarchy[2] and the beginnings of Modern Age[3], the majority centre on the time and the process of construction of the absolute monarchy, particularly during the reigns of D. Pedro II and D. João V[4]. In this chapter, we will try to explain how some of these works specifically interpret the question of the use of religion and sacred language in affirming regal power, and in constructing the image of the king and the foundations of his power through the early modern ages. It is important to note that the majority of these studies do not concentrate exclusively on this perspective, integrating it into an analysis that tries to decode the various instruments and languages of power – sacred or profane. Consequently, we will start by looking at the main studies and the approach they take to this problem, followed by an analysis of some works that propose a different approach: religious power using the rituals and ceremonies of secular power. Finally, we will try to identify some areas that we think deserve some more profound and systematic study, such as the relationship of the protagonist elites of local power with the religious ceremonial universe and the use that they made of this power in their social and political strategies.

An itinerary of the most excellent works on the theme of ceremonies, festivities, art and rituals of regal power shows us the concern of historians when analysing this universe through the basic premise propounded by Roger Chartier, who said that the authority and prestige of an institution or social body largely depends on the representations built of them, and the way they are transmitted[5]. Thus, the study of the exercise of power by the Portuguese monarchs cannot be established without a thorough understanding of their own perception of their role and their political practice (the foundations of their power) and the strategies used to consolidate them.

Political power is viewed as a construction that aimed to transmit, to both the powerful and the common people, an image of the king's power which inherently conveyed image of social organization. In this context, the ceremonies and their rituals are understood as a language, a functional expression of a political message that emphasised "the natural order of social bodies" in the regal perception. This "functional view" justifies the effort made by historians to reconstruct these ceremonies, giving special attention to social position, as well as to the words and gestures of each protagonist, because this role or ritual formalization may be employed as a benchmark of social interaction which opens doors to the understanding of the hierarchies that dominated the organization of power and society in early modern Portugal.

The ceremonies of regal power (proclamations, courts, commemorations, funeral rites) can constitute excellent observation points to observe the exact image that those in power had of themselves, as well as the instruments used to transmit and perpetuate it. One of these instruments was, without a doubt, the use of religion and its rituals, symbols, language and, above all, its capacity to mould mentalities and behaviours. This use is clear throughout the monarch's life, starting with his proclamation as king, and the beginning of his reign. This was an important point in the search for the legitimisation of his natural right to be king, and the blood-line that brought him to the throne – it was important to prove that his ancestors were destined to rule due to their extraordinary character, bravery and pious behaviour. As a result, many new monarchs actively promoted the sanctification of their predecessors – D. Manuel I, whose throne did not come by linear succession (he was the cousin and brother-in-law of D. João II, his predecessor), endeavoured to transfer the mortal remains of his cousin from the Cathedral of Silves to the *Panteão de Avis* in the Monastery of *Santa Maria da Vitória* in Batalha[6], organizing a second funeral, full of state honours. During these ceremonies, the idea that the deceased king should be venerated as a saint was emphasized: his allegedly uncorrupted body apparently being able to promote miraculous cures, earning the devotion of the subjects and of the new monarch[7].

However, D. João II was not the only monarch whose sanctity D. Manuel I intended to reinforce. D. Afonso Henriques, first king of Portugal, was also transferred to a new tomb. This was concluded in 1520. Once more, the chronicles of the time emphasise the state of conservation of the body, which was considered to be the basic mark of sanctity. An official cult to the founder of the nation was thus instituted, culminating with diverse requests made to Rome for his canonization[8]. The pretence of the sanctity of these crucial monarchs was used by D. Manuel I as a strategy to legitimise and consolidate his power as king when assuming his position as the full heir of this pious line.

The religious element was also used in more obvious ways as a tool of power, enabling the strengthening of hierarchies and the justification of decisions. Pedro Cardim, in his important study of Portuguese courts[9] in the 16th and 17th centuries[10], clearly demonstrates this. He emphasizes the fact that the official opening of the courts was carried out using a formal address, the main purpose of which was to state the reasons for that very assembly. This address was given by an ecclesiastic, in a form similar to a sermon, guaranteeing the solemnity of the moment through the introduction of a religious element, and urging the social bodies to fulfil their duties to the kingdom in harmony with its sovereign and his points of view. At the same time, important sermons commanded by the Royal House were given in the Royal Chapel. These sermons invariably concerned the importance of the subjects that were going to be dealt with in the courts, and included explicit instructions regarding the position that the participants in the meeting should assume in the matters that were going to be discussed[11].

The presence of religion, but above all, religion serving the interests of the regal image, was visible in the day-to-day activities of the royal court and its ceremonies. As religion was an important factor of social cohesion, and the ceremonies were a basic tenet of the establishment of hierarchies and social positions, the king controlled these ceremonies and their liturgy, associating his image and his mission with a holy design. As Paula Marçal Lourenço commented, "The magnificent churches, the royal processions, the Patriarchal parades, the richness of the vestments and the cult objects, the canonisations and the solemn *Te Deum*, all contribute to surround the regal figure, patron and demigod, with feelings of collective loyalty, but also of separation, distance, divine intangibility"[12]. For example, the king going to mass was a point when a religious ceremony was used as a place and time to formalise hierarchies, since the proximity of any chosen courtiers to the monarch during the liturgy established their prestige. Hence, the religious space and the solemnity of its function operated as an instrument of exclusion (and inclusion) that the monarch was able to use to maintain harmony in the universe of the court[13].

However, regal power did not confine its use of religion to the appropriation of ceremonies and liturgies. It also emerged in the space of the sacred, moulding or creating spaces where the image and symbols of regal power cohabited with religious symbols, and where regal will was reflected in the organization and functioning of religious hierarchies.

There are two exemplary cases during the reign of D. João V. Firstly, the institution of the Patriarchate with almost pontifical prerogatives that allowed a true "ecclesiastical court" to congregate around the monarch. It was headed by a Patriarch who, while being the primary figure of the Church in Portugal, was also a royal chaplain, responsible for the religious space of the king[14]. The creation of the Patriarchal Basilica of Lisbon, adjacent to the court as the monarch expressly ordered, allowed the king to extend his dominion over the Portuguese ecclesiastical hierarchy. This dominion was achieved though ritual splendour and a careful choice of prelates to key positions in the hierarchy.

The other example is the palace of *Mafra*, the masterpiece of his reign, where the power of men and the power of God are truly joined in an impressive architectural programme[15]. Following other European examples, especially those in Spain, the King set out to build a royal residence on sacred ground adjacent to a convent and a basilica, with the purpose of identifying the duties and attributes of royalty with those of religion through this coexistence of spaces, thus making religion ever more present in the life of the court and the governance of the kingdom.

A further example of the use of religion by the king can be detected in the final act in the process of building the regal image – the farewell of its earthly body – since his memory, as we have seen, would be perpetuated and used in the consolidation of the power of his successors. The regal funeral rites have been the subject of several studies[16] and they all point out the use of the sacred space as the last stage of communication between the monarch and his subjects; a highly ritualised stage, sometimes prepared by the monarch himself beforehand[17]. In the churches where the sculptures were covered by black cloths, altars were raised to the regal memory (*castrum doloris*), regal shields were broken, and sermons eulogized the deceased, in a succession of ceremonies that actively contributed to the consolidation of a certain feeling of "national unity" around the image of the king. The holy space, once more "becomes a place of monarchic exaltation"[18].

We have been exploring the dominant lines of analysis in the works that in some way have studied the theme of ceremony in the context of regal power and its relationship with religion. We have tried to clarify that the interpretative key is importance of religion as an instrument of power and as a tool for building the Portuguese monarchy of the Modern Age. However, some studies reveal an equally interesting perspective – the use of spaces, rituals and ceremonies of political power by the religious powers. Particularly relevant to this field are the studies of José Pedro Paiva on the ceremonial associated with the entrance of bishops into their ecclesiastical dioceses, and other public ceremonies[19].

In the analysis made of these public ceremonies (directed towards an ecclesiastical and lay public), especially the entry of the newly-elected bishops into their dioceses[20], the author makes particular note of the appropriation by the religious powers of secular symbols of prestige, now used for the benefit of the promotion of the Episcopal image. These practices and symbols were, for example, parading on a horse, the construction of triumph arcs, and military guards of honour that presented weapons and saluted the prelate[21]. Throughout this ceremony, there was a flagrant attempt to use the representatives of local power, who were requested to carry the canopy under which the bishop, seated on a horse, crossed the town which was the headquarters of his diocese (a custom that was traditionally reserved for the person of the king[22]). The solemn procession resembled part of the ceremonial used in regal entrances[23], staging a ritual of power that aimed to affirm the bishop's authority and not only consolidate hierarchies of authority inside the ecclesiastical universe (i.e., in the relationship of the bishop with the chapter), but also of this religious universe with regard to the secular universe.

The political assertion mechanisms used by the clergy employed similar strategies to those used to project the image of the monarch. Many prelates adopted programmes of personal and institutional promotion that involved, besides the solemn entrance through the city described above, the involvement of literary academies, book sponsorship, and the organization of festivities, bullfights and processions, all of which were designed to attract popular participation in religious celebrations. Many prelates also used art and architecture as tools of image consolidation, ordering important architectural sets that were meant to impress the public and to eternalise ecclesiastical dignity and power in stone[24].

The majority of the studies analysed or quoted identify ceremonies and rituals as one of the constituent elements of political speech and practice because of the use given to them. While they overflowed with legitimising functions and propaganda, these ceremonies carried a more important purpose, that of establishing a code of communication between the monarch and his subjects. However, the interpretative dimension of the ceremonies, and in our case, of the ceremonies built upon the exploitation of the liturgy, symbols or spaces of religion, also rests on the idea that they were a basic way of understanding social hierarchies and existing or desirable power relationships[25]. We cannot forget that we are analysing a social universe where etiquette played an important role in social organization; the place where an individual was seated or the role he played in a ceremony, for instance, meant that he had a certain social status, and any change made to this place or function could be interpreted as a change in his place in society.

We think that the scope of this last analysis lies in the fact that it can be used as a basic tool to broaden the knowledge of the social relationships and the individual and collective perceptions that moulded the organization and the establishment of social positions. This is especially effective in the understanding of limited social environments, such as those that were strongly hierarchic and codified, like the regal court.

We believe that it is important to widen the perspective of this analysis to other social universes such as the local social organization. The social understanding of the early modern Portuguese communities has been accomplished through a very static analysis based upon the construction of categorizations that are not able to disclose the social complexity and the underlying logic of the local hierarchy.

In our opinion, the ceremonies promoted by the regal power (commemoration of marriages, births, funeral rites of the king and the royal family[26], regal entrances) or the ecclesiastical power (processions[27], solemn entrances of the bishops, *autos-de-fé*, canonisations of saints and so on) constitute basic points of formalisation and public expression of the social position that each individual or group occupied in the local society, and of the way they should relate to those that occupied other positions in the social hierarchy. This analytical perspective allows the historian to draw a more dynamic picture, closer to the perceptions of the social actors, and detect moments when the conflict or the experimentation of new logics may indicate changing processes such as the establishment of upward social movement or loss of importance, prestige and influence in the community.

NOTES

[1]   The majority of the studies that we have mentioned in this article have their origins in the 1990s. Clearly, in this decade of the 20th century, Portuguese historians, especially those working in cultural history, felt attracted to the thematic publishing of sources and articles, where they tried to decode the etiquette of several ceremonies and to understand the processes of communication of the regal power. There are also more extensive works which try to understand the processes of political assertion by the monarchs who were the protagonists of the construction of the modern Portuguese state. See R. Bebiano, *D. João V. Poder e Espectáculo*, Aveiro 1987; A. Pimentel, *Arquitectura e Poder. O Real Edifício de Mafra*, Coimbra 1992; D.R. Curto, *A Cultura Política em Portugal. Comportamentos, Ritos e Negócios*, Lisbon 1994; L.R. Guerreiro, *La Représentation du Pouvoir Royal à l'Âge Baroque Portugais (1687-1753)*, 4 volumes, Paris 1995; P. Cardim, *Cortes e Cultura Política no Portugal do Antigo Regime*, Lisbon 1998 e J. Tendim, *Festa Régia no Tempo de D. João V*, Porto 1999.

[2]   With refence to this subject, we must mention the studies of: P. Merêa, *Sobre a Aclamação dos Nossos Reis*, "Revista Portuguesa de História", X, 1962, pp. 411-417; J. Mattoso, *A Coroação dos Primeiros Reis de Portugal*, in F. Bethencourt - D.R. Curto (eds.), *A Memória da Nação*, Lisbon 1991, pp. 187-200; R. Gomes, *A Corte dos Reis de Portugal no Final da Idade Média*, Lisbon 1995.

[3]   For example, studies such as those of F. Bouza Alvarez, *Retórica da Imagem Real. Portugal e a Memória Figurada de Filipe II*, "Penélope. Fazer e Desfazer a História", 4, 1989, pp. 19-58; R. Araújo, *Lisboa. A Cidade e o Espectáculo na Época dos Descobrimentos*, Lisbon 1990; N. Soares, *O Príncipe Ideal no Século XVI e a Obra de D. Jerónimo Osório*, Lisbon 1994; P.D. Braga - I.D. Braga, *As Duas Mortes de D. Manuel: o Rei e o Homem*, "Penélope. Fazer e Desfazer a História", 14, 1994, pp. 11-22; A. Buescu, *Uma Sepultura para o Rei. Morte e Memória na Trasladação de D. Manuel I (1551)*, in G. Sabatier - R. Gomes (eds.), *Lugares de poder. Europa dos séculos XV a XX*, Lisbon 1998, pp. 185-203; A. Buescu, *Imagens do Príncipe. Discurso Normativo e Representação (1525-1549)*, Lisbon 1996; A. Cardoso, *Um Rei Leva a sua Alma às Sedes Etéreas. Representações do Poder no Portugal de Quinhentos*, Lisbon 1997; P. Cardim, *Entradas Solenes. Rituais Comunitários e Festas políticas, Portugal e Brasil, séculos XVI e XVII*, in I. Jancsó - I. Kantor (eds.), *Festa: Cultura e Sociabilidade na América Portuguesa*, vol. 1, São Paulo 2001, pp. 97-124; J. Paiva, *As Festas de Corte em Portugal no Período Filipino (1580-1640)*, "Revista de História da Sociedade e da Cultura", 2, 2002, pp. 11-38; A. Araújo, *Hagiografia Política e Cerimoniais de Estado no Tempo de D. Manuel I*, "Revista Portuguesa de História", XXXVI, 1, 2002-2003, pp. 319-345.

[4]   Beside the studies quoted in note 1, we also have to mention the studies: A. Barreto Xavier - P. Cardim - F. Bouza (eds.), *Festas que se Fizeram pelo Casamento de Rei D. Afonso VI*, Lisbon 1996; E. Griné, *A Construção da*

Imagem Pública do Rei e da Família Real em Tempo de Luto (1649-1709), Coimbra 1997; A. Araújo, *Ritualidade e Poder na Corte de D. João V .A Génese Simbólica do Regalismo político*, "Revista de História das Ideias", 22, 2001, pp. 175-208 and *Ritual and Power in the Court of King João V. The Symbolic Genesis of Political Regalism*, in J. Paiva (ed.), *Religious Ceremonials and Images,: Power and Social Meaning (1400-1750)*, Viseu 2002, pp. 323-349.

5   R. Chartier, *Pouvoirs et Limites de la Représentation. Sur l'Oeuvre de Louis Marin*, "Annales. Histoire, Sciences Sociales", 2, Paris 1994, p. 413.

6   Burial place of the second dynasty Portuguese monarchs.

7   See Araújo, *Hagiografia Política e Cerimoniais de Estado* cit., pp. 324-326 and Curto, *Ritos e Cerimónias da Monarquia em Portugal* cit., p. 243-245.

8   Official campaigns were registered during the reigns of D. João III and D. Sebastião. See Araújo, *Hagiografia Política* cit., pp. 330-331.

9   Courts being the assembly where the diverse parts of the social body of the kingdom had representation and which were convoked every time the monarch needed to take decisions in certain matters of governance.

10   Cardim, *Cortes e Cultura Política* cit.

11   *Ibid.*, pp. 72-73.

12   P. Lourenço, *Estado e Poderes*, in *Nova História de Portugal*, Vol. VII – *Portugal da Paz da Restauração ao Ouro do Brasil*, Lisbon 2001, pp. 33.

13   Curto, *Ritos e Cerimónias* cit., pp. 228-232; Id., *A Capela Real: um Espaço de Conflitos (Séculos XVI a XVIII)* "Revista da Faculdade de Letras", série Línguas e Literatura, V, 1993, pp. 143-154.

14   The Lisbon Patriarchate was created, after difficult negotiations, by Pope Clement XI in the papal bull *In supremo apostolatus solio*, dated 7th November, 1716. Among the extensive prerogatives it granted, for the fist time in the ecclesiastical history of Portugal, was a position of supremacy over the archbishops and bishops of Portugal, assigned by the king. The monarch went further by granting honours to the nominated Patriarch, and the title of cardinal, even though he did not have the right to do this (1717). It was only in 1737, through the papal bull *Praecipuas apostololici ministeri*, that Pope Clement XIII granted that the "appointed cardinals of Lisbon" could truly be acknowledged as cardinals. See Araújo, *Ritualidade e Poder na Corte de D. João V* cit., pp. 195.

15   With reference to the palace-convent of Mafra and its architectural decoding as an object of power, see the enlightening work of Pimentel, *Arquitectura e Poder. O Real Edifício de Mafra* cit.

16   For example, we quote J. Pereira, *A Morte de D. João V: Ascese e Espectáculo*, "Claro-Escuro, Revista de Estudos Barrocos", 2-3, 1989, pp. 165-176; M. Araújo, *O ritual da morte – As exéquias celebradas na defunção de El-rei D. João V*, in *A Festa. Comunicações Apresentadas no VIII Congresso Internacional*, vol. II, Lisbon 1992, pp. 201-266; M. Hespanhol, *As Cerimónias Religiosas Realizadas na Sé de Évora, no Tempo de D. Teotónio de Bragança, pela Morte de El-rei D. Filipe II de Espanha (1598): Contribuição para a História da Igreja eborense*, in *Actas do Congresso de História no IV Centenário do Seminário de Évora*, Évora 1994, pp. 457-465; Guerreiro, *La Représentation du Pouvoir Royal á l'Âge Baroque Portugais* cit., vol. II, pp. 149-192; Braga - Braga, *As Duas Mortes de D. Manuel: o Rei e o Homem* cit., pp. 11-22; Griné, *A Construção da Imagem Pública do Rei* cit; Buescu, *Uma Sepultura para o Rei* cit., pp. 185-203.

17   As was the case with D. Manuel I, in whose will (7 April 1517) we find detailed specifications for his sepulchre, funeral, suffrages, alms and pious legacies. See Araújo, *Hagiografia Política e Cerimoniais de Estado* cit., pp. 341-345.

18   Griné, *A Construção da Imagem Pública do rei* cit., p. 48.

19   J. Paiva, *O Cerimonial de Entrada dos Bispos nas suas Dioceses: Uma Encenação de Poder (1741-1757)*, "Revista de História das Ideias", 15, 1993, pp. 117-146. Id., *Etiqueta e Cerimónias Públicas na Esfera da Igreja*, in I. Jancsó - I. Kantor (eds.), *Festa: Cultura e Sociabilidade na América Portuguesa*, vol. 1, São Paulo 2001, pp. 75-94 and J. Paiva., *Public Ceremonies Ruled by the Ecclesiastical-clerical Sphere: a Language of Political Assertion (16th-18th centuries)*, in Id. (ed.), *Religious Ceremonials and Images* cit., pp. 415-425.

[20] In Portugal, the bishops were chosen by the monarch and later confirmed by the Vatican, a procedure that provoked several questions and conflicts between the king and the papacy. For the problems raised by the episcopal presentation, see Fortunato de Almeida, *História da Igreja em Portugal*, Vol. II, Lisbon 1967, pp 47-50. The solemn entrance, that assumed the form of a ceremonial procession, passed through the streets of the city diocese headquarters and had, according to José Pedro Paiva, "the function of a rite (...) to give, to know and to recognize a difference, the Episcopal superiority, and to affirm it as a social difference known and recognized by the invested agent, in this case the bishop, and by all the community."; Paiva, *O Cerimonial de Entrada dos Bispos nas suas Dioceses* cit., p. 137.

[21] Paiva, *O Cerimonial de Entrada dos Bispos nas suas Dioceses* cit., pp. 138-142.

[22] The reception of bishops in this manner, with royal support, was opposed by some members of the local government. See Paiva, *O Cerimonial de Entrada dos Bispos nas suas Dioceses* cit., p. 139.

[23] For the ceremonials and rituals of regal entrances see A. Alves, *As Entradas régias portuguesas: uma visão de conjunto*, Lisbon 1986 and Cardim, *Entradas Solenes* cit., pp. 97-124.

[24] One of the best examples is the programme of measures taken by the first Patriarch of Lisbon, D. Tomás de Almeida (1717-1754), in order to establish the new statute, which promoted, beside the solemn entrance, several festivities that celebrated pastoral visits, canonisations or consecrations of works completed throughout his term in office. He also ordered several architectural projects to be carried out, such as the construction of the church of Senhor Jesus da Pedra in Óbidos and the extensive restoration and enlargement of the church, palace and gardens of a property owned by the diocese in Santo António do Tojal (near Lisbon); Paiva, *Etiqueta e Cerimónias Públicas na Esfera da Igreja* cit., pp. 92-93.

[25] With regard to this interpretation, see J. Paiva, *As Festas de Corte em Portugal no Período Filipino (1580-1640)*, "Revista de História da Sociedade e da Cultura", 2, 2002, pp. 19-22.

[26] The commemoration of royal marriages, births of princes and princesses, and funeral rites were locally financed and organized by the city councils. The local officers of the city council and local elites participated very actively, taking advantage of these ceremonies to prove their prestige and social importance using the function and social position that they occupied in these events to exclude or relegate to secondary social positions those individuals that they intended to distance from the opportunity of obtaining a position of power in local society. S. Soares writes, regarding Coimbra: "It is in the political festivities, commemorations of births, marriages and funeral rites of the royal family, proclamations of the new king, celebrations of the victorious battles, peace accords and other diplomatic events, that the highest-ranking members of government position themselves and clarify their relationship with the Crown (...). More than an expression of patriotism by those in government, these acts are used as a tool of assertion of an elite seeking to emphasise their specific, superior and exclusive qualities (...)". S. Soares, *O Município de Coimbra da Restauração ao Pombalismo*, vol. II (*Sociologia do Poder Municipal*), Coimbra 2002, p. 173.

[27] The processions, particularly the procession of the Body of Christ *(Corpus Christi)*, that became an object of thorough regulation during the reign of D. João V, are excellent historical sources as they allow an insight into the logic of local social stratification because the place each one occupied in these religious ceremonies depended upon his "quality" and social positioning. For the procession of the Body of Christ see: M. Genro, *Festa do Corpo de Deus: Procissões Eucarísticas*, Lisbon 1959; L. Couto, *As Origens das Procissões da Cidade do Porto*, Porto 1971; H. Janeiro, *A Procissão do Corpo de Deus na Lisbon Barroca – o Espaço e o Poder*, in *Arqueologia do Estado – 1ᵃˢ Jornadas sobre Formas de Organização e Exercício de Poderes na Europa do Sul, Séculos XIII-XVIII*, Lisbon 1988, pp. 723-742.

BIBLIOGRAPHY

Alves A., *As Entradas régias portuguesas: uma visão de conjunto* Lisbon, 1986

Araújo A., *Hagiografia Política e Cerimoniais de Estado no Tempo de D. Manuel I*, "Revista Portuguesa de História", XXXVI, vol. I, Coimbra 2002-2003, pp. 319-345.

Id., *Ritualidade e Poder na Corte de D. João V. A Génese Simbólica do Regalismo Político*, "Revista de História das Ideias", 22, 2001, pp. 175-208.

Id., *O Ritual da Morte – As Exéquias Celebradas na Defunção de El-rei D. João V*, "A Festa. Comunicações Apresentadas no VIII Congresso Internacional", vol. II, Lisbon 1992, pp. 201-266.

Bebiano R., *D. João V. Poder e Espectáculo*, Aveiro 1987.

Bethencourt F. - Curto D.R. (eds.), *A Memória da Nação*, Lisbon 1991.

Bouza Alvarez F., *Retórica da Imagem Real. Portugal e a Memória Figurada de Filipe II*, "Penélope. Fazer e Desfazer a História", 4, Lisbon 1989, pp. 19-58.

Braga P.D. - Braga I.D., *As Duas Mortes de D. Manuel: o Rei e o Homem*, "Penélope. Fazer e Desfazer a História", 14, Lisbon 1994, pp. 11-22.

Buescu A., *Imagens do Príncipe. Discurso Normativo e Representação (1525-1549)*, Lisbon 1996.

Cardim P., *Cortes e Cultura Política no Portugal do Antigo Regime*, Lisbon 1998.

Cardoso A., *Um rei Leva a sua Alma às Sedes Etéreas. Representações do Poder no Portugal de Quinhentos*, Lisbon 1997.

Couto L., *As Origens das Procissões da Cidade do Porto*, Porto 1971.

Curto D.R., *A Capela Real: Um Espaço de Conflitos (Séculos XVI a XVIII)*, "Revista da Faculdade de Letras", série Línguas e Literatura, V, Porto 1993, pp. 143-154.

Id., *A Cultura Política em Portugal. Comportamentos, Ritos e Negócios*, Lisbon 1994.

Gomes M., *Contribuição para o Estudo da Festa em Lisbon no Antigo Regime*, Lisbon 1985.

Gomes R., *A Corte dos Reis de Portugal no Final da Idade Média*, Lisbon 1995.

Griné E., *A Construção da Imagem Pública do rei e da Família Real em Tempo de Luto (1649-1709)*, Coimbra 1997.

Guerreiro L.R., *La Représentation du Pouvoir Royal á l'Âge Baroque Portugais (1687-1753)*, 4 volumes, Paris 1995.

Hespanhol M., *As Cerimónias Religiosas Realizadas na Sé de Évora, no Tempo de D. Teotónio de Bragança, pela Morte de El-rei D. Filipe II de Espanha (1598): Contribuição para a História da Igreja Eborense*, in "Actas do Congresso de História no IV Centenário do Seminário de Évora", Évora 1994, pp. 457-465.

Jancsó I. - Kantor I. (eds.), *Festa: Cultura e Sociabilidade na América Portugués*, 2 Vols., São Paulo 2001.

Janeiro H., *A Procissão do Corpo de Deus na Lisbon Barroca – o Espaço e o Poder*, in *Arqueologia do Estado – 1ªs Jornadas sobre Formas de Organização e Exercício de Poderes na Europa do Sul, séculos XIII-XVIII*, Lisbon 1988, pp. 723-742.

Lourenço P., *Estado e Poderes*, in *Nova História de Portugal*, Vol. VII – *Portugal da paz da Restauração ao Ouro do Brasil*, Avelino de Freitas Torres (coord.), Lisbon 2001, pp. 17-89.

Merêa P., *Sobre a Aclamação dos Nossos Reis*, "Revista Portuguesa de História", X, 1962, pp. 411-417.

Milheiro M., *Braga: a Cidade e a Festa no Século XVIII*, 2 volumes, Braga 1997.

Paiva J. (ed.), *Religious Ceremonials and Images: Power and Social Meaning (1400-1750)*, Viseu 2002.

Id., *As Festas de Corte em Portugal no Período Filipino (1580-1640)*, "Revista de História da Sociedade e da Cultura", 2, 2002, pp. 11-38.

Id., *O Cerimonial de Entrada dos Bispos nas Suas Dioceses: Uma Encenação de Poder (1741-1757)*, "Revista de História das Ideias", 15, 1993, pp. 117-146.

Pereira J., *A Morte de D. João V: Ascese e Espectáculo*, "Claro-Escuro, Revista de Estudos Barrocos", 2-3, Lisbon 1989, pp. 165-176.

Pimentel A., *Arquitectura e Poder. O Real Edifício de Mafra*, Coimbra 1992.

Sabatier G. - Gomes R. (eds.), *Lugares de Poder. Europa dos Séculos XV a XX*, Lisbon 1998.

Soares N., *O Príncipe Ideal no Século XVI e a Obra de D. Jerónimo Osório*, Lisbon 1994.

Tendim J., *Festa Régia no Tempo de D. João V*, Porto 1999.

Xavier A. - Cardim P. - Bouza Alvarez F. (eds.), *Festas que se Fizeram pelo Casamento do Rei D. Afonso VI*, Lisbon 1996.

Druže Tito, mi ti se kunemo[1].

Ritual and Political Power in Yugoslavia: Tito's Birthday Celebrations (1945-1987)

DIMITAR GRIGOROV
St. Kliment Ohridski University of Sofia

Авторът на това съобщение прави опит да представи основните архивни източници, които биха били от полза при изследването на рождения ден на Йосип Броз Тито като ритуал, който, естествено има важно политическо значение на мобилизационен и интеграционен фактор за югославското социалистическо общество. Предложени са сведения за документалните източници, свързани с празника, подаръците, които Броз е получавал и тяхното символично значение, снимковите и киноматериали, които се съхраняват в Архива на Сърбия и Черна гора и най-вече в Архива на Йосип Броз Тито, който се състои от Фонда на кабинета на Маршала на Югославия (1943-1953), Фонда на Кабинета на президента на Югославия (1953-1980), Архив на Върховния комендант на въоръжените сили на Югославия (1945-1980), Личен архив на Йосип Броз Тито, Фототека с 800 000 негатива, илюстриращи дейността на югославския лидер от 1947 до 1980 г., фонотека, съдържаща 1000 записа с негови изяви и филмотека с повече от 700 филма, най-вече документални. Разбира се, проблема за рождения ден на Йосип Броз е сравнително маргинален и определно не заслужава едно цялостно монографично проучване, но в същото време би могъл да бъде ценен принос в изследването на по-общи въпроси като този за пропагандните образи на балканските политически лидери, отношението водач – народ, или по-ограничения, но също така съществен проблем за написването на основаваща се не толкова на желанието за постигане на абсолютно звучене, колкото на търсенето на полутоновете политическа биография на легендарния ръководител.

Naturally the ambitious and proud man can
not find answer to the question
why another man should command him
to such a degree that his own need makes him feel this.
Only extraordinary events can convince him
that without command he himself could become prey
to a mightier one and that is why
he should like submission as much as he
likes his own life and own tranquility[2].
Louis IX

A huge face from the poster on the wall against the elevator
on each floor was staring at him. The portrait was painted in such a way that the
eyes were followed you wherever you turned around.
BIG BROTHER IS WATCHING YOU read the sign below[3].
George Orwell

And the work was slow and did not move with the times,
with many questions about "the forbidden fruit" [sex] remaining unanswered.
It took a letter [to the *Komsomol*] by comrade Zhivkov [about sex]
to melt the ice of ignorance and pseudo moralizing [...][4].
Yakov Yanakiev

"... others who used to be at the height of their power
and glory now are dishonored and their names resemble looted tombs [...]."
Of course, this should not surprise us, since the only constancy bestowed upon us by the
Heavens is change itself[5].
Victor Pelevin

Josip Broz Tito[6] was one of the most prominent symbols of the Balkans after the Second
World War. Embodying what once has been quite wrongly described as 'national'[7] socialism in what was once imagined to be Eastern Europe, Tito attracted great attention in
the west of the continent and in the USA during his lifetime. He remains a part of some
general Western perceptions of the south-eastern region of Europe and if we compare the
amount of publications in the West dedicated to the Balkan communist leaders we find that
Broz (and maybe Ceausescu[8]) heads the list, followed well behind by the two other prominent contemporary symbols of the peninsula's socialist past – Enver Hoxha and Todor
Zhivkov[9]. Last but maybe not least, it is an interesting fact that the Microsoft Office spelling and grammar tool recognises the name Tito, together with Lenin, Stalin, Khrushchev,
Brezhnev and Mao[10] but considers Dej[11], Zhivkov and Hoxha[12] to be errors. Amongst the
other Balkan leaders, Microsoft has also granted this "honour" to Ceausescu.

Tito still plays an important role in the consciousness of the ex-Yugoslavian people.
Here I suppose that it is worth citing that recently, and not without a trace of irony,
the Yugoslav (Serbian) sociologist Todor Kuljic wrote, "Tell me what you think about
Tito and I'll tell you who are you"[13]. One of the many reasons for this is the spectacular

cult of personality which developed around Tito during his lifetime and continued for several years after his death (4 May1980)[14]. Tito's cult had its roots in the World War II years when he became the powerful leader of a strong, large-scale partisan movement. Tito's popularity was used to strengthen the Communist regime which came to power in 1944-1945 and to expand Soviet influence in the Balkans. Until 1948, the personality cult of Josip Broz in Yugoslavia was overshadowed by that of Josef Stalin[15]. However, the split with the Soviet strongman fuelled the idolisation surrounding the master of Belgrade, and the new independent position of Yugoslavia meant a stronger personality cult. From a wider Balkan perspective, it is possible to conclude that in the countries which were more independent of the Soviet Union there were higher levels of idolisation than in those which were loyal followers of Moscow's policy. In this context, we can add to Yugoslavia the Romanian dictator Nicolae Ceausescu, especially after 1968 when he stood against the Warsaw Treaty intervention in Czechoslovakia, and also Albania, a state which cut its connections with the Soviet Union at the beginning of the 1960s, left the Warsaw Treaty in 1968 and in doing so enabled the Albanian strongman Hoxha to present himself as the one and only bearer and interpreter of communist principles and the true heir of Marx, Lenin and Stalin. The group of countries loyal to the Soviet Union was only represented by the possibly notorious example of Bulgaria. One of the many results was the preservation of the cult of the Soviet Union, and the country's first Bulgarian communist leader George Dimitrov[16] who died in 1949 was not considered responsible for the Stalinist terror of the early 1950s. Blame for this was attached to his heir Valko Chervenkov[17] and an attitude towards leaders was therefore created in Bulgaria which had something in common with that of the USSR. After his death, Dimitrov achieved a cult status similar to Lenin, whilst Chervenkov was condemned as Stalin was and Zhivkov's image varied according to the changing Soviet context – his representations were a mixture of a Bulgarian Khrushchev, a Bulgarian Brezhnev and latterly he tried to act, at least in front of an audience, as a Bulgarian Gorbachov. However, the main task of this short chapter, as the title I hope suggests, is not to provide an overview of cults in the Balkans or to evaluate the objects of this adoration, for it is clear how different they were as people, but to indicate some of the main sources that may be useful in presenting the ritual of 25 May, officially proclaimed Tito's birthday, and its political meaning. Of course I am aware of the fact that this subject is of marginal interest. On the other hand I presume that a study of the topic could be useful as a contribution towards other more important comparative issues such as the propaganda images of the Balkan leaders, the relationship between leaders–subjects in the region or the more limited, but otherwise very significant problem of writing a biography that seeks to uncover nuances rather than provide an absolute and definitive political portrait of Josip Broz. So, after this somewhat lengthy introduction, it is time to get to the point.

DOCUMENTARY SOURCES

As an adherent of the "cult of the written document" I shall start this appraisal by considering this type of source. Very significant documentary data concerning the topic under consideration is held in the Museum of Yugoslavian History – an institution which was actually created in 1996, after the collapse of the real Yugoslavia. This Museum incorporates the ex-Museum of the Yugoslav Nation and National Revolution established in 1959 and the so-called "Josip Broz Tito" Memorial Centre founded in 1982[18]. The latter includes the 25th of May Museum where the archives of the President of Yugoslavia are preserved. The most interesting documents associated with the leader's birthday festivities can be found in the files of the Office of the President of Yugoslavia[19].

One important source is the birthday greetings. These documents are divided into two groups – congratulations from foreign individuals[20] and organizations and letters expressing best wishes from the nation[21]. A large number of them were sent by various official institutions and are distinguished by their formal language. Amongst these documents, the contents of the letters from the members of the Pioneer's organization may be more original, whilst the messages sent by the "common" people are rather different. Some of them have really attractive content and are a relatively good source for the study of popular attitudes towards the leader, which were very closely linked to the mentality of traditional society. Since Tito was a godfather of every ninth child in the family, it may be assumed that the letters from his many godsons and goddaughters also belong to the latter type of greeting[22]. The greater part of Tito's godsons and goddaughters were peasants and "new working-class heroes" who still retained their village mentality. These people were mainly Muslims, Orthodox Serbs and Catholic Croats from Bosnia and Herzegovina and Albanians from Kosovo[23]. Their messages contained a sometimes seemingly irrational, but actually very rational, traditional perception of the leader, expressing on the one hand a measure of financial gratitude, since the godfather had been generous in sending gifts and financial help to the children and, on the other hand, true family pride in being related to the legendary Marshal. The letters reflect Broz's true popularity amongst the masses, even in the 1970s when, in the eyes of some intellectuals and especially some future researchers, he seemed more of an idol than a true leader[24]. Of course the letters were also influenced by the propaganda image of the "initiator of all our victory" as well as by Tito's great charisma as the victorious commander from the "war and the revolution". During his lifetime I suppose that the latter was more important in the popular attitude towards the leader but I believe we should also bear the former in mind, since during and after the collapse of Yugoslavia when strong efforts were made to transform the dead leader into a scapegoat, doubtless very few Yugoslavs were keen to admit that they were Tito's godsons and goddaughters.

Another type of archival document provides scholars with an opportunity to follow almost all of Tito's own activities on his birthdays – as the host of the formal reception and the recipient of gifts and batons bearing birthday wishes from all over the country[25].

A very useful documentary source can be found in the archives of Serbia and Montenegro[26]. The most significant items are the files of the Union of Yugoslav Socialist Youth[27], which was in charge of organising the so-called Tito Baton or Youth Baton. A few words have to be said about this most important mass event which formed part of the celebrations devoted to the leader, in order to clarify what it meant. According to some authors, between 1945 and 1987 probably around 20,000 batons bearing birthday wishes to Tito were "carried"[28]. There were two kinds of batons: local and primary. The latter included six batons from the republics and about a dozen others whose bearers varied and were chosen according to the political climate of the time. They included the Yugoslav People's Army or some of its branches, large towns, builders of important facilities and large companies, as well as sporting and social organizations. Until 1956 Tito received these "primary batons" personally from their final bearers, while local batons were presented to representatives of the authorities in the respective districts and communities and were then forwarded to the depot in Belgrade. From 1957 onwards, only one baton would reach Broz, which he would accept from only one, final bearer[29]. According to Serbian ethnologist Ivan Colovic:

> This "great" baton acquired a new function which essentially set it apart from all the others. It was a sacred object which, from the touch of thousands of hands and thousands of kilometres, had drawn the miraculous energy (love, gratitude and hope) which nourished Tito's political power. But it was now also a symbol of the other batons, the hundreds of "small" batons which did not reach Tito's hands[30].

It seems that from the early 1960s, the "small" or "local" batons gradually lost their significance. This might have been a consequence of the development of television and the possibility of the "magic" baton appearing in every home and "virtually every hand" via the TV screen. Thus the so-called Youth Day became the journey of just one baton and the glamorous ceremony of its presentation to Tito in the Yugoslav National Army Stadium in Belgrade[31].

The files of the Union of Socialist Youth give a good insight into the technology of the sophisticated preparatory work needed for the event. They contain a lot of information on the main executive organ in charge of organising the activities, the Committee for Celebrating Youth Day. There is also a lengthy correspondence preserved in the files between this body and the different political and social institutions and organizations, consisting of a careful accounting of expenses, the requirements for the participants in the competitions filmed for the final event in the Yugoslav army stadium, the texts of the songs that were to be performed, payments to the authors (poets, writers, directors etc), the route of the Baton, and a list of the VIPs in the official boxes at the stadium where most of the legendary revolutionaries of the partisan movement, prominent intellectuals such as Ivo Andric and the leaders of the main faiths in the country could be seen[32]. This extensive documentary source is evidence of the varied nature of the Tito or Youth Baton. It was an ideological event dedicated to one of the few common symbols in the multinational Yugoslav society – Broz himself. Yet this was not all. Particularly in the 1970s and 80s the ideological celebration was also a kind of spectacle, incorporating many modern features and enjoyed by many Yugoslav citizens at the stadium or at home in front of the TV screen. It also represented a profitable business for certain text writers, composers, painters, TV directors and journalists, some of whom acknowledge this fact in their memoirs[33].

Rituals and Implementation of Religious and Political Power

THE GIFTS

The presents Tito received on the occasion of his birthday are another important source of information. In May the Yugoslav leader was the recipient of thousands and thousands of gifts. In the inventories of the Museum of Yugoslav History there are 2,312 entries containing descriptions of birthday presents. The exhibits are catalogued into 6 different types: sculptures, models, children's work, works of art and folk-art, technical instruments and machinery. According to their senders and symbolic meaning, the abovementioned Ivan Colovic divides the gifts into two main groups: those given to the dictator by the official state and party institutions and those sent to the dictator by ordinary citizens. As typical examples of the first group, he mentions the distinctions awarded to Tito by the state: the three honourable tittles of National Yugoslav Hero which he received on the occasion of his birthday, the doctoral degrees awarded by the different science academies of the Republics, the building of the 25th of May Museum, given to him as a present by the city of Belgrade[34], the hunting lodge presented to Broz by the Socialist Republic of Slovenia on his 80th birthday[35] and so on[36]. Here we can also add most of the expensive sculptures usually sent by the higher party or state structures and the models – a typical gift from workers' collectives, trade unions, certain professional associations and so on[37].

The gifts from the common people are different. Many of them were expressions of traditional peasant culture. They include socks, slippers, shoes, hats, handkerchiefs, tablecloths, pillows, pillowcases, and similar hand-made items. Such gifts came from village women, craftsmen and other "ordinary folk", including those to whose children Tito was godfather. Generally such gifts were made by the donors themselves. Messages to comrade Tito were usually embroidered on decorative towels. Colovic suggests that "gifts of this kind had political value because of their modesty and simplicity, which gave the impression that they really were "from the heart"[38]. One of the propaganda editions of the ex-Memorial Centre indicates the same meaning for "ordinary people's" gifts, stressing the fact that Josip Broz himself quite often visited these exhibits in the so-called Old Museum and "supervised their presentation"[39].

In essence, both types of gifts, like the documentary sources, represent the two faces of the Tito cult – the official, formal one, and the unorganized popular admiration for the successful leader. It might be interesting to mention that the examples of "ordinary folk's" presents became rare in the 70s when official adoration in the country was at its peak. Naturally this could be explained by the supposedly diminishing popularity of Broz after the so-called Croatian Spring and the encounter with the "Serbian liberals" within the Union of Yugoslav Communists. However, I believe there is a different reason. The almost complete disappearance of "common" gifts in the Inventory Book from the 1970s onwards could also be explained by the effects of urbanization, the industrialization of the country and the gradual disappearance of crafts. Of course this important change did not immediately free the new citizens from their traditional desire for a strong, powerful leader but it probably did succeed rather more quickly in creating a negative attitude towards the products of peasant culture and the fascination of the masses for industrially produced goods.

PICTURES, AUDIO MATERIALS AND FILMS

Finally I must allude briefly to the photos, tapes and films from the Museum of Yugoslav History depository. These are kept in the picture collection, record library and film library. The collection of photos is particularly valuable, especially bearing in mind the saying that "a picture speaks a thousand words". The Museum has preserved approximately 800,000 pictures from different periods of Tito's life. Photo sessions from all of the Marshal's birthdays are available to researchers, showing many details of the celebration activities. From the pictures of his 68th birthday (1960) for instance, we can get an impression of how the leader received the different kinds of presents, the official reception, with Broz on the grandstand during the celebrations dedicated to the leader, and many details of the various mass performances which took place during the event. The record library holds 1,000 tapes of the Yugoslav dictator's speeches made at his public appearances. Another particularly valuable source is the collection of over 700 films, most of them documentary. Unfortunately, I was unable to see any of these or hear any of the speeches as I was told there were technical problems at the Museum.

CONCLUSION

The sources from the ex-Yugoslav archives and the Museum of Yugoslavian History provide a wealth of information on the problem of the personality cult as a whole and Tito's birthday in particular. Part of the cult included the 25th of May as a political ritual, but its aim was not only to reinforce the leader's propaganda image. The main purpose was to integrate the Yugoslav nations and nationalities behind the Marshal in order to maintain a sense of unity. The official part of the celebrations involved an intense revitalisation of the main images of the Yugoslav leader: Josip Broz the statesman; Tito the leader of the Yugoslav communists, the war hero and military genius, his image of great international importance; Tito the working-class hero; Broz the saviour of the nation. On the other hand, the letters and gifts from the people revealed an important traditional stratum in the attitudes of the "common people" – that of Tito as godfather. This role had been created by the state and party structures but had not been "advertised" by the official propaganda machine. The latter kept silent. It is therefore a good example of how the socialist ideology, which otherwise strived to effect radical changes to the political culture, was actually forced to compromise and adapt to the traditional culture which had, in theory, to be destroyed by the revolutionaries.

Of course I am aware that the archive sources I have attempted to present are somewhat limited. Unfortunately I did not have an opportunity to look at the Slovenia, Croatia, Bosnia and Herzegovina, Macedonia and Montenegro depositories. In addition, the local archives of the ex-Yugoslavian district centres contain important information, and research in these kinds of institutions may reveal differences between the ceremonies in the capital and those in the provinces. These differences could prove rather interesting, as is evident in a not very "scientific" but otherwise fantastic piece of local history dedicated to the May celebration in the south-eastern Serbian district of Leskovac from the end of World War II to the beginning of the 21st century[40].

Naturally the archive materials should be analysed, together with the propaganda editions dedicated to Tito's birthday and especially to the Baton or the events at the People's Army stadium[41]. Another secondary source, and possibly the most important one, is the press. In fact, my work in this area reminds me that the Tito cult and his famous birthday may not have been quite so important in Yugoslav society. In 1977 when the celebrations for the Marshal's 85th birthday and 40 years as a leader of the communists were taking place, as well as articles about the Marshal's glorious life in the Slobodna Dalmacija Split edition, the happy reader was also able to enjoy a picture of a naked Swedish girl on the back page. Obviously newspapers and journals are a "must" in any research into this topic.

NOTES

[1]   *Druže Tito mi ti se kunemo* – "Comrade Tito, We Swear by You" is the title of a famous Yugoslav popular song. The song can be downloaded from the extremely useful site http://www.titoville.com.

[2]   Личността на политика. Сириус 4, Veliko Trinovo 2004, p. 257.

[3]   Д. Оруел, *1984*, Превод от английски Лидия Божилова, Профиздат, Sofia 1989. Quotation from the e-version of the book. Source http://bezmonitor.com

[4]   Я. Янакиев, *Системата действа*, "Здраве", год. XXVII, март, бр. 3, 1982, p. 4. The author mentions in the article Todor Zhivkov (7 September 1911 – 5 August 1998), the most prominent leader of the Bulgarian socialist regime, leader of the Bulgarian Communist Party (1954-1989), Prime Minister (1962-1971) and Chairman of the State Council (1971-1989). See А. Цураков, *Енциклопедия: правителствата на България 1879-2001, Хронология на политическия живот*, Sofia 2001, pp. 325 - 326. For more details see his autobiography Т. Живков, *Мемоари*, Sofia-Veliko Trinovo 1997. Also see И. Баева, *Прагматикът, управлявал България 35 години*, in М. Радева (ed.), *Български държавници 1944-1989*, Sofia 2005, pp. 184-204.

[5]   В. Пелевин, *Записки за търсенето на вятъра*, Диалектика на преходния период (от никъде за никъде), Sofia 2005, p. 289.

[6]   Josip Broz Tito (7.5.1892 – 4.5.1980), leader of the Yugoslav communists (1937-1980), Commander of the Yugoslav military forces (1945-1980), President of Yugoslavia (1953-1980, lifetime president since 1974). Three times National hero of Yugoslavia. A good bibliography listing books and articles about him and by him can be found in Sentić M., *Bibliografija o Josipa Broza Tita*, Rijeka 1981. Also see *Bibliografia, (Selektivna) radova jugoslovenskih i stranih autora o Josupu Broyu Titu (knjige, brošure i članci) – 1937-1987 –*, "Vojnoistorijski glasnik", knj. 4, 1987, pp. 428-492. For recent studies on Tito, the bibliography at the end of Todor Kuljić's book *Tito. Sociološkoistorijska studija*, Institut za političke studije, Belgrade 1998, pp. 373-382 is very useful.

[7]   Actually Tito was always an enemy of any form of nationalism in the different republics that made up the *FNRY* (Federal People's Republic of Yugoslavia) and later the *SFRY* (Socialist Federal Republic of Yugoslavia).

[8]   Nicolae Ceausescu (26 January 1918 - 25 December 1989), leader of the Romanian Communist Party

(until 23rd of July known as the Romanian Workers Party) (1965-1989), Chairman of the State Council (1967-1989), President of Romania (1974-1989). See *Membrii C.C. al P.C.R. 1945-1989. Dicționar*, Bucharest 2004, pp. 140-142. Probably the most valuable study of his personality cult is A. Cioroianu, *Ce Ceaușescu qui hante les Roumains. Le mythe, les representations et le culte du Dirigeant dans la Roumanie communiste*, Bucharest 2004. See also M.E. Fischer, *Nicolae Ceaușescu. A Study in Political Leadership*, Boulder-London, 1989, and the documentary collection A.U. Gabanyi, *The Ceaușescu Cult. Propaganda and Power Policy in Communist Romania*, Bucharest 2000.

9   Enver Hoxha (16 October 1908 - 11 Aprile 1985), as First Secretary of the Communist Albanian Party of Labour, was the leader of Albania from the end of World War II until his death in 1985. He was Prime Minister of Albania from 1944 to 1954 and Minister of Foreign Affairs from 1946 to 1953.

10 It may suffice to type the respective names into the search engine of some of the e-databases providing access to the articles in history periodicals, such as JSTOR or EBSCO, in order to understand what I mean. See http://www.jstor.org, http://search.epnet.com.

11 Gheorghe Gheorghiu Dej (8 November 1901 - 19 April 1965), Secretary General of the Romanian Communist Party / Romanian Workers Party (1945-1954), First Secretary of the Romanian Workers Party (1955-1965), Prime - Minister (1952-1955), Chairman of the State Council (1961-1965). *Membrii C.C. al P.C.R. 1945-1989. Dicționar*, Bucharest 2004, pp. 291-292.

12 This user-friendly tool suggests *Den, Dee, Dew, Jed* or *Deem* instead of Dej, Zhivkov could easily become *Zhukov,* and it would be happy for us to write *Hoax, Hoaxer, Hoaxed, Hoxie* or *Hoo-ha* instead of poor Hohxa.

13 T. Kuljić, *Tito u novom srpskom poredkom sećanja*, "Sociologija", 2, 2003, p. 66.

14 In my opinion the best survey to date of Tito's public representations and the attitude of the people towards Josip Broz, together with other problems of leadership in Yugoslavia, is T. Kuljić, *Tito. Sociološkoistorijska studija*. In 2005, a second "updated" edition appeared: *Tito: sociološko-istorijska studija*, Gradska narodna biblioteka "Žarko Zrenjanin", 2005. On the different aspects of the Tito personality and cult, see also M. Терзић, *Прилог питању стварања Титовог култа*, "Историјски записи", бр. 1, 1995, pp. 88-96; Д. Мојић, *Еволуција култа Јосипа Броза Тита 1945-1990. Анализа штампе*, "Српска политичка мисао", II, бр. 1, 1995, pp. 133-154; T. Kuljić, *Tito – nacrt sociološkoistorijskog istraživanja*, "Srpska politička misao", II, 1, 1995, pp. 49-90; T. Kuljić, *Titova nacionalna politika*, "Istorija" 20. veka. God. 15, br. 2, 1997, str. 141-174; T. Kuljić, *Inetelektualci o Titu. Tri pristupa*, "Sociologija", Vol. XXXIX, 2, 1997, pp. 223-238; Б. Петрановић, *Историографске контроверзе*, Службени лист СРЈ, Belgrade 1998, pp. 105-124; Б. Пејић, *Тито или иконизација једне представе*, in Д. Сретеновић, ејан, *Ново читање иконе*, Belgrade 2002, pp. 107 -157; К. Николић, *Прошлост без историје. Полемике у југословенској историографији 1961-1991. Главни токови.* Институт за савремену историју, Belgrade 2003, pp. 319-373; Х. Мишков, *Приключенията на храбрия войник Броз*, "Минало Година", XI, 1, 2004, pp. 48-56; О.М. Пинтар, *„Тито је стена.“ (Дис)континуитет владарски представљања у Југославији и Србији XX века*, Годишњак за друштвену историју, Година XI, Свеска 2 – 3, 2004, pp. 85-100; Vlastito iskustvo. Past Present. Leposavić, R. (urednik). Samizdat, B92, Belgrade 2004.

15 See for example Д. Мојић, *Еволуција култа Јосипа Броза Тита 1945-1990*, pp. 133-154.

16 G. Dimitrov (18.6.1882 – 2.7.1949), Secretary – General of the Bulgarian Communist Party and Prime – Minister (1946-1949). Цураков, Ангел, *Енциклопедия правителствата на България 1879 – 2001, Хронология на политическия живот*, Sofia 2001, pp. 267-268; also see И. Димитров, *Между идеологията и държавата*, in М. Радева (ed.), *Български държавници 1944 – 1989*, Sofia 2005, pp. 37-58.

17 Valko Chervenkov (6.9.1900 - 21.10.1989), Secretary – General of the Bulgarian Communist Party (1950-1954) and Prime Minister (1950-1956). Цураков, Ангел, *Енциклопедия правителствата на България 1879 – 2001, Хронология на политическия живот*, Sofia 2001, pp. 275-276; also see Л. Огнянов, *Всевластен комунистически лидер*, in Радева (ed.), *Български държавници 1944 – 1989* cit., pp. 100-116.

[18]   V. Kastratović-Ristić, Veselinka, *Fondovi Arhiva Predsednika Republike (Josipa Broza Tita) i Muzeja istorije Jugoslavije*, in *Velike sile i male države u Hladnom ratu 1945-1955: Slučaj Jugoslavije: Zbornik radova sa Međunarodne naučne konferencije*, Belgrade 2003, pp. 381-390.

[19]   Muzej istorije Jugoslavije (MIJ), Kabinet Predsednika Republike (KPR) – V.

[20]   MIJ, KPR – V – 7 b, Čestitke stranih ličnosti i organizacija.

[21]   MIJ, KPR – V – 7 c, Čestitke domaćih ličnosti i organizacija.

[22]   MIJ, KPR – V – 9 a, Dokumentacija o kumovima (kumovanja, materialna pomoć, pozdr. pisma i čestitke).

[23]   But Josip Broz was godfather even of some Slovenian children in the late 1940s and 50s. MIJ, KPR – V – 9 a, br. kutije 601, Kozina – Kulaš.

[24]   MIJ, KPR – V – 9 a, br. kutije 533, br. kutije 601, br. kutije 601.

[25]   MIJ, KPR – V – 7 a, Prijemi ličnosti i organizacija, zahtevi učestnika proslave za fotografia sa prijema kod Predsednika Republike povodom rodjendana; MIJ, KPR – V – 12, Dokumentacija o dnevnim obavezima predsednika republike (dnevni rada, rasporedi rada, beleške i sl.).

[26]   Sufficient information about this institution can be found on its website.

[27]   Fond 114, Savez socialističke omladine Jugoslavije.

[28]   See for instance *Titova Štafeta Štafeta Mladosti*, Memorijalni centar "Josip Broz Tito", Belgrade 1985, M. Stefanović - M. Baljak - D. Petrović - Z. Zoran - B. Borislav, *Titova štafeta mladosti*, Belgrade 1989; *Memorial Center*, Josip Broz Tito Memorial Center, Novi Sad 1991.

[29]   I.Colović, *On Models and Batons*, in *Vlastito iskustvo. Past Present*. edited by R. Leposavić, *Samizdat, B92*, Belgrade 2004, p. 153.

[30]   *Ibid.*, pp. 153-155.

[31]   *Ibid.*, p. 155

[32]   Arhiv Srbije i Crne Gore (ASCG), fond 114 Savez socialističke omladine Jugoslavije (SSOJ), popis I, fascikla 62, Proslave praznika "25 maj"; ASCG, fond 114 SSOJ, popis I, fascikla 63, Proslave "Dana Mladosti", 1961; ASCG, fond 114 SSOJ, popis I, fascikla 64, Proslava "Dana Mladosti", 1962; ASCG, fond 114 SSOJ, popis I, fascikla 65, Proslave "Dana Mladosti", 1963 – 1967; ASCG, fond 114 SSOJ, popis I, fascikla 66, Proslava "Dana Mladosti", 1969; ASCG, fond 114 SSOJ, popis II, fascikla 19, Materijali proslave "Dana Mladosti", 1970; ASCG, fond 114 SSOJ, popis II, fascikla 20, Materijali proslave "Dana Mladosti", 1971; (Dokumentacija odbora za proslavu. Prijave za 1971; ASCG, fond 114 SSOJ, popis II, fascikla 21, Materijali proslave "Dana Mladosti", 1972 -1973; ASCG, fond 114 SSOJ, popis II, fascikla 131, Predsedništvo Konferencije SSOJ, Materijali "Titovog fonda", 1977-79; ASCG, fond 114 SSOJ, popis II, fascikla 132, Predsedništvo Konferencije SSOJ, Materijali o proslave "Dana Mladosti", 1974-77; ASCG, fond 114 SSOJ, popis II, fascikla 133, Predsedništvo Konferencije SSOJ, Materijali o proslave "Dana Mladosti", 1978; ASCG, fond 114 SSOJ, popis II, fascikla 235, Predsedništvo Konferencije SSOJ, Materijali o proslave "Dana Mladosti", 1979-80; ASCG, fond 114 SSOJ, popis II, Savezni odbor za Proslavu "Dana Mladosti", fascikla 406, 1983-986; ASCG, fond 114 SSOJ, popis II, Savezni odbor za Proslavu "Dana Mladosti", fascikla 407, Materijali Saveznog odbora za proslavu "Dana Mladosti": - predlozi za dodelu plaketa i priznanja "25. maj" – organizacija štafete – organizacija proslave – izveštaji o proslavi – dokumentacija odbora 1987-1989.

[33]   *Vlastito iskustvo* cit., p. 177.

[34]   *Memorial Center*, Josip Broz Tito Memorial Center, Novi Sad, 1991, also the leaflet *Muzej "25. maj"*, Belgrade, s.a.

[35]   See *Memorial Center* cit.

[36]   Colović, *On models* cit., p. 149, p. 152.

[37]   MIJ, Muzej "25. maj", Inventarski popis, Depo II, knj. 1, 2.

[38] Colović, *On models* cit., p. 149, p. 152.

[39] *Memorial Center.*

[40] Ж. Стојковић - Х. Ракић, *Мајске свечаности у Лесковцу и околини (1945-2000)*, Општински одбор Савеза удружења бораца Народноослободилаког рата, Лесковац 2003.

[41] *Deset godina Titove štafete*, Belgrade 1956; *Titova štafeta u AP Vojvodini*, Kartografska grada. B.i., B.g.; *Trešnjevka. Prigodno izdanje za "Dan mladosti"*, Zagreb 1962; B. Debeljković, *Dan mladosti. Slikovna grada*, Belgrade 1972; M. Stefanović, *Pozdravi iz srca. Štafeta Titu – Mladost*, Savezni odbor za proslavu Dana mladsoti, Mladost, Belgrade 1977; M. Subotić, *Pletenica djetinja mašta. Literarni radovi učenika osnovnih škola Slavonje i Baranje. Dan mladosti 1978*, Osijek, 1978; A. Trkulja, *Pesnička štafeta 79*, Belgrade 1980; M. Stefanović - M. Baljak - D. Petrović (eds.), *Pozdravi iz srca. Savezni odbor za proslavu Dana mladosti*, Belgrade 1980; *Сунце нас затекло у мају. Мајска песничка штафета. Деца Палилуле*, Belgrade 1980; *Pionirska štafeta. Pozdrav pionira SR Hrvatske drugu Titu 1978. godine*, Savez Društava "Naša djeca", Republički savjet za unapređivanje rada Saveza pionira, 1978; *Pionirska štafeta. Pozdrav pionira SR Hrvatske drugu Titu 1979. godine*, Savez Društava "Naša djeca", Republički savjet za unapređivanje rada Saveza pionira, 1979; *Pionirska štafeta. Pozdrav pionira SR Hrvatske drugu Titu 1980. godine*, Savez Društava "Naša djeca", Republički savjet za unapređivanje rada Saveza pionira, 1981; Степановић, Живадин, *Крагујевачка штафета Титу – Титу*, Крагујевац 1985; G. Rabrenović, *Potrebe i interese omladine i njeno učešće u društveno – političkom zivotu mesne zajednice, Mladi beogradski podstanari. Dan mladosti. Juče, danas, sutra*, Belgrade 1987; M. Stefanović- M. Baljak - D. Petrović- Z. Sekulić - B. Vasić, *Titova štafeta mladosti*, Belgrade 1989.

Bibliography

Documentary Sources

Muzej istorije Jugoslavije (MIJ), Kabinet Predsednika Republike (KPR) – V.

MIJ, Muzej "25. maj", Inventarski popis, Depo II, knj. 1,2.

Arhiv Srbije i Crne Gore (ASCG), fond 114 Savez socialističke omladine Jugoslavije (SSOJ).

Propaganda Issues

Ж.Степановић, *Крагујевачка штафета Титу – Титу*, Крагујевац, 1985.

Сунце нас затекло у мају. Мајска песничка штафета. Деца Палилуле, Народна библиотека Милутин Бојић, Belgrade 1980.

Debeljković B., *Dan mladosti. Slikovna grada*, Belgrade 1972.

Deset godina Titove štafete, Belgrade 1956.

Memorial Center, Josip Broz Tito Memorial Center, Novi Sad 1991, also the leaflet *Muzej "25. maj"*, Belgrade s.a.

Pionirska štafeta. Pozdrav pionira SR Hrvatske drugu Titu 1978. godine, 1978.

Pionirska štafeta. Pozdrav pionira SR Hrvatske drugu Titu 1979. godine, 1979.

Pionirska štafeta. Pozdrav pionira SR Hrvatske drugu Titu 1980. godine, 1981.

Rabrenović G., *Potrebe i interese omladine i njeno učešće u društveno – političkom životu mesne zajednice, Mladi Belgradeski podstanari. Dan mladosti. Juče, danas, sutra*, Belgrade 1987.

Sentić M., *Bibliografija o Josipa Broza Tita*, Rijeka 1981.

Stefanović M., *Pozdravi iz srca. Štafeta Titu – Mladost*, Belgrade 1977.

Stefanović M. - Baljak M. - Petrović D. (eds.), *Pozdravi iz srca. Savezni odbor za proslavu Dana mladosti*, 1980.

Stefanović M. - Baljak M. - Petrović D. - Sekulić Z. - Vasić B., *Titova štafeta mladosti*, Belgrade 1989.

Subotić M., *Pletenica djetinja mašta, Literarni radovi učenika osnovnih škola Slavonje i Baranje. Dan mladosti 1978*, Osijek 1978.

Titova štafeta u AP Vojvodini, Kartografska građa. B.i., B.g.

Trešnjevka. Prigodno izdanje za "Dan mladosti", Zagreb 1962.

Trkulja A., *Pesnička štafeta 79*, Zajednica književnih klubova Srbije, Belgrade 1980.

Selected Literature

Баева И., *Прагматикът, управлявал България 35 години*, in Радева М. (ed.), *Български държавници 1944 – 1989*, Sofia 2005, pp. 184-204.

Димитров И., *Между идеологията и държавата*, in Радева М. (ed.), *Български държавници 1944 – 1989*, Sofia 2005, pp. 37-58.

Мишков Х., *Приключенията на храбрия войник Броз*, "Минало, Година XI", 1, 2004, pp. 48-56.

Мојић Д., *Еволуција култа Јосипа Броза Тита 1945-1990. Анализа штампе*, "Српска политичка мисао", II, бр. 1, 1995, pp. 133-154.

Николић К., *Прошлост без историје. Полемике у југословенској историографији 1961-1991. Главни токови*, Belgrade 2003, pp. 319-373.

Огњанов Л., *Всевластен комунистически лидер*, in Радева М.(ed.), *Български държавници 1944 – 1989*, Sofia 2005, pp. 100-116.

Пејић Б., *Тито или иконизација једне представе*, in Сретеновић Д., *Ново читање иконе*, Belgrade 2002, pp. 107-157.

Петрановић Б., *Историографске контроверзе*, Belgrade 1998, pp. 105-124.

Пинтар О.М., *"Тито је стена." (Дис)континуитет владарски представљања у Југославији и Србији XX века*, "Годишњак за друштвену историју", Година XI, 2-3, 2004, pp. 85-100.

Терзић М., *Прилог питању стварања Титовог култа*, "Историјски записи", бр. 1, 1995, pp. 88-96.

Стојковић Ж., Ракић Х., *Мајске свечаности у Лесковцу и околини (1945-2000)*, Лесковац 2003.

Цураков А., *Енциклопедия: правителствата на България 1879 – 2001, Хронология на политическия живот*, Sofia 2001.

Bibliografia, (Selektivna) radova jugoslovenskih i stranih autora o Josupu Broyu Titu (knjige, brošure i članci) – 1937-1987, Vojnoistorijski glasnik, knj. 4, 1987, pp. 428-492.

Cioroianu A., *Ce Ceaușescu qui hante les Roumains. Le mythe, les representations et le culte du Dirigeant dans la Roumanie communiste*, Bucharest 2004.

Fischer M.E., *Nicolae Ceaușescu. A Study in Political Leadrship*, London 1989.

Gabanyi A.U., *The Ceaușescu Cult. Propaganda and Power Policy in Communist Romania*, Bucarest 2000.

Kastratović-Ristić V., *Fondovi Arhiva Predsednika Republike (Josipa Broza Tita) i Muzeja istorije Jugoslavije*, in: *Velike sile i male drzave u Hladnom ratu 1945-1955: Slučaj Jugoslavije: Zbornik radova sa Medunarodne naučne konferencije*, Belgrade 2003, pp. 381-390.

Kuljić T., *Tito – nacrt sociološkoistorijskog istraživanja*, Srpska politička misao. vol. II, 1, 1995, pp. 49-90.

Id., *Titova nacionalna politika*, "Istorija" 20. veka. God. 15, br. 2 (1997), pp. 141-174.

Id., *Inetelektualci o Titu. Tri pristupa*, "Sociologija", Vol. XXXIX, 2, april – june 1997, pp. 223-238.

Id., *Tito. Sociološkoistorijska studija*, Belgrade 1998.

Id, *Tito u novom srpskom poredkom sećanja*, "Sociologija", 2, 2003.

Membrii C.C. al P.C.R. 1945-1989. Dicţionar, Bucharest 2004, pp. 140-142.

Vlastito iskustvo: Past Present, edited by Leposavić R., Belgrade 2004.

INTERNET RESOURCES

http://www.titoville.com

SOURCES

Greetings to Josip Broz from the pioneers of his native village of Kumrovec on the occasion of his 59th birthday (23 May 1951).

Dragi naš druže Tito,
i mi pioniri Tvog rodnog mjesta pridružujemo se željama naroda Jugoslavije, čestitamo
Ti rođendan i zelimo, da nam još dugo poživiš i, da nas i nadalje vodiš boljem životu.
živio nam naš dragi Maršale!
Pioniri Odreda Maršala Tita
Osmogodišnje škole Kumrovec
Kumrovec 23.V.1951.

Dear our comrade Tito,
We, the pioneers from your homeland, also add to the wishes of the Yugoslav nations in congratulating You on Your Birthday, wishing You a long life with us, that You may continue to lead us towards a better future.
Long live our dear Marshal!
The Pioneers of the Marshal Tito squad
Primary school of Kumrovets
Kumrovec 23 May 1951.

Source: *Muzej istorije Jugoslavije*, Arhiv Kabineta predsednika Jugoslavij.

Greeting of the people from villages Jara and Knespolja on the occasion of Tito's 60th anniversary

Voljeni naš druže Tito,
Zajedno sa svim našim narodima i mi seljaci Jara i Knešpolja, srez Lištica, kličemo Ti i
čestitamo 60-ti rodjendan. Čestitamo Ti ga iz sveg srca i želimo jos dugo da živeš medju
nama. Uvijek si nas vodio pravim putem. Teška je bila četverogodišnja borba i Ti si
njen najsvijetliji lijek. Bio si neustrašiv borac, ušao si uvjek samo naprijed. Naši narodi
su te slijedili i danas Te slijede.
A ovom zgodom obećavamo Ti da ćemo čuvati tekovine Narodno-oslobodilačke borbe,
da ćemo izvršavati zadatke izgradnje naše zemlje i da ćemo odgajati naše djecu da vole
svoju zemlju da budu ponosni na nju, da se ponose sa Tobom, druže Tito!
Još jednom obećajemo Ti, da ćemo biti budni branioci krvlju stečene slobode koju
danas uživamo i po stotinu puta Ti kličemo:

Zivio nam, dragi naš druze Tito, još dugo na našu radost i sreće!
Narod sela Jara i Knešpolja
s[r]eza Lištica.

Beloved Comrade Tito,
Together with all our nations we the peasants from Jara and Knespolja district Listic,
offer You our congratulations on Your 60th birthday. We congratulate You with all
our hearts and wish You to live for many more years among us. You have always lead
us in the right way. The forty year struggle was hard and you are its brightest symbol.
You were fearless fighter You only marched forward. Our nations have always
followed You and today they still follow You.
On this occasion we promise You that we shall defend the achievements of National
Liberation struggle. We shall continue completing its tasks and we shall bring up our
children to love their country, to be proud of it and to feel proud of You, Comrade Tito!
Once again we promise You, that we shall be watchful defenders of the blood shed
for the freedom in which we live today and hundred times we cry out:
Long live our dear comrade Tito, for many years to come, as our joy and
happiness!
People from the Jara and Knespolja villages
District of Listic.

Source: *Muzej istorije Jugoslavije*, Arhiv Kabineta predsednika Jugoslavij.

Greeting of the sick pioneers and nurses from the town of Ohrid, Macedonia to Josip
Broz on the occasion of his 61st birthday

Mnogo sakani naš TITO,
Nije detskite negovatelki, zaedno s pionerite bolesnici pri ovaa bolnica, naj sardečno Ti
go čestitame Rodeniot den, ti ti praćame novi pozdravi i Ti sakame novi pobedi vo
izgradbata na Socijalizmot vo našata zemja.
Bidini ni zdrav i mnogo godini da ziveeš oti nije so tebe se raduvame.
Vetuvame deka nije smelo ke go sledime patot po koj ne vodiš Ti.
Od pionerite i detskite megovatelki vo Ohrid

Our much beloved TITO,
We, the nurses and sick pioneers in this hospital, most cordially
congratulate You on Your birthday and send You new greetings, wishing You
victories in building socialism in our country.
Be healthy and live for many years, for we are happy with you.
We swear we shall bravely follow in the path You lead us along.
From the pioneers and nurses in Ohrid

Source: *Muzej Istorije Jugoslavije*, Arhiv Kabineta predsednika Jugoslavije, V-7-c,
1953.

Greetings of the students and teachers of the Albanian secondary school in Prizren to Josip Broz Tito on the occasion of his 62nd birthday

Voljeni druže TITO,
Učenici I nastavnici Siptarske realne gimnazije u Prizrenu sa praznićnim razpolozenijem Vam čestitaju 62. rodjendan, sa željem da nam jos dugo preživite na srecu svih naroda FNRJ, a posebnonaroda Kosova i Metohije koiji su svoju junaćku proslost i svetlo buducnost su vezali za SKJ na čelo sa Vama.
Saljemo Vam simvoličan poklon bratstva i jedinstva Siptara, Srba i Crnogoraca na Kosmetu kato izraz zadovoljstva sto ste nam omogucili da mirno zivimo, odusevljeno radimo i učimo.
Siptarska gimnazija u Prizrenu prvi put u istoriji siptara Kosova i Metohije izvedi klasu maturanata. To su ljudi koji ce se samopregorno boriti za učvscenje bratstva i jedinstva jer suosetili njegovu vrednost, oni ce visoko dici zastavu jugoslovenskog socijalistiiçeskog patriotiizma i boriti se za mir u svetu. Oni su osetili lepotu zivota i snagu nauke na materrnjem jeziku zato ce se boriti da oçuvaju tradicije NOB-a.
Nasa gimnazija ove godine [?] prvu redovnu polumaturu zenske omladine, to je snaga koja ce skinuti debeo zaostalosti i primitivnosti medju zenama siptarkama.
Mi hocemo, mi moramo pobediti, jer ste sa nama Vi, çovek koji ne zna za umar kad sa u pitanju interesi radnog naroda – çoveka iz naroda.
Prizren, 23 maja 1954
Učenici i nastavnici siptarske realne gimnazije u Prizrenu

Beloved Comrade Tito,
The students and teachers from the Siptarian [Albanian] Secondary School in Prizren, in holiday spirit, congratulate You on Your birthday, with the wish that You will live for many more years ahead, to the joy of all of the Yugoslav nations but especially those in Kosovo i Metohia, which have bound their brave past and bright future to the SKJ [Union of the Yugoslav Communists] led by You.
We send You a symbolic gift from the Kosovo Siptari [Albanian], Serbian and Montenegran brotherhood and union as an expression of our gratitude that You have made it possible for us to live peacefully and work and study enthusiastically.
For the first time in the history of Kosovo and the Metohija Siptari [Albanians], the Siptarian [Albanian] Secondary School in Prizren has produced a class of graduates. These are people who will struggle selflessly to strengthen brotherhood and unity because they understand its value. They will raise high the flag of Yugoslav socialist patriotism and will struggle for peace in the World. They feel the beauty of life and the power of science in their mother tongue and that is why they will fight to protect the legacy of the National Liberation Struggle
This year our secondary school saw the first regular semi-matriculation for young female students. This is the force that will break down the wall of primitive backwardness affecting Sipterian women.
We want to win because You are with us, a man [Tito] who is tireless in championing the interests of the workers and the common man.
Prizren, 23rd of May, 1954
Students and teachers from the Sipterian [Albanian] secondary school in Prizren

Source: *Muzej Istorije Jugoslavije*, Arhiv Kabineta predsednika Jugoslavije, V-7-c, 1954.

Announcement from the meeting of the Presidency of the Union of Yugoslav Youth, 16.V.1970

Na današnoj sednici Predsedništvo Saveza Omladine Jugoslavije je odlučilo da 25. maja na Staduonu JNA Štafetu mladosti sa pozdravima omladine i naroda Jugoslavije drugu Titu preda Žežova (Tudov) [brackets added with a pen] Ljiljana učenica 4 razreda gimnazije „Josip Broz Tito" iz Skoplja. Ljiljana je odličan učenik u svim razredima. Pobednik je na republičkom takmičenji „Nauku mladima" u matematici.
Gimnazija „JosipBroz" slavi 25 – godišnjicu postojanja i naj-bolja je po uspehu u SR Makedoniji.
Belgrade, 16.V.1970. godine
Tanjug 331 – 635
622 – 355
[the name of the Yugoslav news agency and the tel. numbers added with a pen]

As a result of today's meeting, the Presidency of the Union of Yugoslav Youth has decided that on 25th of May on the Stadium of the Yugoslav Army, Zezova (Tudov) Ljiljana, a fourth grade student from Josip Broz Tito Secondary School in Skopje, will hand Comrade Tito the Youth Button containing birthday greetings from the Yugoslav nations and Youth. Ljiljana has been an excellent student in all grades. She is the winner of the "Science for Youth" mathematics competition.
The Josip Broz Tito Secondary School is celebrating its 25th anniversary and has had the best results in the Socialist Republic of Macedonia

Source: *ASCG*, Fond 114, SSOJ, popis II, fasc. 19, Materijali proslave "Dan Mladosti", 1970.

List with the persons to be in the central stand for the Youth Day (1970)
14 +1 [written with a pen]
Raspored centralne tribine za 25. maj [Arrangement of the central stand for the 25th of May][excerpt]
1. *predsednik Savezne Skupštine sa suprugom* [President of the Parliament and wife]
2. *predsednik Saveznog izvršnog veća sa suprugom* √ [President of the Union's Executive council] [mark added in red]
3. *Edvard Kardelj sa suprugom* √ [Edvard Kardelj and wife][underlining and mark added in red]
4. *13 članova izvršnog biroa* [13 members of the Executive Bureau]
5. *6 predsednika republičkih partija* [6 Presidents of the parties in the republics]
6. *6 predsednika republičkih skupština* [6 Presidents of the Parliaments in the Republics]
7. *2 pokrajinska predsednika partija* [2 Presidents of the parties in the autonomous regions]
8. *2 pokrajinska predsednika skupština* [2 Presidents of the Parliaments in the autonomous regions]
9. *predsednik SK Socijalističeskog saveza radnog naroda Jug.* [President of the Committee of the Socialist Union of the working people of Yugoslavia]

10. *predsednik SUBNOR – a* [President of the Alliance of the Unions of fighters from the National – Liberation War]
11. *predsednik Saveza omladine Jugoslavije* [President of the Yugoslav Youth Union]
12. *predsednik Ustavnog suda Jugoslavije* [President of the Yugoslav Constitutional Court]
13. *državni sekretar za inostrane poslove* [Foreign Secretary]
14. *državni sekretar za narodnu odbranu* [Defence Secretary]
15. *predsednik Skupštine grada Belgradea* [President of Belgrade Council]
16. *predsednik odbora Dana mladosti* [President of the Youth Day Celebrations Commitee]
17. *nosilac štafete* [The bearer of the baton]
18. *Dušan Petrović – Šane* [added in ink; also the line below]

LOŽA 20 [Box N 20]
1. *Dragiša Maksimović* √ [mark added in black ink]
2. *Marin Cetinić* √ [mark added in black ink]
3. [the number is enclosed in blue] *Rudi Petovar gen. puk.* [Col. Gen. added in ink] √ [mark added in black ink]
4. [the number is enclosed in blue] *Ante Banina gen. puk.* [Col. Gen. added in ink] √ [mark added in black ink]
5. [the number is enclosed in blue] *Miran Mejak* √ [mark added in black ink]
6. [the number is enclosed in blue] *Ali Šukrija* √ [mark added in black ink]
7. *Čedo Kapor* √ [mark added in black ink]
8. *Milan Vukasović* [struck off the list] *Velibor Gligorić* [added in red ink]
9. [the number is circled in blue] *Ivo Andrić* √ [mark added in black ink]
10. [the number is circled in blue] *Moma Marković s* √ [mark added in black ink]
11. [the number is circled in blue] *Todor Vujasnović* √ [mark added in black ink]
12. *Lepa Pijade* √ [mark added in black ink]
13. *Fanika Salaj* √ [mark added in black ink]
[...]

Source: *ASCG*, Fond 114, SSOJ, popis II, fascikla 19, Materijali proslave "Dan Mladosti", 1970.

Poem *Poklon za Tita* [A Gift for Tito] by the young pioneer Sanela Bazovic from the 4th grade in *Vasa Pelagic* primary school

Када би сунце могло
са неба да се скине
поклонила бих га Титу
чувару мира и истине

И срце бих му дала
с мојy башту са цвећем
нек' вечно живи и нек' се кити
наш драги ковач среће

Нека живи, нека га срећа прати,
Док је он са нама,
У нашем ће срцу
Срећно детињство цвати.

Санела Базовић, IV,
ОШ „Васа Пелагић"

If the sun could
Fall from the sky
I would give it to Tito
The keeper of peace and the truth

And I would give him my heart
From my garden with a flower
Let him live forever
Our maker of happiness

Let him live and let happiness follow him
As long as he is with us
In our heart
A happy childhood will bloom

Sanela Bazovic,
4th grade student, Vasa Pelagic Primary school

Source: *Сунце нас затекло у мају. Деца Палилуле. Мајска песничка штафета.*
1973 – 1979. Народна библиотека „Милутин Боић", Belgrade 1980, p. 81.

Note on Contributors

ALEKSEY KLEMESHOV

Aleksey Klemeshov is lecturer at the Chair of Ancient World and Middle Ages of Moscow State Regional University. His teaching is in areas of Medieval History. The main field of his research is on medieval religious and philosophical thought of Europe with special interest in studies of social and political concepts in 13th-14th centuries.

ANA ISABEL RIBEIRO

Ana Isabel Ribeiro is an assistant teacher in the Department of History (Institute of Economic and Social History) of the Faculty of Letters at the University of Coimbra, Portugal. Her main research subject has been centred around the study of local communities, their social organization and the way they develop in time. She is preparing her doctoral dissertation on the Local Administrative Elites of Coimbra (1777-1820).

BORISLAV MAVROV

Borislav Mavrov was born in 1976, in Sofia, Bulgaria. Currently he is a doctoral student at Sofia University "St. Kliment Ohridski", History Department, Chair of Modern and Contemporary History. His research interests are predominantly focused on Irish and British History at the end of 19th and the beginning of the 20th century.

CHARLES DALLI

Charles Dalli lectures in medieval history at the University of Malta. He studied history at the University of Malta, and specialized in medieval history at the University of Cambridge, UK. His main area of research is the social and economic history of the central Mediterranean region in the later Middle Ages, with special emphasis on island societies and multicultural interaction.

DIETER BERG

Dieter Berg has a chair of Medieval History at the University of Hannover and is also Director of the "Institut für franziskanische Geschichte (Saxonia)" in Münster.

DIMITAR GRIGOROV

Dimitar Grigorov is a Doctoral student in the Department of History at the University of Sofia. His scientific field is Contemporary Balkan History. He is especially interested in the problem concerning the relationship between the leaders and the people in the Socialist regime on the peninsula, the history of political ideas and the development and influence of urban popular culture, urban subcultures and urban mythology on the Balkans after the Second World War.

EMANUEL BUTTIGIEG

Emanuel Buttigieg is the holder of a first class honours degree in history from the University of Malta. His academic interests are now focussed on a Ph.D. about aspects of the history of the Order of St. John in Malta.

EMŐKE HORVÁTH

Emőke Horváth is an Associate Professor and Head of Department at the University of Miskolc (Hungary). She is a medievalist specialized in the Early Middle Ages. Her interest focuses on ecclesiastical and cultural history of the Early Medieval Europe and the history of the Barbarian Kingdoms.

GIULIA LAMI

Giulia Lami is full professor of History of Slavic Countries at University of Milan, member of the editorial board for the international review "Storia della storiografia – Histoire de l'Historiographie – History of Historiography – Geschichte der Geschichtschreibung". She is also a member of AAASS (American Association for the Advancement of Slavic Studies), of AISU (Italian Association for Ukrainian Studies), and of the Bureau of the Commission Internationale d'Etudes Historiques Slaves of the Comité International des Sciences historiques.

IWAN-MICHELANGELO D'APRILE

Iwan-Michelangelo D'Aprile is assistant Professor (*Wissenschaftlicher Assistent*) at the University of Potsdam, Institute for History, Cultural History of Early Modern Times/ Research Centre of European Enlightenment. His interests include Cultural History, Literature and Philosophy of the 18th century.

JEAN-LUC LAMBOLEY

Jean-Luc Lamboley is Professor of History and Archaeology of Ancient Worlds at the University "Pierre Mendès-France" of Grenoble, where he also serves as dean of the

Facolty of Human Sciences. He is promoter of the process of Bologna, Director of the French Epigraphical and Archaeological Mission in Albania (supported by the French Foreign Office), and Director of the European Research Group about the History and Archaeology of Balkans (supported by the French CNRS). His special research interests cover the Greek Mediterranean, and more especially the colonial areas, through the problematics of Cultural Anthropology and Acculturation process.

JOAQUIM CARVALHO

Joaquim Carvalho is professor at the University of Coimbra, Portugal, and member of the Instituto de História e Teoria das Ideias. He has published on the relations between the church and social control in early Modern Portugal.

LUISA TRINDADE

Luisa Trindade is teaching assistant and doctoral student at the History of Art Department of the Faculty of Letters of the University of Coimbra. Her main research interests are: history of urbanism, medieval city, urban life and medieval art.

MARIA PAOLA CASTIGLIONI

Maria Paola Castiglioni is doctoral student at the University " Pierre Mendès-France" of Grenoble and member of the Research Centre CRHIPA (*Centre de Recherche en histoire et Histoire de l'art Italie-Pays Alpins*) and of the Archaeological mission in Apollonia (Albania). Her main research interests are relations and contacts between Greeks and indigenous peoples in Illyria in ancient times, the diffusion and the reception of Greek myths, the concepts of ethnicity, identity, acculturation and frontier in colonial contexts.

MICHAEL REFALO

Michael Refalo is a doctoral student at the University of Malta, currently working on a thesis under the provisional title of *The Social Structure in Malta, 1870-1914*. Main interests include family and gender, poverty and philantropy, social development.

OLGA DEKHTEVICH

Olga Dekhtevich is a doctoral student at the Moscow State Regional University and assistant of the department of History at the Moscow State University of Service. Her main research interests are rationalist and mystic religious sects and movements, problems in particular the relations between the Old Believers and Russian Orthodox Church in 19th and the beginning of the 20th centuries.

Raphaela Averkorn

Raphaela Averkorn taught several years at the Department of History at the University of Hannover, she received in 2005 the Chair of Medieval and Modern History at the University of Siegen. She has published various contributions concerning religious, cultural, social, political and gender history. She has been a Visiting Professor in several countries, is involved in different European projects and also works as an ECTS Counsellor and as a Bologna Promoter.

Rita Ríos de la Llave

Rita Ríos de la Llave teaches History of Middle Ages at the university of Alcalá from 1997. Her main interest is the history of the Mendicant Orders in the Kingdom of Castile during Middle Ages, with special emphasis on the Dominican nuns' communities.

Thomas Ruhland

Thomas Ruhland is research assistant at the Research Centre for European Enlightenment Potsdam/Germany and doctoral student at the University of Potsdam with a grant of the "Gerda Henkel" Foundation. His main research interests are intercultural relations between Europe and Asia, the perception of the cultural "Other", collective identities, religious movements and Protestant missions in the 18th century.

Victor Mallia-Milanes

Victor Mallia-Milanes is Professor of Early Modern History and Director of the Institute for Maltese Studies at the University of Malta, where he served on the University Senate, and as Dean of the Faculty of Arts and Head of the Department of History. He has been Visiting Professor at the universities of Cagliari and Bari in Italy. His special research interests cover the Mediterranean, Venice, and the Order of St John in early modern times, on which he has published extensively.

Index

Under the aegis of CLIOHRES.net

www.cliohres.net

Printed in May 2006
by Industrie Grafiche Pacini Editore S.p.A.
on behalf of Edizioni PLUS - Pisa University Press